Beli

Northern Cayes
p82

Northern Belize
p127

Belize District
p52

Tikal & Flores
p233

Cayo District
p151

Southern Belize
p188

THIS EDITION WRITTEN AND RESEARCHED BY
Alex Egerton, Paul Harding, Daniel C Schechter

PLAN YOUR TRIP

Welcome to Belize 4
Belize Map............. 6
Belize's Top 22 8
Need to Know 18
If You Like 20
Month by Month....... 23
Itineraries 26
Diving & Snorkeling.... 31
Belize Outdoors 38
Travel with Children.... 44
Regions at a Glance.... 48

ON THE ROAD

BELIZE DISTRICT... 52
Belize City 54
Northwest of
Belize City 68
Burrell Boom........... 68
Community Baboon
Sanctuary 69
Rancho Dolores 71
Crooked Tree........... 71
Old Northern Highway.... 73
West of Belize City..... 75
Old Belize............... 75
Hattieville 76
Belize Zoo 77

Monkey Bay............. 79
Along the Coast Road .. 80
Gales Point 80

NORTHERN
CAYES 82
Ambergris Caye
& San Pedro 84
Caye Caulker......... 108
Other Northern Cays.. 122
Cayo Esperanto 122
Turneffe Atoll........... 123
Lighthouse Reef........ 124
Long Caye 125

ANCIENT MAYA RUINS, CARACOL P180

DIVING, LIGHTHOUSE REEF P124

HALF MOON CAYE NATURAL MONUMENT P126

PATRICK ENDRES / DESIGN PICS / GETTY IMAGES ©

RON WATTS / GETTY IMAGES

JEFF HUNTER / GETTY IMAGES ©

Contents

UNDERSTAND

Belize Today. 254
History 256
Ancient Maya 266
People of Belize 273
Rhythms of a Nation . . 277
Beyond Rice & Beans. . 280
Wild Things 284
Land & Environment . . 290

**NORTHERN
BELIZE** 127
Orange Walk District . . **129**
Orange Walk Town 129
Lamanai. 135
Río Bravo Conservation
& Management Area 139
Corozal District. **140**
Corozal Town. 141
Cerro Maya &
Copper Bank. 147
Sarteneja. 149

CAYO DISTRICT 151
Belmopan. **154**
Around Belmopan. **158**
**Hummingbird
Highway** **160**
West of Belmopan **162**
Actun Tunichil Muknal. . . 164
San Ignacio **165**
**Southeast of
San Ignacio** **173**
Cristo Rey &
Chiquibul Roads 174
Mountain Pine
Ridge Area. 178
Caracol. 180
**Northwest of
San Ignacio** **182**
Bullet Tree Falls 182
**Southwest of
San Ignacio** **183**
San José Succotz
& Around 185
Benque Viejo
del Carmen 186

**SOUTHERN
BELIZE** 188
Stann Creek District . . **190**
Dangriga 190
Mayflower Bocawina
National Park 195
Central Cayes 195
Hopkins 199
Sittee Point 203
Sittee River 205
Maya Center 205
Cockscomb Basin
Wildlife Sanctuary 206
Placencia. 208
**Toledo District
(The Deep South).** **217**
Punta Gorda 218
Around Punta Gorda 225
Around the
Deep South 227

**TIKAL & FLORES,
GUATEMALA** 233
Tikal 234
Yaxhá 240
Uaxactun 241
El Remate 241
Flores &
Santa Elena. 243

**SURVIVAL
GUIDE**

Directory A–Z 296
Transportation 305
Index. 313
Map Legend. 319

**SPECIAL
FEATURES**

Diving & Snorkeling. . . . 31
Outdoor Activities 38
Ancient Maya 266
Wildlife-Watching. 284

Welcome to Belize

With one foot in the Central American jungles and the other in the Caribbean Sea, Belize may be small but it's packed with adventure and culture.

Barrier Reef

Belize Barrier Reef is the second largest in the world, after Australia's, and with more than 100 types of coral and some 500 species of tropical fish, it's pure paradise for scuba divers and snorkelers. Swimming through translucent seas, snorkelers are treated to a kaleidoscope of coral, fish and turtles, while divers go deeper, investigating underwater caves and walls and the world-renowned Blue Hole. Add to this island living on the sandy cays, where you can spend your days kayaking, windsurfing, stand-up paddleboarding, swimming, fishing or lazing in a hammock, and you've got the recipe for a perfect tropical vacation.

Jungle Life

Inland, a vast (by Belizean standards) network of national parks and wildlife sanctuaries offers a safe haven for wildlife, which ranges from the industrious parades of cutter ants to the national animal of Belize, Baird's tapir, or the shy jaguar. Birdwatchers aim their binoculars at some 570 species, which roost along the rivers and lagoons and in the broadleaf forest. Keeneyed visitors who take the time to hike can easily spot spider monkeys and howler monkeys, peccaries, coatimundis, *gibnuts* and green iguanas. Even the showy keel-billed toucan, the national bird of Belize, occasionally makes an appearance in public.

Land of the Maya

Belize is home to one of the world's most mysterious civilizations – the ancient Maya. The Cayo District and Toledo's Deep South in particular are peppered with archaeological sites that date to the Maya heyday (AD 250–1000), where enormous steps lead to the tops of tall stone temples, often yielding 360-degree jungle views. Explore excavated tombs and examine intricate hieroglyphs, or descend deep into natural caves to see where the Maya kings performed rituals and made sacrifices to the gods of their underworld. You can appreciate the culture today by staying in village guesthouses and by learning the art of chocolate-making.

Action & Adventure

Whether you're scuba diving the Blue Hole, zip-lining through the jungle canopy, rappelling down waterfalls or crawling through ancient cave systems, Belize is a genuine adventure. Head to Cayo District where you can tube or canoe through darkened river systems or hardcore spelunk in renowned Actun Tunichil Muknal cave. Zip-lining is virtually an art form in Cayo and Southern Belize where you can sail through the jungle at half a dozen locations. Horseback riding is well organised and hiking is superb in national parks, such as Mayflower Bocawina National Park, Cockscomb Basin Wildlife Sanctuary, Shipstern Nature Reserve and Río Bravo.

Why I Love Belize

By Paul Harding, Writer

It's a cliché to say good things come in small packages, but with Belize it just feels right. No bigger than New Hampshire or Israel, Belize doesn't quite fit the mold of Latin America or the Caribbean, but proudly considers itself both. I love the low-key nature of its people and the seamless mix of cultures – Belizean, Creole, *mestizo*, Garifuna, Maya and even expat. I love the fact that you can be snorkeling on the barrier reef one day and hiking in the jungle the next. Belize is endearingly rough around the edges, but thoroughly traveler-friendly.

For more about our writers, see p320

Above: Ambergris Caye (p84)

Belize

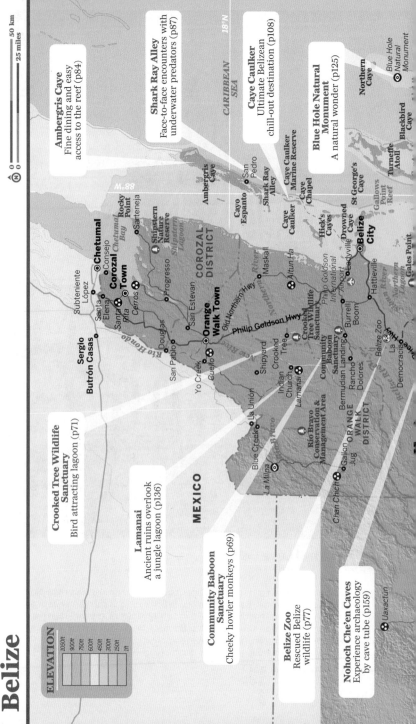

ELEVATION

| 1050ft |
| 900ft |
| 750ft |
| 600ft |
| 450ft |
| 300ft |
| 150ft |
| 1ft |

Ambergris Caye
Fine dining and easy access to the reef (p84)

Shark Ray Alley
Face-to-face encounters with underwater predators (p87)

Caye Caulker
Ultimate Belizean chill-out destination (p108)

Blue Hole Natural Monument
A natural wonder (p125)

Crooked Tree Wildlife Sanctuary
Bird attracting lagoon (p71)

Lamanai
Ancient ruins overlook a jungle lagoon (p136)

Community Baboon Sanctuary
Cheeky howler monkeys (p69)

Belize Zoo
Rescued Belize wildlife (p77)

Nohoch Che'en Caves
Experience archaeology by cave tube (p159)

MEXICO

CARIBBEAN SEA

18°N

0 ————— 50 km
0 ————— 25 miles

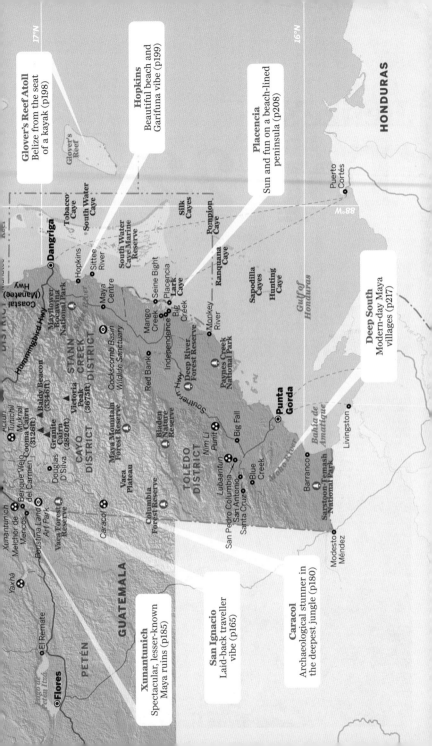

Glover's Reef Atoll
Belize from the seat of a kayak (p198)

Hopkins
Beautiful beach and Garifuna vibe (p199)

Placencia
Sun and fun on a beach-lined peninsula (p208)

Deep South
Modern-day Maya villages (p217)

Caracol
Archaeological stunner in the deepest jungle (p180)

San Ignacio
Laid-back traveller vibe (p165)

Xunantunich
Spectacular, lesser-known Maya ruins (p185)

HONDURAS

GUATEMALA

Belize's
Top 22

Diving the Blue Hole

1 The sheer walls of the Blue Hole Natural Monument (p125) drop more than 400ft into the blue ocean. Although it is half filled with silt and natural debris, the depth still creates a perfect circle of startling azure that is visible from above. The wall of the Blue Hole is decorated with a dense forest of stalactites and stalagmites from times past. A school of reef sharks – as well as plenty of invertebrates and sponges – keeps divers company as they descend into the mysterious ocean depths.

Kayaking Glover's Reef Atoll

2 Lying like a string of white-sand pearls, Glover's Reef Atoll (p198) consists of half a dozen small islands surrounded by blue sea as far as the eye can see. Its unique position, atop a submerged mountain ridge on the edge of the continental shelf, makes it an ideal place for sea kayaking, both between the islands and around the shallow central lagoon. Get a kayak with a clear bottom and you're likely to see spotted eagle rays, southern stingrays, turtles and countless tropical fish swimming beneath as you paddle.

MATTEO COLOMBO / GETTY IMAGES ©

HENRY GEORGI / GETTY IMAGES ©

Ambergris Caye

3 Also known as La Isla Bonita, Ambergris Caye (p84) is the ultimate tropical paradise vacation destination (and that's what Madonna thought, too). Spend your days snorkeling the reef, kayaking the lagoon or windsurfing the straits; pamper yourself at a day spa or challenge yourself at a yoga class; ride a bike up the beach or take a nap at the end of your dock. After the sun sets, spend your evenings enjoying the country's most delectable dining and most happening nightlife.

Snorkeling Shark Ray Alley

4 Local fisherfolk used to come to Shark Ray Alley (p10) to clean their catch, and their discards would attract hungry nurse sharks and southern stingrays. As a result, these predators have long become accustomed to boats, which now bring snorkelers rather than fishers. Shark Ray Alley is the top snorkeling destination in Hol Chan Marine Reserve, a protected part of the Belize Barrier Reef that harbors an amazing diversity of colorful coral and other marine life.

Garifuna Drumming

5 Garifuna culture is strong in Southern Belize and its most obvious cultural impression is music and drumming. Dangriga and Punta Gorda both allow opportunities to study drumming and drum-making with Garifuna drum masters, but for something really special head to the Garifuna village of Hopkins to take part in a drumming ceremony at Lebeha (p199; pictured above). For a really swinging time, come on down when the moon is full. Garifuna Settlement Day (November 19) is an event not to be missed.

Caracol

6 Step out of the modern world and into the ancient realm at Belize's largest Maya site, where you'll spend the day wandering through a city that once rivaled Tikal in political influence and, for many, is more impressive today. Standing in the central area of temples, palaces, craft workshops and markets, you'll feel the power and glory of ancient Caracol (p180). At 141ft, Caana (which means Sky Place; pictured top) is still the tallest building in Belize. In addition to being the country's pre-eminent archaeological site, Caracol also teems with jungle wildlife.

Caye Caulker

7 A brisk breeze is almost always blowing (especially between January and June), creating optimal conditions to cruise across the water on sailboat, windsurfer or kiteboard. The world's second-largest barrier reef is just a few miles offshore, beckoning snorkelers and divers to frolic with the fish. The mangroves teem with life, inviting exploration by kayak. All these adventures await, yet the number-one activity on Caye Caulker (p108) is still swinging in a hammock, reading a book and sipping a fresh-squeezed fruit juice. Paradise.

RELIGIOUS IMAGES / UIG / GETTY IMAGES ©

Altun Ha

8 You've drunk the beer, now visit the ruins that inspired the Belikin beer-bottle label. The most accessible of Belize's ancient ruins, Altun Ha (p74) displays 10 different structures dating from the 6th and 7th centuries, including the Temple of the Masonry Altars (pictured above). It was also the site of some of the richest archaeological excavations in Belize, although the artifacts have long since been removed. You'll get your exercise climbing to the tops of the temples to take in the panorama of the surrounding jungle.

Xunantunich

9 Xunantunich (p185) isn't Belize's biggest archaeological site, but it's still one of the most impressive, especially for its remarkable heiro-glyphics. After taking a hand-cranked ferry across the Mopan River, you'll walk through bird- and butterfly-filled jungle, until you reach a complex of temples and plazas that dates back to the early Classic Maya Period. Once there, you can explore a number of structures and plazas, and even climb to the top of 130ft-high El Castillo (pictured top) for a spectacular 360-degree view.

Lamanai

10 Spanning all phases of ancient Maya civilization, the ruins at Lamanai (p135) are known for their stone reliefs, impressive architecture, and their marvelous set-ting that overlooks the New River Lagoon and is surrounded by some of Northern Belize's dens-est jungle. Arrive at this outpost by boat, allowing up-close observation of birds and wildlife along the New River. While on site, hear the roar of the howler monkeys while climbing the steep facade of the High Temple and admiring the deformed face on the Mask Temple (pictured above).

Crooked Tree Wildlife Sanctuary

11 Belize is for the birds. Nowhere is that truer than at Crooked Tree (p71), a fishing and farming village centered on a picturesque lagoon. The wetlands attract hundreds of bird species (276 to be exact), including dozens of migrants who stop on their way north or south. Birdwatching is best during the drier months (February to May), when the lagoon dries up and the birds congregate around the puddles. Expert guides will lead you by boat or foot to spot and identify your feathered friends.

Jungle Hiking

12 If it's somewhere off the beaten path you're after, take a hike in one of Belize's many protected areas, such as Mayflower Bocawina National Park (p195) or Cockscomb Basin Wildlife Sanctuary (p206; pictured bottom). With jungle, mountains, waterfalls, swimming holes and even some small Maya ruins, you'll feel like you've left civilization and the 21st century behind entirely. Off the tourist trail, you'll be sharing the park with countless birds, mammals, reptiles and, no doubt, a resident squad of black howler monkeys.

Deep-Sea Fishing

13 The Northern Cayes are the base for anglers who are drawn to the flats offshore – a prime spot to pull off a 'Grand Slam' (reeling in a permit, tarpon and bonefish in one outing). The remote Turneffe Atoll (p123) is home to a handful of all-inclusive resorts that cater to folks who are focused on the fish and only the fish. Alternatively, Ambergris Caye (p84) and Caye Caulker (p108) are both perfectly situated for fishing-orientated day trips.

Maya Villages

14 To experience Maya life firsthand, trek through the villages of rural Toledo District, where ancient and contemporary Maya culture exists, and rituals and folklore play an important role in everyday life. From the ruins of Lubaantun (p229) to the cultural circuit through Big Falls, San Miguel and San Pedro Columbia, your trek will take you through some of Belize's most beautiful villages and allow you to interact with a people, such as the Mopan Maya, pictured bottom, whose civilization once surpassed Rome in political influence and grandeur. And they make great chocolate!

JANE SWEENEY / GETTY IMAGES ©

WITOLD SKRYPCZAK / GETTY IMAGES ©

Nohoch Che'en Caves

15 Floating through a darkened cave river on an inflated tube is a remarkably calming experience. Delve even further into the bowels of the earth with an experienced guide to discover some remarkable cave systems. At the Nohoch Che'en Caves (p159; pictured above) you'll float through an underground network, experiencing wonders unseen in the world above. For more adventure, there are jungle zip-lining courses and ATV (All Terrain Vehicle) trails nearby.

Placencia

16 It's hardly off the beaten path, but at the end of a long peninsula there's a reason so many feet beat the path to Southern Belize's most popular beachside resort village. Placencia (p208) is just too chilled out to not spend some time kayaking, sailing or just walking barefoot on the beach by day, and drinking rum cocktails by night. As for dining, it has most of Southern Belize's best restaurants.

Hummingbird Highway

17 Arguably Belize's most beautiful stretch of road, the Hummingbird Hwy (p160) offers unparalleled views of the Maya Mountains as it winds through jungles, citrus orchards and tiny villages. The Hummingbird also offers plenty of reasons to stop for a few hours and there are some fine upmarket lodges and budget guesthouses along the way. Explore St Herman's Cave (p160; pictured above), hike the jungle loop trail or have a dip in the crystal-clear Blue Hole.

ALEX ROBINSON / GETTY IMAGES ©

Hopkins

18 Halfway between the hustle of Dangriga and the tourist vibe of Placencia lies slacked-out Hopkins (p199), a low-key Garifuna village where life hasn't changed much in decades. Children walk the town's one street selling their mothers' freshly baked coconut pies and chocolate brownies; local men catch fish by day and play drums at night; and the pace of life is pleasantly slow. The beach is slender, but on a fine day the view out across the Caribbean is sublime.

Community Baboon Sanctuary

19 The 'baboons' at this sanctuary (p70) are not really baboons but black howler monkeys (pictured top right), an endangered species in Central America. The 'sanctuary' is not exactly a protected area, but rather a network of private properties where the howlers live. Thanks to this community-based, grassroots effort, property owners have agreed to preserve their land for the benefit of the resident monkeys. Encompassing about 20 sq miles, guides take tourists to a small area that offers up-close observation of the funny monkeys.

Belize Zoo

20 Even people opposed to the very concept of caged creatures will approve of this humane earthy and educational zoo (p77). As a halfway house and rehabilitation center for injured, orphaned and rescued Belizean jungle animals including jaguars, pictured above, the Belize Zoo is a fabulous and friendly place to get a good look at 125 species of indigenous animals and birds that are difficult to spot in the wild, such as jaguars (pictured above). The zoo hosts myriad educational programs for kids and adults, including a festive birthday party for April the Tapir, the national animal of Belize.

Half Moon Caye Natural Monument

21 Part of the Lighthouse Reef Atoll, Half Moon Caye (p126; pictured below) provides a nesting ground for the rare red-footed booby bird. Thousands of these rare water fowl make their homes in the treetops, alongside the magnificent frigate bird and 98 other species. Dive the Half Moon Caye Wall (or snorkel the surrounding shallows), enjoy a picnic on the beach, then hike across the island and climb the observation platform to get a good look at the boobies.

San Ignacio

22 Western Cayo's main town (p165) is a relaxed and vibrant community from where you can organise any activity in the region. Saturday is the main market day, where locals sell their produce and wares, but on any day of the week you can chill at a traveler cafe on pedestrian Burns Ave, listen to live music at the Bamboo Bar, stroke green iguanas at San Ignacio Resort Hotel or simply plan your next foray to Mountain Pine Ridge, Caracol or Guatemala. Some of the best-value accommodation in Belize is right here.

21

22

Need to Know

For more information, see Survival Guide (p295)

Currency
Belize Dollar (BZ$)

Language
English, Kriol, Garifuna, Spanish

Visas
For most nationalities, visas are issued upon entry for up to 30 days.

Money
ATMs are widely available; credit cards are accepted at most hotels, restaurants and shops.

Mobile Phones
Local SIM cards can be used in most unlocked international cell phones with the notable exception of phones from some operators in the US.

Time
US Central Standard Time (GMT minus six hours)

When to Go

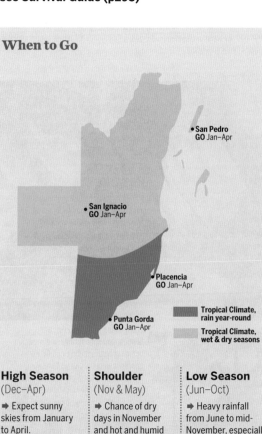

San Pedro
GO Jan–Apr

San Ignacio
GO Jan–Apr

Placencia
GO Jan–Apr

Punta Gorda
GO Jan–Apr

■ Tropical Climate, rain year-round

■ Tropical Climate, wet & dry seasons

High Season
(Dec–Apr)

➡ Expect sunny skies from January to April.

➡ Accommodation prices increase by 30% to 50%.

➡ Extra-high 'peak' prices from mid-December to mid-January; reservations are essential during this period.

Shoulder
(Nov & May)

➡ Chance of dry days in November and hot and humid in May.

➡ Fewer tourists and lower prices.

➡ Most attractions open.

Low Season
(Jun–Oct)

➡ Heavy rainfall from June to mid-November, especially at night.

➡ Hurricanes possible between August and October.

➡ Few tourists; prices for accommodations drop significantly.

Useful Websites

Belizean Journeys
(www.belizeanjourneys.com)
Online magazine covering life
and nature in Belize.

Belize Tourism Board (www.
travelbelize.org) Official tourism
board site.

Belize Forums (www.belize
forum.com/belize) User forum
discussing all topics Belizean.

BelizeNews.com (www.belize
news.com) News and views from
around the country.

Lonely Planet (www.lonely
planet.com/belize) Destination
information, hotel bookings,
traveller forum and more.

Important Numbers

Belize has no regional, area
or city codes, just dial the
seven-digit local number from
wherever you are in the country.

Country code	☑501
Directory assistance	☑113
Emergency	☑90, ☑911
International access code	☑00
Operator assistance	☑115

Exchange Rates

Australia	A$1	BZ$1.38
Canada	C$1	BZ$1.55
Europe	€1	BZ$2.24
Guatemala	Q1	BZ$0.25
Japan	¥100	BZ$1.82
Mexico	M$1	BZ$0.11
NZ	NZ$1	BZ$1.37
UK	UK£1	BZ$2.82
USA	US$1	BZ$2.00

For current exchange rates, see
www.xe.com.

Daily Costs

Budget: less than BZ$150

➡ Camping or dorm bed:
BZ$10–40

➡ Double room in a budget
hotel: BZ$50–100

➡ Street-food stalls or self-
catering: BZ$3–10

➡ One-hour bus ride: BZ$5

Midrange: BZ$150–400

➡ Double room with private
bathroom: BZ$100–200

➡ Dinner and drinks at local
restaurants: BZ$15–35

➡ Adventure and caving
activities: BZ$65–200

➡ Taxis or golf-cart hire:
BZ$20–80

Top end: more than BZ$400

➡ Luxury accommodations
per double: from BZ$300

➡ Fancy restaurants in resort
areas: BZ$30–50

➡ Transportation by rental car or
organized shuttles: BZ$80–100

➡ Shopping, day spas, private
tours: from BZ$100

Opening Hours

Outside of banks, phone
companies and government
offices, you'll generally find most
opening hours to be flexible. Restaurants and bars tend to keep
longer hours during high season,
but will also close early if they
wish (if business is slow etc).

Banks 8am to 3pm Monday to
Thursday and 8am to 4pm or
4:30pm Friday.

Pubs & bars noon to midnight
(or later).

Restaurants & cafes 7am to
9:30am (breakfast), 11:30am to
2pm (lunch) and 6pm to 8pm
(dinner).

Shops 9am to 5pm Monday to
Saturday, some open Sundays.

Arriving in Belize

**Philip Goldson International
Airport** (p305; Belize City)
Many hotels and resorts offer
airport shuttles. Taxis into town
cost BZ$50 for one to two
passengers and BZ$60 for three
to four passengers. No public
buses serve the facility.

Main Bus Terminal (p66;
Belize City) Long-distance
buses from Mexico arrive at
the main bus terminal, a short
distance from downtown Belize
City – although walking is
not recommended. Taxis wait
outside the terminal and charge
BZ$7 to downtown hotels or the
water-taxi terminals.

International Departures Dock
(p107; San Pedro) Boat services
from Mexico arrive at this new
facility in downtown San Pedro.
Collective minivan taxis meet
boats and charge BZ$7 around
town. Rates to hotels outside
the center are negotiable.

For info on **getting
there & around**,
see p305

If You Like...

Sun & Fun

This is the Caribbean, so you'll more than likely spend at least a few days soaking up some rays and dipping your toes in the turquoise blue. Best time: January to April.

Caye Caulker The ultimate chill-out destination, with a laid-back village vibe and easy access to the sea. (p108)

Ambergris Caye If busy San Pedro is too much, head to one of the North Island resorts. (p84)

Placencia Beach-lined peninsula offering ample opportunities for swimming, sunning, snorkeling, scuba diving and offshore island experiences. (p208)

Hopkins Narrow but inviting beaches, village vibe and approximately 20% of the tourist traffic of nearby Placencia. (p199)

Diving & Snorkeling

Life under the sea is dramatic and diverse, from the fantastical coral formations and the kaleidoscopic fish that feed there to the massive and sometimes menacing creatures that lurk in deeper waters.

Glover's Reef On the reef, offering some of the most pristine diving and snorkeling opportunities in Belize. (p198)

Blue Hole Natural Monument Seen from the sky, this national landmark is a perfectly round, perfectly blue bull's eye. (p125)

Turneffe Elbow Attracts huge congregations of cubera snappers, horse eye jacks, spadefish, reef sharks and king mackerel. (p123)

Hol Chan Marine Reserve Shallow waters offer excellent conditions for snorkeling, especially at Shark Ray Alley, but divers will be thrilled by the shipwreck at Amigos Wreck. (p85)

Caves

The erosive action of water on the relatively soft limestone of the Maya Mountains has produced numerous underground rivers and caves. Many of the caves were ritual sites for the ancient Maya, as they were considered to be close to the underworld.

Actun Tunichil Muknal Unforgettable caving experience, where you will see firsthand the evidence of the Maya rituals. (p164)

Nohoch Che'en Caves Branch Archaeological Reserve Combines the mystery of spelunking with river-rafting through an underground network of caves. (p159)

Barton Creek Cave Remote Barton Creek is one of the few caves you can canoe though. (p175)

Wildlife

Wildlife is the star of the show in Belize, thanks to conservation of the forests and reefs, where 25% of the land area is protected. From monkeys to manatees, you can see these creatures in their natural habitat.

Belize Zoo This amazing, privately funded, zoo houses wildlife that have been injured or rescued throughout the country. (p77)

Green Hills Butterfly Ranch An unforgettable experience for animal lovers is meditating among fluttering butterflies and hummingbirds. (p174)

Community Baboon Sanctuary Get up close and personal with black howlers at this community-based, grassroots monkey refuge. (p70)

Swallow Caye Wildlife Sanctuary As many as 30 West Indian manatees inhabit the shallow waters around Swallow Caye. (p108)

Above: Barton Creek Cave (p175)

Right: Chan Chich Lodge (p133)

Birds

Birdwatchers know Belize. For everyone else with a spare pair of binoculars, there are 570 resident and migratory species inhabiting the shores of the rivers and lagoons or deep in the forest. Outstanding.

Crooked Tree Wildlife Sanctuary The lagoon is home to hundreds of bird species, including jabiru storks. (p71)

Red Bank Home to the spectacular scarlet macaw, which feasts on the forest fruits from January to March. (p214)

Río Bravo Conservation & Management Area Spot birds as varied as the collared aricari, oscillated turkey, ruffous hummingbird and turkey vultures. (p139)

Cockscomb Basin Wildlife Sanctuary Jaguars might be hard to spot, but birds are everywhere in this celebrated sanctuary. (p206)

Outdoor Adventure

Come to Belize for action and adventure, to mount seemingly insurmountable temples, to dive to the ocean's darkest depths, and to feel the sticky heat of the jungle and the salty air of the sea.

Deep South Toledo's Deep South features lush jungles, crystal-clear swimming holes, waterfalls and Maya ruins. (p217)

Glover's Reef Islands ideal for hopping. Kayak the limpid waters, admiring the prolific marine life from above. (p198)

Cayo District Around San Ignacio there are opportunities for hiking, horseback riding, caving and Maya ruins. (p151)

Shipstern Conservation Management Area Hiking trails, wildlife spotting and a boat trip on the lagoon make Shipstern an excellent adventure. (p149)

Ecochic Resorts

Ecotourism was practically invented here. Thanks to a progressive populace, Belize offers myriad ways for travelers to tread lightly, from beach resorts powered by solar energy to jungle lodges built from reclaimed hardwoods.

Black Rock Lodge Sweet base for a jungle adventure, surrounded by towering cliffs and protected national park. (p184)

Chan Chich Lodge Chan Chich sits on 200 sq miles of private wildlife preserve on the Guatemala border. (p133)

Turneffe Atoll Resorts on Blackbird Caye are taking steps to preserve the spectacular environment of the atoll. (p124)

Thatch Caye Resort Eco-friendly, rustic-chic and luxurious without being ostentatious, with great beaches, snorkeling and fishing. (p197)

Maya Ruins

For almost 3000 years, the ancient Maya civilization flourished in Belize, building towering temples as tribute to their god-like rulers. The remains of these once-mighty city-states are scattered throughout the country and are prime for exploration.

Xunantunich One of Cayo's prettiest Maya ruins, and definitely among the easiest to get to. (p185)

Caracol Once the most powerful kingdom of the Maya world, Caracol covers a vast, jungle-clad area. (p180)

Lamanai Ruins at Lamanai are among the oldest and the largest Maya sites in the country. (p135)

Lubaantun Among the most complete of Toledo's Maya ruins, Lubaantun is easy to reach. (p229)

Music

A rich diversity is evident in the music of Belize, where you'll hear rhythms and instruments representing Creole and calypso, Maya and Garifuna.

Maroon Creole Drum School Learn traditional drum crafting and playing at Emmeth Young's drum school in Punta Gorda. (p219)

Fido's Among the best places to see live music in San Pedro, Fido's has bands nightly. (p104)

Placencia On weekends the village rocks to the sounds of *punta rock*, reggae and Garifuna drumming. (p208)

Hopkins Garifuna drumming most nights and weekly live music at the excellent Driftwood Beach Bar. (p199)

Month by Month

TOP EVENTS

Fiesta de Carnaval, February

La Ruta Maya Challenge, March

Lobster Season Reopens, June

September Celebrations, September

Garifuna Settlement Day, November

January

Although the dry season hasn't officially started, the holidays bring a huge influx of people and an increase in prices. Visitors might see some rain, but (hopefully) not enough to spoil their good time.

✦ New Year

Burrell Boom hosts a long-standing New Year's Day horse race. Hundreds of spectators cheer on the cyclists who ride from Corozal to Belize City as part of the Krem Annual New Year's Day Classic (www.krembz.com). The biggest NYE party is in San Pedro.

February

The dry season is here, so enjoy sunny skies and warm temperatures day after day. Prices for accommodations remain relatively high.

✈ Birding

Lagoons and rivers begin to dry up and birds become easier to spot, as they congregate around the limited remaining water sources. Migration also significantly increases the number of species you might tick off your list. Prime birding conditions continue through to May.

✦ Fiesta de Carnaval

This festival takes place mainly in San Pedro with costumes, parades, church services, music and dancing.

✕ Closing of the Lobster Season

The lobster's mating and spawning season is from mid-February to mid-June. Belize respectfully gives the crustaceans some privacy, closing the season for trapping lobsters on February 15.

☆ Sidewalk Art Festival

Arts, craft and street music in Placencia. (p211)

March

The dry season rolls on and tourists and residents enjoy perfect blue skies and warm temperatures. Take care to minimize water consumption.

✦ Baron Bliss Day

On March 9 (or the closest Monday), Belize pays tribute to its greatest benefactor. Part of Bliss' legacy is a trust that funds an annual boat race in Belize City, and other towns follow suit by hosting smaller races and regattas.

✈ La Ruta Maya Challenge

Participants from all walks of life join teams to compete in this grueling, four-day canoe race (www.larutamaya.bz). Following the original trade and transport route, the race runs along the Macal and Belize Rivers from San Ignacio to Belize City.

April

The weather is dry and it's beginning to get hot, especially in the southern parts of the country. Expect extra crowds during the weeks before and after Easter.

Holy Week

Various services and processions are held in the week leading up to Easter Sunday. Good Friday and Easter Monday are official state holidays, so most businesses are closed all weekend.

May

Humidity increases and the dry season gradually turns to wet toward the end of May.

Chocolate Festival of Belize

This food and cultural festival in Punta Gorda pays homage to Maya chocolate and music.

June

Dry season becomes rainy season in June. Rivers swell and dirt roads get muddy. Visitors who can tolerate a few raindrops will enjoy the peaceful atmosphere and lower prices.

Lobster Season Reopens

Lobster season reopens on June 15 and the coastal towns and fishing villages celebrate! Fun food festivals take place in Caye Caulker, San Pedro and Placencia, with music, drinking and plenty of seafood. See also www. sanpedrolobsterfest.com and www.placencia.com.

July

The humidity has really kicked in; expect short, sharp heavy showers.

Belize International Film Festival

Screens films from Central America and the Caribbean in Belize City, with additional screenings in Placencia. Traditionally held in July but moved to October for 2016. See www. belizefilmfestival.com.

August

Weather is hot, humid and wet, wet, wet. Belizeans are on the lookout for hurricanes and tourists make themselves scarce.

Costa Maya Festival

People with Maya in their blood or in their souls come from all parts of Central America and Mexico to celebrate Maya coastal culture in San Pedro. See also www.inter nationalcostamayafestival. com.

September

It's the height of hurricane season, but it's also the most festive month in Belize, which celebrates its national holidays with gusto.

September Celebrations

The holidays commence on the Battle of St George's Caye Day on September 10, with ceremonies and celebrations around the country. For the next 10 days, Belize hosts carnival parades and fun competitions. The celebrations culminate with outdoor concerts on September 21, Independence Day.

November

The rain starts to let up. As temperatures drop in the northern hemisphere around Thanksgiving, the trickle of tourists turns into a steady stream.

Garifuna Settlement Day

A celebration of one of the country's richest minority cultures, November 19 commemorates the Garifuna arrival on Belizean soil in 1832. The country gets down with lots of drumming, dancing and drinking, especially in Dangriga, Hopkins and Punta Gorda, where celebrations may last several days.

December

December still brings some rain, but not enough to deter the many travelers who want to spend their holidays in the tropics. Most lodgings are extra expensive in the last two weeks of the month.

Christmas Day

Belizeans celebrate Christmas much like North Americans, decorating their houses with colorful lights weeks ahead. Most people spend Christmas Day sharing meals with family and friends. In some places, festivities continue until January 6, when Garifuna *jonkonu* dancers go from house to house.

Garifuna people celebrating Garifuna Settlement Day, Hopkins (p199)

Itineraries

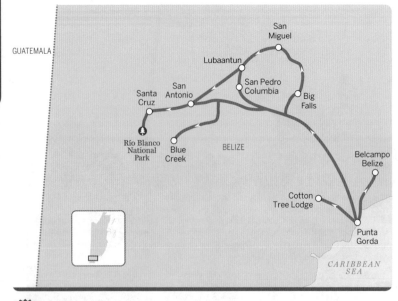

Deep South

Exploring Belize's Deep South can take just a couple of days, but to truly appreciate the village life, allow five days.

Punta Gorda (PG) is a chilled-out, slightly ramshackle coastal town and a natural spot to begin your trek. There are budget digs in PG but if you'd like to experience some luxury, book yourself in at **Cotton Tree Lodge**, **Belcampo Belize** or Lodge at Big Falls within **Big Falls** among the finest ecolodges in Southern Belize.

The true beauty is in exploring the villages, chocolate-making enterprises and cultural tours out of PG. One of the best circuits is from **Big Falls**, then head off the highway to **San Miguel**, where you can sleep cheap, then move on to **San Pedro Columbia** and use it as a base to explore nearby **Lubaantun**. Later, head further still to the small Maya village of **San Antonio**, detouring for a hike and a swim at beautiful **Río Blanco National Park**, or caving at **Blue Creek**.

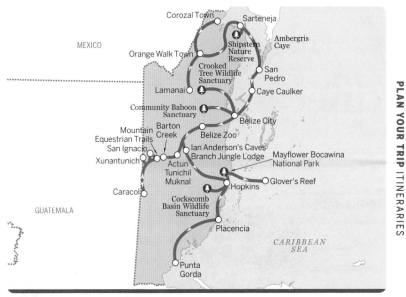

The Whole Enchilada:
Corozal Town to Punta Gorda

4 WEEKS

Belize is small enough that you can see the whole country in a month at express pace. In two months you're practically a resident! This itinerary leads the way, starting in the quaint *mestizo* town of **Corozal Town**, south of the Mexican border. Spend one day in **Orange Walk Town** to cruise the New River and explore the Maya ruins at **Lamanai**, then head east to the fishing village of **Sarteneja** for amazing wildlife watching at **Shipstern Nature Reserve**.

From Sarteneja, catch the fast ferry to **San Pedro**. Stay on either **Ambergris Caye** or **Caye Caulker**, but allow yourself at least four days to chill out in a hammock, kayak out to the reef, frolic with the fish and feast on fresh seafood. When you head back to the mainland, don't bypass the animal-lovers' sights outside **Belize City** in the Belize District, including the **Community Baboon Sanctuary** and the **Belize Zoo**. If you're into birds, spend a night or two around the **Crooked Tree Wildlife Sanctuary**. Further west in Cayo, base yourself in or around **San Ignacio** and take four or five days experiencing regional adventures, whether it be delving deep into the caves at **Actun Tunichil Muknal** or **Barton Creek**, horseback riding at **Mountain Equestrian Trails**, climbing the tall temples at **Caracol** or **Xunantunich**, or all of the above. Backtrack east to the beautiful Hummingbird Hwy, which carries you south across the thickly forested northern foothills of the Maya Mountains. Stop at **Ian Anderson's Caves Branch Jungle Lodge** for some cave exploration, jungle expeditions and abseiling down bottomless sinkholes.

By now you have been away from the Caribbean for way too long, so spend a few days in the coastal village of **Hopkins** to absorb some Garifuna rhythms. From here, you can hike the beautiful jungle trails at **Mayflower Bocawina National Park** or **Cockscomb Basin Wildlife Sanctuary**.

If you're still thirsting for sun and fun, head south to **Placencia** to enjoy lovely sandy beaches, lively bars and lots of water sports, or indulge your tropical-island fantasies at **Glover's Reef**, which has an irresistible low-key vibe and brilliant diving and snorkeling. Finish up in **Punta Gorda**, the southernmost town in Belize from where you can explore the Deep South.

Above: San Pedro
(p84)

Left: Maya site of
Xunantunich (p185)

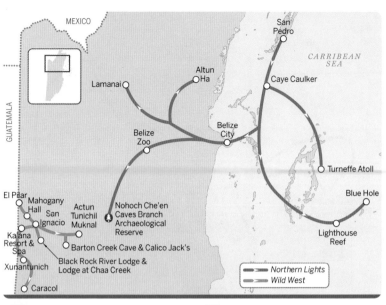

Northern Lights

If you only have a week to spare, make a base on one of the Northern Cayes, where you have access to an impressive array of activities on land and sea.

Choose **Caye Caulker** or **San Pedro**, as they are closest to the mainland. (We prefer Caye Caulker – not only for its easygoing vibe, but also for its easy access to **Belize City**, which is only 45 minutes away by water taxi.) From here, you can take snorkel or dive trips to **Turneffe Atoll** and **Lighthouse Reef**, the latter home to the amazing **Blue Hole**.

You can also use either of these islands as a base for day trips to the mainland. Spend a day in the Belize District to visit **Belize Zoo** or the Maya ruins at **Altun Ha**.

It's also an easy trip to eastern Cayo District, where you can go cave-tubing in the **Nohoch Che'en Caves Branch Archaeological Reserve** or zip-lining through the forest canopy. You can also head north to the Maya ruins at **Lamanai**, enjoying a peaceful boat ride on the New River along the way.

Wild West

On day one head to traveler-oriented **San Ignacio** to get a feel for the town, and visit the Maya site of Cahal Pech and the green iguanas at San Ignacio Resort Hotel. San Ignacio has plenty of good budget hotels and restaurants, so save your money for a night at one of the excellent ecolodges in the region.

Arrange a tour to explore the amazing ritual cave of **Actun Tunichil Muknal**, or the superb Maya ruins at **Caracol**, either of which will take up all of your second day. A third option is canoeing through **Barton Creek Cave** and ziplining at **Calico Jack's**.

On your third day, wake up early and do a half-day trip to either **Xunantunich** or **El Pilar** before checking into one of the better hotels or ecolodges in western Cayo: **Mahogany Hall** is closest to El Pilar, while the fabulous **Ka'ana Resort & Spa** is closer to Xunantunich. Other stand-outs include **Black Rock Lodge** and the **Lodge at Chaa Creek**.

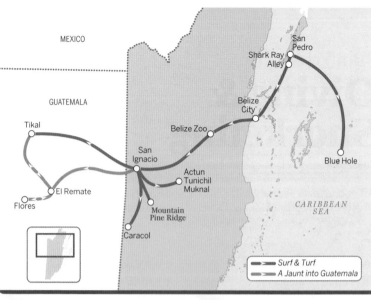

MEXICO

GUATEMALA

Tikal

San Ignacio

El Remate

Flores

Mountain Pine Ridge

Caracol

Actun Tunichil Muknal

Belize Zoo

Belize City

Shark Ray Alley

San Pedro

Blue Hole

CARIBBEAN SEA

Surf & Turf

A Jaunt into Guatemala

2 WEEKS Surf & Turf

This traditional Belize sampler gives you the best of both worlds – a taste of the jungle and a glimpse of the sea – all within your two weeks of vacation time.

Start your trip at holiday central: **San Pedro** on Ambergris Caye. Snorkel or dive among coral gardens and observe the inhabitants of **Shark Ray Alley**. Use San Pedro as your launching pad for dives at **Blue Hole** and other atoll sites.

After a week of sun and fun, make your way to dry land at **Belize City** and head out along the George Price Hwy. Stop on the way to visit the recovering and rescued animals at the **Belize Zoo**.

In Cayo, base yourself at a luxurious jungle lodge or a more affordable hotel in **San Ignacio**. From here, you can explore caves loaded with ancient remains, such as **Actun Tunichil Muknal**; travel by canoe or inner-tube along jungle rivers; dip beneath the waterfalls of the **Mountain Pine Ridge**; or explore Belize's greatest Maya site, **Caracol**. If you have the time and inclination, venture over the border into Guatemala, where you can visit the region's most significant Maya archaeological site at **Tikal**.

5 DAYS A Jaunt into Guatemala

Across the border and within easy reach lie the glory and splendors of the ancient Maya world: scores of ancient ruins surrounded by lush rainforests, and a few really lovely towns thrown in for good measure. Taking it all in would take months, so we suggest a five-day compromise.

Leaving San Ignacio on the morning of the first day, head directly to **El Remate**. The lakefront town makes a lovely base and has accommodations in all budget ranges. Head to **Tikal** early the next morning and spend the day exploring this fascinating ancient Maya city. Having made arrangements to spend the night at one of Tikal's three hotels, you can enjoy the sunset from the top of Temple IV at your leisure. Spend the first half of the third day exploring Tikal further (it's worth it) before heading back to El Remate to relax.

On your remaining days, hang out in **Flores** and soak up the town's island ambience, perhaps taking a half-day trip to one of the parks, villages or smaller ruins that are in the area.

Plan Your Trip
Diving & Snorkeling

Belize is a world-class destination for diving and snorkeling – after all, the world's second-longest barrier reef parallels the country's entire coastline. From North, Central and South Cayes to stunning offshore atolls, whatever your level of underwater experience you'll find a place to explore and indulge in Belize.

Northern Cayes

The two main centers in this northern sector of the barrier reef are Ambergris Caye and Caye Caulker, both of which are a short flight or boat ride from Belize City.

Ambergris Caye is the largest offshore island and the most developed, so it attracts most of the visiting divers. Many choose Ambergris for the variety and quality of its accommodations and nightlife, though it is pretty laid-back compared with other Caribbean destinations. Many of the accommodations along the shoreline have their own dive shops onsite. Ambergris also has the only hyperbaric chamber in Belize.

Caye Caulker, a few miles to the south of Ambergris Caye, is smaller and more laid-back, but also a popular choice. Although prices are generally lower on Caye Caulker than Ambergris, this does not apply to snorkeling and diving, perhaps due to the more limited choices. (There are only three dive shops on Caulker.)

It is also possible to dive the northern reefs and the atolls on a daily basis from a base in Belize City, where there are currently two major dive operators.

The barrier reef is only a few minutes by boat from either island. Diving here is quick and easy, though visibility is not always prime and the water can be somewhat surging. Some divers will put

Planning

When to Go

December to July

What to Read

Reef Creature Identification and Reef Fish: Florida, Caribbean, Bahamas, by Paul Humann and Ned Deloach

www.scubadivingbelize.com

www.ambergriscaye.com/diving

Where to Stay

Glover's Reef (p198), Central Cayes

Caye Caulker (p115), Northern Cayes

Ambergris Caye (p95), Northern Cayes

South Water Caye (p197), Central Cayes

Placencia (p208), Stann Creek

Tobacco Caye (p196), Central Cayes

Best for Snorkeling

Hol Chan Marine Reserve (p85), Northern Cayes

Shark Ray Alley (p87), Northern Cayes

Long Caye (p125), Glover's Reef Atoll

Best for Diving

Blue Hole Natural Monument (p125) & **Half Moon Caye Natural Monument** (p126), Lighthouse Reef

Turneffe Elbow (p123), Turneffe Atoll

Long Caye (p125), Glover's Reef Atoll

up with a longer boat ride to get better visibility and drop-off clarity. Most of the dive shops offer similar deals in terms of the sites they visit and the prices of their packages. All of the dive shops take boats out to Turneffe and Lighthouse Reef Atolls.

Hol Chan Marine Reserve

At the southern end of Ambergris Caye, Hol Chan Marine Reserve (p85) was established more than two decades ago. The profusion of marine life is a testament to the reserve's success. A lot of Hol Chan Marine Reserve is shallow and in many cases the sites are better for snorkeling, but divers have the opportunity to explore a sunken ship at Amigos Wreck. Although the reef is fishier in the south of this section, the north holds more formations, with deep spur-and-groove cuts and interesting terrain.

Central Cayes

Close to the big city but far enough away to be another world apart, the small isles and resorts on the Central Cayes are idyllic and convenient for barrier reef divers. They're normally not as busy as the reefs further north; it is quite possible to go the whole day and not see another dive boat.

If you're staying on the mainland, Hopkins is a good base from which to explore the Central Cayes. A boat ride to the dive sites is about 30 minutes on good days. Beautiful on sunny, calm days with sandy flats, reefs and old staghorns peeking above the surface, the dives are done in the deep passes in the middle of the reef. Nearby are nine passes or cuts; the dive involves a descent to between 35ft and 55ft and then a swim along the deep drop-off looking for denizens.

Alternatively, depart from Dangriga for the resorts on the Central Cayes. Tobacco Caye is a tiny 5-acre island only 10 miles from Dangriga, with the only genuine budget accommodations and a couple of dive outfits. This caye sits right on the edge of the barrier reef, provides excellent snorkeling, and is one of the few beach-diving locations in Belize. South Water Caye is a little larger and offers more expensive accommodations, but also sits on the crest of the barrier reef, offering beach diving and spectacular snorkeling.

South Water Caye Marine Reserve

Encompassing both Tobacco Caye and South Water Caye, this 62-sq-mile marine reserve (http://swcmr.org) protects a unique reef system. A visitor permit (BZ$10) is required but dive and snorkel tour operators will include this.

There is a variety of reef topographies to be explored, ranging from shallow-water coral gardens to spur-and-groove formations, and, of course, the drop-offs from the reef edge. A little further south, the spurs and grooves change to what is known locally as a double-wall reef system. Here there are two separate systems, the first of which slopes sharply seaward from depths of 40ft down to 120ft. This is followed by a wide sand channel with isolated coral outcrops and pillars, and then a second coral reef rising to 60ft before it plunges over the wall beyond scuba-diving depths.

LIVE-ABOARD BOATS

If you are a truly dedicated diver wanting to maximize the number of dives during your trip, then choosing a live-aboard boat is the only way to go. Your 'hotel' moves with you to the dive site, which gives you the opportunity to dive four or five times a day, including night dives. The boats that operate in Belizean waters are comfortable and well equipped, and will even pamper you with hot showers on the dive deck and warm towels to wrap up in. All boats depart from Belize City and operators organize all ground transfers for you. Live-aboard boats in Belize include the *Belize Aggressor III* (www.aggressor.com) and *Sun Dancer II* (www.dancerfleet. com). A seven-night all-inclusive package costs from BZ$5000 per person.

Above: Snorkeling Belize's coral reefs

Right: Belize has the world's second-longest reef

Southern Cayes

The Southern Cayes have developed into a diving hot spot, with excellent sites around the Silk Cayes and Laughing Bird Caye. The base for these dives is the popular resort town of Placencia. The sandy peninsula has some of the best beaches in Belize, while laid-back restaurants and a wide range of accommodations make it an excellent base. Dive shops are scattered around town, as well as being connected with specific resorts.

Gladden Spit & Silk Cayes Marine Reserve

The northernmost point of the southern reef area constitutes the Silk Cayes Marine Reserve. Blue-water action takes the form of whale sharks, bull sharks, hammerheads, dolphins and shoaling fish, all due to the seasonal spawning of cubera snapper. Looking for whale sharks in blue water is hard work, however, and not always fruitful (especially since they are night feeders). But from April to June, the spawning snappers attract the whale sharks and other predators into Gladden Spit, which is only about 12 miles off the barrier reef.

All year-round, dives in the Silk Cayes can produce sightings of spotted eagle rays, turtles, moray eels, southern stingrays, large grouper, barracuda, king mackerel, dolphins and several shark species, as well as many smaller tropical reef fish and invertebrates. Manta rays appear with more frequency during winter months when the water temperatures drop, starting in December and January.

The reef table here is much wider and so it takes a little longer to reach the barrier reef by boat; however, the numerous islands with large expanses of coral reef and connecting channels between them are a bonus, providing a host of alternative dive and snorkeling sites on the way to and from the reef.

Laughing Bird Caye Faro Reef System

Laughing Bird Caye appears to be all that is left of another submerged atoll, its approximately 2.5 acres of land seemingly diminishing with passing storms and wave action. The caye got its name from the many laughing gulls that once nested

---

LEARNING TO DIVE

Have you ever wondered what it would be like to swim along a spur-and-groove reef system, to tunnel through underwater caves or to peer over a drop-off into the blue and watch schools of fish cruise by? Your trip to Belize is a great opportunity to find out. Learning to dive is not as difficult as you might think, and most of the larger dive centers offer 'Discover Scuba' to see if the sport appeals to you.

The Professional Association of Diving Instructors (PADI) system is the most popular certification program worldwide. The first step is the basic Open Water Diver qualification, which usually requires three days of instruction. It is possible to complete the full three-day program while you are in Belize, or you might undertake your basic theory training close to home and complete your dives in Belize under the PADI referral system. Courses include equipment. A Discover Scuba course costs around BZ$350 with two dives, and a three-day PADI Open Water certification course is BZ$900.

Belize's best spots for novice divers include the following:

➡ Mexico Rocks, off Ambergris Caye

➡ Hol Chan Cut, south of Ambergris Caye

➡ Half Moon Caye Wall, in Lighthouse Reef

➡ Faegon's Point and Tobacco Cut, near Tobacco Caye

➡ Long Caye Lagoon and Long Caye Cut, Glover's Reef

➡ any site near Placencia

➡ Silk Cayes or Mosquito Caye South, near Placencia

RESPONSIBLE DIVING

Please consider the following tips when diving and help to preserve the ecology and beauty of reefs:

➡ Never use anchors on the reef, and take care not to ground boats on coral.

➡ Avoid touching or standing on living marine organisms or dragging equipment across the reef. Polyps can be damaged by even the gentlest contact. If you must hold on to the reef, only touch exposed rock or dead coral.

➡ Be conscious of your fins. Even without contact, the surge from fin strokes near the reef can damage delicate organisms. Take care not to kick up clouds of sand, which can smother organisms.

➡ Practice and maintain proper buoyancy control. Major damage can be done by divers descending too fast and colliding with the reef.

➡ Take great care in underwater caves. Spend as little time within them as possible as your air bubbles may be caught within the roof and thereby leave organisms high and dry. Take turns to inspect the interior of a small cave.

➡ Resist the temptation to collect or buy coral or shells, or to loot marine archaeological sites (mainly shipwrecks).

➡ Ensure that you take home all your rubbish and any litter you may find as well. Plastics in particular are a serious threat to marine life.

➡ Do not feed fish.

➡ Minimize your disturbance of marine animals. *Never* ride on the backs of turtles.

here, but most of their nesting areas have since been swallowed by the rising sea. Pelicans and osprey still use the island as nesting grounds, as do sea turtles. Laughing Bird Caye is one of Belize's national parks and a part of the Belize Barrier Reef Reserve System World Heritage site, which includes the island and surrounding reefs.

Within the faro is a system of patch reefs and coral ridges boasting luxuriant hard-coral growth and a variety of sponges and soft coral. The tremendous diversity of fish and invertebrate life in the inshore waters around the island make them ideal for both snorkeling and diving. There are several dive sites at the north and south of the island, all with basically the same marine life and terrain, although in the north it is possible to go a bit deeper.

Offshore Atolls

There are only four atolls in the Caribbean and three of them are right here off the coast of Belize. All three – Turneffe Atoll, Lighthouse Reef and Glover's Reef – lie offshore from the barrier reef, rising from

great depths to just a few feet above sea level. You can dive them on day trips from the main islands, choose one of the atoll-based resorts or take a live-aboard boat that concentrates on diving the atolls.

Turneffe Atoll

Turneffe Atoll is the largest of the offshore trio and comprises a series of islands that runs north–south. Here you will find an area dominated purely by mangrove islands, where juveniles of every marine species are protected until they make their way into the wider waters. Sand flats, shallow gardens and life-filled walls are all highlights of Turneffe dives.

The Elbow is the most beloved Turneffe dive site, with its enormous schools of pelagic fish and pods of dolphins. Visibility varies widely depending mostly on the wind direction. A lot of wave action can stir things up in the mangroves, carrying nutrients into the water and reducing visibility. But more often, the deep water around the atolls guarantees excellent visibility and some of the most thrilling wall-diving you'll find anywhere.

The northwest site moorings such as Sandy Slope and Amber Head normally sit in 35ft to 40ft of water and the reef

PNIESSEN / GETTY IMAGES ©

Top: Butterfly fish on Lighthouse Reef (p124)

Left: Loggerhead sea turtle (p286)

becomes a spur-and-groove system that leads to a vertical wall. This drops to a sandy shelf around 100ft to 120ft at most sites, then falls off again past sport-diving limits. The northwest side is protected from the occasional strong eastern and southeastern winds that sometimes blow in.

When the wind shifts to the north-northwest, blowing down from the US Gulf, conditions are better to dive on the east side, at sites such as Grand Bogue II and Front Porch. This reeftop and wall starts a bit deeper, in the 40ft to 60ft range, and is known for being less of a slope and quite sheer in some spots. The reeftop also has interesting swim-throughs and some tight spurs and grooves.

Being the closest atoll to the coast, Turneffe is a quick trip from Ambergris Caye and Caye Caulker, although there are also resorts on Blackbird Caye (part of Turneffe Atoll).

Lighthouse Reef

At about 50 miles offshore, Lighthouse Reef is the atoll that lies furthest to the east. Lighthouse Reef is probably the best-known atoll in Belize and it is certainly the most popular, due to the Blue Hole. While this icon of Belize diving makes the atoll a major attraction, it is really the stunning walls, many swim-throughs and superb blue water that make it a favorite with both longtime, experienced Belize divers and complete novices.

Lighthouse Reef is home to Half Moon Caye Natural Monument (p126), a national park managed by the Belize Audubon Society, where a colony of rare red-footed boobies can be observed up close. There are a few fantastic dive sites nearby, such as Aquarium and Painted Wall. Other sites in the vicinity include the coral-covered Long Caye Wall.

Dive boats go out to Lighthouse Reef from both Ambergris and Caye Caulker, but the easiest way to see these sites is via a live-aboard boat. The commute from site to site is minimal, and divers can take advantage of early-morning dives and fascinating night dives. Alternatively, there are a few small lodges on Long Caye, while camping is allowed on Half Moon Caye.

Glover's Reef

In southern Belize, divers will find the third of the Belizean atolls. Of the three, Glover's Reef sees the least amount of human contact and remains largely unexplored. Glover's Reef Atoll was named after the 17th-century pirate John Glover, who used the remote islands as a base for raids against treasure-laden Spanish galleons heading to and from the Bay Islands of Honduras.

First recognized as a bird sanctuary in 1954, it has long been atop the conservation list, getting various conservation designations in 1978 before finally being declared a complete marine reserve in 1993, then a Unesco World Heritage site in 1996. There is a marine research station on Middle Caye and the remains of an ancient Maya settlement are being studied on Long Caye.

Located about an hour's boat ride from the mainland, Glover's Reef rises from abyssal depths of well over 2000ft; indeed, a dive site located midway between Long Caye and Middle Caye is known as The Abyss. Oval in shape, the reef is comprised of more than 700 patch reefs within a 100-sq-mile lagoon. Just to the south is one of the Caribbean's deepest valleys, where depths reach 10,000ft.

There are several rustic outpost resorts here for divers and fishers, each occupying its own island and offering an eco-friendly existence. Otherwise, there is day-boat diving from Hopkins and Placencia, and live-aboard boats occasionally cruise this far south.

The chance of seeing dolphins, mantas and whale sharks keep adventurous divers coming back for more. The spectacular walls and hard-coral formations are just a few minutes from the islands that fringe the eastern side of the atoll. If you get the chance, dive the west side of the atoll as well to explore some wonderful swim-throughs and caves.

Plan Your Trip
Belize Outdoors

Forget museums and galleries – Belize is all about the great outdoors. Despite its small land area, an extraordinary array of national parks and wildlife and marine reserves provides an incredible stage for the adventure traveler. Saltwater activities abound along the nation's 240 miles of coastline, while inland the cool waters of Belize's network of rivers enable routes for canoeing and river-tubing. Lush mountains and dense forests provide an exotic setting for jungle treks and wildlife-viewing excursions.

Planning

When to Go

Fishing May to July (also year-round)

Kayaking December to May

Sailing & Windsurfing February to April

Caving January to April

Hiking & Horseback Riding January to May

Resources

Destinations Belize (www.destinationsbelize.com) is a Placencia-based travel agency with useful information on fishing in Belize, including fish guides, tide charts and fishing location descriptions.

Cruising Guide to Belize and Mexico's Caribbean Coast, by Freya Rauscher, provides comprehensive information for anyone navigating these complicated waters.

Best for...

Fishing Ambergris Caye (p84)

Kayaking Glover's Reef (p198)

Sailing Placencia (p208)

Windsurfing Caye Caulker (p108)

Caving Actun Tunichil Muknal (p164)

Hiking Cockscomb Basin Wildlife Sanctuary (p206), Shipstern Nature Reserve (p149)

Horseback Riding Mountain Equestrian Trails, Cayo (p176)

Hiking

In Belize, hiking usually means guided walks in search of birdlife, as well as other flora and fauna. Many lodges have access to trails on their own or nearby properties that you can walk by yourself, but more often lodge walks are with a guide who will show you the animals and plants along the way. Several places offer night walks. Lodges with access to hiking trails include the following:

Chan Chich Lodge (p133) Chan Chich is set on 130,000 acres of protected land and the lodge maintains 9 miles of trails for birding and wildlife-watching, with or without a guide.

Macaw Bank Jungle Lodge (p178) Located on 50 beautiful acres in the foothills of the Maya Mountains, Macaw Bank is ripe for exploration, and includes a trail along the eponymous river.

Black Rock Lodge (p184) Trails departing from the lodge have enticing names like Mountain Summit, Vaca Falls and Vista Loop, promising challenging climbs, waterfalls and wonderful views.

Blancaneaux Lodge (p179) Guided hikes include an early-morning bird walk and a late-night 'jaguar quest,' as well as an all-day jungle trek and a special orchid-hunting walk.

Lodge at Chaa Creek (p184) The 365-acre nature reserve here features the Macal River and a Rainforest Medicine Trail.

Many of the nature preserves and national parks also have well-developed and well-maintained jungle trail networks that you can walk with or without guides:

Cockscomb Basin Wildlife Sanctuary (p206) The well-marked hiking trails are excellent for birding and wildlife-watching, though you'll be very lucky to spot a jaguar.

Mayflower Bocawina National Park (p195) It's only 11 sq miles, but it contains about 7 miles of hiking trails (including the access road) to jungle, mountains, waterfalls and Maya ruins.

Shipstern Nature Reserve (p149) There is a short nature trail that circles the visitors center, but a real appreciation of Shipstern requires taking a longer guided hike to Xo-Pol or along Thompson Trail.

Río Bravo Conservation & Management Area (p139) The country's largest protected area has a network of hiking trails and ranger roads; walks depart from both of the field stations.

Río Blanco National Park (p231) In the Deep South, this 105-acre preserve has marked nature trails and a spectacular waterfall.

Caving

The karstic geology of parts of western Belize has produced many extensive and intricate cave systems, which are fascinating, challenging and awesome to investigate. To the ancient Maya, caves were entrances to Xibalba, the underworld and residence of important gods. Many Belizean caves today still contain relics of Maya ceremonies, offerings or sacrifices, and this archaeological element makes cave exploration doubly intriguing. One of the few caves in the country that you can enter without a guide is St Herman's Cave (p160), but even there you are required to take a guide if you want to go more than 300yd into the cave.

The most thrilling caves in the west of the country include Actun Tunichil Muknal (p164), with its evidence of human sacrifice; Barton Creek Cave (p175), which you explore by canoe; Che Chem Ha (p187), with its vast array of ancient pottery; and the caves in the Nohoch Che'en Caves Branch Archaeological Reserve (p159).

Horseback Riding

Belize has an active equestrian community. A growing number of lodges offer rides to their guests and – in some cases – nonguests.

Backpackers' Paradise (p150) Backpackers has some of the cheapest horseback riding in the country; it's also one of the few places that will let you ride without a guide (as long as you know how!).

Banana Bank Lodge (p159) Near Belmopan, Banana Bank is a highly recommended lodge with a well-tended stable of 100-plus horses, where you can enjoy anything from a two-hour ride to a multiday riding package.

Cotton Tree Lodge (p226) In the Deep South near Punta Gorda, Cotton Tree offers horseback-riding trips for guests and nonguests.

duPlooy's Jungle Lodge (p185) Offers all levels of horseback riding, ranging from a short one-hour excursion to the Belize Botanic Gardens, to a longer journey to Cristo Rey Falls (with river crossings).

Hanna's Stables (p184) Long-running Hannah's offers horseback riding trips from a ride around San Lorenzo farm to the popular half-day tour to Xunantunich (adult/child BZ$144/96).

CAREFUL CAVING

➡ Remember that caves and their contents are extremely fragile. Don't disturb artifacts or cave formations, and try to avoid tours with large groups of people.

➡ For your own well-being, check the physical demands of a cave trip beforehand.

➡ Remember that some caves are subject to flash floods during rainy periods.

➡ An extra flashlight and a spare set of batteries are never a bad idea.

➡ If you have claustrophobic tendencies or are terrified of the dark (or bats), it's no shame to admit that caves are not for everyone!

Above: Horseback riding, Stann Creek District (p190)

Left: St Herman's Cave, Blue Hole National Park (p160)

Outback Trails (p200) This independent ranch near Hopkins offers morning and afternoon trail rides for all levels.

Mountain Equestrian Trails (p176) This rustic resort offers individual rides and riding-based holidays that combine lowland jungles and Mountain Pine Ridge.

Kayaking

The translucent waters of the Caribbean are as inviting for kayakers as they are for divers and snorkelers. It's amazing how much underwater life is visible from above the surface, and you can enjoy snorkeling and birdwatching as you go.

If you fancy some kayaking, consider staying at one of the resorts or hotels on the Placencia peninsula or Ambergris Caye, many of which provide free kayaks for guests. At San Pedro, Caye Caulker, Hopkins, Placencia village and Punta Gorda, you can rent a kayak for anywhere between BZ$30 and BZ$60 per day. Glover's Atoll Resort (p198) rents out single/double touring kayaks by the week for BZ$290/450.

A number of North America- and Belize-based firms offer recommended kayaking holidays:

➡ **Belize Kayak Rentals** (p192) If you want to go it alone on your kayaking expedition, this branch of Island Expeditions rents out kayaks from its base camp in Dangriga. Also offers weekly packages, which include a boat charter out to the cays.

➡ **Island Expeditions** (p192) This ecologically minded Canadian company takes tours departing from Dangriga or Belize City, including weeklong kayaking expeditions and inland trips, which include hiking in the jungle or visiting Maya ruins.

➡ **SeaKunga** (p208) Offers a variety of excellent kayaking tours, including both sea kayaking and river kayaking.

➡ **Slickrock Adventures** (p198) These top-class water-sports holidays are based on Long Caye and Glover's Reef, and combine sea kayaking, surf kayaking, windsurfing, snorkeling and diving. Accommodations are in stilt cabanas.

Canoeing

Canoes are more common than kayaks on inland rivers, especially the Mopan and Macal Rivers near San Ignacio. Both have some rapids, so be sure to choose a stretch of river that's right for your level. Many lodge accommodations in the area rent out canoes, and tour outfits in San Ignacio will also take you out on guided trips.

One of the most unusual canoe trips is the underground river through Barton Creek Cave (p175). Another nice place to use a canoe is the bird paradise of Crooked Tree Lagoon (p71).

River-tubing

River-tubing, where you float down the river in an inflated rubber ring, is a popular pastime in Belize. Depending on the current, it's more relaxing than canoeing or kayaking – naturally you only float downstream and the only technique you need to know is how to avoid getting beached, eddied or snagged on rocks while continuing to face the right direction.

The Mopan River near San Ignacio is a popular spot for river-tubing, as is the Río Grande at Big Falls in Toledo District. Most lodges offer tubes and transportation for their guests, or you can rent tubes at the river's edge and go it alone.

The best of all Belizean tubing adventures is the float in and out of a sequence of caves on the Caves Branch River inside the Nohoch Che'en Caves Branch Archaeological Reserve (p159). People come on day trips from all over Belize for this. Book a tour or just show up and hire a guide at the entrance.

Fishing

This angler's paradise is home to 160 miles of barrier reef, hundreds of square miles of flats, and dozens of jungle-lined rivers and lagoons – all of which teem with a great variety of fish. The best months are May through July, with their hot sunny weather, though every species has its ideal time and place. Spin fishing,

LA RUTA MAYA

One morning in early March the waters of the Macal River beneath San Ignacio's Hawkesworth Bridge are the gathering place for a colorful flotilla of three-person canoes. They are assembled for the start of La Ruta Maya Belize River Challenge, a grueling four-day race down the Belize River to Belize City, where they arrive on Baron Bliss Day, a national holiday in memory of a great Belizean benefactor. From relatively humble beginnings in 1998, the race has grown into Central America's biggest canoe event, attracting international and Belizean teams.

Even though it's all downstream, this is no gentle paddle. The fastest teams cover the river's 170 or so winding miles from San Ignacio to Belize City in around 19 hours, while the slowest take around 36 hours. The race is divided into four one-day stages: Hawkesworth Bridge to Banana Bank Lodge near Belmopan (around 50 miles); Banana Bank to Bermudian Landing (60 miles including Big Falls Rapids); Bermudian Landing to Burrell Boom (35 miles); and Burrell Boom to Belcan Bridge, Belize City (25 miles).

In addition to being Belize's largest competitive sporting event, La Ruta Maya is an impressive conservation effort, as all proceeds are donated to local environmental efforts to revitalize and sustain Belizean waterways. Check out www.larutamaya.bz.

fly-fishing and trolling can all be enjoyed year-round.

Tarpon, snook and jacks inhabit the estuaries, inlets and river mouths, while bonefish, permit and barracuda are found out in the lagoons and flats. The coral reefs support grouper, snapper and jacks, and the deeper waters beyond are home to sailfish, marlin, pompano, tuna and bonito. The flats off the cays and mainland raise realistic hopes of the angler's 'Grand Slam': permit, tarpon and bonefish all in one day. Catch-and-release is the norm for these fish and for most snook. Check with your guide or hotel about the regulations for your area and season.

The most popular fishing bases are in the Northern Cayes, especially San Pedro and Caye Caulker, but there are also fishing outfits in Sarteneja and Belize City.

For tarpon and bonefish, Belize's southern waters, from Placencia to Punta Gorda, are gaining in popularity. It's easy to charter a boat in places such as Glover's Reef, Hopkins, Placencia and Punta Gorda.

River fishing for big tarpon, snook, cubera snapper and 35lb to 100lb goliath grouper is also possible year-round. The Sibun and Belize Rivers and Black Creek are the most frequently fished rivers, but the Deep, Monkey, Temash and Sarstoon Rivers in the south are good, too.

Lodges and guides may have equipment to rent but it's best to bring your own tackle. Fishing charters start from around BZ$800 a day.

Sailing

A day's sailing on crystal-clear Caribbean waters, with a spot of snorkeling or wildlife-watching topped with an island beach BBQ, is a near-perfect way to spend a day. Tours depart from San Pedro, Caye Caulker or Placencia.

Some of these companies offer multiday sailing and camping trips, as well as popular boozy sunset and moonlight cruises. Raggamuffin Tours (p114) and Blackhawk Sailing Tours (p113) both do relatively economical island-hopping sails to Turneffe Atoll, Lighthouse Reef and Placencia.

In San Pedro, Belize Sailing Center (p90) offers sailing lessons and rents boats. It also allows you to rent small craft by the hour or longer for light sailing on your own.

On longer sailing trips you can reach not only Belize's hundreds of islands but also the attractive Guatemalan ports of Lívingston and Río Dulce, the Honduras' Bay Islands and much of the rest of the eastern Caribbean. Several companies offer charters out of Hopkins, Placencia and San Pedro:

Kayaking, South Water Caye (p197)

Under the Sun (p200) The Lodge Hopper's Special is an outstanding eight days of Caribbean cruising on an 18ft Hobie Cat, with plenty of stops for snorkeling, fishing, kayaking and hammocking.

TMM Yacht Charters (p91) Based in San Pedro, TMM has a fleet of three catamarans; custom itineraries include all of the islands and atolls.

Moorings (p210) Luxury catamaran offering customized bareboat (self-charter) sailing from Placencia. Or you can hire a skipper. It's based at Laru Beya marina, 4 miles north of Placencia.

Happy Go Luckie Tours (p200) This Hopkins-based outift offers custom half- and full-day boat charters for up to five people, including snorkeling, fishing and island-hopping.

Stand-up Paddleboarding

Stand-up paddleboarding is gaining popularity, not only in the calm Caribbean Sea but along rivers that drain into it. San Pedro, Caye Caulker and Hopkins all have SUP operators who run tours and rent out boards. The latter does tours down the Sittee River and night tours to see the bizarre bioluminescence.

Windsurfing & Kitesurfing

With a light-to-medium warm easterly breeze blowing much of the time and the barrier reef offshore to calm the waters, conditions on Caye Caulker and Ambergris Caye are ideal for windsurfing. Regulars here boast occasional runs of 10 miles. Beware the boat traffic though, especially at San Pedro. Mellower beaches can be found in Hopkins, home to a small but dedicated group of windsurfers. Winds are biggest (typically 10 to 17 knots) from February through April.

Kitesurfers can do introductory courses on Ambergris Caye or Caye Caulker. If you are a dedicated kitesurfer, you can rent gear from the same operators and head out on your own adventure – there's even a rescue boat if you go too far!

Plan Your Trip
Travel with Children

Belize has some special ingredients for a family holiday. It's both affordable and safe, especially compared to other Caribbean destinations, and it's small and easy to navigate. Belizeans are famously friendly, and families are no exception to this rule. Indeed, kids often break down barriers between tourists and residents, sometimes opening doors to local hospitality.

Best Regions for Kids

Belize District

Many of the Belize District activities and attractions are designed with the cruise-ship passenger in mind. Turns out that cruisers and kids have some of the same criteria: fun stuff that's easy to reach and easy to enjoy in a limited time frame.

Northern Cayes

The boat ride itself is a sort of adventure. Once you reach these paradisiacal islands, the adventure continues with swimming, snorkeling, sailing, kayaking and more traditional beach fare.

Cayo District

Older kids especially will enjoy the wild west and all of its jungle activities.

Belize for Kids

Attractions in Belize – sea life, exploring caves, climbing ruins, watching for birds, wildlife and bugs – will delight kids as much as grown-ups. Most tours and activities can easily accommodate children and teenagers, although they are generally not appropriate for toddlers and babies. With these wee ones, activities might be limited to playing on the beach, swimming in the sea and swinging in the hammock. That's not the worst vacation either.

Most towns and tourist destinations have parks and public beaches where your little ones can frolic with the locals. If your child speaks English, there'll be no language barrier to mixing with local kids.

Be aware that your children may experience a touch of culture shock, especially at the visible poverty.

Children's Highlights

Belize has begun to attract plenty of families for an exciting and exotic adventure vacation.

Action & Adventure

➡ **Cayo District** As long as your kids are not afraid of the dark, they will be thrilled by cave-tubing at Nohoch Che'en Caves Branch Archaeological Reserve (p159) or canoeing into Barton Creek Cave (p175).

➡ **Maya ruins** All of the Maya ruins offer a chance for kids to run, climb and explore.

➡ **Cayo District** Many lodges offer jungle horseback riding, but the best are Banana Bank Lodge (p159) and Mountain Equestrian Lodge (p176).

➡ **Stann Creek** Ride Belize's longest zip-line across the jungle canopy at Mayflower Bocawina National Park (p195).

➡ **Belize District** Besides hiking, biking, kayaking and horseback riding, Bacab Eco Park (p68) also has an amazing swimming pool.

Animal Encounters

➡ **Ambergris Caye** Kids get a kick out of fish. Take them snorkeling at Hol Chan Marine Reserve (p85) near Ambergris Caye.

➡ **Belize District** Sightings (and hearings) of the black howler monkey are practically guaranteed at the Community Baboon Sanctuary (p70).

➡ **Belize District** Children love to get up-close-and-personal with the animals at the Belize Zoo (p77). Even teens are keen on the night safari.

➡ **San Ignacio** Kids come face to face with some scaly monsters at the Green Iguana Exhibit (p167) at the San Ignacio Resort Hotel.

➡ **San Ignacio** Everyone is delighted by the flutter magic at Green Hills Butterfly Ranch (p174).

Beach Retreats

➡ **Around Placencia** For traditional sun-and-sand activities including sandcastle-building, kite-flying and wave-wading, beaches are the best at Hopkins (p199) or Placencia (p208).

➡ **Stann Creek** Snorkeling and kayaking are on your doorstep at family-friendly Thatch Caye (p197).

➡ **Ambergris Caye** Children's yoga classes are just the beginning of the fun at Ak'bol Yoga Retreat (p99).

➡ **Ambergris Caye** The giant waterslide into the sea, floating trampoline and sailing classes are sure to keep little ones entertained at Caribbean Villas (p97).

Jungle Lodges

➡ **Hummingbird Hwy** Many exciting land adventures can be delivered in one handy place at Ian Anderson's Caves Branch Jungle Lodge (p161).

➡ **Bullet Tree Falls** Your family can sleep in a tree house at Parrot Nest Jungle Lodge (p182).

➡ **Cayo District** Trek Stop (p186) is an affordable ecolodge with loads of kid-friendly fun.

➡ **Punta Gorda** Explorers will get lost and found again in the jungle maze at Hickatee Cottages (p223).

➡ **Toledo District** The cool cabins at Cotton Tree Lodge (p226) are connected by a jungle boardwalk.

Rainy Day Destinations

➡ **Belize District** Life-size replicas of Garifuna homesteads and logging camp scenes bring history to life at Old Belize (p75) outside of Belize City.

➡ **Cayo District** Learn about the life cycle of the butterfly and play disc golf at Tropical Wings Nature Center (p186).

➡ **Toledo District** At Ixcacao Maya Belizean Chocolate (p226) kids can learn how to make chocolate with plenty of tasting throughout the process

Planning

Successful travel with children requires some forethought.

Before You Go

Make sure your children are up-to-date on all their routine vaccinations like chicken pox, tetanus and measles, in addition to any special vaccinations recommended for Belize.

When to Go

Kids are less likely to tolerate the tropical showers that occur often during the rainy season. Considering that Belize is an outdoor-activity sort of place, you're better off taking your children during the drier months (December to May).

Above: Water-based fun for kids of all ages

Left: Protected green iguanas

DON'T LEAVE HOME WITHOUT

➡ Child-safe sun block

➡ Child-safe insect repellent

➡ Children's painkillers

➡ Swim diapers

Accommodations

➡ Most hotels, lodges and resorts welcome children – some with special activities and even child care. Many places allow children (usually under the age of 12) to stay for free or at a reduced rate. The icon 🏠 indicates accommodations that are family friendly.

➡ Look for suites, cabins and condos that have the possibility of self-catering (eg in-room kitchenette). Eating at 'home' is an easy way to save money on meals, to make sure everybody gets to eat what they want, and to avoid waiting for tables and the other hassles of dining out with children.

➡ Inquire in advance about the availability of high chairs and cribs at your accommodations. Some resorts and restaurants will be able to provide these upon request but it's worth finding out for certain so you can make alternative arrangements if necessary.

What to Pack

In the towns and tourist destinations, grocery stores are stocked with basic necessities, but you are not guaranteed to find the exact brand your child is accustomed to, so make sure you bring enough supplies. Other more specialized children's items might be difficult to find.

Transportation

If you do not intend to do much traveling around the interior, consider going local. Public intercity transport is usually on old American school buses that have retired to Belize, so your kids will probably be familiar and comfortable (as long as the journey is not too long). Most car-rental companies can provide child seats – usually free of charge – but it's advisable to inquire when you make your reservation. Around the cays, most transportation is by boat, which is a fun activity in itself.

Regions at a Glance

Belize's 9000 sq miles are crammed with diversity, most evident in the geographical contrast between the Caribbean Sea and interior jungle regions. The Northern Cayes and the coastal destinations in Southern Belize are prime destinations for diving, snorkeling and other water sports (not to mention hammock swinging and drinking rum cocktails); the dense forests of Cayo and Belize Districts and inland parts of Northern and Southern Belize are better for birding, wildlife-watching, caving, zip-lining and other jungle adventures.

Ethno-cultural differences are also apparent between regions. The *mestizo* influence is greatest in Northern Belize, while the Maya and Garifuna cultures thrive in Southern Belize. Creole culture is most vibrant in Belize District.

Belize District

Birdwatching
Wildlife
Maya Ruins

Feathered Friends

Crooked Tree Wildlife Sanctuary is undoubtedly the country's top destination for birds and for people who like to watch birds. The lagoon and its environs are home to some 276 species; don't forget your binoculars.

Furry Friends

'Friends' is the operative word here, since the wildlife is not quite as 'wild' as in other parts of the country. Nonetheless, the Belize Zoo is a fabulous place to meet and greet the native species. Sightings are guaranteed!

Tall Temples

Altun Ha is significantly smaller than some of the country's other Maya sites, but it's still an impressive exhibit of ancient craftsmanship and labor. It's also well maintained and easy to access as a day trip from Belize City or the Northern Cayes.

p52

Northern Cayes

Activities
Food
Beaches

Under the Sea

Whether you're a certified diver or a novice snorkeler, the number-one reason to come to the Northern Cayes is to frolic with the fish and admire the colorful coral. This is world-class diving and snorkeling, accessible from any of the northern cays or outer atolls.

Fruits of the Sea

The proliferation of fancy resorts and hotels has at least one positive consequence: amazing food. Thanks to fresh seafood and talented chefs, Ambergris boasts the country's best (and most expensive) eating.

Lounging by the Sea

OK, we admit it: the cays do not have super-fine beaches. The coastline is dominated by mangroves and sea grass, instead of vast stretches of sand. But that doesn't mean that it's not spectacularly beautiful, with picturesque docks providing plenty of places for swimming, sunbathing and hammock swinging.

p82

Northern Belize

Maya Ruins
Wildlife
Food

New River & Old Ruins

The beauty of Lamanai is not only that it's a vast, exquisite archaeological site (the country's second largest), but also that it's surrounded by lush rainforest and accessible primarily by boat. The jungle river cruise combined with the exploration of the ruins makes this one of the most popular and rewarding ways to spend a day in Belize.

Where the Wild Things Are

It's a little-known fact that the wild things are actually in Northern Belize. The remote corners of Corozal and Orange Walk are home to two of the country's most pristine and best-protected nature preserves: Río Bravo Conservation & Management Area and Shipstern Nature Reserve.

Hot & Spicy

We can thank the *mestizo* and Mexican population for spicing up the cuisine in Northern Belize.

p127

Cayo District

Ecolodges
Maya Ruins
Activities

Ecochic

When it comes to natural attractions, Cayo has everything (except the beaches!). The district's ecolodges are among the best in the country, taking full advantage of the region's natural splendors. From remote Black Rock Lodge to the exquisite Blancaneaux Lodge, you'll surely find a perfect setting for your jungle adventure.

Ancient Cities

For almost 3000 years, the ancient Maya civilization flourished in Belize, building towering temples as tributes to their godlike rulers. The remains of these once-mighty city-states are scattered throughout the country, with the most magnificent ones, including Caracol and Xanantunich, in Cayo.

Jungle Adventure

Spelunking, cave-tubing, zip-lining, horseback riding, hiking, river kayaking, birdwatching and more make Cayo an adventurer's paradise. You'll get tired, wet and dirty, but you'll never get bored.

p151

Southern Belize

Beaches
Wildlife
Food

Sun & Sand

Mainland Hopkins and Placencia both have barefoot-perfect beaches, but head out to any of Southern Belize's cays, where you can spend your days beachcombing, snorkeling, kayaking, fishing and, of course, lazing in a beachfront hammock.

Wild & Wonderful

Southern Belize is home to some of the country's finest nature reserves, including Cockscomb Basin Wildlife Sanctuary and Mayflower Bocawina National Park. Your chances of spotting stunning birds, reptiles and small mammals are very high, and you're almost guaranteed to hear the cacophony of howler monkeys.

Sweet & Spicy

Southern Belize is a great place to dine on traditional Garifuna and Maya dishes, not to mention amazing fresh seafood. Don't miss the chance to take a sampling tour of iconic Marie Sharp's (hot sauce) Factory.

p188

Tikal & Flores, Guatemala

Maya Ruins
Jungles
Activities

Archaeological Bliss

The spectacular ruins of ancient Tikal and Yaxhá are the reason most visitors come to the Peten region, but those with a serious interest in the Maya will want to explore further, visiting the many smaller (and not so small) sites that dot the landscape.

Into the Wild

The parts of this region that feature towns and paved roads are small by comparison with the vast majority of the area, which is covered in jungle and accessible only to those willing to trek by foot, horseback or helicopter; Peten is firmly on any off-the-beaten-path traveler's list.

Fun for All

There's more to this region than just the Maya ruins; activities include water sports on beautiful Lake Peten, hiking through nature reserves, zip-lining across jungle canopies and exploring the beautiful island town of Flores.

p233

On the Road

Northern Cayes
p82

Northern Belize
p127

Belize District
p52

Tikal & Flores
p233

Cayo District
p151

Southern Belize
p188

Belize District

Includes ➡

Belize City 54
Burrell Boom 68
Community
Baboon Sanctuary 69
Rancho Dolores 71
Crooked Tree 71
Old Northern
Highway 73
Old Belize 75
Hattieville 76
Belize Zoo 77
Monkey Bay 79
Gales Point 80

Best Places to Eat

➡ Celebrity Restaurant (p62)

➡ The Ice Cream Shoppe (p62)

➡ Nerie's II Restaurant (p62)

Best Places to Sleep

➡ Crooked Tree Lodge (p72)

➡ Maruba Resort Jungle Spa (p75)

➡ Black Orchid Resort (p69)

➡ Tropical Education Center (p78)

Why Go?

What a contrast is the district that shares its country's name! Belize District comprises 1600 sq miles at the heart of the country, and includes its largest population center and some of its most pristine tropical bush.

Belize City gets a bad rap for its impoverished areas, some of which are plagued by crime and violence. But the seaside city also embodies the country's amazing cultural diversity, its neighborhoods packed with people, restaurants and shops that represent every ethnicity.

A few miles out of the city center, the gritty Caribbean urbanism crumbles, revealing a landscape of vast savannah that stretches to the north, dense tropical forest to the west, and lush marshland to the south. There is plenty to see and do in Belize District – so much that a weeklong visitor could spend their entire vacation here, sampling the country's Maya heritage, Creole culture and luxuriant wildlife, all within an hour's drive of the city.

When to Go

➡ **Mar** Baron Bliss Day and Ruta Maya canoe race are both accompanied by colorful parties.

➡ **May** Crooked Tree goes nuts for a weekend during the Cashew Festival.

➡ **Sep** Belize City engages in two weeks of festivities from National Day (September 10).

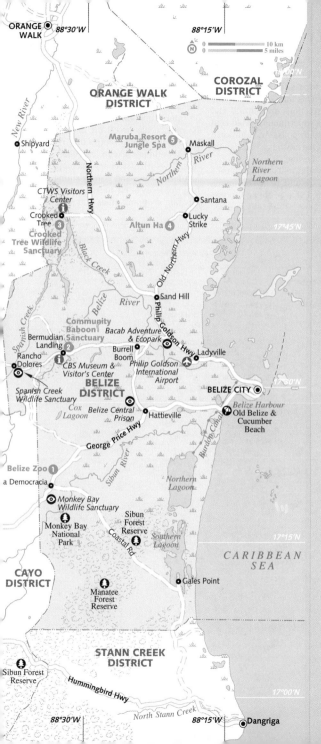

ORANGE WALK · 88°30'W · 88°15'W

ORANGE WALK DISTRICT

COROZAL DISTRICT

Shipyard

Maruba Resort Jungle Spa ⑤ · Maskall

Northern River

Northern River Lagoon

CTWS Visitors Center ℹ

Crooked Tree
Crooked Tree Wildlife Sanctuary ③

Santana

Altun Ha ④ · Lucky Strike

17°45'N

Black Creek

Belize River

Sand Hill

Community Baboon Sanctuary

Bermudian Landing ② ℹ

Bacab Adventure & Edopark

Rancho Dolores

Burrell Boom

Ladyville

CBS Museum & Visitor's Center

Philip Goldson International Airport

Spanish Creek Wildlife Sanctuary

Spanish Creek

BELIZE DISTRICT

BELIZE CITY

17°30'N

Cox Lagoon

Belize Central Prison · Hattieville

George Price Hwy

Belize Harbour
Old Belize & Cucumber Beach

Sibun River

Belize Zoo ①

a Democracia

Monkey Bay Wildlife Sanctuary

Northern Lagoon

Monkey Bay National Park

Sibun Forest Reserve

Coastal Rd

Southern Lagoon

17°15'N

CARIBBEAN SEA

CAYO DISTRICT

Manatee Forest Reserve

Gales Point

Sibun Forest Reserve

STANN CREEK DISTRICT

Hummingbird Hwy

17°00'N

88°30'W · North Stann Creek · 88°15'W · Dangriga

0 ___ 10 km
0 ___ 5 miles

Belize District Highlights

① **Belize Zoo** (p77) Getting a firsthand introduction to all of the zoo's native species.

② **Community Baboon Sanctuary** (p70) Spending a night surrounded by the roar of howler monkeys.

③ **Crooked Tree Wildlife Sanctuary** (p71) Cruising the lagoon and marveling at the birdlife.

④ **Altun Ha** (p74) Admiring the view from atop the Temple of the Masonry Altars.

⑤ **Maruba Resort Jungle Spa** (p75) Indulging in an afternoon of luxurious pampering in the jungle.

BELIZE CITY

POP 60,963

Belize City does not exactly top the list of tourist destinations in Belize. In fact, many visitors choose to bypass the country's only major urban area. This may be because the country's main attractions are natural and nautical, rendering superfluous a prolonged visit to its only metropolis. An additional explanation is that the city has a bad reputation for poverty and crime.

Even those who admire its raffish charms and cultural vibrancy (and, to be fair, there's plenty of this) admit that – unlike the rest of the country – the city is not particularly relaxed. This said, the government has gone to greater lengths in recent years to make visitors feel safer in the city and things on the ground have definitely improved.

Belize City is the historical (if no longer the actual) capital of the nation, making it an interesting place to spend a day or two. Its ramshackle streets are alive with colorful characters who represent every facet of Belize's ethnic makeup, especially the Creoles. The urban scenery encompasses not just fetid canals and grungy slums, but also handsome colonial houses, seaside parks, bustling shopping areas and sailboats that

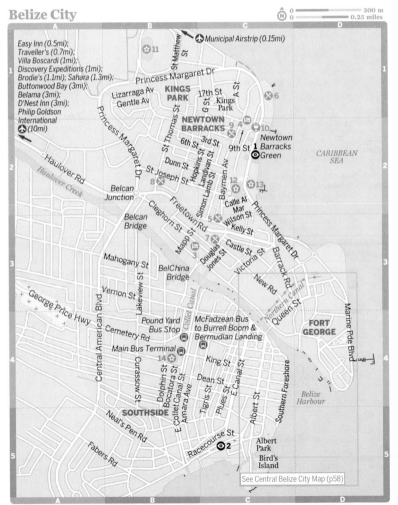

Belize City

See Central Belize City Map (p58)

bob at the mouth of Haulover Creek. You might find Belize City menacing, but you certainly won't find it dull.

Haulover Creek separates the downtown commercial area (focused on Albert St) from the more genteel Fort George district to the northeast. Hotels, guesthouses and places to eat are found on both sides of the creek, with the majority of the city's high-end hotels being in Fort George. The Swing Bridge, which crosses Haulover Creek to link Albert St with Queen St, is the hub of the city, and – some say – the heart of Belize itself.

History

Belize City owes its existence to the harbor at the mouth of Haulover Creek, a branch of the Belize River, down which the Baymen (early British woodcutters) floated lumber from their inland camps. After the rainy season, the Baymen would come to the coast to dispatch their lumber overseas and spend most of the proceeds on rum. Popular lore has it that the settlement – at first just a few huts surrounded by mosquito-ridden swamps – grew on a landfill of mahogany chips and rum bottles, deposited by the Baymen.

The settlement had little significance until 1779, when the Spanish briefly captured St

George's Caye. 'Belize Town' then became and remained the British headquarters in Belize.

During the 19th century, the town grew on both sides of Haulover Creek, with British merchants' homes and buildings of the ruling elite clustered along and near the southern seafront. African slaves and their descendants lived in cabins further inland. By the 1880s the town had a population of around 5000; the great majority were Creoles descended from the British and their slaves, though whites still held all the power and wealth. Belize City witnessed most of the significant events on the long road to Belizean independence, including riots in 1894, 1919 and 1950.

The city was devastated by hurricanes in 1931 and 1961. It was 1961's Hurricane Hattie that spurred the government to build a new capital at Belmopan, 52 miles inland. This left Belize City, and particularly the Creole population, feeling neglected, which led to an increase in emigration by those seeking to escape the overcrowding, unemployment and poor sanitation.

Since the 1980s and 1990s, the city has been plagued by drug use and gang violence, which have contributed to tough conditions for the city's underemployed working class. Middle-class residential areas have developed on the northern and northwestern fringes of the city, while the central areas either side of Haulover Creek remain the country's cultural and commercial hub.

The 21st century has brought about a dramatic transformation in the city – albeit in a tiny corner. Cruise liners anchor off the coast of Belize City and with them come the day tourists, who head for 'Tourist Village' – a large purpose-built facility at the mouth of Haulover Creek. Since 2004, the city has welcomed about 850,000 cruise-ship passengers every year (up from around zero at the turn of the millennium).

◉ Sights

Belize City's main historical sights are all located within walking distance of the Swing Bridge.

★ **Museum of Belize**   MUSEUM
(Map p58; www.museumofbelize.org; Gabourel Lane; admission BZ\$10; ⊙ 9am-5pm Tue-Thu, 9am-4:30pm Fri & Sat) This modern museum in the Fort George District provides an excellent overview of the story of Belize. Housed in the country's former main jail (built of brick in 1857), the museum preserves one cell in

Belize City

◉ **Sights**
1	BTL Park	C2
2	Yarborough Cemetery	C5

⊜ **Sleeping**
3	Bakadeer Inn	B3
4	Bayview Guest House	C2
	Princess Hotel & Casino	(see 13)

⊗ **Eating**
5	Chon Saan Palace	C3
6	Hour Bar	C1
7	Nerie's I Restaurant	C3
8	Pepper's Pizza	B2
9	Sumathi Indian Restaurant	C2

◉ **Drinking & Nightlife**
	Club Elite	(see 13)
10	Thirsty Thursday's	C2
	Vogue Bar & Lounge	(see 13)

◉ **Entertainment**
11	Marion Jones Sporting Complex	B1
12	MCC Grounds	C2
	Princess Cinema	(see 13)
13	Princess Hotel & Casino	C2
14	Rogers Stadium	B4

its original state, complete with inmates' graffiti; if you thought your hotel room was cramped, think again! Fascinating historical photos and documents bear testimony to the colonial and independence eras, and the destruction wrought by hurricanes.

The Maya Treasures section, upstairs, is rather light on artifacts (most of Belize's finest Maya finds were spirited away to other countries), but there are some impressive examples of Maya jade, as well as some ceramics and sculpture. You'll also find plenty of informative models and explanations of the major Maya sites around the country. Other sections of the museum are devoted to Belize's highly colorful postage stamps, and its insect life, with full detail on the disgusting manner in which the human botfly uses living human flesh to nourish its larvae. The museum also has a good little gift shop.

Image Factory GALLERY
(Map p58; www.imagefactorybelize.com; 91 North Front St; ⊙9am-5pm Mon-Fri) FREE The country's most innovative and exciting art gallery stages new exhibitions most months, usually of work by Belizean artists. Opening receptions are mostly held early in the month on the deck, which looks out on Haulover Creek.

★**Swing Bridge** LANDMARK
(Map p58) This heart and soul of Belize City life, crossed by just about everyone here just about every day, is said to be the only remaining manually operated bridge of its type in the world. The bridge, a product of Liverpool's ironworks, was installed in 1923, replacing an earlier bridge that had opened in 1897.

These days it is rarely opened except to allow tall boats to pass in advance of serious storms, but if you're lucky, you might get to watch the procedure that brings vehicles and pedestrians in the city center to a halt.

The Swing Bridge is a favorite hangout for hustlers looking to part tourists from their valuables. You are likely to be approached by seemingly friendly sorts with outstretched hands asking, 'Where you from?' Be advised that the chances of said encounter resulting in a mutually beneficial cultural exchange are slim to none. Downstream from the bridge, Haulover Creek is usually a pretty sight, with numerous small yachts and fishing boats riding at anchor.

★**St John's Cathedral** CHURCH
(Map p58; Albert St; ⊙8am-noon Mon-Fri, 8am-6pm Sat & Sun) Immediately inland of Government House stands St John's Cathedral, the oldest Anglican church in Central America. It was built by slave labor between 1812 and 1820 using bricks brought from Britain as ballast. Notable things to see inside are the ancient pipe organ and the Baymen-era tombstones that tell their own history of

---

BLISS OF BELIZE

Only Belize could have an annual holiday in honor of a national benefactor with a name like Baron Bliss. Born Henry Edward Ernest Victor Bliss in 1869 in Buckinghamshire, England (the title 'Baron' was hereditary), Bliss was a man with a love of the sea and sailing. So much so that he left his wife and his native land for the Caribbean in 1920, spending the next six years living aboard his yacht *Sea King II* off the Bahamas and Trinidad. After a bad bout of food poisoning in Trinidad, the baron took up an invitation from Belize's attorney general, Willoughby Bullock, to drop his anchor off the country on January 14, 1926.

Sadly, Baron Bliss' health took a turn for the worse before he could leave his yacht; his doctors pronounced that the end was nigh. On February 17, 1926, the baron signed a will aboard the *Sea King II*, leaving most of his £1 million fortune to Belize. On March 9 he died. He had, apparently, fallen in love with Belize without ever setting foot on its soil.

The testament decreed that a Baron Bliss Trust be set up to invest his bequest, and that all income from it be used for the permanent benefit of Belize and its citizens, while the capital sum was to remain intact. No churches, dance halls or schools (except agricultural or vocational schools) were to be built with Bliss Trust moneys, nor was the money to be used for any repairs or maintenance to the Trust's own projects.

Over the decades the Baron Bliss Trust has spent more than US$1 million on projects such as the Bliss Centre for the Performing Arts and the Fort George Lighthouse (beside which lies the baron's tomb), both of which are in Belize City, and several health centers and libraries around the country. An annual national holiday, Baron Bliss Day, is celebrated on or close to March 9, the anniversary of the good man's death.

Belize's early days and the toll taken on the city's early settlers.

Court House
HISTORIC BUILDING

(Map p58; Regent St) You can't miss the prominent Court House on Regent St, built in 1926 as the headquarters for Belize's colonial administrators to replace an earlier wooden structure of similar design that was destroyed by fire. It still serves administrative and judicial functions.

BTL Park
PARK

(Newtown Barracks Green; Map p54; Princess Margaret Dr) Fresh from a major makeover funded by the local telecommunications company, BTL Park is now a pleasant waterside recreation area complete with food huts selling local and international cuisine, a playground and a walled-in sandy area with water access, although you'd probably want to avoid swimming here. There is also a stage where concerts and cultural events are held.

Government House
HISTORIC SITE

(House of Culture; Map p58; www.nichbelize.org; Regent St; admission BZ$10; ⊙9am-4pm Mon-Fri) Fronting the sea down at the end of Regent St, this handsome two-story wooden colonial mansion served as the residence of Britain's superintendents and governors of Belize from the building's construction in 1814 until 1996. At the time of research, the building was undergoing renovation and was closed to the public, but will once again serve as the Belizean House of Culture when work is complete.

The house, one of the oldest in Belize, is worth a visit for its historical exhibits, colorful displays of modern Belizean art, spacious colonial ambience and grassy gardens. It was here, at midnight on September 21, 1981, that the Union Jack was ceremonially replaced with the Belizean flag to mark the birth of independent Belize. Displayed in the gardens is the tender from Baron Bliss' yacht.

Temple
HINDU TEMPLE

(Map p58; Albert St) Right in downtown, this simple Hindu temple serves Belize's small but growing Indian community.

Battlefield Park
PARK

(Map p58; Albert St) Battlefield Park is on the right across from the Court House. It's always busy with vendors, loungers, con artists and other slice-of-life segments of Belize City society.

Fort George Lighthouse
LIGHTHOUSE

(Map p58) This diminutive lighthouse guides boats into Haulover Creek and was constructed with funds from the estate of Baron Bliss, who is buried at its foot.

Yarborough Cemetery
CEMETERY

(Map p54; Queen Charlotte St) A narrow graveyard between two roads where you'll see the graves of early citizens of Belize who were not prominent enough to be buried in the nearby St John's Cathedral.

Baron Bliss Tomb
MONUMENT

(Map p58; Fort St) At the tip of the Fort George peninsula lies the granite Baron Bliss Tomb, the final resting place of Belize's most famous benefactor, who never set foot on Belizean soil while alive. Next to the tomb stands the Fort George Lighthouse, one of the many benefits the baron's munificence has yielded the country.

🏃 Activities

Although most divers and snorkelers base themselves out on the cays, it is actually quicker to access some of the best sites directly from Belize City. Some hotels in the city offer their guests diving and snorkeling outings.

The usual destinations are the barrier reef, Turneffe Atoll Marine Reserve and Lighthouse Reef. Prices (including equipment) range from around BZ$250 for a two-tank dive at the barrier reef, to BZ$585 or so for a three-tank dive at Lighthouse Reef (usually including the Blue Hole). A day's snorkeling runs from around BZ$180 to BZ$360. You can also organize sea or river fishing through Belize City adventure outlets.

👉 Tours

Popular day-trip activities and destinations from Belize City include cave-tubing at Nohoch Che'en Caves Branch Archaeological Reserve in Cayo; visits to the Maya ruins at Lamanai in Orange Walk, Altun Ha, Xunantunich in Cayo and even Tikal in Guatemala; birding at Crooked Tree Wildlife Sanctuary; and viewing the animals at the Community Baboon Sanctuary or the Belize Zoo. Several hotels offer tours to their guests.

Many taxi drivers in town are part-time tour guides; they may give you a sales pitch as they drive you around the city. These cabbies/guides can be quite knowledgeable and personable and may suit you if you want a customized tour; in general,

Central Belize City

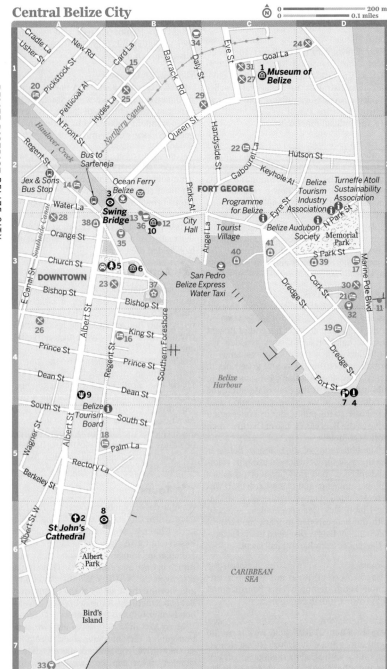

Central Belize City

◎ Top Sights
1 Museum of Belize C1
2 St John's Cathedral A6
3 Swing Bridge B2

◎ Sights
4 Baron Bliss Tomb D4
5 Battlefield Park..B3
6 Court House B3
7 Fort George Lighthouse.......................D4
8 Government House A6
9 Hindu Temple A4
10 Image Factory B3

◎ Activities, Courses & Tours
11 Hugh Parkey's Belize Dive
    Connection D3
12 S&L Travel B3
13 Sea Sports Belize..................................B3

◎ Sleeping
14 Belcove Hotel A2
15 Bella Sombra Guesthouse....................B1
16 Caribbean Palms Inn.............................B4
17 Chateau Caribbean Hotel D3
18 Coningsby Inn A5
19 Great House..D4
20 North Front Street Guesthouse............A1
21 Radisson Fort George Hotel.................D3
22 Sea Breeze Guesthouse C2

◎ Eating
23 Brodie's...B3
24 Celebrity Restaurant.............................D1
25 Dario's Meat Pies...................................B1
26 Dit's Restaurant.....................................A4
27 Ma Ma Chen Restaurant.......................C1
28 Marvas...A3
29 Nerie's II Restaurant C1
30 Stonegrill Restaurant............................D3
31 The Ice Cream Shoppe C1

◎ Drinking & Nightlife
32 Baymen's Tavern....................................D3
33 Bird's Isle Restaurant A7
34 Moon Clusters Coffee House................B1
35 Riverside Patio.......................................B3
36 Spoonaz...B3

◎ Entertainment
37 Bliss Centre for the Performing
    Arts..B3

◎ Shopping
38 Augusto Quan Ltd A3
    Image Factory.............................. (see 10)
39 National Handicraft Center...................D3
40 Tourist Village & Brown Sugar
    Mall..C3
41 Tourist Village Flea Market C3

BELIZE DISTRICT BELIZE CITY

prices for tours to regional attractions start from BZ$200 per day. Hotel staff can often make personal recommendations of cabbies known to them. Make sure your guide has a Belize Tourism Board (BTB) license.

Discovery Expeditions ADVENTURE TOUR
(🗹 671-0748; www.discoverybelize.com; 5916 Manatee Dr, Buttonwood Bay) Specializes in mainland tours to Maya sites, national parks and caves, and offers zip-lining, horseback riding and river kayaking.

Sea Sports Belize ADVENTURE TOUR
(Map p58; 🗹 223-5505; www.seasports belize.com; 83 North Front St; ⊙8am-5pm Mon-Fri) A PADI dive shop that also specializes in wildlife-encounter tours, river cruises, barrier-reef snorkeling and manatee and dolphin spotting.

S&L Travel TOUR
(Map p58; 🗹 227-5145, 227-7593; www.sltravel belize.com; 91 North Front St) A very reputable agency that offers half-day and full-day trips inland, as well as customized trip packages throughout and to Tikal in Guatemala. It specialises in birdwatching. Also offers

air-conditioned internet access (BZ$6 per hour) from its office.

Belize Adventure Lodge ADVENTURE TOUR
(🗹 670-6025; www.belizeadventurelodge.com; Spanish Lookout Caye) On a private island close to Belize City, this well-established adventure lodge has a breezy waterside restaurant and dive shop. It also offers kayaking and a range of other activities to day-trippers. Beware that on cruise days the facilities might be crowded. If you want to stay, there are fan-cooled rooms (BZ$170 per person) perched right over the water. Multiday dive packages available.

Hugh Parkey's Belize Dive Connection ADVENTURE TOUR
(Map p58; 🗹 670-6028, 223-4526; www.hpbelize adventures.com; Radisson Fort George Hotel, Marine Pde Blvd) Offers diving and snorkeling tours to most nearby cays and reefs, as well as kayaking and wildlife tours. Hugh Parkey also operates the highly rated Belize Adventure Lodge on nearby Spanish Lookout Caye. The office is located on the Radisson Marina, but on cruise days it may be unattended, so call in advance.

★ Festivals & Events

September Celebrations CULTURAL
(www.septembercelebrations.com; ☉ Sep 10-21)
Starting on National Day and culminating
on Independence Day, two weeks of city-
wide patriotic celebrations keep the locals
dancing in the streets. The **Belize Carnival**,
a street festival held during this time, sees
Belizeans don colorful costumes and dance
to Caribbean beats.

Baron Bliss Day REGATTA
(☉ Mar 9) Belize City is the end point for the
epic La Ruta Maya canoe race. Other Baron
Bliss festivities include a regatta in front of
Fort George Lighthouse.

Belize International Film Festival FILM
(www.belizefilmfestival.com; ☉ Jul) Showcases
films produced in Belize and in other Central American and Caribbean countries.
Takes place at the Bliss Centre for the Performing Arts.

🛏 Sleeping

Sea Breeze Guesthouse GUESTHOUSE $
(Map p58; ☑ 203-0043; www.seabreeze-belize.
com; 18 Gabourel Lane; r with/without bathroom
BZ$60/50, tr with air-con BZ$80; ❋ 🛜) This little family-run guesthouse is a solid budget
choice, although the razor wire surrounding the place makes it look like the owners
are planning to withstand more than just
the usual crime of Belize City – a zombie
apocalypse, perhaps? The nine rooms are
clean and comfortable for the price; and
the Kalam family offers low-key but accommodating service.

The location in Fort George is safe, convenient and quiet – an easy walk from the
water taxi or from the facilities at Tourist
Village. The place lacks the hangout and
hook-up atmosphere of more popular
backpacker places, but for functionality
and value it's unbeatable.

Belcove Hotel HOTEL $
(Map p58; ☑ 227-3054; www.belcove.com; 9
Regent St; r without bathroom BZ$65, s/d
BZ$69/81, r with air-con BZ$93, deluxe d/tr with
air-con BZ$104/115; ❋ 🛜) Secure and im-
peccably clean, the family-owned Belcove
occupies a bright-yellow-and-burgundy
building overlooking Haulover Creek. Staff
is courteous and accommodating, and
manager Myrna is deeply knowledgeable
about the area. The central location is extremely convenient to transport and all the
sights, while the balcony overlooking the
creek is a great place to unwind.

**North Front
Street Guesthouse** GUESTHOUSE $
(Map p58; ☑ 652-6877; North Front St; dm/r
BZ$30/40) This family-run guesthouse is
basic in the extreme with small rooms
spread around an old house that could do
with a hard-core tidy up. But if you don't
mind missing ceiling panels, the owners
are super-friendly, there is kitchen access,
and the price and location are right.

Bayview Guest House GUESTHOUSE $
(Map p54; ☑ 223-4179; www.belize-guest
house-hotel.com; 58 Baymen Ave; s with/without
bathroom BZ$40/60, d BZ$55/70; ❋ 🛜) There
are no actual water views at this guesthouse
in the quiet residential area of Newtown
Barracks, but it is a short walk from some of
the city's best nightlife. Its eight rooms are
basic – curtains rather than doors separate
the bathroom – but are fairly clean. Some
are poky, so ask to look around and try to
get a window onto the backyard.

Guests get access to the communal kitch-
en. Rooms with air-con go for BZ$10 to
BZ$15 more.

Caribbean Palms Inn GUESTHOUSE $
(Map p58; ☑ 227-0472; 26 Regent St; s/d
BZ$50/100; ❋ 🛜) This downtown option
on busy Regent St does not win any prizes
for character but offers simple, affordable
rooms with good mattresses in a central
location. All have private bathroom, although some are dark and not particularly
appealing.

★ Villa Boscardi B&B $$
(☑ 223-1691; www.villaboscardi.com; 6043
Manatee Dr, Buttonwood Bay; s/d BZ$185/225;
❋ @ 🛜) Set in a secure middle-class sub-
urb, this guesthouse and its charming
hosts will smooth away any stresses that
Belize City's rougher edges might induce.
The eight rooms are large and elegant,
built with Belizean materials and decorat-
ed with fresh, bold colors and prints. Some
rooms have kitchen facilities, while guests
of the other rooms have access to a shared
kitchen. Breakfasts of eggs and pastries are
served in the cozy sitting area. The guest-
house is about 4 miles northwest of the city
center, but there are at least five restau-
rants within walking distance and it's even
safe to walk there.

Bella Sombra Guesthouse
GUESTHOUSE **$$**

(Map p58; ☑223-0223; www.lasbrisasdelmar.net; 36 Hydes Lane; s/d/tr BZ$100/140/180; P ☀ ☎) A fantastic new midrange guesthouse bang in the middle of downtown with large, spotless modern rooms boasting good mattresses and all the mod cons, including huge flatscreen TV. Most rooms have a kitchenette with a sink, microwave and fridge while some have large writing desks. A rooftop terrace was under construction when we visited. Advance reservations essential.

The friendly owner also runs Bella Sombra King's Park, a more homey option targeted at long-term guests a block from the sea in the quiet Kings Park area near the municipal airstrip. Inquires can be made via Bella Sombra Guesthouse.

D'Nest Inn
B&B **$$**

(☑223-5416; www.dnestinn.com; 475 Cedar St, Belama phase 2; s/d/tr from BZ$144/179/214; ☀ ☎) Hosts Gaby and Oty have evidently put a lot of care into this retreat on the northern edge of town. The individually decorated rooms have four-poster beds and Victorian-era antiques, handmade quilts and floral wallpaper. Even more enticing, a lush garden beckons with blooming orchids and allamandas, singing birds and quiet corners.

If you're lucky, you may even spot a manatee in the adjoining canal. It's easy enough to travel the 3 miles into town by taxi or by bus, but in all honesty, you probably won't want to leave this tropical paradise

Princess Hotel & Casino
HOTEL **$$**

(Map p54; ☑223-2670; www.ramada.com; Barrack Rd, Kings Park; s/d BZ$250/275, ste BZ$310, all incl breakfast; P ☀ @ ☎ ☲) This six-story seafront hotel in the north of the city is also an entertainment and social center, with bustling public areas – in fact, a better place to visit for a bit of diversion than a place to stay. Rooms are ample and pretty much what you'd expect for the price at a seaside casino. There's an excellent little coffee shop (and even a movie theater) downstairs.

Coningsby Inn
GUESTHOUSE **$$**

(Map p58; ☑227-1566; coningsby_inn@btl.net; 76 Regent St; r BZ$100; ☀ @ ☎) A friendly and comfortable small hotel in an attractive colonial-style house, the Coningsby is recommended for attentive service and tight security. Rooms are fairly spartan and show some wear, but there is plenty of inviting common space, including a breezy balcony. Also on offer: excellent breakfasts, laundry

service and tours. The location offers easy access to downtown, but it can be noisy.

Bakadeer Inn
GUESTHOUSE **$$**

(Map p54; ☑223-0659; www.bakadeerinn.com; 74 Cleghorn St; r BZ$100; ☀ ☎) This little guesthouse, set along a shady corridor a good distance back from the road, offers clean, quiet and comfortable air-con rooms with fresh fluorescent-green paint jobs. Service is professional, but wi-fi is only available in the lobby area. Unfortunately, the neighborhood feels somewhat dodgy, so avoid walking around here at night.

Chateau Caribbean Hotel
HOTEL **$$**

(Map p58; ☑223-0800; www.chateaucaribbean. com; 6 Marine Parade Blvd; s/d/tr BZ$178/198/218; P ☀ ☎) This converted colonial mansion in the Fort George District offers a spacious lobby, bar and massive dining room overlooking the Caribbean. While some renovation wouldn't go astray, especially on the uneven floors in the common areas, the rooms are mostly breezy, with big beds, large windows and white curtains. Overall the place has an appealing air of faded grandeur. Service is friendly but not particularly professional.

Easy Inn
HOTEL **$$**

(☑223-0380; www.belize-hotel-easy-inn.com; Mile 2 Philip Goldson Hwy; r BZ$120; P ☀ ☎) It's hard to miss this new, bright-orange three-story hotel on the Philip Goldson Hwy offering spacious rooms with all the mod cons. It's distinctly lacking in atmosphere but is reasonably priced for the city.

Radisson Fort George Hotel
HOTEL **$$$**

(Map p58; ☑223-3333; www.radisson.com; 2 Marine Pde Blvd; r BZ$545-621; P ☀ @ ☎ ☲) At the city's top hotel are 102 conservatively decorated rooms with all the comforts. Offering top international-class service, the Radisson avoids the cultural detachment that often comes with such packages, by using local woods, furnishings and decorations conferring genuine Belizean character.

There are three classes of room: Club Tower (the fanciest option, in a glass tower where the marble-floored rooms all enjoy a full sea view); Colonial (in the original hotel structure, with fine wooden furnishings and partial sea views); and Villa (the least expensive, across the street from the main hotel). In addition to the two swimming pools and two bar-restaurants, the hotel also has its own dock.

Great House
GUESTHOUSE $$$

(Map p58; 223-3400; www.greathousebelize.com; 13 Cork St; s/d BZ$366/398; P✳@🛜) This historic colonial-style mansion was built as a private home in 1927 on a piece of prime Fort George real estate. Nowadays, the Great House features 12 graceful rooms that are individually decorated, all with hardwood floors and furniture, ceiling fans and floral prints. Many perks assure your warm welcome, including fresh fruit and hot coffee upon arrival.

The Great House is across the street from the Radisson, so it offers easy access to the big hotel's restaurants and services.

🍴 Eating

★ Nerie's II Restaurant
BELIZEAN $

(Map p58; cnr Queen & Daly Sts; mains BZ$10-18; 7am-9pm, closed Sun) Nerie's offers most accompaniments to rice and beans imaginable, including curried lamb, stewed cow foot, lobster, *gibnut* and deer. Begin with a choice of soups, including chicken, *escabeche* (with chicken, lime and onions), *chirmole* (with chicken and a chilli-chocolate sauce) or cow foot, and finish with cassava pudding. Nerie's has another outlet – Nerie's I Restaurant – on the north side.

The Ice Cream Shoppe
ICE CREAM $

(Map p58; 223-1965; 17 Eve St; 11am-7pm Mon-Thu, 11am-9pm Fri-Sun) When the heat hits unbearable, head to this boutique ice-cream parlor and cool off with delicious homemade ice cream in a variety of great flavors, including some starring local fruits. Order a few scoops and sit back and enjoy the air-con and fast wi-fi.

Nerie's I Restaurant
BELIZEAN $

(Map p54; Douglas Jones St; mains BZ$10-18; 7am-9pm, closed Sun) One of two branches of this local institution serving up budget-friendly quality Creole food.

Dario's Meat Pies
BELIZEAN $

(Map p58; 203-5197; 33 Hydes Lane; meat pies BZ$1; 5am-3pm) Ask any local who makes the best meat pies and they'll tell you without hesitation, Dario's. Get in line and choose from beef or chicken. They're also resold all over the country but it's best to buy them oven fresh at the source. The fillings are piping hot – take care when biting through the crust. Belizean pies are small so grab a few.

Marvas
BELIZEAN $

(Map p58; East Canal St; mains BZ$8-9; 9am-8pm, to 6pm Sun) One of the few places that you'll always find open in downtown, Marvas prepares cheap Creole classics served with a huge plate of rice and beans. The dining rooms is a pretty basic affair but you'll get to watch all kinds of local characters swing by for takeout. The fiery homemade hot sauce is legendary.

Ma Ma Chen Restaurant
TAIWANESE, VEGETARIAN $

(Map p58; 223-4568; 7 Eve St; mains BZ$5-13; 10am-5pm; 🚗) Looking for an antidote to meat-heavy Belizean cuisine? Look no further: Ma Ma Chen's is a genuine Taiwan-style vegetarian restaurant, serving tofu, brown rice and vegetable dishes. The seating area is cozy and bright, and the meals are fresh, filling and healthy.

Dit's Restaurant
DINER, BAKERY $

(Map p58; 50 King St; snacks BZ$3, mains BZ$8-9; 8am-5pm, closed Tue) It doesn't look like much but Dit's is a local favorite and a fine place to get rice-and-beans Belizean standards, sandwiches and Mexican dishes, such as *panades* and *salbutes* (variations on the tortilla). Especially good are the desserts, coconut and lemon pies, milk shakes and juices.

Pepper's Pizza
PIZZA $

(Map p54; 223-5000; 4 St Thomas St; pizza BZ$8.50-34; 11am-10pm; 🚗) One outlet in a chain of pizzerias that you will find throughout the country. It's not gourmet but will fill the hole if you're hankering for a slice. The ambience is pure hospital: there's no windows, white tiles and fluorescent lights – get takeout.

Brodie's
SUPERMARKET $

(Map p58; 2 Albert St; 8:30am-7pm Mon-Thu, 8:30am-8pm Fri, 8:30am-5pm Sat, 8:30am-1pm Sun) This department store has the best downtown groceries. There's another branch (Mile 3 Philip Goldson Hwy; 8:30am-7pm Mon-Thu, 8:30am-8pm Fri, 8:30am-5pm Sat, 8:30am-1pm Sun) northwest of the city center.

Celebrity Restaurant
INTERNATIONAL $$

(Map p58; 223-7272; www.celebritybelize.com; cnr Marine Parade Blvd & Goal Lane; mains BZ$16-40; 11am-11pm) We love Celebrity because it is a semi-swanky place that is not inside a hotel. The place has an extensive menu that includes American favorites, such as steaks and sandwiches, Mexican fare like fajitas and quesadillas, plenty of pasta dishes and a few Mediterranean surprises like hummus, kofta and kebabs.

That said, the chef's specialty is seafood – and you are in Belize, after all – so why not sample the grilled snapper or lobster hollandaise? The ambience is casual with a happening bar as you enter and a large dining room further inside.

Sumathi Indian Restaurant　　INDIAN **$$**
(Map p54; ☑223-1172; 19 Baymen Ave; mains BZ$25-35; ⊙11am-11pm; ✐) Belize City's best Indian restaurant provides a huge range of flavorsome curries, tandooris and *biryanis* (spicy rice with meat or vegetables), with plenty of vegetarian options, all in generous quantities. All curries are served with rice and naan bread, and Bollywood films on the TV intensify the mood. It's not cheap but its good value for the quality involved.

Chon Saan Palace　　CHINESE **$$**
(Map p54; cnr Kelly & Nurse Seay Sts; mains BZ$19.50-33; ⊙11am-11pm; ✐) The Chon Saan has been beloved in Belize City since it opened in the 1970s. The extensive menu includes more than 200 items, including plenty of fresh seafood (which you can see swimming around the tanks). Favorite dishes include chicken in cashew nuts, lobster in black bean sauce and Singapore-style chow mein.

Sahara　　LEBANESE **$$**
(☑203-3031; Vista Plaza, Mile 3.5 Philip Goldson Hwy; mains BZ$13-28) You wouldn't expect to find such quality in a strip mall on the edges of town, but this unpretentious Lebanese diner is hugely popular among expats and visitors alike for its variety of delicious Middle Eastern delicacies.

Hour Bar　　BELIZEAN **$$**
(Map p54; Barrack Rd; mains BZ$23-45) With a fantastic waterside location, this large open-air restaurant is a great place for a meal and is well worth sticking around afterwards for a few drinks.

Stonegrill Restaurant　　GRILL **$$$**
(Map p58; Radisson Fort George Hotel, 2 Marine Pde Blvd; mains BZ$30-46; ⊙11am-10pm; ℗) At this thatched poolside restaurant at the Radisson you get to grill your own meal – steak, fajitas, shrimp, chicken satay and the like – on super-hot volcanic stones. It's fun, tasty and free of added fat.

🍷 Drinking & Nightlife

Top-end hotel bars are one focus of Belize City social life. It's more fun than it might sound, pulling in a range of locals, expats and tourists.

The best of Belize City nightlife is, fortuitously enough, located in the relatively safe Newtown Barracks area in the town's north. The local press publicizes upcoming events.

★Spoonaz　　CAFE
(Map p58; ☑223-1043; North Front St; ⊙noon-10pm Wed, 3pm-midnight Thu-Fri, noon-midnight Sat) An oasis in downtown Belize City, this cosmopolitan cafe serves quality coffee as well as panini and sandwiches. There is a smart air-conditioned lounge area inside but you really want to be under the green cloth umbrellas out the back watching the sailboats bobbing on Haulover Creek and working your way through the cocktail list.

Thirsty Thursday's　　BAR
(Map p54; Barrack Rd; ⊙5pm-2am) A favorite among the young crowd, this hip bar has a large balcony overlooking BTL park. There are early-bird drinks specials from 5pm to 9pm and on Wednesday's there is karaoke.

Club Elite　　CLUB
(Map p54; Princess Hotel & Casino, Barrack Rd, Kings Park; ⊙9pm-late) Located inside the Princess Hotel this is the city's most fashionable disco, which being Belize is still a fairly casual affair. Dress up, but not too much.

Moon Clusters Coffee House　　CAFE
(Map p58; ☑203-0139; 25 Daly St; ⊙1-6pm Mon, 9am-6pm Tue-Sat) The coolest cafe in town, serving up great frappes, espresso, and pastries, donuts and muffins.

Bird's Isle Restaurant　　BAR
(Map p58; Bird's Island; ⊙10:30am-2:30pm & 5:30pm-late Mon-Fri, 10:30am-10pm Sat) Bird's Isle may be the best that Belize City has to offer. An island oasis at the southern tip of town, it manages to defy the urban grit that lies just a few blocks away. Locals and tourists alike flock to the open-air *palapa* to partake of sea breezes, fresh-squeezed juice and cold beers. It has fine views at sunset, but unfortunately at dusk it is engulfed by bloodthirsty mosquitoes – come early or late.

Traveller's　　BAR
(Mile 2 Philip Goldson Hwy) Out on the northern highway, this unpretentious spot is a favorite among middle-class Belizeans who

come for the cheap drinks and karaoke events. There is a small but interesting rum museum in the adjacent building.

Baymen's Tavern BAR
(Map p58; Radisson Fort George Hotel, 2 Marine Pde Blvd; ⊙10am-10pm) The main bar at the Radisson is friendly and sociable, with a pleasant outdoor deck.

Vogue Bar & Lounge LOUNGE
(Map p54; www.princessbelize.com; Princess Hotel & Casino, Newtown Barracks, Kings Park; ⊙noon-late) The lounge bar at the Princess gets lively on Friday nights when a mixed young crowd launches a new weekend.

Riverside Patio BAR
(Map p58; Regent St; ⊙9am-11pm) If you fancy an early beer, join like-minded locals at this bamboo bar hidden behind the commercial center on busy Regent St. It's a bit rough and ready but is an atmospheric place to take a breather and watch the action on Haulover Creek.

☆ Entertainment

For spectator sports, the main venues are the MCC Grounds (Map p54; cnr Barrack Rd & Calle al Mar) for football and cricket; Rogers Stadium (Map p54; Dolphin St) for softball; and the Marion Jones Sporting Complex (Map p54; Princess Margaret Dr), which is used for various events.

**Bliss Centre for
the Performing Arts** PERFORMING ARTS
(Map p58; ☑227-2110; www.nichbelize.org; Southern Foreshore) Operated by the Institute for Creative Arts, the revamped Bliss Centre has a fine 600-seat theater that stages a variety of events throughout the year. Look for concerts of traditional Belizean music and shows celebrating Belize and its culture. Annual events include the Belize Film Festival and the Children's Art Festival in May.

Princess Cinema CINEMA
(Map p54; ☑223-2670; Princess Hotel & Casino, Newtown Barracks, Kings Park; admission BZ$15) The two-screen Princess cinema shows first-run Hollywood films, though usually a bit later than their US release dates.

Princess Hotel & Casino CASINO
(Map p54; Newtown Barracks, Kings Park; ⊙noon-4am) The casino at the Princess Hotel is an informal and fun place to try to boost your budget, with roulette, poker and blackjack

tables, plus hundreds of slot machines and a floor show with dancing girls kicking up their heels at 10pm. You need to show ID such as your passport or driver's license to enter (minimum age is 18).

🛍 Shopping

Image Factory ART, BOOKS
(Map p58; 91 North Front St; ⊙9am-5pm Mon-Fri) This shop at this hip art gallery has the country's best range of books, including international literature, and titles on Belizean and Caribbean society and history. There is also a fine collection of local art for sale.

National Handicraft Center SOUVENIRS
(Map p58; 2 South Park St; ⊙8am-5pm Mon-Fri, 8am-4pm Sat) This store carries the best stock of high-quality Belizean arts and crafts at fair prices. Attractive buys include shade-grown coffee and local chocolate, carvings in zericote and other native hardwoods, slate relief carvings of wildlife and Maya deities, and CDs of Belizean music.

**Tourist Village &
Brown Sugar Mall** SOUVENIRS
(Map p58; Fort St; ⊙8am-4pm cruise-ship days only) This waterfront complex exists for the convenience of cruise-ship passengers, who disembark here on their land trips. Non-cruise tourists may enter from the street with a temporary pass, obtainable on presentation of an identity document. Most of the shops are liquor stores and international jewelers, but there is at least one excellent art gallery and an outlet selling fine carved jade.

Tourist Village Flea Market SOUVENIRS
(Map p58; Fort St; ⊙8am-4pm cruise-ship days only) On the street outside the Tourist Village, local vendors set up tents and tables to sell their wares, which include T-shirts with snappy slogans, original jewelry, woven bags and blankets, and plenty of carved wooden items. Quality varies widely and prices are negotiable.

This is one of the few places in Belize where vendors are not afraid to engage the hard sell. On non-cruise days, the selection is limited, but you might find a few scattered tables.

Augusto Quan Ltd OUTDOOR EQUIPMENT
(Map p58; 13 Market Sq; ⊙8am-6pm Mon-Sat) A large hardware store stocking tools, tarps, bug spray and wet-weather gear. A good place to hit before heading into the bush.

ℹ Information

DANGERS & ANNOYANCES

Not to put too fine a point on it, but Belize City isn't exactly the relaxed place the rest of the country is. Hotel windows are barred and front doors are often kept locked even during the day. While you are likely to spend most of your time in the commercial district (east of Southside Canal around Albert and Regent Sts) and in the Fort George district, both of which are safe during daylight hours, it's worth remaining vigilant.

Most violent crime occurs in the Southside district, south of Haulover Creek and west of Southside Canal. Much of it is violent crime between gang members, but non-intergang crime (both petty and violent) is also an issue. Stay on the main roads or take a taxi when you're going to or from the main bus terminal or other bus stops in this area. Even in the middle of the day these streets can have a threatening atmosphere.

After dark, it's best to take a taxi anywhere you go in the city. If you must walk, stay on better-lit major streets and don't go alone if you can help it. Get advice from your hotel about safety in specific neighborhoods.

Police maintain a fairly visible presence in the main areas frequented by tourists in Belize City, and will intervene to deter hustlers and other shady characters, but you can't rely on them to always be where you need them. Take the commonsense precautions that you would in any major city: be wary of overly friendly strangers; don't flash wads of cash, cameras, jewelry or other signs of wealth; don't leave valuables lying around your hotel room; don't use illicit drugs; and avoid deserted streets, even in daylight.

EMERGENCY

Ambulance (☎90, ☎223-3292 private ambulance)
Crime Stoppers (☎224-4646, ☎922)
Fire Service (☎911)
Police (☎911)

INTERNET ACCESS

King Internet Service (16 King St; per hr BZ$3; ⊗9am-7pm Mon-Sat) Downtown internet access.

S&L Travel (Map p58; ☎227-5145, 227-7593; www.sltravelbelize.com; 91 North Front St) Air-con internet near the water-taxi docks

LAUNDRY

Lavanderia Latinas (☎600-9330; Cran St; per load BZ$5; ⊗7am-6pm) Good cheap laundry service. Wash and dry in about 1½ hours.

MEDICAL SERVICES

Belize City has the best medical facilities in the country with a large public hospital and several good private facilities.

Belize Medical Associates (☎223-0302; www.belizemedical.com; 5791 St Thomas St; ⊗emergency services 24hr) Private hospital in Kings Park District with a good reputation among expats.

Karl Heusner Memorial Hospital (☎223-1671, 223-1548; www.khmh.bz; Princess Margaret Dr; ⊗emergency services 24hr) A public hospital in the north of town.

MONEY

All banks exchange US and Canadian dollars, British pounds and, usually, euros. Most ATMs are open 24 hours, though it's highly recommended that you visit them during daylight hours.

Belize Bank (60 Market Sq; ⊗8am-3pm Mon-Thu, 8am-4:30pm Fri) The ATM is on the north side of the building. There is another Belize Bank **ATM** (North Front St) that is convenient for water taxis.

First Caribbean International Bank (21 Albert St; ⊗8am-2:30pm Mon-Thu, 8am-4:30pm Fri)

Scotia Bank (cnr Albert & Bishop Sts; ⊗8am-3pm Mon-Thu, 8am-4:30pm Fri)

POST

Main Post Office (Map p58; North Front St; ⊗8am-5pm Mon-Thu, 8am-4:30pm Fri)

TELEPHONE

BTL (☎227-7085; 1 Church St; ⊗8am-6pm Mon-Fri) Pick up SIM cards for mobile devices at this downtown shop.

TOURIST INFORMATION

Belize Audubon Society (Map p58; ☎223-4987, 223-5004; www.belizeaudubon.org; 16 North Park St) Offers information and books accommodation for wildlife reserves that it manages throughout the country, including Half-Moon Caye and Crooked Tree.

Belize Tourism Board (BTB; Map p58; ☎227-2420; www.travelbelize.org; 64 Regent St; ⊗8am-5pm Mon-Thu, 8am-4pm Fri) Pick up maps, magazines and all sorts of information relating to travel around Belize. This is also where you will find the cruise-ship schedule, which is published in a handy booklet.

Belize Tourism Industry Association (BTIA; Map p58; ☎227-1144; www.btia.org; 10 North Park St, Belize City; ⊗8am-noon & 1-5pm Mon-Fri) The BTIA is an independent association of tourism businesses, actively defending 'sustainable ecocultural tourism'. The office provides leaflets about the country's regions, copies of its *Destination Belize* annual magazine (free), and information on its members, which include many of Belize's best hotels, restaurants and other tourism businesses. The website has a plethora of information.

Programme for Belize (PFB; Map p58; ☑ 227-5616; www.pfbelize.org; 1 Eyre St; ⊘ 8am-5pm) A Belizean nonprofit organization that works with individual conservationists, private landowners and the Belizean government to demonstrate that the long-term benefits of land preservation outweigh the short-term profits of resource exploitation. PFB manages the massive Río Bravo Conservation and Management Area, and the office can arrange visits to the La Milpa and Hill Bank field stations within the reserve.

Turneffe Atoll Sustainability Association (Map p58; ☑ 670-8272; www.turneffeatoll marinereserve.org; 10 North Park St; ⊘ 8am-5pm Mon-Fri) Manages the Turneffe Atoll Marine Reserve.

TRAVEL AGENCIES

Mundo Maya Travels (☑ 223-1200; www.travelmundomaya.com; Brown Sugar Mall) Sells bus tickets to Guatemala and Mexico.

🛈 Getting There & Away

AIR

Belize City has two airports: Philip Goldson International Airport (BZE), which is 11 miles northwest of the city center off the Philip Goldson Hwy; and the Municipal Airstrip (TZA), around 2 miles north of the city center. All international flights use the international airport. Domestic flights on both local carriers are divided between the two airports, but those using the Municipal Airstrip are cheaper (often significantly).

The following airlines fly from Belize City:

American Airlines (p305) Direct flights to/from Miami and Dallas/Fort Worth.

Avianca (p305) Flights to/from San Salvador, El Salvador.

Copa Airlines (p305) Flies to Panama City with connections all over Latin America and the Caribbean.

Delta Airlines (p305) Direct flights to/from Atlanta.

Maya Island Air (p307) Operates domestic flights to Caye Caulker, Dangriga, Placencia, Punta Gorda, and San Pedro on Ambergris Caye.

Southwest Airlines (p305) Offers some of the best deals to destinations in the US.

Tropic Air (p305) Domestic flights from Belize City to Caye Caulker, Dangriga, Placencia, Punta Gorda, San Ignacio and San Pedro. Also serves Flores, Guatemala; Roatan, Honduras; and Cancún and Merida in Mexico.

United Airlines (p305) Direct flights to/from Houston.

BOAT

There are two water-taxi companies on North Front St offering similar services to Caye Caulker and San Pedro:

Ocean Ferry Belize (Map p58; ☑ 223-0033; www.oceanferrybelize.com; North Front St) New company running boat services to Caye Caulker (one way/round trip BZ$19/29, 45 minutes) and San Pedro (one way/round trip BZ$29/49, 1½ hours) out of the old Caye Caulker Water Taxi terminal. Leaves Belize City for both destinations at 8am, 10:30am, 1:30pm, 3pm and 5pm.

San Pedro Belize Express Water Taxi (Map p58; ☑ 223-2225; www.belizewatertaxi.com; Brown Sugar Mall, Front St) Professionally run water-taxi service with nine departures a day (approximately every hour from 8am to 5pm) to Caye Caulker (one way/round trip BZ$30/50, 45 minutes) and San Pedro (one way/round trip BZ$40/70, 1½ hours). Also operates one daily boat to and from Caye Caulker to Chetumal, Mexico (via San Pedro).

BUS

Belize City's **main bus terminal** (Map p54; West Collett Canal St) is the old Novelo's terminal next to the canal which now sports a faded Rastafarian red, gold and green paint job. Most buses leave from here, although local buses within Belize District to destinations such as Ladyville and Burrell Boom leave from around the corner at the **Pound Yard bus stop** (Map p54; Cemetery Rd).

To judge from the barely legible, handwritten schedules that adorn the walls, the country's intercity bus system is utter chaos. Indeed, there are dozens of companies that ply the main routes out of Belize City – south to Punta Gorda, west to Benque Viejo del Carmen and north to Corozal. It's actually simpler than it seems, since plenty of buses ply the main routes and prices and service do not vary much between companies. Note that there are fewer departures on Sunday and the last buses leave earlier.

Belmopan (BZ$5, 1¼ hours, 52 miles) All southbound buses and all westbound buses pass through Belmopan. Many of the services to the south run express to Belmopan and then make stops after the capital. Any non-express bus heading to Belmopan can drop you anywhere along George Price Hwy.

Benque Viejo del Carmen (BZ$10, 2½ to three hours, 80 miles) Buses depart every half-hour from 5am to 9pm.

Bermudian Landing/Rancho Dolores (BZ$5 to BZ$8, one hour, 27 miles) **McFadzean buses** (Map p54) depart from Amara Ave next to the school at 12:20pm, 3:30pm, 5pm, 5:20pm and 8pm. The 3:30pm and 5pm services continue to Rancho Dolores.

Burrell Boom (BZ$2.50 to BZ$4, 45 minutes, 20 miles) All buses to Bermudian Landing pass through Burrell Boom. There's also a direct bus to Burrell Boom from the Pound Yard bus stop at 4:50pm. Alternatively, catch any bus traveling along the Philip Goldson Hwy, get out at the Burrell Boom turnoff and hitch 3 miles to the village.

Cancún, Mexico (BZ$102, 10 hours, 320 miles) Mexican company ADO runs comfortable air-conditoned buses direct to Cancún nightly from the main bus terminal at 7:30pm. It stops in Tulum, Playa del Carmen and Cancún airport before arriving at the Cancún bus terminal. Buy tickets in advance in the bus terminal.

Chetumal, Mexico (BZ$16, 3½ to four hours, 102 miles) Through buses to Chetumal leave every half-hour or so from 5am to 11:30am. Alternatively, take one of the frequent northbound buses to Corozal, from where there is local transport to the border. An express, air-conditioned tourist service to Chetumal (BZ$50, three hours) leaves from the Brown Sugar Mall at 1:15pm.

Corozal (BZ$10, three hours, 86 miles) Buses run north to Corozal hourly from 5am until 7:30pm.

Crooked Tree (BZ$3.50, one hour, 36 miles) **Jex & Sons** (Map p58) runs buses from the corner of Regent St W and W Canal St at 10:45am from Monday to Saturday, with two additional buses departing at 5pm and 5:20pm from the Pound Yard bus stop. You can also take any northern bus and hitch from the turnoff.

Dangriga (BZ$10 to BZ$14, 2½ to three hours, 107 miles) All southbound buses to Punta Gorda stop in Dangriga.

Flores, Guatemala Fuente del Norte runs a daily luxury bus to Flores (BZ$50, five hours, 145 miles) at 10am. Marlin Espadas runs a smaller bus on the same route at 1pm. Both services depart from the Brown Sugar Mall. From Flores there are connecting services to Guatemala City and and Pedro Sula, Honduras.

Merida, Mexico (BZ$102, 10 hours, 343 miles) ADO runs an air-conditioned express bus direct to Merida three to four times a week leaving from the main bus terminal at 7pm. Alternatively take the Cancún bus and change once across the border in Quintana Roo.

Orange Walk Town (BZ$5 to BZ$7, two hours, 57 miles) Hourly from 5am to 8pm; all buses to Corozal and Sarteneja stop in Orange Walk.

Punta Gorda (BZ$24 to BZ$28, six to seven hours, 212 miles) The terminus for the southern lines – the main one operated by James. Buses depart hourly from 5:15am to 3:45pm.

San Ignacio (BZ$9 to BZ$10, two to 2½ hours, 72 miles) All westbound buses to Benque stop in San Ignacio.

Sarteneja (BZ$15, 3½ hours, 96 miles) Light blue buses depart from Regent St (Map p58)

just northwest of the Swing Bridge at 10:30am, noon, 1:45pm, 4pm and 5pm; runs express to Orange Walk.

CAR & MOTORCYCLE

The main roads in and out of town are the Philip Goldson Hwy (to the international airport, Orange Walk and Corozal), which heads northwest from the Belcan Junction, and the George Price Hwy (to Belmopan and San Ignacio), which is the westward continuation of Cemetery Rd. Cemetery Rd gets its name from the ramshackle Lord's Ridge Cemetery, which it bisects west of Central American Blvd. There are many car-rental firms in Belize City and increased competition has seen prices drop, although they remain somewhat expensive regional standards.

ⓘ Getting Around

Though many of the spots where travelers go are within walking distance of each other, it's always safest to take a taxi after dark.

TO/FROM THE AIRPORTS

Philip Goldson International Airport The taxi fare to/from the international airport is BZ$50 for one to two passengers and BZ$60 for three to four passengers. Alternatively, walk the 1.6 miles from the airport to the Philip Goldson Hwy, where fairly frequent buses pass heading to Belize City. There is no public transport to/from the airport.

Municipal Airstrip Taxis cost around BZ$10 to the center of town. There is no public transport to/from the municipal airstrip.

BUS

Main Bus Terminal Taxis line up outside the bus terminal. They supposedly work on a turn basis but there always seems to be plenty of debate among drivers.

AVOIDING THE CRUISE CROWD

If you intend to explore the sights in Belize District and eastern Cayo District, it's worth planning your itinerary around the cruise-ship schedule. Stop by or call the Belize Tourism Board (BTB; p65) office to find out which dates will have cruise ships at port. On these days you'll want to avoid destinations and tours that are within striking distance of Belize City, as they will be overrun with cruise-ship passengers. The most popular day trips for cruisers are the Maya ruins at Altun Ha and cave-tubing at Nohoch Che'en Caves Branch Archaeological Reserve.

CAR & MOTORCYCLE

Belize City has the heaviest traffic in the country, although it is usually only slow going for a short time in the morning and again in the evening. There's a limited one-way system, which is easy to work with. If you need to park on the street, try to do so right outside the place you're staying. Never leave anything valuable on view inside a parked car.

Car-rental firms in Belize include the following:

AQ Car Rental (☑ 222-5122; www.aqbelizecar rental.com; Mile 5.5 Philip Goldson Hwy; ⊗ 8am-6pm) Locally run outfit that offers the best rates in Belize backed up by top-notch customer service. Free pick-up and drop-off service. It's just past the bridge crossing the Belize River on the Philip Goldson Hwy. There's another branch at Philip Goldson International Airport.

Budget (☑ 223-3986, 223-2435; www.budget-belize.com; Mile 4 Philip Goldson Hwy; ⊗ 8am-5pm) There is also an office at Philip Goldson International Airport and another in Placencia.

Crystal Auto Rental (☑ 223-1600; www. crystal-belize.com; Mile 5 Philip Goldson Hwy; ⊗ 7am-5pm) One of the best local firms; allows vehicles to be taken into Guatemala. Check its website for medium- and long-term rental specials. There's another branch at Philip Goldson International Airport.

Euphrates Auto Rental (☑ 610-5752, 227-5752; www.ears.bz; 143 Euphrates Ave, South-side; ⊗ 8am-5pm Mon-Fri, 8am-2pm Sat) Local firm that offers some good deals.

Hertz (☑ 223-0886, 223-5395; www.hertz.com; 11A Cork St; ⊗ 8am-4:30pm) Also has a branch at Philip Goldson International Airport.

Thrifty (☑ 207-1271; www.thrifty.com; 715 Gibnut St; ⊗ 8am-5:30pm Mon-Sat) Additional outlet at Philip Goldson International Airport.

TAXI

Cabs cost around BZ$7 for rides within the city, give or take; if it's a long trip from one side of town to the other, expect to be charged a bit more. Confirm the price in advance with your driver. Most restaurants and hotels will call a cab for you.

NORTHWEST OF BELIZE CITY

The recently renamed Philip Goldson Hwy is still referred to by many locals as the Northern Hwy. It stretches from Belize City to Orange Walk District, passing the communities of Ladyville and Burrell Boom (west of which you'll find the Community Baboon Sanctuary and Spanish Creek Wildlife Sanctuary). At Sand Hill the road forks. To the west, it continues to Orange Walk, passing the turnoff for the Crooked Tree Wildlife Sanctuary. To the east, the Old Northern Hwy leads to the Maya ruins of Altun Ha.

Burrell Boom

POP 2218

A tranquil and charming village, Burrell Boom occupies a quiet bank of the Belize River, just 19 miles north of Belize City and 3 miles west of the Philip Goldson Hwy. Founded in the 18th century, the village takes its name from the iron chains ('booms') that loggers extended across the river to trap the mahogany logs that were sent from further upriver. You can still see the boom and anchors on display in Burrell Boom Park in the village center.

Burrell Boom is only a few miles from the Community Baboon Sanctuary, but otherwise there are no big tourist draws in the immediate vicinity. Rather, the village's attraction is the exquisite natural setting, ideal for canoeing, birding and croc spotting. Locals take advantage of the lush fruit trees and distill a huge variety of fruit wines, especially sweet berry and cashew wines.

This sleepy village comes to life annually in March when the canoe race, known as La Ruta Maya, passes through. Contestants spend their third night on the banks of the river in town, making Burrell Boom an ideal location for observers to hunker down with a cold drink and watch the fun.

The village's proximity to the international airport and the Philip Goldson Hwy make it a convenient and comfortable base from which to explore the rest of the country. That's the beauty of this place: it may be off the beaten track, but the track is only a few miles away so it's always easy to get back on.

⊙ Sights

Bacab Adventure & Eco Park   ECO PARK
(☑ 225-3537, 225-2587; www.bacabecopark.com; adult/child BZ$10/5, tour prices vary; ⊗ 10am-5pm) 🅟 Part nature reserve, part theme park, Bacab is set on more than 500 acres of jungle through which wind hiking trails and waterways. While it's not a destination for hard-core naturalists, it's a great escape from Belize City, especially for families, who'll appreciate the green environs, huge swimming pool complete with waterfall and the opportunity to check out some animals.

While this place was established with the cruise-ship tourist in mind – days when the ships aren't in (schedules change all the time; call the front desk to find out) are absolutely serene.

A nature hike will reward observers with multiple bird sightings and perhaps a glimpse of resident howler monkeys or crocodiles, while adventurers might wish to explore the reserve on horseback (best scheduled a day in advance), by kayak or even by mountain bike. The staff is warm and friendly and service absolutely top-notch. And while Bacab is loads of fun, its goal is more complex, as management has undertaken an intensive reforestation effort, planting more than 25 species of native trees.

There is also a gift shop onsite and a beautiful *palapa*-roofed restaurant that serves American, Caribbean and Belizean cuisine.

To get to Bacab, turn off the Burrell Boom road into Ridge Lagoon Estates and follow the signs. It claims to be open everyday but has been known to close during inclement weather – call before trekking out here. Bring bug spray.

🛏 Sleeping

While there is one fine resort in Burrell Boom, there isn't much in the way of cheap accommodations around the village. Budget travelers might choose to stay down the road in Bermudian Landing

Black Orchid Resort RESORT **$$$**
(☑ 225-9158; www.blackorchidresort.com; 2 Dawson Lane, Burrell Boom; r BZ$300-450, ste BZ$500-590, villa BZ$700; ⓟ✳🛜🖥) 🥾 Guests rave about the attentive service and comfortable accommodations at this classy riverside

resort. It features spacious rooms with big beds made of mahogany; bedspreads are sprinkled lightly with hibiscus flowers. Mexican-tiled bathrooms and private balconies provide the perfect place to sip your morning coffee and listen to the birds awaken.

Rates are for double rooms, but small discounts may be available for solo travelers. The verdant flower-filled grounds stretch down to the river, where complimentary canoes, kayaks and paddle boats are available for guests' use. Other amenities include a restaurant, small gift shop and plenty of adventure tours. Bonus: free airport transfers.

❶ Getting There & Away

Both Bacab Adventure & Eco Park and Black Orchid Resort will arrange transfers from Belize City or from the international airport, so it's unlikely you will be dependent on public transportation. That said, six buses a day service Burrell Boom from Belize City (although some arrive late in the evening and head back very early in the morning). There are fewer buses on Saturday and one on Sunday. Alternatively, buses ply the Philip Goldson Hwy every half-hour, so if you can get a lift from the village to the highway turnoff, you won't have to wait long.

Community Baboon Sanctuary

No real baboons inhabit Belize; but Belizeans use that name for the Yucatan black howler monkey *(Alouatta pigra)*, an endangered species that exists only in Belize, northern Guatemala and southern Mexico

---

THE MONKEY THAT ROARED

Listen! Up in the sky! It's a jet plane! It's a Harley Davidson! It's a Led Zeppelin! No, it's a howler monkey.

Just how loud is the vociferous simian? The howl of the howler monkey peaks at around 128 decibels, which is louder than a lion's roar, an elephant's trumpet or even a chainsaw. This makes the howler the loudest of all land animals. A hollowed-out bone in the throat gives the 20lb primate the anatomical ability to crank up the volume.

The male monkeys make all the noise. Howler troops, which number about a dozen members, are matriarchal. The females only need one or two mature males around to defend their preferred patch of rainforest from hungry rivals. So early in the morning and late in the afternoon, when the dominant male traipses up to his treetops trapeze to make his booming broadcast, *stay away!*

There are officially nine species of howler, but only one in Belize – the Yucatan Black Howler, which happens to be the largest of its kind. Belizeans refer to it as a baboon, but that is a misnomer. The baboon is an Old World monkey; the howler is strictly New World. Even if you do not see a howler monkey on your trip to Belize, you will likely hear one. Its haunting cry carries as far as 5 miles.

and is one of the largest monkeys in the Americas. The **Community Baboon Sanctuary** (CBS; www.howlermonkeys.org; admission $BZ10; ⊙8am-5pm) is an amazing community-run, grassroots conservation operation that has engineered an impressive increase in the primate's local population.

CBS occupies about 20 sq miles, spread over a number of Creole villages in the Belize River valley. More than 200 landowners in seven villages have signed pledges to preserve the monkey's habitat, by protecting forested areas along the river and in corridors that run along the borders of their property. The black howlers have made an amazing comeback in the area, and the monkeys now roam freely all around the surrounding area.

◉ Sights & Activities

CBS Museum & Visitor's Center   MUSEUM
(☑622-9624, 245-2007, 245-2009; cbsbelize@gmail.com; Bermudian Landing; admission BZ$14; ⊙8am-5pm; P) The CBS Museum & Visitor's Center has a number of good exhibits and displays on the black howler, the history of the sanctuary and other Belizean wildlife. Included with the admission fee is a 45-minute nature walk on which you're likely to get an up-close introduction to a resident troop of black howlers. Along the way the trained local guides also impart their knowledge of the many medicinal plants. The visitor's center also sells maps (BZ$6) of local trails so you an go out and explore on your own. There are also nearly 200 bird species in the area to keep wildlife watchers busy.

Other activities that can be organized here include night hikes, canoe trips and croc-spotting tours. The center can also connect you with local homestays providing both food and lodging.

Note that there is a local business purporting to be the official visitor's center on the road into the village – the real version

is right in front of the Bermudian Landing cricket oval.

🛏 Sleeping

The CBS Museum & Visitor's Center can organize homestay accommodations (single/double including two meals BZ$70/90) in Bermudian Landing and the other villages participating in the sanctuary program. Conditions are rustic (not all places have showers or flush toilets), but there's no better way to experience Creole village life and support the community. There are also private lodges in Bermudian Landing and some of the other villages.

Nature Resort   CABAÑAS $$
(☑223-6115; naturer@btl.net; Bermudian Landing; cabañas s/d BZ$130/150, r with fan BZ$90; P ❀) Right next to the CBS Museum & Visitor's Center, this little resort has six comfortable *cabañas* in a lovely natural setting. It is managed remotely from Belize City and there is not always staff onsite, but you can make bookings through the Visitor's Center.

Howler Monkey Resort   LODGE $$$
(☑607-1571; www.howlermonkeyresort.bz; cabin from BZ$250-270; P ❀ 🛜 ⛲) ✔ Ed and Melissa Turton's beautiful, rustic jungle lodge consists of seven cabins of varying size and proximity to the river, set on 20 jungle-filled acres above a bend in the Belize River. This is the place to come to hear the howler monkeys roar at night and watch birds, agouti, iguana and even the occasional crocodile roam during the day.

Ed and Mel are excellent wildlife guides (and chefs), and their resort has trails to explore, canoes for guest use and even a river-fed swimming pool. All cabin rentals include breakfast and dinner for two at the couple's onsite dining room.

Another surprisingly excellent feature of the Howler Monkey Resort is its newly built bat house; that is, an old cabin that's been converted to a bat sanctuary. The benefit

---

SPANISH CREEK RAINFOREST RESERVE

In one of the most undisturbed corners of Belize, **Spanish Creek Rainforest Reserve** (☑670-0620, 668-3290; www.belizeability.com; Rancho Delores) is a 2000-acre solar-powered farm cultivating the largest collection of noninvasive clumping bamboo in Central America without pesticides, herbicides or energy-intensive irrigation. The farm also has hundreds of tropical fruit trees, including avocados, mangoes and jackfruit. With advanced notice, visitors can take a farm tour to learn all about the sustainable agriculture and community projects here. Long-term volunteer opportunities are also available.

of this to visitors isn't obvious at first, but becomes so once you realize that the bats pay their rent by keeping the area nearly mosquito free.

❶ Getting There & Away

Bermudian Landing is 28 miles northwest of Belize City and 9 miles west of Burrell Boom. Buses depart from the CBS Museum & Visitor's Center to Belize City (BZ$5, one hour) very early in the morning with an additional departure at 3:30pm from Monday to Saturday. Buses leave Belize City from the corner of Amara Ave and Cemetery Rd at 12:20pm, 3:30pm, 5pm, 5:20pm and 8pm.

The CBS Museum & Visitor's Center arranges private transportation between Bermudian Landing and Belize City for BZ$80 round trip.

Rancho Dolores

POP 217

The pristine 5900-acre **Spanish Creek Wildlife Sanctuary** runs 5 miles along the length of the Spanish Creek, beginning by the peaceful Creole/Maya community of Rancho Dolores. The nature here is superb with thick tracts of towering broadleaf forest housing two types of monkeys and scores of bird species.

Like nearby Community Baboon Sanctuary, the Spanish Creek Wildlife Sanctuary is run by a grassroots, community-based group; unlike CBS, it is not well organized. There is a **visitor's center** (☏ 245-2078) on the way into Rancho Dolores in the green building between the bridge and the cemetery, although it's not always staffed. If there's no one around, ask in town for Ms Rosa Joseph or Mr Jude.

In theory, in addition to hiking, local guides take tourists on a boat trip (BZ$100) or canoeing (BZ$20) along Spanish Creek to check out the wildlife; in reality, the wildlife sanctuary does not see enough visitors to keep guides on call – so it might be difficult to make such arrangements.

For those looking for a real adventure, it is possible to travel by boat all the way down Spanish Creek to Crooked Tree, although it's a long trip and it might take a while to sort out the logistics.

Rancho Dolores is located 17 miles west of the junction at Burrell Boom. You will pass through several villages along the way (as well as the Community Baboon Sanctuary) and Rancho Dolores is at the end of the road. Be warned: the last few miles

after Willow Bank are on a dirt track; a 4WD is recommended.

Buses leave Belize City for Rancho Dolores at 3:30pm and 5pm Monday to Friday and 2pm Saturday from the McFadzean bus stop on Amara Ave. They arrive at Rancho Dolores about an hour later. Buses depart Rancho Dolores for Belize City at 5am and 6:30am Monday to Friday, while on Saturday only the 6:30am service operates.

Crooked Tree

POP 805

Founded in the early 18th century, Crooked Tree – 33 miles from Belize City – may be the oldest non-indigenous village in Belize. The story goes that the village got its name from early logwood cutters who boated up Belize River and Black Creek to a giant lagoon marked by a tree that seemingly grew in every direction. These 'crooked trees' (logwood trees, in fact) still grow in abundance around the lagoon. Until the 3.5-mile causeway from the highway was built in 1984, the only way to get here was by boat, so it's no wonder life still maintains the slow rhythm of bygone centuries.

Crooked Tree village is the gateway to the eponymous wildlife sanctuary, quite possibly one of the best birding areas in Belize. It is well worth a visit for anyone who loves nature or anyone who enjoys a peaceful rural community with an interesting history and a beautiful setting. It's best to stay the night so you can be here at dawn, when the birds are most active. Don't forget your binoculars!

The obvious reference point in the village is the 'Welcome to Crooked Tree' sign, at a junction 300yd past the CTWS Visitors Center as you enter the village from the causeway.

◎ Sights & Activities

Crooked Tree Wildlife Sanctuary NATURE RESERVE (CTWS; www.belizeaudubon.org; admission BZ$8; ⊙8am-4:30pm) Between December and May, migrating birds flock to the lagoons, rivers and swamps of the massive Crooked Tree Wildlife Sanctuary, which is managed by Belize Audubon. The best birdwatching is in April and May, when the low level of the lagoon draws thousands of birds into the open to seek food in the shallows. That said, at any time between December and May, birdwatchers are in for hours of ornithological bliss.

Boat-billed, chestnut-bellied and bare-throated tiger herons, Muscovy and black-bellied whistling ducks, snail kites, ospreys, black-collared hawks and all of Belize's five species of kingfisher are among the 276 species recorded here. Jabiru storks, the largest flying bird in the Americas, with wingspans of up to 12ft, congregate here in April and May, and a few pairs nest in the sanctuary in the preceding months.

At the entrance to the village, just off the causeway, stop by the CTWS Visitor Center to browse the interesting displays, books and information materials for sale. It's here that you'll be asked to pay your admission fee. The helpful, knowledgeable staff will provide a village and trail map, as well as information on expert local bird guides.

Walking Trails

A series of walking trails weave along the lakeshore and through and beyond the village. The CTWS Visitors Center supplies maps for self-guided exploration.

Boat Tours

Any of the local hotels can arrange a boat tour of the lagoon (up to four people BZ$200). Tours usually last three to four hours and it's best to plan for an early departure. This activity is particularly worthwhile from December to February, before the level of the lagoon has dropped off dramatically. Expert guides know which birds live in every nook and cranny of the swampland.

South of the lagoon, Spanish Creek and Black Creek harbor plenty of birds all year in their thick tree cover. Black Creek is also home to black howler monkeys, Morelet's crocodiles, coatimundi, and several species of turtle and iguana; Spanish Creek gives access to **Chau Hix**, an ancient Maya site with a pyramid 80ft high.

🎇 Festivals & Events

Crooked Tree Cashew Festival   FOOD
(⊘ May) Crooked Tree is home to a great number of cashew trees and this festival celebrates the cashew harvest in a big way, with music, dancing and lots of cracking, shelling, roasting and stewing of cashews, as well as the making of cashew cake, cashew jelly, cashew ice cream, cashew wine (not unlike sweet sherry) and cashew you-name-it.

🛏 Sleeping

Tillett's Village Lodge   GUESTHOUSE $
(☑ 245-7016, 607-3871; www.tillettvillage.com; r BZ$60-120, lakeside cabin BZ$200; P ❄) The Tilletts are a local Crooked Creek clan who have reared some of the most celebrated bird guides in the country. Their welcoming guesthouse is a good option for those that want to immerse themselves in village life. It has five simple rooms (some with air-con), with comfortable beds, hot showers and an assortment of original artwork featuring the local birdlife.

The thatched-roof upstairs rooms are more atmospheric than the concrete ones below. Wi-fi is available in the front yard area and the little restaurant serves excellent Creole cooking (meals BZ$12 to BZ$20). The Tilletts also have a fully furnished two-bedroom *cabaña* right on the lagoon that sleeps up to six. When its dry you can drive right to the door, but if its raining you might have to reach it by boat.

A pioneering family in Belize's ecotourism field, the Tilletts naturally offer excellent tours around the area, including trips to Altun Ha, Lamani, Belize Zoo and elsewhere. They also lead horseback tours, nature walks and of course, birding trips on the lagoon.

Tillett's is on the main street, 500yd north of the 'Welcome to Crooked Tree' sign.

★ Crooked Tree Lodge   CABAÑAS $$
(☑ 636-3396, 626-3820; www.crookedtreelodge belize.com; campsite per person BZ$20, 1-bedroom cabaña BZ$140-200, 2-bedroom cabaña BZ$400; P 🛜) 🦟 Mick is a British pilot who served for years in Belize; Angie was born and bred in Crooked Tree. This delightful couple has found their little plot of paradise and they welcome visitors! The beautifully crafted wood *cabañas* all have private porches that overlook the lagoon, providing perfect sunrise views. The self-service waterfront bar and open-plan dining room are wonderful and welcoming.

Homemade meals, served family-style, are moderately priced (BZ$20 to BZ$30) and delicious. Mick and Angie will also help you arrange any sort of tour or activity that you wish. The lodge provides reusable water bottles, and campers are welcome to use the fridge.

Note that prices are per *cabaña,* some of which have various beds, and management is quite flexible with squeezing friends together in one room. The lodge is located at the north end of the village; cross the causeway and turn right at the 'Welcome to Crooked Tree' sign.

Bird's Eye View Lodge   HOTEL $$

(☑ 203-2040; www.birdseyeviewbelize.com; campsite per person BZ$20, s BZ$130-200, d BZ$200-300; [P] [✳] [@]) Aptly named, this lodge has an excellent spot for viewing the waterfowl that inhabit the sanctuary's main lagoon. Catering to birdwatchers for almost 15 years, the lodge's 22 rooms are of ample size and include good beds, ceiling fans, Mexican-tile floors and stained-wood wainscoting. The more expensive rooms upstairs have access to the balcony that yields lovely vistas over the lagoon.

Meals (BZ$12 to BZ$30) are served in a bright dining room. The lodge offers lagoon boat tours (BZ$250), nature walks with experienced bird guides (per person per hour BZ$20), horseback riding (per hour BZ$30) and canoe rental (per person per hour BZ$10). There is an onsite gift shop selling local village-made products, including cashew jam, hot sauce and fruit wines. The Bird's Eye View Lodge is about 1 mile south of the 'Welcome to Crooked Tree' sign.

Jacana Inn   HOTEL $$

(☑ 620-9472, 604-8025; jacanainn5@gmail.com; s/d BZ$70/90, r with air-con BZ$130; ☎) Run by the Nicholson family, this friendly hotel sits on a gorgeous spot on the banks of the northern lagoon. While it's still a work in progress, it offers 12 basic but comfortable rooms perfect for birdwatchers visiting Crooked Tree.

Mrs Nicholson will provide breakfast and lunch with advance notice for a small fee, and locally made wines are available for sale.

✖ Eating

Carrie's Kitchen   BELIZEAN $

(mains BZ$3.50-10; ☺ 8am-9pm) Out the back of the village, this small, clean eatery is one of the only places where you can order a meal at any time. It is mostly fast food – burgers, fried chicken and burritos – but there are also sometimes local specialties.

To find it, hang a left at the welcome sign and then take the right fork at the community center before taking the next right all the way to the back.

Nora's   BELIZEAN $

(meals BZ$5; ☺ 8am-8pm) This simple open-air diner serves up good-value Creole plates. There is usually a couple of dishes to choose from and service is very friendly. It's located off the main road to the north of the welcome sign.

ℹ Information

CTWS Visitor Center (☺ 8am-4:30pm) Check in here to pay your entrance to the Crooked Tree Wildlife Sanctuary on arrival in town. You only pay once – no matter how long you are going to stick around. There are interesting books and displays and the friendly staff will give you a map so that you can explore the local trails on your own.

ℹ Getting There & Away

To reach Crooked Tree village, turn off the Philip Goldson Hwy 33 miles north of Belize City and drive across the causeway into the village. The CTWS Visitors Center is immediately on the right. From the 'Welcome to Crooked Tree' sign, other posts will direct you to the various lodges.

Buses leave the village for Belize City (BZ$5, one hour) at 5am, 6am and 6:30am. They return from Belize City at 10:45am, 5pm and 5:10pm, with the first bus leaving from downtown on West Regent St and the afternoon services leaving from the Pound Yard bus stop near the main bus terminal.

Most hotels will arrange vehicle transfers from Belize City (BZ$170) or from the international airport (BZ$150). Alternatively, if your host is willing to fetch you from the Philip Goldson Hwy turnoff, you can take any northbound bus from Belize City.

Old Northern Highway

If you wish to get a sense of what Belize was like before the tourist boom, take a drive along the sleepy Old Northern Hwy, which forks off from the Philip Goldson Hwy about 20 miles north of Belize City. The road was a major thoroughfare during colonial rule, but these days it gets very little traffic, especially to the north of the Maya ruins at Altun Ha.

The Old Northern Hwy is now freshly paved – but still very narrow – from the Philip Goldson Hwy until the turnoff to Altun Ha. It's a scenic drive that traverses dense jungle dotted with tiny villages. North of Altun Ha, the quality of the road declines drastically, and north of Maskall it's all gravel all the time.

Maskall is the only civilization of any note along the Old Northern Hwy, so there's nobody to ask for help if you get a flat tire. Locals advise avoiding the northern part of this highway and approaching Altun Ha from the south (even if you are coming from northerly points such as Orange Walk or Corozal).

◉ Sights

Altun Ha   RUIN
(www.nichbelize.org; admission BZ$10; ⊙ 8am-5pm) Altun Ha, the Maya ruins that have inspired Belikin beer labels and Belizean banknotes, stands 34 miles north of central Belize City, off the Old Northern Hwy. While smaller and less imposing than some other Maya sites in the country, Altun Ha, with its immaculate central plaza, is still spectacular and well worth the short detour to get here.

The original site covered 1500 acres, but what visitors today see is the central ceremonial precinct of two plazas surrounded by temples.

The ruins were originally excavated in the 1960s and now look squeaky clean following a stabilization and conservation program from 2000 to 2004.

Altun Ha was a rich and important Maya trading and agricultural town with a population of 8000 to 10,000. It existed by at least 200 BC, perhaps even several centuries earlier, and flourished until the mysterious collapse of Classic Maya civilization around AD 900. Most of the temples date from around AD 550 to 650, though, like many Maya temples, most of them are composed of several layers, having been built over periodically in a series of renewals.

In Plaza A, structure A-1 is sometimes called the Temple of the Green Tomb. Deep within it was discovered the tomb of a priest-king dating from around AD 600. Tropical humidity had destroyed the garments of the king and the paper of the Maya 'painted book' buried with him, but many riches were intact: shell necklaces, pottery, pearls, stingray spines used in bloodletting rites, ceremonial flints and the nearly 300 jade objects (mostly small beads and pendants) that gave rise to the name Green Tomb.

The largest and most important temple is the Temple of the Masonry Altars (B-4) also known as the Temple of the Sun God. The restored structure you see dates from the first half of the 7th century AD and takes its name from altars on which copal was burned and beautifully carved jade pieces were smashed in sacrifice. This is the Maya temple that's likely to become most familiar during your Belizean travels, since it's the one depicted (in somewhat stylized form) on Belikin beer labels.

Excavation of the structure in 1968 revealed several priestly tombs. Most had been destroyed or desecrated, but one, tomb B-4/7 (inside the stone structure protruding from the upper steps of the broad central staircase), contained the remains of an elderly personage accompanied by numerous jade objects, including a unique 6in-tall carved head of Kinich Ahau, the Maya sun god – the largest well-carved jade object ever recovered from a Maya archaeological site. An illustration of the carving appears on the top-left corner of Belizean banknotes.

A path heading south from structure B-6 leads 600yd through the jungle to a broad pond that was the main reservoir of the ancient town.

At the entrance to the site there is a small museum featuring informative displays covering the history of Altun Ha and a full-scale model of the Kinich Ahau carving.

You can find licensed guides (BZ$20 per visitor) outside the museum building. While

Altun Ha ⊛Ⓝ 0 ▬▬▬ 50 yd

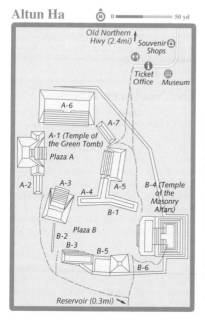

you don't need a guide to find your way around the site, their services are highly recommended as they can show you details you might otherwise miss.

Modern toilets, and drinks and souvenir stands are found near the ticket office, and the site has good wheelchair access.

🛏 Sleeping

Maruba Resort Jungle Spa   RESORT $$$
(📞 225-5555, in US 815-312-1237; www.maruba-belize.com; Mile 40.5 Old Northern Hwy; r BZ$500, junior ste BZ$588, ste BZ$817, 2-bedroom villa BZ$1250; 🅿 ❄ 🛜 🏊) Located in splendid isolation, Maruba takes the jungle-lodge-and-spa concept to extremes of expensive pampering. There are luxurious amenities and a slew of health and rejuvenation treatments. Lush tropical grounds harbor individually designed rooms in a variety of African, Creole, Maya and even Gaudíesque styles – including honeymoon and 'fertility' suites and a jungle treehouse.

There are two pools and a stylish open-air restaurant that serves good seafood and salads. For the active, there are a range of adventures and tours on offer, including horseback riding and jungle excursions.

Nonguests are welcome to visit the restaurant, although reservations are required for dinner service. Visitors can also get access to the lovely waterfall swimming pool with a BZ$70 day pool pass (or by booking a spa treatment).

Maruba is located 2 miles north of Maskall village and 13 miles from Altun Ha.

ℹ Getting There & Away

Many tours run to Altun Ha from Belize City, Caye Caulker, or from San Pedro on Ambergris Caye.

To get here with your own vehicle, turn off the Philip Goldson Hwy 20 miles from Belize City at a junction signed 'Altun Ha,' then drive 11.5 miles along the newly paved Old Northern Hwy to Lucky Strike village, where another paved road heads off west to Altun Ha (2.4 miles).

Irregular buses serve Maskall from Belize City and will drop you at Lucky Strike. Heading back to the city, buses leave only in the early morning, so it makes a day trip to the ruins difficult. Traffic along the jungle-lined Old Northern Hwy tends to be light, so if you're hitchhiking prepare to wait.

WEST OF BELIZE CITY

Formerly the Western Hwy and still referred to as such by many locals, the George Price

Hwy stretches from Belize City through the village of Hattieville, and on to Belmopan and Cayo District. This part of Belize District is mostly agricultural, offering wide vistas of farmland with glimpses of the Mountain Pine Ridge in the distance. At Hattieville, a good, paved road heads north through Burrel Boom to hook up with the Northern Hwy, which is an excellent way to avoid the city when driving around Belize District.

Old Belize

Located just 5 miles outside of Belize City, this strange museum and adventure park was apparently designed to provide hurried cruise-ship tourists with a neatly encapsulated version of Belizean history and culture. Somebody soon realized that most cruisers are looking for sun and fun more than history and culture, so they built a beach (with requisite beach bar). As demand grew for more action and adventure, Old Belize added a giant water slide and a towering swing.

If you are in Belize for one day (as cruise-ship passengers are), Old Belize is a place that you can sample a little bit of everything. If you happen to be here for longer than one day, there are plenty of places where the history and culture, sun and fun, and action and adventure are more authentic and more rewarding. You will, however, have to venture further than 5 miles outside of Belize City.

Any westbound bus will drop you at the Old Belize entrance (BZ$2, 10 minutes from Belize City). A taxi will cost around BZ$30.

⊙ Sights

Old Belize Exhibit   MUSEUM
(📞 222-4129; www.oldbelize.com; Mile 5 George Price Hwy; admission BZ$10; ⊙ 7:30am-4:30pm Tue-Thu, 9:30am-4:30pm Fri-Sun; 🅿) This is the original Old Belize, which manages to pack the country's entire ecological, archaeological, industrial and political history into a 45-minute tour. It starts in the rainforest, with reproductions of the tropical trees and limestone caves that you'll see (for real) just a few miles west. A Maya exhibit has reproductions of some temples and tombs, which you also might see (for real) just a few miles north of here.

The most interesting parts of the museum are the industry exhibits, which display some genuine artifacts, such as a sugarcane press and a steam-powered saw mill. There is also a reproduction of the interior of a Garifuna home, as well as a life-size model of a Belize Town street from the early 20th century.

Your trip through the plastic bowels of Old Belize ends at the gift shop, which is actually pretty well stocked with interesting knickknacks, including T-shirts, rum, chicle gum and Cuban cigars.

Cucumber Beach　　　　　　　BEACH
(www.oldbelize.com; Mile 5 George Price Hwy; admission BZ$20; ⊘7:30am-4:30pm Tue-Thu, 9:30am-4:30pm Fri-Sun) If you are desperate for some beach time but you can't leave the Belize City area, this artificial beach is not a terrible option. It's a 350ft stretch of sand dotted with thatched-roof huts surrounding an artificial lagoon. A massive water slide – also known as Slippery Conch – drops from a 50ft platform into the lagoon and there is a giant rope swing.

The friendly beach bar serves all your favorite fruity cocktails, plus there are showers and changing facilities.

Apparently, back in the 1950s, this plot of land was owned by an American grower and trader, who exported all kinds of vegetables (including cucumbers) to the US. This port was used to package and load the produce-laden boats, and thus earned the name Cumber Beach.

Hattieville

POP 2344

The village of Hattieville – 15 miles southwest of Belize City – takes its name from the infamous Hurricane Hattie that wreaked havoc around the country in 1961. A refugee camp was set up to shelter the many residents of Belize City who were left homeless after the devastating storm. Many residents ended up staying permanently, and so was born the village of Hattieville.

All non-express west-bound buses from Belize City will drop you in Hattieville (BZ$2, 20 minutes).

◉ Sights

Belize Central Prison　　　　　　BUILDING
(Mile 2 Burrell Boom Rd, Hattieville; ⊘9am-3pm) The 'Hattieville Ramada' (as it's called on the streets) is the only prison in Be-

lize and houses criminals of all stripes, from pickpockets to murderers. But don't expect some sort of American-style corporate-owned Supermax with imposing concrete walls topped with electrified razor ribbon. Belize's prison is a low-key affair surrounded by farmland where the inmates work. It's renowned for its prisoner-education programs and the attached gift shop that stocks handicrafts made by the inmates.

🛏 Sleeping

Orchid Garden Eco-Village　　　RESORT $$
(☑225-6991; www.orchidgardenecovillage.com; Mile 14.5 George Price Hwy; d incl breakfast & dinner BZ$280; P🅿🛜🏊) 🍴 Built in a natural setting encompassing 43 acres of jungle savannah (half of which is designated as a protected sanctuary), Orchid Garden is both an ecological and super-convenient place to base yourself during your time on the mainland. The attention in the hotel is top-notch, although the boxish rooms don't take full advantage of the natural surrounds.

In addition to the lodging, the eco-village has nature trails, beautifully cultivated gardens, a swimming hole, butterfly corridor, an iguana reserve, and a small museum with archaeological and geological exhibits.

The excellent Orchid Garden Restaurant features a charming screened bamboo dining room and serves a wide variety of dishes prepared using vegetables and herbs from the family's own organic garden. It specializes in inventive vegetarian cuisine dishes that you won't find elsewhere in Belize.

The location, 15 miles outside of Belize City, makes the Orchid Garden an excellent choice for those looking to avoid staying in Belize City itself. The proprietors offer a wide variety of nature- and culture-oriented day trips all over central Belize, including meals and transportation.

🛍 Shopping

Belize Central
Prison Gift Shop　　　　　HANDICRAFTS
(Mile 2 Burrell Boom Rd, Hattieville; ⊘9am-3pm) The only prison in Belize has a small gift shop (located on the road and outside of the actual prison itself) filled with items from the reformatory's renowned wood workshop, including hand-carved walk-

BELIZE CENTRAL PRISON

Only in a country as laid-back as Belize could a fully functioning prison also be considered a tourist attraction. It's the only prison in Belize (the name 'Hattieville' is to Belizeans what 'San Quentin' is to Americans) and, as such, it houses criminals of all stripes, from pickpockets to murderers.

So what makes the prison worth a visit? Two words: gift shop.

Belize Central Prison (opposite) has a gift shop that sells items from the reformatory's renowned woodshop, including religious items such as crucifixes, statues depicting saints, a host of carved Jesus figures, and even beautifully crafted wooden doors.

This most unusual penal facility is part of the larger vision of an organization called the Kolbe Foundation, which took over the management of the once-notorious government prison and restructured it in a way that was more in line with the foundation's Christian philosophy. Rather than merely punishing criminals by sequestering them from society, the Kolbe approach focuses more on rehabilitation through education and development of skills. In addition to the various craft-making shops inside the prison, there are also a number of small-scale animal farms and gardening operations that supply some of the prison's food. One of the long-term goals of the foundation is for the prison to be self-sustainable; as such, all funds earned by gift-shop sales go back to the maintenance of the prison, meaning that your purchases directly assist in the rehabilitation of Belize's criminal element (who might otherwise wind up robbing you on your next visit to Belize).

ing sticks, traditional masks and religious items meticulously crafted by the prisoners themselves from locally grown woods, such as mahogany, teak and sandalwood.

There's also a fine variety of smaller items, including jewelry, cards, calendars, hammocks, clothing and other assorted knickknacks, all of which have been made inside the facility. The shop is attended by one of the prisoners – complete in jail-issue overalls – who will assist as you as you peruse the selection.

Belize Zoo

You probably won't see a jaguar in the wild, but you will see one at this charming little zoo, which specializes in protecting native species and educating the population about them. Any non-express bus from Belize City heading along the George Price Hwy will drop you at the zoo entrance (BZ$4, 45 minutes).

◉ Sights

★ **Belize Zoo**   ZOO
(☑822-8000; www.belizezoo.org; Mile 29 George Price Hwy; adult/child BZ$30/10; ☉8am-5pm) If most zoos are maximum-security wildlife prisons, then the Belize Zoo is more like a halfway house for wild animals that can't make it on the outside. A must-visit on any trip to Belize District, the zoo has many animals you're unlikely to see elsewhere – there are nine fat tapirs (a Belizean relative of the rhino), *gibnuts,* a number of coatimundi (they look like a cross between a raccoon and a monkey), scarlet macaws, white-lipped peccaries, pumas and many others.

But what really sets Belize Zoo apart is that the zoo itself, and in some cases even the enclosures of individual animals, are relatively porous. This means that the wildlife you'll see inside enclosures are outnumbered by creatures who have come in from the surrounding jungle to hang out, eat, or – just maybe – swap tales with incarcerated brethren.

Among the animals you'll see wandering the grounds are Central American agouti (also called bush rabbits), huge iguanas, snakes, raccoons, squirrels and jungle birds of all sorts. Take a night tour (one of the best ways to experience Belize Zoo, as many of the animals are nocturnal) and you'll be just as likely to see a *gibnut* outside enclosures as in. You'll also be able to hear ongoing long-distance conversations between the zoo's resident black howler monkeys and their wild relatives just a few miles away.

The story of the Belize Zoo began with filmmaker Richard Foster who shot a wildlife documentary entitled *Path of the Raingods* in Belize in the early 1980s. Sharon Matola – a Baltimore-born biologist, former

HURRICANE WATCH

Hurricanes have long bedeviled the Belizean coast, leaving their marks in very visible ways. For example, the Split on Caye Caulker was created when Hurricane Hattie whipped through here in 1961. This is the same storm that motivated the Belizean government to build a new inland capital at Belmopan.

The effects of these tropical storms are not only physical: hurricane season is ingrained in the brains of the residents, who long remember the last evacuation and always anticipate the next one. Any visitor to Belize is likely to engage in at least one conversation about the most recent tempest (more, if it was a bad one). Here are a few of the lowlights from Belizean hurricane history:

Hurricane Five (1931) One of the deadliest seasons in Atlantic-coast hurricane history. Hurricane Five hit the coast of Belize on a national holiday, meaning that emergency services were slow to respond. The entire northern coast of the country was devastated, and around 2500 people were killed.

Hurricane Hattie (1961) This history-making hurricane killed 275 people and destroyed much of Belize City. Afterward, survivors apparently roamed the rubble-strewn streets in search of food and shelter. Many moved to refugee camps, which later morphed into permanent settlements – the origins of the town Hattieville. Hurricane Hattie provides the backdrop for Carlos Ledson Miller's novel *Belize* and Zee Edgell's *Beka Lamb*.

Hurricane Iris (2001) This devastating Category-4 storm made landfall in southern Belize, destroying many rural Maya villages and leaving upward of 10,000 people homeless. Off the coast south of Belize City, a live-aboard dive ship capsized, killing 20 people. Joe Burnworth recounts the tragic tale in his book *No Safe Harbor*.

Hurricane Richard (2010) This Category-1 hurricane made a direct hit on the tiny community of Gales Point severely damaging houses and isolating the village. The only loss of life on land was an expat American who was mauled by a jaguar, which had escaped when a tree fell on its cage.

Recent scientific evidence suggests that the strength of hurricanes increases with the rise of ocean temperatures. So as our climate continues to change, countries such as Belize are likely to experience more frequent and more intense hurricane hits.

circus performer and former US Air Force survival instructor – was hired to take care of the animals. By the time filming was complete, the animals had become partly tame and Matola was left wondering what to do with her 17 charges. So she founded the Belize Zoo, which displays native Belizean wildlife in natural surroundings on 29-acre grounds. The zoo has grown to provide homes for animals endemic to the region that have been injured, orphaned at a young age or bred in captivity and donated from other zoos.

Many of the animals in Belize Zoo are rescue cases, that is, wild animals that were kept as pets by individual collectors. The zoo makes every attempt to recondition such animals for a return to the wild, but only when such a return is feasible. In cases where return is impossible (as is the case with most of the zoo's jungle cats, who have long since forgotten how to hunt, or never learned in the first place), they remain in the zoo: perhaps not the best life for a wildcat, but better than winding up in some closet.

🛏 Sleeping

Tropical Education Center LODGE $
(📞822-8000; tec@belizezoo.org; Mile 29 George Price Hwy; campsite per person BZ$17, dm/s/d incl 2 meals BZ$70/120/150, guesthouse incl 2 meals s/d BZ$141/173; 🅿🛜) 🏵 Run by the Belize Zoo, these rural lodgings are set on 84 acres of tropical savannah with lush gardens and plenty of wildlife. Sleeping options run from dorm-style private rooms – you'll only share with those in your group – in the 'Savannah Castle' to neat, wooden forest *cabañas* on stilts.

Three larger guesthouses are also available, two of which overlook the center's own small lake (home to Morelet's crocodiles). All options have good mosquito screens, hot showers and flush toilets.

A raised viewing platform and savannah nature trails give plenty of opportunities to spot the animals and birds in their natural habitat.

The lodge is just off the Western Hwy, from a signposted turnoff around 1 mile east of the zoo; staff can pick you up from the zoo for a small fee.

★ **Savanna Guesthouse** GUESTHOUSE **$$**
(☑ 822-8005; www.belizesavannaguesthouse.com; Mile 28.5 George Price Hwy; r incl breakfast BZ$120; ☎) ✦ Opened by Richard and Carol Foster, the naturalist filmmaker couple whose productions led to the creation of the original Belize Zoo, Savanna Guesthouse is a fascinating place to stay that sits on the site of the original animal exhibits where it all began. There are just three comfortable rooms, boasting lovely hardwood floors and opening out onto a screened balcony.

While the accommodations are topnotch, perhaps the best reason to choose Savanna is the fascinating hosts who attend their clients with a personal touch. Take a guided walk along the private nature trail, head into the studio to observe firsthand how nature documentaries are made, or just relax and enjoy their amazing tales of jungle shoots in far-flung places.

Monkey Bay

The Monkey Bay Wildlife Sanctuary stretches from the George Price Hwy to the Sibun River, encompassing areas of tropical forest and savannah, and providing an important link in the biological corridor between coastal and inland Belize. Across the river is the remote Monkey Bay National Park, which together with the sanctuary creates a sizeable forest corridor in the Sibun River Valley. The park and the sanctuary get their name from a bend in the river – called a 'bay' in Belize – once noted for its resident black howler monkeys, although now it's rare to see the animals here.

◉ Sights & Activities

Monkey Bay Wildlife Sanctuary WILDLIFE RESERVE
(☑ 822-8032; www.belizestudyabroad.net; Mile 31.5 George Price Hwy) ✦ A natural wonderland located just off one of the country's main highways, this 1.7-sq-mile wildlife sanctuary and environmental education center offers lodging and activities for casual travelers, as well as internship activities for those with a more long-term interest in Belize. A well-stocked library provides plenty of reference and reading matter on natural history and the country.

Activities center around the Sibun River, which attracts sweaty travelers (and other kinds of wildlife) to its inviting swimming hole. Around 230 bird species have been identified at the sanctuary. Larger wildlife, such as pumas and coatimundi, have been spotted on the 2-mile track running down beside the sanctuary to the river. Guided jungle hikes from the lodge to the river cost BZ$50 for one to four visitors. Other activities include canoeing (BZ$90 per visitor) and trips to nearby Tiger Cave. In the dry season, guides take adventurers about 12 miles north to Cox Lagoon, which is home to jabiru storks, deer, tapir, black howlers and lots of crocodiles.

Tiger Cave CAVE
(per person BZ$130) This large cave on a private farm adjoining the Monkey Bay Wildlife Sanctuary can be explored on guided tours.

🛏 Sleeping & Eating

Monkey Bay Wildlife Sanctuary LODGE **$**
(☑ 822-8032; www.belizestudyabroad.net; Mile 31.5 George Price Hwy; campsite per person BZ$22, bunkhouse per person BZ$44, r BZ$65, cabin BZ$109-218; ▣@☎☎) ✦ Accommodations at the sanctuary range from camping out on raised platform decks, to mosquito-screened bunkhouses, to rooms in the field house. All options have shared bathrooms with rainwater showers. It may be rustic, but it's a comfortable and affordable way to spend the night out in the wild. There are also more private *cabañas* with private bathrooms and views to the distant mountains.

The amenities demonstrate ecological principles in action, with biogas latrines (though there are also flush toilets) producing methane for cooking, rainwater catchment and partial solar energy. Meals are prepared for groups, otherwise you'll need to head to one of the restaurants out on the highway.

Cheers AMERICAN, BELIZEAN **$$**
(☑ 822-8014; www.cheersrestaurantbelize.com; Mile 31.25 George Price Hwy; meals BZ$9-24; ⊙6am-7:45pm; ▣✳) This large, airy and friendly restaurant serves hearty meals,

from all-day breakfasts to roast-beef sandwiches to excellent Cuban tilapia. Naturally, rice, beans and stewed chicken are served as well. If you fancy spending the night, there are three simple but spacious *cabañas* (BZ$130) onsite, convenient for an overnight if you are heading further west.

Amigos AMERICAN, BELIZEAN **$$**
(Mile 31.75 George Price Hwy; mains BZ$11-22; ⊙8am-10pm) Amigos serves both American and Belizean cuisine in a distinctly Belizean setting (a mosquito-screened *palapa* house) drenched in pure American whimsy (walls covered in kitschy signs and bumper stickers along with a country music soundtrack). Among the specialties are BBQ pork ribs, as well as some gluten-based veggie options.

ALONG THE COAST ROAD

The Coastal Rd – also known as the Manatee Hwy – heads south from the George Price Hwy, and runs parallel to the coast (appropriately enough) for 36 miles to the town of Dangriga. The Coastal Rd is gravel, which means it is slow going at the best of times, and often impassable during the rainy season. Some car-rental companies advise against driving on the Coastal Rd, which is not really 'a shortcut to Placencia' as it is sometimes called.

Gales Point

POP 296

There's off the beaten track, way off the beaten track and then there's Gales Point. A traditional Creole village, it sits on a narrow peninsula that juts out about 2 miles into the **Southern Lagoon**, one of a series of interconnected lakes and waterways between Belize City and Dangriga. The village was initially founded around 1800 by runaway slaves from Belize City escaping south into jungle and lagoon country.

It remains a very remote and underdeveloped part of the country, but a more beautiful spot you'd be hard pressed to find. To the west, jungle-clad limestone hills rise above the plains that end on the shores of the Southern Lagoon; to the east, also across the lagoon, sits the narrow stretch of forest and mangrove swamp that separates the lagoon from the Caribbean Sea.

Recently, Gales Point has been hit by a series of hardships: hurricanes, an economic downturn, and a complete loss of regular bus services has turned the village into something of a ghost town.

So why come? For the spectacular beauty and superlative wildlife attractions. Gales Point is home to one of the highest concentrations of West Indian manatees in the Caribbean, and the nearby beaches are the primary breeding ground for hawksbill turtles in Belize. The 14-sq-mile **Gales Point Wildlife Sanctuary** (which covers the Southern and adjoining lagoons) offers some of the most amazing birdwatching opportunities in the country.

Getting lost in Gales Point would be difficult – the town's only street runs about 2.5 miles north from the Coastal Rd to the tip of the peninsula, and if you walk too far either east or west you'll be wading in the lagoon. Once you hit town from the south (the only way you can hit town barring an amphibious landing), you'll pass by the police station before coming to the school and a string of basic guesthouses.

🏃 Activities

Nature tours bring most visitors to Gales Point, and for the majority of these you'll need to hire a guide with a boat; all accommodations can set you up with one (your hosts will certainly be able to connect you with a guide, if they aren't guides themselves). In addition to fishing, the lagoons surrounding Gales Point are specifically noted for birding, turtling and, of course, manateeing.

Manatee-Watching
Manatees graze on sea grass in the shallow, brackish Southern Lagoon, hanging out around the **Manatee Hole**, a depression in the lagoon floor near its east side that is fed by a warm freshwater spring. The manatees rise about every 20 minutes for air, allowing spectators views of their heads and sometimes their backs and tails. A 1½-hour manatee-watching boat trip costs BZ$120 to BZ$160 depending on group size. Manatee-watching can also be combined with other activities. (Swimming with the manatees is no longer permitted.)

Turtle-Watching
Around 100 hawksbill turtles, which are protected in Belize, as well as loggerheads, which aren't, lay their eggs on the 21-mile beach that straddles the mouth of the Bar River, which connects the Southern Lagoon

to the sea. For both species, this is one of the main nesting sites in the country. Turtle-watch outings (BZ$350 for up to four guests) involve a boat trip down the river, then a 4-mile nocturnal beach walk to look for nesting turtles.

Birdwatching

In the **Northern Lagoon**, about 45 minutes from Gales Point by boat, is **Bird Caye**, a small island that is home to many waterfowl, including frigate birds, great egrets and toucans. It's possible to visit here on a combined trip with the Manatee Hole for around BZ$200.

Fishing

Large tarpon quite often break the surface of the Southern Lagoon. You can also fish for snook, snapper, jack and barracuda in the lagoon and rivers. A half-/full-day trip for up to three people costs around BZ$350.

🛏 Sleeping & Eating

Yellow Bell Guesthouse   GUESTHOUSE $
(☑ 661-3094, 662-4649; r BZ$50) In front of the school near the entrance to town, Yellow Lodge is the most comfortable of the cheapies. It offers homey rooms complete with worn rugs in a brightly painted wooden house. Owner John Moore offers a variety of tours in his boat, including birdwatching, turtle-spotting and of course manatee observation (BZ$120 to BZ$160).

Ionie's B&B   CABIN $
(☑ 245-8066; r BZ$25-35) This B&B is run by friendly Ionie Samuels (also a justice of the peace, if you've matrimony in mind). This house on stilts has dingy, simple rooms, fans and shared bathrooms with cold showers. Good-sized Belizean meals for under BZ$10 include a drink.

Gentle's Cool Spot   CABIN $
(☑ 668-0102; d/tr BZ$30/55; ℗) Three small rooms with cold-water showers, double bed, a tiny window and little else go for BZ$30. A room with three double beds in a higher house on stilts goes for BZ$55. Meals cost around BZ$7.

Ms Gentle also does hair braiding for BZ$40. Anyone with hair long enough to braid and an hour to kill is welcome. Mr Gentle no longer runs tours himself, but they can organize trips with other local boat owners.

Manatee Lodge   HOTEL $$
(☑ 662-2154; www.manateelodge.com; r BZ$170; ℗ @ 🛜) The only midpriced lodge in the area, Clifton and Nancy Bailey's Manatee Lodge takes up the tip of the Gales Point peninsula and is situated in a beautiful garden surrounded on three sides by the Southern Lagoon. The eight rooms, spread over two floors, are spacious and comfortable, with bathtubs and lots of varnished wood.

There is a large sitting-reading room with a lovely, breezy veranda that overlooks the lagoon. There is also a dining room for guests of the lodge, offering meals (breakfast/lunch/dinner BZ$22/18/32). The lodge is most popular with groups, individual travelers, nature lovers and fishermen. A wide range of activities is on offer, and canoes and a sailboat are provided free for guests.

❶ Getting There & Away

Getting to Gales Point can be quite a mission. The village is located about 1 mile off the Coastal Rd; the turnoff is 22 miles off the George Price Hwy and 14 miles from the Hummingbird Hwy. The Coastal Rd and the road into the village are unpaved and in fairly poor condition and some car-rental companies prohibit driving the route – check before you sign up. The village may be accessible in a normal car during the dry season. In the rainy season, the road floods and a 4WD is essential to avoid getting stuck in the mud.

There are no longer regularly scheduled buses to Gales Point. The best way to travel to or from Gales Point for those who can afford it is by boat via a network of rivers, canals and lagoons stretching from Belize City. The trip takes about two hours, and costs around BZ$400 for up to four people. Arrangements can be made through the Manatee Lodge.

Northern Cayes

Includes ➡

Ambergris Caye
& San Pedro 84

Caye Caulker. 108

Cayo Esperanto 122

Turneffe Atoll. 123

Lighthouse Reef. 124

Long Caye 125

Best Places to Eat

➡ Hidden Treasure (p102)

➡ Habaneros (p121)

➡ Palmilla Restaurant (p102)

➡ Il Pellicano (p120)

➡ Robin's Kitchen (p102)

Best Places to Sleep

➡ Matachica Beach Resort (p99)

➡ Ak'bol Yoga Retreat (p99)

➡ Huracan B&B (p126)

➡ Sea Dreams Hotel (p116)

➡ Caye Casa (p96)

Why Go?

Daydream a little. Conjure up your ultimate tropical island fantasy. With more than 100 enticing isles and two amazing atolls, chances are that one of the northern cays can make this dream a reality.

If you imagined stringing up a hammock on a deserted beach, there is an outer atoll with your name on it. Pining to be pampered? You can choose from an ever-growing glut of ritzy resorts on Ambergris Caye. San Pedro is prime for dancing the night away to a reggae beat, while Caye Caulker moves at a slower pace.

But the islands are only the beginning: the northern cays' richest resource lies below the surface of the sea. Only a few miles offshore, the barrier reef runs for 80 miles, offering unparalleled opportunities to explore canyons and coral, to face off with nurse sharks and stingrays, and to swim with schools of fish painted every color of the palette.

When to Go

➡ **Dec–Apr** Peak season; accommodation prices are high but the weather is wonderful.

➡ **Jun–Aug** Hot, with fewer tourists; lobster season opens.

➡ **Aug** International Costa Maya Festival in San Pedro.

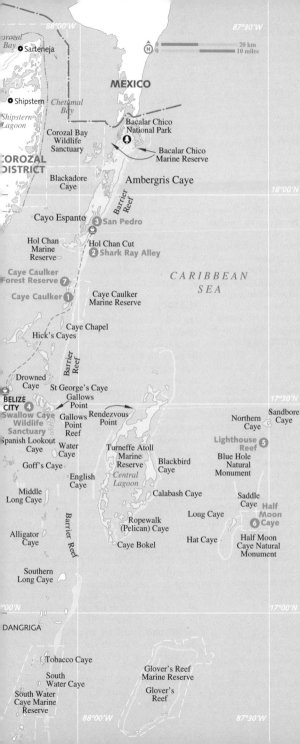

Northern Cayes Highlights

1 Caye Caulker (p108) Availing yourself of the amazing array of aquatic activities – from kitesurfing and paddleboarding to snorkeling and diving.

2 Shark Ray Alley (p91) Being surrounded by nurse sharks and stingrays.

3 San Pedro (p84) Enjoying a sunset cocktail on the deck of a sailboat cruising offshore.

4 Swallow Caye Wildlife Sanctuary (p108) Catching sight of a West Indian manatee frolicking in the shallow waters.

5 Lighthouse Reef (p124) Descending into the darkness of the Blue Hole Natural Monument.

6 Half Moon Caye (p126) Spying a rare red-footed booby.

7 Caye Caulker Forest Reserve (p109) Kayaking into the wilderness to investigate the impressive birdlife.

ℹ Getting There & Away

Scheduled flights and regular passenger boats go from Belize City to San Pedro (on Ambergris Caye) and Caye Caulker; both islands also have flights to Belmopan, San Ignacio and Corozal, near the Mexican border. Northern Caye (Lighthouse Reef) also has an airstrip.

No scheduled boats run to/from the outer islands, but most of the lodges located there provide transportation for their guests.

AMBERGRIS CAYE & SAN PEDRO

POP 16,444

The undisputed superstar of Belize's tourism industry, 'La Isla Bonita' is an enigma that continues to defy the odds by somehow balancing large-scale tourism development with a fun, laid-back atmosphere.

Ambergris Caye remains for many visitors the archetypal tropical paradise where sun-drenched days are filled with fruity drinks and water sports. There are plenty of simple pleasures to be had here from riding a bike along a windswept beach path under the shade of coconut trees to snorkeling in crystal clear waters.

Sure it gets busy – especially in the high season when an endless procession of golf carts takes over its narrow streets – but it's still the kind of place where it's acceptable to stop in the middle of the street and hold up traffic while you catch up with an old acquaintance.

The island is long and thin, measuring 25 miles long and 5 miles across at its widest point, though much of it is less than half a mile across. Although resorts are being erected up and down the coast, its outer reaches are still practically uninhabited. The remote northern extremity abuts Mexican territory, and the Hispanic influence is evident in language, customs, food and fiestas.

Though the entire island is often called San Pedro, technically that's the name of the town that dominates the southern half.

LA ISLA BONITA

When Madonna sang about her dreams of San Pedro, she was referring to the captivating capital of Ambergris Caye, which has since adopted the inevitable nickname 'La Isla Bonita'.

Once a laid-back little village dotted with colorful Caribbean houses, San Pedro is starting to resemble a typical tourist town, lined with souvenir shops and beach bars. The sandy streets have been replaced with concrete, rapidly increasing the number of cars and golf carts on the roads (not to mention the speeds at which they drive). The beach is built up, but while there are plenty of unsightly condos around, there are no massive towers.

Despite complaints about over-development, San Pedro has protected its most valuable asset, the barrier reef, which is only a half-mile offshore. If you are passionate about water sports, San Pedro will seduce you: dive operators lead tours to more than 35 sites, both local and beyond. And if you don't want to look at the fish, surely you'll want to eat them, as San Pedro is home to the country's most imaginative and appetizing dining scene.

History

Once the southern tip of the Yucatán Peninsula, Ambergris Caye was an important Maya trading post. Around 1500 years ago, in order to open up a better trade route between the Yucatán coast and mainland Belize, the Maya dug the narrow channel at Bacalar Chico that now separates Ambergris from Mexico.

As with their counterparts on the mainland, the local Maya inhabitants gradually retreated to the bush as contact with the Europeans became more frequent. Whalers in the 17th century probably gave the island its current name, which derives from the waxy gray substance used in perfume production that comes from the intestines of sperm whales. According to folklore, British, French and Dutch pirates used the island's many coves as hideouts when ambushing Spanish ships, so they may also be responsible for the title. Small treasure troves have been discovered on the island, and gold coins and old bottles have been washed ashore – all evidence of pirates using the island for its fresh water, abundant resources and hidden coves. These swashbucklers turned into mainland loggers who partly depended on manatees and turtles from the Northern Cayes for their survival.

Ambergris Caye was not significantly populated until the War of the Castes, when the war in the Yucatán first forced *mestizos*, and then Maya, across Bacalar Chico and onto the island. The town of San Pedro (named for Peter, the patron saint of fishers) as founded in 1848.

Ownership of the island was bandied about between a group of wealthy British mainlanders. Finally, in 1869, James Hume Blake purchased the land for US$625 with the gold of his wife, Antonia Andrade, a rich Spanish refugee widow from the Yucatán. The Blake family converted much of the island to a coconut plantation, conscripting many of the islanders to work the land.

The coconut business thrived for less than a century. By the 1950s, it had been all but destroyed by a series of hurricanes. In the 1960s, the Belize government forced a purchase of Ambergris Caye and redistributed the land to the islanders.

While the coconut industry declined, the island's lobster industry began to develop. The market for these crustaceans skyrocketed once refrigerated ships came to the island. San Pedro lobster catchers formed cooperatives and built a freezer plant on their island.

Perhaps inevitably, the waters close to Ambergris Caye were over-fished. Fisherfolk looked to supplement their income by acting as tour, fishing and dive guides for the smattering of travelers who visited the island. Today, lobster stocks have partly recovered with the aid of size limits and an annual closed season, but tourism and real estate are the booming businesses on Ambergris.

◉ Sights

★ **Hol Chan Marine Reserve** MARINE RESERVE
(www.holchanbelize.org; admission BZ$20) ✈ At the southern tip of Ambergris, the 6.5-sq-mile Hol Chan Marine Reserve is probably Belize's most oft-visited diving and snorkeling site due to its spectacular coral formations, and abundance and diversity of marine life – not to mention its proximity to the cays. Hol Chan is Mayan for 'Little Channel,' which refers to a natural break in the reef known as Hol Chan Cut (p86). The channel walls are covered with colorful corals, which harbor an amazing variety of fish life, including moray eels and black groupers.

Although the reef is the primary attraction of Hol Chan, the marine reserve also includes sea-grass beds and mangroves. The sea grass provides a habitat for nurse sharks and southern stingrays, which lend

their name to Shark Ray Alley (p87). Snorkelers have the chance to get up close and personal with both species, due mainly to the fact that the animals are used to getting fed by tour boats. All dive operators and nautical tours offer trips to Hol Chan. For information and displays on marine life, visit the **Hol Chan Visitors Center** (Map p92; Caribeña St; ◷ 9am-5pm).

Bacalar Chico National Park & Marine Reserve MARINE RESERVE
(admission BZ$10) ✈ At the northern tip of Ambergris Caye, Bacalar Chico is part of the Belize Barrier Reef Reserve System World Heritage Site, declared in 1996. The park is only accessible by a 90-minute tour-boat ride from San Pedro or Sarteneja in northern Belize, and boats usually make several snorkel stops along the way. Besides the bountiful fish and birdlife, there's a chance of seeing crocodiles and manatees, as well as green and loggerhead turtles. The coral is extra colorful around here, as there is significantly less damage from boats and tourists.

On the way up from San Pedro, boats might stop at Cayo Iguanu, better known as 'bird island,' as it is the nesting ground for the roseate spoonbill and the reddish-brown egret. After visiting the tip, boats motor through the ancient channel that was dug by seafaring Maya about 1500 years ago. Now the narrow channel separates Ambergris Caye from the Mexican mainland.

If the waters are calm, boats go to Rocky Point, notable as one of the only places in the world where land meets reef.

Visitors are required to check-in at the San Juan ranger station at the northern tip of the island, where there is a nature trail and a small museum showcasing Maya artefacts.

In theory, the round trip is on the east side of the island, but this requires a quick detour outside the reef, so in rough seas the boats travel up and down the western side. Not all tour operators run trips to Bacalar Chico, due to the long travel distance, so plan ahead and inquire in advance about trips.

Tres Cocos DIVE SITE
(Map p86) This dive site is a bit deeper than most around San Pedro, with coral heads rising up to 50ft and a wall with spurs that spill out from 90ft to 120ft. The marine life here is wonderful, with thick growth of star corals, big plating corals, red rope sponges and soft sea whips, and gorgonians

Ambergris Caye

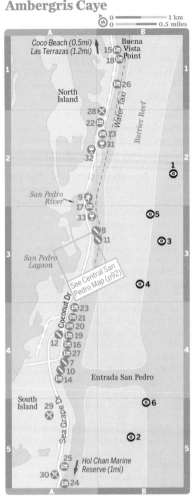

Coco Beach (0.5mi)
Las Terrazas (1.2mi)

North
Island

Buena
Vista
Point

Barrier Reef

Water Taxi

San Pedro
River

San Pedro
Lagoon

See Central San
Pedro Map (p92)

Coconut Dr

Entrada San Pedro

South
Island

Sea Grape Dr

Hol Chan Marine
Reserve (1mi)

on the upper reaches of the spurs. The place is renowned for shoals of schooling fish, including snapper, horse-eye jack and spotted eagle rays.

Tuffy Canyons
DIVE SITE

(Map p86) About 1.6 miles south of San Pedro, this dive site is marked by deep grooves and a long, narrow tunnel. This high-walled passage leads to an opening at 80ft to 90ft onto the reef drop-off. Look for some attractive sponges in the deeper reaches, and the occasional eagle ray passing by. Marauding nurse sharks hang around the entire dive.

Tackle Box Canyons
DIVE SITE

(Map p86) One mile offshore from San Pedro's Tackle Box pier is this great site with big, steep coral grooves. There are swim-throughs in many places along the drop-off on the way to the outer reef. Gray angels, red-band and stoplight parrotfish, and blue chromis hang out along the outer wall, and it's not uncommon to spot marine turtles here.

Cypress Garden
DIVE SITE

(Map p86) This San Pedro dive site is home to resting nurse sharks, turtles, black grouper and tiger grouper. The pronounced under-cuts provide habitat for arrow crabs and various shrimps, as well as drums of all sizes. The coral growth here includes flower coral, thin leaf lettuce coral and some nice stands of the rare pillar coral. There are also some good swim-throughs nearby.

House of Culture
CULTURAL CENTER

(Map p92; Angel Coral Dr; ⊙9am-5pm Mon-Fri) Find out more about the fascinating culture found in San Pedro at this cultural center near the football field. Frequently changing displays celebrate local traditions and events such as Día de Muertos and Garifuna Settlement Day.

Boca del Rio
DIVE SITE

(Map p86) The underwater terrain at Boca del Rio, 2 miles northeast of San Pedro, is a spur-and-groove system, featuring rolling coral hills and sandy channels. This is one of the few sites with healthy staghorn coral as well as plate corals. Around 90ft, there are big coral heads, barrels and tubes, and turtles are often spotted here. Near the mooring is a statue of Christ (now with one arm), which gives this site its alternative name of 'Statue.'

Catholic Church
CHURCH

(Map p92) San Pedro's modern Catholic church has a central location on the waterside and is a local landmark.

Hol Chan Cut
DIVE SITE

Four miles south of San Pedro, this site, part of the Hol Chan Marine Reserve, is famous for its ample sea life, including eagle rays, stingrays and shoaling schools of fish. The channel is lined with large coral, which hides black snapper, chubs, schoolmasters and mutton snappers, as well as moray eels and channel crabs. At the channel mouth, grouper, rays and snapper ride the current. Yellowtails are ubiquitous, but you might also spot

Ambergris Caye

⊙ Sights
1	Boca del Rio	B2
2	Cypress Garden	B5
3	Esmeralda	B3
4	Tackle Box Canyons	B3
5	Tres Cocos	B3
6	Tuffy Canyons	B5

⊙ Activities, Courses & Tours
	Ak'bol Yoga Retreat	(see 13)
7	Belize Pro Dive Center	A4
	Belize Sailing Center	(see 16)
	Bigsup Belize	(see 8)
	Castaway Caye	(see 11)
8	Chuck and Robbie's	A3
9	Go Fish Belize	A2
10	Island Divers Belize	A4
	Just Relax Massage	(see 17)
	Ocean Essence	(see 27)
11	Reef Adventures	B3
12	Scuba School Belize	A4

⊜ Sleeping
13	Ak'bol Yoga Retreat	B2
14	Banana Beach Resort	A4
15	Captain Morgan's Retreat	B1
16	Caribbean Villas Hotel	A4
17	Caye Casa	A3
18	Cocotal Inn & Cabanas	B1

19	Coral Bay Villas	A4
20	Corona del Mar	A4
21	Exotic Caye Beach Resort	A4
22	Grand Caribe	B2
	Hotel del Rio	(see 17)
	Mata Rocks Resort	(see 14)
23	Pedro's Hotel	A4
24	Pelican Reef Villas	A5
25	Victoria House	A5
26	White Sands Cove	B1
27	Xanadu Island Resort	A4

⊗ Eating
28	Aji Tapas Bar & Restaurant	B2
29	Hidden Treasure	A5
	Palmilla Restaurant	(see 25)
	Robin's Kitchen	(see 14)
	Sunrise Island	(see 20)
30	Victoria House	A5

⊙ Drinking & Nightlife
	Crazy Canuck's	(see 21)
	Marbucks	(see 31)
31	Palapa Bar	B2
	Pedro's Sports Bar	(see 23)
	Roadkill Bar	(see 20)
32	Stella's Smile	A2
33	Wayo's Beernet	A3

tarpon. It's a shallow dive that can be quite tricky when there are strong currents.

Shark Ray Alley   DIVE SITE

Only snorkeling is allowed at this perennially popular spot, which is in a shallow part of the Hol Chan Marine Reserve. Shark Ray Alley was traditionally a place for local fishers to clean fish, and the creatures attracted to the fish guts soon became a tourist attraction. As the name implies, the area is known for the big southern stingrays and mooching nurse sharks, which come right up to the boat when it first arrives.

Esmeralda   DIVE SITE

(Map p86) Right in front of the town school, this 50ft to 75ft dive features a spectacular series of deep canyons covered with flourishing soft corals. There is an amazing variety of marine life in the area, including nurse sharks, moray eels and eagle rays, not to mention an astonishing array of tropical fish.

Mexico Rocks   DIVE SITE

This site, 4.5 miles north of San Pedro, is a unique patch reef at the northern end of the island. Snorkelers will find an array of corals, including the *Montastrea annularis*

corals, which are unique to the Northern Shelf Lagoon. Many small creatures inhabit the turtle grass and coral heads, including flounder, walking hermit crabs, conch, stingrays and hogfish. Schooling fish take refuge in the larger corals, while banded shrimp and Pederson shrimp have cleaning stations. The Mexico Rocks area has recently been declared a marine park and a BZ$20 park fee may soon be introduced.

🏃 Activities

If you're into water sports, you'll be in ecstasy on Ambergris. San Pedro is awash with tour companies and individuals organizing scuba diving, snorkeling, windsurfing, sailing, kitesurfing, swimming and fishing trips.

Diving

Many hotels have their own dive shops that rent equipment, provide instruction and organize diving excursions. Numerous dive sites are within a 10- to 15-minute boat trip from San Pedro. Among the most popular (and affordable) are Hol Chan Marine Reserve (p85), south of the island, and Esmeralda, in front of the school.

FEEDING THE FISH

To feed or not to feed? That is the question.

Feeding is common at Shark Ray Alley and other sites, as guides want to guarantee a good time for their guests. Fish feeds usually mean close-up views, more interaction and – sometimes – incredible photographs.

Purists argue that feeding changes a fish's natural behavior; it may alter their natural abilities to forage for food if they become dependent on humans. It certainly makes them more vulnerable to the hand that feeds them as, for example, the wrong kind of food can be harmful. For some people, fish feeds have a tinge of falseness, lessening the thrill of interacting with the creatures in their natural habitat.

This is one controversy that will undoubtedly continue as long as there are snorkel guides and dive masters who want to entertain their clients. One thing that is certain is that feeding should be left to the professionals: lurking barracuda can shred a hand in seconds, poor-sighted moray eels can leave an awful tear in the skin, and aggressive stingrays can give you a mean hickey.

These (and other) fish are inherently dangerous and frequently present at fish-feeding sites. Professional guides know how to look out for fish that could pose a threat – and they know how to respond when somebody scary shows up. So if there is going to be fish feeding taking place during your snorkel or dive outing, leave it to the guide so you can come home with all of your digits working!

Quoted prices sometimes don't include admission to the marine reserves, which is BZ$20 for Hol Chan and BZ$80 for the Blue Hole (p125). Many companies also quote prices without including equipment hire so make sure you confirm what is included.

A one-tank local dive including gear costs from BZ$100 to BZ$150; with two tanks it's from BZ$150 to BZ$200. Night dives are BZ$120 to BZ$140, including a headlamp. Three-day, open-water dive courses cost about BZ$1050 to BZ$1100, including equipment. A one-day Discover Scuba Diving course (offered by most of the dive shops) costs around BZ$340.

Day trips further afield to the Blue Hole and Lighthouse Reef (p124) (three dives) including park fees costs BZ$675 to BZ$700 while Turneffe Elbow (three dives) costs BZ$520 to BZ$540.

There are lots of independent dive operators around town, many of whom also run snorkeling and even mainland tours. Prices are fairly similar but quality varies wildly; diving here is a big investment so it's worth shopping around and spending a little extra if necessary to go with a crew you're comfortable with.

★**Ecologic Divers** DIVING
(Map p92; ☑ 226-4118; www.ecologicdivers.com; single-/double-/triple-tank dives BZ$112/180/247) 🔖 High-end dive shop with great customer service and solid environmental creden-

tials. They offer all of the local dives, multi-day dive charters on luxurious catamarans, fishing expeditions and boat cruises. Management promises small groups with one dive master to every six divers on all immersions. Also recommended for dive courses.

Packages to the Blue Hole including breakfast, lunch, drinks and park fees run at BZ$697, while Turneffe Atoll trips are BZ$540.

Belize Pro Dive Center DIVING
(Map p86; ☑ 226-2092; www.belizeprodivecenter. com; Sea Grape Dr; ☺7am-6pm) Professionally run dive shop with two-tank reef dives and Hol Chan trips departing every morning, as well as offshore dives and dive courses.

Chuck and Robbie's DIVING, SNORKELING
(Map p86; ☑ 226-4425; www.ambergriscayediving. com; Boca del Rio Dr, Wet Willy's Dock) A very popular dive shop with personalized attention and friendly staff who are serious about both safety and diver enjoyment. Also runs recommended snorkeling trips to sites all over the reef.

Scuba School Belize DIVING
(Map p86; ☑ 226-2886; www.scubaschoolbelize. com; Sea Grape Dr) This center specializes in diver training and gets excellent reviews from newbies for the staff's patient and careful approach. Also on offer is a full range of dive and snorkel trips on the reef.

It's located a block back from the water on the main road south just past the bend.

Belize Diving Adventures DIVING
(Map p92; 226-3082; www.belizediving adventures.net) Offers dive trips to the Blue Hole for BZ$695 (including park fee) and single-/double-/triple-tank dives (including gear) for BZ$132/200/279. Discounted multiday dive packages to various sites around the reef are a good deal. Fishing and land tours are also available.

Reef Adventures DIVING
(Map p86; 226-2538; www.reefadventures.net; Wet Willy's Dock; single-/double-/triple-tank dives BZ$156/190/260) A friendly and laid-back dive shop specializing in diving and snorkeling trips to sites around the local reef. It runs snorkel trips (including gear) for BZ$90 and night dives for BZ$170, and also offers fishing excursions.

Island Divers Belize DIVING
(Map p86; 226-4800; www.islanddiversbelize. com; Sea Grape Dr) This knowledgeable and well-organized local dive outfit will tailor dives to individual client interests.

Ramon's Dive Shop DIVING
(Map p92; 226-2071; www.ramons.com; Coconut Dr, Ramon's Village) One of the biggest dive shops on the island this is a good place to arrange offshore dives as they usually have the numbers to get regular trips going.

Amigos del Mar Dive Shop DIVING
(Map p92; 226-2706; www.amigosdive.com) This large operation runs two local dive trips each day, one departing at 9am and another at 2pm. Though it has been PADI certified in the past, it recently lost its accreditation and is not currently recommended.

Ambergris Divers DIVING
(Map p92; 226-2634; www.ambergrisdivers. com) Located on the San Pedro Belize Express pier, this experienced local operator runs trips all over the local reef and also to the offshore atolls. Two-tank dives run from BZ$150 to BZ$180 depending on gear rental and destinations, while Blue Hole trips are BZ$600 to BZ$650.

Snorkeling
The most popular destinations for snorkeling excursions include Hol Chan Marine Reserve and Shark Ray Alley (BZ$90 including park fee) or Mexico Rocks and Tres Cocos (BZ$90). Snorkeling operators usually offer two daily half-day trips (three hours, two snorkel stops), departing at 9am and 2pm.

Full-day snorkeling trips to Bacalar Chico at the northern tip of Ambergris (six hours, three stops) go for around BZ$200.

Many dive boats take snorkelers along if they have room, but snorkelers sometimes get lost in the shuffle on dive boats, so you are better off joining a dedicated snorkel tour whenever possible. Unfortunately, snorkel tours do not often run to Blue Hole, so if you have your heart set on snorkeling around the edge of this World Heritage Site, you'll have to tag along with the divers.

Do not attempt to swim out to the reef from the island as fast boats are unlikely to spot you in the water. You can snorkel around a number of docks around San Pedro including the one at Ramon's Village, but do not venture out beyond the buoys. The docks do not support the extensive life that the reef does, but the snorkeling is free.

Grumpy & Happy SNORKELING
(226-3420, USA 1-888-273-9226; www.grumpy andhappy.com) If you want to enjoy your time with the fish – without having to make conversation with other people – sign up with this husband-wife team who offer private, custom snorkel trips. They cater to special-needs snorkelers with prescription masks and a specially designed, easy-to-climb ladder. There is no storefront, so make arrangements by phone or online.

Manatee-Watching
The most reliable offshore manatee-watching is off Swallow Caye near Belize City. As it is a marine reserve, visitors are not permitted to enter the water and you'll spend the visit watching the animals surface.

Tours from Ambergris Caye usually include a lunch and snorkel stop, in addition to a cruise through the manatee habitat. This trip is slightly cheaper (and travel times are shorter) from Caye Caulker, where folk are also working on manatee conservation.

The all-day tour with Searious Adventures (p90) includes lunch and two snorkel stops, as well as a viewing of the manatees at Swallow Caye. The BZ$180 fee does not include park fees (adult BZ$10, child BZ$5).

With Seaduced by Belize (p93), you can see the manatees at Swallow Caye, have lunch at Goff's Caye, feast at a beach BBQ and snorkel at Coral Gardens all for BZ$210.

When conditions are favorable, it's also possible to spot manatees frolicking in the channel between San Pedro and Caye Caulker. Here it's permitted to dive in and snorkel alongside the animals. Local snorkel guides will know if there are any around and can organize trips to see them.

Swimming

Although there are some sandy beaches around the island, especially in front of big hotels, which truck in sand to furnish their waterfronts, San Pedro is not a classic Caribbean swim-from-the-shore destination. Sea grass at the water line makes entry from the shore unpleasant, so you'll mostly be swimming from piers in waters protected by the reef.

When you do this, watch carefully for boats: there's plenty to see down under if you snorkel, but you often can't see or hear if a boat is coming your way. Have someone look out for you.

Ramon's Village Pier is good for swimming and snorkeling as it has a fairly large area cordoned off for bathers. Of course, the further north or south you go on the island, the fewer people there are on the piers.

All beaches are public and most waterside hotels are generous with deck chairs, but a proprietorial air is developing about the piers, which are also supposed to be public.

Water Sports

Belize Sailing Center　　WATER SPORTS
(Map p86; ☑ 632-4101; www.belizesailing school.com; Caribbean Villas Hotel, Sea Grape Dr) Sign up for sailing lessons for BZ$90 per hour, or if you're already your own captain, rent a Laser Pico or a Hobie and set sail. You can also go kitesurfing – a basic three-hour instructional course costs BZ$400, while rental equipment runs at BZ$240 per half day. Instructors are enthusiastic and highly qualified.

Also on offer are windsurfing lessons and rentals, and kayak and paddleboard rental for BZ$30 per hour.

Searious Adventures　　SNORKELING, SAILING
(Map p92; ☑ 662-8818, 226-4202; www.searious adventuresbelize.com) A long-running and respected outfit that offers a variety of adventures on the water and on the mainland. Combine snorkeling and sailing with the catamaran snorkel tour (BZ$130) which includes three snorkeling stops and a remote BBQ on the route from San Pedro town to Mexico Rocks.

Also runs sailing trips to Caye Caulker (BZ$130), special snorkel trips to Bacalar Chico (BZ$200) and manatee-watching

---

SURF SAFARI BIG FIVE
....

African adventurers have long had their famed 'Big Five' list of must-see big game animals, and the Caribbean now boasts its own version for those who prefer a surf safari. For the wet set, the Big Five includes a selection of the coral reef's most notorious predators. With a couple of trips out to the reef and a little luck, you should be able to complete this checklist. In fact, one visit to Shark Ray Alley will get you nearly halfway home.

➡ **Shark** Even the nurse shark that you are most likely to encounter will on first sight cause a Spielbergian shiver, but that should soon pass after you watch your guide tickle its belly.

➡ **Stingray** These demons of the deep come armed with venomous, spike-tipped tails. The spotted eagle ray is the bigger and badder ray; it cruises the coral in Belize and is rarer to see.

➡ **Barracuda** Reaching 6ft in length and possessing powerful jaws with multiple rows of razor-sharp teeth, meet the pit bull of the reef, capable of a thrusting propulsion when it makes a deadly strike.

➡ **Moray eel** Easily concealing their 5ft-long bodies in a dark pocket of the reef or a crevice in the sea floor, these elongated serpents lie in wait for a quick-strike ambush on passing prey.

➡ **Octopus** With eight arms to hold you, the most cunning of the reef's predators is armed with a sharp beak for biting into fish, and suction cups to pry open shellfish. It is also prey for barracudas, sharks and eels, but can make itself elusive in a cloud of ink.

outings to Swallow Caye (BZ$180). It's located on the beach in front of Ruby's Hotel.

Castaway Caye
WATER SPORTS

(Map p86; ☑671-3000; www.castawaycaye.com; Boca del Rio Dr, Wet Willy's Dock; parasailing BZ$200; ☺8am-6pm) A one-stop water-sports shop offering parasailing, jet-ski rental, banana-boat rides and kayak trips.

Belize Parasail
WATER SPORTS

(Map p92; ☑625-9908; parasailbelize@gmail.com; Fido's Dock; single/tandem flights BZ$158/298) For a panoramic view of the island, take to the air with a parachute pulled behind a speedboat at this parasailing outfit located on Fido's Dock.

Bigsup Belize
WATER SPORTS

(Map p86; ☑602-4447; www.bigsupbelize.com; Boca del Rio Dr; SUP-board rental per hr BZ$30; ☺8am-5pm) Offers SUP-board rentals in addition to instruction and tours. Also offers floating yoga sessions.

San Pedro Watersports
WATER SPORTS

(Map p92; ☑226-2888; www.sanpedrowatersports.com; ☺8am-6pm) Stop by this waterside kiosk for jet skis (BZ$200 per hour), paddleboards and kayaks.

TMM Yacht Charters
SAILING

(☑226-3026, in USA 800-633-0155; www.sailtmm.com; San Pedro; per week BZ$4500-9,900) Based in San Pedro, TMM has a fleet of three catamarans for rent; custom itineraries include all of the islands and atolls.

Sirena Azul
SAILING

(Map p92; ☑226-2326; www.bluetanginn.com; Sandpiper St, Blue Tang Inn) This lovely 40ft wooden yacht crafted from Belizean hardwoods operates out of the Blue Tang Inn and offers snorkeling trips to Hol Chan for BZ$70 and sunset sailing cruises for BZ$100.

Fishing

San Pedro draws fishing enthusiasts who are anxious to take a crack at Belize's classic tarpon flats, which cover over 200 sq miles. The ultimate angling accomplishment is the Grand Slam: catching bonefish, permit (best from March to May) and tarpon (best from May to September) all in one day. In the reef, fishers get bites from barracuda, snapper, jacks and grouper.

Deep-sea fishing is less of a drawcard; most people are here for the reef. There are,

however, stories of giant marlin caught out in the deep beyond.

Fishing is mostly on a catch-and-release basis, but your fishing guide might clean and cut your catch if you intend to eat it. In addition to fishing specialists, some of the dive shops also offer fishing trips.

Go Fish Belize
FISHING

(Map p86; ☑226-3121; www.gofishbelize.com; 7 Boca del Rio) This experienced local operator offers full-day backcountry flats fishing trips (BZ$850) for tarpon, bonefish and permit, and reef fishing outings (half-day BZ$700, full day BZ$850). It also organizes night fishing (BZ$850) and combo fishing/BBQ/snorkeling outings (BZ$950). Prices are per boat, with each boat holding four guests, except for the backcountry trip which holds two.

Tres Pescados
FISHING

(Map p92; ☑226-3474; www.belizefly.com; Barrier Reef Dr; ☺11am-5pm) Get all the gear you need to go fly-fishing at the Ambergris flats or take a guided expedition (full day BZ$900, half-day BZ$700). The fly shop also offers a variety of courses ranging from beginners to advanced fly-fishers.

Cycling

The North Island is a wonderful place for a cycle. With the breeze off the ocean and the palms shading your path, you can ride all the way up to Matachica Beach Resort and beyond. Just follow the sandy path that runs along the beach from the Reef Village Resort in Tres Cocos. There are a few places to stop for a fruit smoothie or an ice-cold Belikin beer along the way. Rent bikes from one of the shops in San Pedro town.

Day Spas

If you have come to Ambergris Caye for a bit of rest and relaxation, you may want to schedule a massage at one of the waterside spas.

Just Relax Massage
MASSAGE

(Map p86; 666-3536; Boca del Rio beachfront) Certified massage therapist Shirlene Santino runs a small beachfront day spa out of a lovely cloth *palapa* tent. Shirlene specializes in Swedish, deep tissue and Belizean-style massage (using coconut oil and incorporating a variety of deep-tissue toxin-releasing techniques). Beachfront massages are BZ$80 to BZ$100 per hour, and house calls are BZ$120 to BZ$140.

Central San Pedro

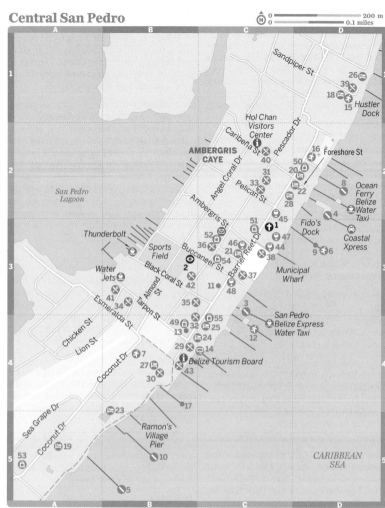

Massage by the Reef   MASSAGE
(Map p92; ☑ 621-8025; Amigos del Mar Dock; massage per hr from BZ$80; ◷10am-5pm) For a massage with a view, head up to this friendly spot above the Amigos del Mar dive shop, with fantastic, uninterrupted panoramas along the full length of the reef in both directions.

Ocean Essence   SPA
(Map p86; ☑ 604-0766, 226-2310; www.amber-grisoceanessencespa.com; Sea Grape Dr; ◷9am-5pm) On a seaside dock a few minutes south of town, this tiny place wins the award for its location – literally *above* the water. In

addition to ear candling (BZ$90), there are plenty of traditional treatments, as well as a romantic oceanside couples massage. Located just south of Xanadu Island Resort.

Delmy's Unique   SPA
(Map p92; ☑ 630-2404, 280-6009; Coconut Dr, Sunbreeze Hotel; massage BZ$150-170; ◷8:30am-5pm) In addition to massages, this recommended spa also offers ear candling, facials, body scrubs, manicures and pedicures.

Oasis Spa   MASSAGE
(Map p92; ☑ 226-4252; oasisspabelize@gmail. com; Fido's Dock; ◷9am-5pm) Head to this

Central San Pedro

⊙ Sights
1 Catholic Church C3
2 House of Culture B3

⊖ Activities, Courses & Tours
3 Ambergris Divers C3
4 Amigos del Mar Dive Shop D2
5 Belize Diving Adventures B5
6 Belize Parasail D3
7 Delmy's Unique B4
8 Ecologic Divers D2
9 Island Dream Tours D3
   Massage by the Reef .... (see 4)
   Oasis Spa .... (see 6)
10 Ramon's Dive Shop B5
11 Reef Runner Glass Bottom Boat C3
12 San Pedro Watersports C4
13 Seaduced by Belize B4
14 Searious Adventures C4
15 Sirena Azul D1
16 Sol Spa D2
17 Tanisha Tours B4
   Tres Pescados .... (see 16)

⊝ Sleeping
18 Blue Tang Inn D1
19 Changes in Latitude A5
20 Conch Shell Inn D2
21 Hostel La Vista C3
22 Hotel San Pedrano D2
23 Ramon's Village B4
24 Ruby's Beachfront B4
25 San Pedro Holiday Hotel C4
26 Sandbar D1
27 Sun Breeze Hotel B4
28 Thomas Hotel C2

⊗ Eating
29 Belize Chocolate Company B4
30 Blue Water Grill B4
31 Caramba! Restaurant C2
32 Celi's Deli B4
33 DandE's Frozen Custard C2
34 El Fogón B3
35 El Patio Restaurant & Grill B3
36 Elvi's Kitchen C3
37 Estel's Dine by the Sea C3
38 Food Stands C3
   Jambel Jerk Pit .... (see 50)
39 Melt D1
40 My Secret Deli C2
41 Neri's Tacos B3
42 Pupuseria Tipico Salvadoreno B3
   Ruby's Café .... (see 24)
43 Wild Mango's B4

⊜ Drinking & Nightlife
44 Big Daddy's Disco C3
45 Fido's C2
46 Jaguar's Temple Club C3
47 Señor Marlins C3
48 Wahoo's Lounge C3

⊚ Shopping
49 12 Belize B4
   Ambar .... (see 45)
   Belizean Arts Gallery .... (see 45)
50 Caribe Creations D2
51 Friki Tiki Toucan C3
52 Gallery of San Pedro, Ltd C3
53 Little Old Craft Shop A5
54 Rum, Cigar & Coffee House C3
55 San Pedro Originals C4

NORTHERN CAYES AMBERGRIS CAYE & SAN PEDRO

well-run spa for massages, manicures, hair brading and facials. It's located over the water at the end of Fido's dock.

Sol Spa SPA
(Map p92; ☑226-2410; www.belizesolspa.com; Front St, Phoenix Resort; ☺9am-6pm Mon-Sat) Sol Spa offers the whole range of body work and facial treatments, as well as yoga classes.

Yoga

Ak'bol Yoga Retreat YOGA
(Map p86; ☑626-6296, 226-2073; www.akbol. com; North Island) With two open, thatch-roof yoga studios (one at the end of the dock), Ak'bol offers daily walk-in classes (BZ$30), in addition to the weeklong yoga retreats that are scheduled throughout the year. It's 1 mile north of the bridge.

☞ Tours

Nautical Tours

Most nautical tours include snorkeling, swimming and sunning; full-day trips also include lunch, and often a beach BBQ. Tours to Caye Caulker and other nearby attractions are often run on sailboats, while those to more remote destinations, such as Bacalar Chico and Swallow Caye, are usually the domain of motor vessels.

Island Dream Tours BOAT TOUR
(Map p92; www.islanddreamtours.com; Fido's Dock) Offers a variety of trips aboard a spacious motorized catamaran including snorkeling trips and an epic sunset cruise that morphs into a full dinner on the water.

Seaduced by Belize BOAT TOUR
(Map p92; ☑226-2254; www.seaducedbybelize. com; Tarpon St, Vilma Linda Plaza; ☺8am-6pm; ☒) Offers a range of sailing trips, including

a sunset cruise and a full-day trip to Caye Caulker. Also runs good-value outings to spot manatees at Swallow Caye (BZ$210), including lunch at Goff's Caye and snorkeling. Other tours include visits to Bacalar Chico and a full-day trip to Robles Beach, complete with snorkel stops and beach BBQ.

El Gato
BOAT TOUR

(☑ 602-8552, 226-2264; www.ambergriscaye. com/elgato; half-/full-day cruise BZ$120/160) Sail to Caye Caulker aboard *El Gato,* stopping to snorkel if you like. Also offers sunset cruises.

Reef Runner Glass Bottom Boat
BOAT TOUR

(Map p92; ☑ 603-0858; Barrier Reef Dr; half-day tour BZ$110; ⊗ 9am & 2pm; ⊕) Here's a way to get a look at the reef without getting wet (if you don't want to). The standard half-day trip visits Hol Chan and Shark Ray Alley. Snorkeling is optional.

Sea Symphony
BOAT TOUR

(☑ 226-2882; www.discoverybelize.com) This strange double-decker houseboat is available for charter trips around the island, including snorkel/scuba trips to Mexico Rocks with open bar and BBQ.

Tanisha Tours
BOAT TOUR

(Map p92; ☑ 226-2314; www.tanishatours.com; inside Hurricane Bar; ⊕) This experienced local tour operator specializes in nature trips. Guide Daniel Nuñez takes his guests to the mouth of the Belize River to see manatees, then continues up the river for sightings of birds, crocodiles and plenty of howler monkeys. He also runs fishing trips and tours to Lamanai. The office is inside Hurricane Bar on the waterfront, south of the dock.

Mainland Tours

Many visitors to Belize use San Pedro as their base and make excursions by plane or

---

SAN PEDRO FOR CHILDREN

San Pedro is among the most 'developed' destinations in Belize, which means the island offers more facilities that cater to demanding tourists. (And let's face it, children are demanding.) There are very few sights, activities and amenities designed specifically for kids in San Pedro, but there are loads of ways to share the joys of surf, sand and sun with your little people.

Sights & Activities

Whether swimming, snorkeling or building sand castles, there's no end to the fun in the sun for your kids. A few pointers for making the most of it:

➡ Frequent the playground just south of the toll bridge.

➡ San Pedro beaches are not ideal for swimming so consider staying in a place with a swimming pool.

➡ Bring lots of books and teach your kids the joy of swinging in a hammock.

➡ Keep a running list of birds, bugs, lizards and other animals spotted (perhaps with illustrations provided by your child).

➡ Dig in the sand. (Pots and spoons work almost as well as shovels and pails.)

➡ Visit the fish! Kids as young as five or six years old enjoy snorkeling. Practice using a mask and snorkel in the bathtub before your trip.

➡ Let older kids paddle around in a kayak or a paddleboat.

➡ Ride bikes. The main roads in town have a lot of traffic, but the North Island is quiet, beautiful and safe. Stick to the road if riding in the sand is too difficult.

➡ Take a family-friendly tour, such as the manatee tour offered by Seaduced by Belize or the Reef Runner Glass Bottom Boat.

Getting Around

The main forms of transportation around San Pedro are boat and golf cart, both of which can be dangerous for children if proper precautions are not taken. Keep small children in the arms of an adult. In town, the narrow roads get congested with traffic, but the beach is a pleasant place to push a stroller. The beach trail on the North Island is only suitable for a heavy-duty baby jogger.

boat to other parts of the country. Mainland trips are operated by many of the dive and boat-tour firms.

Altun Ha (p74), the closest Maya ruin to the cays, is one of the most popular day trips from San Pedro. Trips cost BZ$150 to BZ$220 and go by boat across the San Pedro Lagoon, up the Northern River to Bomba village and then by bus to Altun Ha. Some companies pair Altun Ha with a stop at the exotic Maruba Resort Jungle Spa (p75). The time at Maruba can be filled with lunch, then swimming or spa treatments (at extra cost).

If you're interested in seeing more wildlife, you might combine Altun Ha with a trip to the Community Baboon Sanctuary (p70), Crooked Tree Wildlife Sanctuary (p71) or Belize Zoo (p77), all in Belize District.

Altun Ha is lovely, but it doesn't have the importance or architectural variety of Lamanai (p136). If you want a closer look at Maya history and ruins, consider the Lamanai River Trip (BZ$270 to BZ$310), which takes you up the New River (lots of bird and croc spotting) to the spectacular ruins in Orange Walk. This is a great tour, but it makes for a long day trip in a variety of vehicles – ocean boat, van, river boat and then back again.

Another option is a cave-tubing adventure (BZ$300 to BZ$460) at Nohoch Che'en (Caves Branch) Archaeological Reserve (p159) in Cayo. Tours combine a river-tube float and a tour of a cave, where you'll see stalagmites and stalactites and possibly pottery shards and other evidence of the ancient Maya. At some point during the tour, the group spends a few spooky moments in total darkness. This tour is often packaged with a trip to the Belize Zoo or the Zip-line Canopy Tour at Jaguar Paw Resort.

Tours going all the way west to San Ignacio, Xunantunich and Mountain Pine Ridge are available from San Pedro, but you'll spend most of the day getting to and from these sites. It's better to spend a few days in the west rather than trying to visit from the cays.

★ Festivals & Events

Costa Maya Festival CULTURAL
(www.internationalcostamayafestival.com; ☉ Aug) During the first weekend in August, participants from all over Central America cele-

brate their shared heritage. The streets of San Pedro are filled with music, parades, dancing and drinking, culminating in a bodybuilding contest and the crowning of a festival queen.

San Pedro Lobster Festival CULINARY
(www.sanpedrolobsterfest.com; ☉ Jun) The third week in June is dedicated to the spiny tail. San Pedro reopens lobster season with a block party featuring live music, delicious seafood and the crowning of the Lobsterfest king and queen.

Fiesta de Carnaval CULTURAL
The weekend before Lent is a big party in San Pedro. The parades and costumes of more typical carnival celebrations are replaced with body-painting and flour-fighting – great fun to watch and even more fun to participate in.

🛏 Sleeping

Reservations are recommended for the high (winter) season, between December and May. Almost all hotels accept major credit cards, though you may pay a steep surcharge. For apartments, suites and condominiums, check www.ambergriscaye.com.

San Pedro

Hostel La Vista HOSTEL $
(Map p92; ☎ 627-0831; www.hostellavista.com; Barrier Reef Dr; dm BZ$30-36, r BZ$100-120; ❋) On the site of one of San Pedro's original hotels, in front of the park right in the middle of town, this friendly new hostel has clean and comfortable rooms with air-conditioning. Dorms are fairly spacious while private rooms can fit up to five guests, making them a good deal if you get a group together.

Rooms at the back can be a bit noisy as they are right on Pescador Dr.

Ruby's Beachfront HOTEL $
(Map p92; ☎ 226-2063; www.rubyshotelbelize.com; Barrier Reef Dr; s/d BZ$54/87, r with air-con BZ$130; ❋ 🗦) This white-with-red-trim hotel on the beach near the water-taxi dock is a local landmark and budget favorite. Unfortunately the fan-cooled rooms themselves are pretty tired – but not bad value considering the price and location. Thin walls do little to block out the revelries of your neighbors, so you might as well join the party.

An added bonus here is the downstairs cafe, which guarantees a delicious breakfast every morning. Guests enjoy their coffee on the large terraces that offer sweeping views of the active beachfront.

Pedro's Hotel   HOSTEL, HOTEL $

(Map p86; ☑ 226-3825, 206-2198, 610-5526; www. pedroshotel.com; Sea Grape Dr; s/d without bathroom BZ$30/60, r with air-con BZ$120, deluxe rooms BZ$140; ❄☷☵) One of the cheapest budget options on the island, Pedro's is a longtime San Pedro party-hotel favorite. The original 'hostel' has tiny cell-like rooms with thin walls and shared bathrooms. The best accommodations are near the pool in the deluxe annex, which has 12 rooms featuring flat-screen TVs with 110+ channels, air-con and en-suite bathrooms with hot showers.

Rooms in the slightly older hotel are darker and less appealing, but still have air-con and hot water. The location on a back street south of town is not the most convenient, but you can lounge in hammocks, swim in the above-ground pool or eat pizza at the onsite sports bar, and sleep easy knowing you are saving your money for drinking and diving (and other important things).

Thomas Hotel   GUESTHOUSE $

(Map p92; ☑ 226-2061; Barrier Reef Dr; r with air-con BZ$93; ❄☷) Rooms here are equipped with TV and minifridge. The comfy little balcony out back sports a wonderful view of the building next door. Bit pricey for the ambience.

Hotel San Pedrano   GUESTHOUSE $

(Map p92; ☑ 226-2054; sanpedrano@btl.net; Barrier Reef Dr; s/d BZ$75/85, with air-con BZ$95/105; ❄☷) There are no views from this 2nd-story, streetside hostelry, but you might catch the breeze from the balcony. Relatively spacious rooms have two or three beds.

★ Caye Casa   BOUTIQUE HOTEL $$

(Map p86; ☑ 226-2880; www.cayecasa.com; Boca del Rio; r BZ$250, ste BZ$300, villa from BZ$480; ❄☷☵) At the quiet northern end of San Pedro town, Caye Casa stands out for its simplicity, sophistication and utter loveliness. The sweet colonial-style *casitas* and villas offer thatched-roof porches with wonderful sea views, fully stocked kitchens with stainless-steel appliances and limestone countertops, spacious tiled bathrooms and inviting king- and queen-sized beds.

The hosts go above and beyond to ensure their guests' comfort and convenience. Note the three-night minimum stay during peak periods.

Sandbar   HOSTEL $$

(Map p92; ☑ 226-2008; www.sanpedro hostel.com; Boca del Rio; dm/r BZ$30/120; ❄☷) Rejoice! A tight budget no longer means having to bed down in a stifling room on a back street. San Pedro's only waterfront hostel is also easily its best. The bright private rooms have big sliding doors leading onto a balcony with fine Caribbean vistas, while the air-conditioned dorms are well designed with privacy curtains and individual power sockets for each bed.

Guests can hang out on loungers by the water and use the wooden dock. Downstairs, there is a happening sand-floored bar that serves great pizza.

Conch Shell Inn   HOTEL $$

(Map p92; ☑ 226-2062; 11 Foreshore St; r downstairs/upstairs BZ$148/188; ❄☷) This pink-and-white beauty on the beach offers excellent value smack dab in the middle of town. Recently revamped, the 10 brightly tiled rooms are spacious and comfortable, and the upstairs ones have kitchenettes and hammocks hanging on the shared balcony. The sandy beach area is not great for swimming, but it is decked out with hammocks and lounge chairs from which to watch the comings and goings. Air-con is available for BZ$20 a night but the rooms are designed to take advantage of ocean breezes, so you probably won't need it.

Hotel del Rio   GUESTHOUSE, CABINS $$

(Map p86; ☑ 226-2286; www.hoteldelriobelize. com; Boca del Rio; r BZ$120-150, cabaña BZ$180-300; ❄☷) Just south of San Pedro River, this little lodge is in a perfect spot on a quiet stretch of beach, and provides easy access into town. Rooms vary in size and layout: most enticing are the fan-cooled, thatched-roof *cabañas* (sleeping two to four people) that are clustered around the sandy grounds, which have a central *palapa* that's ideal for socializing or swinging in a hammock.

In the background, the two-story concrete Casa Blanca is less atmospheric but has air-conditioning, while the wooden Palm's building has the cheapest rooms and a large wooden balcony that catches the breeze.

San Pedro Holiday Hotel
HOTEL $$

(Map p92; ☑226-2014; www.sanpedroholiday.com; Barrier Reef Dr; r BZ$268-326, apt BZ$424; ✳🛜) The central location of this place is both a bonus and a shortcoming. Sure, there's great people-watching and easy access to everything, but this is a busy stretch of beachfront and it doesn't get much privacy. Nonetheless, it's a pretty little place, with intricate wooden trim adorning the porches and decks.

The wood-paneled rooms are not particularly spacious and are fairly simple, but they are clean and functional. The suites are not really much of an upgrade.

Blue Tang Inn
GUESTHOUSE $$$

(Map p92; ☑226-2326, in USA 866-881-1020; www.bluetanginn.com; Sandpiper St; r BZ$350-470, deluxe ste BZ$510; ✳🛜🏊) Named for one of the brightest and most beautiful fish on the reef, the Blue Tang lives up to this enticing image. Each of the suites at this beachside retreat includes kitchen facilities, dining furniture and living space. Big windows and vaulted ceilings make the rooms seem even bigger than they are.

Many rooms have good sea views, but for the best views of all, make your way upstairs to the rooftop – one of the highest vantage points on the island – for the true 360-degree panorama.

Ramon's Village
RESORT $$$

(Map p92; ☑226-2071; www.ramons.com; Coconut Dr; cabaña garden/seaside/beachfront BZ$360/450/590, ste from BZ$640; ✳🏊) Guests love the exotic, faux-jungle setting at this luxurious beach resort with a giant Maya mask known as 'Rey Ramon' overlooking the grounds. Thatched-roof *cabañas* are surrounded by lush greenery and flowering hibiscus and bougainvillea, allowing for plenty of privacy. Beachfront *cabañas* are front and center, with uninhibited Caribbean vistas; seaside *cabañas* are set back a bit.

Ramon's boasts one of the best beachfronts on the island, with a dock for swimming and lounge chairs for sunning.

Sun Breeze Hotel
HOTEL $$$

(Map p92; ☑226-2191; www.sunbreeze.net; 8 Coconut Dr; r BZ$376-496; ✳🛜) This reliable hotel is a good choice for those looking for a little comfort without breaking the bank. Located just south of the Belize Tourism Board office, the Sun Breeze has clean and comfortable rooms, featuring two double beds, air-conditioning and hot showers, set around a spacious yard with a fine pool.

Changes in Latitude
B&B $$$

(Map p92; ☑226-2986; www.changesin latitudesbelize.com; 36 Coconut Dr; r BZ$250-350; ✳🛜🏊) Unique in San Pedro for its intimate atmosphere, this B&B is a short block from the beach. The six rooms are small but stylish, with wood and bamboo adding Belizean flair. All rooms overlook a well-tended garden with an exotic flower-covered pagoda – the perfect place for guests to sip fruity cocktails and swap snorkeling tales.

Just across the road and under the same management is the Island Daquiri bar serving refreshing frozen drinks in a garden setting.

🛏 South of San Pedro

If you need a vacation from your vacation, get out of San Pedro. South of town, you can enjoy more peace and privacy, although you still have easy access to the restaurants and facilities in town. If you don't feel like making the trek (more than a mile in some cases), a few restaurants and bars cater to the southerners.

Caribbean Villas Hotel
RESORT $$

(Map p86; ☑226-2715; www.caribbeanvillas hotel.com; Sea Grape Dr; r from BZ$294, suite BZ$424-534; ✳🛜🏊) Boasting one of the widest stretches of beach south of town and two pools, this well-run resort is good value especially for families, who'll love the giant slide into the sea and the floating trampoline. Rooms are simple but comfortable; go for one in the original concrete buildings – they have sea views and get more light than those in the new wooden structure.

The suites are a particularly good deal with some holding up to six guests.

Banana Beach Resort
RESORT $$

(Map p86; ☑226-3890; www.bananabeach.com; Sea Grape Dr; r BZ$287, ste poolside/oceanfront BZ$345/402; ✳🛜🏊) This place may be too motel-like for some tastes and could certainly do with some cosmetic work, but while it is not elegant, it's reasonable value considering the waterside location. Rooms are in a big concrete building and are set either around two swimming pools or facing the water.

★ Victoria House
RESORT $$$

(Map p86; ☑ 226-2067, in USA 800-247-5159; www.victoria-house.com; Sea Grape Dr; r from BZ$400, casitas BZ$670, villas BZ$1950-3950; ❄ 🛜 🏊) This elegant beach resort is one of the oldest on the island, but is meticulously maintained and shines like new. It is fronted by a beautiful, wide beach shaded by a healthy stand of palms, while the grassy grounds center around two excellent pools. Rooms are in thatched-roof *casitas*, or colonial-style 'plantation' houses, with a sophisticated white-on-white scheme that oozes luxury.

Villas are fully furnished with a huge array of top-of-the-line mod cons. It's a bit of a trek into town but complimentary bicycles and four daily shuttles will help get you into town. Considering the beautifully landscaped gardens, huge variety of activities on tap, personalized service and highly touted restaurant, you might never leave the resort!

Coral Bay Villas
HOTEL $$$

(Map p86; ☑ 226-3003; www.coralbaybelize. com; Coconut Dr; r BZ$350; ❄ 🛜 🏊) One of the best deals on the island, this attractive colonial-style hotel is set back from the ocean, leaving a wide, sandy swath shaded by coconut palms free for casual hammock swinging. Six deluxe condos are equipped with full kitchens, wireless internet access, cable TV, and lest you forget where you are, private verandas with sea views. It's accessible to town but the beach gets very little foot traffic this far south, so it feels like you have the whole place to yourself. Bicycles and kayaks are available for guest use.

Xanadu Island Resort
RESORT $$$

(Map p86; ☑ 226-2814; www.xanaduisland resort.com; Sea Grape Dr; studio from BZ$440, 2-bedroom apt BZ$850; ❄ 🛜 🏊) 🍃 If being surrounded by greenery is a priority, it's hard to beat this resort set in lush tropical gardens alive with bird song. Right by the water south of town, rooms have an atmosphere of rustic luxury and are fitted with full kitchens and every amenity. The thatched-roof *cabañas* are clustered around an enticing, solar-heated pool shaded by palm trees.

Bicycles, kayaks, paddleboards and snorkel gear for local explorations are complimentary.

Pelican Reef Villas
HOTEL $$$

(☑ 226-4352; www.pelicanreefvillas.com; Coconut Dr; 2-/3-bedroom ste from BZ$578/998; ❄ 🛜 🏊) At the far south reaches of San Pedro, this intimate resort is a tranquil option for those looking to escape the bustle of downtown without abandoning modern facilities and a touch of luxury. The rooms feature elegant furnishings and excellent kitchens and there is a pool with a cave-like sunken bar and a long dock sheltering a reef that attracts interesting marine life.

Exotic Caye Beach Resort
RESORT $$$

(Map p86; ☑ 226-2870; www.belizeisfun.com; Coconut Dr; 1-bedroom condos BZ$330-430, 2-bedroom condos BZ$470-560; ❄ 🛜 🏊) This small resort has beachfront thatched-roof *cabañas*, a small freshwater swimming pool and a popular beach bar on a pretty, wide stretch of sand. The condos are nothing fancy (certainly not exotic), but the guaranteed views of the Caribbean's sparkling waters make up for this.

Mata Rocks Resort
BOUTIQUE HOTEL $$$

(Map p86; ☑ 226-2336; www.matarocks.com; Sea Grape Dr; r BZ$340-390, ste BZ$445-480; ❄ 🛜 🏊) Modern and minimalist, this intimate 17-room hotel features contemporary design with hardwood or tile floors, stucco walls and high ceilings. Every room gets a bit of an ocean view, however, the property is not particularly big and it can feel a little crowded. Guests can enjoy the complimentary bikes and breakfast.

Corona del Mar
GUESTHOUSE $$$

(Map p86; ☑ 226-2055; www.coronadelmar hotel.com; Coconut Dr; r BZ$298-414; ❄ 🛜) This small hotel has recently taken over the large concrete hotel next door but remains a decent-value waterside option. The rooms in the original Corona building are better equipped than the rundown poolside ones next door, but make sure you get an ocean view; the garden-view ones don't get a breeze and should really be called road view.

🛏 North Island

The North Island is where you should go if you really want to get away from it all. The resorts here are all top end and mainly accessible by boat; you can travel in and out by golf cart or car to at least 5 miles north of the bridge, but the island ferry is probably a more pleasant way to go.

★ **Ak'bol Yoga Retreat**　　　RESORT $$
(Map p86; ☑626-6296, 226-2073; www.akbol.
com; s/d BZ$70/100, cabaña BZ$290-330; ⊠)
Yogis, rejoice! Ak'bol, or 'Heart of the Village,' is a sweet retreat in a near-perfect
location about 1 mile north of town on the
North Island. The seven colorful *cabañas*
have delightful details, such as handcrafted
hardwood furniture and mosaic sinks with
conch shell faucets. Enjoy plantation-style
shutters that open to the sea and mosaic-
tiled showers that are open to the sky.

Alternatively, save your cash and sleep
in the rustic yoga barracks with shared
bathrooms. Either way, you're free to enjoy
the lush grounds and wonderful pool sur-
rounded by greenery. The fabulous food at
the breezy beach bar is worth a trip even if
you're not staying here, as are the daily yoga
classes in the studio surrounded by sea.

Portofino Resort　　　RESORT $$$
(☑226-5096; www.portofinobelize.com; Mile 5.5;
beachfront cabañas BZ$620, ste from BZ$700,
meal plan per person BZ$110; ❋🛜⊠) Who
knew a thatched-roof cabin could be so
chic? With high ceilings and elegant wood
floors, huge picture windows, Mexican tiles
and Guatemalan rugs, these lodgings are at
once primitive and plush. The resort is professionally run and yet remains wonderfully intimate and has personalized check-in
where guests can choose from a selection
of handmade Belizean soaps.

The improved road means that the resort
is now accessible from San Pedro by golf cart,
although the water taxi remains the quick-
est way to arrive. Free pickup on arrival and
drop-off when checking out are included.

Cocotal Inn & Cabanas　　GUESTHOUSE $$$
(☑226-2097; www.cocotalbelize.com; r BZ$290,
casita BZ$350, 2-bedroom apt BZ$520; ❋🛜⊠)
A wonderful antidote to bland condos, the
Cocotal has just half a dozen apartments
offering a cool, colonial atmosphere with
fans hanging from high mahogany ceil-
ings, potted plants, tile floors and wicker
furniture. The most charming unit is the
cupola-topped *casita* with sunlight pouring
through its skylights. It's all very secluded
and sophisticated, and good value to boot.
Complimentary bikes and kayaks available.

Matachica Beach Resort　　RESORT $$$
(☑226-5010; www.matachica.com; Mile 5; r
BZ$650-1500; ❋🛜⊠) Vying for the title of
'swankiest resort,' Matachica is extravagant,
exotic and eclectic. This place is serious
about the idea of tropical luxury, so down
duvets and Frette linens cover the mos-
quito-netted beds, and each thatched-roof
cottage boasts classic furniture and private
patios...hung with hammocks, of course. The
luxury villas have private terraces and outdoor hot tubs.

Other highlights include the excellent
Mambo Restaurant (p103) and the indul-
gent Jade Spa.

X'tan Ha　　　RESORT $$$
(☑in USA 844-360-1553; www.xtanha.com; Mile
7.2; casita BZ$632, villa BZ$690-805; ❋🛜⊠)
Fronted by a fine stretch of white sand
this low-key resort features neat wood-
en *cabañas* trimmed with bright colors.
Rooms strike a good balance between
amenities and tranquillity. Just offshore
there is a large expanse of turquoise water
free of sea grass or you can take a dip in
one of the two pools and watch the iguanas
scurry around the grounds. Some rooms
are a little tight for space, especially the
bathrooms, but all are well finished and
have excellent facilities. Service is top-
notch throughout the resort and the onsite
restaurant serves quality meals.

**El Pescador
Lodge & Villas**　　　RESORT $$$
(☑226-2398; www.elpescador.com; Mile 2.5;
standard r BZ$550, 1-/2-/3-bedroom villas
BZ$800/1250/1700; ❋🛜⊠) 🖉 With the at-
mosphere of a charming old-time fishing
lodge and the amenities of a luxury hotel,
this 21-acre property is a sweet retreat for
anglers and adventurers. Set in an intimate,
colonial-style building, the sea-facing standard rooms have polished hardwood floors
and colorful hand-woven tapestries. The villas are nothing short of vast – perfect if you
have family or friends in tow.

Full fishing packages are also available;
see the website.

White Sands Cove　　　RESORT $$$
(Map p86; ☑226-3528, 602-773-1322; www.white
sandscove.com; 1-bedroom condos BZ$430-510,
2-bedroom condos BZ$630-710; ❋🛜⊠) If you
want to get away from it all without giv-
ing up any of the comforts of home, White
Sands Cove – about 2.5 miles north of San
Pedro – is for you. Condos are furnished
with fully equipped kitchens and spacious
living areas. The beach bar and freshwater
pool are set up for optimal relaxation.

Active types can take advantage of the onsite dive shop or the complimentary bikes and kayaks. White Sands receives rave reviews for exceptional service.

Las Terrazas RESORT $$$
(☎ 226-4249; www.lasterrazasresort.com; Mile 3.5; 1-bedroom villa BZ$725-2250, 2-bedroom villa BZ$1050-2570; ❄ 🛜 ⊞) This stylish resort has a slick, modern design that is big on comfort and service. The wide, coconut-shaded beach is a major selling point, although the manicured resort grounds don't really connect with the surrounding environment. Suites are very well equipped and many boast private balconies with sea views.

Grand Caribe RESORT $$$
(☎ 226-4726; www.grandcaribebelize.com; Mile 2; 1-/2-bedroom condo from BZ$900/1100; ⓟ ❄ 🛜 ⊞) One of the largest resorts on the island, Gran Caribe has around 100 luxurious condos offering sea views and fitted out to the highest levels of comfort. From massive flat-screen TVs to modern American-style kitchens and private wireless routers, the suites have absolutely every modern convenience and are all bright and well furnished.

Even though it's a massive resort, it doesn't feel overcrowded thanks to the spacious grounds and five quality swimming pools. There is also a nice wide dock, complete with loungers and a marked swimming area.

Coco Beach RESORT $$$
(☎ 226-4840; www.cocobeachbelize.com; Mile 3.5; r/ste BZ$805/1265, casita BZ$1035) If you plan to spend a great deal of your trip just lazing in your resort, this large luxury operation is a solid choice. All of the rooms are spacious with modern appliances, big windows and elegant rattan furniture, but Coco Beach's biggest selling point is its two large, brilliant turquoise swimming pools, considered to be the best on the island.

The stretch of beach here is not the best but there's an onsite activity center that organizes trips to the attractions around the island and beyond. It's almost 4 miles north of the bridge. A free boat transfer is included on arrival.

Captain Morgan's Retreat RESORT $$$
(☎ 677-9999; www.captainmorgans.com; casitas/ villas BZ$380/480; ⓟ ❄ 🛜 ⊞) While once it might have been considered a high-end

place, Captain Morgan's now struggles to compete with the newer luxury resorts on the island and could do with an overhaul. Among the many room types, the thatched cabins with private porches overlooking the sea are the most atmospheric.

There are three swimming pools, each with their corresponding bar spread along the waterfront. Beware the time-share sales pitch! There's also an onsite casino featuring slot machines, blackjack, poker and roulette. The resort was the filming location for the first season of reality TV show *Temptation Island*; whether that inspires you or scares you off will depend on what you're looking for in Belize.

✖ Eating

Although there are plenty of options for cheap street food, tacos and fry-jacks, it's hard to sit down at a San Pedro restaurant without paying as much as BZ$50 per person. Dining on Ambergris is expensive, especially in comparison with the rest of Belize. That said, diners usually get their money's worth, as Ambergris is home to the country's freshest seafood and most innovative chefs.

✖ San Pedro

★**DandE's Frozen Custard** ICE CREAM $
(Map p92; www.dande.bz; Pescador Dr; ice cream from BZ$6; ⊙ 2-9pm; 🚶) Don't be confused by 'frozen custard'. It's basically high-quality ice cream, made with eggs for extra richness, then churned as it freezes for extra dense creaminess. The flavors change frequently, often featuring local fruity flavors such as coconut, soursop and mango. Alternatively you can't go wrong with 'not just' vanilla. DandE's also makes sorbet, but you're a fool if you forego the frozen custard.

Belize Chocolate Company SWEETS $
(Map p92; www.belizechocolatecompany.com; Barrier Reef Dr; chocolates BZ$2.50-4; ⊙ 9am-7pm; ❄ 🛜) Run by Chris and Jo Beaumont, the same couple who manufacture the amazing (and Ambergris-produced) Kakaw brand chocolate, this newly opened cafe serves up the finest cacao products on the island.

Come in for a taste of the couple's excellent chocolate, ranging from milk to dark (and everything in between). Especially refreshing in this hot clime is the Chococino, an iced chocolate drink made with French press coffee (BZ$10).

My Secret Deli
BELIZEAN **$**

(Map p92; Caribeña St; meals BZ$8-12.50; ⊙8am-9pm Mon-Sat) This is one secret too good to keep, especially for the budget-conscious traveler looking for good bargain eats. This family-run eatery serves filling Belize favorites such as stew chicken, steak and rice, and chunky chicken vegetable soup. It gets busy but is worth waiting for a table.

Pupuseria Tipico Salvadoreno
SALVADORAN **$**

(Map p92; Pescador Dr; pupusas BZ$2.50-5, mains BZ$10-30; ⊙9am-10pm) For something different that is both cheap and filling, you can't go wrong with this Salvadoran-run *pupusa* shop. The *pupusas* (filled savory maize pancakes) are cooked on a hot plate on the street and brought into the dining room where three old-school TVs blare out three different programs. There is also a good selection of Mexican and local dishes.

Ruby's Café
BAKERY **$**

(Map p92; Barrier Reef Dr; breakfast BZ$2.50-8, pastries BZ$3-5; ⊙4:30am-4:30pm;) This tiny place is packed with locals during the morning hours. Nobody can resist the sweet and sticky cinnamon rolls, chicken-filled Johnny cakes, homemade banana cake, and hot tortillas filled with ham, cheese and beans. There is only one tiny table so grab your breakfast to go and find a shady spot on the beach.

Celi's Deli
FAST FOOD **$**

(Map p92; Barrier Reef Dr; deli items BZ$1-8; ⊙5am-5pm) A fantastic find for breakfast or lunch, Celi's Deli serves great food to go – sandwiches, meat pies, tacos, tamales and homemade cakes.

Neri's Tacos
MEXICAN **$**

(Map p92; Tarpon St; tacos from BZ$0.35; ⊙5am-noon & 5-9pm) For seriously cheap and tasty eats, do as the locals do and head to Neri's, on the back side of the island, for delicious tacos, burritos, fry-jacks and *tostadas*. The large communal tables and laid-back family vibe mean you might make some new friends over dinner.

Food Stands
BELIZEAN **$**

(Map p92; Barrier Reef Dr; snacks BZ$5; ⊙6pm-3am) The fast-food stands around the park are pretty average if you're sober, but are a tasty treat after the bars close when there's not much else open.

Melt
SANDWICHES **$$**

(Map p92; Sandpiper St; meals BZ$10-26; ⊙11am-midnight;) A friendly waterside cafe specializing in artisan grilled cheese sandwiches made with locally baked breads. There are 16 tasty varieties to choose from in addition to gourmet wraps and salads. Also has a good range of breakfast options.

El Fogón
BELIZEAN **$$**

(Map p92; 206-2121; Trigger Fish St; mains BZ$25-40; ⊙11am-9pm) At first glance, the ambience doesn't seem to match the price tag at this backstreet eatery, but once the food arrives you'll not be too worried about the lack of design. El Fogón serves wonderfully prepared classic Belizean Creole cuisine including plenty of fresh seafood cooked to perfection. The conch is especially tasty.

Caramba! Restaurant
BELIZEAN **$$**

(Map p92; 226-3850; www.carambabelize.com; Pescador Dr; burgers BZ$16-20, mains BZ$14-50; ⊙11am-10pm, closed Wed;) Caramba is a busy place due to its excellent food, fun atmosphere and attentive service. Mexican and Creole dishes focus on fresh fish and seafood cooked in at least 10 tasty ways. The tropical decor (including the staff's festive attire) enhances your seafood feast.

Estel's Dine by the Sea
BREAKFAST **$$**

(Map p92; www.ambergriscaye.com/estels; Buccaneer St; breakfast BZ$12-20, mains BZ$15-35; ⊙6am-4pm;) This long-standing breakfast favorite is basically an extension of the beach – complete with sandy floors and ocean breezes. Stop by for a breakfast burrito, fruit-filled jacks or an eye-opening coffee. Breakfasts are served all day but there are also sandwiches, burgers, fish and chips, and burritos on the chalkboard menu.

El Patio Restaurant & Grill
BELIZEAN **$$**

(Map p92; Black Coral St; mains BZ$20-45; ⊙11am-10pm) Potted plants, a flowing fountain and a candlelit interior make this sand-floored *palapa* an inviting setting for a romantic dinner. Grilled meats and seafood are the specialty, accompanied by fresh-squeezed, thirst-quenching fruit juices or ice-cold Belikin beers.

Elvi's Kitchen
BELIZEAN **$$**

(Map p92; 226-2176; Pescador Dr; mains BZ$18-37; ⊙noon-10pm;) This San Pedro institution has been around since the early days, serving up local specialties such as shrimp creole, fried chicken and conch *ceviche*. The funky tropical decor, loud marimba music and T-shirts for sale give it a cruise-line atmosphere, but it's a good place to sample some authentic and filling local cuisine.

Jambel Jerk Pit CARIBBEAN $$
(Map p92; ☑226-3515; Barrier Reef Dr, beachside, Sun Breeze Suites; mains BZ$16-30; ⊙7am-9pm; ⊕) Right on the waterfront, this poolside place serves tasty Caribbean cuisine for lunch and dinner, but most come here for the excellent all-you-can-eat buffet (BZ$40) on Wednesday and Saturday, when you can fill up on conch fritters, jerk chicken, jerk pork and spicy shrimp.

There's another location 5.5 miles north of the bridge at the site of the old Xamanek Resort.

Wild Mango's INTERNATIONAL $$$
(Map p92; ☑226-2859; 42 Barrier Reef Dr; mains BZ$32-48, lunch BZ$16-26; ⊙noon-9pm; ✒) Exuding a carefree, casual ambience (as a beachfront restaurant should), this open-air restaurant manages to serve up some of the island's most consistent and creative cuisine. With a hint of the Caribbean and a hint of Mexico, the dishes showcase fresh seafood, Cajun spices and local fruits and vegetables. The place is usually packed – come early or make a reservation.

Blue Water Grill INTERNATIONAL $$$
(Map p92; www.bluewatergrillbelize.com; Sun Breeze Beach Hotel, Coconut Dr; mains BZ$30-60; ⊙7am-9:30pm; ✒) It's hard to resist the huge open-air restaurant on this beachfront property, and almost everybody who comes to San Pedro ends up eating here at some point. Few are disappointed. The menu is wide-ranging and includes some safe options, such as pizza and pasta, as well as more adventurous dishes with Asian and Caribbean flavors.

On Tuesday and Thursday they offer sushi. The place is always busy, but it's big so you probably won't have to wait for a table.

✕ South of San Pedro

★ **Robin's Kitchen** JAMAICAN $$
(Map p86; ☑651-3583; Sea Grape Dr; mains BZ$15-20; ⊙11am-9pm Sun-Fri, 6-9pm Sat) At his simple, small roadside restaurant south of town, Jamaican BBQ king Robin prepares the best jerk chicken and fish this side of Kingston. Dishes are spicy without overbearing the subtle flavors, and his sauc-

es are also to die for. If you catch your own fish, Robin will prepare it for you any way you like and will only charge for sides.

He also prepares vegetarian dishes. It's a fair hike from town, opposite the Royal Palms Resort, but well worth the trip.

Sunrise Island BELIZEAN $$
(Map p86; Coconut Dr; mains BZ$25-40; ⊙11am-9pm) Tucked away in the back of a residential building, this simple diner serves up high-quality Caribbean fare to match any gourmet restaurant on the island. Everything is prepared from scratch, so it might take a little while; order a couple of drinks and chat with gregarious waitress Margie, safe in the knowledge that when it comes out, your meal will be delicious.

★ **Hidden Treasure** CARIBBEAN $$$
(Map p86; ☑226-4111; www.hiddentreasure belize.com; 4088 Sarstoon St; mains BZ$29-68; ⊙5-9pm Wed-Mon; ✒) Living up to its name, Hidden Treasure is a gorgeous open-air restaurant set in an out-of-the-way residential neighborhood (follow the signs from Coconut Dr). Lit by candles, the beautiful bamboo and hardwood dining room is the perfect setting for a romantic dinner, which might feature almond-crusted grouper, snapper wrapped in a banana leaf, or spare ribs marinated in a Garifuna spice rub.

When you make your reservation, inquire about free transportation from your hotel.

★ **Palmilla Restaurant** INTERNATIONAL $$$
(Map p86; ☑226-2067; www.victoria-house.com; Coconut Dr; mains BZ$40-78; ⊙7am-10pm; ❄✒) The classy, candlelit restaurant at Victoria House is overseen by New York-trained chef José Luis Ortega, who prepares high-quality cuisine for his discriminating guests. At lunchtime, you might prefer Admiral Nelson's Beach Bar, the hotel's casual, open-air cafe on the beachfront.

Black Orchid INTERNATIONAL $$$
(☑206-2441; www.blackorchidrestaurant.com; South Coconut Dr; mains BZ$40-60) Fine dining in San Pedro is still a fairly relaxed affair as demonstrated by this attractive restaurant in the deep south of the island that serves up high-quality meals made from fresh local ingredients in a semi-formal dining room. Alongside the fine cuts of beef, you'll also find pasta dishes and, of course, plenty of fresh seafood.

During the day, burgers, sandwiches and light meals are served. Reservations are recommended.

North Island

Aji Tapas Bar
& Restaurant   MEDITERRANEAN $$$
(Map p86; ☑ 226-4047; North Island; tapas BZ$14-28, mains BZ$28-60; ⊗ 11am-10pm; ☑) If you're in the mood for romance, book one of the six tables at this magical Mediterranean hideaway. Surrounded by blooming flowers and swaying palms, the dining area is only steps from the sea. The menu features a few classic tapas (such as garlic shrimp or bacon-wrapped dates), as well as some delectable seafood dishes (including highly recommended paella). Personalized service completes the delightful experience.

Portofino Restaurant   EUROPEAN, CARIBBEAN $$$
(El Bistro; ☑ 220-5096; www.portofinobelize.com; Portofino Resort; mains BZ$40-70; ⊗ breakfast, lunch & dinner) With a chef trained in French and Italian cuisine, and a brilliant Belizean setting, the European-Caribbean fusion cuisine at Le Bistro makes perfect sense. The menu features freshly caught snapper, lobster and other seafood prepared with diverse (and delectable) sauces. If you're feeling really romantic, inquire about private dining on the pier.

A complimentary shuttle boat leaves Fido's Dock at 6:30pm; reservations recommended.

Mambo Restaurant   MEDITERRANEAN $$$
(☑ 220-5011; www.matachica.com; Matachica Beach Resort; mains BZ$56-68; ⊗ 8am-10pm) Matachica Beach Resort's award-winning restaurant is as eclectic and exotic as the resort itself. Specializing in Mediterranean fare such as pasta and paella, the menu does not skimp on fresh seafood and local seasonal produce. While here, be sure to stroll around the grounds to thoroughly appreciate this tropical fantasy. Reservations required.

Rain   INTERNATIONAL $$$
(Gran Caribe, North Island; mains BZ$32-72; ⊗ noon-10pm) The swankiest place to eat on the North Island is this smart rooftop restaurant in the Grand Caribe complex that serves sophisticated international plates with a view. Prices are some of the highest on the island, but both the service and quality of the dishes is up there. Try the chef's recommended wine pairing menu.

O Restaurant   INTERNATIONAL $$$
(Las Terrazas, Mile 3.5, North Island; light meals BZ$18-30, mains BZ$34-62) Located inside a high-end resort, this modern restaurant feels more Miami than Belize so it's no surprise that the menu goes beyond rice and beans to include everything from curry to risotto. It's a bit pricey, but the quality fare hits the spot if you're looking for something different. Go for a table on the rooftop terrace.

Drinking & Nightlife

Stella's Smile   WINE BAR
(Map p86; ☑ 602-6574; Mile 1, Tres Cocos, North Island; ⊗ 4-9pm Wed-Sat, 8am-2pm Sun) A fantastic addition to the North Island entertainment scene, Stella's is a classy but unpretentious wine bar set in a lovely garden on the edge of the San Pedro Lagoon that affords fine sunset views. Sit on lounge chairs under the trees or at a table in the open-air *palapa* and work your way through the 14 reds and 14 whites on the menu.

There are also rotating wine specials and bottomless sangria (BZ$22) for those who don't have to drive their golf cart home. For eats, there is a small menu of quality appetizers, and meals are prepared by a different guest chef each night – a fantastic concept that allows clients to try some of the best food on the island without going into town. On Sunday morning it's all about the crepes.

Marbucks   COFFEE
(Map p86; coffee BZ$4-15) The North Island's only real coffee shop serves up all kinds of caffeinated beverages – both hot and cold – using quality Guatemalan beans. Also sells excellent breakfasts. It's just off the main road at the Palapa Bar turnoff.

Palapa Bar   BAR
(Map p86; www.palapabarandgrill.com; North Island; ⊗ 10am-9pm) This over-the-water *palapa*, about a mile north of the San Pedro bridge, is a popular place to hang out. It serves good burgers and decent tacos, and is a fantastic place for tropical drinks at any time of day. There are no laws against drinking and floating, so when it's really hot you are invited to partake of a bucket of beers while relaxing in an inner tube.

Wayo's Beernet   BAR
(Map p86; Boca del Rio; ⊗ 10am-midnight) You'll usually find a social crowd gathering at this laid-back bar on the pretty Boca del Rio

waterfront just north of San Pedro's center. Pull up a stool at the well-stocked bar or grab one of the picnic tables across the road by the water and admire the view.

Señor Marlins   BAR

(Map p92; Foreshore St; ⊘9pm-2am) A popular pre-disco hangout, this small open-air bar with a sand dance floor gets packed with locals and visitors alike. The soca soundtrack inside is set to maximum volume, but there is also a large sandy area out front offering a more mellow experience.

Crazy Canuck's   BEACH BAR

(Map p86; www.belizeisfun.com; Exotic Caye Beach Resort, Coconut Dr; ⊘11am-midnight) Open to the cooling sea breezes, staff here are friendly and regular patrons welcoming. Sunday is the big day, with crowd-drawing live music from 3pm. There's also live reggae music on Monday nights, crab races and a live band on Tuesday, and trivia on Friday, which is often followed by karaoke.

Jaguar's Temple Club   CLUB

(Map p92; www.jaguarstempleclub.com; Barrier Reef Dr; ⊘9pm-4am Thu-Sat) You can't miss this surreal Maya temple, complete with jaguar face, across from the central beachside park. The place does its very best to create a 'wild' atmosphere, with jungle dioramas setting the stage and lighting effects keeping it spooky.

Fido's   CLUB

(Map p92; www.fidosbelize.com; 18 Barrier Reef Dr; ⊘11am-midnight) This enormous *palapa* – decorated with seafaring memorabilia – attracts crowds for drinking, dancing and hooking up. There's plenty of seating, an extensive food menu and an ample-sized dance floor. Live music is on every night at 8pm – classic and acoustic rock, reggae and the occasional record spin.

Big Daddy's Disco   CLUB

(Map p92; Barrier Reef Dr; ⊘11pm-4am) Right next to San Pedro's church, this entertainment complex pulls a crowd once most of the bars around town have closed. There is a bar by the water and a cavernous disco behind.

Pedro's Sports Bar   SPORTS BAR

(Map p86; 📞206-2198; www.pedroshotel.com; Sea Grape Dr) A little out of the way, this bar inside the hotel of the same name is a popular place to eat pizza and watch sports on the big screen. There are also regular karaoke nights, if that's your thing.

Wahoo's Lounge   BEACH BAR

(Map p92; Barrier Reef Dr; ⊘11am-midnight) This otherwise innocuous sports bar has made a name for itself by hosting the weekly 'Chicken Drop' (6pm Thursday). Sort of like bingo with chickens, it gives new insight to the origin of the term 'chicken shit.' The sand is divided by numbered squares and a chicken is put in the middle of it; participants place bets on where it will drop a turd.

Give people enough alcohol and they are amused by anything.

Roadkill Bar   BEACH BAR

(Map p86; Coconut Dr) Feels like a beach bar, but it's actually on the roadside a block back from the water. It's a welcoming place that is difficult to fly past without stopping for a drink.

🛍 Shopping

Plenty of gift shops in the hotels and on and around Barrier Reef Dr sell T-shirts, beachwear, hammocks, jewelry and ceramics. But there are also interesting boutiques, fancy gift stores, art galleries and woodwork shops. Prices are high but you might find unique and artistic souvenirs.

Sometimes artisans sell their woodwork and handicrafts from stalls on the street near the central park, and you can often find Maya merchants selling locally made handicrafts along the waterfront north of Fido's dock.

12 Belize   GIFTS

(Map p92; www.12belize.com; Tarpon St, Vilma Linda Plaza; ⊘9am-4pm) If the cheesy offerings on the front street aren't really your style, head up the stairs to this small shop to find a selection of interesting, locally made gifts including handmade soaps, Maya bags and local sauces.

Little Old Craft Shop   ARTS

(Map p92; Coconut Dr; ⊘8am-8pm) Talented and friendly local artist Ricardo Zetina crafts beautiful jewelry and figurines, as well as wonderful wood carvings. If your purchase is too big for your suitcase, he will arrange shipping for you.

Gallery of San Pedro, Ltd   ARTS

(Map p92; Pescador Dr; ⊘9am-6pm) Maintains one of the largest collections of paintings by Belizean artists in the country, in addition to a wide variety of other quality arts and crafts including tapestries, hammocks and masks.

Belizean Arts Gallery ARTS
(Map p92; www.belizeanarts.com; 18 Barrier Reef Dr; ⏰9am-10pm Mon-Sat) This is one of the country's best shops for local art and handicrafts, selling ceramics, wood carvings, Garifuna drums and antiques alongside

TYING THE KNOT IN BELIZE

Getting married in Belize is popular, and surprisingly easy and affordable. Most upscale resorts and hotels offer wedding packages/services, which simplifies the planning process enormously. For a more customized approach, there are a few wedding planners working in the most popular destinations – Caye Caulker, San Pedro, Hopkins and Placencia.

Resources

WEDDING PLANNERS

Hopkins Weddings (www.hopkinsbelizeweddings.com)

I Do (www.idobelizeweddings.com)

Mayan Ruins Weddings (www.mayanruinsweddings.com)

Romantic Travel Belize (www.romantictravelbelize.com)

Sandy Point Weddings (www.belizeweddings.com)

Secret Garden (www.secretgardenplacencia.com)

Signature Belize Weddings (www.signaturebelizeweddings.com)

PHOTOGRAPHERS

Conch Creative (www.conchcreative.com)

Jose Luis Zapata (www.joseluiszapata.com)

Demian Solano (www.demiansolano.com)

Olivera Rusu (www.oliverarusuphoto.com)

Leonard Melendez (www.leonardomelendez.com)

Legal Requirements

Five days, two passports and one justice of the peace is all it takes to get married in Belize. The government bureaucracy that oversees such things is the Belize General Registry. Here's what it takes to make your marriage legal:

➡ Obtain your application for a marriage license from the Register General (available by fax or in person).

➡ Complete the application and have it notarized by a justice of the peace (the Register General can provide contacts for JPs in your area).

➡ Both parties must be in Belize for three days before submitting your application to the Register General.

➡ Submit your application, along with photocopies of your passports showing your photograph and your arrival date. If either party has been married before, proof of divorce or widowhood is also required.

➡ For overnight service, the application costs BZ$500, plus a BZ$10 administrative fee. If you don't need expedited service, the fee is only BZ$200 plus administrative fee.

➡ When it's ready, pick up your marriage license and go get married! The marriage ceremony must be performed by a justice of the peace, a minister of a registered church or a boat captain. Two witnesses (one male and one female) must be present.

➡ After the ceremony, the marriage must be registered in the **Belize Registry Department** (☎227-7377; www.belizejudiciary.org; Treasury Lane, Belize City; ⏰8am-noon & 1-5pm Mon-Fri). Your marriage is legal and valid anywhere in the world. Congratulations!

affordable and tasteful knickknacks. You'll also find a decent selection of paintings by local and national artists. Rainforest-flora beauty products, including soaps, are on sale, too. It's inside Fido's.

San Pedro Originals ARTS
(Map p92; ☑ 226-4075; islandexcursion@btl.net; Barrier Reef Dr; ⊙ 10am-9pm) Displaying the works of eight local artists, this tiny gallery is chock-full of colorful island-inspired paintings. They arrange shipping.

Rum, Cigar & Coffee House DRINK
(Map p92; ☑ 226-2020; saul.rums@gmail.com; Pescador Dr; ⊙ 9am-9pm; ☎) Catering to all of your vices with a good selection of freshly roasted coffee beans, local rums and cigars from all over the Caribbean. Stop by for a taste test, which will give you the chance to sample several coffee and fruit-flavored liqueurs. The coffee can't be beat, and there's even free wireless so you can check your email.

Ambar ACCESSORIES
(Map p92; 18 Barrier Reef Dr; ⊙ 9am-9pm Mon-Sat) Beautiful handmade jewelry in diverse styles, including plenty of options from the namesake stone. Custom designs made while you wait! It's inside Fido's (p104).

Friki Tiki Toucan SOUVENIRS
(Map p92; Barrier Reef Dr; ⊙ 8am-10pm) Sure, this place has loads of stuffed toucans and 'You better Belize it' T-shirts, but it also has a selection of music by Belizean artists, the full range of Marie Sharp's hot sauces, delicious locally grown coffee beans and decadent rum cake packed to travel. You might even find a T-shirt or a baseball cap that you'd like to show off to your friends at home.

Caribe Creations CLOTHING
(Map p92; Barrier Reef Dr; ⊙ 9am-5pm) Take a bit of Belizean style home with you: here you'll find custom-made clothes with Caribbean flair, ranging from beach cover-ups and do-rags to silky sarongs and wedding gowns, all in free-flowing fabrics with a distinctive island design. Its motto is 'from cloth to clothes in 24 hours,' so if you don't see what you like, you can have it custom-made.

ⓘ Information

EMERGENCY
Police (☑ 206-2022; Pescador Dr)

INTERNET ACCESS
Dominio's Internet (Barrier Reef Dr; per hr BZ$10; ⊙ 9am-11pm) Centrally located internet cafe.

INTERNET RESOURCES
Gay Travel Belize (☑ 635-0518) An LGBT-focused travel agency based in San Pedro. Its Facebook page has useful tips for gay travelers.

LAUNDRY
Esmeralda Laundry (Esmeralda St; per lb BZ$2; ⊙ 8am-7pm)
Tradewinds Laundry (☑ 206-2855; Pescador Dr; per lb BZ$2.50; ⊙ 8am-4:30pm Mon-Sat)

MEDIA
Two rival media outlets keep readers informed about news and events.
Ambergris Today (www.ambergristoday.com) Online news service.
San Pedro Sun (www.sanpedrosun.net) Online news as well as weekly printed newspaper.

MEDICAL SERVICES
San Pedro has both private and public health facilities, but for serious conditions you would want to get to Belize City.
Hyperbaric Chamber (☑ 226-3195, 684-8111, 226-2851; Lion St; ⊙ 24hr) Center for diving accidents – it's in front of the Maya Island Air terminal.
San Carlos Medical Clinic, Pharmacy & Pathology Lab (☑ 226-2918, emergencies 614-9251; 28 Pescador Dr; ⊙ 24hr) Private clinic treating ailments and performing blood tests.
San Pedro Policlinic (☑ 226-2536; Sea Grape Dr; ⊙ 24hr) A 24-hour public health clinic.

MONEY
You can exchange money easily in San Pedro, and US dollars are widely accepted. Most accommodations accept card payment.
Atlantic Bank (Barrier Reef Dr; ⊙ 8am-3pm Mon-Fri, 8:30am-noon Sat)
Belize Bank (Barrier Reef Dr; ⊙ 8am-3pm Mon-Thu, to 4:30pm Fri)

POST
Post Office (Map p92; Pescador Dr; ⊙ 8am-5pm Mon-Thu, to 4pm Fri)

TOURIST INFORMATION
Ambergris Caye (www.ambergriscaye.com) Excellent island information and a lively message board.

Belize Tourism Board (Map p92; 🖉 226-4532; Barrier Reef Dr; ⊙ 8am-5pm Mon-Fri) Goverment tourism office with limited practical information.

Hol Chan Visitors Center (Map p92; Caribeña St; ⊙ 9am-5pm) Information and displays on marine life.

❶ Getting There & Away

AIR

The San Pedro airstrip is just south of the town center on Coconut Dr. The Tropic Air terminal is at the north end of the strip, right on Coconut Dr, while the Maya Island Air terminal is on the west side of the strip. All flights depart between 6am and 5pm.

Maya Island Air (🖉 226-2485; www.maya islandair.com) Runs regular flights to Belize International (20 minutes, one way BZ$169, round trip BZ$306) and Belize Municipal (20 minutes, one way BZ$102, round trip BZ$186) airports with some services stopping on Caye Caulker. Also has four flights daily to Corozal and two to Orange Walk.

Tropic Air (🖉 226-2012; www.tropicair.com; Coconut Dr) Operates around 20 flights a day to Belize City's Philip Goldson International Airport (one way BZ$178, round trip BZ$315, 20 minutes), as well as around a dozen flights to the Belize City Municipal Airstrip, 12 miles closer to town (one way BZ$109, round trip BZ$192, 20 minutes). There are also four flights a day to Caye Caulker (one way BZ$106, round trip BZ$186, five minutes, six daily). Other destinations include Corozal, Orange Walk and San Ignacio.

BOAT

There are two water-taxi companies running the route between San Pedro and Belize City via Caye Caulker, both departing from docks on the reef side of the island.

Ocean Ferry Belize (Map p92; 🖉 226-2033; www.oceanferrybelize.com; Caribeña St) Leaves San Pedro for Caye Caulker (one way BZ$19, round trip BZ$29, 40 minutes) and Belize City (one way BZ$29, round trip BZ$49, 1½ hours) at 6am, 8am, 10am, 1pm and 4pm.

San Pedro Belize Express Water Taxi (Map p92; 🖉 226-3535; www.belizewatertaxi.com; Black Coral St) Departs San Pedro for Caye Caulker (one way BZ$30, round trip BZ$50, 40 minutes) and Belize City (one way BZ$40, round trip BZ$70, 1½ hours) at 6am, 6:30am, 7:30am, 8:30am, 10am, 11:30am, 1pm, 3pm and 4:30pm.

Thunderbolt (Map p92; 🖉 631-3400; Black Coral St; one way/round trip BZ$50/90) Operates a daily service between San Pedro and Corozal in northern Belize (one way BZ$50, round trip BZ$90, two hours) departing from

behind the football field on the lagoon side of the island.

There are also departures every morning at 8am for Chetumal, Mexico (one way BZ$100 to BZ$110, two hours), from the International Departures Dock on the lagoon side of town with companies **Water Jets** (Map p92; 🖉 226-2194; www.sanpedrowatertaxi.com; Tarpon St) and San Pedro Express taking turns to make the run.

❶ Getting Around

You can walk into the center of town from the airport terminals in five minutes and the walk from the boat docks is even shorter. Minivan taxis ply the streets looking for customers. Official rates are BZ$7 during the day and BZ$10 at night to anywhere in the town center. For hotels outside the center, negotiate the rate before hopping in.

There is a small toll bridge over the San Pedro river. Pay a ridiculous BZ$5 for each 20m crossing on a golf cart. Bicycles cross for free.

BICYCLE

Many hotels and resorts provide bikes for their guests for a small fee or for free. Otherwise, you can rent a bike at a couple of places in town, such as **Beach Cruiser** (🖉 651-1533; solenyancona@ gmail.com; Pescador Dr; per day BZ$18; ⊙ 9am-7pm Mon-Thu, to 9pm Fri & Sat) and **Joe's Bicycle Rentals** (🖉 226-5371; cnr Pescador Dr & Caribeña St; per day BZ$15; ⊙ 8am-6pm).

BOAT

The **Coastal Xpress** (Map p92; 🖉 226-2007; www.coastalxpress.com; Caribeña St; per trip BZ$10-28, day pass BZ$50, week pass BZ$250; ⊙ 5am-10pm) operates a regular scheduled passenger boat service between San Pedro town and the resorts on the North Island. Boats leave from the Amigos del Mar pier roughly every two hours from 5:30am to 10pm. Charter services are also available to destinations outside their normal route or schedule. Tickets costs BZ$10 to BZ$28 depending on distance traveled, but if you are staying on the North Island you may want to consider a weeklong pass (BZ$250).

Many resorts and restaurants also offer a water-shuttle service into town for clients.

GOLF CART

These days, traffic jams are not unusual in San Pedro due to the glut of golf carts cruising the streets. Note that some golf carts are battery-powered and others run on gas; the former being more ecologically sound and the latter having greater endurance. Expect to pay between BZ$140 and BZ$160 per day, although when things are slow you can negotiate a sizeable discount. Most rental outlets will drop the cart off at your hotel.

Gulf Karts (☑615-5278; www.belizebuggies. com; Lion St; ☺8am-6pm) A laid-back place with good prices and attentive service.

Island Adventures (☑226-4343; www. islandgolfcarts.com; Coconut Dr) Has good new carts and a central location.

Moncho's Cart Rentals (☑226-4490; www. sanpedrogolfcartrental.com; 11 Coconut Dr; ☺8am-5pm) A professional operator with a large fleet of quality vehicles.

Polo's Golf Carts (☑226-3542; Barrier Reef Dr; ☺7am-7pm)

Rocks Golf Cart Rentals (☑226-2044; Pescador Drive; ☺8am-9pm) Located inside the Rocks Grocery Store; significant discounts are available during slower times.

CAYE CAULKER

POP 1763

'No Shirt, No Shoes...No Problem.' You'll see this sign everywhere in Belize, but no place is it more apt than Caye Caulker. Indeed, nothing seems to be a problem on this tiny island, where dogs nap in the middle of the dirt road and suntanned cyclists pedal around them. The only traffic sign on the island instructs golf carts and bicycles to 'go slow,' a directive that is taken seriously.

Local residents have traditionally made their living from the sea, specifically the spiny lobsters and red snapper that inhabit its warm waters. It has also long been a budget traveler's mecca, but in recent years, tourists of all ages and incomes have begun to appreciate the island's unique atmosphere.

On Caye Caulker, there are no cars, no fumes and no hassles, just balmy breezes, fresh seafood, azure waters and a fantastic barrier reef at its doorstep. The easygoing attitude is due in part to the strong Creole presence on the island, which pulses to a classic reggae beat and is home to a small community of Rastafarians.

While the increase in visitors has resulted in more construction and a strain on the islands fledgling infrastructure, the surrounding nature remains both accessible and enthralling.

The island is an ideal base for snorkeling and diving adventures at the nearby reef. The northern part of the island – a tempting destination for kayakers – is mostly mangroves, which are home to an amazing variety of birdlife. Other than that, all visitors should be sure to schedule in plenty of time for swinging in hammocks and enjoy-ing the breeze (which is indeed a legitimate activity on Caye Caulker).

History

Caye Caulker was originally a fishing settlement. It became popular with 17th-century British buccaneers as a place to stop for water and to work on their boats. Like its neighbor Ambergris Caye, it grew in population with the War of the Castes. It was purchased in 1870 by Luciano Reyes, whose descendants still live on the island. Reyes parceled the land out to a handful of families, and to this day, descendants of those first landowners still live in the general vicinities of those original parcels. These islanders were self-sufficient, exporting turtle meat until the turtle population was decimated.

During much of the 20th century, coconut processing, fishing, lobster trapping and boat building formed the backbone of the island's economy. Caulker was one of the first islands to establish a fisherfolk cooperative in the 1960s, allowing members to receive fair prices for the lobster and other sea life pulled from their waters.

Caye Caulker remains a fishing village at heart, and fishing (as well as boat design and construction) continue. Tourism, which began as a small part of Caulker's economy in the late 1960s and 1970s (when small numbers of hippies found their way to the island), has become its prime economic mover, and the idea of Caulker without tourism would strike most Belizeans as ludicrous. Today, many islanders operate tourism-related businesses, but there are no plans for large-scale development. Caulker residents enjoy the slow rhythm of life as much as visitors do.

⦿ Sights

Swallow Caye
Wildlife Sanctuary　　　　MARINE RESERVE
(☑226-0567; www.swallowcayemanatees.org; adult/child BZ$10/5) ⬤ About 19 miles southwest of Caye Caulker, the vast Swallow Caye Wildlife Sanctuary spans nearly 9000 acres, including Swallow Caye and some parts of nearby Drowned Caye. Here the ocean floor is covered with turtle-grass beds, which support a small population of West Indian manatees.

After tireless efforts on the part of conservationists and guides, a wildlife sanctuary was established here in 2002.

Swimming with manatees is forbidden by the Belizean authorities, while education programs dissuade boat operators from using their motors near the manatees and from speeding through the area (propeller injuries are one of the chief causes of manatee deaths.) There is a permanent caretaker in these waters, although some complain that this is not enough to adequately enforce regulations.

Patient visitors are usually rewarded with several sightings of breaching and feeding manatees, often including a mother and calf swimming together.

Caye Caulker
Marine Reserve　　　　MARINE RESERVE

🐟 Declared a marine reserve in 1998, the 61-sq-mile Caye Caulker Marine Reserve includes the portion of the barrier reef that runs parallel to the island, as well as the turtle-grass lagoon adjacent to the Caye Caulker Forest Reserve. It is rich with sea life, including colorful sponges, blue-and-yellow queen angel fish, Christmas tree worms, star coral, redband parrotfish, yellow gorgonians and more.

Between April and September, snorkelers and divers might even spot a turtle or manatee. All local snorkel and dive operators lead tours to the Caye Caulker Marine Reserve.

The Split　　　　BEACH
A narrow channel that splits Caye Caulker into two, the Split has clean, deep waters free of seaweed, making it one of the island's best swimming areas. The loud music and rowdy crowd at the adjacent bar will either enhance or dampen your experience, depending on what you're looking for.

Public Beach　　　　BEACH
There is not much in the way of sand at Caye Caulker's main swimming area, just before the Split, but sun-lovers make use of the crumbing sea wall to take a rest between dips in the crystal clear Caribbean waters.

Caye Caulker
Forest Reserve　　　　NATURE RESERVE

🐟 The northernmost 100 acres of the island constitute the Caye Caulker Forest Reserve, declared in 1998. Birdlife is prolific in the reserve, particularly wading birds, such as the tricolored heron, and songbirds, including the mangrove warbler. Somewhat rare species that can be spotted include the white-crowned pigeon, rufus-necked rail

and black catbird. Inland lagoons provide habitat for crocodiles and turtles, five species of crab, boa constrictors, scaly tailed iguanas (locally called 'wish willies'), geckos and lizards.

The littoral forest on Caye Caulker is mostly red, white and black mangrove, which grows in the shallow water. The mangroves' root systems support an intricate ecosystem, including sponges, gorgonians, anemones and a wide variety of fish. Besides the mangroves, the forest contains buttonwood, gumbo-limbo (the 'tourist tree'), poisonwood, madre de cacao, ficus and ziracote. Coconut palms and Australian pines are not native to this region, but there is no shortage of them.

The forest reserve is an excellent, but very challenging destination for kayakers. You may prefer to paddle up the calmer, west side of the island to avoid strong winds and rough seas.

Assembleas de Dios Church　　　　CHURCH
(Estella St) A small local church serving the island's Spanish-speaking residents.

Catholic Church　　　　CHURCH
(Middle St) The island's Latin roots can be observed at the simple Nuestra Señora de la Asunción church, which serves the Catholic community.

🏃 Activities
Activities on the island focus on water sports and sea life.

Diving
There are enough top-class dive sites in the surrounding area to inspire divers of all levels to stick around for a while.

Common dives made from Caye Caulker include two-tank dives to the local reef (BZ$170 to BZ$200) and two-tank dives to check out the wide variety of aquatic life at Esmeralda off San Pedro (Ambergris Caye, BZ$230). You can also organize three-tank dives off Turneffe Atoll (BZ$300 to BZ$400) and three-tank trips to the Blue Hole Natural Monument and Half Moon Caye (BZ$480 including park fees) but these are often subcontracted out to bigger operators from San Pedro, so make sure you know who you are going with before you sign up.

Belize Diving Services　　　　DIVING
(☑ 226-0143; www.belizedivingservices.net; Chapoose St) Professional and highly

Caye Caulker

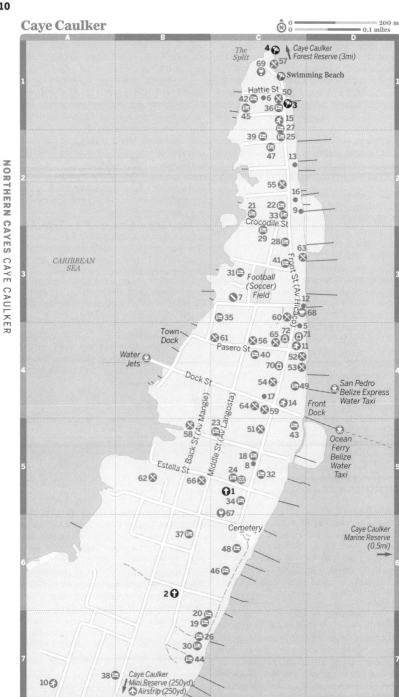

Caye Caulker

⊙ Sights
1 Assembleas de Dios Church C5
2 Catholic Church B6
3 Public Beach.. C1
4 The Split.. C1

⊕ Activities, Courses & Tours
5 Anda De Wata Tours C4
6 Anglers Abroad C1
  Barefoot Fisherman
    Expeditions .... (see 50)
7 Belize Diving Services C3
  Blackhawk Sailing Tours..............(see 25)
8 Carlos Tours C5
9 Caveman Tours... C2
10 Coco Plum Gardens................................. A7
11 Contour C4
12 E-Z Boy C3
13 Frenchie's Diving...................................... C2
14 Healing Touch Day Spa C4
15 Kitexplorer.. C1
16 Raggamuffin Tours C2
  Reef Watersports......................... (see 36)
  Spearfishing Shack.......................(see 21)
17 Stressless Tours C4
  Tsunami Adventures....................(see 27)

⊙ Sleeping
18 Amanda's Place C5
19 Anchorage Resort.................................... B7
20 Barefoot Beach Belize............................ B7
21 Bella's Hostel... C2
22 Blue Wave C2
  Caye Caulker Condos.................. (see 36)
23 Caye Caulker Plaza Hotel C5
24 Caye Caulker Rentals.............................. C5
25 Caye Reef.. C2
26 Colinda Cabanas...................................... B7
27 Costa Maya Beach Cabanas C1
28 De Real Macaw Guest House C3
29 Dirty McNasty's Hostel C3
30 Ignacio Beach Cabins............................. B7
31 Iguana Reef Inn C3
32 Island Magic... C5
33 Jerimiah's Inn... C2
34 Juan in a Million....................................... C5
35 Leeside Rooms... C3

36 Mara's Place... C1
37 Maxhapan Cabanas B6
38 Oasi B7
39 Ocean Pearl Royale Hotel.....................C2
40 Pancho's Villas... C4
41 Rainbow Hotel... C3
42 Sea Dreams Hotel C1
43 Seaside Cabanas...................................... C5
44 Shirley's Guest House.............................. B7
45 Sophie's Guesthouse.............................. C1
46 Tree Tops Guesthouse C6
47 Tropical Oasis C2
48 Tropical Paradise Hotel C6
49 Yuma's House Belize C4

⊗ Eating
50 Aladdin's C1
51 Amor Y Café C5
52 Bambooze C4
53 Barrier Reef Sports Bar &
   Grill..C4
54 Belizean Flava...C4
55 Coconut Reef C2
56 Errolyns House of Fry Jacks C4
57 Gelato Italiano.. C1
58 Glenda's Café... B5
59 Habaneros C4
60 Happy Lobster C3
61 Il Pellicano C4
62 Little Kitchen Restaurant B5
  Pasta per Caso..............................(see 18)
63 Rainbow Grill & Bar C3
64 Rose's Grill..C4
65 Roy's Blue Water Grill C4
66 Syd's.. B5

⊙ Drinking & Nightlife
  Barrier Reef Sports Bar
    & Grill.. (see 53)
67 I&I Reggae Bar C5
68 Ice & Beans C3
69 Lazy Lizard C1

⊙ Shopping
70 Caribbean Colors......................................C4
71 Cooper's Art Gallery................................C4
72 Little Blue Gift Shop C4

recommended dive shop that runs PADI-certification courses and offers immersions around the local reefs, as well as offshore dives at Turneffe Elbow and the Blue Hole. They also offer advanced technical dive training and organize trips to local cave systems.

Frenchie's Diving　　　　　　DIVING
(☑226-0234;　www.frenchiesdivingbelize.com; Front St) Well-regarded local dive operator offering a full range of dives throughout the region, including full-day trips (three dives) to Blue Hole and Turneffe, and half-day trips (two dives) to Esmeralda and Spanish Bay. Night dives at Caye Caulker Marine Reserve cost BZ$130.

It also runs overnight dive adventures, which include six immersions and a night on Half Moon Caye.

Snorkeling

It is possible to snorkel around the Split and off the pier near the airstrip, but to really experience life under the sea it's necessary to sign up with a tour operator and go out to the reef.

The most popular destinations for snorkeling trips are Hol Chan Marine Reserve (p85) and Shark Ray Alley (p87). Full-day tours cost BZ$120 to BZ$140 and visit around four different snorkelling sites; some include a stop in San Pedro for lunch (not included in the price), but between disembarking, eating and digesting your meal, you are losing time in the water. Some trips also include a visit to a sunken barge near the northern tip of Caye Caulker and, in season, manatee spotting in the channel.

Alternatively half-day snorkeling trips visit the Caye Caulker Marine Reserve (BZ$70) just in front of the island, and include Coral Gardens, the Swoosh (a stand of coral near an opening in the reef where the current and swells attract a good variety of marine life) and Shark Ray Village (Caulker's own shark and ray habitat).

Some tour operators also take snorkel groups to Turneffe Atoll if there is demand, a longer trip that promises a more pristine reef and an even greater variety of fish. Dedicated snorkel tours to Blue Hole and Lighthouse Reef are rare, although snorkelers are usually welcome to tag along with dive boats if space permits.

All of the tour operators in town take groups snorkeling, as do the sailing companies. Shop around for an operator you are comfortable with and find out about group size and what is included before signing up.

Even though it is only a short boat ride offshore, only licensed guides are permitted to take snorkelers out to the reef, which helps protect this fragile ecosystem. To get the most out of your trip, it's important to hunt around for a quality guide – the best guides are knowledgeable about the reef and adept at spotting and identifying many hidden creatures.

★ **Caveman Tours** SNORKELING

(☑ 226-0367; www.cavemansnorkelingtours.com; Front St; ⊙ 8:30am-5:30pm) Larger-than-life captain Caveman offers extremely popular snorkeling trips throughout local waters, as well as manatee-watching expeditions to Swallow Caye and visits to sandy Goff Caye. He is serious, safety conscious and very attentive to customer needs. His office is inside the handicraft market.

★ **Stressless Tours** SNORKELING, FISHING

(☑ 624-6064; www.stresslesstours.com; Dock St) 🏄 This professional new operation stands out in the crowded snorkeling market for its great customer service, focus on sustainability and passionate guides. They offer a condensed version of the classic Hol Chan/Shark Ray Alley trip with a focus on exploring a variety of experiences in the water rather than non-snorkeling extras. They also run fishing trips and charter excursions.

Carlos Tours SNORKELING

(☑ 600-1654, 226-0458; carlosayala10@hotmail.com; Front St; ⊙ hours vary; 🖶) Popular local guide Carlos is an accomplished underwater photographer and offers all of his guests a CD for BZ$30 featuring photographs from their snorkel outing. He is usually out on the boat but leaves a sign-up board on his front door.

Manatee-Watching

Tours are available to observe manatees in the Swallow Caye Wildlife Sanctuary (p108), and are followed by one or two snorkeling stops and a lunch break at Sergeant's Caye or Goff's Caye. If you don't have any luck spotting manatees in the morning, the boat might return to Swallow Caye in the afternoon to give it another go. The tour usually lasts from 9am until 4pm and costs around BZ$170 per participant.

Note that visitors are not permitted to enter the water within the sanctuary and even if you are lucky enough to spot manatees, you will possibly only see the animals briefly as they surface for air.

When temperatures are high, many manatees leave the mud around Swallow Caye and can be observed frolicking in the channel near Caye Caulker, where you can get a better view of the majestic animals. If manatees are around, many companies include a visit here as part of their snorkeling trips.

Sailing

Several companies organize day sailing trips, most of which visit two or three different snorkeling sites – usually around Caye Caulker Marine Reserve (p109) or Hol Chan Marine Reserve (p85). At around BZ$140 the price is similar to a regular snorkel tour, but the difference is that your journey will be wind powered. While it is a more pleasant way to travel, note that you'll probably spend more time traveling between sites and less time in the water. In general, the sailboats are large, meaning they can take larger groups than the little motorboats other tour operators might use.

In addition to the snorkeling trips, sailing companies also offer sunset cruises (BZ$70) and moonlight sailing trips. Island-hopping trips include overnight excursions to Lighthouse Reef or Turneffe Atoll, as well as multiday trips to the southern cays and Placencia (BZ$700). These tours usually involve one or two nights camping on the beach, as well as plenty of snorkel stops.

Blackhawk Sailing Tours   SAILING
(✒607-0323; www.blackhawksailing.com; Front St) Locally owned and operated, Blackhawk offers sailing/snorkeling tours; overnight sailing trips, where guests sleep under the stars on sandy isles; and sunset reggae cruises complete with fresh *ceviche*.

Swimming
Hurricanes Mitch and Keith in 1998 and 2000, respectively, left some strips of hard sand on Caye Caulker where there once were sea shrubs, and local authorities have also attempted to build up sandy stretches.

However in reality Caye Caulker doesn't really have a real beach where you may be enticed to throw your towel down and soak up some rays. Furthermore, sea grass lies under the water along much of the shore, which doesn't make for pleasant wading or swimming; you'll find the best swimming is off the end of the docks that line the east side of the island. Many of the docks are supposed to be public, but some hotel owners have become proprietorial, putting up gates to give privacy to their guests, who use the sun lounges and deck chairs provided.

Caye Caulker's official public beach (p109) is at the northern end of the village right by the Split. The beach is small and scattered with debris – sunbathers lounge on a broken seawall that is crumbling into the ocean – but the water is cool and clean, thanks to the currents that pass through the Split. You might prefer to get into the water at the tip of the Split itself, where you can jump right into the deep waters in front of the bar or wade in the roped-off shallow area. You can snorkel around here, but beware of boats cruising through deeper water on the north shore.

The surf breaking on the barrier reef is easily visible from the eastern shore of Caye Caulker. Don't attempt to swim out to it, as powerful boats speed through these waters. Crocodiles live in the waters on some parts of the west side of the island.

Water Sports
★Contour   WATER SPORTS
(✒653-8515; www.contourbelize.com; Front St; rentals per hr/half day/full day BZ$30/80/120; ⊗8am-6pm) This well-run shop brings something different to Caulker's aquatic recreation: taking visitors through mangroves or on sunset tours on paddleboards. It also runs scenic yoga sessions on paddleboards and rents out quality equipment.

Kitexplorer   KITESURFING
(✒626-4613; www.kitexplorer.com; Front St; equipment rental per hr/half-day/day BZ$120/200/300; ⊗8am-6pm) Offers a two-hour introductory course (BZ$360) or a six-hour basic course (BZ$980), as well as equipment rental. Also offers windsurfing classes and has SUP boards. Located at the northern end of the island near the Split.

Reef Watersports   WATER SPORTS
(✒635-7219; www.reefwatersports.com; Av Hicaco) This high-adrenaline outfitter right by the Split offers jet-ski rentals (BZ$140 per half-hour). It also offers various packages including wakeboarding and waterskiing. Check their website for package details.

Fishing
Just about any skipper will take you fishing in the deep water, flats or reef, and it's cheaper from here than from Ambergris Caye. Grand Slams are not unusual (catching permit, tarpon and bonefish all in one day); other fish often caught include snook, barracuda, snapper and shark, usually on a catch-and-release basis. If you venture out for deep-sea fishing, look for wahoo, sailfish, kingfish, snapper, grouper, jacks, shark and barracuda.

Half-/full-day fly-fishing or deep-sea fishing trips for two to three people run at BZ$500/700.

Spearfishing Shack   SNORKELING, FISHING
(Captain Jacob; ✒666-4654; Crocodile St) A favorite among backpackers, Captain Jacob and sidekick Shorty lead full-day snorkeling tours leaving from the dock behind Bella's Hostel. For an extra BZ$20 they will add a spot of spearfishing to the end of the trip.

NORTHERN CAYES CAYE CAULKER

Anglers Abroad

FISHING

(📞 226-0602; www.anglersabroad.com; Hattie St) Experienced and professionally run outfit offering adventurous fishing trips throughout the region. Head to the office inside Sea Dreams Hotel to arrange your tour.

Barefoot Fisherman Expeditions

FISHING

(📞 226-0405; www.barefootfishermanexpeditions. com; Front St) A serious operation dedicated to all kinds of fishing excursions, including catch-and-release sportfishing (half-day BZ$500, full day BZ$600). It also rents kayaks and SUP boards.

Tsunami Adventures

ADVENTURE, FISHING

(📞 226-0462; www.tsunamiadventures.com; Front St; ⏱ 8am-6pm) Bring home some barracuda, grouper or snapper on one of the many fishing tours run by this established local company. Tsunami also offers a wide range of other activities including flyovers of the Blue Hole, snorkeling trips, island-hopping sightseeing outings and tours on the mainland.

Hiking, Cycling & Birdwatching

Swim or paddle across the Split to reach the **north side**, as it is called, which is still untouched by the tourist boom. Only a handful of residents live along the main road, meaning there is plenty of opportunity for exploring the more remote parts, and spotting birds and even crocodiles. Alternatively, arrange boat transport all the way up to the northern end of the island to the Caye Caulker Forest Reserve (p109), which has a short trail that leads through the mangrove forest. It is an excellent place to spot water birds, including rails, stilts and herons, as well as ospreys and mangrove warblers.

The southern part of the island is also relatively undeveloped, especially in the interior, despite the fact that houses are being built along the coastline south of the airstrip. A rough trail suitable for hiking or biking follows the perimeter of the **southern tip**, beginning and ending at the airstrip. The airstrip is flanked by swampy marshland, making it a fantastic place to spot birds, including the killdeer, the black-necked stilt, the common black hawk and herons of all kinds. Be on the lookout for airplanes that fly in and out of here without paying much heed to who or what might be on the airstrip.

Just north of the airstrip, the **Caye Caulker Mini Reserve** is run by the Caye Caulker

branch of the Belize Tourism Industry Association (BTIA). There is a short interpretative trail that runs through the littoral forest.

Day Spas

After swimming, snorkeling and sunning, you may be in need of a little hands-on healing.

Healing Touch Day Spa

SPA

(📞 206-0380; www.healingtouchbelize.com; Front St; ⏱ 9am-7pm) Ms Eva McFarlane can take care of all your beauty and body needs, including manicures and pedicures; Reiki, reflexology, body scrubs and aromatherapy.

Coco Plum Gardens

SPA

(📞 226-0226; Back St; ⏱ 8am-5pm) Offering a variety of massages, this day spa is set amid lush gardens south of town.

🎫 Tours

Although most tour operators have their own specialties, many offer similar versions of the same trips, with similar prices. Most tour operators work closely together, consolidating tours on slow days and juggling overflow at busier times. Snorkel gear, water and fruit are included in the price of most boat trips.

Aside from the boat tours, some companies also organize trips to the Belizean mainland, including those involving ziplining, cave-tubing and visiting Maya sites at Lamanai and Altun Ha.

Raggamuffin Tours

BOAT TOUR

(📞 226-0348; www.raggamuffintours.com; Front St) Runs popular three-day sailing and camping trips to Placencia, departing every Tuesday and Friday, that pass through some less visited islands and areas of reef. Advance reservations are essential. Also runs snorkeling tours to Hol Chan and sunset sailing cruises.

E-Z Boy

TOUR

(📞 226-0349; www.ezboytoursbelize.com; Front St) Runs the full gamut of tours and activities, including snorkeling tours, manatee watching at Swallow Caye and sportfishing trips (BZ$500 per boat).

Anda De Wata Tours

ADVENTURE TOUR

(📞 624-9536, 607-9394; www.snorkeladw.com; Front St) Does floating on an inner tube pulled behind a slow-moving boat sound like a dream come true? The 90-minute boat-and-float tour (BZ$60) may be your own personal paradise! It also offers a variety of interesting snorkeling tours around local reefs and fly-overs to check out the Blue Hole.

★ Festivals & Events

Lobsterfest FOOD
Caulker hosts the original Northern Cayes Lobsterfest, which marks the opening of lobster fishing season on June 15, although the festival is usually held a couple of weekends later so there's enough lobster to go around. The streets are filled with *punta* drumming, Belikin beer and grilled lobster.

Other activities include a fishing tournament, canoe races, dance performances and, of course, the Lobster Festival Pageant.

🛏 Sleeping

Golf-cart taxis meet boats and flights upon arrival; if you don't have a reservation they will take you around to look at a few places to stay. It's best to book in advance if you're coming at Christmas or Easter.

Take care with belongings left in hotel rooms – especially in some of the more rustic accommodations south of town – as room robberies have been reported. If your room doesn't lock properly, ask for another and make use of the hotel safe if one is available.

🛏 Central Area

As you wander up Front St you will see that there is an endless array of accommodation options, including many budget digs, stretching from the water-taxi docks all the way to the Split.

Caye Caulker Rentals ACCOMMODATION SERVICES
(☑630-1008; www.cayecaulkerrentals.com; Estella St) Manages many rental properties on the island including some lovely secluded homes in the southern reaches.

**Caye Caulker
Accommodations** ACCOMMODATION SERVICES
(☑226-0382; www.cayecaulkeraccommodations.com) Manages a large number of rental houses all over the island.

Yuma's House Belize HOSTEL $
(☑206-0019; www.yumashousebelize.com; Front St; dm/s/d BZ$35/70/85; 🛜) This fun and freshly painted hostel is just a few steps from the water-taxi dock, giving it a prime location in the center of town and at the water's edge. It takes full advantage of the choice positioning with a dock for guests

and a breezy, palm-shaded garden complete with hammocks and picnic tables from which to admire the view. Guests have access to a well-equipped kitchen.

Ocean Pearl Royale Hotel HOTEL $
(☑226-0074; oceanpearl@btl.net; Park St; r with/without air-con BZ$90/65, cabaña BZ$100; ❄🛜) Located on a quiet side street, this small hotel is surrounded by sandy grounds strewn with palms and flowering trees that attract hummingbirds and other beauties. The 10 clean rooms are remarkably good value, with brightly painted walls and simple wood furnishings. A big, airy lobby offers space for guests to congregate and swap island stories. There are also good-value *cabañas* onsite for those planning to stay a week or more.

Juan in a Million GUESTHOUSE $
(Pirates of the Caribbean; Front St; dm BZ$15, s with/without air-con BZ$44/39, d with/without air-con BZ$49/44) On the quiet southern end of Front St, this small, friendly guesthouse is popular with budget travelers thanks to its cheap, comfortable air-conditioned dorms and neat private rooms. For value, its hard to beat.

Bella's Hostel HOSTEL $
(☑635-4265; bellas.hostel@yahoo.com; Crocodile St; dm with/without air-con BZ$35/25, s/d/tr BZ$35/60/75; 🛜) On the back side of the island, Bella's is a hideaway for the backpacker set, who appreciate the good-value dorms in the elevated wooden house. There is a chilled-out vibe here aided by laid-back management and good tunes. You are likely to see travelers sharing a meal in the kitchen, playing cards on the balcony and taking advantage of free rentals, such as canoes and bikes.

Sophie's Guesthouse GUESTHOUSE $
(besophiesguesthouse@gmail.com; Almendra St; r BZ$73) This laid-back budget option near the Split on the back side of the island has five simple but neat rooms in an elevated wooden house. It's close to all the action but in a supremely tranquil setting and there is a decent swimming spot just in front. All rooms share bathrooms.

Jerimiah's Inn HOTEL $
(☑625-2618; Front St; d with/without bathroom BZ$55/44; 🛜) A good budget choice, fan-cooled rooms at this small hotel right on the main drag are comfortable enough (though somewhat spartan), surrounding a

shared courtyard. A central location assures that you're never more than a stone's throw from Caulker's many aquatic attractions. Management has plans to offer new air-con rooms.

Tropical Oasis
HOSTEL $

(☑ 629-0511; karianne_mokkelbost@hotmail. com; La Poza St; dm BZ$25, cottage BZ$50) Basic but centrally located and well suited to hardy backpackers, this low-key place has a ramshackle collection of semi-open huts and dorms covered in mosquito mesh that let in plenty of fresh air. There is also an outdoor kitchen, as well as hammocks hung around the ample yard, which is dominated by a mysterious large trailer that somehow arrived on the island.

Dirty McNasty's Hostel
HOSTEL $

(☑ 636-7512; Crocodile St; dm with/without air-con BZ$43/32, d BZ$76; 🛜) The ongoing construction work at this large hostel takes away from the paradise vibe, and many of the rooms feel like budget university dorms or even a bush penitentiary, with the only decoration being the fire extinguishers. Even so, the place remains popular for its free breakfast and rum punch, which guarantees a social atmosphere.

★ Sea Dreams Hotel
B&B $$

(☑ 226-0602; www.seadreamsbelize.com; Hattie St; r BZ$230, apt BZ$330-430; 🌀🛜) A lovely guesthouse on the north side of the island, Sea Dreams offers a rare combination of easy access and sweet tranquillity. Spend the day lounging around the Split, then retreat to the cozy accommodation just a few steps away. Original paintings by local artists adorn the colorful walls of the rooms and apartments, which are elegant and comfortable.

The small dock on the back side gives access to one of the best swimming areas on the island – it's deep, free of sea grass and affords glorious sunset views. For even better panoramas, head up to the rooftop lounge. Breakfast, and bike, paddleboard and canoe use are included.

Seaside Cabanas
RESORT $$

(☑ 226-0498; www.seasidecabanas.com; Dock St; r BZ$258-358, ste BZ$398; 🌀🛜🏊) Sun-yellow stucco buildings shaded by thatched-palm roofs exude a tropical atmosphere at this beachfront beauty. The interior decor features desert colors, rich fabrics and plenty

of pillows. Most of the rooms occupy the main building facing the ocean; closer to the sea, the comfortable *cabañas* take advantage of the location with private rooftop decks and terrace hot tubs.

Amanda's Place
GUESTHOUSE $$

(Casita Cariñosa; ☑ 226-0547; www.cayecaulker casita.com; Front St; apt BZ$190, house BZ$200-390; 🌀🛜🏊) Amanda offers a variety of accommodations on leafy grounds with a nice pool a block from the beach. On one side of the property there is a modern three-bedroom house with a rooftop terrace. The main house looks over the road to the water and has two art-filled apartments with kitchenettes downstairs and a traditional Belizean-style *casita* upstairs.

Leeside Rooms
GUESTHOUSE $$

(☑ 634-4046; leesiderooms@gmail.com; r with/ without air-con BZ$180/120; 🌀🛜) This charming, small guesthouse offers a pair of elegant air-conditioned rooms with small verandas that overlook the water, as well as cheaper fan-cooled rooms upstairs. Located on the lagoon side behind the football field, there is less noise and less light than on Front St. The stylish interior design features high beds, tiled floors and walls hung with old maps.

Blue Wave
GUESTHOUSE $$

(☑ 206-0114; www.bluewaveguesthouse.com; Front St; r BZ$44, cabañas with/without air-con BZ$109/65, deluxe r BZ$164; 🌀🛜) Look for the attractive log-cabin–style house overlooking Front St, and you'll know you've arrived at the Blue Wave, an inviting guesthouse with several different accommodation options. 'Deluxe' rooms are spacious and stylish, with air-con, TV, private bathrooms and breezy balconies. Beneath the owners' clapboard house, there are three cheaper rooms with shared facilities.

Caye Caulker Condos
HOTEL $$

(☑ 226-0072; www.cayecaulkercondos.com; Front St; ste BZ$198-278; 🌀🛜🏊) Inside this attractive, salmon-colored concrete block on Front St sit eight sweet retreat suites. Each has a fully equipped kitchen, satellite TV and fancy bathroom with a romantic two-person shower made of stone. Suites each have a private balcony, and the rooftop terrace – with its 360-degree views – is a key selling point.

Caye Caulker Plaza Hotel HOTEL $$

(✆ 226-0780; http://cayecaulkerplazahotel.com; cnr Middle St & Calle Al Sol; r BZ$196-240; ❄ 🛜) This 32-room hotel offers good amenities including private bathrooms with hot showers, cable TV, in-room safes and mini refrigerators in every room. More expensive rooms also have private balconies, while cheaper ones are on the ground floor. The beautiful rooftop terrace is open to all. Staff are friendly, and the location is central.

Island Magic HOTEL $$

(✆ 226-0505; www.islandmagicbelize.com; Front St; r BZ$220-280, penthouse 1-bedroom/2-bedroom ste BZ$370/570; ❄ 🛜 ☒) Offering excellent value for its accommodations and amenities, Island Magic has 10 spacious, earth-toned rooms with fully equipped kitchens and dining areas, with more expensive rooms offering glorious ocean views from their private balconies. Island Magic's two penthouse suites offer even lovelier views of the sea and surrounding island.

The swanky swimming pool is an added bonus although the bar area blocks the view of the sea.

Pancho's Villas HOTEL $$

(✆ 226-0304; www.panchosvillasbelize.com; Pasero St; d with/without kitchenette BZ$180/130; ❄ 🛜) Resembling a big square wedding cake with lemon-yellow frosting, Pancho's Villas is a little out of place on this quiet side street. The new building is decked out with modern amenities, such as kitchenettes, cable TV and the rest. It's not particularly stylish, but it's convenient and pretty good value.

Costa Maya Beach Cabanas GUESTHOUSE $$

(✆ 226-0432; www.costamayabelize.com; Front St; r BZ$130-180, ste BZ$260-400; ❄ 🛜) This well-run guesthouse has a new building out the back with six spacious, air-conditioned rooms featuring large fridges and two queen beds, as well as a large rooftop terrace. In front, the cheaper original units can be a bit gloomy, but each has a porch for catching sea breezes. Guests enjoy beach chairs, a swimming dock and complimentary canoes.

Rainbow Hotel HOTEL $$

(✆ 226-0123; www.rainbowhotel-cayecaulker.com; Front St; r BZ$200-230; ❄ 🛜) Bright blue paint, a couple of rainbows for decoration and upgraded rooms make this bunker-like concrete building relatively appealing. Bottom-floor rooms open right onto the street so you can sit out front and enjoy the street life. For privacy, choose a room on the top floor or rent one of the cottages (BZ$220 to BZ$250) at the back.

All rooms have flat-screen TVs, mini fridges and coffee makers.

Mara's Place GUESTHOUSE $$

(✆ 600-0080; maras_place@hotmail.com; Front St; d BZ$109; @ 🛜) The eight guest rooms spread over a number off two-story wooden *cabañas* are simple but spotless, not cramped but comfortable. Not exactly luxurious, they nonetheless include a few perks you would not expect, such as a private veranda complete with hammock, lightning quick wi-fi and reading material.

There is a communal kitchen on the premises, and the main town beach is right across the street, where Mara also runs the Sip & Dip – the most popular place for waterside socializing among islanders and Belizean visitors.

De Real Macaw Guest House GUESTHOUSE $$

(✆ 226-0459; www.derealmacaw.biz; Front St; r BZ$100-140, apt BZ$260; ❄ 🛜) All the rustic lodgings dotting the leafy grounds here are inspired by the jungle, from *cabañas* built from pimenta sticks to the beachfront rooms with thatched-roof verandas. The decor continues the theme with swinging hammocks and woven tapestries, but the rooms are also equipped with modern conveniences such as TVs, fridges and coffee makers.

★ Caye Reef BOUTIQUE HOTEL $$$

(✆ 226-0381; www.cayereef.com; Front St; 1-bedroom apt BZ$346-420, 2-bedroom apt BZ$420-494; ❄ 🛜 ☒) The six apartments at Caye Reef have been designed with the utmost attention to detail – from the original art hanging on the walls to the swinging hammocks hanging on the private balconies. Room prices rise with the floor, with the most expensive rooms being on the 3rd floor.

As comfortable and classy as they are, the apartments are not the main attraction to staying at Caye Reef: that would be the roof deck, complete with hammocks, hot tub and 360-degree sea views.

Iguana Reef Inn RESORT $$$

(✆ 226-0213; www.iguanareefinn.com; Calle Aguado; standard r BZ$358-398, deluxe r BZ$418-458; ❄ 🛜 ☒) Set on sandy grounds fringed with palms, the Iguana Reef is both upscale and informal. It's the kind of place you can roam around barefoot by day, but you might dress up for dinner. Bamboo furniture, Mexican tapestries and local artwork adorn the jewel-toned rooms. Outside, you can lounge poolside or pull up a lounge chair on the fantastic waterside area by the dock.

At the end of the day, take your pick from the extensive menu of tropical cocktails in the *palapa* bar and watch the sunset. A continental breakfast is included.

South of Town

South of the cemetery, Caye Caulker is noticeably quieter and the beach sees much less foot traffic. Most of the accommodation south of town are in the midrange price bracket. The back streets are known as 'Gringo Heights,' for this is where many expats have bought property and built houses. Sporting names such as 'Hummingbird Hideaway' and 'Canuck Cottage,' many of them are available for longer-term rentals (three days or more) via Caye Caulker Rentals (p115).

Ignacio Beach Cabins
CABIN **$**

(✆ 226-0175; http://aguallos.com/ignaciobeach; r BZ$30-40; 🖌) In the far south of town, Ignacio offers very basic waterfront lodging in weathered cabins on stilts. Here you are giving up a bit of comfort but the reward is tranquillity; there is little foot traffic this far south, so it feels private and pristine. The cold-shower cabins all have easy access to the beach, but the pricier ones are at the water's edge, catching cool breezes.

★ Oasi
GUESTHOUSE **$$**

(✆ 623-9401; www.oasi-holidaysbelize.com; Back St; apt BZ$190-210; 🖌🖌🖌) Set around blooming tropical gardens featuring an inviting pool, this excellent guesthouse has just four elegant apartments with lovely wide verandas (hung with hammocks, of course). Tapestries and warm hues enrich the interiors, which are equipped with full kitchens, sofas and quality bathrooms. There's also a small bar that hosts regular low-key concerts and a fine BBQ area.

Hosts Luciana and Michael go above and beyond to ensure you enjoy your stay, offering expert opinions about local snorkel and dive trips. The guesthouse is away from town and away from the waterfront, but free bikes make for an easy trip.

Colinda Cabanas
CABAÑA **$$**

(✆ 226-0383; www.colindacabanas.com; Playa Ascension; r from BZ$118-298; 🖌🖌) It's hard to miss Colin and Linda's brightly colored yellow-and-blue property, which sits south of the cemetery. Both the *cabañas* and suites are appointed with fridges, hot showers and comfy beds alongside value-adding extras such as coffee makers with a stash of gourmet Belizean coffee beans and binoculars for wildlife spotting. The suites have a full kitchen and air-conditioning.

Out the front there is a fine dock with a *palapa* throwing shade on a pair of swinging hammocks.

Barefoot Beach Belize
GUESTHOUSE **$$**

(✆ 226-0205; www.barefootbeachbelize.com; r BZ$138-158, ste & cottages BZ$258; 🖌🖌) Painted in candy colors, this perky place is on a quiet stretch of beach at the southern end of the village. Suites and cottages have kitchens and living space, with direct access to beach breezes; rooms are smaller but still spacious, with fridges, air-con and coffee makers. The whole place has a tropical theme, with plenty of floral prints and sea-themed artwork.

There are also some well-appointed new huts (BZ$170) a block further back. Hammocks hang under a thatched-roof *palapa* at the end of a long dock, offering the perfect place to while away an afternoon, while bicycles are provided to explore the island.

Maxhapan Cabanas
CABIN **$$**

(✆ 226-0118; maxhapan04@hotmail.com; 55 Av Pueblo Nuevo; s/d/tr BZ$120/140/160; 🖌🖌) In an unexpected location south of town, Maxhapan has just three sweet, yellow *cabañas* clustered around a sandy yard complete with an elevated *palapa* with hammocks and a bring-your-own bar, where guests can gather. Natural light floods the spotless, modern cabins, which are equipped with fridge, air-conditioning and TV. Your host, Louise, guarantees your comfort and happiness throughout your stay.

The only drawback is that it's not on the water, which explains why it's such a bargain. Free bikes are a bonus.

Anchorage Resort
HOTEL **$$**

(✆ 206-0304; www.anchorageresort.com; Playa Asuncion; r BZ$172; 🖌🖌) This is not the place to come for style or swank, but if you're in search of reasonably priced accommodations right by the water then it's a fairly good deal. The resort boasts one of the widest stretches of sand on the island and the rooms, while a little generic, are equipped with plenty of perks, such as king-size beds, cable TVs and private balconies.

Tree Tops Guesthouse GUESTHOUSE **$$**
(📞 226-0240; www.treetopsbelize.com; Playa Asuncion; r with/without bathroom from BZ$196/152, ste BZ$261; ✳ @ 🛜 ☀) For years Doris has been winning accolades for her hospitality and helpfulness. The spacious, cool and clean rooms are very comfortable and are decorated with original artistic touches. Set back from the beach, the three-story building is fronted by a pleasant palm-shaded garden, while a roof terrace with panoramic vistas towers over the treetops, giving the place its name.

There is also a new sandy area by the waterside with recliners for guest use.

Shirley's Guest House CABIN **$$**
(📞 226-0145; www.shirleysguesthouse.com; Playa Asuncion; r BZ$130-150, with air-con BZ$180; 🛜) At the far end of the island, just north of the airstrip, is this secluded spot featuring classic Caribbean wood cottages in a large yard. The grounds are fenced off from the beach, which might increase security but it does detract from the island's easygoing vibe.

Tropical Paradise Hotel RESORT **$$**
(📞 226-0124; www.tropicalparadise.bz; Front St; r with/without air-con BZ$100/90, cottage BZ$120, ste BZ$150; ✳ 🛜) With an ideal location on the waterside just south of the cemetery, Tropical Paradise Hotel is Caulker's 'original beach resort.' It was one of the first places to clean out a stretch of sand, furnish it with painted lounge chairs and entice guests with fruity cocktails. These days there are plenty of more stylish places to stay, but these colorful clapboard cottages still offer decent value.

Low-season discounts are available. They have another branch on Front St near the docks.

🍴 Eating

Gelato Italiano ICE CREAM **$**
(The Split; ice cream BZ$5-10; ⊙ 11am-6pm) Long overdue on Caye Caulker, Gelato Italiano has brought first-class ice cream to the island. Choose from over a dozen varieties of genuine Italian gelato and head outside to pull up a stool on the long balcony overlooking the vivid blue Caribbean. The perfect way to cool off.

Errolyns House of Fry Jacks BELIZEAN **$**
(Middle St; BZ$1.50-5; ⊙ 6am-3pm & 6-9pm Tue-Sun) Who said Belize had to be expensive? Locals and travelers alike descend on this neat, board takeout hut to chow down on the island's best-value breakfast – delicious golden fry-jacks (deep-fried dough) filled with any combination of beans, cheese, egg, beef or chicken. Cheap, filling and delicious.

Amor Y Café BREAKFAST **$**
(Front St; breakfast BZ$6-12.50; ⊙ 6am-noon; 🖋) There's no contest when it comes to the most popular breakfast spot on the island – this place is always busy, but you won't have to wait long for a table on the shaded porch overlooking Front St. Take your pick from freshly squeezed juices, scrambled eggs or homemade yogurt topped with fruit – and don't miss out on the freshly brewed coffee.

If you have to pack a lunch, sandwiches are available to go.

Glenda's Café BELIZEAN **$**
(Back St; mains BZ$9-12; ⊙ 7am-1pm Mon-Fri) Glenda's serves traditional Belizean food in a clapboard house on the island's west side. It boasts some of the best breakfasts in town, from cinnamon rolls and orange juice to full cooked breakfasts of bacon or ham, eggs, bread and coffee. Burritos, tacos, sandwiches and chicken with rice and beans are offered for lunch. Arrive early for breakfast.

Roy's Blue Water Grill BELIZEAN **$$**
(Pasero St; mains BZ$18-25; ⊙ 6-10pm) Former Habaneros (p121) chef Roy has branched out on his own with this simple open-air restaurant just off the main drag. The menu features plenty of fresh seafood, but there are also interesting chicken and pork dishes, all of which are imbued with rich Caribbean flavors.

Belizean Flava SEAFOOD **$$**
(Front St; ⊙ 6-11pm) The most popular grill restaurant and rightly so. Take your pick from the fantastic selection of lobster, snapper or conch, which will then be expertly grilled on the street before being served up with tasty sides of your choice.

Service is super-friendly and there is a great, laid-back atmosphere throughout the casual dining area – no doubt aided by the generous amounts of free rum punch.

Pasta per Caso
ITALIAN $$

(Front St; mains BZ$25-27; ⊙6-9pm Mon-Thu) Pull up a stool at one of the long tables on the deck and dig into some of the best pasta in Belize, prepared the traditional way by the Milanese owners. There is usually just one vegetarian and one nonveg sauce served with a healthy portion of one of the many varieties of fresh pasta made onsite. Garden fresh salads also make an appearance.

Little Kitchen Restaurant
BELIZEAN $$

(☑667-2178; off Luciano Reyes St; mains BZ$15-25; ⊙noon-10pm) Elisia Flower's Little Kitchen is a 3rd-floor, open-air restaurant on Caulker's southwestern side serving traditional (yet artfully done) Belizean dishes such as curry shrimp, coconut red snapper and excellent conch fritters (just to name a few). Portions are big and it's outstanding value, although we have some concerns about immature lobsters on the menu – make sure yours is legal size.

Its unique vantage point makes it a fine spot to watch the sun go down with a cocktail made with local rum, a wine or a fresh juice.

Happy Lobster
SEAFOOD $$

(Front St; mains BZ$20-30; ⊙6:30am-9:30pm; ☑) The lobster at this Caulker institution is actually not that happy, but you will be after eating big plates of fresh fish, spiced with Creole flavoring or sweetened with coconut. The place also has a popular breakfast menu, and the front porch is a pleasant place to catch the breeze off the ocean and watch the activity on Front St.

Syd's
BELIZEAN, MEXICAN $$

(Middle St; mains BZ$15-30; ⊙11am-3pm & 5:30-9pm Mon-Sat) Syd's is a long-standing favorite for its good-value meals and convivial atmosphere. Out back, there is a flower-filled patio where you can dine to the soothing sounds of a gurgling fountain. Otherwise, the dining room is rather nondescript. No matter where you sit, you will be sated by the big plates of Belizean and Mexican food.

Coconut Reef
ITALIAN $$

(☑206-0333; Front St; mains BZ$27; ⊙5-9:30pm) This casual Italian restaurant across the road from the beach has a wide menu of pizzas, pastas and international dishes, with a focus on fresh seafood. Finish off with some real coffee from the espresso machine.

Aladdin's
MIDDLE EASTERN $$

(Front St; mains BZ$20-27; ⊙11am-7:30pm Tue-Sun) Nestled behind a couple of rental shops, this tiny restaurant doesn't look like much, but sit down at one of the three picnic tables and enjoy great Middle Eastern cuisine prepared by the Belizean owner, who trained in Jordan. The hummus is top notch.

Barrier Reef Sports Bar & Grill
INTERNATIONAL $$

(Front St; mains BZ$10-25; ⊙9am-midnight; ☎) This unlikely spot is a no-holds-barred expat hangout but has surprisingly delicious food. If you don't like the multiple TVs blaring sports interviews into the atmosphere, take a seat out front and enjoy the breeze off the ocean.

Rose's Grill
SEAFOOD $$

(Dock St; mains BZ$20-30; ⊙5-11pm; ☑) Take your pick from the selection of fresh fish and lobster on display at this friendly streetside grill restaurant. Then head back to the shade of the *palapa* while they grill it up for you. Family-style seating at big picnic tables makes for a fun, lively atmosphere. A free rum drink is included with all meals.

Bambooze
SEAFOOD $$

(waterfront; mains BZ$14-25; ⊙noon-late; ☑) In one of the best locations on the island, this casually cool bar and grill sits right on the waterside, with swings hanging from the rafters and tables set up in the sand. Besides the Cajun specialties, you can feast on a huge seafood burrito or a grilled fish sandwich, washed down with a fruit smoothie.

Rainbow Grill & Bar
SEAFOOD $$

(waterfront; mains BZ$10-25; ⊙10:30am-10pm Tue-Sun; ☑) Perched on a deck over the turquoise waters, this local favorite is evidence of Caulker's agreeable temperatures. By day, nibble on vegetarian plates, burgers, quesadillas, burritos and sandwiches. At night, fancier fare includes fish, shrimp, conch and lobster cooked how you like it, from simple lemon with butter to Jamaican jerk or Oriental-style.

★ Il Pellicano
ITALIAN $$$

(☑226-0660; Pasero St; mains BZ$25-42; ⊙5-9pm) Head to the lagoon side of the island to find this wonderful garden restaurant preparing a small, but constantly changing, selection of outstanding classic Italian dishes including flavorful homemade pastas and the best pizza on the island. Accompany your meal with Italian wine served by the glass or bottle, and be sure to sample the excellent desserts.

⭐ Habaneros   INTERNATIONAL **$$$**
(☑ 626-4911; habanerosdream@gmail.com; cnr Front & Dock Sts; mains BZ$32-58; ⊙ 6-11pm) Caulker's 'hottest' restaurant, named for the habanero chili, is located in a brightly painted clapboard house in the center of town. Here chefs prepare gourmet international food, combining fresh seafood, meat and vegetables with insanely delicious sauces and flavors. Wash it down with a fine wine or a jug of sangria.

Sit in the funky bar and sip a fruity cocktail or enjoy the buzz and eat by candlelight at the tables on the veranda. Reservations are recommended.

🍷 Drinking & Nightlife

Lazy Lizard   BEACH BAR
(The Split; ⊙ 10am-late) The Lazy Lizard is described as a 'sunny place for shady people' – and there is no shortage of the latter hanging about. It mainly serves beer to swimmers and sunbathers, but the seafood is also recommended.

I&I Reggae Bar   BAR
(Luciano Reyes St; ⊙ 6pm-midnight) I&I is the island's most hip, happening spot after dark, when its healthy sound system belts out a reggae beat. Its three levels each offer a different scene, with a dance floor on one and swings hanging from the rafters on another. The top floor is the 'chill-out zone,' complete with hammocks and panoramic views. A great place for a sunset drink.

Barrier Reef
Sports Bar & Grill   SPORTS BAR
(Front St; ⊙ 9am-midnight) Perennially popular with expats and international visitors alike, this waterfront beach bar serves fantastic international food and all kinds of drinks. There is often live music and major sporting events are shown on the many flat-screen TVs. It's pretty much the only place on the island that you are always guaranteed to find a social atmosphere.

Ice & Beans   COFFEE
(Front St; ⊙ 6:30am-6pm) If the heat is getting too much, pick up an iced coffee, iced tea or flavored crushed ice at this friendly coffee shop and take a stool on the breezy balcony overlooking the water. They also sell delicious, fresh mini-donuts. Be warned: they'll get you in with the free samples then you'll keep coming back for more.

🛍 Shopping

Caulker has a few shops selling T-shirts, beach gear and souvenirs, but this is not the best place for shopping. Keep your eye out for colorful paintings and handmade jewelry by local artists.

Little Blue Gift Shop   GIFTS
(Front St; ⊙ 9am-4pm Mon-Sat) This excellent gift shop near the dock sells handcrafted artisanal products made from local ingredients, including non-chemical bug spray made with coconut oil, and a variety of interesting works by local artists.

Cooper's Art Gallery   ARTS
(Front St; ⊙ noon-8pm Wed-Sun) Debbie Cooper's primitive painting style is a huge hit with tourists, who appreciate her colorful depictions of island life. The gallery also sells works by other talented local artists.

Caribbean Colors   ARTS
(www.caribbean-colors.com; Front St; ⊙ 6am-3pm; ☎) This shop stocks a collection of silk-screened fabrics, jewelry and paintings by the owner, artist Lee Vanderwalker, as well as pieces by other Belizean artists. While you browse you can treat yourself to a hot coffee (the best on the island, some say) or a cool smoothie at the onsite cafe, which also prepares breakfasts and salads.

ℹ Information

EMERGENCY
Police (☑ 226-0179, 911; Front St)

INTERNET ACCESS
Cayeboard Connection (Front St; per hr BZ$12; ⊙ 8am-9pm) Internet access and printing; sells coffee and books.
Island Link (Front St; per hr BZ$9) This is not an internet cafe, but rather an internet ice-cream parlor – a concept that's long overdue.

LAUNDRY
Caye Caulker Coin Laundromat (Dock St; per wash/dry cycle BZ$4; ⊙ 7am-9pm)

NORTHERN CAYES CAYE CAULKER

Marie's Laundry (Middle St; per 8lb BZ$10; ⊘8am-8pm)

Ruby's Laundry (🖉 226-0137; Dock St; per load BZ$12; ⊘8am-5pm Mon-Sat, 8am-noon Sun)

MEDICAL SERVICES

There is a basic health center on the island, but if you really need medical attention, you're better off heading directly to Belize City.

Caye Caulker Health Center (🖉 226-0166, emergency 668-2547) Just off Front St, two blocks south of Dock St.

MONEY

Atlantic Bank (Middle St; ⊘8am-2pm Mon-Fri, 8:30am-noon Sat) Has a pair of fairly reliable ATMs, although make sure you have some cash before you arrive in case they are out of service.

POST

Post Office (Estella St, Caye Caulker Health Center Bldg; ⊘8am-noon & 1-4:30pm Mon-Thu, to 4pm Fri)

TOURIST INFORMATION

Caye Caulker BTIA (www.cayecaulker vacation.com) The official site of the Caye Caulker branch of the Belize Tourism Industry Association (BTIA).

GoCayeCaulker.com (www.gocayecaulker. com) General information for visitors.

ⓘ Getting There & Away

AIR

Both **Maya Island Air** (🖉 226-0012; www. mayaislandair.com) and **Tropic Air** (🖉 226-0040; www.tropicair.com) connect Caye Caulker with San Pedro and Belize City. The airline offices are at Caye Caulker's newly renovated airstrip at the southern end of the island.

BOAT

There are two companies running boats from Caye Caulker to Belize City and San Pedro.

Ocean Ferry Belize (🖉 226-0033; www. oceanferrybelize.com) boats depart for Belize City (one way BZ$19, round trip BZ$29, 45 minutes) at 6:30am, 8:30am, 10:30am, 1:30pm and 4:30pm, and for San Pedro (one way BZ$19, round trip BZ$29, 40 minutes) at 8:45am, 11:15am, 2:15pm, 3pm and 5pm.

San Pedro Belize Express Water Taxis (🖉 226-0225; www.belizewatertaxi.com) depart for San Pedro (one way BZ$30, round trip BZ$50) at 7am, 8:45am, 9:45am, 11:15am, 12:45pm, 2:15pm, 3:45pm, 4:45pm, 5:15pm and 6:15pm, and Belize City (one way BZ$30, round trip BZ$50) at 6:30am, 7am, 8am, 9am, 10:30am, noon, 1:30pm, 3:30pm and 5pm.

The docks are a couple of blocks apart on the reef side of the island.

San Pedro Belize Express Water Taxis also runs a daily service to Chetumal, Mexico via San Pedro. **Water Jets** (🖉 226-2194; www.sanpedro watertaxi.com; lagoon dock) runs the same service on alternate days.

ⓘ Getting Around

Caulker is so small that most people walk everywhere. A couple of golf-cart taxis hang out around Front St and charge BZ$5 to BZ$7 per short trip around town.

You can rent a golf cart at **Buddy's Golf Cart Rentals** (🖉 628-8508; buddys_carts@ hotmail.com; Middle St; per hr/day/24hr BZ$25/100/150) but bicycle rental is far cheaper and just as fast a way to get around. You can rent bikes at grocery stores, tour operators and hotels.

OTHER NORTHERN CAYS

Cayo Esperanto

The coconut-covered Cayo Espanto is just 3 miles or a seven-minute boat ride from San Pedro but feels a world away.

The island was christened Cayo Espanto or 'Frightening Caye' by local fisherman, who claimed it was populated by elves who would put out their fires and throw rocks at them until they pulled up anchor and left.

It seems the elves have since gone into retirement because most modern visitors who set foot on this tropical paradise never want to leave. It's not uncommon for celebrities to frequent the island, which has hosted the likes of Robert De Niro, Harrison Ford and Tiger Woods. Leonardo DiCaprio loved it so much that he bought neighboring Blackadore Caye to build his own environmentally friendly island resort.

🛏 Sleeping & Eating

The entire island is part of the Cayo Espanto resort, which offers a variety of exclusive high-end villas.

Cayo Espanto　　　　　　　　　RESORT $$$
(🖉 in US 910-323-8355; www.aprivateisland.com; villas incl all meals from BZ$1595; ✴ 🛜 ⓧ) Billed as 'a private island,' this ultimate romantic retreat boasts seven delightful villas, each designed for maximum privacy and panoramic views. Each *casa* has a private dock

ⓘ GETTING TO CHETUMAL, MEXICO BY BOAT

Many travelers chose to exit Belize by sea using either Water Jets (p107) or San Pedro Belize Express Water Taxi (p107), which offer a fairly efficient ferry service on alternating days between Caye Caulker, San Pedro and Chetumal, Mexico. Daily boats leave Caye Caulker at 7am and stop in San Pedro to pick up passengers and clear immigration. Though theoretically the boat should leave San Pedro by 8:30am, the immigration line can move more slowly than at land borders. In addition to the BZ$37.50 exit fee, passengers may also be charged a BZ$10 'port fee'.

The trip between San Pedro and Chetumal takes around two hours. Once you've cleared immigration in San Pedro you'll be unable to leave the dock. There is usually a money-changer hanging around to change your left over Belizean currency into Mexican pesos or US dollars.

Upon entering the port of Chetumal, you'll be greeted by soldiers and your luggage will be inspected by drug-sniffing dogs before you are asked to pay the Mexican tourism tax of US$18 (MXN320); save your receipt to avoid paying this tax again when exiting Mexico.

fantastic views from the upstairs master bedroom.

One of the highlights of staying at Cayo Espanto is the exceedingly attentive service (all packages include the services of a personal house attendant). Prior to arrival, guests are invited to fill out a preferences survey, which is used to prepare for all aspects of the visit, including the menu. Chefs create artistic dishes according to your personal tastes and serve them in the privacy of your villa.

ⓘ Getting There & Away

Hotel guests have access to scheduled motor-boat transport to and from San Pedro town on Ambergris Caye.

Turneffe Atoll

Belize's newest protected marine area, Turneffe Atoll, is the largest and most biologically diverse atoll in the Americas.

At 30 miles long and 10 miles wide, Turneffe Atoll is alive with coral, fish and large rays, making it a prime destination for diving, snorkeling and catch-and-release sport fishing. After lobbying by environmental organizations, the area was protected in 2012 as the 506-sq-mile Turneffe Atoll Marine Reserve which is administered by the Turneffe Atoll Sustainability Association in Belize City. The atoll is dominated by mangrove islands. Mangroves are what make Belize diving special, as they are the nurseries on which almost all marine life depends to ensure juvenile protection and biological productivity. Although the atoll is best known for its walls, there are also many shallow sea gardens and bright sand flats inside the reef that are excellent sites for novice divers and snorkelers.

If you plan on going ashore on any of the islands of the atolls bring some good repellent as insects can be a real menace here.

Though there are not currently any entry fees to enter the marine reserve, plans are on the table to introduce an admission charge in line with other protected areas. Most likely the fee will be collected at the ranger station on Calabash Caye.

🏃 Activities

The best dive spots are in the southern reaches of the atoll, which are less visited by big dive boats, and have more live coral coverage and a wider variety of marine

complete with loungers under cloth umbrellas and private waterside plunge pools.

Luxurious and stylish yet unpretentious, the overall vibe here is shipwreck chic – the kind of outcome you'd expect if a couple of talented interior designers and architects had washed up along with Gilligan and his team.

Each villa has polished concrete or bright tile floors and king-size beds dressed in high-thread-count designer sheets. There is an abundance of comfortable cane furniture and the TVs and other mod cons are carefully hidden in elegant wooden cupboards so as not to clash with the castaway vibe. Many rooms also have alfresco showers sheltered by coconut trees and mangroves.

The most unusual option is Casa Ventanas, which is perched out at the end of a long dock, surrounded by 360 degrees of crystal blue loveliness, while two-storey Casa Estrella is extra spacious and affords life. The highlight of Turneffe Atoll diving is a spot called the Turneffe Elbow, where the current attracts big hungry fish in large numbers and affords one of the only drift dives in Belize. Other sites include Myrtle's Turtle, named for the resident green turtle that appears annually, and Triple Anchor, marked by three anchors remaining from a wreck. Fishing enthusiasts are attracted by the flats, which are ideal for saltwater fly-fishing.

🛏 Sleeping & Eating

Lodging is available on the Turneffe Islands at all-inclusive resorts, which offer diving, snorkeling and/or fishing packages.

Turneffe Island Resort   RESORT **$$$**
(☑ 532-2990, in USA 800-874-0118; www.turneffe resort.com; 3-night resort/diving/fishing packages BZ$2680/3480/4180; ❋ @ 🛜 ☒) At the southern tip of the atoll, the fanciest of the Turneffe resorts offers gorgeous *cabañas* with screened porches, wooden floorboards, and indoor and outdoor showers, all set amid coconut palms just yards from the beach. Proximity to the famous Elbow dive site means trips from the resort go there frequently; some of the best tarpon fishing is a three-minute boat ride away.

Blackbird Caye Resort   RESORT **$$$**
(☑ in USA 888-909-7333; www.blackbirdresort. com; Blackbird Caye; 3-night resort/dive packages from BZ$1920/2950; ❋ 🛜 ☒) This large resort has a range of comfortable accommodations including thatched-roofed *cabañas* right on the sand, complete with screened porches strung with hammocks from which to admire the sea views. The resort offers complete snorkeling and dive packages, and is popular with kayakers as it has coral gardens, uninhabited islands and mangrove creeks all ripe for exploration.

There is a pool with Caribbean views, which comes in handy as the sea in front of the resort is not the best for swimming. Meals are served in a huge *palapa* restaurant near the main dock.

Turneffe Flats Lodge   RESORT **$$$**
(☑ 232-9022, in USA 888-512-8812; www.tflats. com; Blackbird Caye; 3-night resort/diving/fishing packages from BZ$1920/2220/3424; ❋ 🛜 ☒) 🤿 Although its principal fame is as a fishing retreat with expert guides, this lodge on Blackbird Caye also offers dive trips that are often far less crowded than those from other resorts (because most of the other guests are out fishing). Accommodations are in spacious, terracotta-tiled duplex apartments, each with balcony and dramatic views of the waves crashing on the nearby reef.

The owners of the lodge are particularly active in local conservation efforts.

Oceanic Society Field Station   CABIN **$$$**
(☑ in USA 800-326-7491; www.oceanic-society. org; Blackbird Caye; 5-day research programs BZ$5400) 🤿 This conservation field station about five-minutes' walk from Blackbird Caye Resort is currently closed for renovations, but once work is complete will again host the society's recommended 'scientific voluntourism' tours. Participants help with natural history research, collecting data on the diverse wildlife (manatees, crocodiles, bottle-nosed dolphins and hawksbill sea turtles among others) around Turneffe.

Family education programs are especially worthwhile.

❶ Getting There & Away

Of Belize's three coral atolls, the Turneffe Atoll is the closest to the mainland and the most accessible.

It is usually visited by day trip, as it's within easy reach of Caulker, Ambergris and Belize City to the north, and Glover's Reef and Hopkins village to the south. Even Placencia dive boats occasionally make the trip to Turneffe Elbow, at the southern tip of the islands. On rough days it's favored by San Pedro dive operators because much of the trip can be made behind the barrier reef, protecting passengers from choppy open seas.

Turneffe Atoll resorts run a scheduled boat service to and from Belize City on Wednesday and Saturday. A private boat transfer costs at least US$450 one way.

Lighthouse Reef

At 50 miles from the mainland, Lighthouse Reef is the furthest of the three atolls from the coastline. But it is probably the most visited, thanks to the allure of the mysterious Blue Hole Natural Monument. While this icon of Belize diving makes the atoll a major attraction, it is the stunning walls, heavily adorned with swim-throughs, and clear blue water that make it a favorite of both longtime divers and complete novices.

In addition to Half Moon Caye and Long Caye, uninhabited islands in the atoll in-

BLUE HOLE

At the center of Lighthouse Reef is the world-famous **Blue Hole Natural Monument** (www.belizeaudubon.org; entrance fee BZ$60; ☉8am-4:30pm), an incomparable natural wonder and unique diving experience. It may not be the best dive in Belize, but it certainly ranks among the most popular. The image of the Blue Hole – a deep blue pupil with an aquamarine border surrounded by the lighter shades of the reef – has become a logo for tourist publicity and a symbol of Belize.

Deep blue in the center, the hole forms a perfect 1000ft-diameter circle on the surface. Inside, it is said to be 430ft deep, but as much as 200ft of this may now be filled with silt and other natural debris.

Divers drop quickly to 130ft, from where they swim beneath an overhang, observing stalactites above and, sometimes, a school of reef sharks below. Although the water is clear, light levels are low, so a good dive light will enable divers to appreciate the sponge and invertebrate life. Because of the depth, ascent begins after eight minutes; the brevity of the dive does disappoint some divers.

This trip is usually combined with other dives at Lighthouse Reef. Experienced divers will tell you that those other dives are the real highlight of the trip. But judging from its popularity – most dive shops make twice-weekly runs to the Blue Hole – plenty want to make the deep descent.

On day trips the Blue Hole will be your first dive, which can be nerve-racking if you're unfamiliar with the dive master and the other divers, or if you haven't been underwater lately. It may be worth doing some local dives with your dive masters before setting out cold on a Blue Hole trip. An alternative is to take an overnight trip to Lighthouse Reef.

Snorkelers can enjoy a trip to the Blue Hole, too, as there's plenty to see around the shallow inner perimeter of the circular reef. But it's an expensive trip and you'll probably have to tag along on a dive boat.

Note: this trip involves two hours each way by boat in possibly rough, open waters. Also, there's a BZ$60 marine-park fee for diving or snorkeling at the Blue Hole, that is usually on top of the dive fees.

clude Northern Caye, Sandbore Caye, Saddle Caye and Hat Caye, some of which are popular with mosquitoes and crocodiles.

🏃 Activities

Besides the Blue Hole, there is no shortage of fantastic dive sites in Lighthouse Reef, including **Painted Wall**, named for the plethora of painted tunicates found here; the **Aquarium**, often visited as a second stop after the Blue Hole; and the **Cathedral**, known for its amazing variety of sponges. **Half Moon Caye Wall** is probably the best of the lot for its variety of coral formations along the wall and within canyons and swim-throughs. Of particular interest is a field of garden eels found on the sand flats near the wall.

Snorkelers don't despair: the shallows around these sites are interesting as well.

Long Caye

Long Caye at Lighthouse Reef (www.belizeisland.com) is an idyllic private island, 2.5 miles long and 3.25 miles wide, with white sandy beaches and plentiful coconut palms. There have been plans to develop it as a resort, but the isolation and costs involved in running businesses here mean that the vision never really took off.

These days the island has a bit of a 'ghost island' feel about it, with no permanent residents and just two accommodation options. The crumbling state of some of the infrastructure, including the western dock, just adds to the feeling of an abandoned paradise.

That said, it is close to some of Belize's best diving sites and if you don't mind being alone in your resort, it is definitely a more spacious option than being holed up on a live-aboard dive boat. Overnighting here means you'll make it to the Blue Hole before the big dive boats arrive from San Pedro and have the site to yourself.

You can snorkel right from the shore here but the main reason to travel all the way to Long Caye is for diving – some of Belize's best dive spots are a short boat ride away.

HALF MOON CAYE

A nesting ground for the rare red-footed booby bird, **Half Moon Caye Natural Monument** (www.belizeaudubon.org; park fee BZ$20; ⊙ 8am-4:30pm) is the most oft-visited of the Lighthouse Reef islands.

As well as providing nesting grounds for the rare red-footed booby bird, there is a lighthouse, excellent beaches and spectacular submerged walls that teem with marine flora and fauna. Underwater visibility can extend more than 200ft here.

Rising less than 10ft above sea level, the cay's 45 acres hold two distinct ecosystems. To the west is lush vegetation fertilized by the droppings of thousands of seabirds, including some 4000 red-footed boobies, the magnificent frigate bird and 98 other bird species. The east side has less vegetation but more palms. Loggerhead and hawksbill sea turtles, both endangered, lay their eggs on the southern beaches.

A nature trail weaves through the southern part of the island to an observation platform that brings viewers eye level with nesting boobies and frigate birds. Along the path you'll see thousands of seashells, many inhabited by hermit crabs.

The Belize Audubon Society has a visitors center where you must register and pay a BZ$20 park fee on arrival.

Based out of Canada, **Island Expeditions** (⏎ in US 1-800-667-1630; www.island expeditions.com) runs the Kayaking, Reef and Rainforest Adventure Vacation through Belize, which includes a recommended kayaking trip to Half Moon Caye. Check its website for more details.

🛏 Sleeping & Eating

Huracan B&B
B&B $$$

(⏎ in USA 954-802-5005; www.huracandiving. com; 4-night package s/d from BZ$1385/2500; 🛜) ✐ This small dive lodge is a sweet little escape with lots of dark stained wood and simple tropical decor. It's not right on the water, but is only a short walk away. There are four rooms all featuring king-size beds draped in mosquito nets and colorful throw pillows. Delicious gourmet meals are served on the front deck. The owner is an artist and his paintings can be found hanging throughout the property.

Packages include transportation by boat from Belize City, all meals and three days of glorious diving. Nightly rates are also available, as are seven-day dive packages. Check the website for current deals.

Itza Lodge
LODGE $$$

(⏎ in USA 305-600-2585; www.itzalodge.com; 3-day resort package US$735-1035; 🛜) ✐ The biggest place to stay on the island has 12 hardwood rooms with ocean views and private bathrooms in the main lodge and 12 smaller rooms with shared bathrooms in a smaller wing. Meals are served in a lovely thatched open-air dining room with views over the Caribbean to nearby Half Moon Caye.

The social heart of the lodge is the large common area, which has a large map of the atoll painted on the floor and is filled with folk art and musical instruments from around the globe. There are SUP boards and kayaks for guest use, as well as a DVD collection for those quiet island evenings.

ℹ Getting There & Away

Lodges on the island organize scheduled boat transport (US$250 round trip) on Wednesday and Saturday. This is sometimes included in package prices.

A private boat charter can be arranged from around US$650 one way. It's also possible to arrive by private helicopter transfer for around US$2000 per trajectory.

Northern Belize

Includes ➡

Orange Walk Town . . .129

Lamanai 135

Río Bravo
Conservation &
Management Area 139

Corozal Town 141

Cerro Maya &
Copper Bank 147

Sarteneja 149

Best Places to Eat

➡ Maracas Bar &
Restaurant (p133)

➡ Nahil Mayab (p134)

➡ Patty's Bistro (p145)

➡ Cocina Sabo (p134)

➡ Venky's Kabab
Corner (p145)

Best Places to Sleep

➡ Cerros Beach
Resort (p148)

➡ Serenity Sands (p143)

➡ Chan Chich Lodge (p133)

➡ Almond Tree
Resort (p145)

➡ Backpackers
Paradise (p150)

Why Go?

Many travelers save a chunk of change by flying into Cancún and bussing or driving down to their final destination. Passing through the flat farmland and provincial towns of Northern Belize, they may not be inspired to linger.

But what are they missing? This is a chilled-out stretch of Belize that is entirely void of crowds, with unbeaten paths, abundant wildlife and prices a fraction of those in the rest of Belize.

Northern Belize comprises two districts: Corozal and Orange Walk, both traversed by the straight, flat Philip Goldson Hwy. Off the main road, adventurous travelers will find pretty fishing villages, pristine jungles, ancient Maya cities and anachronistic Mennonite communities.

Then there's the food. Exhibiting influences from Mexico, Northern Belizean cuisine is more diverse and more daring than its southern counterpart. If you're ready to trade rice and beans for seafood *ceviche*, you've come to the right place.

When to Go

➡ **Jan–Apr** The dry season opens up top trekking opportunities throughout the region.

➡ **Mar–Jun** Spot flocks of water birds while cruising in a canoe on stunning Shipstern Lagoon.

➡ **Sep** Residents from all over Belize come to party at Orange Walk's famous Carnival.

Northern Belize Highlights

1 **Lamanai** (p136) Taking a riverboat tour along the New River to these magnificent Maya ruins.

2 **Shipstern Nature Reserve** (p149) Spotting crocs and other lagoon inhabitants.

3 **Orange Walk Town** (p129) Chowing down on Belize's best tacos.

4 **Sarteneja** (p149) Chilling in this laid-back fishing town.

5 **Cerro Maya** (p147) Enjoying panoramic ocean views from this waterfront Maya temple.

6 **Río Bravo Conservation & Management Area** (p139) Discovering unexcavated ruins and undisturbed wildlife.

7 **Corozal Town** (p141) Soaking up the saltwater breezes while sipping cocktails.

History

Located on the eastern fringe of the ancient Maya heartland, Northern Belize supported many settlements through history without producing any cities of the size or grandeur of Caracol, which lies further south in Belize, or Tikal in Guatemala. It was home to important river trade routes that linked the interior with the coast: the north's major Maya site, Lamanai, commanded one of these routes and grew to a city of up to 35,000 people during the Maya peak, known as the Classic Period. The city at Lamanai continued to serve as a Maya center until the Spanish arrived in the 16th century.

Meanwhile, another city grew up further west at La Milpa. During the late Classic Period, La Milpa was home to 46,000 people, but archaeologists believe the city came to an abrupt end in the 9th century AD, possibly due to environmental and economic stresses brought on by drought.

A Spanish expedition into Northern Belize from the Yucatán in 1544 led to the conquering of many of the region's Maya settlements and, later, the creation of a series of Spanish missions distantly controlled by a priest at Bacalar in the southeastern Yucatán. Maya rebellion was fierce, and after a series of battles the Spanish were driven out of the area for good in 1640.

British loggers began moving into the region in search of mahogany in the 18th century. They encountered sporadic resistance from the now weakened and depleted Maya population, which had been ravaged by European-introduced diseases.

In 1847 the Maya in the Yucatán rose up against their Spanish-descended overlords in the War of the Castes ('Guerra de Castas' in Spanish), a vicious conflict that continued in diminishing form into the 20th century. Refugees from both sides of the conflict took shelter in northern British Honduras (as Belize was then called), with people of Spanish descent founding the towns of Orange Walk and Corozal, and the Maya moving into the forests and countryside. It wasn't surprising that intermittent hostilities took place in British Honduras. One group of Maya, the Icaiché, was repulsed from Orange Walk after fierce fighting in 1872. The border between Mexico and British Honduras was not agreed upon between the two states until 1893.

Caste War migrants from the Yucatán laid the foundations of modern Northern Belize by starting the area's first sugarcane plantations. Despite the sugar industry's many vicissitudes, it is now the backbone of the Northern Belize economy, with some 900 cane farms in the region.

❶ Getting There & Around

The Philip Goldson Hwy links Belize City with the Mexican border via the region's two main towns: Orange Walk Town and Corozal Town. Several bus companies service the route, with some going as far as Chetumal, 7 miles into Mexico. Approximately 30 daily buses run each way from Belize City to Corozal Town and beyond. There are also daily buses connecting Orange Walk Town with Sarteneja (though the nicest way to get to Sarteneja is by boat from Corozal Town). There is a regular boat service that connects Corozal Town and Sarteneja with San Pedro on Ambergris Caye. Both Corozal Town and Orange Walk Town also have direct air links to San Pedro.

ORANGE WALK DISTRICT

Orange Walk is one of the more spread out and thinly populated districts in Belize. The Philip Goldson Hwy cuts through the district's population center in its far northeast, and most of the communities and attractions west of this are connected by a network of (mostly) unpaved roads, although the main westward highway has recently been paved and is now one of the best roads in Belize. A casual glance at the government-produced Belize travel map shows fairly extensive grid roads west of the Philip Goldson Hwy that stretch out into towns with names like Yo Creek and August Pine Ridge. Though this gives the impression of larger communities in rural Orange Walk, these are actually farming communities; the neatly drawn lines represent farming roads and boundaries created by the farmers themselves, and not major towns bustling with activity.

Further west and to the south, these grid roads disappear entirely, and you're in what Belizeans refer to as 'deep bush,' the backwoods jungle country that makes up most of Orange Walk District. It's here you'll find the vast Río Bravo Conservation & Management Area and, further out still, the village of Gallon Jug and the ultra-exclusive Chan Chich Lodge.

Orange Walk Town

POP 13,687

Orange Walk Town is many things to many people: agricultural town, economic hub,

Mennonite meeting place, street-food paradise...but it is not generally considered a tourist town. And the chances are pretty good that this won't change any time soon. This town of 14,000 souls – just 57 miles from Belize City – doesn't have much to keep travelers around for more than a day or two. Having said that, it is a useful base from which to make the superlative trip to the ruins of Lamanai and longer excursions into the wilds of Northern Belize. Orange Walk has a fine location beside the New River, which meanders lazily along the east side of town, and there are a few very nice (and reasonably priced) hotels and restaurants for visitors who choose to hang around for a bit.

History

Orange Walk Town was born as a logging camp in the 18th century, from where mahogany was floated down the New River to Corozal Bay. It began to develop as a town around 1850, when Mexican refugees from the War of the Castes arrived. These migrants, whose agricultural experience was welcomed by the British colonial authorities, started Northern Belize's first sugar boom (which lasted from the 1850s to the 1870s).

Meanwhile, tensions were on the rise between the settlers and the local Icaiché Maya. British loggers had been encroaching on lands that the Icaiché considered their own around the Río Hondo (which today forms Belize's border with Mexico). Moreover, British Honduras had been supplying arms to the Cruzob Maya (bitter enemies of the Icaiché). In 1872 the War of the Castes came to Orange Walk when a force of some 150 Icaiché Maya attacked the town's British garrison. After several hours of fierce fighting, the Icaiché were repelled, and their leader Marcos Canul was fatally wounded. The attack went down in history as the last significant armed Maya resistance in Belize.

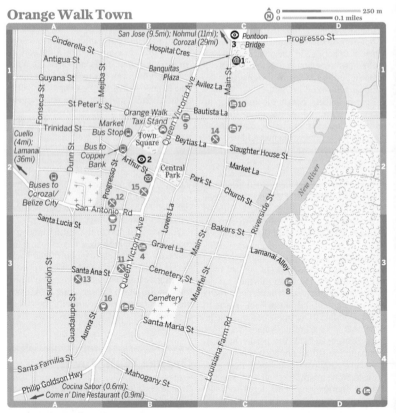

Orange Walk Town

⊙ Sights

Nohmul   RUIN

FREE For a taste of how Belize's many majestic ruins may have looked to early explorers before being excavated and landscaped, head to this vast jungle-covered Maya site just off the Philip Goldson Hwy. Meaning 'Great Mound' in Maya, Nohmul (noh-mool) was a town of 3000 people during the late Classic Period. The ruins – and Belize – made headlines in 2013 when a construction company bulldozed one of the site's main temples in order to obtain material for road construction.

While the temple was damaged beyond repair, many other structures remain buried, forming jungle-covered outcrops surrounded by a sea of sugarcane. The ruins themselves aren't spectacular – at first glance they look just like a series of hills – but with some imagination and a sense of adventure it is a rewarding place to visit as you scramble up mounds sheltering untold archaeological riches below.

You'll almost certainly have the place to yourself, which adds to the sense of discovery. Scramble to the top of the lofty main tower and through the thick jungle you'll catch glimpses over the endless sugar fields of Orange Walk District. Keep your eye out for exposed steps on the peaks of the mounds and a hidden, partially excavated section of walls that form a deep stone nook shaded by thick jungle.

From the northern edge of Orange Walk, drive 9.6 miles north on the Philip Goldson Hwy to the village of San Jose. Turn west at the north end of the village and drive 1.3 miles west to Nohmul. The site is not well marked so you'll probably have to ask for directions through the maze of sugar roads. A taxi from Orange Walk is about BZ$60, round trip.

Cuello   RUIN

(📞320-9085; Yo Creek Rd; ⊙9am-5pm) **FREE** Close to Orange Walk Town, Cuello (*kway-yo*) is one of the earliest known settled communities in the Maya world, probably dating back to around 2400 BC, although there's not much left to show for it. Archaeologists have found plenty here, but only Structure 350, a nine-tiered pyramid, is of much interest to the non-expert. The pyramid was constructed around AD 200 to AD 300, but its lower levels date from before 2000 BC.

The site is on private property owned by Cuello Distillery, 4 miles west of Orange Walk (take San Antonio Rd out of town). It is not really open to the public, although the distillery usually allows access if you turn up during office hours. It's a good idea to call and make advance arrangements. A taxi to Cuello from Orange Walk costs about BZ$25, round trip.

Flagpole Plaza   LANDMARK

(Arthur St) A small plaza behind the Town Hall that was once the site of Fort Cairnes, a British military post during the War of the Castes conflict.

Independence Plaza   HISTORIC SITE

(Main St) This rundown plaza near the bridge over the New River marks the site of Fort Mundy, a strategic British military position.

Banquitas House of Culture   MUSEUM

(📞322-0517; Banquitas Plaza; ⊙8:30am-5:30pm Mon-Fri) **FREE** Modern Banquitas House of Culture has an attractively displayed exhibit on Orange Walk's history. It's especially good on the local Maya sites, and has artifacts, maps and illustrations, as well as exhibits that change monthly. It's set in a pleasant, small, riverside park with an amphitheater.

NORTHERN BELIZE ORANGE WALK TOWN

Orange Walk Town

⊙ **Sights**
1 Banquitas House of
  Culture.....................................C1
2 Flagpole Plaza B2
3 Independence Plaza..................C1

⊙ **Activities, Courses & Tours**
  Lamanai River Tours ....(see 6)

⊜ **Sleeping**
4 Akihito Hotel.............................B3
5 D'Victoria Hotel........................B3
6 El Gran Mestizo D4
7 Hotel de la Fuente....................C2
8 Lamanai Riverside Retreat...................C3

9 Orchid Palm Inn.......................B1
10 St Christopher's Hotel............C1

⊗ **Eating**
11 Juanita's B3
12 Lee's Chinese Restaurant.....................B2
  Maracas Bar & Restaurant............(see 6)
13 Nahil Mayab A3
14 Panificadora La Popular......................C2
15 Torta Hut B2

⊜ **Drinking & Nightlife**
16 Hi 5 ....B3
  Lamanai Riverside Retreat...........(see 8)
17 Natural Balance.......................B3

👉 Tours

Sugarcane and street tacos aside, the main reason travelers come to Orange Walk is to head out to the Maya ruins at Lamanai. Tour companies offer full-day trips (from 9am to 4pm) by riverboat that give visitors a chance to see the prolific birdlife along the New River and to learn about the history and archaeology at Lamanai. Any hotel can help make arrangements for this tour. The price includes a picnic lunch served by the New River lagoon at the entrance to the temple complex. These companies usually require a minimum of four people to make the trip. You should probably reserve your place the day before, although you may be lucky on the morning you want to go.

Reyes & Sons   TOUR
(☎ 610-1548, 322-3327; Tower Hill Bridge, Philip Goldson Hwy; per person BZ$80) Reyes & Sons keeps its boat docked by the Philip Goldson Hwy bridge over the New River, 5 miles south of town, but staff will pick you up at your hotel with advanced notice.

Lamanai River Tours   TOUR
(☎ 302-1600, 670-0700; 1 Naranjal St; per person BZ$100) Located inside Maracas Bar, this is the only Lamanai tour company based in Orange Walk Town. Its boat will pick you up at your hotel dock or at the Casa de Cultura. Tour price includes admission and lunch at the site.

Dave's Eco Tours   TOUR
(☎ 205-5597, 627-7955, 607-9929; www.daveseco tours.com; 3 Pelican St, Maskall Village) Travelers rave about David Chan's trips to Altun Ha, Lamanai, Cahal Pech and other Maya sights around Belize. David also does cave-tubing, horseback riding and various nautical trips. Though based in Maskall (just outside of Altun Ha), Dave travels throughout the country.

Lamanai Eco Adventures   TOUR
(☎ 610-2020; www.lamanaiecoadventures.com; Tower Hill Bridge) One of several tour operators based by the toll bridge just south of Orange Walk, Lamanai Eco Adventures has good boats and its knowledgeable guides get top reviews.

Lamanai Eco Tours   TOUR
(Tower Hill Bridge) This experienced tour operator runs boat trips from near the Tower Hill Bridge just outside Orange Walk and has professional and attentive guides. Not to be confused with Lamanai Eco Adventures right next door.

🛏 Sleeping

St Christopher's Hotel   HOTEL $
(☎ 302-1064; www.stchristophershotelbze.com; 10 Main St; r with fan/air-con BZ$80/110; P ❄ @ 🛜) The flowering gardens and riverside setting make this otherwise nondescript hotel an attractive place to stay. The rooms themselves are spacious but plain. River-boat trips to Lamanai pick you up right from the hotel grounds and your hosts – the Urbina family – are attentive and welcoming, in a low-key, unassuming sort of way.

Orchid Palm Inn   HOTEL $
(☎ 322-0719; www.orchidpalminn.com; 22 Queen Victoria Ave; s/d BZ$77/94; P ❄ @ 🛜) Set on a busy corner in the center of all the action, the friendly Orchid Palm Inn is a tiny island of tranquility. It has eight well-furnished and nicely decorated rooms that offer excellent value. Avoid room one if you need wi-fi.

Lamanai Riverside Retreat   GUESTHOUSE $
(☎ 302-3955; Lamanai Alley; r BZ$90; P ❄ @ 🛜) Located right on the river, this place is about 24 miles from the namesake ruins. It has only three rustic wooden rooms, with breezy balconies and mosquito-netted beds, and is far from the fanciest digs in town, but the jungly atmosphere and accommodating service are excellent.

The owner is involved in the cataloging and protection of the area's crocodile population, and will be glad to tell you all about the crocs and other animals that call the river home. Adjoining the retreat is one of Orange Walk's more picturesque eating and drinking spots, so come for a beer even if the rooms are booked.

D'Victoria Hotel   HOTEL $
(☎ 322-2518; 40 Queen Victoria Ave; r BZ$130-170; P ❄ 🛜 ▨) The fresh paint does not do too much to brighten up this concrete hotel right on a busy road. Rooms are clean but basic and some are rather musty. The biggest selling point is the pool, which is a great option for cooling off in the Orange Walk heat.

Akihito Hotel   HOTEL $
(☎ 302-0185; philosophy.dude@gmail.com; cnr Queen Victoria Ave & Gravel Lane; r with/without air-con BZ$65/45, tr BZ$45; ❄ @ 🛜) The cheapest of the bunch, the Akihito has a collection of very plain rooms with small bathrooms in

CHAN CHICH LODGE

In the far western corner of Orange Walk District, in the middle of a 200-sq-mile private reserve, Chan Chich Lodge (☑ in US 800-343-8009, 223-4419; www.chanchich.com; Gallon Jug; r BZ$763-915, villa with air-con BZ$1362; 🅿 @ 🛜 ⛱) is one of the country's original ecolodges. The remote setting and pristine environs make this a picture-perfect location for a jungle lodge. It is also a destination itself: many bird- and wildlife enthusiasts arrive via charter flight from Belize City and spend the whole of their Belize visit right here.

Luxurious thatched *cabañas* surround the partly excavated ruins of an ancient Maya plaza. The *cabañas* are gorgeous – built from local hardwoods and furnished with ceiling fans, comfy king- or queen-size beds and rustic yet modern decor. The lodge's distance from anywhere deters drop-ins, and the limited number of *cabañas* (not to mention the price) also keeps the crowds away.

Chan Chich lies within a private reserve known as the Gallon Jug Estate, which has been maintained by Belizean businessman Barry Bowen since his purchase of the BEC's lands in the 1980s. Be sure to obtain detailed driving instructions and a permit to enter the reserve from lodge management before setting out.

a large concrete building on the main road. They are all different with some significantly better than others, so ask to look around. The family who runs the hotel is very friendly and a treasure trove of local information.

El Gran Mestizo
CABAÑAS $$

(☑ 322-2290; www.elgranmestizo.com; 1 Naranjal St; r BZ$130-150; 🅿 ✴ 🛜) Perched on the banks of the New River south of town, these new *cabañas* are a great choice for those looking to be surrounded by nature but want to be close to town. On the far side of the river there is a wall of jungle that is a riot of birdlife and iguanas laze around on the hotel grounds.

The rooms are modern and comfortable, though not particularly spacious, and don't make a feature of the lush surroundings. Management arranges free transfers to and from town for guests, which is necessary as the onsite restaurant isn't always open. Boat trips to Lamanai will pick up here.

Hotel de la Fuente
HOTEL $$

(☑ 322-2290; www.hoteldelafuente.com; 14 Main St; r BZ$80-170, ste BZ$130-170; 🅿 ✴ @ 🛜) This family-run hotel is smack dab in the center of Orange Walk, but most of the rooms are in a new building set back from the hustle and bustle (and noise) of the road. The clean, cozy rooms – all equipped with fridge and coffee maker – are probably the best in town, while the suite has a full kitchen.

✖ Eating

Although there aren't many 'five-star eateries' in this working-class town, Orange Walk is known for its street food. Surrounding

the town plaza are tiny cafes, snack stalls, fruit stands and pushcarts offering a veritable smorgasbord of Northern Belizean and Mexican foods, including rice and beans, tacos, tamales, stewed chicken, ice cream and more. Piped-in music and enticing aromas create an irresistible atmosphere, especially on Saturday afternoons. Everything is supercheap and hygiene standards are generally good. Some folks come from as far away as Corozal 'just to hang out and eat.'

Maracas Bar & Restaurant
BELIZEAN $

(☑ 322-2290; 1 Naranjal St; mains BZ$8-22; ⊙ 11:30am-10pm Thu & Sun, til midnight Fri & Sat) For good eats in a fantastic natural setting, take a taxi down to this restaurant at the El Gran Mestizo on the banks of the New River south of town. For the full experience, pick a table in one of the waterside *palapas* and choose from Belizean- and Mexican-inspired dishes on the ample menu. Also a fantastic spot for a cool drink, but bring bug spray.

Come n' Dine
Restaurant
BREAKFAST, BELIZEAN $

(Philip Goldson Hwy; dishes BZ$8-30; ⊙ 7am-10pm) Unassuming and unexpected, this roadside restaurant serves some of the best Belizean food around. Located right next to the gas station on a crook on the Philip Goldson Hwy just a couple of miles south of town, it's well placed for road-trippers (but also worth the trip if you are staying in town). Look for excellent stews, steaks and stir-fries. Daily specials run at BZ$8 to BZ$10 and are a great way to try some more unusual local dishes.

NORTHERN BELIZE ORANGE WALK TOWN

PARTY TIME, SPANISH STYLE

One of the more colorful features of multi-ethnic Belize is the diversity of feasts and celebrations. Holidays in Northern Belize reflect a strong Mexican influence, with old-style Catholic Spanish roots.

A Northern Belizean Christmas is a distinctive festival. While Maya are gearing up for animistic deer dances and Brits are planning Boxing Day football parties, the north gets ready for Las Posadas. The tradition is more than 400 years old, and is practiced still in Mexico and Guatemala as well. It is based on Mary and Joseph's unsuccessful search for accommodation – Las Posadas means the 'the lodging.' For nine days, beginning on December 16, people participate in candlelit processions, singing hymns, stopping at designated homes, in a loose re-enactment of the Bible story that culminates in a big Christmas Eve ceremony. In a secular spin-off to the tradition, Northern Belizeans still go around to each others' houses at Christmas time, being treated to holiday dishes, cakes and drinks.

The other big event in the north is Orange Walk Carnival held on Independence Day in September when the whole town turns out for dancing, parades and concerts.

Lee's Chinese Restaurant   CHINESE $
(11 San Antonio Rd; dishes BZ$7.50-20; ⊘11am-midnight; ▣) Orange Walk's most popular Chinese eatery, Lee's serves up a superior range of Hong Kong–style dishes. Aside from the blaring TV and the plastic tablecloths, the atmosphere is festive and welcoming, with the stylish dragon-theme decor kept cool by whirring ceiling fans. The menu is extensive, including excellent seafood and vegetarian options.

Juanita's   BREAKFAST, BELIZEAN $
(8 Santa Ana St; breakfast BZ$4-6, mains BZ$6; ⊘6am-2pm & 6-9pm) You can tell from the number of dedicated locals who flock to this place that the food here is satisfying. Simple, clean and very well priced, Juanita's serves eggs and bacon for breakfast, and rice and beans and other local favorites, such as cow-foot soup, during the rest of the day.

Torta Hut   FAST FOOD $
(Queen Victoria Ave; sandwiches BZ$4-6; ⊘4pm-midnight Thu-Sun) Not exactly street food, but certainly not a restaurant, the tiny Torta Hut is a food truck that parks at a busy intersection in the center of Orange Walk. There are picnic tables out the back but most locals just hang out on the street enjoying the fat sandwiches stuffed with chicken, beef or pork.

Panificadora La Popular   BAKERY $
(Beytias La; pastries BZ$2-8; ⊘6:30am-8pm Mon-Sat, 7:30am-noon & 3-6pm Sun) Should you find yourself in Orange Walk during daylight hours, *do not pass go, do not collect $200;* go *directly* to this amazing bakery, grab a tray and a pair of tongs, and take your pick from the spread of sticky buns, cinnamon rolls, croissants and meat pies, which make for a perfect breakfast or lunch for the road. Good luck trying to decide.

★**Cocina Sabor**   BELIZEAN $$
(▣322-3482; Philip Goldson Hwy; mains BZ$18-40, light meals BZ$12-25; ⊘11am-10:30pm, closed Tue) Hugely popular among expats, this welcoming place on the highway has a large menu of local and international fare, including good pasta and steak served in the spotless air-conditioned wooden dining room. During the day it serves light meals, such as tasty burgers and wraps. Service is prompt and courteous, and there's a well-stocked bar.

Nahil Mayab   BELIZEAN, MEXICAN $$
(www.nahilmayab.com; cnr Santa Ana & Guadalupe Sts; mains BZ$14-25; ⊘11am-3pm Mon, 11am-10pm Tue-Thu, 11am-2am Fri & Sat; ☻▣) Decked in exotic greenery and faux Maya carvings, the dining room evokes the district's surrounding jungles, as does the pleasantly shaded patio. It's a fun, kitschy atmosphere in which to sample some Yucatecan-inspired food, like Ke'Ken (salt pork in tomato sauce) or Cham Cham (empanadas).

🍷 Drinking & Nightlife

Orange Walk is a town where farmers from all over northern Belize (including the area's sizable Mennonite population) come to swap tales, sell produce and feast at Chinese restaurants, which also function as bars during the day when traditional nocturnal establishments are closed.

There are also a couple of lovely bars surrounded by nature on the banks of the New River.

Natural Balance   CAFE
(San Antonio Rd; coffee & tea from BZ$5; ⊘ 9am-5:30pm; 🛜) This Taiwanese-owned cafe is an oasis of tranquility and serves fresh-brewed coffee drinks (iced and hot), as well as bubble milk tea (popular in Asia but almost unknown in Belize). Light vegetarian snacks are also available.

Hi 5   CLUB
(Aurora St; ⊘ 6pm-late Thu-Sun) Orange Walk's best late-night option, Hi 5 is in fact two venues, one with a lounge bar opening from 6pm onwards and an air-conditioned disco next door. The music is better in the bar but sooner or later all punters end up next door.

Lamanai Riverside Retreat   BAR
(Lamanai Alley; ⊘ 8am-10pm) With its breezy deck and tables with lovely river views, this restaurant-bar gets crowded on weekends. The menu (mains BZ$12 to BZ$25) is pretty extensive, but the place is recommended mainly for drinking and socializing.

ℹ Information

Belize Bank (34 Main St) Accepts all major credit cards, with BZ$4 fee and a limit of BZ$500 per day.

Loz Internet (Cinderella St; per hr BZ$4; ⊘ 8:30am-9pm) Internet and ice-cream parlour in one; a great concept in hot Orange Walk.

Northern Regional Hospital (☑ 322-2072; Philip Goldson Hwy; ⊘ emergency services 24hr) Located just off the highway on the northern edge of town.

Police Station (☑ 322-2022; Hospital Cres) Across from the library.

Post Office (cnr Queen Victoria Ave & Arthur St; ⊘ 8am-5pm Mon-Thu, until 4pm Fri)

Scotia Bank (cnr Park & Main Sts) Accepts all cards with BZ$4 fee; limit per day BZ$800.

ℹ Getting There & Away

BUS

Orange Walk is the major Northern Belize bus hub for buses plying the Corozal–Belize City route. There are half a dozen companies servicing this route and around 30 buses a day going in each direction. All long-distance buses, including services to Belize City, Corozal, Chetumal and Sarteneja, stop at the makeshift bus terminal west of the cemetery. It is supposed to be a temporary facility but it has an air of

starting to feel permanent as there has been no progress on a replacement.

Buses to rural destinations around Orange Walk District, such as Copper Bank, leave from various points around the market. Schedules are subject to change, so you'll want to ask in advance around the market or at your hotel.

Buses heading north from Orange Walk begin at 6:45am and run until around 9:15pm. Heading south to Belize City, buses begin at 4:45am and run until 8:30pm. The trip to Belize City takes around two hours, and costs BZ$5 to BZ$7; the trip to Corozal is slightly quicker and cheaper.

There's also direct services to Belmopan at 4:15am and 4:45am that bypass Belize City.

The bus to Indian Church near Lamanai (BZ$8, 1½ hours) departs from the market at 3:45pm on Monday and Friday.

Bus to Copper Bank Buses to Copper Bank via Progresso leave from near the market.

Buses to Corozal/Belize City (Temporary Bus Station; Dunn St) This lot is marked as the 'Orange Walk Temporary Bus Station' but it appears to be all but permanent now with locals holding out little hope of getting a real bus station. Buses between Belize City and Corozal all pull in here, as do Sarteneja services.

Market Bus Stop Buses to local and regional destinations, including the irregular service to Indian Church.

TAXI
Orange Walk Taxi Stand Taxis park by the town plaza.

Lamanai

One of the biggest and best excavated Maya sites in northern Belize, Lamanai lies 24 miles south of Orange Walk Town up the New River (or 36 miles by unpaved road). The ruins are known both for their impressive architecture and marvelous setting, surrounded by dense rainforest overlooking the New River Lagoon. The translation of the word *lamanai* – which means 'submerged crocodile' in Maya – gives a pretty good indication of the local residents of this jungly setting. Bring plenty of bug spray – the jungle surrounding the ruins is home to vicious mosquitos.

History

Lamanai not only spans all phases of ancient Maya civilization but also tells a tale of ongoing Maya occupation and resistance for centuries after the Europeans arrived, equaling the longest known unbroken

Lamanai

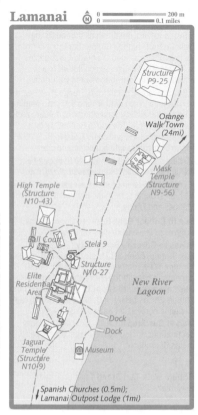

occupation in the Maya world. Lamanai was inhabited at least as early as 1500 BC, and was already a major ceremonial center, with large temples, in late Preclassic times.

It seems to have surged in importance (perhaps thanks to its location on trade routes between the Caribbean and the interior) around 200 or 100 BC, and its major buildings were mostly constructed between then and AD 700, although additions and changes went on up until at least the 15th century. At its peak it is estimated to have had a population of around 35,000.

When the Spanish invaded Northern Belize from the Yucatán in 1544, one of the most important of the missions they set up was Lamanai, where they had found a thriving Maya community. But the Maya never readily accepted Spanish overlordship, and a rebellion in 1640 left the Lamanai mission burned and deserted. Maya continued to live here until the late 17th or 18th century,

when they were decimated by an epidemic, probably smallpox.

Archaeological excavations commenced as early as 1917, but large-scale digging, by David Pendergast of Canada's Royal Ontario Museum, only began in 1974. The painstaking work of uncovering more than 700 structures found here will take several lifetimes, not to mention huge amounts of funding.

⊙ Sights

Arriving at Lamanai by boat, you'll probably first be brought to the small museum, which exhibits some beautiful examples of pottery, and obsidian and jade jewelry. Then you'll head into the jungle, passing gigantic guanacaste (tubroos), ceiba and *ramón* (breadnut) trees, strangler figs, allspice, epiphytes and examples of Belize's national flower, the black orchid. In the canopy overhead you might see (or hear) some of the resident howler monkeys. A tour of the ruins takes a minimum of 90 minutes, but can be done more comfortably in two or three hours.

Lamanai   ARCHAEOLOGICAL SITE
(www.nichbelize.org; admission BZ$10; ⊙8am-5pm) Perhaps the most fascinating Maya site in northern Belize, the ruins are known both for their impressive architecture and marvelous setting overlooking the New River Lagoon. Climbing to the top of the 125ft High Temple to gaze out across the vast jungle canopy is an awe-inspiring experience that is not to be missed.

Most visitors approach Lamanai by guided river trip from Orange Walk not just to avoid the long and bumpy road, but to take advantage of the river trip itself, which goes deep into the home of the countless colorful and unusual birds that live in the area. Many guides who do the 1½-hour river trip are experts in both archaeology and the area's wildlife, making it an especially worthwhile experience. The river voyage passes through some of the most beautiful jungle and lagoon country in northern Belize, and the Mennonite community of Shipyard, before reaching Lamanai itself. There are a number of excellent tour guides in Orange Walk who specialize in the journey.

Mask Temple   RUIN
The Mask Temple (Structure N9-56) was begun around 200 BC and was modified several times up to AD 1300. It has two

13ft stylized masks of a man in a crocodile headdress emblazoned on its west face to the north and south of the main stairs. Dating from about AD 400, these are considered some of the finest big masks in the Maya world.

What you actually see are fibreglass replicas that have been crafted in front of the original limestone masks in order to protect them. Deep within the building archaeologists found the tombs of a man adorned with shell and jade jewelry, and a woman from almost the same date. The pair are thought to be a succession of leaders – perhaps a husband and wife, or brother and sister.

High Temple   RUIN
North of the ball court, across a plaza shaded by trees, is Structure N10-43, the highest at Lamanai, which rises 125ft above the jungle canopy. Few large buildings in the Maya world were built as early as this one, which was initially constructed around 100 BC. You can climb to its summit for fabulous panoramas over the rest of Lamanai, the New River Lagoon, and plains and forests stretching out on all sides. This grand ceremonial temple was built from nothing on a site that had previously been residential, which indicated a dramatic surge in Lamanai's importance at the time.

Jaguar Temple   RUIN
This temple (Structure N10-9), fronting a 100yd-wide plaza, was built in the 6th century AD and modified several times up to at least the 15th century – a fine example of the longevity of the Lamanai settlement. The stone patterning on the lowest-level turns depicts two cleverly designed jaguar faces, dating from the initial 6th-century construction. On the opposite (north) side of the plaza is a set of buildings that were used as residences for Lamanai's royal elite.

Lamanai Museum   MUSEUM
(☉8am-5pm) In the main administrative building where you pay your entrance fee, this small museum features artifacts unearthed throughout the Lamanai complex, including the original Stele 9, the most detailed of three main carved stone slabs found here. In addition to pottery and jewelry, there are also some informative displays covering all aspects of Maya civilization.

Maya Structures   RUIN
At the far north end of the Lamanai site, and often missed by tour groups, this large platform, 120yd by 100yd in area, supports several large buildings up to 92ft high. Next to it is a river inlet that once formed an ancient harbor.

Ball Court   RUIN
Not far west of Stela 9 is Lamanai's ball court, one of the smallest in the Maya world – but with the largest ball-court marker found yet! A ceremonial vessel containing liquid mercury, probably from Guatemala, was found beneath the marker.

Stela 9   RUIN
North of the elite residential complex, this temple was the original site of the intricately carved standing stone erected in AD 625 to commemorate the accession of Lord Smoking Shell in AD 608, which is now on display in the site museum. A faithful replica has been placed in front of the temple in the original position.

The stone shows the leader in ceremonial regalia, wearing a rattlesnake headdress with quetzal feathers at the back, and holding a double-headed serpent bar diagonally across his body, with a deity emerging from the serpent's jaw at the top. The remains of five children – ranging in age from newborn to eight – were buried beneath the stela. Archaeologists believe the burial must have been highly significant, since offerings are not usually associated with the dedication of monuments.

Spanish Churches   RUIN
Some 400yd south of Jaguar Temple are the remains of the thick stone walls of two Spanish colonial churches, which were built by Maya forced labor from the remains of a temple. The southern church was built in 1544, and the northern one in the 1560s. Both were destroyed by the Maya, the second one in the 1640 rebellion.

Unknown to the Spanish, the Maya placed sacred objects such as crocodile figurines inside the churches while building them. A 300yd path opposite the churches leads to the partly overgrown remains of a 19th-century sugar mill, which some say directly contributed to the final abandonment of Lamanai by bringing new diseases into the area.

👉 Tours

Most visitors approach Lamanai by guided river trip from Orange Walk Town, not just to avoid the long and bumpy road, but to take advantage of the river trip itself. The

CHURCHES OF LAMANAI

Lamanai is one of the few Maya sites in Belize with clearly identifiable Spanish colonial ruins within the indigenous city. The road from the southern entrance to the site passes what remains of a large stone church. These ruins provide evidence of the Spanish practice of demolishing indigenous structures and using the materials to create Christian places of worship.

The first church in Lamanai was constructed in 1544 on top of an existing Maya temple. Archaeologists believe that Spanish priests didn't reside permanently in Lamanai but rather visited as part of an established circuit of indigenous settlements.

While there is evidence that some of the residents of Lamanai embraced Christianity, including the discovery of a Christian burial site, overall the Maya of Lamanai didn't take kindly to the Spanish demolishing sacred places and imposing their beliefs, and burnt the church to the ground in 1610.

Not to be diverted from their mission, the stubborn Spanish built another, much larger church on the site – the famed Indian Church, which gives its name to the adjacent village. The scale and form of the church suggest that the Catholic leaders had grand plans for the Lamanai area. The church continued to function until 1640 when a major Maya rebellion saw the community abandon Christianity and revert to an indigenous belief system. This time the church wasn't destroyed but rather reworked into a traditional place of worship with the placement of a stela around the church entrance accompanied by an offering of zoomorphic figurines and animal bones.

majority of tours set out from docks near the Tower Hill Bridge around 4 miles south of Orange Walk and cost BZ$80 per visitor. Most companies will include a free vehicle transfer from Orange Walk on request. It's also possible to travel by boat all the way from downtown Orange Walk Town to Lamanai for BZ$100 per person; this trip involves another 20 minutes on the New River.

Whichever tour you take, the boat ride is an opportunity to observe the river's prolific and colorful birdlife, as well as crocs, iguanas, monkeys and other wildlife. Most guides who do the 1½-hour trip are experts in local archaeology and ecology, making this tour a two-for-the-price-of-one experience. Besides the beautiful jungle and lagoon, the river voyage passes the Mennonite community of Shipyard before reaching the ruin site.

Most tours leave around 9am and return to Orange Walk around 3pm. Tours include lunch, which is usually served in the lagoon-side *palapas* at the archaeological site upon arrival.

🛏 Sleeping & Eating

Guesthouse Olivia GUESTHOUSE $
(☑ 668-8593; Indian Church; r per person BZ$40) This no-frills guesthouse has the only cheap beds near the Lamanai site. Don't expect luxury, but rest easy knowing you'll have the archaeological site all to yourself in the morning. Call first to make sure there is a

room ready. It's next to the Gonzalez Store in the heart of Indian Church.

Lamanai Outpost Lodge LODGE $$$
(☑ 670-3578, in US 954-636-1107; www.lamanai.com; r from BZ$315; ⓟ @ 🛜) For those who can afford it, the best option for fully exploring Lamanai is one of the package tours offered by this place. About 1 mile south of the ruins, this classy lodge is perched on a hillside just above the lagoon, and boasts panoramic views from its bar and gorgeous open-air dining room (meals BZ$36 to BZ92).

The 17 thatched-roof bungalows, each with fan, private bathroom and veranda, are lovely and perfectly suited to the casual jungle atmosphere. Two of the rooms have air-con. Packages include meals, transfers to/from Belize City and two guided small-group activities per day. The list of activities ranges from visiting the ruins to observing howler monkeys, sunrise canoeing and nocturnal crocodile encounters. Birding is big here: almost 400 species have been documented within 3 miles of the lodge.

ℹ Getting There & Away

If you decide to go without a guide, you can get to the village of Indian Church (next to Lamanai) from Orange Walk, but the bus goes only twice a week on Monday and Friday. You'll need to find somewhere to spend a few nights while waiting for your return bus.

Alternatively if you have a vehicle, Lamanai is a fairly straightforward 90-minute drive along an unpaved road from Orange Walk Town.

Río Bravo Conservation & Management Area

If you're looking for true, wild tropical rainforest, this is it. Encompassing 406 sq miles in northwest Belize, the Río Bravo Conservation & Management Area (RBCMA) takes up 4% of Belize's total land area and is managed by the Belizean nonprofit organization Programme for Belize (PFB; p66). The RBCMA harbors astonishing biological diversity – 392 bird species (more than two-thirds of Belize's total), 200 tree species and 70 mammal species, including all five of Belize's cats (jaguar, puma, ocelot, jaguarundi and margay). Río Bravo is said to have the largest concentration of jaguars in all of Central America.

Parts of the territory of the RBCMA were logged for mahogany and other woods from the 18th century until the 1980s, but distance and inaccessibility helped to ensure the survival of the forest as a whole. The area also contains at least 60 Maya sites, including La Milpa, the third-largest site in Belize.

At the RBCMA, the PFB seeks to link conservation with the development of sustainable land uses. Programs include tree nurseries, extraction of nontimber products such as chicle, thatch and palm, experimental operations in sustainable timber extraction, and ecotourism.

History

Maya lived in this area as early as 800 BC. When Spanish expeditions first journeyed here, the Maya were still using the same river trade routes, though by then their population was seriously depleted. Mahogany loggers moved into the area by the mid-18th century but were subject to intermittent attacks by the Maya for at least a century. By the late 19th century, the Belize Estate and Produce Company (BEC) owned almost all of the land in northwestern Belize. The company carried out major timber extractions, floating mahogany and Mexican cedar out through the river system to the coast. With the advent of rail systems and logging trucks, operations flourished until overcutting and a moody market finally prompted the BEC to stop cutting trees in the early 1980s.

Intensive chicle tapping also took place throughout the 20th century, and you can still see slash scars on sapodilla trees throughout the RBCMA.

Belizean businessman Barry Bowen, owner of the Belikin brewery and the country's Coca Cola distribution rights, bought the BEC and its nearly 1100 sq miles of land in 1982. He quickly sold off massive chunks to Yalbac Ranch (owned by a Texan cattle farmer) and Coca Cola Foods. Meanwhile the Massachusetts Audubon Society was looking for a reserve for migrating birds. Coca Cola donated 66 sq miles to support the initiative (a further 86 sq miles followed in 1992), and Programme for Belize was created to manage the land. Bowen also donated some land, and PFB, helped by more than US$2 million raised by the UK-based World Land Trust, bought the rest, bringing its total up to today's 406 sq miles.

◉ Sights & Activities

La Milpa   RUIN

FREE In the northwestern corner of the RBCMA, La Milpa is the third-largest Maya site in Belize, believed to have had a population of 46,000 at its peak between AD 750 and AD 850. Its 5-acre Great Plaza, one of the biggest of all Maya plazas, is surrounded by four pyramids up to 80ft high. Now the structures are all covered with jungle and inhabited by howler monkeys, evoking the mystery and history of the ancient ruins.

Guides from La Milpa Field Station can accompany your hike to shed light on the function of the various structures, and to point out the stelae and other moss-covered artifacts that still remain in the area.

Birdwatching

Considering the link to Mass Audubon, it's no surprise that Río Bravo is one of the country's prime birding areas. The conservation area may attract fewer birders than more accessible destinations like Crooked Tree, but it attracts more birds – more than 390 species to be exact. Due to its remote location and vigilant protection measures, Río Bravo is home to dozens of species that are rarely spotted in other parts of the country. Case in point: in 2005 the RBCMA was selected as the release site for the restoration of the amazingly majestic and globally threatened harpy eagle. Although you're unlikely to spot a harpy eagle, other large avian species are not uncommon, including the oscillated turkey, the crested guan and the ornate hawk eagle. The open area around La Milpa Lodge attracts fly-catchers, mannekins, redstarts, orioles, tanagers, trogons and hummingbirds, so you can lounge in your hammock with your binoculars and watch the show. Alternatively, guides organize early-morning bird walks around the grounds.

☞ Tours

In addition to exploring the nature trails, from Hill Bank Field Station you can make arrangements to tour the lagoon by canoe or by boat, including nighttime croc-spotting, while from La Milpa Field Station you can visit the adjacent Maya Ruins.

🛏 Sleeping & Eating

La Milpa Lodge LODGE **$$$**
(☑ 227-5617, 227-5616; www.pfbelize.org; s/d from BZ$212/350, without bathroom BZ$187/325; 🅿🛜) ✇ The four lovely hardwood thatched *cabañas* at La Milpa Lodge are in tune with the natural surroundings and feature big comfortable beds, ceiling fans, spacious bathrooms, writing desks and power outlets. There are also fan-cooled dormitory-style rooms with shared bathrooms.

Hill Bank Field Station LODGE **$$$**
(☑ 227-5617, 227-5616; www.pfbelize.org; s/d BZ$212/350, without bathroom BZ$162/275; 🅿@) ✇ Guests at Hill Bank stay in spacious hardwood *cabañas* built on a clearing adjacent to the New River lagoon. There is also ecologically sound dormitory-style

accommodations with shared bathrooms featuring composting toilets. Rooms have wide balconies with hammocks perfect for watching the abundant birdlife in the area. Add BZ$130 per visitor to the prices for meals packages.

ℹ Getting There & Away

Most visitors rent a vehicle to get to either field station. La Milpa is about one hour from Orange Walk Town (via Yo Creek, San Felipe, Blue Creek and Tres Leguas). Hill Bank is about two hours from Belize City (via Burrell Boom, Bermudian Landing and Rancho Dolores), although it's also possible to travel from Orange Walk by road or boat via Lamanai.

Call Programme for Belize (p66) or check the website for detailed directions and advice on road conditions (the later stages of both trips involve sections on unpaved roads, which can be impassable after heavy rains). PFB can also help arrange transfers from Orange Walk, Belize City or Lamanai.

COROZAL DISTRICT

The country's northernmost district, Corozal is wedged in between Orange Walk District and the border. Its proximity to Mexico lends it a certain Spanish charm, and also offers easy access to travelers coming from Cancún or Chetumal. In recent years, Corozal has been 'discovered' by outsiders, who are racing to buy up the affordable seaside property and build retirement homes on their little plots of paradise. However,

---

LITTLE BELIZE

Located on the eastern shore of Progresso Lagoon, Little Belize is an Old Order Mennonite community of approximately 2000 residents. Among the more traditional Mennonite groups, these folks look as thought they've come straight from the prairie, driving around in horse-drawn carriages, with men wearing broad-brimmed hats and overalls and women in long dresses and bonnets.

Like most Mennonite villages, Little Belize is an industrious place, with an economy thriving on farming. One of the largest employers in the village is Belize Exports Ltd, which grows papayas for export to North America.

Old Order Mennonites are typically an insular group, interacting with outsiders just enough to sell their wares. Tentatively opening itself up to rural tourism, Little Belize offers visitors a rare opportunity to get a closer look inside this enigmatic community. With advanced arrangements, visitors can tour the village in a horse-drawn buggy, visiting the papaya packing plant, a poultry farm, a wood workshop and other local industries. Make arrangements in advance through the Shipstern Nature Reserve (p149). A visit to Little Belize can be combined with a visit to the *mestizo* community of Chunox and the Maya ruins at Cerros in a full-day tour for BZ$150.

Little Belize is a 40-minute drive from Sarteneja, Corozal or Orange Walk. There is no public transportation available, but the Shipstern Nature Reserve can organize transfers.

this district is still relatively unknown to Belize-bound tourists, who don't often venture off the Philip Goldson Hwy.

The chunk of land that spreads south and eastward across the bay from Corozal Town is at once one of the least-visited and most visitworthy spots in Belize. It's more compact than Orange Walk District, and most of the sights are within striking distance by boat or road of Corozal Town itself. Though topographically not as dramatic as the west or the south (most of Northern Belize is fairly flat), this part of the country is sparsely populated and filled with pristine jungle, as well as the cool seaside town of Sarteneja and the amazing coastal Maya ruins at Cerros.

❶ Getting There & Away

Corozal District is the first taste of Belize for many travelers after crossing the border from Mexico at Santa Elena. Local buses and minivans connect the border with Corozal Town.

The main bus route between Corozal District and the rest of Belize runs the length of the Philip Goldson Hwy connecting Corozal Town with Belize City via Orange Walk Town. Another major bus line connects Belize City and Sarteneja via Orange Walk Town.

There is an airport south of Corozal Town with regular flights to and from San Pedro. It's also possible to travel between San Pedro and Corozal Town or Sarteneja by boat.

Corozal Town

POP 11,722

Just 9 miles south of Mexico and 29 miles north of Orange Walk Town, Corozal has a vibe different from any other town in Belize. The Mexican influence is palpable on the streets of this provincial town, where you are likely to hear Spanish and eat tacos. Though it feels prosperous (especially by Belizean standards), most of the town's wealth comes from its position as a commercial and farming center – not from tourism. In fact, the town's fledgling tourism sector has been hit hard by the direct boat service between San Pedro and Chetumal, which has seen many travelers bypass Corozal altogether and several tourist-orientated businesses close.

But Corozal remains a fine place to be a tourist as it escapes the holiday-ville atmosphere that haunts some other places in Belize. With ocean breezes, affordable hotels, fine food and easy access to the rest of the district, Corozal is worth a stop on the way to or from Mexico – if not a detour from your Belizean itinerary further south. The whole town is situated on Corozal Bay, and the waterfront is lined with parks, picnic tables and the odd waterside *palapa* (thatched-roof open-air hut).

The town center is arranged around a town square, encompassing the plaza (Central Park), post office and police station. The main highway passes through town as Santa Rita Rd and 7th Ave, briefly skirting the sea at the south end of town.

History

The ruins of the Postclassic Maya trading center, now called Santa Rita (probably the original Chetumal), lie beneath parts of modern Corozal. Across the bay, Cerros was a substantial coastal trade center in the Preclassic Period.

Modern Corozal dates from 1849, when it was founded by Mexicans fleeing the War of the Castes. The refugees named their town Corozal after the Spanish word for cohune palm, a strong symbol of fertility.

For years Corozal had the look of a typical Mexican town, with thatched-roof homes. Then Hurricane Janet roared through in 1955 and blew away many of the buildings. Much of Corozal's wood-and-concrete architecture dates from the late 1950s. Like Orange Walk, the Corozal economy is based on sugarcane farming, although there's also quite a bit of trade with nearby Chetumal in Mexico as well.

◉ Sights

★ **Old Customs House** HISTORIC SITE
(cnr 2nd St South & 1st Ave; ⊙9am-5pm Mon-Fri) **FREE** Built in 1886, this fine old Spanish Colonial building once housed a bustling market and customs house. It was one of only 11 buildings spared by Hurricane Janet in 1955. Today the historic building houses a cultural center and museum with exhibits of local artifacts. It's a good place to catch up on what's going on in Corozal during your visit.

Santa Rita RUIN
(admission BZ$10; ⊙8am-6pm) **FREE** Santa Rita was an ancient Maya coastal town that once occupied the same strategic trading position as present-day Corozal Town, namely the spot between two rivers – Río Hondo (which now forms the Belize–Mexico border) and New River (which enters Corozal Bay south of town). Much of Santa Rita remains unexcavated, but it's worth a short excursion out of town to explore the site.

NORTHERN BELIZE COROZAL TOWN

Corozal Town

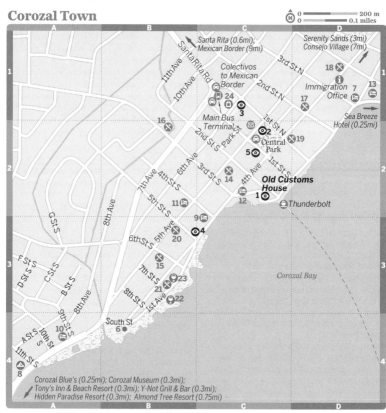

To reach the Maya site, head out of town on Santa Rita Rd. Continuing north on the main highway toward Mexico and turn left at the Super Santa Rita store. Some 350yd past the store you'll find a wooded area on the right and in it is a partially restored pyramid offering an amazing view across the surrounding town to the bay. Apply liberal amounts of bug spray before making the trip. A taxi from downtown costs BZ$5.

Clock Tower
LANDMARK
This Corozal landmark dominates central park.

St Paul's By-the-Sea
LANDMARK
This simple waterside church is the largest Anglican place of worship in Corozal.

Corozal Museum
MUSEUM
(☑ 402-3314; 129 South End; admission by donation; ⊙ 9-11:30am & 2-4:30pm Mon-Fri, 9-11:30am Sat) Called 'A Window to the Past,' the exhibit at this little museum focuses on the expe-

rience of the East Indian population, who arrived around 1838 as indentured servants working on the sugar plantations, but also features traditional items from other ethnic groups. It's located about a half-mile south of town right on the Philip Goldson Hwy.

Fort Barlee
HISTORIC SITE
At the center of town, this fort was built in 1849 by Caste War refugees for protection from attacks by hostile Maya. Remains of the brick corner turrets are still visible on the fort site.

Town Hall
NOTABLE BUILDING
(☑ 422-2072; 1st St South; ⊙ 9am-noon & 1-5pm Mon-Fri) FREE A colorful and graphic mural by Belizean-Mexican artist Manual Villamor Reyes enlivens the lobby of the town hall. The mural depicts episodes from Corozal history, including the War of the Castes, with the talking cross and the fall of Bacalar; the flight of refugees into Brit-

Corozal Town

◉ Top Sights
  1 Old Customs House C2

◎ Sights
  2 Clock Tower.. C2
  3 Fort Barlee...C1
  4 St Paul's By-the-Sea B3
  5 Town Hall C2

◎ Activities, Courses & Tours
  6 Our Island Tour B4

◎ Sleeping
  7 Bayside Guesthouse D1
  8 Caribbean Village................................. A4
  9 Hok'ol K'in Guest
     House C3
  10 Hotel Maya.. A4
  11 Las Palmas Hotel.................................. B2

  12 Mirador Hotel..C2
  13 Scotty's Bay Inn...................................... D1

◎ Eating
  14 Al's Cafe...C2
  15 Cactus Plaza B3
  16 Chico's Tortilla Factory.........................B2
  17 Patty's Bistro D1
  18 RD's Diner D1
  19 The 1..C2
  20 Venky's Kabab Corner...........................B3
  21 Wood House Bistro B3

◎ Drinking & Nightlife
  22 Jamrock..B3
  23 Primo's Casita Bar B3

◎ Shopping
  24 Gabrielle Hoare Market C1

ish Honduras; the founding of Corozal; and Hurricane Janet.

🏃 Activities

Our Island Tour　　　　　　　　　　TOUR
(☑ 402-2401, 633-9372, 633-0081; www.our islandtour.com; 1st Ave) Offers a tour by boat to the ruins at Cerro Maya (BZ$50 per person, minimum three people), as well as fishing trips and other adventures.

🎉 Festivals & Events

Art in the Park　　　　　　　　　　　ART
(www.corozal.com/culture/artinpark; ⊙ 5:30-10pm) On one Saturday of every month, downtown Corozal hosts an outdoor art exhibition and mini music festival, known as Art in the Park. Artists congregate in the central park to display their wares, with paintings, photography, woodwork and more. Music is performed live or piped in over the loud speakers and the whole town comes out to socialize. Check the website for the schedule.

🛏 Sleeping

Bayside Guesthouse　　　　GUESTHOUSE $
(☑ 625-7824; baysideguesthouse@live.com; 31 3rd Ave; s/d/tr BZ$80/90/100, d with air-con BZ$105) A welcoming and homey option just off the waterfront with just four big, well-equipped rooms and an ample terrace upstairs offering bay views. Everything here is spotless and well maintained. Breakfast is included and other meals are available on request.

Hotel Maya　　　　　　　　　　　HOTEL $
(☑ 422-2082; hotelmaya@btl.net; 7th Ave, South End; s/d BZ$70/85, with air-con BZ$85/95; ❄️☎️) Run by the very friendly Rosita May, the Hotel Maya is a long-time favorite of budget-conscious travelers. Rooms are clean and homey, and enlivened by colorful bedspreads and paintings done by local artists. Apartments are available for long-term rentals. In addition to being a licensed travel agent, Rosita is also a great source of local information.

Scotty's Bay Inn　　　　　　GUESTHOUSE $
(www.scottysbelize.com; 1st Ave; r from BZ$50; ❄️☎️) Cheap, clean and right by the water, Scotty's has some of the best budget digs in town. The upstairs social area has inside and outside seating and is perfect for gazing out at Corozal Bay. Air-con costs BZ$20 extra.

Caribbean Village　　　　　CAMPGROUND $
(☑ 422-2725; www.belizetransfers.com; 7th Ave; campsite per person BZ$10, RV site BZ$40; @☎️) You can't miss this place; it's the plot of land right off the main road at the south end of town with all the RVs parked on it. Lot spaces include all connections (water, electricity, sewage). There's also a camping ground with toilets and cold showers. The owners, Henry and Joan Menzies, are licensed travel agents who rent vehicles (per day BZ$160) and book tickets throughout Central America.

★ Serenity Sands　　　　　　　B&B $$
(☑ 669-2394; www.serenitysands.com; Consejo Rd; d BZ$190-200, house BZ$220; 🅿️❄️@☎️)
🏖 Located about 3 miles north of Corozal

Town, this B&B is off the beaten track, off the grid and out of this world. The remote beachside setting offers the perfect combination of isolation and accessibility (though you'll need a vehicle to get here), and the four spacious tiled rooms are decorated with locally crafted furniture and boast private balconies. There is also a self-contained two-bedroom house with kitchen for rent behind the main building.

Hok'ol K'in Guest House
GUESTHOUSE $$

(☎ 422-3329; www.corozal.net; 89 4th Ave; s/d with fan BZ$77/104, with air-con BZ$92/120; ✳@🛜) With a Maya name meaning 'rising sun,' this modern, well-run, small hotel overlooking the bay may well be the best value in town. The large, impeccably clean rooms are designed to catch sea breezes. Each has two double beds, a bathroom and a balcony with hammock. Hok'ol K'in also serves meals at reasonable prices (breakfasts are particularly good).

Hidden Paradise Resort
RESORT $$

(Corozal Bay Inn; ☎ 636-9355; www.corozal bayresort.com; Almond Dr; cabañas BZ$100; P✳🛜🏊) With a new name and under new managment, these 10 cozy, colorful *cabañas* are set around a broad sandy area that faces the sea at the far southern end of town. Tucked in under thatched roofs, the *cabañas* are nicely decorated and fully equipped. Alas, the resort's restaurant and bar has closed, but its outdoor pool is still a good place to chill out.

Tony's Inn & Beach Resort
RESORT $$

(☎ 422-2055, 422-3555; www.tonysinn.com; Almond Dr; s/d BZ$160/180, deluxe r BZ$240; P✳@🛜) This southside resort is the largest in town, with uniform rooms on two floors surrounding a small garden. Spacious and comfortable rooms offer all necessities, such as hair dryers and cable TV, and there's free wi-fi throughout the property. Tony's Y-Not ('Tony' backwards, get it?) Grill & Bar is a lovely seaside spot for food and drinks.

Las Palmas Hotel
HOTEL $$

(☎ 602-5186, 422-0196; www.laspalmashotel belize.com; 123 5th Ave; s/d BZ$100/120; P✳🛜) This centrally located, renovated hotel has simple, clean rooms with fresh white paint jobs. The accommodations have all the basics covered but are distinctly lacking in character and seem a bit pricey for what you get. There is plenty of gated parking onsite.

Mirador Hotel
HOTEL $$

(☎ 422-0189; www.mirador.bz; cnr 4th Ave & 3rd St South; r BZ$70-120, with air-con BZ$100-180; ✳@🛜) Resembling a miniature Belizean version of New York City's famed Flatiron Building, the four-story Mirador is a local landmark. The staff are friendly and many rooms are enhanced by lovely ocean views,

COROZAL FREE ZONE

Straddling the Belize–Mexico border at Santa Elena–Subteniente López, 9 miles north of Corozal Town, is a curious experiment in global capitalism going by the moniker 'Free Zone.' Though the name implies a kind of free-market free-for-all, with shops and stalls selling goods from both sides of the border at discounted rates to consumers from both sides of the border, the reality is, well...different.

In practice, the Free Zone resembles a shopping mall comprising loads of high-turnover small shops selling second-rate consumer goods from China, India and other export nations. Shops are staffed by both Belizean and Mexican workers, which apparently is where the notion of 'free' comes in, as both Belizeans and Mexicans are free to work there.

But not to shop. Unlike their Mexican counterparts, Belizeans can't just show up, shop and go home, due to restrictive import regulations and duties on the Belizean side of the border. In essence, the Free Zone is a bargain-basement shopping mall for consumers on the Mexican side of the border – one that Belizean customers can only utilize with some degree of bureaucratic wrangling.

So, the Free Zone is not open to Belizeans (or non-Belizean residents of Belize) but it is open to nonresident foreigners, eg tourists, who can shop duty-free. Shoppers can get excellent deals on alcohol, household appliances and brand-name shoes and clothing. It's cheap – *very* cheap – leading folks to speculate about the authenticity of those brand names. But there are good deals to be had nonetheless.

Here's the catch: the duty-free goods are for sale for use outside of Belize; if you bring your loot back into Belize, you are obliged to pay all applicable taxes.

although they could do with a makeover. The rooftop patio affords tremendous views of the bay.

★ **Almond Tree Resort** RESORT **$$$**
(☑422-0006; www.almondtreeresort.com; 425 Bayshore Dr; r BZ$196-338; P ❄ ❋ 🗪 ☀) The town's most luxurious lodging, this gorgeous seaside inn offers spacious, stylish rooms with wonderful sea views, Caribbean-style furniture and tempurpedic beds. Deluxe suites have full kitchenettes. The whole place is centered on lush grounds and a glorious swimming pool.

✕ Eating

The 1 MEXICAN **$**
(4th Ave; tacos BZ$2; ⊘8am-8pm) Right on the corner of Central Park, this popular little shop serves authentic Mexican-style tacos and *tortas* (Mexican pressed sandwiches) with a great variety of sauces.

Venky's Kabab Corner INDIAN **$**
(☑402-0546; 5th St South; dishes BZ$10-15; ⊘9am-9:30pm) Chef Venky is the premier – and, as far as we know, only – Hindu chef in Corozal, cooking excellent Indian meals, both meat and vegetarian. The place is not much to look at on the inside, in fact there is just one table that is usually covered in assorted clutter, but the food is excellent and filling. Two main dishes and a few sides easily serve three people.

Wood House Bistro ASIAN **$**
(1st Ave; dishes BZ$12-25; ⊘noon-10pm) A dime a dozen in Belize, cookie-cutter Chinese restaurants are barely worth mentioning, which is why we're especially pleased that Corozal now has the quirky and pretty darn good Wood House Bistro at the southern end of town.

You'll notice the difference the moment you arrive. Unlike most restaurants of the genre, the dining area here is open air and there is a fine reggae soundtrack. But the differences are not just superficial: the food is eclectic, offering more than the usual fried chicken. Singapore-style noodles (BZ$12) are especially good, as are the Rangoon crab puffs (BZ$8).

Corozo Blue's PIZZA, BELIZEAN **$**
(Philip Goldson Hwy; mains BZ$12-24; ⊘10am-midnight Sun-Thu, 10am-2am Fri & Sat; ☑) Located on an inviting curve of beach just where the road turns south out of town, this semi-enclosed restaurant has indoor and beachfront seating with a spectacular view of the bay. (On a clear day you can see the ruins at Cerros!) It has an outdoor stone oven for pizzas, as well as Belize standards like rice and beans and *ceviche*.

Patty's Bistro BELIZEAN **$**
(cnr 2nd St North & 4th Ave; meals BZ$8-15; ⊘10:30am-8pm, closed Sun; ❋) Though the location has shifted two blocks, management of this Corozal favorite has not changed, nor has its friendliness or overall decor. The yellow walls are hung with hokey beach art, and the tables are covered in plastic tablecloths, but the atmosphere is so welcoming that the informal interior only adds to the charm.

The place is best known for its conch soup (BZ$15), a thick potato-based chowder with vegetables, rice and chunks of conch meat, but more adventurous diners may want to go for the cow-foot soup (BZ$10). You'll also find more Mexican and Belizean fare on the menu, not to mention burgers, sandwiches and other standards.

RD's Diner BELIZEAN **$**
(25 4th Ave; mains BZ$20-25; ⊘noon-10pm, closed Sun; ❋) Rick and his staff go above and beyond to ensure a good time at this innocuous-looking eatery. The interior might be nondescript but it's an excellent place to sample some local specialties like *gibnut* stew or rice and beans. Otherwise the menu offers a mix of Belizean, Mexican and straight-up continental fare, such as burgers, salads and fried seafood. Service is a bit slow but exceedingly friendly.

Cactus Plaza MEXICAN **$**
(6 6th St South; snacks BZ$3-5, mains BZ$8-20; ⊘6am-late Fri-Sun) You can't miss this building, which looks a bit like a cross between a Christmas tree and a Mexican fruitcake. On the menu you'll find tacos, *salbutes* and *panuchos* (fried corn tortillas with fillings), as well as shrimp, sea-snail or mixed-seafood *ceviches*. Beware the habaneros! There are also plenty of good drinks, including *licuados con leche* (milkshakes) and fresh fruit juices.

Al's Cafe DINER **$**
(5th Ave; snacks BZ$1-2, mains BZ$6-8; ⊘9am-4pm Mon-Sat & 6-9pm Sat) This tiny local place is popular for tasty Mexican snacks and cheap daily lunch specials. Try the burritos with beans, chicken and cheese (and very hot habanero sauce)!

Chico's Tortilla Factory
BAKERY $

(25 7th Ave; tortillas per dozen BZ$1.25; ⊙6am-5pm) Not a sit-down restaurant, but a fun place to go to watch flour tortillas being made.

Y-Not Grill & Bar
INTERNATIONAL $$

(☑422-2055; www.tonysinn.com; Almond Dr; mains BZ$11-38; ⊙11am-10pm) The waterfront restaurant at Tony's Inn offers a delightful setting and decent grub served under a breezy thatch-roofed *palapa* right on the waterfront, with dockside seating stretching out into the bay. The bar offers a fine selection of tropical fruity cocktails and other drinks.

🍷 Drinking & Nightlife

Corozal's best bars are found in town along the waterfront. For an early start, the waterside hotels and restaurants on the southern edge of town serve up cold beers with a view.

Jamrock
BAR

(1st Ave; ⊙11am-midnight, closed Tue) In a park right by the bay, this open-air watering hole catches plenty of breeze and is popular with expats and locals alike. Tasty meals are served from noon to 10pm and the bar is very well stocked.

Primo's Casita Bar
BAR

(Front St; ⊙noon-midnight Tue-Sun) Have a seat at this open-air bar and restaurant and enjoy the Corozal Bay breeze with a cold Belikin or an even colder margarita or piña colada. Also has an extensive list of cocktails.

🛍 Shopping

If you're really desperate for retail therapy, your best bet might well be a quick trip up to the 'Free Zone' on the Belize–Mexico border.

Gabrielle Hoare Market
SOUVENIRS

(6th Ave; ⊙6:30am-5:30pm Mon-Sat, until 3pm Sun) Amid the fruit, vegetables and fish, you'll also find a few local craftspeople selling art, woodwork and tapestries. The 2nd floor has stores selling food and locally made clothing. You'll certainly find a greater selection further south (especially in the more tourism-focused towns).

ℹ Information

Atlantic Bank (cnr 4th Ave & 3rd St North; ⊙9am-4pm Mon-Fri) Has a reliable ATM accepting all major cards.

Belize Bank (cnr 5th Ave & 1st St North; ⊙9am-4pm Mon-Fri) Situated on the plaza; ATM accepts all international credit cards.

Corozal Hospital (☑422-2076) This hospital is located northwest of the center of town on the hill in Santa Rita.

Immigration Office (☑402-0123; 4th Ave; ⊙8:30am-noon & 1-4pm Mon-Fri) Provides 30-day visa extensions for most nationalities.

J&M Printing (☑422-0106; 7th Ave; per hr BZ$3; ⊙8am-9pm)

Post Office (5th Ave; ⊙8:30am-noon & 1-4:30pm Mon-Thu, until 4pm Fri) On the site of Fort Barlee, facing the plaza.

Scotiabank (4th Ave; ⊙8am-3pm Mon-Thu, 8am-4:30pm Fri) Currency exchange and cash advances; ATM accepts all international cards.

ℹ Getting There & Away

AIR

Corozal's airstrip is a couple of miles south of the town center in Ranchito. Taxis (BZ$10) meet incoming flights. Both **Tropic Air** (☑226-2012; www.tropicair.com; Airport, Ranchito) and **Maya Island Air** (☑422-2333; www.mayaislandair.com; Airport, Ranchito) fly in and out of Corozal with direct flights to San Pedro.

BOAT

Corozal is the natural jumping-off point for trips to Cerros, Sarteneja and San Pedro, and the town's only water-taxi service is **Thunderbolt** (☑631-3400, 610-4475; 1st Ave). The advent of the Chetumal to San Pedro boat has made this journey less popular, but crossing the border by bus and taking this boat is significantly cheaper.

It leaves Corozal at 7am, returning from San Pedro at 3pm. It stops at Sarteneja (upon request). The trip to Sarteneja takes 30 minutes and costs BZ$25/50 one way/round trip; San Pedro is two hours away and will cost you BZ$50/90 one way/round trip.

BUS

Corozal's main bus terminal is a key stop for nearly all of the myriad bus lines that ply the Philip Goldson Hwy down to Orange Walk and Belize City. At last count, 30 buses daily were doing the 2½-hour run from Corozal Town to Belize City, from 3:30am until 7pm; there are half a dozen buses in the other direction on the 15-minute run to the Mexican border, with the last coming through around 4pm. There are a couple of very early direct buses to Belmopan via Orange Walk at 3am and 3:30am.

In Chetumal, Mexico, buses from Corozal stop at the Nuevo Mercado (New Market), about 0.75 miles north of the town center. A taxi from the Nuevo Mercado to the intercity bus station or town center is around US$1. From Chetumal to

NORTHERN BELIZE CERRO MAYA & COPPER BANK

ⓘ GETTING TO MEXICO

The border crossing at Santa Elena (Belize) and Subteniente López (Mexico) is 9 miles north of Corozal and 7 miles west of Chetumal. If you are crossing from Mexico to Belize, you will have to hand in your Mexican tourist card to Mexican immigration as you leave.

If you are one of the many travelers who has flown into Cancún, be aware that unscrupulous Mexican immigration officials may try to charge you the tourist card fee again even though it was most probably included in your air ticket. Carry a printout of your ticket receipt showing all the taxes paid – the tourist card will be listed under the code 'UK.'

If you entered Mexico by land or on a charter flight, the tourist card fee may be pending, in which case you'll need to pay at the onsite bank. If you plan on taking the night bus to Belize, you'll probably end up paying the officials directly in order to get on your way even though you technically are required to wait for the bank to open.

Travelers departing from Belize by land have to pay BZ$37.50; this includes both the exit fee and a government-imposed conservation fee. Bus travelers, heading in either direction, have to get off the bus and carry their luggage through customs.

Corozal, buses leave from the north side of the Nuevo Mercado from around 4:30am to 6pm.

There are two buses daily, except Sunday, from Corozal to Copper Bank running along the edge of Corozal Bay leaving from the pier at 11am and 4pm.

TAXI

Colectivos (Corozal United Taxi Cooperative; Santa Rita Rd) to the Mexican border depart for the Belizean immigration post (BZ$5, 20 minutes) from outside the main bus terminal from 7am to 7pm. Once you complete border formalities, Mexican *colectivos* and private taxis run into Chetumal. If you are in a hurry, these minivans will run a private transfer for BZ$25 to the border post or BZ$60 all the way to the ADO intercity bus terminal in Chetumal.

Regular city taxis charge around BZ$30 to the border or BZ$70 to the ADO bus terminal; you can find them outside Corozal Town's main bus terminal or around the central park.

Cerro Maya & Copper Bank

POP 500

The small fishing (and lobstering) village of Copper Bank (called San Fernando on some maps) is set on the shores of a brackish lagoon known as Laguna Seca (which is anything but dry). The village is a tiny place, consisting of just 500 souls, with a lazy, hazy, crazy tropical charm.

Although Copper Bank is only 9 miles from Corozal, it's isolated due to the poor condition of the roads and the necessity of crossing the New River by hand-cranked cable ferry. Nonetheless, this tranquil little hamlet has just enough going on to make it an ideal place to hole up for a spell. The Maya ruins at Cerro Maya (also known as Cerros) are 2.5 miles north, overlooking Corozal Bay; and the New River and the surrounding jungles are ideal for fly-fishing, birdwatching and other outdoor adventures.

◉ Sights

Cerro Maya   RUIN
(Cerros; admission BZ$10; ⊘8am-5pm) The ruin at Cerro Maya is the only Maya site in Belize that occupies beachfront property. It is composed of a series of temples built from about 50 BC. While the site is mostly a mass of grass-covered mounds, the center has been cleared and two structures are visible. Be warned: Cerro Maya can get very very buggy, especially during the rainy season; cover up and don't skimp on the bug spray!

In late Preclassic times, its proximity to the mouth of the New River gave Cerro Maya a key position on the trade route between the Yucatán coast and the Petén region. The temples are larger and more ornate than any others found in the area, and archaeologists believe Cerro Maya may have been taken over by an outside power at this time, quite possibly Lamanai. Cerros flourished until about AD 150, after which it reverted rapidly to small, unimportant village status.

Climbing **Structure 4** (a funerary temple more than 65ft high) offers stunning panoramic views of the ocean and Corozal Town just across the bay. Northwest of this, **Structure 5** stands with its back to the sea. This was the first temple to be built and may have been the most important. Large stucco masks flanking its central staircase have been covered with modern replicas for

DON'T MISS

CONSEJO

About 7 miles north of Corozal, Consejo is a sweet small fishing village set on Chetumal Bay, offering little more than a pristine stretch of beach and lovely sunrise views. Bring a book and your binoculars and you might be content to stay here for quite a while.

There aren't many amenities for tourists in Consejo. But there is a handful of folks who like the place so much that they decided to stay, setting up a sort of outpost for expats at Consejo Shores at the southern end of the village. Although there are no gates, it does have the exclusive atmosphere of a gated community.

Located around 2 miles northwest of Consejo, family-run **Smuggler's Den** (☑ 629-9460; smugglersdenbelize.tripod. com; Consejo Village; r/bungalow/house BZ$70/120/220; [P] [?]) has spacious thatched bungalows with kitchenettes and a lounge area set around a grassy yard that runs down to a tranquil stretch of sand. The food here gets rave reviews, especially the owner's special roast beef.

The road between Corozal and Consejo is paved but pot-holed. There are no longer any public buses on this route, so if you don't have transport, you'll need to negotiate a taxi from Corozal – about BZ$30.

protection, but the new material looks out of place and the models are not as well executed as those at Lamanai.

Southwest of Structure 5, a third structure remains unexcavated, protected by an army of mosquitoes. Apparently Structure 6 exhibits a 'triadic' arrangement (one main temple flanked by two lesser ones, all atop the same mound), which is also found in Preclassic buildings at Lamanai and El Mirador in the Petén.

🛏 Sleeping & Eating

There are good hotels in Copper Bank but the nicest places to stay are nestled on the edge of Corozal Bay just to the east of Cerro Maya.

★ **Cerros Beach Resort**   RESORT, CABAÑAS **$$**
(☑ 623-9763, 623-9530; cabaña BZ$120; [P] [?]) About 3.5 miles north of Copper Bank, on the coast and surrounded by jungle, this rustic little beach resort is perhaps our favorite spot in northern Belize. A self-contained chunk of tranquility, it has everything a great getaway should, including a top location on the crystal-blue side of Corozal Bay, fantastic ecofriendly facilities, and genuine, welcoming hosts.

The four beautiful, hardwood, thatched-roof *cabañas* are equipped with hot solar showers and come with free use of kayaks, bicycles and fishing gear. Just behind the accommodations there are nature trails and it's possible to walk to the Cerro Maya ruins through the bush. But perhaps the biggest reason to book an extended stay here is the highly recommended food (mains BZ$10 to BZ$21) prepared by the owner, a former pastry chef from Miami who makes tangy, to-die-for *ceviche* and delicious, decadent chocolate cake as well as homemade fruit wine and beer. Many ingredients are grown onsite in the organic garden and the owner even hunts his own deer to prepare gourmet smoked sausages.

The Thunderbolt boat service between San Pedro and Corozal will drop you at the resort if you have a group of four or more.

Copperbank Inn   GUESTHOUSE **$$**
(☑ 662 5281; www.copperbankinn.com; r incl breakfast BZ$130; [P] [❄] [?] [≋]) Under new management, this gracious plantation-style home stands out in the middle of modest little Copper Bank. With its wraparound veranda and comfortable rooms, it's a fine base from which to explore the surrounding area. There's also an outdoor pool, but it was empty when we visited. Top gringo-style meals are available at the onsite bar-restaurant.

❶ Getting There & Away

An unpaved road runs from Corozal to Copper Bank, punctuated by a river that needs to be forded by a hand-cranked cable ferry, and on to Cerros. During the dry season you can pass in a regular vehicle, but when it's wet you'll need a 4WD.

Buses leave from near the pier in Corozal for Copper Bank (one hour) at 11am and 4pm, returning from Copper Bank at 1pm and and 6:30am.

Cerro Maya is about 2.5 miles north of the village of Copper Bank. Bus schedules to Copper Bank don't facilitate day trips to Cerros; if you don't have your own vehicle, you can organize a private boat transfer from Corozal (BZ$40 per person) or hire a taxi (typically costing around BZ$100 per vehicle including an hour wait at the site).

Sarteneja

POP 2000

If you came to Belize in search of sparkling blue waters, delicious fresh seafood, fauna-rich forests and affordable prices, look no further than Sarteneja (sar-ten-*eh*-ha). The tiny fishing and shipbuilding village, located near the northeastern tip of the Belizean mainland, is a charming base from which to explore both the nautical and jungle treasures of the region.

The village spreads just a few blocks back from its long, grassy seafront. It's a delicious place to chill out for a few days. From this lovely seaside setting, visitors can also head out to the Shipstern Nature Reserve and take birding, fishing and wildlife-watching trips all along the fabulous coast of northern Belize, including to Bacalar Chico National Park & Marine Reserve, on the northern tip of Ambergris Caye.

◉ Sights

Stroll along the shoreline to admire the wooden sailboats that are still constructed in workshops around town.

Shipstern Conservation Management Area   NATURE RESERVE
(☑ 660-1807; www.visitshipstern.com; admission BZ$10; ☺ 8am-5pm) 🍃 Run by a nonprofit organization, this large nature reserve, which protects 43 sq miles of semideciduous hardwood forests, wetlands and lagoons and coastal mangrove belts, has its headquarters 3.5 miles southwest of Sarteneja on the road to Orange Walk. Lying in a transition zone between Central America's tropical forests and a drier Yucatán-type ecosystem, the reserve's mosaic of habitats is rare in Belize.

All five of Belize's wildcats and scores of other mammals can be found here, and its 250 bird species include ospreys, roseate spoonbills, white ibis and a colony of 300 pairs of American woodstorks, one of this bird's few breeding colonies in Belize.

Admission allows access to both a small museum and butterfly house at the headquarters, as well as a short botanical trail that leads to an observation tower over the treetops. There are several other longer hiking trails, including Thompson Trail, which goes to the shore of the lagoon and along which you may spot agouti and peccari in addition to plenty of bird species. It's accessible only in the dry season.

Of course, the best way to see the lagoon and its birdlife is by taking a full-day boat tour, which costs BZ$450 for up to three people (including lunch).

About a 40-minute drive from the headquarters, Xo-Pol has a treetop hide overlooking a large forest-surrounded pond where you might see crocodiles, waterfowl, peccaries, deer and tapirs. Half-day birding tours are BZ$70 per visitor. Rangers also take adventurers on overnight expeditions to Xo-Pol for BZ$250.

Another interesting tour is the 'Ranger Experience' where visitors tag along and accompany the reserve rangers on their daily rounds assisting in patrols and research tasks.

Call ahead to check on conditions and book tours. Don't forget your long sleeves, pants and bug spray!

🏃 Activities

Sarteneja Tour Guide Association   ADVENTURE TOUR
(☑ 621-6465; North Front St; ☺ 9am-5pm) A cooperative of enthusiastic young guides that rents kayaks (per hour/day BZ$10/50) and runs tours around Sarteneja and to the ruins at Cerro Maya. They also organize boat trips to remote Bacalar Chico at the northern trip of Ambergris Caye (BZ$160 per visitor). The office is on the main waterfront.

HAND-CRANKED FERRIES

If you're driving or riding through the back bush of Corozal District between Corozal Town and Sarteneja, you'll wind up fording two rivers in a distinctly Belizean way – via hand-cranked ferries that run along thick cables strung from riverbank to riverbank. This throwback to the early days of industrialization owes its existence to the low traffic density plying the roads. With too few vehicles to make building a bridge feasible, the low-tech (and low-impact) human-powered cable ferry was seen as a fine way to ensure that cars, bikes and motorcycles could get where they needed to go (even if only two at a time). The first is between Corozal and the town of Copper Bank, and the second on the way out of Copper Bank toward Sarteneja. They're slow and fun and, according to locals, they run 24 hours a day. Best of all, they're free.

🛏 Sleeping

Shipstern Nature Reserve Bungalows
LODGE **$**

(☑ 660-1807; www.visitshipstern.org; Shipstern Conservation Management Area; dm/s/d BZ$40/78/98) Located at the Shipstern Nature Reserve headquarters 3 miles out of town, these four new bungalows are a great choice for visitors intending to take early nature tours or are looking to be surrounded by wilderness. The air-con rooms have private bathroom and open out onto a screened porch to enjoy the sounds of the jungle.

There are also two spacious dormitories offering value budget accommodations. The large onsite restaurant serves all meals (BZ$10 to BZ$20) and can prepare takeout packages for those going on tours.

Backpackers Paradise
CABAÑAS, CAMPGROUND **$**

(☑ 607-1873, 423-2016; http://cabanasbelize.wordpress.com; Bandera Rd; campsite BZ$12, s/d BZ$30/40, without bathroom BZ$26/34, little house BZ$50-60, family house BZ$60-80; 🛜) Peaceful, sustainable and affordable, this laid-back spot set on lush grounds is a bit of a hike from the beach, but is one of the best places for budget travelers in northern Belize. All sorts of travelers (not just backpackers) will enjoy spending a few days here, walking on jungle trails, swimming in the nearby ocean, or just lounging in the comfy communal spaces.

The *cabañas* are screened-in huts with thatched roofs and king-size beds, and two charming Mennonite-built houses sleep four to six. There's high-speed internet, a communal kitchen, horses and bicycles for rent, and plenty of other activities in the area. Breakfast costs BZ$10, while lunch and dinner costs BZ$20.

Candelie's Sunset Cabanas
CABAÑAS **$**

(☑ 660-7519; candelies.cabanas@yahoo.com; North Front St; cabaña with fan/air-con BZ$100/120; 🅿 ❄ 🛜) At the west end of the waterfront street, Candelie's has two big, breezy *cabañas* with spacious bathrooms and a dining room with an amazing mural that depicts Sarteneja's history.

Oasis Guest House
GUESTHOUSE **$**

(☑ 601-3401; Verde St; r BZ$100; 🅿) One block back from the bay, this small place has clean and comfortable suites and a rooftop patio with a fine view, although it's partially blocked by the large phone tower next door.

Fernando's Seaside Guesthouse
GUESTHOUSE **$$**

(☑ 423-2085; www.fernandosseaside.com; North Front St; d BZ$100; ❄ 🛜) This colorful family-run hotel has five spacious rooms, each with two double beds, private bathrooms with hot showers, and ceiling fans. Go for one of the two at the front, which have fine sea views. Meals are served and internet is available in the common areas. Fernando also arranges snorkeling, fishing and other trips around the area.

🍴 Eating

Crabby E's
BELIZEAN **$$**

(North Front St; mains BZ$12-30; ⊘ 9am-10pm) This welcoming open-air bar-restaurant on the 2nd floor has great great views of the waterfront and serves up tasty seafood, Belizean classics and ice-cold beers.

ℹ Information

@Do's Cyber Cafe (Caracol St; per hr BZ$3; ⊘ 9am-4:30pm & 6-9pm; 🛜) Also offers wi-fi connection to get online with your own devices.

ℹ Getting There & Around

BICYCLE

You can rent bicycles at guesthouses or at **Brisis Rental** (La Bandera St; per day BZ$10; ⊘ 6am-6pm) in town.

BOAT

With advance notice, the **Thunderbolt** (☑ 610-4475, 631-3400) ferry will stop in Sarteneja en route between Corozal and San Pedro. The ride to Corozal takes 30 minutes and sets you back BZ$25; to San Pedro you're looking at 1½ hours at sea and a cost of BZ$50.

BUS

Four buses daily run between Belize City and Sarteneja (BZ$14, three hours) leaving from next to the Swing Bridge in Belize City at 10:30am, noon, 4pm and 5pm. They return from Sarteneja at 3:30am, 4:30am, 5:30am and 6:30am. You can also pick them up in Orange Walk around 1½ hours after they depart from Belize City. On Sunday there's no service.

CAR & MOTORCYCLE

Sarteneja is 40 miles northeast of Orange Walk by a mostly unpaved all-weather road that passes through the village of San Estevan and the scattered Mennonite community of Little Belize. Drivers from Corozal Town can reach Sarteneja (43 miles) by driving to Copper Bank and then crossing the river and heading to the town of Chunox on the Orange Walk Town–Sarteneja road.

Cayo District

Includes ➡

Belmopan 154

Hummingbird Hwy . . .160

Actun Tunichil
Muknal 164

San Ignacio 165

Cristo Rey &
Chiquibul Roads 174

Mountain Pine
Ridge Area 178

Caracol 180

Bullet Tree Falls 182

San José Succotz
& Around 185

Best Places to Eat

➡ Running W
Steakhouse (p172)

➡ Benny's Kitchen (p186)

➡ Blancaneaux Lodge (p179)

➡ Guava Limb Cafe (p172)

➡ Corkers (p156)

Best Places to Sleep

➡ Black Rock Lodge (p184)

➡ San Ignacio Resort
Hotel (p170)

➡ Ian Anderson's Caves
Branch Jungle Lodge (p161)

➡ Trek Stop (p186)

➡ El-Rey Hotel (p154)

Why Go?

Cayo District is Belize's premier adventure and eco-activity region. The lush environs of the Wild West are covered with jungle, woven with rivers, waterfalls and azure pools, and dotted with Maya ruins ranging from small, tree-covered hills to massive, magnificent temples. Cahal Pech, Xunantunich, El Pilar and the mother of all Belizean Maya sites, Caracol, are all in Cayo.

Travelers leave the coast and head inland to tube through river caves, zip-line over the jungle canopy or horseback ride through the Maya Mountains. From a base at San Ignacio or Belmopan, tour operators can easily get your adventure started. This region teems with nature too, from botanic gardens and butterfly houses to primeval jungles and rainforests, where the only thing coming between you and the wildlife is a pair of binoculars.

Accommodations range from camping and budget hostels to some of the most luxurious jungle and mountain lodges in Belize. Head to Cayo with a sense of adventure and you won't be disappointed.

When to Go

➡ **Jan–Mar** Sun-drenched days, cooler nights and dry roads make these months a great time to explore Cayo.

➡ **Apr & May** The height of the hot, dry season.

➡ **Jun–Nov** Plenty of rain and muddy roads.

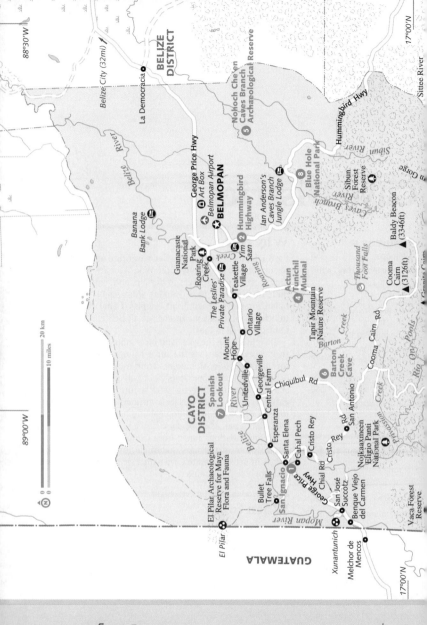

Cayo District Highlights

1 San Ignacio (p165) Hanging out in this traveler-friendly town, especially during market day on Saturday.

2 Hummingbird Highway (p160) Bridging the gap between Cayo and coastal Southern Belize along the region's most scenic highway.

3 Caracol (p180) Exploring these remote and ancient Maya ruins.

4 Actun Tunichil Muknal (p164) Serious spelunking in Belize's most dramatic cave.

5 Nohoch Che'en Caves Branch Archaeological Reserve (p159) Cave-tubing, jungle zip-lining and exploring a

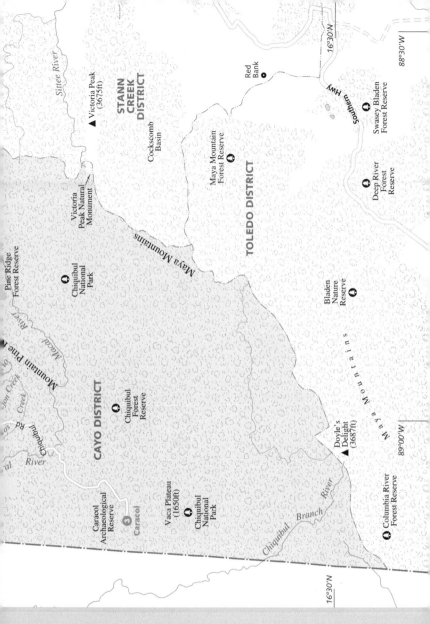

unique underground system.

6 Barton Creek Cave (p175) Canoeing through a remote cave river.

7 Spanish Lookout (p164) Seeing a different side of Belize in this industrious Mennonite community.

8 Blue Hole National Park (p160) Hiking through jungle from Herman's Cave to the Blue Hole.

Sittee River

▲ Victoria Peak (3675ft)

STANN CREEK DISTRICT

Red Bank

Southern Hwy

Swasey Bladen Forest Reserve

Cockscomb Basin

Maya Mountain Forest Reserve

Deep River Forest Reserve

TOLEDO DISTRICT

Victoria Peak Natural Monument

Maya Mountains

Pine Ridge Forest Reserve

Chiquibul National Park

Macal River

Mountain Pine Ridge

Bladen Nature Reserve

CAYO DISTRICT

Chiquibul Forest Reserve

Chiquibul Rd

Privassion Creek

River

Caracol Archaeological Reserve

3 Caracol

Vaca Plateau (1650ft)

Chiquibul National Park

Doyle's Delight (3687ft)

M a y a   M o u n t a i n s

Columbia River Forest Reserve

Chiquibul Branch

River

16°30'N

89°00'W

89°00'W

88°30'W

16°30'N

ℹ️ Getting There & Around

AIR
There are two airstrips in Cayo District, both served by daily Tropic Air flights: Belmopan and the tiny Maya Flats airstrip about 7 miles from San Ignacio.

BUS
Buses run along the George Price Hwy between Belize City and Benque Viejo del Carmen, stopping in Belmopan and San Ignacio. For destinations in southern Belize, change in Belmopan.

BELMOPAN

POP 19,460

Like many purpose-built capital cities around the world, Belmopan can seem a bit dull at first glance. Ordered streets, empty urban parklands and drab government buildings conspire to give it a desolate feel. The exception is the vibrant central market area, where cheap food stalls and incoming buses provide some welcome activity.

But this is the national capital, a major transport hub, a place to extend your visa and an easygoing university city with a decent range of restaurants and shopping. More importantly, it's a useful base for exploring nearby caves, national parks, the Hummingbird Hwy and most of the attractions in eastern Cayo.

History

Belmopan was conceived after Hurricane Hattie all but destroyed Belize City in 1961. Certain that a coastal capital would never be secure from further terrible hurricanes, the government decided to move and built the new capital here in 1971.

A grand new National Assembly was built to resemble a Maya temple and plaza, with government offices around it. Government needs have since outgrown these core buildings and an assortment of less-uniform government offices are spread out around the central green. Many government ministries and other organizations are based here, as are a few embassies, giving the place an unexpected international atmosphere.

⊙ Sights

The main market days are Tuesday and Friday, when stallholders come from all over the district to sell produce.

George Price Center for Peace & Development
MUSEUM

(☎ 822-1054; www.gpcbelize.com; Price Blvd; ⊙ 8am-6pm Mon-Thu, 8am-5pm Fri, 9am-noon Sat) **FREE** This museum and conference center celebrates the life of Belize's beloved statesman and first prime minister after independence, George Price, who passed away in 2011. As well as photographs and information panels, there's an archive of documents and letters written by Price.

Belize Archives Department
MUSEUM

(☎ 822-2247; www.archives.gov.bz; 26-28 Unity Blvd; ⊙ 8am-5pm, closed 2nd & 4th Fri of the month) Under renovationwhen we were there, this local history collection has rotating displays on hurricanes, the Garifuna, Belmopan, Baron Bliss and other subjects. You can stop by and chat with the researchers on anything to do with Belizean history.

🏃 Activities

Several companies offer local tours, notably cave-tubing and trips to Maya sites in Cayo District.

Belize Inland Tours
ADVENTURE TOUR

(http://belizeinlandtours.com; Mile 42 Hummingbird Hwy, Armenia) Based just out of Belmopan in Armenia, Belize Inland Tours runs cave-tubing trips, guided tours of Blue Hole National Park and tours all over the Cayo District.

🛏️ Sleeping

Belmopan suffers from a lack of good budget accommodation but there are a few decent midrangers in town and more upmarket lodges in the surrounding region.

⭐ El-Rey Hotel
HOTEL $

(☎ 822-3438; www.elreyhotel.com; 23 Moho St; r BZ$80, with air-con BZ$120-160; P ❄ 🤖) Northeast of town, El-Rey is Belmopan's best budget offering, an affordable and welcoming place with 12 plain, clean ground-floor rooms equipped with private bathroom, TV, wi-fi and fans. All rooms have air-con but you can pay the budget price not to use it. Tours can be booked here.

⭐ Hibiscus Hotel
HOTEL $$

(☎ 822-0400, 633-5323; www.hibiscusbelize.com; Market Sq; s/d BZ$110/120; ⊙ reception from 11am; P ❄ 🤖) 🌿 Close to Belmopan's lively market place, this neat little place has just six chalet-style rooms. Comforts include king and twin-sized beds, flat-screen cable TV, bathtubs, and tea and coffee facilities. There's an eco angle – some of the profits go to support local avian conservation and rescue projects – and the excellent Corkers restaurant and bar is upstairs.

Villa San Juan
B&B $$

(☑822-0958; www.villasanjuanbelmopan.com; 3639 Tangelo St; s/d BZ$190/210; P❄🛜🏊) The three comfortable rooms in this family-run Spanish-style villa orbit a homey communal lounge-dining area and overlook a large inground pool. Rooms are individually decorated and furnished, with cable TV and air-con. It's in a quiet part of town near the hospital.

Bull Frog Inn
HOTEL $$

(☑822-2111; www.bullfroginn.com; 25 Half Moon Ave; s/d BZ$180/213; P❄🛜) The Bull Frog is a cheerful, if nondescript, place on the eastern edge of town. The 26 rooms are spacious and comfortable enough with cable TV, fridge and two double beds (kids under 12 years stay free). There's a playground and a popular restaurant and bar.

Yim Saan
HOTEL $$

(☑822-1356; Hummingbird Hwy; s/d BZ$120/160; P❄🛜) If you really can't be bothered driving into Belmopan, this high-rise Chinese-run hotel is easily spotted on the outskirts of town. It's squarely aimed at business travelers but the rooms are spacious and ruthlessly clean. Ground-floor rooms are motel style, while those in the main building have tiny balconies. The downstairs restaurant serves decent Chinese food.

✖ Eating

★ Market Food Stalls
STREET FOOD $

(Market Sq; from BZ$2; ⊙6am-6pm) For a cheap meal, you can't beat the food stalls in the market square. They serve quick-fire Mexican snacks such as burritos and *salbutes* (mini-tortillas, usually stuffed with chicken), as well as Belizean standards such as beans and rice and cow-foot soup, or omelets and fry jacks for breakfast.

Scotchies
JAMAICAN $

(☑832-2203; 7753 Hummingbird Hwy; mains BZ$7-15; ⊙11.30am-8.30pm, until 9.30 Fri & Sat) Scotchies is a Jamaican transplant serving smoky jerk chicken and pork, sausage, wings and ribs, along with sides such as

mashed sweet potato, yam and breadfruit. Dining is in a cool garden beneath one of the octagonal thatched *palapas*.

Caladium Restaurant
BELIZEAN, SEAFOOD $

(☑822-2754; Market Sq; mains BZ$8-12; ⊙7:30am-8pm Mon-Fri, 7:30am-7pm Sat; ❄) In the market area, the Caladium is one of Belmopan's oldest family businesses. The intimate dining room goes well with the menu of Belizean favorites, such as fried fish and coconut rice, conch soup and BBQ chicken. Well-made burgers sit comfortably alongside Belizean treats such as lobster creole.

Moon Clusters Coffee House
CAFE $

(☑602-1644; 4 Shopping Center, E Ring Rd; coffee & drinks BZ$3-11; ⊙noon-7pm Mon-Sat; ❄) The Aguilar family's excellent little old-school coffee shop serves some of the best Java in Belize, from Cuban Dark Roast to the attitude adjustment, a five-shot espresso that will keep you up all night. It's all about the drinks here with a variety of smoothies and shakes, but they can whip up a quesadilla too.

Casa Cafe
CAFE $

(☑822-2098; 43 Forest Dr; snacks BZ$3-10; ⊙8am-6pm; 🚫) With excellent coffee, waffles, ice cream and breakfast snacks, Casa is a great place to start the day, but also dishes up vegetarian Asian dishes such as egg rolls and noodles for lunch.

Pasquale's
PIZZA $

(☑822-4663; Forest Dr; calzones from BZ$15, pizza BZ$25-60; ⊙11am-9pm Mon-Thu, 11am-9:30pm Fri & Sat, noon-9pm Sun; ❄🛜) In a log cabin just off Constitution Dr, this Chicago-style pizza joint has a wide range of pizzas, but if you're still not satisfied you can 'build-your-own'. Also great calzones, burgers, hot subs and pasta.

Veggie Garden
VEGETARIAN $

(☑602-1644; off Hummingbird Hwy; mains BZ$8-18; ⊙8am-6pm Mon-Sat; 🚫) This sweet Taiwanese vegetarian restaurant serves excellent ova-lacto dishes from noodles to dumplings, as well as fresh juices and smoothies. It's down a lane off the Hummingbird Hwy on Belmopan's outskirts.

Wing Stop
AMERICAN $

(Mountain View Blvd; meals from BZ$5; ⊙9am-midnight) If wings are your thing, this is the place. Try buffalo (six pieces for BZ$10) or a range of flavors up to the mind-bendingly spicy 'atomic'. Also burgers

Belmopan

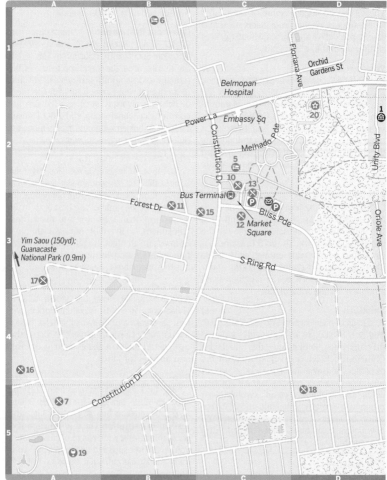

and carrot sticks. The semi-open-air bar is convivial and said to be open 24 hours if enough drinkers stick around.

Breads & Drinks   CAFE $
(📞624-6095; lunch BZ$12; ⊙10:30am-2pm) This new place near the basketball stadium has no menu and offers just one lovingly prepared meal – a changing daily lunch special such as fish or pork chops with a free soft drink or coffee. The name is a little misleading as there's no alcohol.

Brodies   SUPERMARKET $
(⊙8am-7pm Mon-Sat, 9am-1pm Sun) Well-stocked supermarket with beer and wine.

Corkers   INTERNATIONAL $$
(📞822-0400; Hibiscus Plaza, Melhado Pde; mains BZ$16-30; ⊙11am-9pm Mon-Wed, 11am-late Thu-Sat; 🛜🍴) This breezy upstairs restaurant and bar has a 'Brit-pub in the tropics' feel with a welcoming atmosphere and a mélange of seafood, meat and pasta dishes from tortillas to steak and veggies. There are good-value lunch dishes and snacks, and happy hour at the bar is a generous 4pm to 10pm Thursday to Saturday.

Belmopan

◉ Sights
1 Belize Archives Department..............D2
2 George Price Center for Peace
   & Development F3

🛏 Sleeping
3 Bull Frog Inn E2
4 El-Rey Hotel E1
5 Hibiscus Hotel...................................C2
6 Villa San Juan.................................... B1

✖ Eating
7 Blue Moon A5
8 Breads & Drinks E2
9 Brodies E2
  Bull Frog Inn .... (see 3)
10 Caladium Restaurant C2
11 Casa Cafe B3
  Corkers....................................(see 5)
12 Everest C3
13 Market Food Stalls C2
14 Moon Clusters Coffee House............. E2
15 Pasquale's C3
16 Scotchies...A4
17 Veggie Garden A3
18 Wing Stop..D5

🍷 Drinking & Nightlife
19 La Cabaña A5

✪ Entertainment
20 Screen on the Green D2

pasta. The *ceviche* and fried chicken are reliable, while the steaks (BZ$45 to BZ$67) push well into the top-end price category.

Bull Frog Inn INTERNATIONAL **$$**
(☏822-2111; www.bullfroginn.com; 25 Half Moon Ave; mains BZ$12-25; ◷7am-10pm; 🛜🖥) This popular and breezy hotel-restaurant serves up good steaks and seafood. The adjoining bar is lively on weekends with karaoke and live mariachi music.

🍷 Drinking & Nightlife

For a capital city, nightlife is somnolent in Belmopan but Corkers and Bull Frog Inn have reliably lively bars with occasional live music.

La Cabaña NIGHTCLUB
(☏822-1577; Hummingbird Hwy; cover charge after 10pm BZ$10; ◷11am-3am) If you're wondering where the nightlife is in Belmopan, it's out at this Latin-themed dance club most nights. Tuesday, Friday and Saturday are dance nights, Thursday and Sunday see a bit of karaoke. It's a dingy bar and

Everest NEPALESE **$$**
(☏662-2109; mains BZ$15-20; ◷8am-9am Mon-Sat, 9am-6pm Sun; 🖥) Belmopan's (and probably Belize's) only Nepalese restaurant is in a cute blue shack opposite the market area. Authentic mutton, chicken and vegetarian curries and biryanis, along with Indian specialties such as masala tea. The menu even has pictures for the uninitiated.

Blue Moon INTERNATIONAL **$$**
(☏822-4433; 1533 Constitution Dr; mains BZ$16-56; ◷11am-9pm Tue-Sun; 🅿🛜🖥) A decent family restaurant serving a wide range of dishes from burgers to steaks and tacos to

restaurant by day, out on the highway just south of the roundabout.

☆ Entertainment

Screen on the Green CINEMA
(http://belize.usembassy.gov; ⊙ 2nd Thu of month) **FREE** The US embassy hosts free outdoor movie nights once a month at Governor General Field. Movies start when it gets dark; if it's raining, the screening moves to the George Price Center from 6pm.

❶ Information

Belize Bank (Constitution Dr) and **Scotiabank** (Constitution Dr) keep regular banking hours and have 24/7 ATM access.

Belmopan Hospital (☎ 822-2264; off N Ring Rd) Just north of the city center, this is the only emergency facility between Belize City and San Ignacio.

BTL Telephone Office (Bliss Pde; ⊙ 8am-noon & 1-5pm Mon-Fri) The place to buy Digicell SIM cards.

Darah Travel (☎ 822-3272; www.belizetravel services.com; 23 Moho St) This Belmopan-based travel agency can organise flights, transfers and adventure tours throughout Cayo and Southern Belize.

Immigration Office (☎ 822-3860; Dry Creek St; ⊙ 8am-noon & 1-5pm Mon-Thu, to 4:30pm Fri) Cayo's only immigration office offers 30-day visa extension stamps for BZ$50. It's often busy so you'll probably need to queue.

PC.com (per hr BZ$5; ⊙ 8am-8pm) Internet access and computer repairs.

Post Office (⊙ 8am-noon & 1-5pm Mon-Thu, to 4:30pm Fri) Near the market square.

UK High Commission (☎ 822-2146; http://ukinbelize.fco.gov.uk; Embassy Sq, Belmopan; ⊙ 8am-noon & 1-4pm Mon-Thu, 8am-2pm Fri) The British High Commission provides consular service, including advice on general travel, lawyers and overseas voting, and helps with the usual visa and passport dilemmas.

US Embassy (☎ 822-4011; http://belize.us embassy.gov; Floral Park Rd; ⊙ 8am-noon & 1-5pm Mon-Fri) From visa and passport information to marriage advice and hurricane preparedness tips, the US embassy can help. The embassy also hosts a program of events such as Screen on the Green; see the website for details.

❶ Getting There & Away

AIR
Belmopan's tiny airstrip is just a few miles east of the city.

Tropic Air (☎ 226-2012; www.tropicair.com) has four daily flights to San Pedro (BZ$243, 55 minutes), Belize City Domestic (BZ$134, 25 minutes) and Belize City International (BZ$178, 25 minutes).

BUS
Belmopan's **bus terminal** (☎ 802-2799; Market Sq) is Cayo's main transit hub, and all buses (regardless of company) heading south or west from the Belize District, as well as north and west from Dangriga (and points south), stop in Belmopan. Along the George Price Hwy, buses head east to Belize City (BZ$5, one hour) and west to San Ignacio (BZ$5, one hour) and Benque Viejo del Carmen (BZ$6, 1½ hours) every half-hour from 6am to 7pm. Along the Hummingbird Hwy, buses go south to Dangriga (BZ$6, two hours) once or twice an hour from 6:45am until 7:15pm. From Dangriga, most buses continue on to Punta Gorda (BZ$19, 5½ hours).

Transfers to Hopkins and Placencia-bound buses can be made in Dangriga.

❶ Getting Around

The city center, within the ring road, is compact and easily negotiated on foot. Taxis gather outside the bus terminal. A short fare around town is BZ$5.

AROUND BELMOPAN

West of the Belize District, the sealed George Price Hwy speeds along for about 50 miles to Belmopan – probably the country's most heavily trafficked road. This region gets busy with island-based tourists and cruise-ship passengers heading to inland adventures, such as cave-tubing, zip-lining and horseback riding.

◉ Sights

Guanacaste National Park NATIONAL PARK
(George Price Hwy; admission BZ$5; ⊙ 8am-4:30pm) Belize's smallest national park was declared in 1990 and is named for the giant guanacaste tree on its southwestern edge. The tree survived the axes of canoe-makers but has now died naturally, though it still stands in its jungle habitat. The 51-acre park, off the highway at the Belmopan turnoff, is framed by Roaring Creek and the Belize River, with 2 miles of hiking trails that will introduce you to the abundant local trees and colorful birds.

Birding is best here in winter, when migrants arrive from North America. On the short Guanacaste Trail there's a timber deck leading down to the river where you can swim in a deep waterhole. Don't leave bags or valuables unattended here while swimming.

🏃 Activities

★ Nohoch Che'en Caves Branch Archaeological Reserve   CAVE ACTIVITIES

(admission BZ$10; ⊙7am-4pm) This extensive network of limestone caves northwest of Belmopan is super-popular for cave-tubing, kayaking and spelunking. The Caves Branch River flows through nine caves, providing ideal conditions for floating through on a rubber tube or allowing for exploration of side passages, which lead to other caves, such as the spectacular Crystal Cave.

A number of operators run tours – you can only enter the caves with a licensed guide (minimum one guide per eight people). The basic 1½-hour tour includes a jungle walk and a gentle float through the caves, witnessing (with the help of your headlamp), schools of eyeless cave fish, stalactites and strange Maya paintings high on the cave ceilings. The cost (BZ$90) includes life vest and helmet, and the tubes are linked together for safety. Tours can be customized to explore further into the cave system – the ultimate full-day tour includes Crystal Cave.

The turnoff for Nohoch Che'en Caves Branch Archaeological Reserve is at Mile 37 on the George Price Hwy, then it's 6 miles down a sealed road to the reserve entrance. The reserve has toilets, snack shops and numerous tour operators.

Vital Nature & Mayan Tours   CAVE ACTIVITIES

(☑602-8975; http://cavetubing.bz; per person from BZ$90, with zip-lining BZ$130) One of the pioneers of cave-tubing in Belize, Vitalino Reyes is still a reliable and recommended operator. There are a variety of cave-tubing trips (including equipment and lunch), up to the full-day Crystal Cave (BZ$180) and 'sunset tubing' (last entry is at 4pm). Vital also has a zip-line course and ATVs (quad bikes). A combo with all three activities is BZ$200 per person. Add BZ$40 per person for transfers from Belize City or Belmopan.

Butt's Up!   CAVE ACTIVITIES

(☑605-1575; www.cave-tubing.com; tubing per person from BZ$90) This outfit runs cave-tubing trips as well as zip-lining and ATV adventures. It specializes in cruise-ship passengers from Belize City. Lunch included.

Zip-Line Canopy Tour   ADVENTURE SPORTS

(☑602-8975; http://cavetubing.bz; per person from BZ$110) This zip-line canopy tour, just outside Nohoch Che'en, is a professional operation where you zoom through the treetops from platform to platform on nine linked cable runs up to 200ft long. Trained guides give you a safety briefing and help you into your harness. Zip-lining can easily be combined with cave-tubing and ATV rides.

Banana Bank Lodge   HORSEBACK RIDING

(☑820-2020; www.bananabank.com; Banana Bank Rd; 2/4hr jungle tour BZ$120/180) Set on a jungle- and pasture-covered property of more than 6 sq miles, Banana Bank has more than 100 well-tended horses enjoying an extensive grazing area and state-of the-art stables. Besides miles of jungle and riverside trails, facilities include a round pen and a large arena for training and exercising the horses. Combined accommodation and riding packages are available.

The turnoff to Banana Bank is at Roaring Creek, then it's 4 miles on a signposted dirt road. If you're not driving, inquire about the hand-cranked boat across the Belize River.

🛏 Sleeping

A couple of high-end lodges are just north of the Belize River.

Banana Bank Lodge   RESORT $$

(☑832-2020; www.bananabank.com; Banana Bank Rd; d/tr chalet BZ$100/150, s/d/tr cabaña BZ$230/290/340, s/d/tr ste BZ$300/350/400; P ✳ ⓢ ☰) This old-fashioned lodge and equestrian center is ensconced in lush gardens on the banks of the Belize River, north of Belmopan, and offers mahogany-and-thatch *cabañas* with a unique two-bedroom design with a sitting room, ceiling fans and wrought-iron or carved-mahogany bedsteads. Suites have air-con while, the budget 'chalet' rooms sleep up to five people. The lodge has a bird observation tower overlooking a lagoon, an orchid garden with more than 50 species of orchids and some small Maya ruins onsite. Lunch/dinner is available for BZ$20/30. To get here, turn off at Roaring Creek village and follow the signs for 4 miles.

Belize Jungle Dome   RESORT $$$

(☑822-2124; www.belizejungledome.com; Banana Bank Rd; r standard/junior/ste/upper terrace BZ$190/250/290/330; P ✳ @ ⓢ ☰) 🌿 This retreat is an architectural oddity, with a signature dome allowing sunlight to filter in, reflecting the polished mahogany interior. Standard rooms, suites and terraces are fully equipped with modern conveniences, such as air-con, cable TV and wi-fi, and have easy access to the central swimming pool.

There's also an organic fruit orchard and an enticing treetop cafe from which to survey the domain. Drive to Belize Jungle Dome via the village of Roaring Creek (follow the signs to Banana Bank Lodge).

Shopping

Art Box   ARTS & CRAFTS

(☑822-2233; www.artboxbz.com; Mile 46 Western Hwy; ☺8am-6pm Mon-Sat; ☎) It's hard to miss this cube-like two-story purple building on the highway just before the Belmopan airstrip. It's a combination gallery, store and cafe, with locally made furniture, jewelry, crafts and stationery, as well as a bookstore heavy on bibles; the staircase to the mezzanine is a sight to behold. The attached cafe specializes in strong organic coffee and frappacinos.

HUMMINGBIRD HIGHWAY

The lyrically named Hummingbird Hwy is one of the prettiest drives in Belize, winding its way through jungle and citrus orchards and impossibly small villages as it skirts the northern edges of the Maya Mountain range between Belmopan and Dangriga. Passing caves and jungle adventures, on a clear day the road affords plenty of postcard-perfect vistas. You can drive the 55-mile length of it in two hours, but along the way are some excellent ecolodges and budget accommodations, just begging for an overnight stay.

Sights

Blue Hole National Park   NATIONAL PARK

(admission BZ$8; ☺8am-4:30pm) The 575-acre Blue Hole National Park contains St Herman's Cave, one of the few caves in Belize that you can visit independently. The visitors center (where flashlights can be rented for BZ$3) is 11 miles along the Hummingbird Hwy from Belmopan. From here, a 500yd trail leads to St Herman's Cave. A path leads 200yd into the cave alongside an underground river – to go any further you'll need a guide.

Return via the Highland Trail, steep in places but with rope guides, for some nice views. Carry a strong flashlight and good insect repellent. If you're keen on a longer hike, there's a three-hour trail from here via Crystal Cave.

The Blue Hole, a 25ft-deep swimming hole, is about a mile further along the highway. Drive there, or take the 45-minute jungle trek from the visitor center. Admission is with the same ticket as St Herman's Cave.

Buses will drop you at the visitor centre or the entrance to the Blue Hole.

Barquedier Waterfall   WATERFALL

(Hummingbird Hwy; admission BZ$8; ☺9am-4pm) This magnificent waterfall cascades into a cool swimming hole located a 15-minute walk off the Hummingbird Hwy (signposted). If there's no one there to take your entry fee, it may be risky leaving a vehicle unattended.

Activities

Caves Branch Adventures   ADVENTURE TOUR

(☑610-3451; www.cavesbranch.com; Mile 41½ Hummingbird Hwy; tours per person BZ$150-500) At Ian Anderson's, the signature adventures include jungle treks, river cave and waterfall caves expeditions, and the Black Hole Drop. Adventure activities are exclusive and depart from the excellent lodge just off the Hummingbird Hwy.

Maya Guide Adventures   TOUR

(☑600-3116; www.mayaguide.bz; overnight tours from BZ$320) Highly experienced Kekchí Maya guide Marcos Cucul runs jungle survival tours ranging from overnight to multiple nights. Tours feature trekking, leadership and survival skills with the night spent suspended in Hennessy hammocks. With over a decade's experience as an area guide, Cucul enjoys an excellent reputation.

Sleeping

Some fine mountain and jungle lodges are complemented by a couple of excellent budget eco-guesthouses.

Hummingbird Haven
Lodge & Hostel   HOSTEL $

(☑626-4599; www.hummingbirdlodge.com; Mile 29.5 Hummingbird Hwy; campsite BZ$20, dm/d BZ$30/80, 2-bedroom lodge BZ$150; ℗☎) ✈ Hummingbird Haven enjoys a sublime location in a quiet patch of forest just off the highway and surrounded by a split in the creek. The 100-acre property features a double-story timber lodge with two large dorms, and a few private rooms in another building, as well as plenty of space to camp.

There are a couple of chill-out areas, a self-catering kitchen, eco credentials such as solar power and organic gardens, and plenty of opportunities for jungle hikes and swimming in the river.

T.R.E.E.S
CABIN $

(Toucan Ridge Ecology & Education Society; ☑ 669-6818, 665-2134; www.treesociety.org; Mile 27.5 Hummingbird Hwy; bunkhouse BZ$30, s/d cabin BZ$125/140, without bathroom BZ$85/100; 🛜) 🌿 T.R.E.E.S is part field station and part ecofriendly lodge, welcoming research students, interns, birdwatchers and passing backpackers alike. The operation is nonprofit, with proceeds going into community conservation projects and ecotourism. There are lectures in biodiversity, field courses and guided activities, along with yoga, hiking and village tours.

Accommodation is in simple but comfortable cabins away from the main lodge, and meals are available (breakfast/lunch/dinner cost BZ$26/28/30).

Yax'che Jungle Camp
CABAÑAS $

(☑ 600-3116; www.mayaguide.bz; Hummingbid Hwy; campsite BZ$20, bunkhouse BZ$30, d cabañas BZ$140; Ⓟ🛜) 🌿 Adventure guide Marcos Cucul runs this little camp just off the highway. Spacious cabañas on stilts have sunken bathrooms and verandas. There's a communal dining area and a great range of jungle activities on offer.

Kantara Ku
CABAÑAS $$

(☑ 818-903-1999; www.kantaraku.com; Mile 34 Hummingbird Hwy, St Margaret's; cabañas per person BZ$70, villa BZ$150-300, 3-bedroom cottage BZ$400; Ⓟ🛜🏊) Kantara is an intimate midrange resort, with just a few cabañas, villas and cottage rooms in grounds of fruit trees, backed by verdant rainforest. There's an inviting little pool and bar area, and easy access to excellent jungle hikes.

★ Ian Anderson's Caves Branch Jungle Lodge
LODGE $$$

(☑ in Belize 610-3452, toll free from USA & Canada 866-357-2698; www.cavesbranch.com; Mile 41.5 Hummingbird Hwy; d cabaña & bungalow BZ$340-$492, d ste & treehouse BZ$588-$1182; Ⓟ🛜🏊) 🌿 Hidden away in dense jungle off the Hummingbird Hwy, Ian Anderson's is a 90-sq-mile private estate that acts as a base for a variety of exclusive jungle activities on the property. Accommodations are superb jungle-chic, and guests can indulge themselves in the beautiful riverside pool and hot tub, and enjoy meals and cocktails at the family-style restaurant overlooking the river.

Most exclusive of the accommodations are the canopy treehouses overlooking the Caves Branch River, featuring beautifully carved four-poster beds, screened decks, outdoor tropical showers and views to die for. More humble but no less lovely are the wooden *cabañas* closer to the river, and there's a range of lodge rooms in between. The lodge also has an onsite artisanal cheese factory and organic soap-making facilities.

Most guests to the lodge book multiday packages, including tours, accommodations, meals and more. Check the website for current deals.

Sleeping Giant Rainforest Lodge
BOUTIQUE LODGE $$$

(☑ 1-786-472-9664, 1 954-707-6986; www.vivabelize.com/sleeping-giant; Mile 36.5 Hummingbird Hwy; r from BZ$400; Ⓟ❄🛜🏊) 🌿 The swanky new Sleeping Giant has 20 rooms either garden-facing in the main lodge or in vast individual cottages, *casitas* or suites scattered around a lush garden. They feature mod cons such as air-con, espresso machine and local hardware furniture, while the best have gorgeous bathrooms with skylight tubs or Jacuzzis.

The property, split by the Sibune River, features mountain views, abundant birdlife and guided hikes, and there's a lovely

---

UNIVERSAL HEALING INSTITUTE & RETREAT

The unique **Universal Healing Institute & Retreat** (Map p174; ☑ 677-7878; www.universalhealinginternational.com) is spread out over a 150-acre organic jungle farm near the village of Unitedville on the George Price Hwy. Operators Yosiah and Linda offer medium- and long-term retreats focusing on health and nutrition, yoga and spirituality, as well as courses in organic gardening and sustainability.

A 30-day workshop starts at BZ$1600 per person, a 30-day assisted healing retreat is BZ$5000, or just book the farmstay (per night s/d BZ$90/135) and get a feel for the place. Check the website for more details.

two-story restaurant-bar and pool area as its centerpiece.

✕ Eating

Country Barn   ICE CREAM **$**
(☑636-0031; Mile 31 Hummingbird Hwy; ⊘ Mon-Sat) Stop in at this roadside dairy near St Margaret's village for homemade ice cream, flavored milk and fresh yogurt. It's run by a Christian ministry, which employs local youth and trains them in farm skills.

Café Casita De Amour   CAFE **$**
(☑660-2879; Mile 16.5 Hummingbird Hwy; meals BZ$4-14; ⊘7:30am-5pm Tue-Sun) Café Casita De Amour – the House of Love – is an architectural oddity and a worthwhile pit stop on the Hummingbird drive. Inside is a cafe with a simple menu of crepes, sandwiches, burgers, coffee and smoothies. It's a mile or so past the Barquedier waterfall, before the village of Pomona.

WEST OF BELMOPAN

The George Price Hwy continues for 22 miles from the Belmopan turnoff to San Ignacio through verdant, well-shaded countryside, with a number of villages, lodges and resorts strung along the road. The single main attraction out here is remote Actun Tunichil Muknal cave – best accessed on guided tours from San Ignacio or Belmopan. The dirt road to Actun Tunichil Muknal heads south at Teakettle Village, 8

miles west of Belmopan. At Mount Hope, a sealed road heads northwest to the industrious Mennonite community of Spanish Lookout, while at Georgeville, the unsealed Chiquibul Rd turns south off the highway, heading to Barton Creek and the Mountain Pine Ridge.

🏃 Activities

Hot Mama's   TOUR
(Map p174; ☑824-0444; www.hotmamasbelize.com; Mile 60 George Price Hwy, Unitedville; tour BZ$10; ⊘shop 8am-4pm Mon-Fri, tour Tue-Fri by appointment) Take a tour of the chili gardens and the factory producing hot sauces at Hot Mama's, not far out of San Ignacio. You can visit the shop, or arrange a guided tour of the factory and gardens.

🛏 Sleeping

**Lower Dover Field Station
& Eco Lodge**   CABIN **$**
(Map p174; ☑834-4200; www.lowerdoverbelize.com; Mile 59 Western Hwy; campsite per tent BZ$20, bunk house per person BZ$30, cabaña BZ$118-130, air-con cabin BZ$200; Ⓟ🛜) 🌿 Located on 99 acres of prime jungle and virtually on top of extensive and largely unexcavated Maya ruins, Lower Dover is an intriguing eco place where you can sleep cheap and and explore some serious archaeological history. If you have your own tent you can camp, or take a bed in the bunkhouse.

The private *cabañas* range from basic with open-sky shower to extremely comfort-

CAYO DISTRICT WEST OF BELMOPAN

VOLUNTEER WITH WILDLIFE

With a mission statement including the goals of establishing and managing a state-of-the-art veterinary clinic for wildlife and domestic animals in Belize, the **Belize Wildlife & Referral Clinic** (Map p174; ☑632-3257; www.belizewildlifeclinic.org) provides educational opportunities and training for students, professionals and interested individuals. This nonprofit organization offers ongoing internships in wildlife medicine, rescue and rehabilitation.

Internships focus on wildlife medicine, rescue and emergency medicine and conservation, and are designed to provide students with real-world experience while supporting wildlife rescue and conservation in the field. Some interns are pre-veterinary or animal-science students, while others are veterinary students seeking clinical rotation credit in wildlife medicine.

Short-term internships ranging from two to six weeks for non-veterinary students are available from BZ$1900 per week (including lodging, breakfasts and airport pickup and drop-off), with reductions after the first two weeks. Various courses are available, and the clinic is interested in speaking with sincere potential interns and long-term volunteers.

Contact internship coordinator Justin Ford (jford@belizewildlifeclinic.org) or check out the website.

able cabins on stilts. There are self-guided walks to Maya ruins (the dogs will help you find the way) or hire a guide for BZ$10 donation. Other activities include canoeing, swimming in one of the seven river-fed swimming holes, fishing and birdwatching. There's also a homemade wine sourced from the roselle hibiscus – ask Justin for a taste or buy a bottle.

Leslies' Private Paradise   RESORT $$

(Map p174; ☑822-2370; http://lesliesprivate paradise.com; Mile 51.5 Western Hwy; cabins BZ$200; P🛜❄) On 60 acres of jungle-covered property a short drive from Belmopan, this welcoming retreat is run by Robert and Bernadette Leslie. The three timber cottages are well separated for privacy and are self-contained with king-sized beds, kitchenette, modern bathroom and soothing verandas. There's a pool, bar area (BYO) and dining-barbecue area, or head up to the serene hilltop meditation hut.

It's family friendly – kids stay for free on fold-out sofa beds. The Leslies are a charming couple who treat guests like family.

Orange Gallery   GUESTHOUSE $$

(Map p174; ☑824-2341; www.belizegifts.com/guesthouse; Mile 60 George Price Hwy; s/d/tr/q BZ$140/160/170/180 plus tax; P✳🛜) The guesthouse behind the Orange Gallery gift shop offers simple but clean and comfortable en-suite rooms and easy access to the excellent Orange Cafe.

Wolf's Place   CABIN $$

(Map p174; ☑605-4640; www.explore-belize. com; Mile 57 Western Hwy, Blackman Eddy; cabins BZ$98-138; 🛜) There are three huts on a hillside at this 1.5-acre resort in the unsignposted Western Hwy village of Blackman Eddy. Cabins are well furnished with queen-sized beds, a futon and cold-water shower. The best is the 'Eco-*cabaña*', an octagonal cabin with wraparound screened windows offering a good view of the surrounding countryside.

On the roadside is **McWolf's Restaurant** (Map p174; Western Hwy; mains BZ$5-10; ⊙11am-7pm), a tiny diner serving burgers, steaks and Wiener schnitzel.

Amber Sunset Jungle Resort   RESORT $$$

(Map p174; ☑824-3141, 824-3142; www.amber sunsetbelize.com; Mile 59 George Price Hwy; d/q treehouse cabañas BZ$300/600; P🛜❄) 🖉 Set atop a mountain with brilliant views of the surrounding Cayo District, this ecoresort is spread over 28 hilly acres, with five unique *cabañas* (three doubles and two family *cabañas*), each named after one of the cultures that makes up the tapestry of Belizean life. Each *cabaña* is built and furnished with locally sourced and crafted materials.

The Garifuna features a king-sized bed suspended from ropes, indoor rock-tiled shower and an outdoor stone pool for bathing beneath the stars. Other rooms also have their own outdoor tubs and screened lounge areas that immerse you in the surrounding jungle. There's a beautiful onsite restaurant and a hilltop pool with an attached bar.

Pook's Hill Lodge   LODGE $$$

(Map p174; ☑832-2017; www.pookshilllodge.com; s/d cabañas from BZ$320/400; P🛜) Off the dirt road that leads to Actun Tunichil Muknal, approximately 8 miles south of Teakettle Village, this is a gorgeous lodge on the site of a small Classic Period Maya residential complex. Round, thatch-and-stucco *cabañas* sport wraparound windows and immaculate natural-stone bathrooms. They are well spaced, allowing plenty of privacy. Breakfast/lunch/dinner for BZ$16/24/40 is also offered.

Set within a 300-acre private reserve, the grounds are lush with life, excellent for swimming, river-tubing, birdwatching and horseback riding.

Dream Valley   RESORT $$$

(Map p174; ☑665-1000; www.dreamvalleybelize. com; Young Gal Rd, Teakettle Village; d/ste BZ$360/500; P✳🛜❄) The spectacular log cabin–style rooms and suites overlook a broad section of the Belize River in the vast grounds of Dream Valley. Spacious cabins are rustic luxury, with hand-carved timber four-poster beds and furniture, private veranda, and mod cons including air-con, flat-screen TV, fridge and wi-fi. The stunning split-level suites feature a Jacuzzi.

The property features a popular restaurant (open to nonguests), pool, day spa, nature trails and kayaks.

🍴 Eating

Ham's Barbecue in a Bun   BARBECUE $

(Map p174; Mile 60 George Price Hwy, Unitedville; mains $5-12; ⊙10am-4pm) This hole-in-the-wall highway diner, in the same complex as Hot Mama's hot sauce factory, does delicious pit-smoked pork, beef and chicken in rolls, as well as baked potatoes. A great place for a drive-by snack.

Casa Sofia ITALIAN $$
(Map p174; Mile 59 George Price Hwy, Unitedville; mains BZ$18-34; ⊙11am-5pm Tue-Sat, dinner Wed-Sat by appointment) Stop in at tiny Unitedville to savour the Italian delights of elegant Casa Sofia. Lovingly crafted antipasti, pizza and pasta feature on the menu, with homemade sauces and garden-fresh salads. It's all served in a uniquely quirky churchlike dining room or garden patio.

🛍 Shopping

Orange Gallery GIFTS
(Map p174; ☑824-3296; www.orangegifts.com; Mile 60 George Price Hwy; ⊙7:30am-5:30pm) On the highway, east of Georgeville, Orange Gallery is a quality gift shop and gallery showcasing a wide selection of Belizean souvenirs and handicrafts, including fine hardwood furniture, kitchen wares and sculptures made in the family's own workshop. The owner and founder – Caesar Sherrard – designed the ergonomic folding 'clam chair' that now furnishes just about every resort in Belize.

Actun Tunichil Muknal

Actun Tunichil Muknal (Cave of the Stone Sepulchre; Map p174; admission BZ$30) is one of the most unforgettable and adventurous underground tours you can make in Belize. The guided trip into ATM takes you deep into the underworld that the ancient Maya knew as Xibalba. The entrance to the 3-mile-long cave lies in the northern foothills of the Maya Mountains. Most people arrive on a guided tour from San Ignacio, Belmopan or the coastal resorts, but it's also possible to arrange a guide and self-drive.

SPANISH LOOKOUT

A thriving Mennonite community, Spanish Lookout (population 2250) is a fascinating place about 5 miles north of the Western Hwy, and a good day trip from San Ignacio.

With its broad, ordered streets, neat farmland, huge factories and modern stores (hardware is popular here!), Spanish Lookout appears a little incongruous in this part of Cayo, but it's a great place to see Mennonites' industriousness in action. They are the country's primary producers of dairy, meat, poultry and produce: here in Spanish Lookout you will find Quality Chicken, the biggest poultry producer, as well as Western Dairy, the only commercial dairy. They're also renowned builders – many of the cabins and *cabañas* you might stay in were probably built right here. Although Mennonites are known for eschewing modern conveniences, you'll see more cars and tractors here than horse and carts.

In 2005, commercial quantities of oil were discovered on land in Spanish Lookout. Subsequent drilling proved controversial in the conservative community, but the prospect of oil production and export was too tempting. The Mennonites came to an agreement to share profits with the landowner and oil company, Belize Natural Energy Ltd. Crude oil exports have since netted around BZ$1.5 billion, with some BZ$5 million going to the landowners. Oil money was partly responsible for the new paved road into Spanish Lookout.

Getting here can be half the fun. The shortest route from San Ignacio crosses the Belize River by hand-cranked vehicle ferry. Alternatively, take the new road from Mount Hope on the George Price Hwy.

Western Dairies (Map p174; ☑823-0112; www.westerndairies.com; Center Rd; scoop from BZ$2; ⊙7am-5pm Mon-Thu, 7am-7:30pm Fri & Sat) Famous for its ice cream but also producing cheese, flavored milk and other dairy products, WD's is a must-stop on the main street in Spanish Lookout. It also does pizzas and burritos.

Sista's Diner (Map p174; ☑624-9436; Center Rd; dishes from BZ$5; ⊙9am-9pm) Styled like an American diner, open-air Sista's does a fine line in burgers, pizzas, Tex-Mex and Philly cheesesteak.

Reimers Health Food (Map p174; ☑823-0096; Bee Lane; ⊙8am-5pm Mon-Sat) Looking to stock up on vitamins or locally grown chia products? Reimers, in Spanish Lookout, is a dedicated health-food store stocking a similar selection of vitamins, supplements and other health products as you'd find at a good American supermarket.

The experience is moderately strenuous, starting with an easy 45-minute hike through the lush jungle and across Roaring Creek (your feet will be wet all day). At the wide, hourglass-shaped entrance to the cave, you'll don your helmet, complete with headlamp. To reach the cave entrance, you'll start with a frosty swim across a deep pool (about 15ft across), so you must be a reasonably good swimmer. From here, follow your guide, walking, climbing, twisting and turning your way through the blackness of the cave for about an hour.

Giant shimmering flowstone rock formations compete for your attention with thick, calcium-carbonate stalactites dripping from the ceiling. Phallic stalagmites grow up from the cave floor. Eventually you'll follow your guide up into a massive opening, where you'll see hundreds of pottery vessels and shards, along with human remains. One of the most shocking displays is the calcite-encrusted remains of the woman whom Actun Tunichil Muknal is named for. In the cave's Main Chamber, you will be required to remove your shoes; wear socks to protect the artifacts from the oils on your skin.

The trip takes about 10 hours from San Ignacio, including a one-hour drive each way. A number of San Ignacio–based tour companies do the trip for BZ$180 per person, including transportation, admission, lunch and equipment. You must be accompanied by a licensed guide. Cameras are no longer allowed inside the cave due to an incident (p265) involving a clumsy traveler, a dropped camera and the breaking of priceless artifacts.

🛈 Getting There & Away

Actun Tunichil Muknal cave is about 8 miles south of the George Price Hwy along an unsealed road that turns off at Teakettle Village. It's possible to drive yourself if you arrange a guide in advance, but most travelers join a tour from San Ignacio or Belmopan.

SAN IGNACIO

POP 20,580

San Ignacio is the heart and soul of the Cayo District, a vibrant traveler center from where all roads and activities fan out. Together with twin-town Santa Elena, on the east bank of the Macal River, this is the main population center of Cayo, with lots of good budget accommodation, decent restaurants and frequent transport.

But San Ignacio is no inland San Pedro, existing only for tourism. It has a very positive and infectious local vibe, with a bustling market and a steady influx of immigrants. Residents are *mestizos*, Maya and Garifuna, as well as a bunch of free-spirited expats from Europe and North America. San Ignacio is on the west bank of the Macal River, a couple of miles upstream from its confluence with the Mopan River – a meeting of waters that gives birth to the Belize River.

Pedestrianized Burns Ave, running north–south, is San Ignacio's main thoroughfare, with the central plaza and market area a block to the east.

◉ Sights & Activities

Most activities – and there are many – happen outside of San Ignacio but can be organised here. Swimming is possible in the Macal and Mopan Rivers, or head to the pools at Midas Resort or Cahal Pech Village Resort.

Cahal Pech   RUIN
(Map p174; ☑ 824-4236; admission BZ$10, 2hr tours BZ$20; ⊙ 6am-6pm) High atop a hill about a mile south of San Ignacio, Cahal Pech is the oldest known Maya site in the Belize River valley, having been first settled between 1500 and 1000 BC. Less impressive than Xunantunich and Caracol, it's still a fascinating example of Preclassic Maya architecture and an easy uphill walk from town. It was a significant Maya settlement for 2000 years or more. Drop into the small visitors center, which explains some of the history of Cahal Pech.

Cahal Pech is Mopan and Yucatec Mayan for 'Place of Ticks,' a nickname earned in the 1950s when the site was surrounded by pastures grazed by tick-infested cattle. Today it's a pleasantly shady site with plenty of trees and few tourists. Its core area of seven interconnected plazas has been excavated and restored since the late 1980s. Plaza B is the largest and most impressive complex; Structure A-1, near Plaza A, is the site's tallest temple. Two ballcourts lie at either end of the restored area.

The earliest monumental religious architecture in Belize was built here between 600 and 400 BC, though most of what we see today dates from AD 600 to 800, when Cahal Pech and its peripheral farming settlements had an estimated population of

San Ignacio

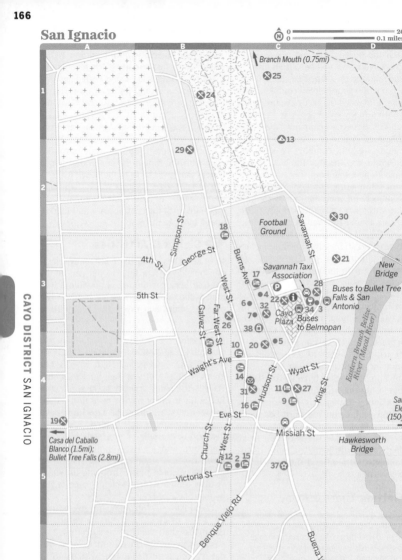

↑ Branch Mouth (0.75mi)

Football Ground

Savannah Taxi Association

Buses to Bullet Tree Falls & San Antonio

New Bridge

Cayo Plaza

Buses to Belmopan

Santa Elena (150yd) →

Hawkesworth Bridge

Casa del Caballo Blanco (1.5mi); Bullet Tree Falls (2.8mi) ←

Green Iguana Conservation Project

↙ Guatemala Border (9mi)

San Ignacio

⊚ Top Sights
1 Green Iguana Conservation
   Project D6

✛ Activities, Courses & Tours
2 Ajaw Chocolate C5
3 David's Adventure Tour C3
4 Maximum Adventure Tours C3
5 Mayawalk Tours C4
6 Pacz Tours C3
7 River Rat Expeditions C3

🛏 Sleeping
8 Bella's Backpacker's B4
9 Casa Blanca Guest House C4
10 Hi-Et Guest House C4
11 Hotel Mallorca C4
12 J&R's Guest House B5
13 Mana Kai Camp & Cabins C2
14 Martha's Guesthouse C4
   Old House Hostel .... (see 37)
15 Rainforest Haven Inn C5
16 Rosa's Hotel C4
   San Ignacio Resort
   Hotel .... (see 1)
17 Venus Hotel C3
18 Western Guesthouse B2

✴ Eating
19 Coaba A4
20 Eva's C4
21 Farmers Market D3
22 Fuego Bar & Grill C3
23 Great Mayan Prince B6
24 Guava Limb Cafe B1
25 Hode's Place C1
26 Ice Cream Shoppe B3
27 Ko-Ox Han-nah C4
   Martha's Kitchen .... (see 14)
28 Mike's C3
29 Mr. Greedy's B2
30 New French Bakery D2
31 Pop's Restaurant C4
   Running W Steakhouse .... (see 1)
32 Serendib C3
33 Sweet T'ing A7

☕ Drinking & Nightlife
34 Bamboo Bar C3
35 Thirsty Thursdays C7

✦ Entertainment
36 Princess Casino D7
37 Soul Project C5

🛍 Shopping
38 Back to My Roots C3

between 10,000 and 20,000. The place was abandoned around AD 850.

★ Green Iguana Conservation Project
GARDENS

(Map p166; ☎824-2034; www.sanignaciobelize. com; 18 Buena Vista St; tour BZ$18; ⊙8am-4pm, tour every hr; ♠) ✐ On the lush Macal Valley grounds of the San Ignacio Resort Hotel, this excellent program collects and hatches iguana eggs, raising the reptiles until they are past their most vulnerable age. The iguanas are then released into the wild. On the guided tour you'll get plenty of opportunities to stroke and handle the adorable iguanas and learn much about their habits and life cycle. The tour also follows the medicinal jungle trail that winds through the forest.

Branch Mouth
PARK

(Map p174; Branch Mouth Rd) Branch Mouth is the meeting place of the Mopan River, coming from Guatemala, and the Macal River, flowing down from Mountain Pine Ridge. The confluence of these rivers forms the beginning of the Belize River, which flows northeast to the sea. It's a cool spot for a swim on a hot day. A rope-pulled boat can take you across to the opposite bank. To get there, cycle or walk 1.5 miles north of town past Midas Resort.

★ Ajaw Chocolate
TOUR

(Map p166; ☎635-9363; ajawchocolatebze@ gmail.com; Victoria St; demonstration only per person BZ$24, with farm tour BZ$50; ⊙9am-6pm Mon-Sat, tours hourly; ♠) Adrian and Elida, Kekchí Mayans from Toledo, bring their chocolate-making expertise to San Ignacio with excellent demonstrations that can be combined with a tour of their small cacao farm. The tour includes grinding and creating your own chocolate drink and chocolate bar from roasted beans.

☞ Tours

San Ignacio, or the lodges around it, are the natural base for visiting the cultural and natural riches of the Cayo region. There are numerous tour operators on Burns Ave and most hotels organize the same tours working with the same operators.

Trips to Actun Tunichil Muknal and Barton Creek Cave can only be done with a guide, while Caracol must be visited by vehicle convoy.

Typical day-trip prices per person are BZ$190 for Actun Tunichil Muknal (p164), BZ$90 to BZ$160 for a half-day trip to Barton Creek Cave (p175), BZ$190 to BZ$220 to Caracol (p180), BZ$170 for a cave-tubing trip to Nohoch Che'en (p159), BZ$160 for Mountain Pine Ridge (p178) and BZ$290 (plus border fees) for Tikal in Guatemala.

David's Adventure Tour ADVENTURE TOUR

(Map p166; ✔804-3674; www.davidsadventure tours.com; Savannah St; canoe tours BZ$40-90) Based just across the street from the Saturday market, David's is an experienced operator offering ecofriendly tours to sites throughout the area, specialising in river canoe trips, cave adventures and overnight jungle treks.

Pacz Tours GUIDED TOUR

(Map p166; ✔824-0536; www.pacztours.net; 30 Burns Ave; tours BZ$80-290) Offers reliably excellent service and knowledgeable guides to Actun Tunichil Muknal and Tikal, as well as shuttle transfers all over Cayo.

Belize Nature Travel CAVE TOUR

(✔824-3314; www.experiencebelize.com; Santa Elena) Belize Nature Travel specializes in cave tours such as Actun Tunichil Muknal and Barton Creek, and trips to Caracol. Check the website for other tour packages.

Belizean Sun CAVE TOUR

(✔665-2808; www.belizeansun.com) Based in San José Succotz, Belizean Sun provides personalized caving experiences to some of Cayo's lesser-known caves, including Actun Chapat and Halal Cave, as well as birdwatching, jungle camping and archaeology.

River Rat Expeditions ADVENTURE TOUR

(Map p166; ✔661-4562; www.riverratbelize.com; Burns Ave) Specialist in kayaking, river-tubing and cave trips, including Che Chem Ha near Benque Viejo del Carmen. Enjoy a relaxing paddle down the Mopan River near Clarissa Falls, or take on some white water near Paslow Falls.

Paradise Expeditions BIRDWATCHING

(✔820-4014, 610-5593; www.birdinginbelize.com; Crystal Paradise Resort) Run by the accomplished local bird guide Jeronie Tut, Paradise Expeditions does trips for both the casual and serious birdwatcher from its base at Crystal Paradise Resort.

Mayawalk Tours ADVENTURE TOUR

(Map p166; ✔824-3070; www.mayawalk.com; 19 Burns Ave) One of San Ignacio's original tour companies does recommended trips to Caracol (BZ$190), Actun Tunichil Muknal (BZ$190), Tikal (Guatemala) and many other adventure tours geared toward travelers of all levels and interests. Also operates a shuttle service all over Belize.

Maximum Adventure Tours ADVENTURE TOUR

(Map p166; ✔623-4880; http://maximum adventuretours.com; 27 Burns Ave) Runs tours to caves and Maya ruins, and offers hiking expeditions. Also operates shuttle services throughout Belize.

Carlos the Caveman CAVE TOUR

(✔669-7619; www.carloscaveman.com) Cayo native Carlos Panti has a high level of cave and cultural knowledge, and specializes in small-group spiritually themed journeys into the Actun Tunichil Muknal cave.

🛌 Sleeping

San Ignacio has the best range of good-value budget accommodation (including camping) in Belize, with a few excellent midrange places as well. More luxurious options – some of the best in Belize – are the jungle and mountain lodges out of town.

Casa Blanca Guest House GUESTHOUSE $

(Map p166; ✔824-2080; www.casablancaguest house.com; 10 Burns Ave; s/d/tr BZ$50/65/80, with air-con BZ$80/100/120; ❄🛜) Intimate, immaculate and secure, the Casa Blanca is everything you need from a budget guesthouse. Decent-sized rooms have clean white walls and crisp fresh linens. Guests have a comfy sitting area, a clean kitchen and a breezy balcony from which to watch the world go by.

Old House Hostel HOSTEL $

(Map p166; ✔623-1342; https://www.face book.com/hostelbelize; 3 Buena Vista St; dm/d BZ$25/70) There's a lot to like about this hostel above the sometimes-happening Soul Project. The two eight-bed dorms are clean and spacious with lockers and wi-fi, and there's a neat common room, self-catering kitchen and street-view balcony. There's only one private double room so book ahead.

Bella's Backpacker's HOSTEL $

(Map p166; ✔824-2248; www.bellasinbelize.com; 4 Galvez St; dm BZ$25, d with/without bathroom BZ$66/60; 🛜) Bella's is a classic backpackers,

CAYO DISTRICT SAN IGNACIO

with rustic charm, bohemian travelers of all ages floating about and a sociable rooftop chill-out area with hammocks and couches. Well-laid-out dorms with sturdy timber bunk beds and bathrooms are complemented by a few private rooms with screened-in windows and a rock-motif bathroom. Breakfast is available for BZ$10. Bella also has a farm at Cristo Rey.

Venus Hotel   HOTEL $
(Map p166; ☎824-3202; 29 Burns Ave; d/tr BZ$66/82, with air-con BZ$93/115; P ❋ 🛜) The three-story Venus is something of a landmark on Burns Ave, drawing in wandering travelers like a tractor beam. It's not flash but it's friendly and good value, and the variety of rooms are clean and comfy – the best are the spacious air-con rooms with shared balcony overlooking the marketplace. A bonus is free use of the large adjacent car park.

Western Guesthouse   GUESTHOUSE $
(Map p166; ☎824-2572; www.westernguesthousebelize.com; 54 Burns Ave; s/d with fan BZ$66/76, with air-con BZ$86/106, f ste BZ$152; P ❋ 🛜) The Urbina family's guesthouse is above a hardware store on San Ignacio's quiet west side. Big pluses are the family atmosphere and access to a fully furnished kitchen. The eight clean and comfortable guestrooms each have two beds, TV and hot shower, and there is also a large family suite with three double beds and full bathroom.

Hotel Mallorca   HOTEL $
(Map p166; ☎824-2960; mallorcahotel@gmail.com; 12 Burns Ave; s/d BZ$50/60) Colorful quilts on firm beds in compact rooms with cable TV and hot showers are the main selling points of Hotel Mallorca. Management lives onsite and guests have access to a small kitchen, a pleasant lounge area and a tiny balcony overlooking Burns Ave.

Mana Kai Camp & Cabins   CAMPGROUND $
(Map p166; ☎624-6538; http://manakaibelize. weebly.com; Branch Mouth Rd; campsite per person BZ$10, s/d cabin BZ$30/40, with bathroom BZ$50/60, with air-con BZ$100/110; P ❋ 🛜) One of the best urban camping grounds in Belize, Mana Kai is a big swath of flat grassy land with an open-air communal kitchen, *palapa* with hammocks and free wi-fi. Even if you're not camping there are several log cabin–style cottages, some with air-con. There's a great feeling of space here, just a short walk from the town center.

Hi-Et Guest House   GUESTHOUSE $
(Map p166; ☎824-2828; thehiet@yahoo.com; 12 West St; s/d BZ$25/30, d with bathroom BZ$50; 🛜) Friendly, family-owned and budget-friendly, Hi-Et occupies two connected houses, each with its own veranda overlooking the busy street below. The cheaper rooms have shared bathrooms, but all are clean, comfy and good value for money.

River Park Inn   CAMPGROUND $
(Map p174; ☎824-2116; www.riverparkinnbelize. com; Branch Mouth Rd; campsite per person BZ$10, RV site BZ$35, d cabin BZ$85, r BZ$100; P ❋ 🛜) This large property backs on to the Macal River just north of the town center, with plenty of space for campers and RVs. There are also two comfortable timber *cabañas*, and neat double rooms with bathroom, cable TV and air-con in the main building.

J&R's Guest House   GUESTHOUSE $
(Map p166; ☎632-8877; 20 Far West St; s/d without bathroom BZ$25/30, d with bathroom BZ$45) This six-room guesthouse up the hill from the town center has a family atmosphere, a guest kitchen and a porch out front. Three rooms have private bathroom and three share facilities, so it's an all-round good deal for budget travelers.

Rosa's Hotel   HOTEL $
(Map p166; ☎804-2265; http://rosashotelbelize. com; 65 Hudson St; d with fan/air-con incl breakfast BZ$75/84; ❋ 🛜) Rosa's is a little nondescript but it's friendly, central and decent value, especially if you value air-con.

Midas Resort   HOTEL $$
(Map p174; ☎824-3172; www.midasbelize. com; Branch Mouth Rd; cottage/cabaña/casita BZ$152/166/370, d/f BZ$235/320; P ❋ 🛜 🏊) In a budget town, Midas stands out as one of San Ignacio's better midrange choices. The large pool, funky bar and friendly staff complement an interesting array of accommodations from hotel-style rooms in the main building to cottages, *cabanas* and a two-bedroom *casita* at the back of the property. It's in a quiet location a five-minute walk north of the market.

Cahal Pech Village Resort   RESORT $$
(Map p174; ☎824-3740; www.cahalpech.com; Cahal Pech Hill; d/cabaña/ste BZ$232/232/326; P ❋ @ 🛜 🏊) Atop Cahal Pech hill, half a mile up from the town center, you can enjoy San Ignacio's finest views from this upscale family resort. The resort has 21 bright,

tile-floored, air-con rooms, nine family suites and 27 dreamy thatch-roof *cabañas* dotted around the property. The amazing two-level cascading pool (nonguests BZ$10) is a great place to cool off.

The onsite restaurant serves good international, Belizean and Maya food with a view. The resort also has its own onsite tour service, booking trips to Caracol, Tikal, Xunantunich and any place else in Belize.

Rainforest Haven Inn HOTEL $$
(Map p166; ☏ 674-1984; www.rainforesthavens. com; 2 Victoria St; r & cabaña BZ$100, 2-bedroom apt BZ$130; ▣ @ ☎) Rainforest Haven is a good find if you're looking for midrange comfort at an almost budget price. The five rooms have air-con, flat-screen TV with cable, fridge, wi-fi and hot-water showers. The *cabaña* has a kitchenette and the two-bedroom apartment boasts a full kitchen – a steal for families or groups. There's a cool chill-out spot on the 2nd floor.

Martha's Guesthouse HOTEL $$
(Map p166; ☏ 804-3647; www.marthasbelize. com; 10 West St; d BZ$150, ste BZ$170-190; ▣ ☎) This family-run guesthouse has 10 bright, sparkling-clean rooms, each with a private balcony and a cut above most in the town center. Woven Maya tapestries accent the mahogany walls and furniture, while tile floors keep the rooms cool. Hotel amenities include a laundry, shuttle bus and an excellent restaurant.

San Ignacio Resort Hotel HOTEL $$$
(Map p166; ☏ 824-2034; www.sanignaciobelize. com; 18 Buena Vista St; s/d from BZ$336/382, regal BZ$368/442, f ste BZ$550; ▣ ▣ @ ☎ ☎) The most upscale hotel in San Ignacio by a considerable margin (Queen Elizabeth stayed here in 1994, as the photos in the lobby attest), this is boutique luxury but with welcoming, professional staff and a serene location just uphill from the town center. Beyond the pool area, the property is backed by jungle and home to the excellent Green Iguana Conservation Project.

Rooms are understated but exquisite; family-sized suites comfortably house six, while standard rooms are more cozy, but all have private balconies with views of the pool or the hotel's lush garden. If you're in the mood for an in-town splurge, this is the place (ask for the Queen's room).

✖ Eating

San Ignacio's compact center is packed with eateries, street-food stalls and mini supermarkets. True to its traveler vibe, most places are good value and a few open very early to feed adventurers heading out on tour.

Farmers Market MARKET $
(Map p166; ☻ from 5am Sat) Saturday is the big market day in San Ignacio when traders come from all over Cayo to sell fresh bargain produce, handicrafts and clothing. The dozen or so food stalls set up in the middle of the action serve quick-fire street food – cheap and tasty. Smaller versions of the market happen most other days of the week.

Pop's Restaurant DINER $
(Map p166; West St; breakfast BZ$4-13; ☻ 6:30am-2pm) You may feel like you're in a *Seinfeld* episode at this friendly six-booth, hole-in-the-wall diner. Best omelets in town and bottomless cups of coffee make this San Ignacio's worst-kept breakfast secret and a great place to meet other diners. Good burritos at lunchtime.

Mike's BREAKFAST $
(Map p166; dishes BZ$3-8; ☻ 5-9am) This unsignposted green shack opposite the market is a local legend for breakfast and fresh Johnnycakes (cornmeal flatbread). Go early or miss out.

New French Bakery BAKERY $
(Map p166; ☏ 804-0054; baked goods BZ$1.50-5; ☻ 6:30am-6pm Mon-Sat) Best place in town for French bread, cinnamon rolls, croissants, apple turnovers and good coffee. It's in an open space just north of the market – get here early for the freshest, straight-out-of-the-oven stuff.

Great Mayan Prince BELIZEAN $
(Map p166; ☏ 824-2588; 28 Benque Viejo Rd; mains BZ$8-15, Sun brunch adult/child BZ$15/7; ☻ 7am-9pm Mon-Thu, 7am-10pm Fri & Sat, 7am-3pm Sun; ☎ ☏) Great Mayan Prince is worth the short hike up Benque Viejo Rd for the sweeping balcony view of San Ignacio and an honest (not overpriced) menu of Belizean and Mexican dishes. A good spot for breakfast and Sunday brunch.

Ice Cream Shoppe ICE CREAM $
(Map p166; ☏ 634-6160; 24 West St; ☻ 11am-8:30pm Mon-Thu, 11am-9:30pm Fri-Sun; ☎ ☎) This is the place for excellent homemade ice cream with some deliciously offbeat flavors,

such as pumpkin cheesecake, s'mores and fudge brownie.

Sweet T'ing
BAKERY **$**

(Map p166; ☑ 610-4174; 96 Benque Viejo Rd; cakes BZ$2-5, coffee from BZ$2; ☺ noon-9pm) A tiny bakery at the top of the hill with an exceptional variety of local chocolates (including made-in-Belize favorites Cotton Tree and Goss) and coconut cream pie, Sweet T'ing is worth the walk.

Eva's
BREAKFAST, BELIZEAN **$$**

(Map p166; Burns Ave; mains BZ$10-24; ☺ 6am-10pm) Open early for breakfast, Eva's is a popular traveler hangout on Burns Ave, serving good breakfast and tasty Belizean and Western favorites. Tex-Mex, rice and beans, burgers, steaks and curries.

Fuego Bar & Grill
LATIN AMERICAN **$$**

(Map p166; ☑ 663-3663; Cayo Plaza; mains BZ$16-40; ☺ noon-10pm Wed, Thu & Sun, noon-midnight Fri & Sat; P⟨⟩) One of central San Ignacio's more upscale restaurants, Fuego is a chic but casual fusion of Latin American, Belizean and international flavors done with flair. Curry-shrimp tacos, plantain-encrusted fish burger and coffee-molasses glazed pork chops are some of the interesting twists on old classics. It takes drinks seriously too, with margaritas, martinis and mojitos among the specialty mixes.

Hode's Place
BELIZEAN, AMERICAN **$$**

(Map p166; Branch Mouth Rd; mains BZ$10-28; ☺ 9am-10pm; ⟨⟩) Locals love this rambling barn-sized place north of the city center. A large terrace restaurant opening onto a citrus orchard and kids' playground, it's a popular spot for families or for an evening drink. Friendly service and satisfying food – from burritos and fajitas to steaks, seafood and rice and beans – complete the recipe.

Coaba
INTERNATIONAL **$$**

(Map p166; ☑ 824-3300; cnr Bullet Tree Rd & Joseph Andrews Dr; mains BZ$10-35; ☺ 10am-10pm) The cool semi-open-air dining space, friendly service and tasty Central American–style food – from Maya to Tex-Mex – make this a good choice. The BZ$10 daily specials include cow-foot soup and *pilbil* (Mexican pulled pork stew), or go for steak, burgers, wings or burritos.

Serendib
SRI LANKAN **$$**

(Map p166; ☑ 804-2302; Burns Ave; mains BZ$14-22; ☺ 11am-10pm) San Ignacio's only Sri Lankan restaurant serves excellent curries with

> ### STREET FOOD & FARMERS MARKET
>
> To experience the true cultural tapestry of Belize first-hand, head down to the Farmers Market on Saturday, when San Ignacio's open-air market draws farmers and food producers from all ends of Belize (culturally and geographically) to buy and sell all manner of fruits, vegetables, jams and dairy products. The food stalls here are superb – cheap, tasty, fast and offering a wide variety of choice. For street food when the market is not on, try the taco and quesadilla stands on Savannah St or head over the bridge to Santa Elena.

a choice of yellow, fried or savoury rice, spicy chicken tandoori, and other delicacies from the Indian subcontinent. Friendly owners, sensational food and streetside or peaceful courtyard dining areas.

Ko-Ox Han-nah
BELIZEAN, INDIAN **$$**

(Map p166; ☑ 623-0019; 5 Burns Ave; breakfast BZ$8-12, Belizean mains BZ$10-12, Indian mains BZ$28-32; ☺ 6am-9pm; ☑) The name means *let's go eat* in Mayan, but Han-nah's is far from just another Belizean restaurant. The schizophrenic menu features an intriguing range of Indian dishes, such as lamb curry and the likes of Mozambique peri-peri chicken, with all food sourced from local farms. Breakfasts are good, while lunch and dinner are a mix of Mexican, burgers and Indian.

Cahal Pech Restaurant
BELIZEAN **$$**

(Map p174; ☑ 824-3740; Cahal Pech Village Resort, Cahal Pech Hill; mains BZ$5-22; ☺ 7am-10pm; ⟨⟩) If it's food with a view you're after, you won't get better than this unless you have your own chef and a zeppelin. From the dining room, with its Maya jungle motifs, you can enjoy sweeping views over San Ignacio and Cayo while enjoying a menu of Belizean faves, such as Maya pork chops, or burgers and pasta.

Martha's Kitchen
BREAKFAST, INTERNATIONAL **$$**

(Map p166; ☑ 804-3647; 10 West St; mains BZ$8-30; ☺ 7am-10pm; ⟨⟩) Highlights run the gamut from tasty pizza and delicious fish burritos to juicy steaks and vegetarian kebabs. Take a seat inside the wood-accented dining room or outside on the foliage-fronted terrace. Good spot for breakfast.

Tolacco Smokehouse   MAYA $$

(Map p174; Cristo Rey Rd, Santa Elena; mains BZ$10-30; ⊙4-10pm) Across the river in Santa Elena, this family-run open-sided thatch restaurant makes a welcome change from downtown San Ignacio. Pork ribs, chops and grilled chicken and fish are the specialties, along with juicy steaks. There's a bar and a friendly atmosphere. Dinner only.

Mr. Greedy's   PIZZA $$

(Map p166; ☑664-7375; 60 West St; mains BZ$7-20; ⊙11am-10pm) Greedy's is an industrial-sized pizzeria, bar and burger joint with a takeout window and sports-bar feel. Occasional DJs and party nights make it a potential go-to spot if the night is right.

★ Guava Limb Cafe   INTERNATIONAL $$$

(Map p166; ☑824-4837; 79 Burns Ave; mains BZ$14-38; 🛜☑) 🎜 One of San Ignacio's newest and trendiest restaurants, boutique Guava Limb is set in an adorable turquoise two-story building with a serene outdoor garden area. Fresh organic ingredients are sourced from the owners' farm or local providers to create an eclectic international menu that might include Indonesian *gado gado,* Thai chicken and lettuce wraps, or Hawaiian teriyaki chicken burgers.

Vegetarians will enjoy the range of fresh salads, and breakfast is also well covered with Belgian waffles, crepes and huevos rancheros. It's at the north end of Burns Ave.

★ Running W Steakhouse   INTERNATIONAL, STEAKHOUSE $$$

(Map p166; San Ignacio Resort Hotel, 18 Buena Vista St; mains BZ$20-70; ⊙7am-10pm) One of San Ignacio's top dining splurges, this restaurant at the San Ignacio Resort Hotel is named for the owner's Running W ranch that supplies most of the best meat in western Belize. Steaks are a specialty, including the signature Maya steak, but there's also a wide range of thoughtfully prepared international and Belizean dishes.

Dine in the air-conditioned restaurant or out on the romantic, candlelit balcony patio overlooking the pool and jungle. There's an attached bar with slick service.

🍷 Drinking & Nightlife

Bamboo Bar   BAR

(Map p166; South side, Market Sq; ⊙9am-midnight; 🛜) In a town with low-key nightlife, Bamboo Bar is a standout, smack in the market square and with welcoming staff,

regular live music and a guaranteed crowd most nights.

Thirsty Thursdays   CLUB

(Map p166; ☑824-2727; www.thirstythursdays belize.com; Buena Vista Rd; ⊙5pm-midnight Wed-Sun, till 2am Fri & Sat) The go-to place after (or before) other bars in town close, semi-open-air Thirsty Thursdays has regular live DJs, party nights, drink specials, bar food and a mixed crowd. Sunday is karaoke. It's up the hill past San Ignacio Resort Hotel.

☆ Entertainment

Soul Project   ARTS VENUE

(Map p166; ☑653-1855; Buena Vista Rd; ⊙4-10pm Wed & 6-11pm Fri; 🛜) 🎜 Soul Project is a sweet bar and venue where local artist, filmmaker and conservationist Daniel Velazquez works hard to create a space for local and visiting artists and musicians. And he makes his own herbal fruit wine. At the time of writing it was only open Wednesday and Friday, but with a hostel upstairs and a bit of prodding, this may change.

Princess Casino   CASINO

(Map p166; ⊙noon-4am Mon-Fri, noon-5am Sat & Sun) Belize isn't a big casino destination but you can spend your money here on a handful of live gaming tables (black jack, poker) or slot machines, or drink at the Next Lounge Bar till late. Security is tight – ID, webcam photo and bag checks.

🛍 Shopping

Jungle Remedies   HEALTH

(Map p174; ☑663-0248; miracle@btl.net; Orange St; ⊙by appointment) From gastric distress and asthma to high blood pressure, gall stones and gout, Dr Harry Guy claims his jungle remedies can cure nearly any ailment. Many locals swear by his potions, made from locally harvested roots, barks and leaves. His place, off Bullet Tree Rd, is hard to find – call ahead for an appointment.

Back to My Roots   ARTS & CRAFTS

(Map p166; ☑824-2740; 30 Burns Ave) Offers cool handmade jewelry, including silver, amber and other semiprecious stones. The name of the place refers to the drums and other Rasta gear for sale.

ℹ Information

Belize Bank (16 Burns Ave), **Scotiabank** (cnr Burns Ave & King St) and **Atlantic Bank** (Burns

Ave) have ATMs that accept international Visa, MasterCard, Plus and Cirrus cards.

Cayo Welcome Center (Map p166; ☑ 634-8450; Savannah St, Cayo Plaza; ☺ 8am-5pm Mon-Fri, 8am-4pm Sat) The only tourist office in the Cayo District, this is a helpful, air-conditioned modern place in the central plaza opened in 2013. As well as some local exhibits, a short film about the region runs on a loop.

La Loma Luz Hospital (☑ 804-2985, 824-2087; http://lalomaluz.org; Western Hwy; ☺ emergency services 24hr) This Adventist hospital in Santa Elena is one of the best in the country.

Post Office (Map p166; ☑ 824-2049; West St)

San Ignacio Hospital (☑ 824-2761; Bullet Tree Rd)

Tradewinds Internet (Hudson St; per hr BZ$5; ☺ 7am-11pm Mon-Sat, 10am-10pm Sun) A friendly internet spot with free coffee.

Getting There & Away

AIR

The nearest airstrip is tiny Maya Flats on Chial Rd, about 7 miles from San Ignacio. Tropic Air has three daily flights to/from Belize City (from BZ$183). A taxi to/from town costs around BZ$40.

BUS

San Ignacio (surprisingly) has no bus station. Buses stop in the market plaza en route to/from Belize City (regular/express BZ$9/10, two hours), Belmopan (BZ$5, one hour) and Benque Viejo del Carmen (BZ$2, 30 minutes). Buses run in both directions about every half-hour from 3:30am to 7pm, with a less frequent service on Sunday.

From a vacant lot on Savannah St, buses leave for Bullet Tree Falls (BZ$1, 15 minutes) roughly hourly from 10:30am to 5pm Monday to Saturday. From the same spot, buses go to San Antonio (BZ$3, 35 minutes) five or six times a day, Monday to Saturday.

Several tour companies also run charter shuttle buses around Cayo and further afield. Sample fares include Guatemala border (BZ$50) and Belize City (BZ$150).

CAR & MOTORCYCLE

To really explore Cayo, a car is useful, preferably with good off-road capabilities and high clearance. Don't even think about heading to Caracol without a 4WD.

There is a convenient central gas station next to the bridge out of San Ignacio.

Cayo Auto Rentals (☑ 824-2222; www.cayo autorentals.com; 81 Benque Viejo Rd) Daily rates start at BZ$140 for an economy or BZ$140 for a 4WD Jeep Patriot.

GETTING TO GUATEMALA

There are no direct government buses between Belize and Guatemala, but the **Marlin Espadas** (www.marlinespadas. com) shuttle runs daily between Chetumal (Mexico) and Flores (Guatemala) via Belmopan and San Ignacio.

Otherwise, getting into Guatemala from San Ignacio isn't too challenging. *Colectivos* (charging per person and leaving when they have a full car) head from a vacant lot on Savannah St to Benque Viejo del Carmen (BZ$4) and then directly to the Guatemalan border (BZ$6). Once you've crossed the border, you'll need to walk about a mile or hop on a taxi to get to the *colectivo* stand in Melchor de Mencos for Q10, from where you can catch a ride to Flores or El Remate.

Matus Car Rental (☑ 663-4702, 824-2005; www.matuscarrental.com; 18 Benque Viejo Rd) Rates start at BZ$135 per day up to BZ$150 for a 4WD such as a Jeep or Suzuki.

TAXI

Several taxi stands are dotted around the town center; **Savannah Taxi Association** (Map p166; ☑ 824-2155; ☺ 24hr) is San Ignacio's main central taxi stand. Sample fares are BZ$25 to the Guatemalan border (9 miles), BZ$60 round trip to Xunantunich, and BZ$80 to BZ$100 one way to the Mountain Pine Ridge lodges. Taxis to Bullet Tree Falls (colectivo/private BZ$4/20) go from Wyatt St, just off Burns Ave.

Getting Around

San Ignacio is small enough that you can easily walk to most places of interest. If you're driving, note that parking can be difficult in the city center. Also pay attention to the one-way traffic system; Hawkesworth Bridge is one way leaving San Ignacio, while New Bridge enters town north of the market.

Short taxi rides around town cost BZ$5.

SOUTHEAST OF SAN IGNACIO

Forming a loop encircling a large, beautiful swath of the Cayo District and leading into both the Mountain Pine Ridge Forest Reserve and Caracol, unsealed Cristo Rey Rd winds southeast of San Ignacio (via

CAYO DISTRICT SOUTHEAST OF SAN IGNACIO

Around San Ignacio

Santa Elena), eventually linking up with Chiquibul Rd (sometimes called Pine Ridge Rd), which runs 9 miles up to Georgeville on the George Price Hwy.

The only major population center on the loop is San Antonio (population 2000). Settled by Mayas from the Yucatán, the village gets its name from the statue of St Anthony in the town church.

Apart from the exhilarating forest drive, there are numerous cultural and adventure activities along the way.

Buses run from San Ignacio to San Antonio village (BZ$4, 45 minutes) and back three or four times from Monday to Saturday. Tours out of San Ignacio go to Barton Creek Cave and other attractions in the region.

Cristo Rey & Chiquibul Roads
◎ Sights

★ **Green Hills Butterfly Ranch**　　BUTTERFLY FARM

(Map p174; ☑ 834-4017; http://biological-diversity.info/greenhills.htm; Mile 8 Chiquibul Rd; adult/child BZ$20/10; ☺ 8am-4pm, last tour 3:30pm) This amazing butterfly ranch offers a unique opportunity to see 50-plus exquisite native species in flight. Biologists Jan Meerman and Tineke Boomsma breed the butterflies for research and educational purposes, with research activity including tracking interaction between different species and compiling a field guide, as well as cultivating a botanical garden that supports the butterfly population. The ranch also boasts 13 species of hummingbird. Guided tours are hourly, with a minimum of two people required.

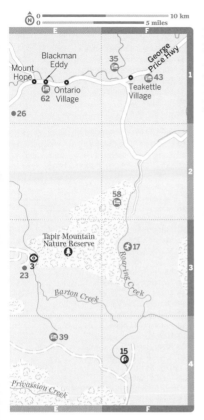

Blackman
Eddy

Mount
Hope

Ontario
62 Village

●26

Teakettle
Village

George
Price Hwy

35

43
1

58

Tapir Mountain
Nature Reserve

17

●
23

Barton Creek

Roaring Creek

39

15

Privassion Creek

0 ─────── 10 km
0 ─────── 5 miles

Rd passes through the scattered traditional Mennonite farming community of Upper Barton Creek and fords both Barton Creek itself then one of its tributaries. The second route along 7 Mile El Progresso Rd (follow the signs for Mike's Place) involves possibly the steepest road in Belize with a series of tight switchbacks descending into the valley.

García Sisters' Place
CULTURAL CENTER

(Map p174; ☑669-4023; artistmai1981@gmail.com; Cristo Rey Rd, San Antonio; ⊙7am-6pm) The García sisters display and sell a wide assortment of beautiful black-slate carvings. These five sisters – born and raised near San Antonio – developed this craft, which is now widely imitated around Belize. Their carvings, selling for between BZ$10 and BZ$200, depict a variety of subjects, including local wildlife and Maya deities and calendars.

Today their home and gallery is part museum of Maya culture, part art center and shop, and part healing center. Various herbal and healing treatments cost from BZ$40. Outside is a garden where medicinal and herbals tours (BZ$20) are held, along with lectures and workshops on Maya culture, meditation and spiritual healing.

Sa'c Tunich
MUSEUM

(Map p174; ☑662-1253; Cristo Rey Rd; tours BZ$10; ⊙8am-8pm) Many refer to Sa'c Tunich as 'the living Maya site' because at first glance it looks like an excavated ruin. However, Sa'c Tunich is actually the museum-workshop of Maya artists Jose and Javier Magaña, who create contemporary Maya artworks from stone and clay, both for exhibition and for sale. Tours of the site include the nearby *gibnut* (small, brown-spotted rodent similar to a guinea pig) breeding program and the lookout tower.

🏃 Activities

Calico Jack's
ZIP-LINING

(Map p174; ☑820-4078, in USA 301-792-2233; www.calicojacksvillage.com; 7 Mile El Progresso; per person BZ$80-170; ⊙8am-4pm) This 365-acre property boasts the largest state-of-the-art zip-lining setup in Western Cayo, a nine-run, 15-platform zip-line; various packages take you on different runs ranging from a 45-minute 'explorer' to a 90-minute 'ultimate adventure.' Adventurous visitors can try the jungle swing (BZ$50), which offers a trip across a canyon combined with a 55ft free-fall, or the cable walk.

Barton Creek Cave
CAVE

(Map p174) Barton Creek rises high in the Mountain Pine Ridge and flows north to join the Belize River near Georgeville. Along the way it dips underground for a spell, flowing through the Barton Creek Cave. During the Classic Period, the ancient Maya interred at least 28 people and left thousands of pottery jars and fragments and other artifacts on 10 ledges. Today the cave is only accessible by canoe on excellent guided tours.

Peaceful canoe trips take you (in groups of six or fewer) about 750ft into the cave so you can get a look at the crystal cave formations, as well as the spooky skulls, bones and pottery shards that remain from the Maya. Numerous tours operate out of San Ignacio, or head to Mike's Place (p177) just outside the cave entrance.

There are two routes to the cave, both very rough and both turning off Chiquibul Rd. The main route on Upper Barton Creek

176

Around San Ignacio

CAYO DISTRICT CRISTO REY &CHIQUIBUL ROADS

Top Sights

1 Green Hills Butterfly Ranch D3
2 Xunantunich...B3

Sights

3 Barton Creek Cave E3
Belize Botanic Gardens...............(see 36)
4 Benque Viejo House of Culture B3
5 Big Rock Falls D4
6 Branch Mouth C2
7 Cahal Pech C2
8 Chaa Creek...B3
Chaa Creek Natural History
Center & Butterfly Farm ....(see 44)
9 Che Chem Ha...C4
10 El Pilar..B1
11 Five Sisters Falls D4
12 García Sisters' Place C3
13 Poustinia Land Art Park B4
14 Sa'c Tunich..C3
15 Thousand Foot Falls F4
16 Tropical Wings Nature Center B3

Activities, Courses & Tours

17 Actun Tunichil Muknal..........................F3
18 Belize Wildlife & Referral Clinic D2
19 Calico Jack's D3
20 Chaya Garden Ashram...........................B3
21 Hanna's Stables.....................................B3
22 Hot Mama's..D1
23 Mike's Place E3
24 Mountain Equestrian Trails D3
25 Ocean Spirit Fire Temple C2
Rainforest Medicine Trail............(see 44)
Spa at Chaa Creek.......................(see 44)
26 Universal Healing Institute &
Retreat..E1

Sleeping

Amber Sunset Jungle
Resort...(see 26)
Benque Resort & Spa....................(see 4)
27 Black Rock Lodge C4
28 Blancaneaux Lodge D4
29 Cahal Pech Village Resort....................C2
30 Calico Jack's Village D3
31 Casa del Caballo Blanco B2
32 Ceiba Jungle Camp D2
33 Cool M Farm...C2
34 Crystal Paradise Resort C3

35 Dream Valley F1
36 duPlooy's Jungle Lodge.........................C4
37 Gaïa River Lodge D4
Garcia Sisters' Homestay.............(see 12)
38 Gumbolimbo Village Resort D2
39 Hidden Valley Inn E4
40 Hotel El Pilar...B2
41 Inn the Bush...C3
42 Ka'ana Resort & Spa B3
43 Leslies' Private Paradise......................F1
44 Lodge at Chaa Creek B3
45 Log Cab-Inn B2
46 Lower Dover Field Station & Eco
Lodge D1
47 Macal River Camp at Chaa
Creek..C3
48 Macaw Bank Jungle Lodge.....................C3
49 Mahogany Hall.......................................B2
50 Mariposa Jungle Lodge.........................D3
Maxim's Palace...............................(see 4)
51 Maya Mountain Lodge C2
52 Maya Vista B3
53 Midas Resort C2
54 Moonracer Farm D3
55 Mystic River C3
56 Orange Gallery D1
57 Parrot Nest Jungle Lodge......................B2
58 Pook's Hill Lodge F2
59 Rawspa...B2
60 River Park Inn C2
61 Table Rock Jungle Lodge.......................C3
Trek Stop ....(see 16)
62 Wolf's Place...E1

Eating

63 Benny's Kitchen B3
Cahal Pech Restaurant ....(see 29)
64 Casa Sofia D1
Chef Charly's .... (see 4)
Ham's Barbecue in a Bun ....(see 64)
McWolf's Restaurant ....(see 62)
Sista's Diner.................................(see 68)
Tel-esh ....(see 4)
65 Tolacco Smokehouse C2
66 Western Dairies.....................................D1

Shopping

67 Jungle Remedies....................................C2
Orange Gallery.............................(see 56)
68 Reimers Health Food D1

Mountain Equestrian Trails HORSEBACK RIDING (Map p174; ☑669-1124, in USA 800-838-3918; www.metbelize.com; Mile 8 Chiquibul Rd; 6-day horseback tours s/d BZ$3060/5524) For equestrians, nothing beats exploring the area from the back of a horse. MET has highly professional six- and seven-day riding packages, including accommodation in rustic cabañas (no electricity) and meals. For less committed riders, half-day and full-day local rides can also be organised. Expert guides can also arrange birdwatching, caving and vehicle tours.

Chaya Garden Ashram YOGA (Map p174; ☑652-9642; http://chayagarden ashram.com; ☉yoga 10am Tue-Fri & Sun) Set on lush grounds next to a series of stunning natural waterfalls with an amazing swimming hole, Chaya Gardens offers yoga classes, massage treatments, natural healing, and excellent vegan and vegetarian meals. Drop-in yoga classes are BZ$20, massage is BZ$100 for an hour treatment, and the ashram also hosts workshops and musical events.

Mike's Place
GUIDED TOUR

(Map p174; ☑670-0441; www.bartoncreekcave.com; Barton Creek Cave; cave tour adult/child BZ$260/130) Mike's is based near Barton Creek Cave and offers guided canoe trips into the cave, as well as rock climbing and a short zip-lining course. You can camp here for BZ$20, and there's a restaurant serving burritos and Belizean rice and beans. Transfers are available from San Ignacio for an extra BZ$60. The steep road here is atrocious.

Ocean Spirit Fire Temple
SPIRITUAL

(Map p174; ☑675-3721; http://oceanspiritfiretemple.com) Not far from the small Cayo village of Cristo Rey, Ocean Spirit Fire Temple is home to spiritual healer and artist Winsom Omiala. Initiate of many rituals in Africa, Cuba, and Central and North America, Winsom acts as a reader and spiritual healer, and offers workshops and classes, which incorporate yoga, dance and shiatsu massage.

🛌 Sleeping

Garcia Sisters' Homestay
HOMESTAY $

(Map p174; ☑669-4023; Cristo Rey Rd; campsite per person BZ$10, r BZ$35) Just out of San Antonio village, the Garcia Sisters offer rooms behind their Maya gallery and spots to pitch a tent. Traditional meals are BZ$15.

Ceiba Jungle Camp
CAMPGROUND $

(Map p174; ☑673-5286; Chiquibil Rd; tent BZ$10, tent hire BZ$10) This is rustic camping at its best at Kim and Craig's property along the Chiquibil Rd, about 5 miles south of George Price Hwy. Composting toilets, bucket showers and organic gardens – Kim is a master herbalist – make this a Zen place to chill out for a while.

Calico Jack's Village
VILLA $$

(Map p174; ☑820-4078; www.calicojacksvillage.com; 7 Mile El Progresso; s/d/tr/q BZ$160/280/320/360; P❄🛜🏊) Best known for its zip-lining course, Calico Jack's also has a range of comfortable one- two- and three-bedroom villas with kitchen facilities, wi-fi and cable TV. The onsite restaurant serves breakfast, lunch and dinner overlooking the pool.

Cool M Farm
FARMSTAY $$

(Map p174; ☑824-2276; cool.m.farm@gmail.com; Mile 0.25 Cristo Rey Rd; cabañas d/f BZ$100/110, per extra person BZ$20) 🍃 Cool M is an offbeat place to stay for a few days on a genuine Mennonite farm. The Lǒhr family's 75-acre garden-filled dairy farm, on Cristo Rey Rd about a 20-minute walk from San Ignacio, has two lovely fan-cooled cabañas – one double and one family with two double beds – each with modern bathroom and a sun porch overlooking the valley.

The welcoming family offers a light breakfast and can provide farm-fresh dinners, boxed lunches and even baby-sitting on request. Minimum two-night stay.

Gumbolimbo Village Resort
RESORT $$

(Map p174; ☑650-3112; www.gumbolimboresort.com; Mile 2 Chiquibul Rd; d cabañas BZ$210-270; P🍃🛜🏊) 🍃 Perched high atop a hillside covered in gumbo-limbo trees (also known as the tourist tree due to its red, peeling bark), this resort offers modern cabañas, as well as the romantic hexagon room with cool white interiors and large glass doors offering mountain and jungle views. The ecoresort runs completely on solar and wind power. Meals available.

Maya Mountain Lodge
RESORT $$

(Map p174; ☑824-2164; www.mayamountain.com; Mile 0.75 Cristo Rey Rd; r small/standard/family BZ$138/178/258, cottage BZ$218-258; P❄🛜🏊) Lush gardens with a trail leading to a small, ancient Maya ceremonial site and the eight air-conditioned cottages with tile floors and porches hung with hammocks keep visitors coming back. Family units are like apartments with complete kitchenettes, and all units have wi-fi. There's also a medicinal trail and a wellness centre onsite.

Maya Mountain Lodge is easily reached, less than 1.5 miles from San Ignacio on Cristo Rey Rd.

Crystal Paradise Resort
RESORT $$

(Map p174; ☑834-4016, 820-4014; www.crystalparadise.com; Cristo Rey Rd; s/d/tr from BZ$146/190/234; P@) The Tut family's resort is spread out over well-tended gardens just above the Macal River, and offers utilitarian but comfortable cabañas. Most guests come here on packages that incorporate preplanned tours, including birdwatching, horseback riding, canoeing, Maya ruins and other activities. Breakfast and dinner are included.

CAYO DISTRICT CRISTO REY &CHIQUIBUL ROADS

Moonracer Farm
CABAÑAS $$

(Map p174; ☑667-5748; www.moonracerfarm. com; Mile 9 Mount Pine Ridge Rd; cabañas d/q BZ$150/280; ⓟ@🛜🐾) Intimate, rustic Moonracer occupies the former grounds of a wild feline rehabilitation center. There's just one jungle cabin with two separate double rooms, each with two queen-size beds, bathroom with hot shower, and screened-in porches with hammocks. Kerosene lamps provide ambience for the rooms, but the communal *palapa* kitchen and dining room has electricity and wi-fi.

The location is good for birdwatchers and explorers looking to head out early to explore Caracol. For a truly relaxing homestay experience, book the whole cabin.

Table Rock Jungle Lodge
RESORT $$$

(Map p174; ☑834-4040; www.tablerockbelize. com; Cristo Rey Rd; campsites BZ$60, cabañas d BZ$290-450; ⓟ🛜) ✎ This exquisite little resort boasts five classy *cabañas*, each furnished with custom-made four-poster beds, tile floors and thatched roofs, and equipped with 24-hour electricity and hot showers. Budget travelers can make use of the riverside camping and still enjoy free activities, such as canoeing, cave-tubing and mountain biking.

The owners of Table Rock produce their own electricity, grow their own fruits and vegetables, and use purified rainwater. Nonguest diners are welcome at the Table Rock restaurant with 24 hours' notice.

Mystic River
CABIN $$$

(Map p174; ☑834-4100; www.mysticriverbelize. com; Mile 6 Cristo Rey Rd; d from BZ$450; ⓟ🛜) This beautiful ecolodge on the bank of the Macal River features six beautifully furnished *cabañas* with Mexican tiled floors and high wooden ceilings, and three one-bedroom suites. All feature spacious living areas and bathrooms, and river-facing verandas. Hang out on the river with tubes, boogie boards and canoes, or hike the jungle trails that wind through Mystic River's 180 acres.

The lodge also has the new Jasmine Spa and a yoga deck, the open-sided restaurant serves organic foods, and there's an onsite artisanal cheese house.

Inn the Bush
CABIN $$$

(Map p174; ☑670-6364; www.innthebush belize.com; Cristo Rey Rd; 1-/2-bedroom cabins BZ$250/450; ⓟ🐾) Sitting atop a small hill, intimate Inn the Bush has two large cabins with massive four-poster mahogany beds, couches, full-sized bathrooms with hot showers and porches bigger than most hotel rooms, and a two-bedroom family cabin with living room. A large *palapa* bar and dining area overlooks a swimming-pool deck with jungle views.

Meals featuring locally sourced meats and vegetables are served all day, but advance notice is requested. It's 2 miles south of Cristo Rey Rd.

Mariposa Jungle Lodge
LODGE $$$

(Map p174; ☑670-2113; www.mariposa junglelodge.com; Cristo Rey Rd; d/tr/q from BZ$390/470/550, treehouse BZ$850; ⓟ✳️🛜🐾) This luxurious jungle lodge is a cut above some of the more rustic nearby places in terms of comfort with seven beautiful cabins, each named for a jungle creature or flower and featuring king-size canopy beds dressed with Egyptian linens and mosquito nets, hardwood furniture and hand-thatched roofs. Rooms also come with mini-fridge, optional air-con and hot showers.

With views of the rainforest or the mountain ridge, the screened porch is a perfect place to hang a hammock. There's a pool complete with bar stools and a waterfall, and a full-service bar and restaurant.

Macaw Bank Jungle Lodge
LODGE $$$

(Map p174; ☑603-4825; www.macawbankjungle lodge.com; off Cristo Rey Rd; d cabañas BZ$360-400; ⓟ🛜) ✎ Deep in the jungle about 3 miles south of Cristo Rey Rd and spread out along the Macal River Macaw Bank is a 50-acre wildlife wonderland, teeming with birds and other animals. The six rustic but spacious *cabañas* are decorated with hand-hewn furniture, mosaic-tile floors and woven tapestries. A restaurant serves locally sourced meals (order in advance).

Eco credentials are good, including solar power, recycling projects, organic gardening and water-conservation efforts.

Mountain Pine Ridge Area

South of San Ignacio and the Western Hwy, the land begins to climb toward the heights of the Maya Mountains, whose arching ridge forms the border separating Cayo District from Stann Creek District to the east and Toledo District to the south.

In the heart of this highland area, 200 sq miles of submontane (ie on the foothills or lower slopes of mountains) pine forest is the Mountain Pine Ridge Forest Reserve. The sudden switch from tropical rainforest to pine trees as you ascend to the Mountain Pine Ridge – a broad upland area of multiple ridges and valleys – is a little bizarre and somewhat startling. The reserve is full of rivers, pools, waterfalls and caves; the higher elevation means relief from both heat and mosquitoes.

⊙ Sights

The pine forest is a thriving ecosystem, covered with flora, traversed by river systems and replete with birds and other wildlife. The Macal River, Río Frio, Barton Creek and Roaring Creek all start up in Mountain Pine Ridge. From here they flow north to the Belize River and out to the sea, cascading across rocky cliffs and verdant hillsides along the way.

Big Rock Falls   WATERFALL
(Map p174) The small but powerful Big Rock Falls on Privassion Creek are, for many, more impressive than the Thousand Foot Falls – not least because you can get up close and swim in the pools below. Take the road toward Gaïa River Lodge (signposted) and, 1.5 miles past Blancaneaux Lodge, turn along a track to the left marked 'Big Rock'. From the parking area it's a steep walk down (even steeper back up!), aided by timber steps.

Five Sisters Falls   WATERFALL
(Map p174) The pools at tranquil Five Sisters Falls are only accessible to guests or diners at Gaïa River Lodge. A cable tram can take you down and back up.

Thousand Foot Falls   WATERFALL
(Map p174; ⊙ lookout point 8am-6pm) Ten miles off Chiquibul Rd, the Thousand Foot Falls are reckoned to be the highest in Central America, a ribbon of water cascading down a mountainside that you can view from a distant lookout point. Access them by turning onto Cooma Cairn Rd (follow the Hidden Valley sign), then turn left after 7 miles at the '1000 Ft Falls' sign. Walk around the lookout area for views over the pine-covered valley out toward Belmopan.

The falls are in fact around 1600ft high, but since you can't get any closer to them it's a long drive for this sort of scenery. Birdwatchers should keep their eyes peeled for the rare orange-breasted falcon.

Río On Pools   WATERFALL
Just off Chiquibul Rd, 2.5 miles north of Douglas D'Silva (Augustine), Río On Pools is a series of small waterfalls connecting pools that the river has carved out of granite boulders. It's a beautiful spot: the pools are refreshing for a dip and the smooth slabs of granite are perfect for stretching out on to dry off. It's remote but a popular spot for tour groups on their way back from Caracol.

Río Frio Cave   CAVE
In Douglas D'Silva (Augustine), on the way to or from Caracol, look for the signed turnoff to Río Frio Cave, less than 1 mile away. The river gurgles through the sizeable cave, keeping it cool while you go off and explore.

🛏 Sleeping

★**Blancaneaux Lodge**   RESORT $$$
(Map p174; ☑ 866-356-5881, 824-3878, in USA 800-746-3743; www.blancaneaux.com; cabañas BZ$700-1140, 2-bedroom villas BZ$1400; P 🛜 ☀ 🌊) 🗐 Owned by movie director Francis Ford Coppola (who keeps a personal villa, 'the Francis Ford Coppola Villa,' complete with attendant and private pool, yours for BZ$1718 per night here), this indulgent 78-acre lodge offers 20 thatched *cabañas* and luxury villas, spread around beautifully manicured gardens, with some looking right over the picturesque Privassion Creek.

The lodgings feature beautiful tiled bathrooms, with open-air living rooms in the villas, and handicrafts from Belize, Guatemala, Mexico and Thailand. Luxury *cabañas* feature their own plunge pools and outdoor showers, as well as indoor-style Japanese baths. There's also the Enchanted Cottage, a secluded one-bedroom stone cottage with fireplace, private pool, attendant and majestic view. Two onsite restaurants serve Italian and Guatemalan cuisine; nonguests are welcome with advance reservations.

Gaïa River Lodge   CABAÑAS $$$
(Map p174; ☑ 834-4024, 834-4005; www.gaiariverlodge.com; d cabañas BZ$400-450, ste BZ$630, villa BZ$790) The former Five Sisters has been transformed into the stylish Gaïa River Lodge, beautifully perched on a ridge above Privassion Creek. Luxurious *cabañas* and villas are well spaced out in the lodge grounds, creating a sense of privacy; the best are the waterfall-view rooms and the riverside lodge.

From the restaurant and bar, with its outdoor terrace, there are fine views down to Five Sisters Falls, which can be reached in style by the lodge's hydropowered tram. Nonguests are welcome to eat here with advance notice – lunch with a view is unbeatable.

Hidden Valley Inn RESORT **$$$**
(Map p174; ☑822-3320, 866-443-3364; www.hiddenvalleyinn.com; 4 Common Cain Rd; d estate r/ste BZ$670/890; 🅿🛜🏊) Secluded Hidden Valley Inn is set on 11 gorgeous sq miles of Mountain Pine Ridge, all strictly for the exclusive use of its guests. The grounds straddle pine and tropical forest ecosystems, and have access to 90 miles of signposted trails, waterfalls, inviting swimming spots and spectacular lookouts. The 10 cottage-style estate rooms and two suites feature earth-toned tapestries, brick fireplaces and mahogany furniture.

The lodge also offers a plethora of amenities, including free mountain bikes, yoga classes and more. It is situated 4 miles off the Chiquibul Rd, along Cooma Cairn Rd.

Caracol

Beyond Mountain Pine Ridge, to the southwest, are the ruins of Belize's largest and most important Maya site, **Caracol** (admission BZ$30; ⊙8am-4pm, convoy departs 9am). Once among the most powerful cities in the entire Maya world, this ancient city now lies enshrouded by thick jungle near the Guatemalan border, a 52-mile (much of this very rough) drive from San Ignacio that takes anywhere from three to four hours.

Sitting high on the Vaca Plateau, 1650ft above sea level, it's postulated that Caracol may have stretched over 70 sq miles at its peak (around AD 650). Nearly 40 miles of internal causeways radiate from the center to large outlying plazas and residential areas, connecting different parts of the city. At its height, the city's population may

Caracol

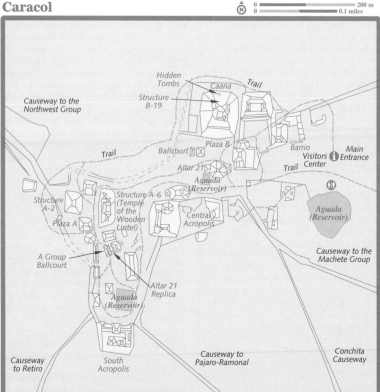

EXCAVATION HISTORY OF CARACOL

In 1937 a logger named Rosa Mai first stumbled upon the ruins. In 1938 commissioner of archaeology AH Anderson named the site Caracol (Spanish for snail), perhaps because of all the snail shells found in the soil. In 1950 Linton Satterthwaite from the University of Pennsylvania recorded the visible stone monuments, mapped the site core, and excavated several tombs, buildings and monuments. Many stelae were removed and sent to Pennsylvania.

Since 1985, Drs Diane and Arlen Chase have led the Caracol Archaeological Project (www.caracol.org), with annual field seasons conducting surveys and excavations that have revealed Caracol's massive central core and complex urban development. From 2000 to 2004, the Tourism Development Project carried out an excavation and conservation program led by Belizean archaeologist Jaime Awe, which also improved road access to the site.

have approached 150,000, more than twice as many people as Belize City has today. Though they had no natural water source, the people of Caracol dug artificial reservoirs to catch rainwater and grew food on extensive agricultural terraces. Its central area was a bustling place of temples, palaces, busy thoroughfares, craft workshops and markets. Caracol is not only the pre-eminent archaeological site in Belize but also exciting for its jungle setting and prolific birdlife.

At the ticket office, a small visitors center outlines Caracol's history and has a helpful scale model, and a new museum houses much of the sculpture found at Caracol.

A system of trails meanders through Caracol, but Plazas A and B are the most excavated. The highlight is Caana (Sky-Place), which rises from Plaza B, and at 141ft is still the tallest building in Belize! Caana underwent many construction phases until its completion in about AD800. It supports four palace compounds and three temples. High steps narrowing up to the top probably led to the royal family's compound, where Structure B-19 housed Caracol's largest and most elaborate tomb. It contained the remains of a woman, possibly Lady Batz' Ek from Calakmul, who married into Caracol's ruling dynasty in 584. Climb to the top of Caana to feast upon one of the most magnificent views in all of Belize. On the way down, don't miss the hidden tombs around the back on the left side.

South of Plaza B, the Central Acropolis was an elite residential group with palaces and shrines. To its west, Plaza A contained many stelae, some of which are still in place. Atop Structure A-2 is a replica of a stela found here in 2003 that is engraved with the longest Maya inscription found in Belize.

Structure A-6, the Temple of the Wooden Lintel, is one of the oldest buildings at Caracol. One of its lintels (the one to the left as you enter the top chamber) is original.

South of the Temple of the Wooden Lintel is the A Group Ballcourt, where the all-important Altar 21, telling us so much about Caracol's history, was found. A replica of the 'altar,' actually a ballcourt marker, sits in the middle. Further south is one of Caracol's many *aguadas* (reservoirs), and beyond that the South Acropolis, a Classic Period elite residential complex where you can enter two tombs.

🛏 Sleeping & Eating

Camping isn't permitted at Caracol. The nearest accommodations are the lodges at Mountain Pine Ridge.

ℹ Getting There & Away

Most people come on a guided tour but it's possible to drive yourself with a 4WD. Note that some car-hire companies prohibit driving this route. The road to Caracol, once the stuff of rugged travel legend, is now graded and no worse (and in many places better) than other unpaved roads in the area. All visitors – individuals and groups alike – travel to Caracol in a convoy that departs Douglas D'Silva Ranger Station in the Mountain Pine Ridge area at 9:30am every morning. On the return trip, the convoy departs at 2pm. Each car must sign in and out. The convoy is accompanied by two park ranger vehicles to ensure the safety of all passengers. This system was instituted after several reported incidents of tourist vehicles being stopped by armed robbers some years ago, but it also safeguards against breakdowns and accidents.

The 52-mile drive from San Ignacio can be done in around 2½ hours, depending on road conditions.

NORTHWEST OF SAN IGNACIO

Bullet Tree Falls

Bullet Tree Falls is a quiet and quaint little village, home to a few laid-back lodges overlooking the Mopan River. Activities include hiking in the nearby forests, river-tubing down the Mopan River and exploring the remote ruins of El Pilar.

◉ Sights

El Pilar   RUIN
(El Pilar Archaeological Reserve for Maya Flora and Fauna; Map p174; admission BZ$10; ⊙8am-4pm) Remote El Pilar, about 7 miles from Bullet Tree Falls, was occupied for at least 15 centuries, from the middle Preclassic Period (around 500 BC) to the late Classic Period (about AD 1000). Long before present-day political borders, El Pilar stretched to modern-day Pilar Poniente in Guatemala, and the two countries are now working as partners to preserve the area.

With 25 plazas and 70 major structures, El Pilar was more than three times the size of Xunantunich. Despite excavations since 1993, not much of El Pilar has been cleared; this has been to avoid the decay that often follows the clearing of ancient buildings. While appreciating El Pilar's greatness requires some imagination, this may help to give you the feeling that you're discovering the place rather than following a well-worn tourist trail.

Six archaeological and nature trails meander among the mounds. The most impressive area is Plaza Copal, which has four pyramids from 45ft to 60ft high. A partly visible Maya causeway runs 500yd west from here to Pilar Poniente.

The rough road to El Pilar heads off to the left, 400yd past the bridge in Bullet Tree Falls. Be prepared for a bumpy ride: if it's wet, a 4WD is required. If you have your own vehicle, it's an incredible, remote and rewarding place to wander on your own – you might have the entire site to yourself. Otherwise, you can hire a taxi (BZ$50 from Bullet Tree Falls) or take a tour. Local guides can be sourced through accommodation in Bullet Tree Falls or tour operators in San Ignacio.

Masewal Forest Garden   GARDENS
(admission BZ$10) Just past the village of Bullet Tree Falls, Masewal Forest Garden is an herbal and botanical garden created by renowned local healer Hilberto Cocom.

🛏 Sleeping

Bullet Tree Falls is home to a few laid-back lodges overlooking the Mopan River.

Hotel El Pilar   HOTEL $
(Map p174; ☑824-3059; http://hotelelpilar.aguallos.com; Main Rd; s/d BZ$60/95, with air-con BZ$95/120; [P][✲][🕏]) A bright-yellow two-story building right in town offers clean tiled rooms with fan, air-con, cable TV and hot showers. It's a dull choice compared with nearby lodges and cabins, but rooms are spacious and clean.

Rawspa   CABAÑAS $$
(Map p174; www.rawspabelize.com; camping per person BZ$20, cabañas BZ$110-160; [🕏]) This jungle riverside lodge is a great place to kick back and relax. Budget travelers can pitch a tent, or go for one of the cozy, well-designed en-suite *cabañas*. Next level up is the two-story riverfront '7th Heaven'; you can rent either the upper or lower level or the whole thing (BZ$240). Meals are available, along with a communal *palapa* with hammocks.

Parrot Nest Jungle Lodge   CABAÑAS $$
(Map p174; ☑669-6068, 660-6336; www.parrotnest.com; treehouse or cabin without bathroom BZ$100, q cabañas with bathroom BZ$150; [P][🕏]) Individually designed *cabañas* – some on stilts, some in trees, one in a 100ft guanacaste tree – all have sturdy wood construction, tin roofs and shared bathrooms; four larger *cabañas* have private bathrooms and inviting verandas. The lush jungly grounds are a relaxed haven for wildlife-watching, river swimming and hammock swinging. Guests enjoy free use of kayaks, tubes and bicycles.

Casa del Caballo Blanco   CABAÑAS $$
(Map p174; ☑824-2098; www.casacaballoblanco.com; Bullet Tree Rd; s/d/tr incl breakfast BZ$122/176/214; [P][🕏]) ∅ About a mile out of San Ignacio on the way to Bullet Tree Falls, the 'House of the White Horse' is a concrete yellow ecolodge set on 23 acres of rolling hills and forest overlooking the Mopan River valley. Guests stay in spacious thatched-roof *cabañas* that are sparingly decorated with hardwood furniture and Maya fabrics.

Aside from the sweeping views, the highlight of the White Horse is the impressive bird sanctuary, used for the rehabilitation and release of native species. Lunch and dinner is available BZ$24/40.

⭐ **Mahogany Hall** BOUTIQUE HOTEL $$$
(Map p174; ☎844-4047; www.mahoganyhall belize.com; d/ste BZ$470/880; ❄️🛜🏊) This beautiful three-story eight-room colonial mansion sits on the eastern bank of Mopan River, about a mile from Bullet Tree Falls village. Rooms feature dark mahogany floors and beds, classic French doors, and bathrooms with exquisite brass fixtures. All rooms have air-con and LCD-screen TV with cable. There's even a small, chic pool and a patio overlooking the rushing river.

Onsite restaurant Rico's Restaurant and Bar offers breakfast, lunch and dinner, and cocktails with a traditional colonial West Indies feel.

ℹ️ Getting There & Away

Bullet Tree Falls is 2.5 miles from San Ignacio on a good sealed road. Seven buses run daily (except Sunday) from San Ignacio (BZ$1, 15 minutes) and back. Alternatively, *colectivos* (shared taxis) run frequently between San Ignacio and Bullet Tree Falls (BZ$4). A private taxi costs BZ$20.

SOUTHWEST OF SAN IGNACIO

Southwest from San Ignacio, the George Price Hwy runs across rolling countryside toward Benque Viejo del Carmen and the Guatemalan border. There is a variety of places to stay strung out along the highway and along diversions such as Chial Rd.

👁 Sights

Belize Botanic Gardens GARDENS
(Map p174; ☎824-3101; www.belizebotanic.org; per person self-guided/guided tour BZ$15/30, child under 10yr BZ$3; ⊙7am-4pm, last entry 2:30pm) 🍃 The magnificent Belize Botanic Gardens, accessed from the grounds of duPlooy's Jungle Lodge, hold samples of roughly one-quarter of the approximately 4000 species of plants in Belize. The bountiful 45-acre zone boasts 2 miles of trails, many fruit trees and four different Belizean habitats: wetlands, rainforest, Mountain Pine Ridge (with a lookout tower) and medicinal plants of the Maya.

Two ponds attract a variety of waterfowl; Hamilton Hide allows birdwatchers to spy on various species. The garden's native orchid house is the largest of its kind in Belize. The self-guided tour includes a 56-page guidebook, while specialty tours from duPlooy's include Plants of the Maya (per person BZ$100), which starts at 6am and includes the entrance fee, shuttle from San Ignacio, a traditional knowledge tour, with lunch and lessons in cooking or crafting with a local Maya guide; and a Day at the Gardens (per person BZ$100), which includes transportation, guided tour and lunch.

Chaa Creek NATURE RESERVE
(Map p174) Set along the banks of the Macal River, beautiful Chaa Creek is a 365-acre nature reserve offering extensive facilities to lodge guests and nonguests alike. Running through the jungle just above the river, the Rainforest Medicine Trail (p183) was established by Dr Rosita Arvigo. This is just one of a series of projects that aim to spread knowledge of traditional healing methods and preserve the rainforest habitats, from which many healing plants come. It identifies about 100 medicinal plants used in traditional Maya and/or modern medicine.

Chaa Creek Natural History Center & Butterfly Farm NATURE CENTRE
(Map p174; guided tours BZ$10; ⊙tours hourly 8am-4pm) Hike up the tree-covered hillside above the Macal River to reach the Chaa Creek Natural History Center & Butterfly Farm, a small nature center with displays on Belize's flora and fauna, as well as the early Maya. The highlight is the butterfly farm, which breeds the dazzlingly iridescent blue morpho (*Morpho peleides*) for export. Tours are offered from the lodge.

🏃 Activities

Spa at Chaa Creek SPA
(Map p174; ☎824-2037; www.chaacreek.com; spa treatments BZ$50-210, 1-day package BZ$474) The luxurious hilltop Spa at Chaa Creek overlooks the Macal River and the Lodge at Chaa Creek. Treatments range from facials and manicures to aromatherapy massage.

Rainforest Medicine Trail WALKING TOUR
(Map p174; guided tours BZ$10; ⊙tours hourly 8am-5pm) Running through the jungle just above the Macal River, the Rainforest Medicine Trail was established by Dr Rosita Arvigo. This is just one of a series of projects, which aim to spread knowledge of traditional healing methods and preserve

the rainforest habitats, from which many healing plants come. It identifies about 100 medicinal plants used in traditional Maya and/or modern medicine.

Hanna's Stables HORSEBACK RIDING

(Map p174; ☑661-1536; www.hannastables.com; Mile 71 George Price Hwy; adult/child from BZ$96/74) Long-running Hanna's offers horseback-riding trips from a ride around San Lorenzo farm to the the popular half-day tour to Xunantunich (adult/child BZ$144/96).

🛏️ Sleeping

Log Cab-Inn CABAÑAS $$

(Map p174; ☑670-0711, 824-3367; www.logcabinn-belize.com; Mile 68 Western Hwy; d BZ$180, d cabañas BZ$220, 3-bedroom house BZ$560; P✳🛜🏊) The name says it all, with 20 well-designed *cabañas* built from mahogany logs and furniture crafted at the onsite carpentry workshop. All *cabañas* have air-con, hot showers and cable TV, and the whole property is set on a citrus and palm-dotted hillside. Meals are served in an open-air restaurant and bar overlooking a pool area.

Macal River Camp at Chaa Creek CABIN $$

(Map p174; Macal River Camp; cabin per person BZ$130) 🌿 A half mile from the Lodge at Chaa Creek, the Macal River Camp at Chaa Creek offers rustic screened-in wooden cabins on stilts with comfy cots inside and a shady veranda. The place is not landscaped, but rather inhabits the jungle without disturbing the environs. All cabins share clean bathrooms and hot showers. Rates include breakfast and dinner.

To reach the Camp at Chaa Creek, you'll have to park in the designated area and hike in through the jungle for about half a mile. Rates include canoeing, guided bird walks, and visits to the onsite rainforest medicine trail, natural history center and butterfly farm.

★Black Rock Lodge RESORT $$$

(Map p174; ☑834-4049, 834-4038; www.blackrocklodge.com; cabins BZ$220-370, ste BZ$430; P🛜) 🌿 High up the Macal in beautiful Black Rock Canyon, this is a stunning setting for a jungle adventure. Slate-and-wood cabins are fan-cooled and have lovely verandas overlooking the river and up toward towering cliffs. Black Rock is all about the location and activities; you can hike pristine

trails, ride a horse to Vaca Falls or canoe down the Macal River.

The inviting dining area and deck, covered by a *palapa*, is fantastic for birding, and you may also spot howler monkeys, otters and iguanas. An onsite organic farm provides produce for some of the meals served in the restaurant, and all electricity is solar and hydro powered. Black Rock Lodge is at the end of a rugged, well-signposted, 6-mile unpaved road that leaves Chial Rd 0.8 miles off the Western Hwy.

★Ka'ana Resort & Spa RESORT $$$

(Map p174; ☑824-3350; www.kaanabelize.com; Mile 69 George Price Hwy; ste from BZ$570, casitas BZ$770-900, pool villas 1-/2-bedroom BZ$1600/2400; P✳🛜🏊) 🌿 A touch of understated luxury, this unique boutique resort and spa (Ka'ana means 'Heavenly Place' in Kekchi Maya) offers luxurious rooms and *casitas* fully equipped with high-thread-count sheets, down comforters, LCD TVs and iPod docking stations. Decor is contemporary Maya, with artwork by local Belizean artists. The private pool villas offer the peak of both privacy and luxury. Private terraces overlook the lush grounds. The gourmet restaurant (breakfast BZ$16 to BZ$24, lunch and dinner BZ$40 to BZ$60) offers innovative, organic local cuisine and is open to nonguests with advanced reservations. Equally tempting is the Caribbean Spa, with treatments ranging from facials and pedicures to mud wraps and coffee massage.

Lodge at Chaa Creek ECOLODGE $$$

(Map p174; ☑824-2037; www.chaacreek.com; cottage per person BZ$360, d villa BZ$1080, ste BZ$830-1080; P@🛜🏊) 🌿 Consistently rated among the best lodges in Belize, and with good reason, Chaa Creek's tropical gardens and beautifully kept thatched cottages are spread across a gentle slope above the Macal River. Chaa Creek blossomed from an overgrown farm more than 40 years ago. The cottages, decorated with Maya textiles and local crafts, have decks, fans and private bathrooms.

For the last word in luxury, check out the three-level treetop Jacuzzi suite, the amazing garden suite and the spa villa, which has three bedrooms and sleeps up to seven people. An array of tours and activities is offered, or just laze around the infinity pool in tropical bliss. A state-of-the-art hilltop spa (p183) provides all levels of pampering.

duPlooy's Jungle Lodge RESORT $$$

(Map p174; ☑824-3101; www.duplooys.com; r/ bungalow BZ$410/520, treehouse BZ$360, ste or casita from BZ$720; ℗☺🗑) Family-run du-Plooy's occupies large and lovely grounds above the Macal River. One of the original Cayo lodges, duPlooys has a wide range of accommodations from breezy, spacious lodge rooms and private bungalows to a six-bedroom house sleeping up to 16 people. The secluded stilted treehouse is perfect for honeymooners. Rooms are fan-cooled, with private verandas overlooking the jungle grounds.

The superbly located lodge restaurant and bar serves breakfast, lunch and dinner (a light breakfast is included with room rates); a raised timber walkway leads out to fine views of the river and jungle canopy. Guests can enjoy swimming and canoeing in the river, hiking along the jungle trails, horseback riding and free visits to the adjacent Belize Botanic Gardens.

San José Succotz & Around

San José Succotz is 6.5 miles west of San Ignacio on the way to the Guatemalan border. The main reason to stop here is to visit the exceptional ruins of Xunantunich across the Mopan River, but there are a handful of other nearby attractions. Though Xunantunich can easily be done as a day trip from San Ignacio, you may prefer to use this slow-paced *barrio* as your base for exploring Cayo or along the way to Guatemala.

⊙ Sights

★Xunantunich RUIN

(Map p174; San Jose Succotz; admission BZ$10; ⊙7:30am-4pm) Set on a leveled hilltop, Xunantunich (shoo-nahn-too-neech) is one of Belize's most easily accessible and impressive Maya archaeological sites. Getting here is half the fun with a free hand-cranked cable ferry taking you (and vehicles) across the Mopan River. Xunantunich may have been occupied as early as 1000 BC but it was little more than a village. The large architecture that we see today began to be built in the 7th century AD.

From AD 700 to 850, Xunantunich was possibly politically aligned with Naranjo, 9 miles west in Guatemala. Together, they controlled the western part of the Belize River valley, although the population probably never exceeded 10,000. Xunantunich

partially survived the initial Classic Maya collapse of about AD 850 (when nearby Cahal Pech was abandoned), but was deserted by about AD 1000.

The site centers on Plazas A-2 and A-1, separated by Structure A-1. Just north of Plaza A-2, Structure A-11 and Plaza A-3 formed a residential 'palace' area for the ruling family. The dominant El Castillo (Structure A-6) rises 130ft high at the south end of Plaza A-1. El Castillo may have been the ruling family's ancestral shrine where they were buried and/or represented in sculpted friezes. Structures A-1 and A-13, at either end of Plaza A-2, were not built until the 9th century and would have had the effect of separating the ruling family from the rest of the population, possibly a response to the pressures that came with the decline of Classic Maya civilization at that time.

You can climb to the top of El Castillo to enjoy a spectacular 360-degree view. Its

Xunantunich

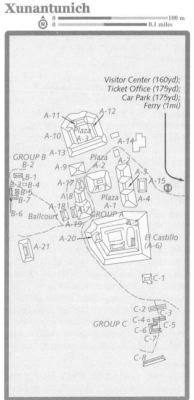

upper levels were constructed in two distinct phases. The first, built around AD800, included an elaborate plaster frieze encircling the building; the second, built around AD900, covered over most of the first and its frieze.

The frieze on the east end of the building and part of the western one have been uncovered by archaeologists; these depict a series of Maya deities, with Chaac, the rain god, probably the central figure at the east end. The friezes you see today are replicas, with the originals underneath for safekeeping.

South of El Castillo is a partly overgrown area of lesser structures (Group C) that were abandoned as the city shrank after AD900, leaving El Castillo (formerly at the center of the ancient city) on the southern edge of the occupied area.

There's a visitor center (opened in 2014) just past the ticket office. Inside are archaeological finds from the site, including pottery and jewellery, an interesting burial site and explanations of the El Castillo friezes.

To reach the ruins, take the ferry in San Jose Succotz village, then it's about 1 mile uphill to the parking lot and ticket office. Any bus from San Ignacio can drop you at the ferry point.

Tropical Wings Nature Center GARDENS
(Map p174; ☑823-2265; www.thetrekstop.com; Mile 71 Western Hwy; adult/child BZ$10/5; ☉8am-5pm; 🖐) This interactive ecology exhibit is aimed at kids, but even adults will enjoy the butterfly house and medicinal gardens. It's on the grounds of the Trek Stop just outside San Jose Succotze.

🛏 Sleeping & Eating

★**Trek Stop** LODGE, CAMPGROUND $
(Map p174; ☑823-2265; www.thetrekstop.com; Mile 71 Western Hwy; camping per person BZ$14, s/d without bathroom from BZ$30/48, d/tr/q with bathroom BZ$76/100/120; 🅿@🛜) 🌱 Trek Stop is a great option if you want to get out of San Ignacio on a budget and be close to Xunantunich. The ecolodge and backpackers' outpost consists of well-made timber cabins in a jungle setting just off the highway. There's an eco-vibe but it has mains electricity and wi-fi. Plenty of hangout space, a self-catering kitchen and a cool little restaurant.

Maya Vista RESORT $$
(Map p174; ☑823-3020, in USA 609-828-1163; www.mayavistabelize.net; Mile 70 Western Hwy; cabañas from BZ$200; 🅿❄🛜) This family-run resort is set on 70 acres of working farm and garden-filled jungle savannah with a killer view of El Castillo in Xunantunich. Eight comfortable *cabañas* have tile floors, air-con, private bathrooms with hot showers and beautiful Maya carvings. Call ahead for pickup or to make sure that someone is there to meet you when you arrive.

Benny's Kitchen BELIZEAN $
(Map p174; ☑823-2541; Mile 72 Western Hwy; meals BZ$10-16; ☉8am-9pm Mon-Thu, 8am-11pm Fri & Sat, 8am-10pm Sun; 🛜🖐) Benny's is a local institution in San Jose Succotz – the turnoff is opposite the Xunantunich ferry so it's convenient for a post-ruin meal. Local specialties include tangy *escabeche* (spicy chicken with lime and onions), fiery BBQ and cow-foot soup. The semi-open-air dining area has a bar, gift store, children's playground and an internet cafe.

Benque Viejo del Carmen

POP 6500

About a mile from the Guatemalan border and 7 miles from San Ignacio, Benque Viejo del Carmen is a small town with some interesting cultural attractions in the vicinity.

The George Price Hwy passes through, becoming George Price Blvd through town. Most places of interest, including the bus terminal, market, hotels and Centennial Park, are west of the highway and south of the Mopan River.

◉ Sights

The centerpiece of the town is Our Lady of Mount Carmel Church. On Good Friday the church hosts a dramatic procession through town, culminating in a rendition of the Passion Play. In mid-July, Benque breaks out of its tropical somnolence, when the Benque Viejo del Carmen Fiesta celebrates the town's patron saint with several days of music and fun.

Another central landmark is Centennial Park, which hosts the biennial International Festival of Culture in early December (odd years).

Poustinia Land
Art Park PUBLIC ART
(Map p174; ☑822-3532; Mile 2.5 Mollejon Rd; by appointment only BZ$20) Created by Benque brothers Luis and David Ruiz, this highly unexpected avant-garde sculpture park is one of the hidden artistic gems of Western

Belize. Set in 60 acres of rainforest about 2 miles southeast of Benque, the park displays some 35 works by Belizean and international artists. Poustinia was conceived as an environmental art project, where, once in place, the exhibits – including a car, a greenhouse and a strip of parquet flooring – become subject to the action of nature.

One piece, *Stone Labyrinth,* is set on top of an unexcavated Maya mound with views to Xunantunich. Poustinia is best enjoyed if you have time to contemplate the art and the natural environment it's set in. Allow at least two hours. Buy your admission ticket at the Benque Viejo House of Culture in Benque Viejo del Carmen (if it's the weekend, when House of Culture is closed, call the park direct). The House of Culture can give directions or arrange a taxi (BZ$25). Otherwise, turn south off George Price Blvd onto unpaved Mollejon Rd (beside the Long Luck Super Store), and drive 2 miles to the park (signposted but hard to spot).

Che Chem Ha   CAVE

(Map p174; ☑ 653-0799; Mile 8 Mollejon Rd; tour per person BZ$70) William Morales' dog was busy chasing down a *gibnut* on his lush property one day in 1989, when the dog seemingly disappeared into a rock wall. Morales pressed into the 'wall' and found it was a cave mouth; inside he came upon probably the largest collection of Maya pottery ever discovered. This was Che Chem Ha (Cave of Poisonwood Water). Morales' family has been farming this land since the 1940s, and today they also conduct tours through the cave.

The cave, about 800ft long, was used by the Maya for many centuries for food storage and rituals. Narrow passages wind past ceremonial pots, many of them intact, to a stela at the end of the tunnel. Short ladders enable you to climb up rock ledges. Bring strong shoes, water and a flashlight. There are usually two daily tours lasting about 90 minutes, following an uphill jungle walk of about 30 minutes to the cave mouth.

You can also make tour arrangements through River Rat Expeditions (p168) in San Ignacio or Benque Viejo del Carmen (BZ$170 per person).

Benque Viejo

House of Culture   MUSEUM

(Map p174; ☑ 823-2697; 64 St Joseph St; ⊙ 9am-4pm Mon-Fri) On the southeast corner of Centennial Park, Benque Viejo House of Culture hosts regular traveling exhibits of art and music and provides a space for local artists and musicians to gather and perform. For travelers it's also a de facto tourist office and a good source of local information.

🛏 Sleeping

Although not awash with accommodations, Benque has a couple of good options if you need to crash this side of Guatemala.

Benque Resort & Spa   HOTEL $

(Map p174; ☑ 632-0688; www.benque-resort.com; 22 Riverside; dm BZ$35, s/d BZ$60/80, d with air-con BZ$100; ❋ ﹫) This charming three-story home on the south bank of the Mopan River offers unexpected B&B-type amenities, including beautiful woodwork and colorful tiled bathrooms with hot showers, as well as popular budget dorm accommodation. There's a professional-quality onsite massage studio. Larger rooms offer more space and a veranda with a river view.

Maxim's Palace   HOTEL $

(Map p174; ☑ 603-8322; cayobenque@yahoo.com; 41 Church Hill St; d with fan/air-con BZ$65/85; ❋) Spacious rooms, warm hospitality and affordable rates make Maxim's a popular crashpad on the way to the Guatemalan border.

🍴 Eating

Tel-esh   CAFE $

(Map p174; ☑ 628-5938; Churchill St; meals BZ$5; ⊙ 8am-2pm; ﹫) This hole-in-the-wall cafe serves up cheap and tasty Belizean dishes, such as chicken, rice and beans, good coffee, fruit drinks and breakfasts.

Chef Charly's   AMERICAN $$

(Map p174; ☑ 660-7480; George Price Blvd; mains BZ$8-25; ⊙ 5-10pm Tue-Sun) Chef Charly's is an American-style diner, pub and beer garden on the highway through town, serving big burgers, pizzas and the like – comfort food on the way to Guatemala.

CAYO DISTRICT BENQUE VIEJO DEL CARMEN

Southern Belize

Includes ➡

Dangriga 190

Mayflower Bocawina
National Park 195

Central Cayes 195

Hopkins 199

Sittee Point 203

Maya Center 205

Cockscomb Basin
Wildlife Sanctuary . . 206

Placencia 208

Punta Gorda 218

Best Places to Eat

➡ Rumfish (p215)

➡ Jungle Farm Restaurant
(p227)

➡ Mojo Lounge & Bartique
(p215)

➡ Loggerheads Pub & Grill
(p204)

➡ Chef Rob's (p204)

Best Places to Sleep

➡ Belcampo Belize (p226)

➡ Thatch Caye Resort (p197)

➡ Maya Beach Hotel (p213)

➡ Coconut Row (p201)

➡ Tobacco Caye Paradise
(p196)

Why Go?

Southern Belize is the country's most absorbing cultural melting pot, with a strong Garifuna influence around Dangriga and Hopkins, and Belize's largest Maya population down in Toledo. Nature is rich here too, where open savannah and citrus-filled farmland give way to forested hills dotted with Maya villages and ruins.

Adventurers will find no shortage of opportunities to get off the beaten path in Toledo's jungles. Trekkers with deep pockets can choose from a number of five-star jungle lodges tucked away in remote corners, or you could stay at local guesthouses in the small villages and communities of the Deep South.

Then there's the beaches of villagey Hopkins and chilled-out Placencia, with opportunities for diving, fishing and slacking. The south also has an alluring string of offshore cays all boasting stunning coral reefs, where snorkeling, boating and diving enthusiasts can experience Belize's nautical wonders while avoiding the crowds (and the significantly higher price tags) of the Northern Cayes.

When to Go

➡ **Dec–Apr** Rainfall ends and weather is at its mildest.

➡ **May–Jul** Shoulder season sees fewer tourists and you can eat lobster starting June 15.

➡ **Aug–Sep** Dog days of summer, with hot weather, occasional showers and bargains galore.

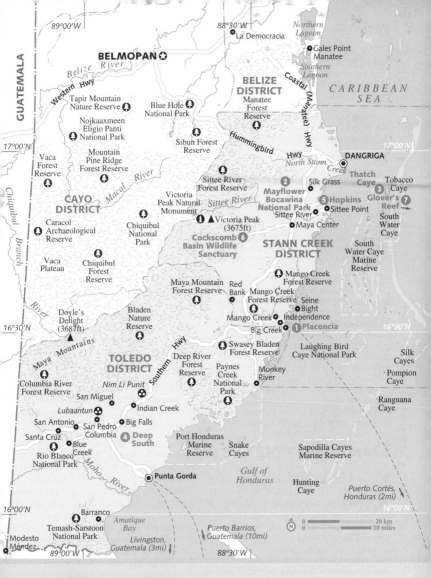

Southern Belize Highlights

1 Placencia (p208)
Eating, drinking, slacking and snorkeling at the mainland 'cay you can drive to'.

2 Mayflower Bocawina National Park (p195) Hiking, zip-lining and waterfall rappelling in the jungle.

3 Thatch Caye (p197) Living like a posh castaway on this idyllic eco island resort.

4 Deep South (p217) Immersing yourself in the Maya culture and chocolate-making in remote Toledo District.

5 Hopkins (p199) Listening to Garifuna drumming under the full moon in this laid-back beach village.

6 Cockscomb Basin Wildlife Sanctuary (p206) Mountain-biking or jaguar-spotting on the trails with a Maya guide.

7 Glover's Reef Atoll (p198) Kayaking and diving at this wonderfully remote atoll.

❶ Getting There & Away

AIR
Daily flights operate from Belize City (international and municipal airports) to Punta Gorda, via Dangriga and Placencia.

BOAT
Scheduled boat services link Placencia with Puerto Cortés in Honduras, and Punta Gorda with Puerto Barrios and Lívingston in Guatemala.

BUS
Clapped-out buses from Belize City and Belmopan head down the Hummingbird Hwy to Dangriga then on to the Southern Hwy to Independence and Punta Gorda. Less frequent services run from Dangriga to Hopkins and Placencia, and from Punta Gorda to the villages in the far south. Two main companies (James and Ritchie's) operate on the main routes and schedules fluctuate, but are reasonably frequent and cheap.

CAR & MOTORCYCLE
Two roads connect Southern Belize to the Belize District and Northern Belize: the Hummingbird Hwy (which runs from Belmopan to the start of the Southern Hwy near Dangriga) and the Coastal (Manatee) Hwy, an unpaved road that stretches from the Belize District just south of the zoo to the Hummingbird Hwy west of Dangriga (along the way stretching the very definition of the term 'highway.') Though shorter in terms of miles, unless you're planning to visit Gales Point Manatee on your way down south, the Manatee isn't worth the chiropractic trauma and some hire-car companies prohibit customers traveling on it.

STANN CREEK DISTRICT
POP 39,865

Bordering the Belize District to the north, Cayo to the west and Toledo to the south, the Stann Creek District covers the coastal towns of Dangriga, Hopkins and Placencia, some of Belize's least-visited cays and the amazing inland parks and jungle sanctuaries west of the Southern Hwy.

Dangriga
POP 39,865

Dangriga is the largest town in Southern Belize, and the spiritual capital of the country's Garifuna people. Dangriga has a funky coastal vibe about it – tumbledown and mildly untidy. Despite sharing a similar ramshackle exterior with Belize City, Dangriga doesn't have a big-city feel and is generally a safe place to explore. This is a proud, festive town, one that does its best to make the most of its vibrant Garifuna heritage, but apart from a handful of worthwhile cultural sights it's not a tourist hangout like Hopkins or Placencia, most travelers are either changing buses or getting a boat out to the Central Cayes.

The name Dangriga comes from a Garifuna word meaning 'sweet water' – the town's name having been changed from Stann Creek Town in the 1980s. This is the birthplace of *punta* rock (a fusion of acoustic Garifuna and electric instruments), and home to a number of notable Garifuna artists, artisans and festivals.

◉ Sights

Central Dangriga is an interesting place to wander, but its best sights are a little way west of the town center.

Pen Cayetano Studio Gallery　　GALLERY
(☑628-6807; www.cayetano.de; 3 Aranda Cres; adult/student BZ$5/3; ◐9am-5pm Mon-Fri, Sat & Sun by appointment) Renowned throughout Belize for his art and music, Pen Cayetano's workshop and gallery displays Garifuna artifacts and crafts. It also has works of art and music by Pen, and the textile artwork of his wife, Ingrid, available for sale. Among the most unusual items are drums made of turtle shells, which sell for around BZ$50.

There are also occasional musical shows by Pen and drum workshops led by local drummers. The gallery is west of town down a small side street.

Gulisi Garifuna Museum　　MUSEUM
(☑669-0639; www.ngcbelize.org; Hummingbird Hwy, Chuluhadiwa Park; admission BZ$10; ◐10am-5pm Mon-Fri, 8am-noon Sat) This museum, operated by the National Garifuna Council (NGC), is a must for anyone interested in the vibrant Garifuna people. The museum is 2 miles out of town; ask any bus heading out of Dangriga to drop you here or hire a bicycle. It brings together artifacts, pictures and documents on Garifuna history and culture, including an exhibit on the life and music of the late Garifuna musician Andy Palacio. A free guided tour is included with admission.

Marie Sharp's Factory　　FACTORY
(☑532-2087; www.mariesharps-bz.com; 1 Melinda Rd; ◐7am-4pm Mon-Fri) The super-hot bottled sauces that adorn tables all over Belize and beyond are made from habanero peppers here at Marie Sharp's Factory, 8 miles northwest of town on Melinda Rd. Free tours are usually offered during business hours (by

Dangriga

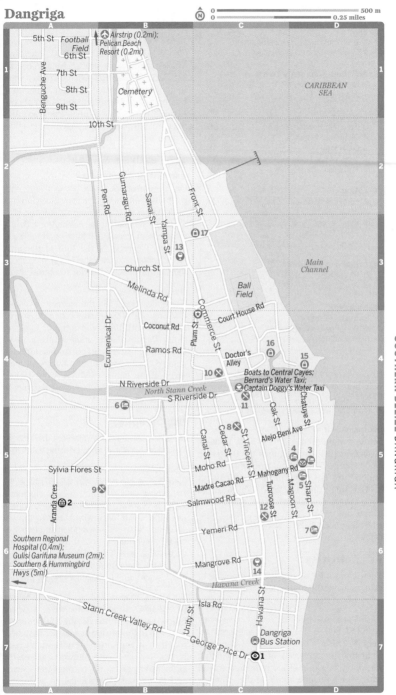

Dangriga

◎ **Sights**
1 Drums of Our Father's Monument C7
2 Pen Cayetano Studio Gallery..............A5

➕ **Activities, Courses & Tours**
Belize Kayak Rentals ....(see 7)
Island Expeditions ....(see 7)

🛏 **Sleeping**
3 Bonefish Hotel D5
4 Chaleanor Hotel D5
5 D's Hostel D5
6 Jungle Huts Hotel B4
7 Ruthie's Cabanas D6

🍴 **Eating**
8 Family Restaurant C5
9 Ivy's..B5
10 King Burger C4
11 Riverside Café C4
12 Steph's C6

🍷 **Drinking & Nightlife**
13 Roxy Club B3
14 Wadini Shed C6

🛍 **Shopping**
15 Austin Rodriguez D4
16 Dangriga Central Market C4
17 Marie Sharp's Factory Store..............C3

advance reservation), and the factory shop sells hot sauces and jams at outlet prices. If you can't make it to the factory, Marie Sharp's also has a store (p194) in Dangriga.

**Drums of Our
Father's Monument** LANDMARK
(George Price Dr) This monument in the traffic circle south of Dangriga's main bus station underscores the importance of percussion in Garifuna (and Belizean) life, with its large bronze representations of ritual dügü drums and *sisira* (maracas). It was sculpted by Stephen Okeke, a Nigerian resident of Dangriga.

🏃 Activities

There's not a lot of scope for swimming in Dangriga, but the southern cays and reef are a short boat ride away.

Island Expeditions WATER SPORTS
(☑ in USA 800-667-1630; www.islandexpeditions. com) 🚣 This ecologically minded Canadian company runs a variety of tours including weeklong kayaking expeditions and inland trips, which include hiking in the jungle or

visiting Maya ruins. Tours also depart from Belize City.

Belize Kayak Rentals KAYAKING
(☑ 522-3328, in USA 800-667-1630; www.belize kayaking.com; single/double kayak per day BZ$70/110, per week BZ$420/700) If you want to go it alone on your kayaking expedition, this branch of Island Expeditions rents out kayaks from its base camp in Dangriga. Also offers weekly packages, which include a boat charter out to the cays.

🎉 Festivals & Events

Garifuna Settlement Day CULTURAL
On November 19, Dangriga explodes with celebrations to mark the arrival of Garifuna in Dangriga in 1832. Dangrigans living elsewhere flock home for the celebrations. Drumming, dancing and drinking continue right through the night of the 18th to the 19th, while canoes re-enact the beach landing in the morning. Book ahead for accommodation.

Día de los Reyes CULTURAL
(Three Kings' Day) On the nearest weekend to January 6, Dangrigans celebrate Día de los Reyes with the *wanaragua* or *jonkonu* (John Canoe) dance: male dancers wearing bright feather-and-paper headdresses, painted masks representing European men, and rattling bands of shells around their knees move from house to house dancing to Garifuna drums.

🛏 Sleeping

Decent accommodation choices are slim in Dangriga. Book way ahead during festivals.

D's Hostel HOSTEL $
(☑ 502-3324; 1 Sharp St; dm/d BZ$25/100; @ 🛜) Dangriga's one and only hostel (formerly Val's) is a local institution. A large porch faces a desolate park with views to the sea and leads to an eight-bed dorm and two spacious, hotel-quality private rooms sleeping up to three, with TV and fridge.

There's a communal kitchen as well as movies, wi-fi and luggage lockers for guests.

Ruthie's Cabanas GUESTHOUSE $
(☑ 502-3184; 31 Southern Foreshore; s cabaña BZ$54, additional person BZ$10) Ruthie's comprises four tumbledown, seaside, thatched-roof huts on the north side of Havana Creek. It has hot and cold showers, an earthy ambience, plenty of coconut-tree shade and home-cooked meals for an additional charge.

Jungle Huts Hotel　　　　　HOTEL $$
(☑ 665-8966, 522-0185; junglehutsresort@gmail.com; 4 Ecumenical Dr; d from BZ$86, cabaña & ste BZ$158; P❄️🌐) Philip Usher's riverside resort is just a little way out of town but its location is a blessing, offering a peaceful (even jungle) vibe away from the Commercial Rd scene. There are good-value rooms, suites and three *cabañas*, all with one double and one single bed, en-suite bathrooms with showers, and air-con. Only suites and *cabañas* have TV with cable.

There are free canoes for river paddles and bikes for rent, and the garden restaurant serves Belizean food with advance notice.

Bonefish Hotel　　　　　HOTEL $$
(☑ 522-2243; www.bluemarlinlodge.com/bonefish-hotel; 15 Mahogany Rd; r BZ$180-210; P❄️🌐) Upper floors are not without charm, but the ones on the lower floor are darker and somewhat less cheery, though no less functional. All rooms have two double beds, fan, air-con and cable TV. Pay a bit extra for breakfast or a lot more for full board.

Pelican Beach Resort　　　　　RESORT $$
(☑ 522-2044; www.pelicanbeachbelize.com; 1st St; s/d with fan BZ$188/247, with air-con BZ$210/270, ste s/d BZ$235/293; P❄️@🌐) The Pelican is the only 'upmarket' choice in Dangriga but still it has a faded 1950s air about it. The hotel is close to the airport and has clean, but uninspiring rooms with TV, air-con and colorful local artwork. Most rooms have beach-facing porches with hammocks.

The beachside restaurant has a good vibe and sea views, though most of the dishes are pricey for Dangriga.

Chaleanor Hotel　　　　　HOTEL $$
(☑ 522-2587; www.chaleanorhotel.com; 35 Magoon St; s/d/tr/q BZ$116/165/198/227, without bathroom BZ$33/55/73; P❄️🌐) This old-style family-run hotel straddles the budget divide with clean air-con rooms of a midrange standard (upstairs rooms have views). The cheaper units without bathroom are fairly rundown but would suit committed budget travelers. The owners can help you arrange any trips or boat charters.

✖️ Eating

Most of Dangriga's restaurants appear to be in an advanced state of decay, but the food is pretty good and even dodgy-looking streetside shacks on the main drag serve up decent stews, fish, rice and beans, BBQ and Garifuna dishes. Dangriga also has several supermarkets.

Riverside Café　　　　　SEAFOOD $
(S Riverside Dr; mains BZ$8-15; ⊙ 7am-9pm) Just east of the Stann Creek bridge, this cafe is the place to meet fishers and the boat captains who offer tours and transport to the outlying cays. The food is inexpensive, the fish is always fresh and the Belikin is cold.

Steph's　　　　　BELIZEAN $
(St Vincent St; mains BZ$5-10; ⊙ 7am-10pm Wed-Mon) There's no menu, but tasty Belizean classics such as baked pork or chicken with rice and beans are a steal at this clean shack restaurant on the main street.

King Burger　　　　　BELIZEAN $
(Commerce St; dishes BZ$4-15; ⊙ 7am-3pm & 6-10pm Mon-Sat) Serves reliably fresh breakfasts of eggs, beans and fry-jacks, as well as hamburgers and plates of fried shrimp. The coffee is instant, but juices are fresh.

Ivy's　　　　　CHINESE $$
(☑ 522-3922; Ecumenical Dr; mains BZ$10-24; ⊙ 10:30am-11pm; ❄️) Next to the huge Family City Supermarket west of the center, this reliable Chinese place has a bright air-conditioned dining room and a popular takeout window on the side. Veg dishes, seafood, chow mein and noodle dishes are served in generous portions.

Family Restaurant　　　　　CHINESE $$
(Commerce St; mains BZ$5-20; ⊙ 10am-11pm) This clean, fun and efficient Chinese restaurant serves both Sino-Belizean fare and dishes catering to the tastes of local Chinese who still remember what Chinese food is supposed to taste like. Check out the swinging tables and chairs in the back.

🍷 Drinking & Nightlife

Dangriga's main-street bars can get lively, especially during festivals when Garifuna drumming takes center stage.

Wadini Shed　　　　　BAR
(St Vincent St; ⊙ 4pm-midnight) One thatched roof, no walls and a mainly local clientele make this a great spot to have a stout and get down with Dangriga culture.

Roxy Club　　　　　BAR
(Commerce St; ⊙ 5pm-late Tue-Sun) At the north end of Commerce St, the Roxy is an unassuming but enduringly popular bar.

🛍 Shopping

Marie Sharp's Factory Store FOOD
(🗹 522-2370; 3 Pier Rd; ⊘ 8am-noon & 1-5pm Mon-Fri) In an unsigned white building down a lane off the main street, this is Dangriga's outlet store for Marie Sharp's iconic hot sauces.

Austin Rodriguez ARTS
This master artisan carves Garifuna drums from mahogany, cedar and mayflower wood in his outdoor workshop by the water's edge (southeast of Dangriga Central Market). Though Austin's drums are sold all over Belize, you can buy them straight from the maker himself. Mr Rodriguez can usually be found working away and is happy to talk about the drum-making process.

Dangriga Central Market MARKET
(behind Doctor's Alley; ⊘ 6am-4pm) The Dangriga Central Market is a microcosm of Dangriga society with traders selling shoes, clothing, crockery and Maya crafts alongside farmers and fishmongers.

ℹ Information

Belize Bank (St Vincent St), **Scotia Bank** (St Vincent St) and **First Caribbean International Bank** (Commerce St) all have 24-hour ATMs that accept international Visa, MasterCard, Plus and Cirrus cards. The latter charges an outrageous US$5 fee for transactions.

Immigration Office (🗹 522-3412; St Vincent St; ⊘ 8am-5pm Mon-Thu, 8am-4:30pm Fri) Offers 30-day visa extension stamps for BZ$50.

Post Office (🗹 522-2035; Mahogany Rd) Next to the Bonefish Hotel.

Southern Regional Hospital (🗹 522-2078; Stann Creek Valley Rd) Good-standard public hospital on the outskirts of town.

ℹ Getting There & Away

AIR
From Dangriga airport (DGA), **Maya Island Air** (🗹 522-2659; www.mayaislandair.com) and **Tropic Air** (🗹 226-2012) fly direct to Belize City, Placencia and Punta Gorda several times daily.

BOAT
Dangriga is the departure point for trips to Belize's Central Cayes, as well as for chartered trips along the coast. The best spot to arrange boat transport is outside the Riverside Café on South Riverside Dr. Stop by before 9am, or the afternoon before, to check when boats will be leaving. The more people you can get for one trip (within reason), the cheaper it works out per person.

Boats usually go daily to Tobacco Caye (BZ$40 per person) but can also be chartered to Thatch Caye, South Water Caye and Glover's Reef; the upmarket lodges on these islands will organize your boat for you.

Captain Doggy (🗹 627-7443; captaindoggy@gmail.com) has a colorful 25ft boat that travels between Dangriga and all of the cays. He also does custom day trips with spearfishing, island stops and lunch for BZ$100.

Bernard's Water Taxi (🗹 633-0160; dalila56@yahoo.com) also offers trips out to all the cays, as well as fishing and other privately chartered trips.

BUS
A major transit point for all bus companies servicing southern Belize, Dangriga's main **bus station** (St Vincent St) is near the roundabout at the southern end of town. There are frequent buses to Belize City (regular/express BZ$10/12, two hours), Belmopan (BZ$6, 1½ hours), Punta Gorda (BZ$13, 2½ hours), and San Ignacio (BZ$11, 2¼ hours), and a handful of direct services to Hopkins (BZ$5, 30 minutes) and Placencia (BZ$10, 1½ hours).

HOT SAUCE QUEEN

If there's one thing that defines Belize from a culinary perspective, it's Marie Sharp's hot sauces. On every table in every restaurant and cafe across the country, you'll find at least two, maybe three, bottles of Marie's iconic habanero chili sauces. From mild green pepper to eye-watering 'Belizean Heat', Marie has managed to occupy a national market more successfully than any product since Coca-Cola.

Marie started out in 1980 bottling peppers and preserves from her farm for friends and family. Encouraged by positive feedback and a high demand for good sauce, she went into business and the rest is history. Today, the factory (p190), about 1 mile off the Hummingbird Hwy and 8 miles from Dangriga, offers tours, tastings and sales, and exports sauces and preserves around the world. Even if you curl your tongue at spicy hot sauce, it's a unique opportunity to see a family business that started around a cooking pot and turned into a national institution.

Mayflower Bocawina National Park

Easily reached from Hopkins or Dangriga, this beautiful 11-sq-mile park offers high-adrenaline adventure activities or plain old-fashioned DIY jungle hiking to mountains, waterfalls, swimming holes and small Maya sites. It's remote enough that you might find yourself alone (apart from the birdlife) on some spectacular walking trails

◉ Sights & Activities

Mayflower Bocawina National Park   NATIONAL PARK
(admission BZ$10; ⊘ 8am-4pm) This beautiful 11-sq-mile park of jungle, mountains, waterfalls, walking trails, swimming holes and small Maya sites lies about 16 miles southwest of Dangriga and 12 miles northwest of Hopkins. The walks here are at least as good as the trails most people do at nearby Cockscomb Basin, and you'll encounter far fewer tourists. You'll see lots of birds, and the park is home to troops of black howler monkeys.

A 4-mile unpaved access road heads west from the Southern Hwy, 2 miles north of Silk Grass village, to the park visitors center, where you pay the park fees. Here you'll also find the partly excavated Mayflower Maya site, with two pyramids and nine other structures, occupied in the late 9th and early 10th centuries. The Antelope Trail leads down over Silk Grass Creek to the larger, unexcavated, partly tree-covered Maintzunun temple mound, 250yd away (built around AD800). Continue on a further 1.7 miles – steep and strenuous in places – to the beautiful 100ft-high Antelope Falls, with great panoramas. The less demanding Bocawina Hill Trail (1.4 miles) leads to the lower and upper Bocawina Falls: there's a cool swimming pool at the foot of the 50ft upper falls. Branch trails, for which a guide is recommended, lead to Peck Falls and Big Drop Falls.

Bocawina Adventures   ADVENTURE TOUR
(☑ 670-8019; www.bocawinaadventures.com) At the Mayflower Bocawina National Park this outfit, based at the Rainforest Resort, features Belize's longest zip-line (BZ$130), and rappelling down either the 1500ft Antelope Falls (BZ$250) or the smaller 125ft Bocawina Falls (BZ$130). Also available are hiking, birdwatching tours, night flying (zip-lining at night) or combination packages.

🛏 Sleeping & Eating

Bocawina Rainforest Resort   RESORT $$$
(☑ 670-8019, USA 1-844-894-2311; www.bocawina. com; d BZ$238, cabaña BZ$358, ste BZ$438; P 🛜)
⬧ Within Mayflower Bocawina National Park, this ecoresort is the base for some of the most exciting adventure activities in Southern Belize. Accommodation ranges from six lodge rooms with timber floors and mountain views, to traditional thatch *cabañas,* to spacious suites with separate lounge and jungle views. All have hot showers and wi-fi, and breakfast is included.

Power is solar and hydroelectric, and the vibe is rustic ecochic. There are lots of easily accessible jungle walks around the property and a good restaurant onsite.

Wild Fig Restaurant   CAFE $$
(☑ 670-8019; Mayflower Bocawina National Park; BZ$18-35; ⊘ 11am-3pm & 6-10pm; 🛜) This casual screened-in thatch restaurant and bar on the grounds of Bocawina Rainforest Resort is a good place to stop for lunch after walking in the national park or rappelling down local waterfalls. Lunch features tacos, burgers and sandwiches, while dinner is a changing menu of Belizean, Creole and BBQ grill dishes using locally sourced ingredients.

ℹ Information

Visitors Center (⊘ 8am-4pm) At the entrance to the Mayflower Bocawina National Park, this is where you pay the park entry fee and pick up information on walks and activities.

Central Cayes

Less crowded, lesser known and often less costly than the cays in the north, the Central Cayes – most of them private islands – off Belize's central coast are smack in the middle of some of the country's most amazing diving, snorkeling and fishing sites.

ℹ Getting There & Away

In most cases the resorts will arrange boat transfers. The Central Cayes are best reached from Dangriga, but charters also run from Hopkins and Placencia.

Tobacco Caye

Sitting right on the barrier reef, 12 miles from Dangriga, tiny Tobacco Caye is the budget destination among the Central Cayes – and it shows. While there are some bright new *cabañas*, many of the timber buildings on the island are in an advanced state of dilapidation. Mainly composed of sand, palm trees and guesthouses, and at just 200yd long and 100yd wide, the cay can be walked around in 10 minutes.

Part of the South Water Caye Marine Reserve, Tobacco Caye is a fabulous place for snorkeling, diving, fishing or hanging out on a hammock. Sociable and friendly, it's ideal for travelers on a limited budget looking for that *Gilligan's Island* experience.

Boat transfers operate out of Dangriga every morning (BZ$40 per person), or ask your accommodation to arrange transport.

🛏 Sleeping & Eating

While there are half a dozen places to stay on the island, it's best not to show up looking for a bed; book ahead.

Tobacco Caye Paradise   CABIN $

(☑ 532-2101; http://tobaccocaye.com; cabaña per person BZ$70; 🛜) This is the best deal on Tobacco. Paradise has six lovely *cabañas* perched on stilts over the water with private baths and cold-water showers. Verandas, with chairs and hammock, look out towards the reef where the water is shallow enough to wade right in. Meals are served in the classroom-like dining room (breakfast/

lunch/dinner BZ$20/20/30). Wi-fi is BZ$5 per day, per cabin.

Fairweather Place   HOTEL $

(☑ 802-0030, 660-6870; hevf7@yahoo.com; per person BZ$30) The cheapest of the Tobacco Caye guesthouses, Fairweather has four rooms in a rickety wooden building, each with one double bed and fan. There's a shared bathroom with a cold-water shower, and a sea-facing porch with a couple of chairs and hammocks out the front. The first-floor kitchen is open for use by guests; bring supplies.

Joe Jo's by the Reef   CABIN $$

(☑ 601-1647; www.joejosbythereef.com; r & cabaña incl meals per person BZ$150-180; 🛜) The flashiest and priciest *cabañas* on Tobacco Caye are right here. The seven sturdy, brightly painted cabins come with private bathroom, fans, balcony deck and, in most cases, clear ocean views. There are four more rooms just back from the beach in the main building. Hot and cold water, free wi-fi, kayak rental, transfer and three meals a day.

Tobacco Caye Lodge   RESORT $$

(☑ 532-2033; www.tclodgebelize.com; per person incl meals BZ$110) This lime-green waterfront place has six simple but clean, fairly spacious rooms with private bathrooms, fans and inviting verandas. There's generator

---

THE CAY THAT'S RIGHT FOR YOU

Stann Creek District has offshore cays to suit every vacationer's need.

Tobacco Cay

Pros Cheapest of the southern cays to get to and stay on. You'll never be lonely on Tobacco Caye and it won't bust your budget.

Cons With half a dozen accommodations in a small space, Tobacco can feel a bit cramped and cheap. Also, the coral around the island isn't as healthy as it once was.

South Water Caye

Pros Excellent diving and snorkeling opportunities and great space-to-resort ratio make this a good choice for visitors looking for a sublime island experience.

Cons Lack of cheap accommodations keeps South Water Caye off-limits to travelers on a budget.

Glover's Reef

Pros The best of both worlds, Glover's is surrounded by amazing coral, provides access to good dive sites, and the resorts along the atoll offer the full spectrum of budget accommodations.

Cons The boat ride out takes between 1½ and three hours. Glover's remoteness makes it a less-than-ideal choice for those looking to spend just a couple of days – most packages are a minimum of one week.

power in the evenings. Nonguests can dine here with advance notice.

Reef's End Lodge LODGE **$$$**
(☑ 676-8363, 522-2419; www.reefsendlodge.com; 3-night s/d BZ$546/780, beachfront cabaña BZ$630/900) At the south end of the island, Reef's End has lodge-style rooms plus a couple of ramshackle *cabañas*, available on all-inclusive packages for a minimum of three nights. It's pretty simple stuff for the price, but the over-water restaurant is the best on the island.

South Water Caye

Three times as big as Tobacco Caye, but with half as many resorts, the 15-acre South Water Caye has excellent sandy beaches and an interesting combination of palm and pine trees. Like Tobacco Caye, it's part of the South Water Caye Marine Reserve. A seemingly bottomless 8-mile-long underwater cliff on the ocean side of the reef makes for excellent wall diving, usually with good visibility, and there's a dive resort on the island. Snorkelers will find healthy coral reefs in the lagoon. Trips to Belize's offshore atolls are possible from here and there's excellent fishing, too. Bring insect repellent; the sand flies are voracious.

🛏 Sleeping & Eating

⭐ **Pelican Beach Resort** CABINS **$$$**
(☑ 522-2044; www.pelicanbeachbelize.com; s/d incl meals BZ$460/700, s/d cottages incl meals BZ$650/880; 🛜) 🏊 The solar-powered Pelican's eight comfortable wooden cottages at the south of the island are well spaced among the palms, giving a feeling of seclusion. Heron's Hideaway is the pick of the bunch, with a big porch and two hammocks looking out to the reef. The main building (once an island retreat for Belize's Sisters of Mercy) houses the dining room and five guest rooms opening onto long verandas. If you want to dive from here, book at least a week ahead. Kayaks are available free of charge.

IZE Belize RESORT, CABINS **$$$**
(☑ 580-2000, in USA 1-508-655-1461; www.ize belize.com; packages per person per night from BZ$320; 🛜) Massachusetts-based IZE (International Zoological Expeditions) operates this site in the middle of the island with dorms (primarily for students) and beautiful, spacious log-cabin shoreline cottages for other guests. The main building incorporates

a field station, an attractive wood-furnished dining room and bar.

The basic package (minimum three nights) includes meals, transfers to/from Dangriga, snorkeling and sightseeing boat trips, as well as use of kayaks and sports equipment.

Blue Marlin Lodge RESORT **$$$**
(☑ 522-2242, in USA 800-798-1558; www.blue marlinlodge.com; r from BZ$420, cottage BZ$510; ❄🛜) At the northern end of South Water Caye, Blue Marlin is a popular dive destination with its own full-service PADI dive center. The resort has a series of *cabañas* and rather odd (but cool-looking) igloo-shaped 'dome cottages', as well as free kayaks and an excellent over-water restaurant serving fresh seafood. Nonguests should call ahead for dining reservations.

The complicated rate sheet published on their website gives the lowdown on the dozens of offered packages, including longer stays, meals, transits and diving. The Dangriga office is inside the Bonefish Hotel (p193).

Thatch Caye & Plum Caye

Thatch Caye, and neighboring Plum Caye, are stunning twin private islands with an air of exclusivity and a luxury-meets-castaway vibe. Activities on offer at the resorts include swimming, diving, snorkeling, fishing and kayaking, or just hanging out on the islands' white sands.

🛏 Sleeping & Eating

Thatch Caye and Coco Plum resorts both have excellent restaurants and bars. Day-trippers can eat here but advanced reservations are recommended.

⭐ **Thatch Caye Resort** RESORT **$$$**
(☑ 603-2414; www.thatchcaye.com; all-inclusive d BZ$1190; ❄🛜) 🏊 The most luxurious of the South Caye private island resorts, Thatch Caye has 13 beautiful thatched-roof, air-conditioned *cabañas* built from local hardwoods and set on stilts over the ocean, connected by paths winding through native mangroves. The resort features an excellent social-hub bar-restaurant (meals and drinks included), the over-water Starfish Bar and a dazzling array of activities.

For all its luxury, Thatch has a strong eco philosophy with power generated from solar and wind sources, with a single diesel generator kept as backup. Nonguests can dine here with 24 hours' notice.

Coco Plum Caye
CABINS $$$

(☑1-800-763-7360; www.cocoplumcay.com; 4-day package from BZ$2480; ❄ ☎) Coco Plum is the laid-back but luxurious little sister to flashy Thatch Caye, just a Frisbee throw away – you can wade across at low tide and mingle with your neighbors. The colorful Caribbean-style *cabañas* offer air-conditioning and sea views. All packages – and there are many variations from honeymoon to diving adventures – include meals, full use of the private island and transportation from Dangriga.

Glover's Reef

If you're serious about getting away from it all, Glover's Reef is the place. Named after the 18th-century English pirate John Glover (who attacked Spanish merchant ships from here), the atoll is 16 miles long and 7 miles wide, and is pretty much as far from mainland Belize as you can get. Lying like a string of pearls in a blue sea, Glover's consists of half a dozen small cays of white sand, palm trees, and a handful of low-key resorts, diving and kayaking bases.

🏃 Activities

The reef's unique position atop a submerged mountain ridge on the edge of the continental shelf makes it home to some of the world's finest dive sites. Divers here regularly see spotted eagle rays, southern stingrays, turtles, moray eels, dolphins, several shark species, large groupers, barracudas and many tropical reef fish. In the shallow central lagoon, 700 coral patches brim with marine life – brilliant for snorkelers. Turtles lay eggs on the beaches between June and August. Glover's Reef is included in the Belize Barrier Reef World Heritage listing, and it's also a marine reserve with a no-take zone covering most of the southern third of the atoll. As a protected marine reserve, guests at all resorts pay a park fee of BZ$30 per week.

Slickrock Adventures
WATER SPORTS

(☑in USA 800-390-5715; www.slickrock.com; 5-/6-/9-night package US$1395/1565/2250) These top-class water-sports holidays are based on Long Caye, Glover's Reef, and combine sea kayaking, surf kayaking, windsurfing, snorkeling and diving. Accommodations are in stilt *cabañas*, and packages include all meals and drinks.

🛏 Sleeping & Eating

Glover's Long Caye is home to camps and resorts for North American–based Slickrock Adventures and Island Expeditions (p192). Resorts have restaurants and meals are usually included in the package. For snacks and alcohol, stock up on the mainland.

★ Glover's Atoll Resort
CABINS $

(☑520-5016; www.glovers.com.bz; per person per week campsite BZ$198, dm & onsite tents BZ$298, cabins BZ$498-598; ☎ ⛵) Occupying the Glover's northeast cay, this ramshackle backpackers' paradise is the perfect, affordable island getaway. The private 10-acre island has 16 cabins (over the water and on the beach), a basic dorm and eight private campgrounds. Most travelers take the weekly deal, which includes boat transfers from Sittee River, but nightly 'drop-in' rates are also available, starting from BZ$24 for camping.

There's an open-air thatched restaurant (breakfast/lunch/dinner BZ$24/24/36), or you can make your own meals – a few basic groceries plus fish, lobster and conch are available on the island, but the rest (including any alcohol) you must bring over yourself. Activities on the island include a PADI dive center, snorkeling, kayaking, catamarans and fishing, all at an additional cost. The free transfer leaves from Glover's Guest House (p205) in Sittee River at 9am every Sunday, returning the following Saturday or you can charter a boat for BZ$700 one way (up to six people).

Off the Wall
RESORT $$$

(☑532-2929; www.offthewallbelize.com; Long Caye; per person per week from BZ$2990; ☎) 🐚 On beautiful Long Caye, close to the reef, the solar- and wind-powered Off the Wall is a small and intimate PADI five-star island resort offering a variety of weeklong packages. Rates include meals and non-alcoholic drinks, use of kayaks and stand-up paddleboards, a couple of snorkeling trips and transfer. Scuba diving and gear rental (for diving, fishing or snorkeling) are extra.

The five cozy oceanfront *cabañas* come with queen-size beds with Egyptian high-thread linens, verandas and hammocks. Other touches include yoga mats, and the owners strive to make this a personalized and intimate island experience. Boat transfers are from Dangriga every Saturday.

Isla Marisol Resort
RESORT $$$

(☑532-2399, 610-4204, in USA 866-990-9904; www.islamarisolresort.com; cabañas 3-/4-/7-night per person incl meals BZ$1750/2150/3050; ❄ ☎) The atoll's 18-acre southernmost island (called Usher Caye by some) is home to Glover's most upscale resort. Eleven sturdy and comfortably furnished wooden cabins with zinc roofs, hot showers, fans and air conditioners are laid out along the island, while two family-size reef houses provide accommodations for six closer to the water.

There's also an excellent restaurant and a bar on stilts over the water. Prices include boat transfers to and from Dangriga, with boats running on Wednesday and Saturday. Activities at Marisol include snorkeling, kayaking, sunbathing, fishing and, of course, diving.

Hopkins

POP 1500

The friendly, slightly scruffy, coastal village of Hopkins attracts travelers looking to soak up sea breezes and Garifuna culture. It's an unpretentious place to meet other travelers and makes a good base for explorations to the cays, reefs and islands to the east, and the jungles, mountains and parks to the west.

Founded in 1942 by people from Newtown, a nearby Garifuna settlement that was destroyed by a hurricane, the village is named for Frederick Charles Hopkins, a Catholic priest who (perhaps as a cautionary tale to future travelers) drowned in the waters here in 1923.

Hopkins stretches about 1.5 miles along the coast and is divided by the 4.5-mile sealed Hopkins Rd from the Southern Hwy into North Side and South Side. Streets in the village are unpaved.

Activities & Tours

Hopkins is a fine place from which to access some of Belize's best dive sites. The barrier reef is less than a 40-minute boat ride away, and Glover's Reef is about 90 minutes on a fast skiff. Diving and snorkeling can be arranged through several outfits in Hopkins and nearby Sittee Point.

Lebeha   DRUMMING
(☑665-9305; North Side; lessons per hr BZ$30) Set up by local drummer Jabbar Lambey and his wife Dorothy, Lebeha functions both as an educational and cultural center for locals and as a general happening spot for travelers interested in Garifuna drumming. Lessons for individuals and groups are available, and there's drumming most nights

Hopkins & Sittee Point

SOUTHERN BELIZE HOPKINS

Hopkins & Sittee Point

Activities, Courses & Tours
1 Belize Underwater B7
2 Happy Go Luckie Tours........................A3
3 Hopkins Standup Paddleboard A6
Lebeha ....(see 29)
4 Motorbike Rentals & Alternate
Adventures..A3

Sleeping
5 All Seasons Guest House A5
6 Beaches & Dreams...............................B7
7 Buttonwood Lodge A2
8 Castille Beach A5
9 Coconut Row Guesthouse A3
10 Cosmopolitan Guesthouse A7
11 Funky Dodo A2
12 Hamanasi Adventure & Dive
Resort B6
13 Hopkins Inn A3
14 Jaguar Reef Lodge & Spa....................B7
15 Jungle Jeanie by the Sea B6
16 Latitude Adjustment A5
Lebeha ....(see 29)
17 Parrot Cove Lodge B7
18 Solution Guest House A2
19 Tipple Tree Beya....................................A4
20 Windschief Cabanas.............................A3

Eating
Barracuda Bar & Grill .... (see 6)
Chef Rob's ....(see 17)
21 Driftwood Beach Bar & Pizza
Shack B1
22 Frog's Point Cafe A5
23 Gecko's..A2
24 Loggerheads Pub & Grill A7
Love on the Rocks ....(see 17)
25 Sandy Beach Bar &
Restaurant..B5
26 Swinging Armadillo..............................B2
27 Thongs Cafe A3

Drinking & Nightlife
28 Herbal Healer Tea Bar A3
Windschief ....(see 20)

Entertainment
29 Lebeha...A1

Shopping
30 David's Woodcarving............................A4
31 Sew Much Hemp A5

from 7pm. Full-moon drumming parties are an especially great reason to visit.

Woogie Buggy BUGGY RENTAL
(☑ 665-5533; www.woogiebuggy.com; per hr/day BZ$30/130) Hire one of these go-anywhere dune buggies for a fun spin around the Hopkins region. Minimum two hours.

Happy Go Luckie Tours BOAT TOUR
(☑ 635-0967; www.hgltours.com; half-/full-day charters BZ$470/700) Happy Go Luckie offers custom half- and full-day boat charters for up to five people, including snorkeling, fishing and island-hopping. Also does transfers to the southern cays and Glover's Reef. The office is in Hopkins village but the boats leave from Sittee Point marina.

Seemore Adventures DIVING, SNORKELING
(☑ 602-4985, 667-6626; http://seemore adventures.com) Run by local dive instructor Elmar 'Boo' Avila, Seemore offers customized snorkeling, fishing or just cruisey trips out to the reef, as well as scuba-diving trips.

Outback Trails HORSEBACK RIDING
(☑ 650-9083; www.outbacktrails.com; Mile 13 Southern Hwy, Kendal; ☺ trail rides 8.30am & 2pm) Trail rides head out from this friendly ranch through the forest and make a stop at the Sittee River. Suitable for riders of all abilities from seven years old. It just off the Southern Hwy about 10 miles from Hopkins.

Under the Sun SAILING
(☑ 970-270-3556; www.underthesunbelize.com; 8-day trip per person BZ$4400) The Lodge Hopper's Special is an outstanding eight days of Caribbean cruising on an 18ft Hobie Cat, with plenty of stops for snorkeling, fishing, kayaking and hammock-based relaxing. Instruction is provided for novice sailors. Accommodations in lodges on the cays, food, guide and support boat are all included in the price.

Lloyd Nunez FISHING
(☑ 662-0873, 603-2970) Lloyd is a professional fly-fisherman who leads expeditions into both the inner and outer cays.

Hopkins Kulcha Tours TOUR
(☑ 661-8199; http://hopkinskulchatours.weebly. com; tours BZ$50-380) Charlton Castillo will take you birdwatching, hiking or on a tour of Maya ruins. Tours explore Stann Creek, Cayo and beyond.

Motorbike Rentals & Alternate Adventures SELF-GUIDED TOURS
(☑ 665-6292; www.alternateadventures.com; South Side) MR&AA rents 200cc dirt bikes (BZ$118 per day, BZ $598 per week) and 250cc cruiser motorcycles (BZ$150 per day, BZ$750 per week) for self-guided motorcycle touring. Emma, the owner, offers helpful suggestions for independent-minded travelers and is a wealth of local knowledge.

🛏 Sleeping

Guesthouses and hotels are spread out along the dusty main street and the beaches north and south of the main road into the village. More upmarket lodges are further south in Sittee Point.

⭐ Funky Dodo   HOSTEL $
(☎ 676 3636; www.funkydodo.bz; South Side; dm/d without bathroom BZ$22/51, d/tr/q with bathroom BZ$66/90/120; ☎) Hopkins' only hostel is indeed a funky place, with a tightly packed village of rustic timber cabin rooms and dorms inhabiting a leafy garden. Backpackers swing in hammocks reading books, while others roll out the yoga mats. Upstairs the Tree Top Bar is a good place to socialize or find a cheap meal. There's also a communal kitchen and tour desk.

Solution Guest House   GUESTHOUSE $
(☎ 668-7594; elaineortiz_37@yahoo.com; r with/without bathroom BZ$66/56; P ☎) Across the road from the Funky Dodo, this five-room guesthouse is an excellent deal if you're after a clean, private room in the village center. Elaine is a cheerful host who can book tours and cook meals, and will let you use the downstairs kitchen.

Lebeha   CABIN $
(☎ 665-9305; North Side; cabañas BZ$30-50, cabins from BZ$90-160; ☎) You'll get a warm welcome at these beachfront cabins and *cabañas* attached to a Garifuna drumming school.

Windschief Cabanas   CABIN $
(☎ 523-7249; www.windschief.com; South Side; small/large cabaña BZ$60/90; P @ ☎) There are just two basic, but comfy stilted *cabañas* with private bathrooms and hot showers here in this seafront location. Oliver and Pamela's beachfront bar is a happening spot on Friday and Saturday. Oliver was busy building a minigolf course out front when we visited.

Castille Beach   CAMPGROUND $
(☎ 660-2413; per tent BZ$10) You can pitch a tent on this private bit of beach between Hopkins and Sittee Point. Shared bathrooms and canoes available.

⭐ Coconut
Row Guesthouse   GUESTHOUSE $$
(☎ 670-3000, in USA 518-223-9775; www.coconutrowbelize.com; beachside; d BZ$230, cabins BZ$250, apt BZ$260; P ❄ ☎) The colorfully painted Coconut Row boasts some of the finest beachfront rooms in Hopkins. The

five main rooms are spacious and spotless, and come with air-conditioning, fridge and coffee-maker, and two of them are full two-bedroom apartments. Rooms are beautifully designed for maximum comfort with tile floors and king-sized beds. In the adjoining property are three free-standing beachfront log cabins.

⭐ All Seasons
Guest House   GUESTHOUSE $$
(☎ 523-7209; www.allseasonsbelize.com; South Side; r BZ$86-150, family cabins BZ$196; P ❄ ☎) With its colorful two-bedroom *cabañas* and cozy guesthouse rooms, All Seasons may just be the cutest accommodations in town. All rooms have air-con, coffee-makers and hot showers. There's a great patio out front with a grill and picnic area. The location is good, at the south end of town and a short walk over the road to the beach.

Buttonwood Lodge   GUESTHOUSE $$
(☎ 670-3000; r BZ$240-270, apt BZ$280) The four spacious suites and single two-bedroom self-contained apartment at Buttonwood all face the sea. This high-quality accommodation is located at the north end of town and the rooftop deck has some of the best views in Hopkins.

Tipple Tree Beya   HOTEL $$
(☎ 615-7006; www.tippletreebelize.com; South Side; r BZ$80-110, 1-/2-bedroom apt BZ$196/360; ☎) 🖉 This sturdy wooden beachside place rents three cozy, clean, fan-cooled rooms sharing a sociable veranda beneath the owner's quarters upstairs. In an adjacent buildings are some excellent self-contained apartments that would suit a family or group. The owner, Tricia, implements a number of sustainable practices including composting, recycling and keeping the place as energy-efficient as possible.

Latitude Adjustment   CABAÑAS $$
(☎ 670-1705; www.latitudeadjustment.bz; d BZ$210; ☎ 🏊) A block west of the main street, these raised timber cabins are beautifully finished with dark-wood interiors, king-size beds, kitchenettes, cable TV and immaculate bathrooms. The five units orbit a small saltwater pool and there are security cameras and laundry facilities onsite.

Jungle Jeanie by the Sea   CABIN $$
(☎ 533-7047; www.junglebythesea.com; d cabañas BZ$120-240; ☎) 🖉 About a 10-minute walk south of Hopkins village, Jungle Jeanie's is

a little ecoresort with beautiful hardwood single and duplex cabins on stilts, some with sea views and easy beach access. This is a place where serenity meets spirituality meets action – there's a yoga *shala* with regular classes, but also kitesurfing, kayaks and stand-up paddleboards for rent.

Hopkins Inn HOTEL **$$**
(☑ 501-665-0411; www.hopkinsinn.bz; South Side; cabaña incl breakfast BZ$199; ℙ) The four stylish and spacious *cabañas* here are in a good location right by the beach.

Hopkins Bay Resort RESORT **$$$**
(☑ 523-7284, in USA 305-433-8394; www.hopkins baybelize.com; North Side; 1-/2-/3-bedroom villas incl breakfast BZ$300/550/750; ℙ✳🛜🏊) This flashy resort at the far northern end of Hopkins feels worlds away from the village life, with two pools, an absolute beachfront position and luxurious villas. Take out a free kayak or relax under the Rum Shack, an inviting sea-facing *palapa*-style bar and restaurant.

✖ Eating

Hopkins has a surprisingly good range of traveler-oriented restaurants and food shacks, mostly in the budget and midrange categories.

Gecko's BELIZEAN **$**
(☑ 629-5411; North Side; mains BZ$6-15; ⊙ noon-9pm Mon & Wed-Sat; 🛜🍴) One of Hopkins' newer places, Gecko's gets ticks for cheap tacos; vegetarian, vegan and gluten-free dishes; an interesting range of specials and a breezy open-air dining space located just north of the main intersection.

Sandy Beach Bar & Restaurant GARIFUNA **$**
(South Side beachfront; meals BZ$10-15; ⊙ 11am-9pm Mon-Sat) The ladies of the Sandy Beach Women's Cooperative serve up daily Garifuna specials such as *hudut* (a creamy fish stew served with mashed plantain), chicken stew, and rice and beans. It's also a cool beachfront bar.

★ Driftwood Beach Bar & Pizza Shack PIZZA **$$**
(North Side; pizza BZ$16-25, tacos BZ$10; ⊙ 11am-10pm Thu-Tue) On a decent stretch of beach at the northern end of Hopkins, Driftwood serves excellent pizza and tacos beneath a thatched roof. This is a popular social hub and party place: Tuesday is the big night

with Garifuna drumming, but there are also weekend events and beach BBQs.

★ Swinging Armadillo SEAFOOD **$$**
(☑ 635-5404; North Side; mains BZ$12-25; ⊙ 10am-10pm Sun-Fri) The Swinging Armadillo has one of the most enviable locations in Hopkins with a sweet little veranda hanging over the water. Ted and his crew back it up with generous portions of fresh seafood and an ever-changing blackboard menu.

Frog's Point Cafe INTERNATIONAL **$$**
(☑ 665-7589; South Side; mains BZ$13-25; ⊙ 7-10am & 5-9pm) Open for breakfast and dinner, Frog's Point has an inviting main street deck and bar with crisp tablecloths and a European flair. The German owners offer a wide-ranging menu that includes locally caught seafood, pasta, steak and tasty breakfasts. Highly regarded.

Thongs Cafe CAFE **$$**
(Main St; mains BZ$7-22; ⊙ 7am-3pm Wed-Sun) This cute Euro-style cafe is a cool spot for breakfast or a light lunch of salad, wraps and specials such as quesadillas or meatballs. Smoothies are good – if you're detoxing try the Green Fusion with spinach, cucumber and pineapple. Service can be slow, so browse the gift shop with designer T-shirts and vintage clothing while you wait.

🍷 Drinking & Nightlife

Garifuna drumming and singing can be heard most nights in season. Hopkins has a few good beach bars that attract travelers, expats and locals.

Herbal Healer Tea Bar TEAHOUSE
(South Side; tea & drinks BZ$5-10; ⊙ 8am-6pm) With 22 types of homegrown tea, smoothies and juices, this is a zen place to nurse a cuppa. There's a gift shop with herbal remedies and an organic garden out the back.

Windschief BAR
(☑ 523-7249; South Side; ⊙ 11am-10pm Mon-Wed & Fri & Sat) The small bar at this local waterfront place is a good spot to meet expats and visitors. They also serve light snacks, such as burgers and nachos, and are an internet cafe.

☆ Entertainment

Lebeha LIVE MUSIC
(☑ 608-3143; North Side; admission BZ$10) This drumming center is one of the coolest spots to be in Hopkins on any given evening from about 7pm, when local Garifuna drummer

Jabbar Lambey hosts drum-ins for friends, students and travelers alike. Drop in during the day to see what's going on.

🛍 Shopping

Hopkins is an especially good place to buy local crafts. Some restaurants and hotels carry items made by local craftspeople, but you can go to the source at stalls along the main street.

Sew Much Hemp   HANDICRAFTS
(☑ 668-6550; ☺ daylight hrs) Between Hopkins and Sittee Point, follow the signs toward the beach and stop at the old bus that Barbara calls home. This is Sew Much Hemp, a classic hippie outpost where Barbara makes and sells bags and clothing from hemp, as well as concocting various balms, bug repellents and essential oils from natural ingredients including hemp oil, beeswax and citronella.

David's Woodcarving   ARTS
(South Side) David makes exquisitely carved staffs, masks, canes, mortar-and-pestle sets and wooden jewelry in a workshop behind his shop, a block west of the main street.

ℹ Information

Wi-fi is available at most accommodations and cafes, but there's also **Hopkins Internet** (☑ 523-7249; per hr BZ$8; ☺ 1-9pm Fri-Wed), a rare internet cafe next to Windschief's.

There's a **Belize Bank ATM** (☺ 24hr) at the main intersection in the town center.

ℹ Getting There & Away

Two buses a day leave Hopkins for Dangriga (BZ$5, 30 minutes) from Monday to Saturday from the main intersection in town. Many travelers hitch or take a taxi (BZ$20) the 4 miles to the Southern Hwy junction and pick up any passing bus going north or south from there. A taxi to Hopkins from Dangriga costs BZ$80.

ℹ Getting Around

Hopkins is walkable but it's well spread out from north to south and it helps to have some form of wheels. You can rent bikes at numerous places in town including **Fred's Bike Rental** (per hr/day BZ$5/20). Head to Sittee Point to rent golf carts.

Sittee Point

About 1.5 miles south of Hopkins, Sittee Point is a small community where high-end beachfront resorts and a few interesting independent restaurants gather. Just where Hopkins ends and Sittee Point begins is the subject of mild debate locally, but it's generally considered to be at the junction with the Sittee River Rd. The *actual* Sittee Point is about 2.7 miles further south at the mouth of the Sittee River, while the marina is about 1.5 miles south.

🏃 Activities & Tours

Sittee Point is home to a couple of dive outfits, SUP tours and the marina.

Hopkins Standup Paddleboard   WATER SPORTS
(☑ 650-9040; www.suphopkins.com; Sittee Point; paddleboarding tours BZ$110-150) Stand-up paddleboarding has arrived in Sittee Point in a pretty special way. This outfit offers SUP tours on the Sittee River with a mind-blowing two-hour evening bioluminescence paddle or a half-day paddle in search of wildlife. Combination paddle and snorkel tours are also available. The office is at the junction at Sittee Point.

Sittee River Marina   TOURS
(☑ 520-7888; Sittee Point Rd; ☺ 6am-5.30pm) Boats head out to the reef and cays or on fishing trips from this full-service marina near the mouth of the Sittee River. Reef snorkeling and Land Rover tours can also be arranged here, and there's a gas station and popular bar-restaurant.

Belize Underwater   DIVING
(☑ 633-3401; www.hopkinsunderwateradventures.com; Sittee Point) Belize Underwater is a PADI-certified dive shop offering scuba instruction and trips to South Water Caye, Thatch Caye and Glover's Reef.

🛏 Sleeping

Sittee Point is home to the most upmarket resorts in the region, as well as holiday rentals and the odd guesthouse.

Cosmopolitan Guesthouse   GUESTHOUSE **$$**
(☑ 673-7373; www.cosmopolitanbelize.com; Sittee River Rd; cabaña BZ$150, d BZ$180; ℗ ❄ 🤶 ⛵) This traditional comfort guesthouse has four spotless rooms in the two-story main house and three, slightly smaller, private *cabañas* at the side, facing the small pool. All have air-con and verandas.

⭐ **Beaches & Dreams**   BOUTIQUE HOTEL **$$$**
(☑ 523-7259; www.beachesanddreams.com; Sittee River Rd; tree house BZ$242, d cabaña BZ$322, ste BZ$440; ℗ ❄ 🤶 ⛵) Beaches & Dreams is run

by Tony and Angela Marsico, professional chefs who traded catering in Alaska for running this high-quality boutique inn on the Belizean shore. They haven't given up on food, though, also running the adjacent Barracuda Bar & Grill. The 'Bird's Nest', with a loft area, sleeps five, while the beachfront *cabañas* have sea views and hammocks on the veranda.

The newest part of the operation is the three-story boutique hotel with six spacious suites each boasting sea-facing balconies, cable TV and air-conditioning, and sharing a private pool and rooftop deck. Bikes and kayaks are available for guests, and discounts are available during the low season and for stays longer than three days.

Parrot Cove Lodge   RESORT $$$
(☑523-7225; www.parrotcovelodge.com; Sittee River Rd; d from BZ$338, apt BZ$800; P✳︎🅰︎🛜🏊︎) This beachfront lodge has eight beautifully appointed rooms with air-con, full bathrooms with hot showers, TVs and coffee-makers. There's also a beach house next door with apartment suites sleeping up to six. These suites are fully furnished and have DVD-equipped TVs.

The lodge has its own dock, a courtyard pool with a small waterfall, and an excellent beachfront bar. It's also the home of Chef Rob's restaurant and Love on the Rocks stone grill.

Jaguar Reef Lodge & Spa   RESORT $$$
(☑520-7040, in USA 800-289-5756; www.jaguarreef.com; cabañas BZ$320-400, beachfront ste BZ$460; P✳︎@🛜🏊︎) Part of the Viva Belize trio (along with nearby Almond Beach and Villa Margerita resorts) this 'cash-free' luxury resort has a long, sandy beachfront and ample amenities and activities on land and water. The breezy and beautifully furnished *cabañas* here feature king-size beds, full bathrooms with tiled tubs, and end tables made from traditional Garifuna drums.

As well as snorkeling, birding, diving, jungle hiking, fishing and river kayaking, guests can enjoy a wide variety of other activity packages available through the resort.

Hamanasi Adventure
& Dive Resort   RESORT $$$
(☑533-7073, in USA 877-552-3483; www.hamanasi.com; r BZ$796-1380; P✳︎@🛜🏊︎) The premier resort of the area, Hamanasi (Garifuna for 'almond tree') combines the amenities of a top-class dive resort with an array of inland tours and activities, all on a gorgeous 400ft

private beachfront. All of Hamanasi's rooms and suites face the sea, except for the popular wood-floored tree houses, which hide among the foliage behind the beach.

The best deals at this exclusively priced resort are available as packages including room, meals and tours. Hamanasi's professional PADI dive operation can carry divers out to all three of Belize's atolls (Lighthouse, Turneffe and Glover's), as well as to the barrier reef's best dive spots; it is also equipped with the latest in nitrox dive technology.

🍴 Eating & Drinking

★ Loggerheads Pub & Grill   BURGERS
(☑650-2886; burgers BZ$12-20; ⊙11am-10pm Thu-Mon) The best burgers in town are served here on homemade rolls. Try the pulled pork or the gorgonzola-stuffed beef burger with bacon. The breezy upstairs dining area is the place for a cold beer.

★ Chef Rob's   SEAFOOD $$$
(Sittee Point Rd; mains BZ$37-59; ⊙5-9pm Tue-Sat) Well known locally for his sublime seafood creations, Chef Rob presents a changing menu that might include rum-flavored lobster bisque and sauteed grouper with lobster sauce, as well as rib-eye steak or Thai-style pork. Put together a four-course meal from BZ$59. The waterfront dining area at Parrot Cove is suitably romantic.

Love on the Rocks   INTERNATIONAL $$$
(☑672-7272; Sittee Point Rd; mains BZ$29-55) At Parrot Cove, Love on the Rocks is a hot-stone restaurant, where meat and seafood are grilled on hot stones right at your table. The lobster (in season) is said to be the best in town, or choose from chicken satay or beef tenderloin. Chef Rob also has a gourmet cafe next door.

Barracuda Bar & Grill   INTERNATIONAL $$$
(Sittee Point Rd; ⊙4-10pm) Tony and Angela, the chefs formerly of the fine-dining Two Rivers Restaurant in Alaska, bring their culinary skills to this intimate place attached to Beaches & Dreams (p203). Seafood is a specialty here, including local lobster, along with steaks and homemade pastries.

Curve Bar   INTERNATIONAL
(☑675-8525; Sittee River Rd; ⊙11am-8:30pm Tue-Sun) At Sittee River Marina, this lovely riverside thatch-roof restaurant and bar is worth the trip from Hopkins for the fine location, friendly atmosphere and bar snacks, such as lobster fritters, nachos and sliders. Happy

hour is from 4pm to 6pm. It's about 1.5 miles south of the Sittee Point junction.

ℹ Information

Diversity Cafe (☑ 661-7444; golf carts 2/5/24hr BZ$50/90/120; ⊙7am-6pm) Information, drinks and golf-cart rental.

ℹ Getting There & Away

Sittee Point is closer to Hopkins than to Sittee River village (with which it should not be confused); it's about a 20-minute bike ride from Hopkins or BZ$10 in a taxi.

Sittee River

The tranquil Creole village of Sittee River, with its increasing population of North American expats, stretches alongside the beautiful jungle-lined river of the same name, about 3 miles by unpaved road southwest of Hopkins. Sittee River is known for its spectacular river, plethora of birds and other wildlife, and notorious for its nigh-invisible and perpetually ravenous sand flies.

🏃 Activities & Tours

Nearby Boom Creek (inhabited by otters, a few crocodiles and plenty of birds) and Anderson's Lagoon make for good canoeing.

Belize by Horace   TOUR
(☑ 603-8358; www.belizebyhorace.com; Sittee River) Offers tours out to the cays and through the lagoons and rivers around Sittee River on a 26ft skiff, as well as land trips to Mayflower, Cockscomb and Red Bank.

🛏 Sleeping

There are just a couple of isolated places to stay in Sittee River.

Glover's Guest House   GUESTHOUSE $
(☑ 532-2916; campsite per person BZ$8, dm BZ$18, r/cabin per person BZ$24/38; P) Most visitors come to Glover's Guest House on Saturday night prior to catching the boat to Glover's Atoll Resort (p198), but the riverside guesthouse is a peaceful, slightly isolated budget place with free kayaks and bikes for rent. It has one large bunkhouse and two cabins on stilts; bring insect repellent.

River House Lodge   HOTEL $$
(☑ 533-7799; www.riverhouselodgebelize.com; r BZ$140-170; P❄@🛜🛝) With a lovely secluded riverside setting, River House Lodge

has six comfortable air-con rooms with screened verandas in two-story wooden houses. There's also a quirky restaurant-bar with a small indoor pool. Bikes and kayaks are free for guests, and meals and tour information are available by request.

Maya Center

POP 300

Maya Center, at the junction of the Southern Hwy and the access road to Cockscomb Basin Wildlife Sanctuary, was established in the 1980s to relocate Mopan Maya villagers when the sanctuary was proclaimed. Many of the villagers now make their living from the sanctuary, running tourist accommodations or tours, selling handicrafts or working as park staff.

If you're not staying in the sanctuary itself, this is the best base.

◉ Sights & Activities

Most traveler's head straight to the wildlife sanctuary (p206), but there are a couple of cultural attractions in the village including a chocolate factory, women's craft shop and herbal clinic and cooking classes.

Che'il Chocolate Factory   CULTURAL TOUR
(☑ 660-3903; juliosaqui@gmail.com; Southern Hwy; tours per person BZ$30; ⊙ shop 7am-5:30pm, tours 9am, 11am, 1pm & 3pm or by appointment) Julio Acqui is a master chocolate maker who offers two-hour farm-to-factory tours including a trip to the cacao plantation. The full process is explained right through to the finished bar of dark chocolate. There's a shop selling cacao products and a separate Maya cultural museum. Call ahead to book a place on a tour.

Aurora's Herbal Clinic   HEALTH & FITNESS
(☑ 533-7043; Sanctuary Rd; private reading or group healing per person BZ$20) Niece and apprentice of the legendary Maya healer Eligio Panti, Aurora performs consultations at her clinic at Nu'uk Che'il Cottages using locally harvested herbal medicines, treating everything from the common cold and gastric distress to spiritual and emotional

MAYA VILLAGE HOMESTAY PROGRAM

There are two guesthouses in the village, as well as the Maya homestay program.

SOUTHERN BELIZE SITTEE RIVER

issues. She also maintains a medicinal plant trail (BZ$5 per person with a self-guiding leaflet, BZ$20 per group for 30-minute guided tours).

🛏 Sleeping & Eating

★ **Aurora & Ernesto's Nu'uk Che'il Cottages**   CABIN $

(📞 670-7043; www.nuukcheilcottages.com; campsite per person BZ$7, dm BZ$20, d & tr BZ$60; ⊗ restaurant 7am-8pm; 🅿 🛜) Spread around a verdant garden about 500yd along the sanctuary road, Nu'uk Che'il is owned by Ernesto and Aurora Saqui. Ernesto is a knowledgable guide who was director of the Cockscomb Sanctuary from 1988 to 2004. There's a range of rooms for all budgets, a large screened *palapa* restaurant serving Maya meals, and lots of resident bird (and insect) life.

Among her many talents, Aurora is a great cook and has published a Maya cookbook. She offers farm-to-table cooking classes (BZ$20 per person).

Tutzil Nah Cottages   CABIN $

(📞 533-7045; www.mayacenter.com; s/d without bathroom BZ$28/36, d with bathroom BZ$44, house BZ$110; 🅿 🛜) On the Southern Hwy, 100yd north of the Maya Centre junction, the Chun brothers offer four clean rooms in houses on stilts decked out in basic Maya style. Rooms have shared bathrooms, but there is a fifth with its own bathroom. The brothers lead guided hikes throughout the area and sanctuary.

IGNACIO'S BIKE TRAIL

Ignacio's Bike Trail (per person BZ$50, bike hire BZ$50; ⊗ Jan-May) is a new mountain-biking trail in Cockscomb Basin Wildlife Sanctuary, winding 7.5 miles from the park office to the campsite at the start of the Victoria Peak hiking trail. The ride takes about four hours return and is only accessible in dry conditions between January and May. Serious riders should bring their own bikes, but there is a limited number of bikes for hire at the park office.

The trail is named for Ignacio Pop, a pioneer of the sanctuary and former warden who used to ride his bike 6.5 miles up from Maya Center to work, before the access road was fully constructed.

Cockscomb Diner   BELIZEAN $

(📞 660-3903; mains BZ$8-12; ⊗ by reservation) Above the Che'il Chocolate Factory, this balcony restaurant is open only for advance orders (usually groups), offering Belizean and Maya dishes for lunch.

🛍 Shopping

Maya Center Women's Craft Shop   HANDICRAFTS

(Southern Hwy; ⊗ 7:30am-5pm) At the junction of the Southern Hwy and the road to Cockscomb Basin Wildlife Sanctuary, this shop stocks locally made Maya arts and crafts including jewelry, carvings, baskets and textiles. You can arrange taxi transport and guides, and buy sanctuary tickets here.

Cockscomb Basin Wildlife Sanctuary

The Cockscomb Basin Wildlife Sanctuary is Belize's most famous jaguar sanctuary; at 200 sq miles, it's also one of its biggest protected areas.

As the sanctuary is part of the eastern Maya Mountain range, most visits to the sanctuary are restricted to a small eastern pocket, which contains a visitors center, the sanctuary's accommodations and a network of excellent walking trails.

Early mornings are the best time for wildlife-watching, as most animals seek shelter in the heat of the day. Many visitors come as part of large (and inevitably noisy) tours arranged through nearby lodges or travel agencies, but your best bet for viewing more elusive wildlife is to come alone or in as small and quiet a group as possible.

⊙ Sights

Cockscomb Basin Wildlife Sanctuary   WILDLIFE RESERVE

(admission BZ$10) The Cockscomb Basin Wildlife Sanctuary is Belize's most famous sanctuary and one of its biggest protected areas. This great swath of tropical forest became the world's first jaguar sanctuary in 1984, thanks to the efforts of American zoologist Alan Rabinowitz. Today, this critical biological corridor is home to an estimated 40 to 50 jaguars and a vast array of other animal, bird and botanical life.

The unpaved, 6-mile road to the sanctuary starts at the village of Maya Centre, on the Southern Hwy, 5 miles south of the Hopkins turnoff. The sanctuary office, where you pay admission, is at the end of the road that begins at Maya Centre. The office has trail maps (BZ$5) plus a few gifts, soft drinks and chocolate bars for sale. You can also rent binoculars (BZ$5 per day).

The visitor sighting book records instances of people spotting jaguars (often on the drive in), so it is possible. But, despite its size, the sanctuary itself isn't big enough to support a healthy breeding population of jaguars, although its position adjacent to other reserves and swaths of jungle make it part of a biological corridor that, many believe, offers promise for the jaguar's future in Central America.

Belize's four other wild cats, the puma, ocelot, margay and jaguarundi, also reside in and pass through the sanctuary, as do tapirs, anteaters, armadillos (the jaguar's favorite prey: crunchy on the outside, but soft and chewy on the inside), brocket deer, coatimundis, kinkajous, otters, peccaries, tayras iguanas, local rodents such as *gibnuts*, and other animals native to the area. The sanctuary is also home to countless birds: more than 290 feathered species have been spotted. Egrets, hummingbirds, the keel-billed toucan, king vulture, great curassow and scarlet macaw are just a few that live in or pass through the park.

There's also a thriving community of black howler monkeys living close to the visitors center. If you don't see them near the center, you'll definitely hear their eerie, cacophonous howling if you stay overnight. Large boa constrictors, small (and deadly poisonous) fer-de-lances and tiny coffee snakes are some of the snakes that call the sanctuary home.

Activities

Though a guide is useful, the well-maintained 12-mile network of trails that fans out from the park office is pretty user friendly. Most of the walks are flat along the bottom of the basin, but the moderately strenuous Ben's Bluff Trail (1.25 miles and steep in parts) takes you up to a lookout point with fantastic views over the whole Cockscomb Basin and the Cockscomb Mountains.

An easy 1.4-mile self-guided nature walk, looping together the Curassow Trail, Rubber Tree Tail and River Path, can be followed with the trail map from the park office. The River Path (0.4 miles) and the Wari Loop (a 2.3-mile loop from the office) are good early-morning bets for seeing a variety of birds. Jaguar tracks are often spotted on the Wari Loop and the Victoria Peak Path. The Antelope Loop (a 3.4-mile loop from the office) rises and falls through a variety of terrain and vegetation, and offers walkers a good overview of the basin's geological features The visitor center also rents **tubes** (BZ$5) for hour-long river-tube floats down South Stann Creek from the River Overlook on Wari Loop.

Guides

Villagers who formerly lived in the park area now make their living from the sanctuary, running accommodations or tours, or working as park staff. A typical day tour to the sanctuary from Maya Center costs around BZ$100 per person and includes transportation, a couple of guided walks, lunch and maybe river-tubing. An interesting option is a **night tour** (per person BZ$50), which offers increased chances of seeing nocturnal animals.

Sleeping & Eating

To truly appreciate Cockscomb Basin Wildlife Sanctuary, especially its night-time jungle noises, you need to stay the night and there's a decent range of accommodation close to the park office. There are three campgrounds with raised tent platforms (one near the visitor center and two on park trails; per person BZ$20), a lodge with five six-bed dormitories (per person BZ$40) and various standards of cabins (from BZ$109 to BZ$300). Cabins range from a basic hut with composting toilet and shower, to the two-room 'Bird House' and the self-contained two-story 'White House' near the entrance gate. There's a functional self-catering kitchen and dining area close to the main lodge buildings. To make bookings, contact the **Belize Audubon Society** (☑ 223-5004; www.belizeaudubon.org).

There's a basic snack shop but you'll need to bring all of your own food and drinks and use the barbecues or communal kitchen. Maya Center has a couple of grocery stores selling basic supplies, but you're better off shopping in Placencia or Hopkins.

Information

Cockscomb Basin Wildlife Sanctuary Office (www.belizeaudubon.org; ⊘ 7:30am-4:30pm, night warden on duty after hours) Call into the visitor center to register, buy your ticket, and peruse the displays and visitor book (for recent jaguar sightings). You can arrange park accommodation and hire river-tubes here, but you can't hire guides – do that in Maya Center.

❶ Getting There & Away

Any bus along the Southern Hwy will drop you at Maya Center, but there is no public transportation into the sanctuary. Most of the Maya Center tour guides offer taxi services to the sanctuary for around BZ$60 round trip. Otherwise, it's a two-hour walk over flat terrain.

Placencia

POP 1500

Placencia, a true beach-holiday strip on the mainland, is enduringly popular with North American expats and tourists. Perched at the southern tip of a long, narrow, sandy peninsula, the village has long enjoyed a reputation as 'the cay you can drive to'. A fully-paved 27-mile road heads off the Southern Hwy via Maya Beach and Seine Bight to the tip of the peninsula.

Placencia can be a lot of fun, but how you feel about it really depends on what you're looking for. If it's laid-back ambience, varied accommodations and some of the best restaurants in Southern Belize, this beachfront hangout is for you. If it's off-the-beaten-path adventure and cheaper living you're after, it might serve better as a place to check out for a day or two, organize a tour and move on.

High season in Placencia begins the week before Christmas and lasts until late April. During the full moons of May and June, the town hops as whale sharks come to spawn in the nearby waters.

❶ Orientation

The village of Placencia occupies the southernmost mile of the peninsula. On the eastern side is a sandy beach; between the beach and the road is a narrow, pedestrian-only footpath known as the Sidewalk.

Placencia's airport is about 1 mile north of the village; 6 miles beyond that is the Maya Beach. Between the village and the airport lies an increasing number of accommodations, including some of the swankiest in Belize and a growing number of luxury housing units.

🏃 Activities

Diving, snorkeling, fishing, kayaking and trips to inland adventures are all available from Placencia and there are plenty of operators who can organise activities.

Placencia is close enough to a plethora of cays, reefs and dive sites to make it a good base for diving and snorkeling. The more distant the area, the more expensive the trip. Most operators will charge around BZ$250 per person for a two-tank dive on an inner reef site such as Laughing Bird Caye. Longer outings to spots such as Glover's Reef or the Sapodilla Cayes should be around BZ$350.

For some sites you may need to add admission fees of between BZ$8 and BZ$30. March, April, May and June are especially good months to see whale sharks in the area. Most dive operators also run snorkeling trips. A snorkeling day trip to nearby cays, often with a beach BBQ included, costs from BZ$75.

Opportunities for fishing are equally amazing, and in the waters off Placencia you can troll for barracuda, kingfish or tuna; spincast or fly-fish for tarpon, bonefish or snook; and bottom-fish for snapper or jack. Sailing is also popular in the waters around Placencia. In addition to Belize's cays and other ports, Río Dulce in Guatemala and Honduras' Bay Islands are close enough to sail to.

As the whole town is geared toward tourism and aquatic fun, any hotel in Placencia can arrange your tour for you. Most beachside accommodations, particularly the mid-priced ones north of the village, have free kayaks or canoes for guests' use, and some will even provide fishing poles and bait to use on their private docks.

⭐ **Splash Dive Center**   DIVING, TOURS
(☑ 523-3058; www.splashbelize.com; Main St) Splash teaches PADI courses to divers of all levels, as well as offering diving and snorkeling tours to islands and reefs throughout the area. Owner Patty Ramirez is a patient and professional instructor, making her suitable for first-time divers and experts alike. As Quest Tours, Patty and partner Ralph also lead tours inland, including trips to Maya ruins and jungles.

Seahorse Dive Shop   DIVING
(☑ 523-3166; www.belizescuba.com; snorkeling BZ$170, 2-tank dive BZ$260) Seahorse runs regular diving and snorkeling trips to the reef (from BZ$260), South Water Caye, Glover's, Blue Hole and (in season) to see whale sharks. Also offers Discover Scuba courses (from BZ$350) and PADI open-water courses (BZ$900).

Seakunga Adventure   ADVENTURE TOUR
(☑ 523-3644; www.seakunga.com; Seine Bight, Peninsula; 1-/4-day kayaking tours BZ$160/2400) On the peninsula, just past Seine Bight, Seakunga runs fully supported multiday river and ocean kayaking tours and a range

Placencia

of adventure trips. They rent windsurfing equipment (per day BZ$80, lessons BZ$160) and the only kitesurfing equipment (per day BZ$160) in Placencia. They also have farm tours with riverside camping (BZ$30) at Redbank.

Jaguar Lanes Bowling BOWLING
(☑664-2583; Maya Beach; per person per game BZ$7, shoe rental BZ$3; ☺4-10pm Mon-Fri, 11am-10pm Sat & Sun) A cool distraction from the beach, this four-lane bowling alley is a lot of fun. Apart from knocking down the pins, there's a lively bar and cafe area serving pizzas, wings, burgers and fries (BZ$5 to BZ$7).

It's about 50m south of the Maya Beach Hotel.

Book it @ Barefoot TOUR
(☑523-3515) At Barefoot Bar, this tour desk is the booking agent for D-Tourz (offering tours to Cockscomb, Maya ruins and Red Bank) and the ticketing agent for the D-Express ferry to Honduras.

Captain Jak's Rentals BICYCLE RENTAL
(☑628-6447; www.captainjaks.com; Main St; ☺7am-5pm) From his office on the main street, Captain Jak rents bikes (BZ$20 per day) and golf carts (BZ$100 a day).

Placencia

🟠 Activities, Courses & Tours
Book it @ Barefoot	(see 39)
1 Captain Jak's Rentals	B2
2 Joy Tours	B4
3 Nite Wind Tours	D5
4 Ocean Motion Services	D4
5 Seahorse Dive Shop	C5
6 Secret Garden Massage & Day Spa	C4
Splash Dive Center	(see 38)
7 Trip 'n Travel	C4

🔵 Sleeping
8 Anda Di Howse	D4
9 Captain Jak's	B2
10 Colibri House	B1
11 Deb & Dave's Last Resort	B3
12 Julia's Guesthouse	C3
13 Lydia's Guesthouse	B2
14 Manatee Inn	B1
15 Michelo Hotel	B1
16 Miramar Apartments	C2
17 Omar's Guesthouse	B4
18 One World Rentals	C4
19 Paradise Resort	C5
20 Ranguana Lodge	C3
21 Sea Glass Inn	C5
22 Seaspray Hotel	C2
23 Seaview Suites	C4
24 Serenade Guesthouse	C3

🔴 Eating
25 Above Grounds	C4
26 Dawn's Grill	B4
27 De-Tatch Restaurant	C2
28 Dolce Vita	C4
29 Friends	D4
30 Mojo Lounge & Bartique	C4
31 Mr Q	C5
Omar's Creole Grub	(see 17)
32 Radi's Fine Food	B3
33 Rick's Cafe	C4
34 Rumfish	C4
Secret Garden Restaurant	(see 28)
35 Shak	D4
36 Sweet Dreams	C4
37 Tutti Frutti	C4
38 Wendy's Creole Restaurant & Bar	C4

🟢 Drinking & Nightlife
39 Barefoot Bar	C3
40 Brewed Awakenings	B2
41 J-Byrds	C5
42 Pickled Parrot	C4
43 Street Feet	C4
44 Tipsy Tuna Sports Bar	C3
45 Yoli's	C5

🟤 Shopping
46 Made in Belize	C3

Cayequest Tours　　　　　　　　TOUR
(☑ 633-6330; http://cayequestadventures.blogspot.com) Cayequest, run by local guide Mark Leslie, runs some offbeat tours to an organic chocolate farm and banana plantations, as well as culinary-oriented trips to the cays.

Trip 'n Travel　　　　　　TOUR, FISHING
(☑ 523-3205; www.tripntravel.bz; Main St; tours BZ$140-450; ⊙ 8am-6pm Mon-Fri, 8am-2pm Sat) Reliable company offering all the usual tours, plus fly-fishing and regular tours into Maya country in Toledo. Most tours will go with only two people.

Moorings　　　　　　　　　　SAILING
(☑ in USA 888-952-8420; www.moorings.com) Luxury catamaran offering customized bareboat (self-charter) sailing from Placencia or you can hire a skipper. It's based at Laru Beya marina, 4 miles north of Placencia.

Secret Garden Massage & Day Spa　SPA
(☑ 523-3420; www.secretgardenplacencia.com; per hr BZ$110; ⊙ by appointment) Beside the garden restaurant of the same name (p215), US-trained and licensed massage therapist Lee Nyhus offers a soothing range of Swed-

ish massages, hot-stone massages, facials, Reiki and physical therapy.

Ocean Motion Services　　　　　TOUR
(☑ 523-3162, 523-3363; www.oceanmotionplacencia.com; Sidewalk; tours BZ$70-400; ⊙ 7:30am-6pm Mon-Sat, to 5pm Sun) Arranges fishing and snorkeling trips, as well as cave-tubing.

Joy Tours　　　　　　　　　　TOUR
(☑ 523-3325; www.belizewithjoy.com; Main St) Joy is a reliable outfit offering a variety of local fishing, snorkeling and diving activities, as well as arranging hiking tours to Maya ruins around Southern Belize.

Permit Pow　　　　　　　　　FISHING
(☑ 523-3132; www.permitangling.com) Renowned local fishing guide 'Pow' Cabral will take you fly-fishing or on customized trips in search of permit fish (among others).

Nite Wind Tours　　　　　　　　TOUR
(☑ 660-6333, 503-3487; Main St; tours BZ$45-385; ⊙ 7am-5.30pm) Offers a variety of land and nautical tours including snorkeling on nearby cays and day trips to Monkey River and Cayo District.

✨ Festivals & Events

Lobsterfest FOOD
(☺ last weekend of Jun) Celebrates the opening of the lobster-fishing season with music, boat races, a fishing contest, a huge variety of lobster dishes to eat and a lot of fun.

Sidewalk Art Festival ART
(☺ mid-Feb, nearest weekend to Valentine's Day) Features art, crafts and music, with scores of participants from all over Belize.

Mistletoe Ball DANCE
(☺ Dec) Organised by the Belize Tourism Industry Association (BTIA), this popular party of dancing and music takes place at one of Placencia's resorts each December.

🛏 Sleeping

Many of Placencia's accommodations span the budget and midrange spectrum, while more upmarket resorts are further north around Maya Beach and the airport. Places fill up fast, especially in high season, so book ahead or expect to pay a premium. During low season some places close, but others offer discounts of 25% or more.

In the Village

★ Anda Di Howse HOSTEL $
(☏ 523-3306, 631-1614; pandora_gaudino@ yahoo.com; dm BZ$25; 🛜) 'Under the House' is Placencia's only genuine hostel. Owner Pandora has designed a beautiful 10-bed dorm beneath her stilt home, with timber floors, spring mattresses, individual fans, lockers and spotless bathrooms. Best of all, it's right on the beach at the southern end of the Sidewalk.

It's a cozy space with an immaculate full kitchen and small veranda – you can't help but meet other travellers here!

Lydia's Guesthouse GUESTHOUSE $
(☏ 523-3117; www.lydiasguesthouse.com; r BZ$60, apt BZ$70; 🛜) Lydia's is a good budget option on a quiet stretch of Sidewalk on the northern side of town. The eight rooms share bathrooms and there's one studio apartment with a full kitchen. There's also a laundry service, communal kitchen with purified drinking water and hammocks on the verandah.

Manatee Inn HOTEL $
(☏ 523-4083; www.manateeinn.com; s/d/tr BZ$70/80/90; 🅿🛜) Built by Slavek Machacka in 1999, this classical wooden hotel is the best in the budget category. Down a lane in a quiet spot, the Manatee puts you close enough to the beach to feel a constant breeze. Rooms are airy with high ceilings, hardwood floors, refrigerators and private bathrooms with hot-water showers.

Omar's Guesthouse GUESTHOUSE $
(☏ 605-7631; Main St; d BZ$45; 🛜) Omar's has moved from the beach to the main street and he was busy rebuilding his popular budget guesthouse at the time of writing. The four spacious but simple rooms are fan-cooled with shared bathrooms. It's behind Omar's Creole Grub (p215).

Deb & Dave's Last Resort GUESTHOUSE $
(☏ 523-3207; debanddave@btl.net; r without bathroom BZ$55; 🛜) A reliable central cheapie in the town centre, D&D offers four compact rooms (two twins, two doubles) with fans, surrounded by a leafy garden. A screened-in space offers a communal chill-out spot with a coffee-maker, but no kitchen. The outdoor pool is not for guests!

Casa Placencia APARTMENT $$
(☏ 630-7811; www.casaplacencia.com; r BZ$110, apt per week BZ$1300; 🅿❄🛜🏊) On the quiet northern end of town, Casa Placencia offers beautifully decorated rooms with kitchenettes, cable TV and wi-fi. There's an organic garden with bananas, mangoes and papayas, and a chill-out spot with an above-ground pool and BBQ at the back. The one- and two-bedroom apartments come with full kitchen and are perfect for families. Free bikes.

One World Rentals APARTMENT $$
(☏ 620-9975, 523-3103; www.oneworldplacencia. com; Main St; studios from BZ$130, cabaña BZ$180, apt from BZ$200; 🅿❄🛜) These clean, colorful, fully equipped studios and apartments come with kitchenettes, ample parking and a leafy central courtyard. Run by a gregarious Swiss woman named Claudia, it's behind the gift shop of the same name, and there's also a laundry onsite.

Michelo Hotel HOTEL $$
(☏ 523-3519; www.belize.net84.net; Harbour Place 21; d BZ$180, with air-con BZ$210; 🅿❄🛜) This small hotel on the north end of town has four spotless suites with queen-sized bed and futon, cable TV, wi-fi, and full kitchenettes with microwave and fridge. The owners have built a beautiful circular temple and meditation space around the back, open to guests and nonguests alike.

Colibri House APARTMENT **$$**
(☑605-0586; www.colibrihouseplacencia.com; Sidewalk; downstairs/upstairs apt per week BZ$1080/1460; ❈ 🛜 ☲) The one-of-a-kind, octagonal Colibri house is built from a mix of hardwoods and is fully furnished with treasures from Tibet, Bali, Italy and India. Of the two apartments, the upper suite features a downstairs bedroom and living room and a 2nd-floor loft space, while the downstairs studio is ideal for couples.

Gregarious Stefano (the Italian-born manager of Colibri house) also manages a number of other properties around Placencia; call him for more information.

Captain Jak's CABIN **$$**
(☑628-6447; www.captainjaks.com; Main St; cabañas BZ$190, cottage BZ$250; ℗ 🛜) The Captain offers three *cabañas* and two larger cottages surrounding a quiet garden (weekly rates are available). All rooms are fan-cooled and come with kitchenettes, hot water and private bathrooms. There is also an immaculately furnished, very airy, two-story private villa that sleeps up to eight for BZ$630 a night.

Ranguana Lodge CABAÑAS **$$**
(☑523-3112; www.ranguanabelize.com; garden/ seaview cabins BZ$180/200; ❈ 🛜) Ranguana offers five good-sized mahogany cabins on a piece of happening beach (next to Barefoot Bar). The garden cabins have kitchens; the smaller beachfront cabins have sea views and air-con. All have two double beds, hot-water bathrooms, cable TV and microwaves, not to mention lovely verandas. Prices are for up to three people.

Serenade Guesthouse HOTEL **$$**
(☑523-3113; http://serenadeplacencia.com; Sidewalk; d BZ$125-150; ℗ ❈ 🛜) This big two-story house on the Sidewalk looks a bit creaky from the outside, but the nine brightly painted rooms are spacious and well-appointed with air-con, microwave, mini-fridge, cable TV and bathrooms with hot showers. The upper-floor rooms have sea views. Of course, the beach is just steps away.

Sea Glass Inn HOTEL **$$**
(☑523-3098; www.seaglassinnbelize.com; d/tr BZ$158/188, per additional person BZ$20; ❈ 🛜) The welcoming Sea Glass Inn offers unobstructed ocean views and endless sea breezes thanks to its position on Placencia's southern shore. Renovated rooms have coffee-makers, microwaves, fridge and air-con.

The wide, wood-floored veranda has chairs and hammocks for long-term lounging.

Julia's Guesthouse GUESTHOUSE **$$**
(☑503-3478; www.juliascabanas.com; r BZ$90-200; 🛜) A beachfront place on the tightest packed part of the shore (next to Barefoot Bar), Miss Julia has three cabins, four duplexes and one apartment, all painted in Julia's signature tropical yellow and orange, and offering TVs, hot showers, private bathrooms and sea views. Laundry facilities are available, and guests can use the beachside hammocks and lounge chairs.

Seaspray Hotel HOTEL **$$**
(☑523-3148; www.seasprayhotel.com; Sidewalk; r BZ$60-160; ❈ 🛜) Owned and operated by the Leslies (one of Placencia's most established families), this lovely hotel has seven grades of room in varying sizes, luxury and proximity to the ocean. All come with private hot-water bathrooms, but the budget rooms can be pokey. De-Tatch Restaurant (p215) is next door.

Seaview Suites HOTEL **$$**
(☑523-3777; www.seaviewplacencia.com; r BZ$172; ❈ 🛜) A great location at the southern end of the Sidewalk and six immaculate rooms make this a good deal. Rooms have either a king or two double beds and come with air-con, fridge, microwave and coffee-maker.

Paradise Resort HOTEL **$$$**
(☑523-3179; www.belize123.com; r BZ$178-398; ℗ ❈ 🛜) This semi-upmarket, 12-room hotel enjoys a peaceful location on the peninsula's southern edge, offering clean and comfortable rooms with air-con, flat-screen TVs and comfy beds – the best are the upper-floor seaview rooms with balconies. The popular nautical-themed bar and restaurant is a good meeting place and there's an over-water burger bar in season.

There's also free use of kayaks and bicycles for guests, and golf carts for hire.

Miramar Apartments APARTMENT **$$$**
(☑523-3658; www.miramarbelize.com; studio BZ$220, ste BZ$400, 3-bedroom apt BZ$550; ❈ 🛜) These fully furnished apartments with bathrooms suit longer stayers. They're spacious enough with TV, fridge and microwave, and the location is good on a lively part of the Sidewalk. There's a three-night minimum and beach towels are provided.

Around Placencia

If laid-back Placencia town is too busy for you, a range of hotels and swish resorts line the beach on the peninsula north of the village toward Maya Beach.

Singing Sands Inn
BOUTIQUE HOTEL **$$$**

(☑533-3022; www.singingsands.com; 714 Maya Beach Rd; r BZ$260-600, cabañas BZ$260-320; P✳︎☎︎⊛) Tucked away in a beautifully landscaped garden at Maya Beach, Singing Sands offers an affordable oceanside tropical oasis. Choose from thatched-roof *cabañas* or garden-view rooms with hardwood floors, custom-designed doors and furniture made by local craftspeople. Dine in the poolside Bonefish Grill, and take a sunset cocktail at the bar on the end of the private pier.

Energy-efficient LED lighting gives the Sands a warm night-time glow. There's also a great swimming pool, beach, and free kayak use for guests.

Robert's Grove
Beach Resort
RESORT **$$$**

(☑523-3565, in USA 800-565-9757; www.roberts grove.com; r from BZ$400, villa from BZ$1500; P✳︎☎︎⊛) 🍴 From the Grecian fountain in the front driveway to the beautiful beachfront patio bar and restaurant, Robert's Grove is classy all the way. Rooms range from studios with ocean or garden views to one- and two-bedroom suites or spacious three- and four-bedroom villas sleeping up to eight people. Eat in at the fine-dining Seaside Restaurant or the more casual Sweet Mama's or Habanero Cafe.

Located about 4.5 miles north of town, amenities include a marina, day spa, three pools, use of bikes, kayaks and Hobie Cats.

Maya Beach Hotel
HOTEL **$$$**

(☑533-8040; www.mayabeachhotel.com; Maya Beach; r BZ$218-600; P✳︎@☎︎⊛) The Maya Beach has 10 delightful, individually furnished and decorated rooms facing the beach. The smallest is cozy but most are spacious and thoughtfully designed, all with air-conditioning, custom-made furniture, kitchenettes and balconies or verandas. There's a cool little pool and swimming off the private jetty, and guests have free use of kayaks and stand-up paddleboards.

Owners John and Ellen also manage a number of beautiful beachfront houses ranging from one to three bedrooms.

Green Parrot
Beach Houses
CABAÑAS **$$$**

(☑533-8188, in USA 734-667-2537; www.greenparrot-belize.com; 1 Maya Beach; d BZ$340; P☎︎) Green Parrot offers six quirky timber beach houses with a loft space and two stilted *cabañas*, all on the beach. All-wood interiors, high ceilings and huge screened-in windows maximising breezes are features. *Cabañas* have thatched roofs and open-air showers with a tropical feel. Guests have free use of bicycles, snorkeling equipment, kayaks and glass-bottom canoes, and the restaurant serves breakfast, lunch and dinner.

SEINE BIGHT

Most visitors to Placencia just breeze through Seine Bight, the Garifuna village in the center of the peninsula, which, with its shacks, shanties and cheap restaurants, sticks out like a Rastafarian at a GOP fundraiser. But as the home of many of the folks who keep the surrounding resorts running, Seine Bight is worth a stop. In addition to offering some of the cheapest food on the peninsula, Seine Bight is home to renowned artists. A new Garifuna museum was under development in the village when we visited.

Seine Bight is worth the trip just for the cheap Garifuna street food. Any of the roadside BBQ shacks are good bets, especially on a Saturday afternoon. There's also a great pub and easy access to excellent resort restaurants along the peninsula.

A new place called **Global Freehouse** (☑673-3733; www.globalfreehouse.com; mains BZ$22-32; ⊙11am-11pm; ☎︎) was about to open when we visited and looks like an exciting addition to this part of the peninsula. Billing itself as a gastropub, the menu is indeed global, with bacon sliders, Canadian poutines, Indian curry, Austrian chicken and steak tacos.

If it's some souvenirs you're after, local painter and sculptor Lola Delgado runs **Lola's Art** (☑601-1913; http://lolasartinbelize.blogspot.com.au), which sells some of the same paintings, handcrafted jewelry, sculpture and assorted crafts you'll find adorning (and being sold at higher prices in) hotels and resorts around the area.

Turtle Inn   LODGE $$$
([☑]523-3486, in USA 800-746-3743; www.turtleinn.
com; cottages BZ$638-2038, villas BZ$1300-3858;
[P][🛜][🐾]) The last word in ultra-chic luxury
(with a price tag to match), this Balinese-
themed lodge is owned by the family of
Francis Ford Coppola, where the director
himself maintains his own Belizean villa.
The thatch-roofed cottages and villas are a
combination of opulence with a hint of the
rustic, while signature Italian fine dining
can be found at the Mare Restaurant.

Facilities include a private beach and
jetty, two pools, a fully equipped PADI dive
shop, and day spa staffed with Thai mas-
seurs. The most exclusive accommodations,
Francis' Family Pavilion and Sofia's Beach
House, top out at BZ$6700 and BZ$7840
respectively! From January to April there's
a three- or four-night minimum. It's just un-
der 2 miles north of town.

🍴 Eating

Placencia stands out as having the best
restaurants and diversity of cuisine in
Southern Belize, from street BBQs and Ital-
ian gelati to high-quality resort restaurants.
If you're looking to stock up on supplies,
there are a number of good Chinese-run
supermarkets.

Tutti Frutti   ICE CREAM $
(Main St; from BZ$5; ⊙9am-9pm Thu-Tue) If you
don't like the ice cream here, you won't like
ice cream anywhere. It's that simple. The
Italian gelato is even better and the flavours
are constantly changing.

Above Grounds   CAFE $
([☑]634-3212; www.abovegroundscoffee.com;
Main St; coffee from BZ$3-5, snacks BZ$2-7;
⊙7am-4pm Mon & Thu-Sat, 8am-noon Sun; [🛜])
This coffee-shop stilt shack offers great
coffee drinks, bagels, muffins and people-
watching from the raised wooden veran-
da deck. All coffee is Guatemalan organic,
sourced directly from the farmers. They also
have organic chocolate drinks, fresh juice,
free wi-fi and good tunes.

Mr Q   BBQ $
(Main St; plates BZ$10; ⊙noon-9pm) One of sev-
eral good Belizean BBQ places at the south-
ern end of the peninsula, Mr Q serves up
BBQ and fried chicken with rice and beans
on Styrofoam plates, along with ice-cold
beer. Cheap and filling.

Radi's Fine Food   BELIZEAN $
(Main St; lunch specials BZ$10; ⊙11am-3pm)
What you see is what you get: a shack, a
porch, a kitchen and three daily specials
cooked by Creole chef Radiance, aka Radi.
Shrimp dishes are a given, and the other two
dishes can be anything from conch soup to
meatloaf. All are delicious, and portions are
always more than ample.

Dawn's Grill   BELIZEAN $
(Main St; meals BZ$9-15; ⊙7am-3pm & 5:30-9pm)
Good things come in small packages, and
good food comes from a small kitchen at
Dawn's Grill. Changing daily specials include
chicken, pork roast and fish fillets. Saturday
is BBQ day, while breakfast is available daily.

Shak   CAFE $
([☑]622-1686; dishes BZ$10-15; ⊙7am-6pm Sun &
Mon, 7am-9pm Wed-Sat) This ocean-facing res-
taurant is one of the best places in town for
a healthy smoothie – there are 28 varieties –
or an all-day breakfast. They also serve
seafood, tacos and other Mexican dishes.
The vibe is mellow and the people-watching
fine.

RED BANK'S SCARLET MACAWS

What brings people to the remote Maya
village of **Red Bank**, just south of the
Placencia turnoff on the Southern Hwy?
It's the rare and spectacularly plumaged
scarlet macaws who gather in the trees
surrounding the village for around three
months of the year (January to March,
though sometimes they will arrive as
early as December) to feast on the fruits
that grow in the area. Lush, verdant
and almost entirely off the tourist trail,
the surrounding jungles are filled with
brooks, rivers and swimming holes. A
group of villagers manage the area and
lead guided tours deep into the sur-
rounding jungles (with some strenuous
hiking) to see not just the macaws, but
other unique animals that inhabit the
area, including tapirs, jaguars, *gibnuts*
and agoutis.

It's a truly unique experience, and as
both the guesthouse and local tours are
locally owned and operated, all money
spent stays in the village of Red Bank.
For more information, contact Red
Bank native **Florentino** ([☑]660-6320;
scarletmacawb3d@gmail.com), who helps
coordinate experiences.

Friends   BREAKFAST $
(Sidewalk; meals from BZ$10-15; ☉8am-2pm; 🛜)
This bright yellow shack at the southern end
of Sidewalk has friendly service and holds
church services on Sunday morning. Breakfast features pancakes, French toast and
lobster-and-cheese omelets, while lunch is
mainly sandwiches.

Sweet Dreams   BAKERY $
(Sidewalk; baked goods from BZ$5; ☉from 6am;
🛜) Freshly baked mini pizzas, multigrain
breads, cinnamon rolls and baked goods of
all sorts are served all day at this family-run
Swiss bakery.

★**Mojo Lounge & Bartique**   CAFE $$
(☎628-7974;   www.mojoloungeplacencia.com;
Main St; starters BZ$10-12, mains BZ$24-30; ☉5-
9pm Mon-Sat; ✳🛜) Since opening in 2013,
little Mojo has made a big name for itself
with an imaginative menu, fresh local ingre-
dients, impressive cocktails and the ultimate
in cozy lounge vibe. From 5pm till 6pm it's
happy hour, so get in early and grab a space
on the balcony for half-price cocktails and
starters.

The global menu features caramelized
pear and brie bruschetta, stuffed baked
chicken, stir-fry and lobster linguine. Read
about the Canadian owner's story at the end
of the handwritten menu.

★**Omar's Creole Grub**   SEAFOOD $$
(☎605-7631; Main St; mains BZ$10-45; ☉7am-
9pm Mon-Thu & Sun, 7am-5pm Fri, 6-9pm Sat)
Omar's has been around a long time and
still serves some of the freshest seafood in
town. Step into the small and rustic streetside shack and choose from crab, lobster,
shrimp or conch prepared either traditional Creole style, Caribbean curry or coconut
curry. There's also burgers and burritos. No
alcohol.

★**Rumfish**   FUSION $$
(☎523-3293; www.rumfishyvino.com; Main St;
tacos BZ$9, mains BZ$22-38; ☉noon-midnight,
kitchen closes at 10pm) Rumfish is a gas-
tro-style wine bar done Central American
style. Head up to the balcony of the beautiful
old timber building and simple starters such
as Peruvian *ceviche* or specialty mains such
as Yucatán chicken or Caribbean fish stew.
Gourmet tacos are BZ$9 a pop. Imported
wines, beers and cocktails, and a breezy co-
lonial veranda complete the picture.

Dolce Vita   ITALIAN $$
(☎678-1089; Main St; mains BZ$27-30; ☉from
5:30pm; 🖉) Upstairs next to Secret Garden
(p210), Dolce Vita is a classic Italian restaurant in the tropics with peach-colored walls,
traditional furniture and authentic antipas-
ta, handmade gnocchi and pasta dishes. Ingredients such as cheese, olives and wine are
imported.

**Wendy's Creole
Restaurant & Bar**   CARIBBEAN $$
(☎523-3335; Main St; BZ$9-45; ☉7am-9:30pm;
✳🛜🖐) Wendy's is a traditional-style
air-conditioned restaurant serving a wide
range of dishes from burgers and burritos
to seafood specialties such as Caribbean jerk
snapper fillet and Creole fish. There's a full
bar and cheap beer (BZ$4).

Rick's Cafe   PIZZA $$
(Sidewalk; mains BZ$14-32; ☉11am-9:30pm; 🛜)
This cool little veranda cafe on the Sidewalk
is best known for its pizza and pasta, but
Rick also whips up sandwiches, quesadillas
and *ceviche*.

Secret Garden Restaurant   CARIBBEAN $$
(☎634-9789;   mains BZ$24-38;   ☉11am-9pm
Mon-Sat) In a lush patch of garden hidden
away from the main street, this low-key res-
taurant and bar offers up an eclectic menu
with Caribbean gumbo, chicken Maya and
spicy jambalaya.

De-Tatch Restaurant   CARIBBEAN $$
(Sidewalk; breakfast & lunch dishes BZ$10-15, din-
ner mains BZ$30-45; ☉7am-9:30pm Thu-Tue)
This popular thatched-roof, open-air beachfront place specialises in tasty shrimp and
seafood dishes in a range of styles: Caribbean, Belizean and North American food are
De-Tatch signatures and service is snappy.
The specials board might include coconut
shrimp curry, chicken in mango-rum sauce
or whole fried snapper. It's also a good spot
for breakfast and lunch.

★**Maya Beach Bistro**   INTERNATIONAL $$$
(☎533-8040; www.mayabeachhotel.com; Maya
Beach; lunch BZ$18-39, dinner BZ$28-58; ☉7am-
9pm) Maya Beach Hotel's popular bistro is
a veritable Placencia landmark, offering ex-
cellent international dishes using fresh local
ingredients. This is the restaurant where
folks who run the restaurants in town come
to eat seafood and coconut chowder, lobster
bread pudding or cacao pork on their days
off. The waterfront view is fine, service is

friendly and you can swim in the small pool or off the pier.

Tranquilo
BELIZEAN, SEAFOOD $$$

(☑ 620-7763; www.tranquilobelize.com; Placencia Caye; mains BZ$24-32; ☺ 3-10pm Mon & Wed-Fri, noon-10pm Sat & Sun) Don't feel like you're really on an island in Placencia? Call ahead for the free boat shuttle and head across to Placencia Caye, where the beautifully located dockside Tranquilo is one of the most romantic places for lunch or a sunset dinner in Southern Belize. Dine on conch stew or lobster Creole and drink in the view. Reservations recommended.

Fusion Beach
INTERNATIONAL, FUSION $$$

(☑ 523-3197; Mile 22.5 Placencia Rd; lunch BZ$18-24, dinner BZ$32-50; ☺ 11:30am-10pm; P ☎ ♨) Placencia's newest dining experience, stylish Fusion Beach boasts a roomy seafront restaurant and outdoor deck with infinity swimming pool. The innovative international menu features shrimp papaya salad, teriyaki chicken in banana leaf and lobster tail in jasmine-tea sauce, with a natural emphasis on fresh seafood. Or just drop in for a cocktail and plate of 'light bites'.

🍷 Drinking & Nightlife

Placencia is the best place in Southern Belize for partying, with some good beach bars and a nightclub.

Brewed Awakenings
CAFE

(Main St; coffee BZ$3.50-6.75, shakes BZ$7-8; ☺ 6am-5pm Mon-Sat) The imaginative name extends to the drinks with perfectly brewed espresso coffee and a range of flavored seaweed shakes (the seaweed acts as a thickener and is said to contain various healthy vitamins). Great for an early morning caffeine fix.

Barefoot Bar
BAR

(☑ 523-3515; Sidewalk; ☺ 11am-midnight; ☎) Occupying prime beach real estate, Placencia's most happening spot for drinking and entertainment has live music five nights a week, fire dancing on Wednesdays, full-moon parties and more. Happy hour is from 5pm to 6pm, with bitters and cheap rum. The menu has a big range of Mexican snacks, pizza and burgers.

Tipsy Tuna Sports Bar
BAR

(www.tipsytunabelize.com; Sidewalk; ☺ 11am-midnight) Brightening up the beach with its multicolored sun loungers, Tipsy Tuna provides occasional action with live music (Garifuna drumming on Wednesday), along with big-screen TV, pool tables, rooftop deck and happy hour from 5pm to 7pm. The food is reasonably priced: standard issue burgers, tacos, wings and the like.

Yoli's
BAR

(☑ 624-3807; ☺ 7am-8pm, till late Fri) This thatched bar over the water at the south end of the village is especially popular on Fridays, when there's a live band and Yoli's BBQ grill, and again on Sunday afternoons.

Pickled Parrot
BAR

(☑ 636-7068; ☺ 11am-midnight Wed-Mon) This thatched-roof Caribbean-style bar and restaurant, tucked down a lane off the main street, is a cool spot for a drink and the food is top notch. Head in for the bargain BZ$10 specials (meatloaf Monday, shrimp Saturday) or trivia on Thursday.

Street Feet
CLUB

(☑ 523-3515; Main St; ☺ 10pm-late Fri & Sat) Placencia doesn't party like San Pedro, but with DJs and dance parties this lounge and nightclub keeps things going after the beach bars close.

J-Byrds
BAR

(☺ 10am-midnight or later) This dockside bar can get pretty lively with locals and visitors, especially at the Friday dance party.

🛍 Shopping

Made in Belize
HANDICRAFTS

(Sidewalk; ☺ 7am-9pm) Leo handcrafts exquisite wooden sculptures from rosewood, mahogany and driftwood at his workshop on the Sidewalk and displays and sells them in his little shop. Birds (such as toucans) and marine life (dolphins and turtles) are featured. Small pieces start at BZ$50.

ℹ Information

Free wi-fi is widespread in Placencia but if you've lost your phone, check your email at **Placencia Office Supply** (☑ 523-3205; internet per hr BZ$8; ☺ 8am-6pm Mon-Fri, 8am-2pm Sat), next to the post office.

Belize Bank and **Scotiabank** (☺ 8:30am-2:30pm Mon-Thu, to 4pm Fri) are both on the main drag and have 24/7 ATM access. There's an Atlantic Bank branch on the far north end of town.

There's no shortage of info on Placencia, both on the web and around Belize. In town, head to the **Placencia Tourism Center** (☑ 523-4045; www.

placencia.com; ⊙ 8am-5pm Mon-Fri), down a lane opposite Scotia Bank (look for the sign). This private BTIA (Belize Tourism Industry Association) office has friendly staff who can offer local information such as transport info. While you're there, pick up a copy of the monthly *Placencia Breeze* (also online at www.placenciabreeze.com). Or try your luck at the erratically staffed **Information Booth** (Main St; ⊙ 9-11am & 2-4pm Mon-Fri).

The immigration office for visa extensions (BZ$50) is at the deep-water port in Independence. Take the Hokey Pokey Water Taxi from Placencia; it's a 2-mile taxi ride away.

🛈 Getting There & Away

AIR

Between them, from Placencia airport (PLJ), **Maya Island Air** (☑ 523-3443; www.maya islandair.com; Maya Island air terminal) and **Tropic Air** (☑ 523-3410; www.tropicair.com) fly 21 times daily to Belize City (one way BZ$250, 35 minutes), eight times to Dangriga (BZ$120, 15 minutes) and five times to Punta Gorda (BZ$120, 15 minutes). The airstrip is just north of town.

BOAT

The **Hokey Pokey Water Taxi** (☑ 665-7242; one way BZ$10; ⊙ approximately hourly from 6:45am to 6pm, or 5pm Sunday) runs skiffs between the southern tip of Placencia and the town of Independence/Mango Creek; from Independence bus station you can connect with any of the buses that traverse the Southern Hwy.

The 45-passenger **D Express** sails from Placencia municipal pier to Puerto Cortés, Honduras, (BZ$130, 4½ hours including immigration time) at 9am on Friday. Tickets are sold at **Book it @ Barefoot** (p209). The return trip leaves Puerto Cortés at 11am on Monday.

BUS

Ritchie's (☑ 523-3806; www.ritchiesbusservice. com) bus line has one daily bus to Belize City at 6:15am (BZ$20, 4½ hours) and three buses to Dangriga (BZ$10, 1¾ hours) Monday to Saturday, from where you can transfer to Belmopan and points beyond. Buses to Dangriga leave at 7am, 12:45pm and 2:30pm (2:30pm only on Sunday) from the bus stop on Main St opposite the Hokey Pokey Water Taxi.

To get to Hopkins, ask to be let off at the Hopkins junction and hitch or call a taxi from there.

Travelers heading to Toledo should take the Hokey Pokey Water Taxi to Independence and pick up a south-bound James Line service.

🛈 Getting Around

Many accommodations north of the village offer free airport transfers and free use of bicycles for guests.

Taxis meet flights. The ride to or from the village costs BZ$10. A taxi from the village costs around BZ$20 to Seine Bight or BZ$30 to Maya Beach.

Cars, motorbikes and golf buggies can be hired along the Placencia peninsula; try **Barefoot Services** (☑ 523-3066; www.barefootservicesbelize. com; ⊙ 8am-5:30pm Sun-Fri), near the airport.

TOLEDO DISTRICT (THE DEEP SOUTH)

POP 34,900

Bordering Guatemala to the south and west and the Stann Creek and Cayo Districts to the north, the 1669-sq-mile Toledo District encompasses an area most Belizeans refer to lovingly as 'The Deep South.' The only major town is Punta Gorda, and about half the district is under protection as national parks, wildlife sanctuaries, forest reserves or nature reserves.

Visitors to Belize's Deep South have a unique opportunity to simultaneously experience both ancient and contemporary Maya culture. Over 60% of the population of Toledo District is Maya and these people, with more than 30 villages, have done a great deal to keep their culture alive and intact. The Maya of Southern Belize who survived European diseases were mostly driven into Guatemala by the British in the 18th and 19th centuries. But two groups crossed back from Guatemala to Southern Belize in the late 19th and early 20th centuries, fleeing taxes, forced labor and land grabs by German coffee growers. The Mopan Maya settled in the uplands of Southern Belize, while the Kekchi Maya, from the Alta Verapaz area of Guatemala, settled in the lowlands. The Mopan and Kekchi speak distinct Maya languages, as well as English and sometimes Spanish.

While Maya men generally adopt Western styles of dress, most women still wear plain, full-length dresses with bright trimmings, or calf-length skirts teamed with embroidered blouses. Rituals and folklore continue to play an important role in Maya life, with masked dances such as the Cortés Dance and Deer Dance performed in some villages at festivals, including All Saints' and All Souls' Days (November 1 and 2) and Easter week.

Toledo's attractions – jungle trails, lagoons, wetlands, rivers, caves, waterfalls, countless birds – and its archaeological heritage are much less trumpeted than those of Belize's other districts, which makes them all the more magnetic to those looking to get off the beaten path.

The Deep South

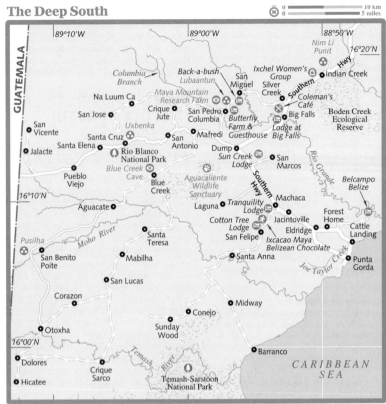

The sealing of the Southern Hwy through to Guatemala has made this area much more accessible and many villages can be visited without leaving the main road, but you'll need to delve a little further to experience the best of the Deep South.

❶ Getting There & Around

Frequent James Line buses run along the Southern Hwy from Belize City and Dangriga to Punta Gorda. Less frequent local buses connect villages.

Any north-bound bus leaving Punta Gorda will drop you off at the Dump or Lubaantun intersections, from where people often hitchhike to many of the villages.

One daily bus leaves Punta Gorda at 6am, stopping at the villages of Eldridge, Dump, Mafredi, San Antonio, Santa Cruz, Santa Elena and Pueblo Viejo before reaching Jalacte. On Monday, Wednesday, Friday and Saturday there is another service at 11:30am and 4pm.

The Barranco bus leaves at noon on Monday, Wednesday, Friday and Saturday. Another goes to San Jose at 11:30am or noon, leaving San Jose at 4pm and 5pm.

To get to Lubaantun, take one of the morning buses to Silver Creek.

Schedules fluctuate; stop by the BTB office in Punta Gorda for the latest (printed in the Toledo Howler). Village buses cost between BZ$2 and BZ$6, depending on distance. All village buses leave from Jose Maria Nunez St, in Punta Gorda (just north of Tate's Guest House).

Punta Gorda

POP 5910

Punta Gorda (or PG as it's known) is a slightly ramshackle coastal settlement down in the Deep South of Toledo. Once known to travelers mainly as a port to get the boat across to Guatemala, it's increasingly attracting visitors looking to chill out in the south and as a base for exploring surrounding Maya villages and culture, and the remote Southern Cayes.

PG spreads along the Gulf of Honduras, its compact downtown area stretching lazily for several blocks just in from the coast. The town center is a triangular park with a distinctive blue-and-white clock tower; the airstrip is northwest, on the inland edge of town. Wednesday, Saturday and, to a lesser extent, Monday and Friday are market mornings, when villagers from the mostly Maya settlements of southern Toledo come to town to buy, sell and BBQ around the central park and Front St.

Though it lacks the beaches of Placencia, there are plenty of docks from which to take a dip in the calm waters. A good part of PG's charm lies in its unassuming character.

☉ Sights

Clock Tower   LANDMARK
The clocktower is a useful landmark in the center of Punta Gorda's downtown.

🏃 Activities

Punta Gorda is a cool place to chill out for a few days, but outside of eating, lounging around the park and swimming off various docks, it isn't exactly activity central.

In the town's immediate environs, however, it's a different story: you can kayak on Joe Taylor Creek, which enters the sea at the eastern end of town, hike in the jungle or take kayak trips on other rivers in the area, where you may see monkeys, crocodiles and even manatees or dolphins.

Offshore, some of the islands of the Port Honduras Marine Reserve (p225), northeast of Punta Gorda, offer good snorkeling and diving, especially the Snake Cayes (named for their resident boa constrictors), 16 miles out, with white-sand beaches. The beautiful Sapodilla Cayes (p225) on the barrier reef, some 38 miles east of Punta Gorda, are even better, with healthy coral reefs, abundant marine life and sandy beaches. A day trip for four costs around BZ$500 to the Port Honduras Marine Reserve or BZ$650 to Sapodilla Cayes.

Fishing for bonefish, tarpon, permit, snook, barracuda, kingfish, jacks and snapper is superb in the offshore waters and some coastal lagoons and inland rivers: fly- and spin-fishing and trolling can be practiced year-round. Any of the tour operators in town can help you arrange fishing and sailing trips, as well as other activities.

★ Cotton Tree
Chocolate Factory   FOOD
(www.cottontreechocolate.com; 2 Front St; ☉ 8am-noon & 1:30-5pm Mon-Fri, to noon Sat) 🅿 **FREE**
Cotton Tree is a good opportunity to buy some local chocolate and learn a bit about the process. Beans are sourced from Toledo Cacao Growers Association, promoting both fair trade and local production. The owner happily offers tours of the small factory, and there's a gift shop selling only locally made (and some chocolate-themed) handicrafts, including soaps, cacao-bean jewelry and, obviously, chocolate bars.

Maroon Creole Drum School   MUSIC
(☏ 632-7841, 668-7733; methodsdrums@hotmail.com; Joe Taylor Creek; ☉ by appointment) Those looking to study with a master will find the trip to Emmeth Young's drum school well worth it. When he's not touring the country performing, one of Belize's most respected Creole drummers hosts drum-making workshops and group presentations. It costs BZ$25 an hour for drum lessons, or for around BZ$250 you can spend a few days learning both drumming and drum making, leaving with your own handcrafted drum.

Open hearth cooking classes can also be arranged here. Appointment only.

Warasa Garifuna
Drum School   MUSIC
(☏ 632-7701; www.warasadrumschool.com; New Rd; drum lessons BZ$25, half-day package BZ$125; ☉ by appointment) Local drummer Ronald

RANGER FOR A DAY

The unique 'Ranger for a Day' program enables travelers to experience the life and work of jungle rangers of the **Ya'axché Conservation Trust** (☏ 722-0108; www.yaaxche.org) as they go about their daily activities in the Golden Stream Corridor Preserve, protecting the area from illegal activity and monitoring biodiversity. To the untrained eye, it's a pile of poop, but to a ranger, the scat tells many a tale.

Participants in the program have a unique chance to learn various skills such as species recognition, identifying edible and medicinal plants, and jungle survival in general while exploring a 15,000-acre wildlife reserve with local park rangers. For more information, contact Ya'axché Conservation Trust.

Punta Gorda

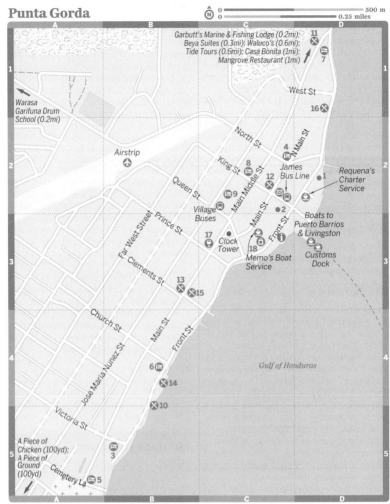

Garbutt's Marine & Fishing Lodge (0.2mi);
Beya Suites (0.3mi); Waluco's (0.6mi);
Tide Tours (0.6mi); Casa Bonita (1mi);
Mangrove Restaurant (1mi)

West St

Warasa
Garifuna Drum
School (0.2mi)

North St

King St

Airstrip

Queen St

Village
Buses

Clock
Tower

Memo's Boat
Service

James
Bus Line

Requena's
Charter
Service

Boats to
Puerto Barrios
& Livingston

Customs
Dock

Gulf of Honduras

Church St

Victoria St

A Piece of
Chicken (100yd);
A Piece of
Ground
(100yd)

Cemetery La

SOUTHERN BELIZE PUNTA GORDA

Raymond (Ray) McDonald teaches Garifuna beats at his Warasa Garifuna Drum School on New Rd (about 15 minutes' walk out of town). There are one-on-one lessons and group classes. McDonald also performs and lectures about Garifuna culture at Hickatee Cottages (p223).

☞ Tours

Ideally located for exploring Belize's Deep South, Punta Gorda has a number of certified tour guides who lead day trips and longer expeditions, both terrestrial and nautical, as well as renting out canoes, kayaks and other gear.

Garbutt's Marine &
Fishing Lodge   FISHING, DIVING
(☏ 722-0070;   www.garbuttsfishinglodge.com;
Front St; fishing charters per day US$450) Garbutt's is an experienced and highly professional fishing charter company and dive outfit, with exclusive access to private island Lime Caye in the Sapodillas and accommodation and kayak rental in Punta Gorda.

Punta Gorda

⊕ Activities, Courses & Tours
1 Cotton Tree Chocolate Factory D2
2 Wild Thing C2

⊕ Sleeping
3 Blue Belize Guest House B5
4 Charlton's Inn C2
5 Coral House Inn A5
6 Nature's Way Guest House B4
7 Sea Front Inn D1
8 St Charles Inn C2
9 Tate's Guest House C2

⊗ Eating
10 Asha's Culture Kitchen B4
  Fajina Maya Food .... (see 18)
11 Gomiers D1
12 Grace's Restaurant C2
13 Hang Cheong Restaurant B3
14 Marian's Bayview Restaurant B4
15 Olympic Bar & Grill B3
  Snack Shack .... (see 2)
16 Waterfront Italian Restaurant D1

⊕ Drinking & Nightlife
17 PG Sports Bar C3

⊕ Shopping
18 Fajina Crafts Center C3

Tide Tours GUIDED TOUR
(☑722-2129; www.tidetours.org; Hopeville) 🎣 Ecofriendly Tide runs tours throughout the Toledo area, including inland adventures to caves and waterfalls, birding trips to Payne's Creek National Park and cultural tourism to local Maya villages. Tide also does boating adventures out to the Southern Cayes including snorkeling, sport fishing and diving tours.

Wild Thing ADVENTURE TOUR
(☑663-1028; Snack Shack, Main St) Offers custom tours around the Toledo District, including snorkeling trips, temple expeditions, kayaking, fishing and more. Head to the Snack Shack and ask for Roberto.

Toledo Cave & Adventure Tours GUIDED TOUR
(☑604-2124; http://tcatours.com) Bruno Kuppinger has been running adventure tours for more than 15 years. He's based out near Manfedri village.

Wild Encounters GUIDED TOUR
(☑620-3499, 636-1028) Experienced tour operator in Punta Gorda offering cultural and adventure tours in the Toledo District.

🎉 Festivals & Events

Chocolate Festival of Belize FOOD
(http://chocolatefestivalofbelize.com; ⊙May) Celebrating all things to do with cacao and chocolate – the Maya food of the gods – this festival is held on the Commonwealth Day holiday weekend, mainly in Punta Gorda. As well as tastings, demonstrations and music, there's a street fair.

TIDE Fish Fest FOOD
(⊙Oct) The Fish Fest weekend celebrates the town's favorite natural resource with seafood feasts and live music.

🛏 Sleeping

There's a sprinkling of accommodations in PG's downtown, but some of the best places are on the northern and southern fringes of town.

A Piece of Ground HOTEL $
(☑665-2695; www.apieceofground.com; 1050 Pelican St; dm/d BZ$30/70; ❄️🛜) Better known locally as Backa Jama's, this funky, sociable four-story place has a new ground-floor hostel with two dorms (one with air-con) and four spotless guesthouse rooms with attached bathroom on the 2nd floor. Keep going up the stairs to the popular restaurant, serving chicken dishes and American-style burgers and fries, and the rooftop bar with pool table.

It's tricky to find at the southern end of town. Call ahead or ask locally.

Tate's Guest House GUESTHOUSE $
(☑722-0147; tatesguesthouse@yahoo.com; 34 Jose Maria Nunez St; r BZ$70-80, apt BZ$125-150; P❄️🛜) Former postmaster Mr Tate keeps his guesthouse in immaculate condition and it's the best budget deal in the town center. The six rooms inside the mauve two-story facade, set in a little garden with a gazebo, are good value at these rates. Two are self-contained, with kitchenettes and air-con, and all come with cable TV and hot showers.

Casa Bonita GUESTHOUSE $
(☑623-0497; johnharrisbze@gmail.com; Front St; s/d BZ$50/75; 🛜) At the north end of town facing the sea, the two rooms and two-bedroom apartment at this family home (also home to Mangrove Restaurant; p224) are a great deal for long stayers, with cheap weekly and monthly rates. Plenty of home comforts, wi-fi and free use of kayaks.

SOUTHERN BELIZE PUNTA GORDA

TRAVEL WITH TEA

A unique opportunity to be welcomed into local villages and experience village life first-hand is provided by the **Toledo Ecotourism Association** (TEA; ☑ 702-2119; www.tea belize.org). TEA is a community organization that manages guesthouses in several Maya villages. Currently, villages with TEA guesthouses are San Jose, Santa Elena, San Antonio, Laguna and San Miguel.

Although these are guesthouses, not homestays, you get the opportunity to mix with local families by having meals in different village homes. Main meals usually consist of tortillas and *caldo*, a stew made from root vegetables and meat, usually chicken. If you're vegetarian, be sure to specify this clearly and in advance. Rates vary depending on the guesthouse, starting from BZ$25 per person, and meals are around BZ$10.

Most of the funds collected through the programs go directly to the villages themselves, benefiting many Maya communities. Organised activity programs range from guided hikes, caving, canoeing and birdwatching to classes in textiles, basket weaving and cooking, as well as village tours and after-dinner storytelling. Performances of traditional dance and music (using the harp in Kekchi villages, marimba among the Mopan) can also be arranged.

To get specific contact information for key people in individual villages, call Reyes Chun or stop by Nature's Way Guest House in Punta Gorda, which has a booking desk.

Nature's Way Guest House
GUESTHOUSE **$**
(☑ 702-2119; natureswayguesthouse@hotmail.com; 82 Front St; dm BZ$18, s/d/tr/q without bathroom BZ$28/38/48/58, s/d with bathroom BZ$30/40) Rustic and ramshackle, this place has been a longtime backpacker bolthole in Punta Gorda. Simple, screened-in, ocean breeze–cooled wooden rooms are upstairs, and a large sociable communal area with TV, music and free wi-fi is below. Nature's Way also rents bikes and kayaks for BZ$15 per day.

Charlton's Inn
HOTEL **$**
(☑ 722-2197; www.charltonsinn.com; 9 Main St; s/d/tr BZ$80/100/110, apt s/d per month BZ$900/1000; ❄ @) With 25 clean rooms with air-con and cable TV, not to mention a good location at the north end of town, Charlton's is a decent choice for those looking for a place in the upper level of the budget category. Triples are more like suites, with two stand-alone bedrooms. There are also five apartments for long-term stayers.

St Charles Inn
HOTEL **$**
(☑ 722-2149; 23 King St; s/d/tr BZ$50/60/70; ❄ 🛜) Lilac-colored walls, verandas with hammocks, and budget rooms are the main draws of this aging guesthouse in downtown Punta Gorda. Rooms come with private bathrooms, coffee-makers and cable TV.

★ Coral House Inn
BOUTIQUE HOTEL **$$**
(☑ 722-2878; www.coralhouseinn.net; 151 Main St; d incl continental breakfast BZ$196-218, ste BZ$272;

❄🛜🌊) This sublime seaside inn at the southern end of town boasts a lovely garden and in-ground swimming pool. Enormous rooms are clearly decorated by someone with an eye for style, giving the place a classic (but not at all pretentious) colonial feel. A spacious veranda overlooks the sea on one side and a quaintly picturesque old cemetery on the other.

Chilling at the quiet poolside bar and exploring the area by bicycle (provided free) are just some of the bonuses for guests.

Garbutt's Marine & Fishing Lodge
CABINS **$$**
(☑ 604-3548, 722-0070; www.garbuttsfishing lodge.com; Front St, Joe Taylor Creek; r BZ$160-200; P ❄🛜) Although primarily for guests on fishing or dive charters, Garbutt's awesome seafront rooms and stilt *cabañas* are available to anyone if they're available. It's a low-key setup, but this is the only absolute waterfront accommodation in PG, and the spacious lodge rooms and private cabins with air-con, TV and over-water balconies are excellent value. Also a dive shop and kayak rental.

Beya Suites
HOTEL **$$**
(☑ 722-2188; www.beyasuites.com; 6 Hopeville; s/d/tr from BZ$142/175/208; P ❄🛜) Brightly colored (it's the garish two-story pink building) and breezy, this seaside hotel about half a mile north of PG is a good find for those looking to balance comfort and economy. The eight rooms and two suites

are well appointed and supremely comfortable for this price. The cozy dining room serves breakfast and there's a small bar.

Hickatee Cottages RESORT **$$**
(☑ 662-4475; www.hickatee.com; cottages BZ$130-200, d BZ$160, ste BZ$240-260; [P] 🛜 🌊) 🏊 Serene Hickatee Cottages is a beautiful and unique solar-powered resort that leaves as light an ecological footprint as possible. There are three fully furnished cottages, two spacious suites and the Hickatee Den, a small detached unit that sleeps two and overlooks the tiny plunge pool. The property features both garden and wild jungle space, and a 3-mile trail network.

Activities at Hickatee include nature walks and tarantula spotting, and Ronald Raymond McDonald gives drumming performances and lessons here at 6:30pm every Wednesday. Hickatee has a remote feel, located down a rugged dirt road, but it's only 1.25 miles from town – call ahead for a free pickup.

Sea Front Inn HOTEL **$$**
(☑ 722-2300; www.seafrontinn.com; 4 Front St; s/d/tr BZ$150/180/185, apt per month BZ$1900; [P] ❄ 🛜) One of the quirkiest looking hotels in Southern Belize, this four-story gabled stone, wood and concrete construction is a comfortable and hospitable place. There are sea views from the front rooms and self-contained apartments at the back for long-term stayers.

⭐**Blue Belize Guest House** B&B **$$$**
(☑ 722-2678; www.bluebelize.com; 139 Front St; ste BZ$184, honeymoon ste BZ$270, 2-bedroom ste BZ$370; @ 🛜 🌊) 🏊 It's impossible not to feel a calming sense of space and relaxation at Blue Belize, with its waterfront location, lush garden and enormous rooms in a pair of connected two-story houses. The six breezy and beautifully decorated suites are more like serviced apartments than hotel rooms, offering well-furnished living rooms and kitchenettes, in addition to a comfortable master bedroom.

✖️ Eating

⭐**Snack Shack** CAFE **$**
(Main St; mains BZ$6-12; ⊙ 7am-3pm Mon-Sat) Tucked away off the main street among a group of shack restaurants, this is the best spot in town for Western or Belizean breakfasts. Lunchtime is 'build you own burrito' served alongside brain-freezing slushies. The open-air deck is breezy and inviting.

⭐**Gomiers** VEGETARIAN **$**
(☑ 620-1719; 5 Alejandro Vernon St; meals BZ$6-17; ⊙ 8am-10pm; 🛜 🍴) There's a laid-back bohemian vibe at this small open-air restaurant where excellent organic vegetarian cuisine, veg and conch fritters, fresh juices and a variety of tofu-based creations are the order of the day. Friday night's live reggae is a PG institution.

Olympic Bar & Grill TEX-MEX **$**
(☑ 629-1699; cnr Main & Clements Sts; mains $7-22; ⊙ 7am-11pm Mon-Sat) This popular little spot serves spicy hot wings, burritos and burgers, along with ice-cold beer. Happy hour is from 5pm to 7pm and Thursday is 'wings night'.

Fajina Maya Food MAYA **$**
(Front St; mains BZ$5; ⊙ 6am-noon Mon-Sat) Above the Fajina Crafts Center (p224), this small restaurant serves interesting Maya soups and stews with vegetables and poultry from farms in the outlying communities. The specialty of the house is *caldo*, a chicken soup colored red with annatto, a local vegetable. Lack of ambience is compensated for by the sea breeze and ocean view.

Marian's Bayview Restaurant CARIBBEAN **$**
(76 Front St; mains BZ$8-14; ⊙ 11am-9pm) This nondescript 3rd-floor outdoor eatery on the southern waterfront has a good local reputation and great views. Marian serves up excellent east Indian cuisine. Lunch and dinner are served buffet-style.

Grace's Restaurant SEAFOOD **$**
(16 Main St; mains BZ$7-22; ⊙ 7am-10pm; 🛜) A longtime favorite of locals and travelers alike, Grace's offers a wide range of dishes, from Belizean specialties such as chicken stew, fry fish, and rice and beans, to more exotic seafood fare and good breakfast. The decor is simple but breezy.

Hang Cheong Restaurant CHINESE **$**
(☑ 722-2064; cnr Main & Clements Sts; dishes BZ$6-16; ⊙ 10:30am-2:30pm & 5pm-midnight; ❄) Hang Cheong does a brisk lunchtime trade and some good vegetarian dishes such as chow mein.

Waterfront Italian Restaurant PIZZA **$$**
(☑ 663-8994; 18 Front St; pizzas BZ$12-30; ⊙ 10am-9pm Mon-Thu, 10am-midnight Fri-Sun; 🛜) If you're just dying for a pizza or calzone, come to this takeaway place. There's also a sea-facing dine-in area with plastic tables and chairs.

A Piece of Chicken
AMERICAN $$

(1050 Pelican St; mains BZ$8-14; ☺ 5pm-midnight)
The main ingredient here is chicken – in
burgers, sandwiches or with rice and beans.
Also hand-cut fries and nachos. The food is
good and the 3rd-floor bar is a great place to
hang out.

Asha's Culture Kitchen
SEAFOOD $$

(☑ 722-2742; Front St; mains BZ$15-30; ☺ 4-10pm)
Twisted lobster, baked barracuda, whole snapper and lionfish finger – and the best waterfront deck in PG. There's a lot to like about
Asha's, where seafood is the specialty and
the sea breezes are fine. A standard meal includes a choice of main from the blackboard
menu and two sides (garlic mash potato is a
winner). Service slow but it's worth the wait.

Mangrove Restaurant
SEAFOOD $$

(☑ 623-0497; Milestone One, Cattle Landing; mains
BZ$12-20; ☺ 5-10pm Mon-Sat) Chef Iconie is
well known locally for her fusion Belizean
meals, incorporating locally caught seafood,
curries and pasta dishes. Choose from a
small selection of mains and sides on the
changing blackboard menu. It's across from
the waterfront north of PG.

🍷 Drinking & Nightlife

Punta Gorda has a number of bars along
Front St and downtown. The town is also
home to some top performers, such as
brukdown (19th-century Creole music)
queen Leela Vernon, and local *punta* rock
favorites, the Coolie Rebels.

Waluco's
BAR

(☑ 702-2129; Front St, Hopeville; ☺ 11:30am-
midnight Tue-Sun; 🐾) This big, breezy *pal-
apa*, a mile northeast of town, is a popular
weekend spot, especially for Sunday ses-
sions when the BBQ fires up and everyone
goes swimming off the pier opposite. There's
cheap bar food and Garifuna drummers
sometimes play here.

PG Sports Bar
BAR

(cnr Main & Prince Sts; ☺ 8pm-midnight Tue-Thu,
to 2am Fri & Sat) This bar is incongruously
enhanced by a staggering collection of US
sports photos and posters. There's usually
a DJ or live music on Friday and Saturday.

🛍 Shopping

Fajina Crafts Center
ARTS

(Front St; ☺ 8am-11:15am Mon, Wed, Fri & Sat) Op-
erated cooperatively by a women's associa-
tion with members from 13 villages around
southern Toledo, the Fajina Crafts Center
sells handmade necklaces, belts, bracelets,
baskets, clothing, bags, earrings, wood carv-
ings and many other items made by Toledo's
indigenous peoples. Proceeds earned at the
shop go directly back to the craftspeople
themselves.

❶ Information

Belize Bank (30 Main St) Exchanges cash; ATM
accepts most international cards.

Customs & Immigration (☑ 722-2022; Front St;
☺ 9am-5pm Mon-Fri) This is your first port of
call when coming to Punta Gorda by boat from
Guatemala or Honduras; it should also be your
last stopping place when leaving by sea (there's
a departure tax of BZ$40). Head here for visa
extensions too.

Post Office (Front St; ☺ 8am-noon & 1-5pm
Mon-Thu, 8am-noon & 1-4:30pm Fri) PG's post
office.

Punta Gorda Hospital (☑ 722-2026; Main St)
The hospital is south of the town centre.

Punta Gorda Tourism Information Center
(☑ 722-2531; Front St; ☺ 8am-5pm Mon-Fri)
PG's little BTIA tourist office can answer general
questions and has village bus timetables. Pick
up a free copy of the local tourist paper *Toledo
Howler*.

Scotia Bank (1 Main St) ATM accepts most
international cards.

TIDE (☑ 722-2274; www.tidebelize.org; One Mile
San Antonio Rd) The Toledo Institute for Devel-
opment and Environment (TIDE) is responsible
for a range of community conservation projects
in the Deep South, both in the inland forests and
the marine parks.

❶ Getting There & Away

AIR

Tropic Air (☑ 722-2008; www.tropicair.com)
has five daily flights to Belize City (BZ$296, one
hour) and Belize City International (BZ$348,
one hour), and one to Placencia (BZ$135, 20
minutes) and Dangriga (BZ$214, 40 minutes).

Maya Island Air (☑ 722-2856; www.maya
islandair.com) flies four times daily to Belize
City, Placencia and Dangriga for similar prices.
Specials are often available, and ticket offices
are at the airstrip (PND).

BOAT

There are four daily boat services to Puerto
Barrios in Guatemala at 9:30am, 1pm, 2pm and
4pm. There is also one daily boat to Livingstone.
Boats depart from the municipal pier in front of
the customs and immigration office.

Memo's Boat Service (☑ 651-4780; memos
boatservicandtours@yahoo.com; Front St)

DON'T MISS

THE CAYS OF THE DEEP SOUTH

If the northern or central cays are too crowded for you, head seriously off the beaten path to the seldom-visited cays of the Deep South.

About a two-hour boat ride from Punta Gorda (and right on the barrier reef) is the **Sapodilla Cayes Marine Reserve**. A protected reserve (visitors pay a daily BZ$20 conservation fee), the Sapodillas offer superlative opportunities for swimming, snorkeling and diving. Lime Caye, the most popular of the Sapodillas, has wonderful white-sand beaches, a basic Gilligan's Island bunkhouse (BZ$40 per person), beach camping (BZ$30) and meals for BZ$20. A round-trip fare to Lime Caye is around BZ$600 per boat (maximum of six passengers). Trips to other cays in the chain are also available. Contact Garbutt's Marine (p220) in Punta Gorda.

Closer to Punta Gorda, the **Port Honduras Marine Reserve** contains 130+ mangrove cays and is managed by the Toledo Institute for Development and Environment, aka TIDE (p224). There's a daily fee of BZ$10.

Trips to the Port Honduras reserve begin at Abalone Caye, where a short presentation is given by the rangers in charge. Visitors will then be brought to different cays in the reserve, including West Snake Caye (known for its white-sand beaches), East Snake Caye (excellent snorkeling) and Frenchman Caye (a prime spot for manatee-watching). Depending on the trip, you may also get to see Wild Cane Caye, an ancient Maya center of obsidian trade and production.

To arrange trips to either Sapodilla or Port Honduras, contact Garbutt's Marine & Fishing Lodge (p220). Garbutt's also arranges a variety of marine tours around the area, including fishing, scuba and snorkeling trips, with price dependent on distance.

departs Punta Gorda daily at 12:45pm for Livingston (BZ$50, 30 minutes) and Puerto Barrios, Guatemala (BZ$60, 45 minutes). Returning, Memo's boat leaves Livingston at 2pm and Puerto Barrios at 3pm, with identical prices. The office is across from Customs & Immigration.

Requena's Charter Service (☑ 722-2070; 12 Front St) operates the *Mariestela*, departing Punta Gorda at 9:30am daily for Puerto Barrios, Guatemala (BZ$50, one hour), and returning at 2pm. Tickets are sold at the office and the customs dock down the street.

BUS

James Bus Line (☑ 702-2049, 722-2625; King St) has hourly buses from Punta Gorda to Belize City (regular/air-con BZ$22/24, seven hours) from 4am to 4pm. Buses stop at Independence (BZ$9/11, two hours), Dangriga (BZ$13/15, 3½ hours) and Belmopan (BZ$19/22, 5½ hours). All buses leave from the main bus station on King St and cruise around PG a bit before heading north.

ⓘ Getting Around

Aliram Auto Rental (☑ 722-2753; aliram@btl. net; Far West St) rents cars for use in the Toledo area.

Taxis congregate around Central Park.

The main stop for buses to villages around Punta Gorda is on the corner of Queen St and Jose Maria Nunez St. Timetables are available from the tourist office.

Around Punta Gorda

The Southern Hwy heads northwest from Punta Gorda to the intersection at Dump (we didn't name it!), where there's a gas station. Along the way are detours to some of the region's best ecolodges and there are several interesting places on the rugged road to remote Barranco village.

◉ Sights

**Aguacaliente
Wildlife Sanctuary**   NATURE RESERVE
(Laguna) About 13 miles northwest of Punta Gorda and 2 miles off the Southern Hwy, the village of Laguna is the starting point for the 8.6-sq-mile Aguacaliente Wildlife Sanctuary, an extensive wetland area. The lagoon, at the heart of the park, is home to flocks of ibis and woodstork, many raptors including ospreys, plenty of kingfishers and herons and the odd jabiru stork. There's a visitors center on the trail from the village.

The two-hour hike in can be wet and muddy and is sometimes impossible at the height of the rains.

**Temash-Sarstoon
National Park**   NATIONAL PARK
(☑ 604-8564, 626-7684; egbertvalencio@yahoo. com) The tiny Garifuna fishing community of

Barranco (population 160), about an hour's drive from Punta Gorda, is the access point for Temash-Sarstoon National Park, a remote 64-sq-mile protected reserve of rainforest, wetlands, estuaries and rivers lined by towering mangroves and stretching all the way to Guatemala. The park harbors a huge variety of wildlife, from jaguars, tapirs and ocelots to birdlife and manatees in the estuaries.

Two Barranco natives deeply involved in both local tourism and park conservation are Egbert Valencio and Alvin Loredo; both lead land and river tours (around BZ$200 per day) into the nearby park given at least a few days' notice.

🏃 Activities

Ixcacao Maya Belizean Chocolate   FOOD
(📞 742-4050; www.ixcacaomayabelizeanchocolate.com; San Felipe village; tours per person from BZ$60; ⊙9am-5pm) 🌿 Learn all about the Maya chocolate-making process at Juan and Abelina's beautiful cacao farm and chocolate factory in the off-track village of San Felipe. There's a variety of tour options, including farm tours, factory tours and traditional Maya lunch. Juan will walk you through the traditional chocolate-making process – from harvest and fermentation to drying and roasting, to deshalling and grinding, tasting as you go. Reserve a day in advance; group discounts are available. The family also has a small homestay bunkhouse next to the factory (BZ$50 per person including breakfast and dinner) as well as camping (BZ$10) and farmstay (BZ$50).

🛏️ Sleeping

A number of excellent ecolodges can be found in the jungles around Punta Gorda.

Sun Creek Lodge   RESORT $$
(📞 607-6363; www.suncreeklodge.de; d cabaña with/without bathroom from BZ$140/80, villas BZ$180-240) As jungle lodges in Belize go, Sun Creek is a real bargain. Thomas and Marisa run this rustic, eco-oriented lodge in a fine patch of jungle near the village of San Marcos about 13 miles from Punta Gorda. In the tropical garden are four individual thatched-roof *cabañas*, two with bathroom outside and open-sky shower, and two beautifully appointed family villas, all made from dark tropical hardwoods.

Villas are a comfortable blend of modern and rustic, with a spacious living area, kitchenette with fridge, and private bathrooms with open-sky shower.

ℹ️ RURAL TRAVEL ON THE FLY

While tourism in rural Toledo is picking up, aside from the TEA program (p222) and a few independent hotels and fancy ecolodges, there just aren't many hotels in the Deep South. This doesn't mean you'll wind up sleeping in the jungle (although that can be arranged), it just means that outside swanky jungle lodges you'll have to look a bit harder to find a bed. Plan ahead (there are five villages with TEA guesthouses) or, if you get stuck, ask at the local village store or 'cool spot' – someone should find you a bed.

★ Belcampo Belize   LODGE $$$
(📞 722-0050; www.belcampobz.com; ste incl breakfast BZ$1050-1300; P❄️🛜🏊) 🌿 The fabulous Belcampo Belize enjoys a superb hilltop setting overlooking miles of protected jungle stretching down to the Gulf of Honduras. This beautiful lodge offers 16 spacious and luxurious suites with solid wood furniture, queen- or king-size beds, full-length windows and private verandas overlooking jungle and sea.

There's a day spa and two cable tramways, one leading down through the jungle to the Río Grande and hotel gym. The excellent restaurant serves food sourced from the organic farm. Tours on offer include fly-fishing, birding, snorkeling and trips to Maya ruins. Belcampo feels remote but is only 2.5 miles off the Southern Hwy, and about 5 miles from Punta Gorda.

Cotton Tree Lodge   RESORT $$$
(📞 670-0557, in USA 866-480-4534; www.cottontreelodge.com; d cabañas BZ$392-700, incl meals, activities & transfers BZ$918-1228; P❄️@🛜🏊) 🌿 Luxury, environmentalism and intense beauty meet on the banks of the Moho River a few miles north of the village of San Felipe. All of Cotton Tree's 11 thatched-roof cabins on stilts are luxuriously furnished in a superb jungle/hardwood motif – while they're all screened in, there's an exhilarating feeling of sleeping in the open.

The resort's power is partially provided by solar panels, while most of the food served in the lodge's excellent restaurant is bought locally or sourced from the onsite organic garden. Activities include hiking, horseback riding, kayaking, canoeing, caving and birdwatching (included in all-inclusive packages, extra if you take room-only). The 100-acre property offers amazing views of the nearby Maya Mountain Range on the western horizon.

Tranquility Lodge   RESORT $$$
(☑ 677-9921, 665-9070, in USA 800-819-9088; www.tranquility-lodge.com; r & cabañas BZ$250-290; P ❄ 🛜 🌊) Tranquility Lodge is just off the highway 8 miles from Punta Gorda and offers three rustic, thatched-roof *cabañas* and four lodge rooms set amid pretty gardens and jungle. Rooms are equipped with air-con and flat-screen TVs, while the *cabañas* are big, breezy, fan-cooled and TV-free.

There's a regulation pool table and a shuffleboard deck in the lodge dining-common room, not to mention an excellent swimming hole on the property.

✖ Eating

The best restaurants are in the upmarket lodges, where nonguests are welcome (usually with advanced reservation).

**★ Jungle Farm
Restaurant**   INTERNATIONAL, BELIZEAN $$$
(Wilson Rd, Belcampo Belize; lunch BZ$18-24, dinner BZ$42-48; ⏱ 6am-9pm) If you have only one dining splurge in Southern Belize, the restaurant at Belcampo is not a bad place to do it. The location, high on a jungle hilltop, is superb and the restaurant is a delight with its large, open deck, expansive views and attentive service. Food is expertly prepared with a farm-to-table philosophy combining uniquely Belizean and international flavors.

Much of the produce comes from Belcampo's own farm and gardens or from local farmers and fishers. Light lunch might consist of tacos, salads or lionfish *ceviche*. Dinner is a daily changing menu that might feature Gulf snapper, roast suckling pig or vegetarian rice and beans. Downstairs is the sociable Rum Bar and there's a coffee shop at the hotel. Reservations recommended, especially for dinner.

Around the Deep South

Big Falls & Around
POP 1100
On the Southern Hwy, about 20 miles from Punta Gorda, Big Falls is a small village with a number of cultural and adventure attractions. This is a good starting point for the Toledo cultural circuit taking in San Miguel and San Pedro Columbia.

Further north are the Kekchi villages of Silver Creek (population 320), Indian Creek (population 570) and Golden Stream (population 320).

⊙ Sights

**★ Living Maya
Experience**   CULTURAL CENTER
(☑ Chiacs 632-4585, Cals 627-7408; livingmaya experience@gmail.com; Big Falls; tours per person BZ$20-30; ⏱ by appointment) Two Kekchi families in Big Falls village have opened up their homes as a cultural experience for visitors and both are excellent. The Cal family demonstrates ancient Maya lifestyle from tortilla- and chocolate-making to traditional instruments and an exploration of their self-sufficient garden. With the Chiac family you can learn to make woven Maya crafts – baskets, hammocks or bags.

Nim Li Punit   RUIN
(☑ 822-2106; admission BZ$10; ⏱ 8am-5pm) The Maya ruins of Nim Li Punit stand atop a natural hill half a mile north of the Southern Hwy, near the village of Indian Creek. The site is notable for the 26 stelae found in the southern Plaza of the Stelae. Four of the

Nim Li Punit

finest are housed in the stela house beside the visitors center.

Stela 14, at 33ft, is the second-longest stela found anywhere in the Maya world (after Stela E from Quiriguá, Guatemala). It shows the ruler of Nim Li Punit in an offering or incense-scattering ritual, wearing an enormous headdress, which is responsible for the name Nim Li Punit ('Big Hat' in Kekchi Maya).

Rediscovered in 1976 by oil prospectors, Nim Li Punit was inhabited from some point in the middle Classic Period (AD 250–1000) until sometime between AD 800 and 1000. It was probably a town of 5000 to 7000 people at its peak, and likely was a political and religious community of some importance in the region.

The most interesting part of the site is the south end, comprising the Plaza of the Stelae and the Plaza of Royal Tombs. The Plaza of the Stelae is thought to have acted as a calendrical observatory: seen from its western mound, three of the small stones in front of the long eastern mound align with sunrise on the equinoxes and solstices. The Plaza of Royal Tombs, with three open, excavated tombs, was a residential area for the ruling family. Archaeologists uncovered four members of this family in Tomb 1, along with several jadeite items and 37 ceramic vessels.

Nim Li Punit has a good visitors center where you can view various items preserved from earlier excavations, as well as hire tour guides or get general information. Buses along the highway will drop you off or pick you up at the turnoff.

WORTH A TRIP

MAYA CULTURAL TRAIL

A good short loop of the central Maya villages starts in Big Falls, where you can visit the Cal and Chiac families as part of the Living Maya Experience (p227). Next head to Silver Creek and stop by Miguel Choco's cacao farm. It's another 3.5 miles to the village of San Miguel where there's a TEA guesthouse (p222). Ask around about Maya harpist Florendo Mess. Stop in to visit the ancient Maya ruins of Lubaantun on the way to San Pedro Columbia, where you can tour another cacao farm with Eladio Pop (p230) and learn about the art of chocolate making.

🏃 Activities

Big Falls Extreme Adventures ADVENTURE SPORTS
(☑ 634-6979; http://bigfallsextremeadventures. com; Big Falls; zip-lining & tubing BZ$100, with lunch BZ$120) The six-line zip-lining course will have you flying through the jungle on a 45-minute adventure. It can be combined with tubing down the Río Grande, including a stop at hot springs and lunch at a riverside restaurant. Reserve a day in advance.

Belize Spice Farm FARM TOUR
(☑ 732-4014; www.belizespicefarm.com; Golden Stream; adult/child BZ$20/free; ⊙ tours hourly 8am-4pm) Spices more commonly associated with India and Asia – black pepper, nutmeg, vanilla, cardamom and clove – grow in abundance at this large farm. Take a 45-minute vehicle tour and learn the full spice story.

Miguel Choco's Farm Tours FARM TOUR
(☑ 630-4075; Silver Creek; per couple BZ$50) Tour Miguel's organic cacao farm and learn how to make a traditional chocolate drink.

🛌 Sleeping

There are a couple of places to stay here. Ask at Coleman's about self-contained rooms.

Big Falls Cottages GUESTHOUSE $
(☑ 605-9985; www.bigfallscottages.com; Esperanza Rd; s/d BZ$75/85; 🅿 🛜) These two lovely, family-run cottages are set in a magnificent garden. They come with a kitchenette and bathroom (with hot showers).

Lodge at Big Falls RESORT $$$
(☑ 610-0126, 732-4444; www.thelodgeatbigfalls.com; Big Falls; s/d/tr cabaña incl breakfast BZ$296/412/458; 🅿 @ 🛜 🏊) On a bend in the jungle-clad Río Grande, 18 miles from Punta Gorda, Lodge at Big Falls is a meticulously maintained property where tiled-floor, palm-thatched cabins are spread around beautiful gardens. Popular with birdwatchers and butterfly enthusiasts, the lodge is also a fine place from which to enjoy a host of activities and tours, from caving to kayaking and river-tubing.

The hardwood *cabañas* come with air-con and kitchenette, while the thatch *cabañas* are fan-cooled with screened windows catching the breeze. The lodge also has a fine restaurant and bar serving breakfast, packed lunches and dinner (BZ$80). Transfers to or from Punta Gorda are BZ$100 for up to four people.

✖ Eating

Coleman's Café · BELIZEAN
(☑ 630-4069; Big Falls; buffet BZ$15; ⊘ 10:30am-4:30pm; P ⊜ ♨) Something of an institution for travelers driving the Southern Hwy, Coleman's offers a self-serve lunch buffet with three or four dishes plus rice, beans and salad. Pile up your plate! Dinner is by reservation and you can also get beer, soft drinks and local chocolate. It's just off the highway north of Big Falls.

NorVilly's · BELIZEAN $
(☑ 622-2598; mains BZ$10-15; ⊘ 10am-6pm) This family-owned local restaurant near the river in Big Falls is a great spot to stop for lunch beneath the thatched roof. Traditional Belizean meals include chicken with rice and beans, pork stew, and fried or steamed fish – you might even find *gibnut* (*paca*) on the menu. Call ahead for a reservation.

🛍 Shopping

Marigold Women's Cooperative · HANDICRAFTS
(☑ 620-6084; marigoldwomen@gmail.com; Southern Hwy, Indian Creek) In Indian Creek village, Marigold is a cooperative of local Kekchi Maya women working to preserve their culture through cooking. Traditional Maya food including breads and cakes are available, along with arts and craft. Call ahead to check that it's open.

Ixchel Women's Group · HANDICRAFTS
(☑ 632-7938; www.indiancreekvillage.info/ixchel.html; Indian Creek; ⊘ 7am-5:30pm) Operating from a hut in Indian Creek village, the Ixchel Women's Group is run by a small cooperative of Kekchi Maya women who produce traditional handicrafts and sell them throughout the area. Among the items you'll find here are bracelets, bags, necklaces and *kalaba* shakers (a local instrument). Free craft demonstrations are also given.

San Miguel

POP 400
Just up the road from San Pedro Columbia, this Kekchi village is on the unsealed loop road past the Lubaantun ruins and off the Southern Hwy. You can walk to Lubaantun (2 miles) or trek to **Tiger Cave**, 1½ hours'

walk away, returning by canoe along the Río Grande.

🛏 Sleeping

San Miguel offers the basic budget options of Back-a-bush and a TEA guesthouse (p222).

Back-a-bush · HOSTEL $
(☑ 631-1731; www.back-a-bush.com; camping per tent BZ$10, dm BZ$25, d without bathroom per person BZ$30, s/d with bathroom BZ$70/100; ⊜) In the village of San Miguel, just a few miles from Lubaantun, is this simple, chilled-out jungle guesthouse and farm with a lovely Dutch owner. Accommodations are very rustic but peaceful – there's one private cabin with attached bath and porch – and guests can enjoy meals made with cacao, coffee and vegetables grown on the farm.

San Pedro Columbia

POP 1500
Around 20 miles northwest of Punta Gorda is the village of San Pedro Columbia, the largest Kekchi Maya community outside Guatemala. Columbia (as locals call it) was established by Kekchi families who left Pueblo Viejo to look for new farmland around 1905. The village has seen boom and bust, with mahogany and cedar felling, chicle collection and, in the 1970s and 1980s, marijuana cultivation. There are several shops where handicrafts and food can be bought.

Two miles up the river is the source of the Columbia Branch of the Río Grande, where water bubbles out from beneath the rocks. Local guides can take you to see the source; it's a 45-minute walk from the center of town. Behind the village, up in the hills, is the Columbia Forest Reserve, which has thousands of acres of forest, sinkholes, caves and ruins hidden in the valleys. There are also local guides who can take you there.

⊙ Sights & Activities

Ask locally about hiring a *dory* (dugout canoe) for paddles on the Columbia Branch of the Río Grande, or join a chocolate-making tour.

Lubaantun · RUINS
(admission BZ$10; ⊘ 8am-5pm) The Maya ruins at Lubaantun, 1.3 miles northwest of San Pedro Columbia, are built on a natural hilltop and display a construction method unusual in the ancient Maya world of mortar-less,

SOUTHERN BELIZE AROUND THE DEEP SOUTH

neatly cut, black-slate blocks. Archaeologists postulate that Lubaantun, which flourished between AD 730 and 860, may have been an administrative center regulating trade, while nearby Nim Li Punit was the local religious and ceremonial center. The Maya site comprises a collection of seven plazas, three ballcourts and surrounding structures.

At the entrance is a small visitors center displaying pottery, ceramic figurines, maps and panels detailing the controversial 'crystal skull', said to have been found here in the 1920s by 17-year-old Anna Mitchell-Hedges. Lubaantun is known for the numerous mould-made ceramic figurines found here, many of which represent ancient ball players.

In 1924, Belize's chief medical officer Thomas Gann, an amateur archaeologist, bestowed the name Lubaantun (Place of Fallen Stones) on these ruins. More professional archaeological work has taken place since 1970 and much of the site is now cleared and restored.

There are two entry points to Lubaantun from the Southern Hwy, either via Silver Creek (signposted just north of Big Falls) or San Pedro Columbia. Either way it's around 23 miles from Punta Gorda along dirt roads once you leave the highway. Village buses running between San Pedro Columbia and San Miguel can drop you at the turnoff to the site, then it's about half a mile further.

Chaos Oasis　　　　　　　ARCHITECTURE
(www.facebook.com/TheChaosOasisBelize; Lubaantun Rd; by donation) One of the more bizarre things you're likely to see in Belize is this 'Earth Ship' structure, made even more incongruous because it's so close to the entrance of the Lubaantun ruins. The strange construction is made from recyclable materials such as old tires and glass and plastic bottles (a lot of Crystal Head vodka was consumed in the process), all plastered together.

It's a three-year labor of love for British expats Alisa and Richard, who hope to turn it into a living art gallery and juice bar. Stop in for a chat and admire their work. Donations go to help local schools.

Eladio's Chocolate Adventure　　　FOOD
(✆ 624-0166; eladiopop@gmail.com; per person BZ$60) In San Pedro Columbia village, Eladio Pop will take you on a tour of his cacao farm, followed by a traditional chocolate-making demonstration and Maya lunch.

🛏 Sleeping

Ask locally about village rooms or head over to San Miguel.

**Butterfly Farm
& Guesthouse**　　　　　　HOSTEL $
(✆ 632-5949; www.columbiarivercooperative.com; San Pedro Columbia; dm BZ$20, breakfast BZ$10; 🛜) Lisa runs this offbeat farm and butterfly house just out of San Pedro Columbia. The four dorm-style rooms are in a large wooden bunkhouse with clean beds and one shared bathroom with cold shower. It's as basic as you would expect out here, but there's wi-fi and the butterfly house and farm are quite cool. Breakfast is included and other meals can be provided.

San Antonio

POP 1200

The largest Mopan Maya community in Belize, San Antonio was founded in the

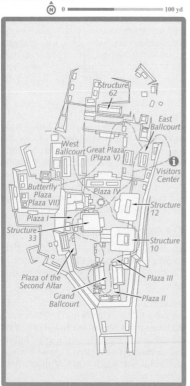

Lubaantun

0 ——————— 100 yd

Structure 62

East Ballcourt

West Ballcourt

Great Plaza (Plaza V)

Visitors Center

Butterfly Plaza (Plaza VII)

Plaza IV

Structure 12

Plaza I

Structure 33

Structure 10

Plaza of the Second Altar

Grand Ballcourt

Plaza III

Plaza II

MAYA MOUNTAIN RESEARCH FARM

A 70-acre organic farm and registered NGO, **Maya Mountain Research Farm** (Map p218; ✎ 630-4386; www.mmrfbz.org) offers internships for those interested in learning about organic farming, permaculture, biodiversity and alternative energy. Located in a beautiful jungle valley 2 miles upriver from San Pedro Columbia, the farm is run by permaculture teacher Christopher Nesbitt, with the philosophy of promoting fully sustainable food production.Accommodations in a series of rustic dorm-style *cabañas* and thatched-roof *palapas* cost BZ$350 a week, or BZ$1200 a month, all inclusive.

Interns take part in every stage of meal preparation, from harvesting fruits, vegetables, nuts and herbs to cooking over a wood-burning stove inside the farm's outdoor kitchen (hand-built with stones from the river). MMRF also offers short-term courses lasting between one and three weeks in both permaculture design and renewable energy. Rustic and beautiful in the extreme, the farm is pretty remote, with no road access. To get there you need to walk or take a *dory* (dugout canoe) from San Pedro Columbia village

mid-19th century by farmers from San Luis Rey in the Petén, Guatemala. A wooden idol (of San Luis) was taken from the church in San Luis Rey by settlers who returned to Guatemala to retrieve their saint. The idol remains in the beautiful stone church in San Antonio, which has wonderful stained-glass windows with Italian and Irish names on them (because the glass was donated by parishioners from St Louis, Missouri).

San Antonio has a large concentration of cacao farmers growing cacao for export and use in Belizean-made chocolate products.

◉ Sights

Río Blanco National Park　　　NATIONAL PARK
(admission BZ$10; ⊙ 7am-5pm) The 105-acre Río Blanco National Park is a compact protected wildlife area that's home to a variety of flora and fauna. The highlight for visitors is definitely Río Blanco Falls, a beautiful 20ft-high waterfall leading into a clear swimming hole just a five-minute walk from the ranger station. Other attractions include birdwatching, hiking and kayaking (the ranger station has one kayak at BZ$5 per hour).

There's also a basic dorm bunkhouse at the ranger station (BZ$20), which has a small stove for cooking, or you can camp in the park itself (BZ$10).

Uxbenka　　　RUIN
FREE The Maya ruins of Uxbenka are close to the village of Santa Cruz on the road from San Antonio. The site is mostly undeveloped and the visible part is merely the center of a larger, yet-to-be-excavated city. Archaeologists believe Uxbenka dates back to the Classic Period, with stelae erected in the 4th century.

There is evidence that it had a close relationship with Tikal to the north. The open site has a large plaza with some excavated tombs and sweeping views to the sea. On a clear day it is possible to see the mountains of Honduras and Guatemala. There's no visitor center for Uxbenka; a local guide can take you, or you can make your own way there.

✸✸ Festivals & Events

Feast of San Luis　　　RELIGIOUS
The Feast of San Luis, a harvest festival where the famous Deer Dance is performed, is celebrated in town from about August 15 to 25.

⌂ Sleeping

San Antonio has a TEA guesthouse, a bunkhouse at Río Blanco National Park and the excellent Farm Inn.

Bol's Hilltop Hotel　　　HOTEL **$**
(r without bathroom BZ$20) This TEA guesthouse in San Antonio has very basic rooms. Meals can be obtained next door at Clara Bol's house.

Farm Inn　　　FARMSTAY **$$**
(✎ 732-4781; www.thefarminnbelize.com; San Antonio; campsite BZ$20, d incl breakfast BZ$214-320; P ✿ ⛵) ✿ Even in the back blocks of the Deep South you can uncover a few hidden gems. On the highway between Santa Cruz and San Antonio, the family-owned Farm Inn is set on 52 acres of jungle and organic farmland (with 7000 cacao trees). Accommodation consists of a *cabaña* with two comfortable en-suite rooms and the superb four-room inn by the creek.

The double-story inn has spacious rooms with porch or balcony, kitchenette and

THE ROAD AHEAD

By the time you read this, Southern Belize may have a legal border crossing with Guatemala. The US$8 million, 23-mile road extension from Dump to the border began in 2011 and was due to be completed in 2014 but, in true Belizean style, by the end of 2015 it was still 6 miles short of the border. Nevertheless, this continuation of the Southern Hwy has opened up the Deep South with villages such as Mafredi, San Antonio, Santa Cruz, and Santa Elena now easily accessible. (Jalacte, which used to be an unofficial crossing point via a swing bridge, has been bypassed by the new road.)

It's difficult to say what changes the road will bring to these communities, and what effect an official border crossing will have on the flow of visitors in the south, but one thing is certain: the Deep South's days as a quiet, dead-end backwater are numbered.

lounge areas. The sociable restaurant and bar is open all day but reserve ahead for lunch or dinner; meals are Belizean with an African influence. Power is solar with a backup generator.

Blue Creek

POP 250

This village, part Kekchi and part Mopan, is split by the pretty, blue-green namesake river. Howler monkeys inhabit the surrounding hilly jungles, otters live along the creek and green iguanas are plentiful. For travellers, Blue Creek is an appealing destination for its cave, zip-lining and jungle walks.

Near Blue Creek is the Tumul'kin School of Learning, a Maya boarding school that hosts students from throughout Toledo and other parts of Belize, providing a learning venue that inculcates pride in being Maya and gives students an education that values traditional knowledge.

◉ Sights

Blue Creek Cave CAVE
(Hokeb Ha Cave; guided tours from BZ$30) About a 20-minute walk along a jungle path from the bridge is Blue Creek Cave, which you can only enter with a guide. The cave has a 'wet side,' where you swim and wade up to an underground waterfall (about one hour in the cave), and a 'dry side' where you can try a more difficult venture involving some climbing and emerge at a different entrance. Guides and caving equipment can be hired in the village or at the zip-lining office.

⭐ Activities

Blue Creek Canopy Tours ADVENTURE SPORTS
(☑ 653-6533; www.bluecreekbelize.com; Blue Creek; per person BZ$130, per person with group BZ$110) One of Belize's more remote zip-lining adventures has nine lines and 15 platforms traversing thick jungle over the namesake Blue Creek. Numbers are limited to 35 per day so call or book ahead.

🛏 Sleeping

There are a couple of homestays in the village and a cool riverside lodge.

Blue Creek IZE Lodge LODGE $$
(☑ 655-1461; www.izebelize.com; d incl meals BZ$140) This IZE (International Zoological Expeditions) property enjoys a gloriously remote rainforest location on the banks of Blue Creek, deep in rural Toledo District but close to Blue Creek village. There are five rustic, river-facing timber cabins and two cool new tree houses, all with verandas, fans and shared bathroom.

It's primarily for school and study groups but travelers are welcome with advance reservation.

❶ Getting There & Away

Blue Creek is 23 miles from Punta Gorda and 5 miles down a rough dirt road off the Southern Hwy. Two village buses (11:30am and noon) head to Blue Creek from Punta Gorda on Monday, Wednesday, Friday and Saturday, returning on the same day.

Tikal & Flores, Guatemala

Includes ➡

Tikal 234
Yaxhá 240
Uaxactun 241
El Remate 241
Flores &
Santa Elena 243

Best Places to Eat

➡ Las Orquideas (p243)

➡ Las Mesitas (p249)

➡ Terrazzo (p249)

➡ Cool Beans (p249)

Best Places to Sleep

➡ Tikal Inn (p239)

➡ Alice Guesthouse (p242)

➡ Posada del Cerro (p242)

➡ Hotel Santa Barbara (p247)

➡ Hotel Isla de Flores (p248)

Why Go?

The glory and splendors of the ancient Maya world await you, just over the border in the lush rainforests of Eastern Guatemala. The region is especially important to the Maya people, being home to many temples, pyramids and ruins with significance to the alignment of 12/21/2012, which recently completed a major cycle of the Maya calendar and began another.

The most fabled (and easiest to reach) of Guatemala's slice of La Ruta Maya is Tikal. Larger and more completely restored than any of the Maya sites in Belize, Tikal offers visitors the unique opportunity to spend the night at the ruins, waking up in the middle of the jungle, thanks to its in-park campground and lodges. Alternatively, the nearby lakeside villages of Flores and El Remate are peaceful, picturesque places to recover from some intensive archaeological exploration.

When to Go

➡ **Jan–Mar** Few bugs and little rain make for optimum jungle travel conditions.

➡ **Dec** The Unificación Maya Festival takes place at Maya sites throughout the area.

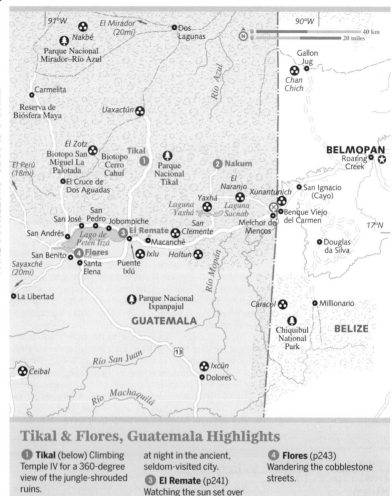

Tikal & Flores, Guatemala Highlights

❶ Tikal (below) Climbing Temple IV for a 360-degree view of the jungle-shrouded ruins.

❷ Yaxhá (p240) Camping

at night in the ancient, seldom-visited city.

❸ El Remate (p241) Watching the sun set over Lago de Petén Itzá.

❹ Flores (p243) Wandering the cobblestone streets.

Tikal

The most striking feature of **Tikal** (☏ 2367-2837; www.parque-tikal.com; Q150; ⊙ 6am-6pm) is its towering, steep-sided temples, rising to heights of more than 144 feet, but what distinguishes it is its jungle setting. Its many plazas have been cleared of trees and vines, its temples uncovered and partially restored, but as you walk from one building to another you pass beneath the dense canopy of rainforest amid the rich, loamy aromas of earth and vegetation. Much of the delight of touring the site comes from

strolling the broad causeways, originally built of packed limestone to accommodate traffic between temple complexes. By stepping softly you're more likely to spot monkeys, agoutis, foxes and ocellated turkeys.

Tikal is a popular day trip from Flores or El Remate, so is much quieter in the late afternoon and early morning, which makes an overnight stay an attractive option.

❶ Orientation

The archaeological site is at the center of the 212-sq-mile Parque Nacional Tikal. The road from Flores enters the park 12 miles south of the ruins.

From the parking lot at the site, it's a short walk back to the junction where there's an information kiosk. Immediately south of this junction, a visitor center sells books, maps, souvenirs, hats, insect repellent, sun block and other necessities; it also houses a restaurant and museum (p245). Near the visitor center are Tikal's three hotels, a campground, a few small *comedores* (cheap eateries) and a modern research center containing a second museum (p239). It's a five-minute walk from the ticket control booth to the entry gate. Just beyond, there's a large map posted. From here, it's a 1-mile walk (20 minutes) southwest to the Gran Plaza. From the Gran Plaza west to Templo IV, it's more than 1950 feet.

⊙ Sights

Gran Plaza

The path comes into the Gran Plaza around the **Templo I**, the Templo del Gran Jaguar (Temple of the Grand Jaguar). This was built to honor – and bury – Ah Cacao. The king may have worked out the plans for the building himself, but it was actually erected above his tomb by his son, who succeeded him to the throne in AD 734. The king's rich burial goods included stingray spines, which were used for ritual bloodletting, pearls, 180 jade objects and 90 pieces of bone carved with hieroglyphs. At the top of the 144-foot-high temple is a small enclosure of three rooms covered by a corbeled arch. The sapodilla-wood lintels over the doors were richly carved; one of them was removed and is now

in a Basel museum. The lofty roofcomb that crowned the temple was originally adorned with reliefs and bright paint. When it's illuminated by the afternoon sun, it is still possible to make out the figure of a seated dignitary.

Although climbing to the top of Templo I is prohibited, the views from **Templo II** just across the way are nearly as awe-inspiring. Templo II, also known as the Temple of the Masks, was at one time almost as high as Templo I, but it now measures 125 feet without its roofcomb.

Nearby, the **Acrópolis del Norte** (North Acropolis) significantly predates the two great temples. Archaeologists have uncovered about 100 different structures, the oldest of which dates from before the time of Christ, with evidence of occupation as far back as 600 BC. The Maya built and rebuilt on top of older structures, and the many layers, combined with the elaborate burials of Tikal's early rulers, added sanctity and power to the temples. The final version of the acropolis, as it stood around AD 800, had more than 12 temples atop a vast platform, many of them the work of King Ah Cacao. Look especially for the two huge, powerful wall masks, uncovered from an earlier structure and now protected by roofs. On the plaza side of this acropolis are two rows of stelae. These served to record the great deeds of the kings, to sanctify their memory and to add power to the temples and plazas that surrounded them.

---

① TRANSITIONING: BELIZE TO GUATEMALA

Language

Spanish is the main language in Guatemala. Most Tikal tour guides speak English, as do the staff of some upscale hotels. But most hotel and restaurant employees, bus drivers, taxi drivers and other people on the street are unlikely to speak English, so brush up on your Spanish before arriving. For all your language needs in Guatemala, pick up a copy of Lonely Planet's Latin American Spanish phrasebook.

Money

The unit of currency in Guatemala is the quetzal (Q). Money changers hang around the border, but there are no ATMs or banks on either side. The nearest ATMs are in Santa Elena and Flores. US dollars are widely accepted.

Visas & Fees

Citizens of the USA, Canada, EU countries, Norway, Switzerland, Australia, New Zealand, Israel, Iceland, South Africa and Japan are among those who do not currently need visas to visit Guatemala. (Regulations can change, so check with your travel agent or a Guatemalan embassy or consulate before your trip.)

There's a BZ$37.50 departure tax when you leave Belize, and even if you're only going to Tikal for the day, you'll have to pay it. Belizean and US dollars are both accepted. And on the way back, Guatemala will expect their cut; there's a Q250 departure tax if you're flying and a mere Q20 if leaving by land.

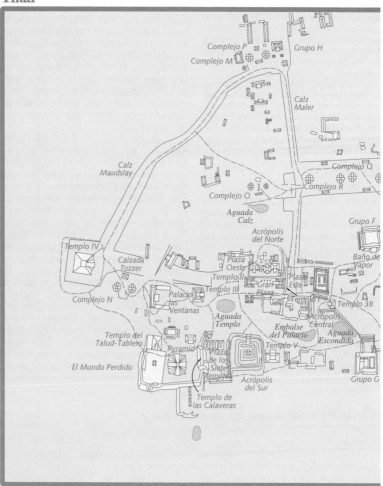

Acropolis Central

South and east of the Gran Plaza, the maze of courtyards, rooms and small temples is thought by many to have been a palace where Tikal's nobles lived. Others think the tiny rooms may have been used for sacred rites and ceremonies, as graffiti found within them suggests. Over the centuries the configuration of the rooms was repeatedly changed, suggesting that perhaps this 'palace' was in fact a noble or royal family's residence and alterations were made to accommodate groups of relatives. A hundred years ago, one part of the acropolis provided lodgings for archaeologist Teobert Maler when he worked at Tikal.

Templo III

West of the Gran Plaza, across the Calzada Tozzer (Tozzer Causeway) stands **Templo III**, still undergoing restoration. Only its upper reaches have been cleared. A scene carved into the lintel at its summit, 180 feet high, depicts a figure in an elaborate jaguar suit, believed to be the ruler Dark Sun. In front of it stands stela 24, which marks the date of its construction, AD 810. From this point, you can continue west to Templo IV along the Calzada Tozzer, one of several sacred byways between the temple complexes of Tikal.

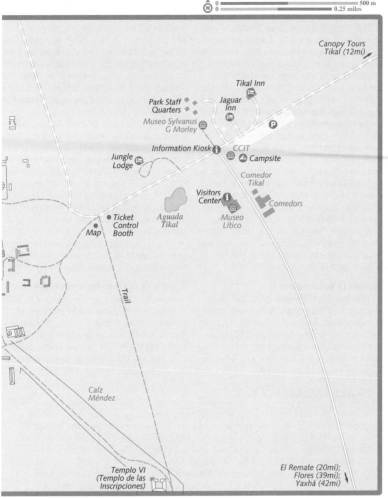

0 _____ 500 m
0 _____ 0.25 miles

Canopy Tours
Tikal (12mi)

Tikal Inn

Park Staff
Quarters

Jaguar
Inn

Museo Sylvanus
G Morley

P

Information Kiosk

CCIT

Campsite

Jungle
Lodge

Comedor
Tikal

Visitors
Center

Comedors

Ticket
Control
Booth

Aguada
Tikal

Museo
Lítico

Map

Trail

Calz
Méndez

El Remate (20mi);
Flores (39mi);
Yaxhá (42mi)

Templo VI
(Templo de las
Inscripciones)

Templo V & Acrópolis del Sur

Due south of the Gran Plaza, **Templo V** is a remarkably steep structure (187 feet) that was built sometime between the 7th and 8th centuries AD. It consists of seven stepped platforms and, unlike the other great temples, has slightly rounded corners. A recent excavation of the temple revealed a group of embedded structures, some with Maya calendars on their walls. Tempting as it may seem, you are not allowed to scale the broad central staircase. Excavation has hardly even begun on the mass of masonry just west of the temple, known collectively as the **Acróp-olis del Sur** (South Acropolis). The palaces on top are from the late Classic Period (the time of King Moon Double Comb), but earlier constructions probably go back 1000 years.

Plaza de los Siete Templos

To the west of the Acrópolis del Sur is this broad grassy plaza, reached via a path to its southern edge. Built in the late Classic Period, the seven **temples** with their stout roofcombs line up along the east side of the plaza. On the south end stand three larger 'palaces'; on the opposite end is an unusual **triple ballcourt**.

El Mundo Perdido

About 430 yards southwest of the Gran Plaza is El Mundo Perdido (Lost World), a complex of 38 structures with a huge pyramid in its midst, thought to be essentially Preclassic (with some later repairs and renovations). The pyramid, 105 feet high and 260 feet along the base, is surrounded by four much-eroded stairways, with huge masks flanking each one. The stairway facing eastward is thought to have functioned as a platform for viewing the sun's trajectory against a trio of structures on a raised platform to the east, a similar arrangement to the astronomical observatory at Uaxactún. Tunnels dug into the pyramid by archaeologists reveal four similar pyramids beneath the outer face; the earliest (Structure 5C-54 Sub 2B) dates from 700 BC, making this pyramid the oldest Maya structure at Tikal.

A smaller temple to the west, dating from the early Classic Period, demonstrates Teotihuacán's influence, with its *talud-tablero* style of architecture.

Templo IV & Complejo N

At 213 feet high Templo IV is the highest building at Tikal and the second-highest pre-Columbian building known in the western hemisphere, after La Danta at El Mirador. It was completed about AD 741, probably by order of Ah Cacao's son, Yax Kin, who was depicted on the carved lintel over the middle doorway (now in a museum in Basel, Switzerland), as the western boundary of the ceremonial precinct. A steep wooden staircase leads to the top. The view east is almost as good as from a helicopter – a panorama across the jungle canopy, with (from left to right) the temples of the Gran Plaza, Temple III, Temple V (just the top bit) and the great pyramid of the Mundo Perdido poking through.

Between Templo IV and Templo III is Complejo N, an example of the 'twin-temple' complexes erected during the late Classic Period. This one was built in AD 711 by Ah Cacao to mark the 14th *katun*, or 20-year cycle, of *baktún* 9. (A *baktún* equals about four centuries.) The king himself is portrayed on the remarkably preserved stela 16 in an enclosure just across the path. Beside the stele is altar 5, a circular stone depicting the same king accompanied by a priestly figure in the process of exhuming the skeleton of a female ruler.

Templo de las Inscripciones (Templo VI)

Templo VI is one of the few temples at Tikal to bear written records. On the rear of its 40-foot-high roofcomb is a long inscription – though it will take some effort to discern it in the bright sunlight – giving us the date AD 766. The sides and cornice of the roofcomb

TIKAL'S REDISCOVERY

No doubt the Itzáes, who occupied Tayazal (now Flores), knew of Tikal in the late Post-classic Period. Perhaps they came here to worship at the shrines of old gods. Spanish missionary friars who moved through El Petén after the conquest left brief references to these jungle-bound structures, but their writings moldered in libraries for centuries.

It wasn't until 1848 that the Guatemalan government sent out an expedition, under the leadership of Modesto Méndez and Ambrosio Tut, to visit the site. This may have been inspired by John L Stephens' bestselling accounts of fabulous Maya ruins, published in 1841 and 1843 (though Stephens never visited Tikal). Like Stephens, Méndez and Tut took an artist, Eusebio Lara, to record their archaeological discoveries. An account of their findings was published by the Berlin Academy of Science.

In 1877 the Swiss Dr Gustav Bernoulli visited Tikal. His explorations resulted in the removal of carved wooden lintels from Templos I and IV and their shipment to Basel, where they are still on view in the Museum für Völkerkunde.

Scientific exploration of Tikal began with the arrival of English archaeologist Alfred P Maudslay in 1881. Others continued his work, Teobert Maler, Alfred M Tozzer and RE Merwin among them. Tozzer worked at Tikal on and off from the beginning of the 20th century until his death in 1954. The inscriptions at Tikal were studied and deciphered by Sylvanus G Morley.

Archaeological research and restoration was carried on by the University of Pennsylvania and the Guatemalan Instituto de Antropología e Historia until 1969. Since 1991, a joint Guatemalan–Spanish project has worked on conserving and restoring Templos I and V. The Parque Nacional Tikal (Tikal National Park) was declared a Unesco World Heritage Site in 1979.

bear glyphs as well. Its secluded position, about a 25-minute walk southeast of the Gran Plaza along the Calzada Méndez, makes it a good spot for observing wildlife. From here, it's a 20-minute hike to the main entrance.

Northern Complexes

About half a mile north of the Gran Plaza is **Complejo P**. Like Complejo N, it's a late-Classic twin-temple complex that probably commemorated the end of a *katun* (20 year cycle in the Maya calendar). **Complejo M**, next to it, was partially torn down by the late-Classic Maya to provide building materials for a causeway, now named after Alfred P Maudslay, which runs southwest to Templo IV. **Grupo H**, northeast of Complexes P and M, with one tall, cleared temple, had some interesting graffiti within its temples.

Complejo Q and **Complejo R**, about 330 yards north of the Gran Plaza, are very late-Classic twin-pyramid complexes with stelae and altars standing before the temples. Complex Q is perhaps the best example of the twin-temple type, as it has been partly restored. Stela 22 and altar 10 are excellent examples of late-Classic Tikal relief carving, dated to AD 771.

Museums

Museo Sylvanus G Morley　　　　MUSEUM
(Museo Cerámico, Museum of Ceramics; Q30, also valid for Museo Lítico; ☺8am-4pm) This museum exhibits a number of superb ceramic pieces from excavations, including incense burners and vases, with descriptions of their uses and significance (in Spanish). The usual museum building is under restoration indefinitely, during which time the ceramics are displayed at the CCIT.

Two of the most highly prized items, the elaborately carved Stela 31 dedicated to the ruler Stormy Sky-Double Comb, and the simulated tomb of King Moon Double Comb with the precious items unearthed from his burial site beneath Temple I, remain inside the museum, and the guard can show them to you on request.

CCIT　　　　MUSEUM
(Centro de Conservación e Investigación de Tikal; ☺8am-noon & 1-4pm) ᴹᴿᴱᴱ This Japanese-funded research center is devoted to the identification and restoration of pieces unearthed at the site. The 14,000-sq-foot facility has a huge cache of items to sort through, and you can watch the restorers at work. Though not strictly a museum per se, it features an excellent gallery on the

different materials used by Maya craftsmen. The center will house the Museo Sylvanus G Morley for an indefinite period while that museum is under restoration.

🏃 Activities & Tours

Multilingual guides are available at the information kiosk. These authorized guides display their accreditation carnet, listing the languages they speak. Before 7am, the charge for a half-day tour is Q80 per person with a minimum of five persons. After that you pay Q475 for a group tour.

Canopy Tours Tikal　　　ADVENTURE TOUR
(☑5615-4988; www.tikalcanopy.com; Q230; ☺7am-5pm) By the national park entrance this outfit offers a one-hour tour through the forest canopy, with the chance to ride a harness along a series of cables linking trees up to 980 feet apart and to cross several hanging bridges. The fee includes transportation from Tikal or El Remate.

Roxy Ortiz　　　　TOURS
(☑5197-5173; http://tikalroxy.blogspot.com) Archaeologist Roxy Ortiz has 32 years' experience trekking throughout the Maya world and does early-morning tours around Tikal from her base at the Tikal Inn. She also does personalized treks to Uaxactún, Yaxhá and other less-visited sites with her 15-seat military vehicle.

🛌 Sleeping

Staying overnight enables you to relax and savor the dawn and dusk, when most of the jungle birds and animals can be seen and heard (especially the howler monkeys). Other than camping, there are only three places to stay, and tour groups often have many of the rooms reserved. Almost any travel agency in Guatemala offers Tikal tours, including lodging, a meal or two, a guided tour and transportation. There's no need to make reservations if you want to stay at Tikal's **campground** (campsite per person Q50, hammock with mosquito net Q85), behind the research center. This is a large, grassy area with a clean bathroom block and *palapa* (thatched-roof shelters) for hanging hammocks.

Tikal Inn　　　HOTEL **$$**
(☑7861-2444; www.tikalinn.com; s/d Q500/730; P🅿@🛜🏊) Built in the late '60s, this resort-style lodging offers rooms in the main building and thatched bungalows alongside the pool and rear lawn, with little porches

out front. All are simple, spacious and quite comfortable. The most secluded accommodations are the least expensive, in a handful of cabins at the end of a sawdust trail through the forest.

Jungle Lodge HOTEL $$$
(☑ 7861-0446; www.junglelodgetikal.com; s/d Q695/810, without bathroom Q370/385; P @ ≋) Nearest of the hotels to the site entrance, this was originally built to house archaeologists working at Tikal. Self-contained bungalows, plus a bank of cheaper units, are well spaced throughout rambling, jungle grounds. Some newer suites feature jungle-chic decor and outdoor rain-showers. The restaurant-bar (mains Q80 to Q100) serves veggie pastas, crepes and other international dishes in a tropical ambience.

Jaguar Inn HOTEL $$$
(☑ 7926-2411; www.jaguartikal.com; campsite per person Q50, with tent Q115, s/d/tr Q580/695/925; P ✳ @ ☎) The inn of choice for youthful, independent travelers has duplex and quad bungalows with thatched roofs and hammocks on the porches, plus a smart little restaurant with a popular terrace out front. For those on a tight budget there are tents for rent on a platform.

✖ Eating

Comedor Tikal RESTAURANT $$
(Visitor Center; mains Q60-70; ⊙ 6:30am-8:30pm) This is one of a series of little open-air *comedores* (cheap eateries) along the right-hand side of the access road to Tikal, all offering bland versions of standards like grilled chicken or grilled steak (Q40 to Q50). All are open similar hours.

❶ Information

Everyone must purchase a ticket at the entry gate on the road in; tickets purchased after 3pm are valid for the whole next day. Those staying more than one day can purchase additional tickets at the ticket control booth along the path to the site entrance. Seeing the sunrise from Templo IV at the west end of the main site is possible from about October to March, but to enter the park before or after visiting hours you must purchase an additional ticket for Q100, presumably to pay the guide who must accompany you.

The core of the ancient city takes up about 6 sq miles, with more than 4000 structures. To visit all the major building complexes, you must walk at least 6 miles, so wear comfortable shoes with good rubber treads that grip well. The ruins here can be slick from rain and organic material, especially during the wet season. Bring plenty of water, as you'll be walking around all day in the heat.

Please don't feed the coatis (*pisotes*) that wander about the site.

Visitor Center (⊙ 8am-4pm)

❶ Getting There & Away

Six microbuses by **Asociación de Transportistas Imperio Maya** (ATIM; ☑ 5905-0089) depart Flores between 6:30am and 3pm (Q30, 1½ hours), the last returning at 5pm. They return from Tikal at noon, 1:30pm, 3pm and 6pm. You could also take the Uaxactún-bound bus from the market of Santa Elena at 3:30pm, which goes a bit slower. San Juan Travel (p251) runs five shuttles daily from Flores (one way/round trip Q50/80, including guide Q150) between 4:30am and 1pm, the last returning at 6pm.

From El Remate a collective shuttle departs at 5:30am for Tikal, starting back at 2pm (one way/round trip Q30/50). Any El Remate accommodations can make reservations.

If traveling from Belize, get a Santa Elena–bound microbus to Puente Ixlú, sometimes called El Cruce, and switch there to a northbound microbus for the remaining 22 miles to Tikal. Heading from Tikal to Belize, start early and get off at Puente Ixlú to catch a bus or microbus eastward. Be wary of shuttles to Belize advertised at Tikal: these have been known to detour to Flores to pick up passengers!

Yaxhá

The Classic Maya sites of Yaxhá, Nakum and El Naranjo form a triangle that is the basis for a national park covering more than 91,000 acres and bordering the Parque Nacional Tikal to the west. Yaxhá, the most visited of the trio, stands on a hill between two sizable lakes, Lago Yaxhá and Lago Sacnab. The setting, the sheer size of the site, the number of excellently restored buildings and the abundant jungle flora and fauna all make it particularly worth visiting. The site is 6.5 miles north of the Puente Ixlú–Melchor de Mencos road, accessed via unpaved road from a turnoff 20 miles from Puente Ixlú and 20 miles from Melchor de Mencos.

🛌 Sleeping & Eating

El Sombrero Eco-Lodge (☑ 4215-8777; www.elsombreroecolodge.com; s/d/tr Q544/880/1216, without bathroom Q144/288/416; P) ✿ offers comfortable lodging 1 mile from the archaeological site. On the lake shore below the Yaxhá ruins is Campamento Yaxhá, where you can camp for free on raised platforms with thatched roofs. Outbuildings have showers and toilets. Drinking water can be purchased at a store, but you must bring food. There's no need to purchase another admission ticket if you'd like to stay another day or two.

ℹ Getting There & Away

Agencies in Flores and El Remate offer organized trips to Yaxhá, some combined with Nakum and/or Tikal. Horizontes Mayas in El Remate runs tours (Q125 per person, minimum three persons), including guide and entrance fee, at 7am and 1pm, returning at 1pm and 6:30pm. Otherwise, take a Melchor de Mencos–bound microbus and get off at Restaurante El Portal de Yaxhá, opposite the Yaxhá turnoff, and they can arrange transportation to the site by pickup truck or motorcycle (Q65 return).

Uaxactun

Uaxactún (wah-shahk-*toon*), 14 miles north of Tikal along an unpaved road through the jungle, was Tikal's political and military rival in late Preclassic times. It was conquered by Tikal's Chak Tok Ich'aak I (King Great Jaguar Paw) in the 4th century, and was subservient to its great sister to the south for centuries thereafter, though it experienced an apparent resurgence during the Terminal Classic, after Tikal went into decline.

Villagers make an income from collecting chicle, *pimienta* (allspice) and *xate* (low-growing palm, exported to Holland for floral arrangements) in the surrounding forest. In the *xate* warehouse on the west end of town, women put together bunches of the plants for export.

Much of the attraction here is the absolute stillness and isolation. Few visitors make it up this way.

El Remate

This idyllic spot at the eastern end of Lago de Petén Itzá makes a good alternative base for Tikal-bound travelers – it's more relaxed than Flores, and closer to the site. Just two roads, really, El Remate has a ramshackle vibe all of its own.

El Remate begins half a mile north of Puente Ixlú, where the road to the Belize border diverges from the Tikal road. The village strings along the Tikal road for half a mile to another junction, where a branch heads west along the north shore of the lake.

El Remate is known for its wood carving. Some fine examples of the craft are sold from stalls along the main road.

You can change US dollars and euros, or check your email, at **Horizontes Mayas** (☑5825-8296; www.horizontesmayas.com; Ruta a Tikal), adjacent to Hotel Las Gardenias (p242).

🏃 Activities

Biotopo Cerro Cahuí   NATURE RESERVE
(Q40; ⊙7am-4pm) Comprising a 3-sq-mile swath of subtropical forest rising up from the lake over limestone terrain, this nature reserve offers mildly strenuous hiking and excellent wildlife-watching, with paths to some brilliant lookout points. As a bonus, there's an adjacent lakeside park with diving docks for a refreshing conclusion to the tour.

More than 20 mammal species roam the reserve, including spider and howler monkeys, white-tailed deer and the elusive Mesoamerican tapir. Birdlife is rich and varied, with the opportunity to spot toucans, woodpeckers and the famous ocellated turkey, a big bird resembling a peacock. Trees include mahogany, cedar, *ramón*, and cohune palm, along with many types of bromeliads, ferns and orchids.

A network of loop trails ascend the hill to three lookout points, affording views of the whole lake and of Laguna Sacpetén to the east. The trail called Los Escobos (2.5 miles long, about 2¼ hours), through secondary growth forest, is good for spotting monkeys.

The admission fee includes the right to camp or sling your hammock under small thatch shelters inside the entrance. There are toilets and showers. The reserve is 1 mile west along the north-shore road from El Remate.

Project Ix-Canaan   VOLUNTEERING
(www.ixcanaan.com) This group supports the improvement of health, education and opportunities for rainforest inhabitants. Operating here since 1996, they run a community clinic, women's center, library and research center. Volunteers work in the clinic, build and maintain infrastructure, and assist in various other ways.

☞ Tours

La Casa de Don David (p242) offers tours to Yaxhá (Q460 per person, minimum two people) and Tikal (Q479). Prices include an English-speaking guide and lunch but not admission to the site. Horizontes Mayas has slightly cheaper tours and runs collective excursions to Yaxhá at 7am and 1:30pm (Q100 per person, minimum three people).

🛏 Sleeping

Most hotels are set up for swimming in – and watching the sun set over – the lake.

Casa de Doña Tonita   HOSTEL $
(☑5767-4065; dm/s/d Q30/40/80) This friendly family-run place has four basic, adequately ventilated rooms, each with two single beds and screened windows, in a two-story clapboard *rancho* (small house), plus a dorm over the restaurant, which serves tasty, reasonably priced meals. There's just one shower. Across the road is a pier's-end hut for sunset gazing.

Hotel Las Gardenias   HOTEL $
(☑5936-6984; www.hotelasgardenias.com; Ruta a Tikal; s/d from Q90/150, with air-con Q150/200; ✲@🛜) Right at the junction with the north shore road, this cordial hotel-restaurant-shuttle-operator has two sections: the wood-paneled rooms at the front are bigger, those in the rear are appealingly removed from the road. All feature comfortable beds with woven spreads, attractively tiled showers and porches with hammocks.

Hotel Sun Breeze   HOTEL $
(☑5898-2665; sunbreezehotel@gmail.com; Main Rd; s/d Q80/120; 🅿) The nearest place to the junction, this excellent-value homey guesthouse has neatly kept and well-ventilated rooms with screened windows and porches. Rear units are best, at the back of a pleasant patio. It's a short stroll to the public beach.

Posada Ixchel   HOTEL $
(☑3044-5379; hotelixchel@yahoo.com; s/d Q90/120) This family-owned place near the village's main junction is a superior deal, with spotless, wood-fragrant rooms featuring fans and handcrafted mosquito nets. The cobbled courtyard has inviting little nooks with tree-log seats.

★Posada del Cerro   BUNGALOW $$
(☑5376-8722; www.posadadelcerro.com; dm/s/d/tr Q100/220/330/450; 🅿🛜) 🍴 This ecologically sound option blends brilliantly into its jungle setting, close enough to the Cerro Cahui nature reserve to hear the monkeys howl the evening in. Ten thoughtfully furnished rooms occupy stone-and-hardwood houses and solitary huts scattered over the hillside; one is open to the woods with its own lake-view deck. There's also an eight-bed hut for groups. Herbs from the forest are stirred into local recipes in the neat, thatched-roof restaurant.

★Alice Guesthouse   BUNGALOW $$
(☑3087-0654; alice.gwate@gmail.com; dm Q60, bungalow Q200) As in Wonderland, that is. Fruit of the budding imaginations of a Franco-Belgian pair, this slightly remote spread looks not at the lake but a swath of jungle. Free-form, friendly and fun, it has dorms in fanciful huts with conical thatch roofs, a pair of neat colorful cabins and a tropical shower in a roundhouse, all connected by pebbly paths.

An open-air kitchen is the domain of a chef imported from Nantes. To reach Alice, go down the Jobompiche road about 1 mile; a signed track on the right angles uphill.

Gringo Perdido Ecological Inn   RESORT $$
(☑5804-8639; www.hotelgringoperdido.com; Jobompiche Rd; campsite Q40, s/d with breakfast & dinner Q380/760; 🅿) 🍴 Ensconced in a paradisaical lakefront setting within the Cerro Cahui biosphere reserve, this jungle-style lodge offers a bank of rooms with full-wall roll-up blinds to give you the sensation of sleeping in the open air. few lakeside bungalows offer a bit more seclusion. There's also a grassy campground with thatched-roof shelters for slinging hammocks, and a Maya sauna.

The Gringo Perdido is 2 miles along the north shore from the main Tikal road.

La Casa de Don David   HOTEL $$
(☑5306-2190; www.lacasadedondavid.com; Jobompiche Rd; s/d incl breakfast or dinner from Q273/436; ✲@🛜) Just west of the junction, this full-service outfit has spotless, modern rooms with Maya textiles for decor. All feature verandas and hammocks facing the broad garden that's been cultivated into an incredible aviary. Whether or not you're staying here, don't miss the ceiba tree and Maya calendar arrangement in the rear garden designed by owner David Kuhn (the original Gringo Perdido).

Hostal Hermano Pedro   HOSTEL $$
(☑5164-6485; www.hhpedro.com; Calle Camino Biblico 8055; dm/s/d incl breakfast Q96/152/208; 🛜) About 500 feet from the north shore junction, this two-level wooden structure has a relaxed environment, with plenty of hammocks in the patio and along the verandas. Recycled elements are cleverly incorporated into the decor of the spacious rooms,

which feature big fans and lacy curtains. Guests can use the kitchen.

Hotel Mon Ami HOTEL $$
(2 3010-0284; www.hotelmonami.com; Jobompiche Rd; dm/s/d Q75/150/200, s/d without bathroom Q100/150; 🎧) A 15-minute walk from the Tikal road, Santiago's place maintains a good balance between jungle wildness and Euro sophistication. Quirkily furnished cabins and dorms with hammocks are reached along candlelit paths through gardens bursting with local plant life. And the pier opposite is a delight. Fans of French cuisine will appreciate the open-air restaurant.

Hotel Palomino Ranch HOTEL $$
(2 3075-4189; hotelpalominorancho@gmail.com; Km 30 Carretera a Tikal; s/d Q300/448; P❄🎧🏊) An incongruous slice of the old west in El Remate, this hotel has air-conditioned rooms with a cowpoke motif. There's a swimming pool and stable: guests are allowed to ride around the grounds for free from 7am to 4pm, and trail rides can be arranged as well. Food and beverages are served all day long in the vintage saloon.

Pirámide Paraiso HOTEL $$$
(http://hotelgringoperdido.com/hotel-piramide-paraiso; Jobompiche Road; r from Q1550; P🎧) Built in time for the dawn of the new *bak-tún* of the Maya calendar (in 2012) is this glitzy addition to the Gringo Perdido Ecological Inn, a smooth white structure that rises surreally from the forest like a Maya temple. Each of the eight huge, luxuriously decorated suites features its own exterior Jacuzzi.

✕ Eating

Most hotels have their own restaurants and there are simple *comedores* (cheap eateries) scattered along the main road.

Desayunos El Árbol CAFE $
(2 5950-2367; breakfast Q30; ⊙5am-1pm) This gringo-friendly shack sports a lovely, lake-view terrace, a fine setting for healthy breakfasts, including granola, pancakes and omelets. Sandwiches come with a side of fruit salad, and the smoothies are just grand. It's on the lake side of the Tikal road, 165 feet south of the crossroads.

La Casa de Don David INTERNATIONAL $
(mains Q45; ⊙7am-8:30pm; 🅿) This splendid open-air dining hall serves a good breakfast, including banana pancakes (Q30), fruit and granola, and a collection of *National Geo-*

graphic articles on Maya sites to browse over coffee. Nightly prix-fixe specials include vegetarian fare – reserve your meal by 4pm.

La Piazza CAFE $
(2 5951-7338; mains Q30-40; ⊙5am-9pm) Stop into this breezy open-air pavilion any time for espresso and tasty snacks. Run by sweet-tempered staff who make brilliant papaya milkshakes and mighty fine pineapple cake. It's right at the junction.

★**Las Orquídeas** ITALIAN $$
(2 5819-7232; Jobompiche Rd; pastas Q55-80; ⊙noon-9pm Tue-Sun) Almost hidden in the forest, a 10-minute walk down the north shore from the Tikal junction, is this marvelous open-air dining hall. The genial Italian owner-chef blends *chaya*, a local herb, into his own tagliatelle and *panzarotti* (smaller version of calzones). There are tempting desserts, too.

Mon Ami FRENCH $$
(mains Q35-55; ⊙6am-9pm) Down the north shore road, here's the French jungle bistro you've dreamed of, a peaceful palm-thatched affair. Try the lake whitefish or the big *ensalada francesa* (French salad).

ℹ Getting There & Away

El Remate is linked to Santa Elena by frequent minibus service (Q20) till around 7pm.

For Tikal, a collective shuttle departs at 5:30am, starting back at 2pm (one way/round trip Q30/50). Any El Remate accommodations can make reservations. Or catch one of the ATIM (p240) or San Juan Travel shuttles (p251) (Q20) passing through from Santa Elena to Tikal from 5am to 3:30pm.

For taxis, ask at Hotel Sun Breeze (p242). A one-way ride to Flores costs about Q300; round trip to Tikal costs Q350.

For Melchor de Mencos on the Belizean border, get a minibus or bus from Puente Ixlú, 1.2 miles south of El Remate (Q20, 1¼ hours). Additionally, Horizontes Mayas (p241) offers daily departures to Belize City (Q150) via Melchor at 5:30am and 8am.

Flores & Santa Elena

POP 85,000

With its cubist houses cascading down from a central plaza to the emerald waters of Lago de Petén Itzá, the island town of Flores evokes a Mediterranean ambience. A third of a mile long causeway connects Flores to its humbler sister town of Santa Elena on the lake shore, which then merges into the even

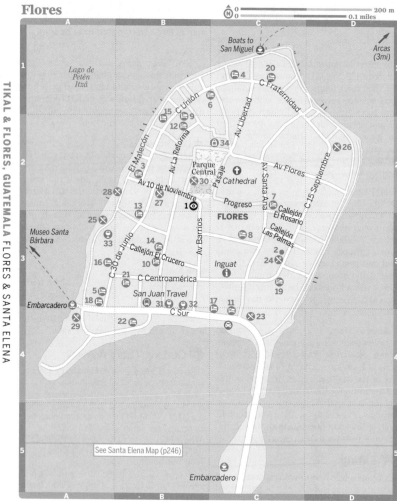

homelier community of San Benito to the west. The three towns actually form one large settlement, often referred to simply as Flores.

Flores proper is by far the more attractive base. Small hotels and restaurants line the streets, many featuring rooftop terraces with lake views. Residents take great pride in their island-town's gorgeousness, and a promenade runs around its perimeter.

Flores does have a twee, built-up edge to it, though, and some Tikal-bound budget travelers opt for the tranquility of El Remate, just down the road. Santa Elena is where you'll find banks, buses and a major shopping mall.

⊙ Sights

Flores is great for strolling, especially now that the lakefront promenade that rings the islet is complete – though rising lake levels have submerged much of the northern section. In the center, atop a rise, is the Parque Central, with its double-domed cathedral, Nuestra Señora de los Remedios.

Cathedral   CATHEDRAL
(Map p244; Flores) The double-domed Nuestra Señora de los Remedios (the Spaniards' original name for the isle of Flores) stands at the isle's summit, anchoring the Parque Central.

Flores

⊙ **Sights**
1 Municipalidad.........................B2

⊕ **Activities, Courses & Tours**
2 Mayan Adventure C3

⊜ **Sleeping**
3 Casa Amelia B2
4 Casazul.................................C1
5 Green World Hotel A3
6 Hospedaje Doña Goya..........C1
7 Hostal Frida.........................C2
8 Hostel Los Amigos...............C3
9 Hotel Aurora........................B2
10 Hotel El Peregrino................B3
11 Hotel Flores de Petén..........C4
12 Hotel Isla de Flores.............B2
13 Hotel La Casona de la Isla B3
14 Hotel La Mesa de los Mayas ...B3
15 Hotel La Unión B2
16 Hotel Petén..........................A3
17 Hotel Petenchel C4
18 Hotel Santana A3
19 Hotel Villa del Lago C3

20 La Posada de Don José.........C1
21 Posada de la Jungla B3
22 Ramada Tikal........................B4

⊗ **Eating**
23 Antojitos Mexicanos C4
24 Café Arqueológico Yaxha C3
25 Café/Bar Doña Goya.............A3
26 Cool Beans...........................D2
27 La Luna.................................B2
28 Las Mesitas..........................B2
29 Raíces...................................A4
30 Restaurante El Mirador.........B2
Restaurante El Peregrino ....(see 10)
Terrazzo.....................................(see 15)

⊙ **Drinking & Nightlife**
31 El Trópico..............................B3
32 Jamming B3
33 Qué Pachanga A3

⊝ **Shopping**
34 Castillo de Arizmendi............C2

Museo Santa Bárbara MUSEUM
(☑ 7926-2813; www.radiopeten.com.gt; Isle of Santa Bárbara; Q20; ⊙ 8am-noon & 2-5pm) On an islet to the west of Flores, this little museum holds a grab bag of Maya artifacts from nearby archaeological sites, plus some old broadcasting equipment from Radio Petén (88.5 FM), which still broadcasts from an adjacent building. Phone ahead and they'll pick you up at the dock behind Hotel Santana (p248) (Q20 per person).

After browsing the museum, take a wander round the islet, watch birds poking round the twigs off the banks, then enjoy chilled coconuts at the cafe by the dock.

Museo Lítico MUSEUM
(Stone Museum; Q30, also valid for Museo Sylvanus G Morley; ⊙ 8am-4:30pm Mon-Fri, 8am-4pm Sat & Sun) The larger of Tikal's two museums is in the visitor center. It houses a number of carved stones from the ruins. The photographs taken by pioneer archaeologists Alfred P Maudslay and Teobert Maler of the jungle-covered temples, in various stages of discovery, are particularly striking. Outside is a model showing how Tikal would have looked around AD 800.

Municipalidad NOTABLE BUILDING
(Town Hall; Map p244; Flores) Flores' stately town hall, just below the Parque Central,

is the place where citizens go to conduct official business.

🏃 Activities

Arcas VOLUNTEERING
(Asociación de Rescate y Conservación de Vida Silvestre; ☑ 7830-1374; www.arcasguatemala.com/volunteering) This Guatemalan NGO has a rescue and rehabilitation center for wildlife on the mainland northeast of Flores, where volunteers 'adopt' and feed animals, such as macaws, parrots, jaguars and coatis, that have been rescued from smugglers and the illegal pet trade. The fee of Q1335 a week covers food and accommodation.

☞ Tours

Boats can be hired for lake tours at the *embarcaderos* (docks) opposite Hotel Petenchel and beside the Hotel Santana (p248) in Flores, and in the middle of the Flores–Santa Elena causeway. Prices are negotiable. An hour-long jaunt runs around Q150. A three-hour tour, which might include the Petencito Zoo, the isle of Santa Bárbara and its museum and the ruins of Tayazal should cost Q350, with stops and waiting time included.

Explore TOUR
(Map p246; ☑ 7926-2375; www.exploreguate.com; 2a Calle 4-68, Santa Elena) Professionally managed agency offering custom-designed tours and accommodations in Santa Elena.

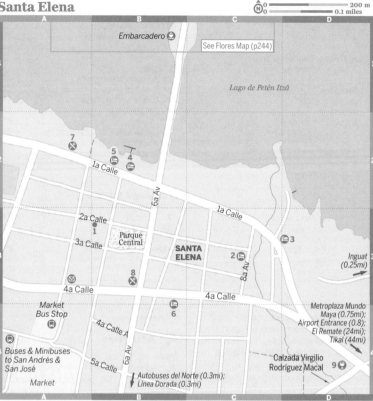

Santa Elena

Santa Elena

Activities, Courses & Tours
1 Explore B3

Sleeping
2 Hotel del Patio.......................................C3
3 Hotel Maya Internacional....................D3
4 Hotel Petén Espléndido B2
5 La Casona del Lago B2
6 Mayaland Plaza Hotel..........................B4

Eating
7 Restaurante El Puerto..........................A2
8 Restaurante Mijaro...............................B3

Drinking & Nightlife
9 Mi Disco.. D4

Mayan Adventure ARCHAEOLOGICAL TOUR
(Map p244; ☎ 5830-2060; www.the-mayan-adventure.com; Calle 15 de Septiembre, Flores) Coordinated by a German Mayanologist, this outfit offers 'scientific' tours to sites currently under excavation, with commentary by participating archaeologists or architects. Some of these are available year-round, such as to Naranjo, a huge site being restored and excavated by more than 100 scientists; others only part of the year. In either case, tours should be reserved well in advance.

🛏 Sleeping

Except for a few upscale properties along Santa Elena's waterfront, Flores makes a far more desirable place to stay, unless you have a liking for traffic and dust.

Hostal Frida HOSTEL $
(Map p244; ☎ 7926-5427; fridahostel@gmail.com; Callejón El Rosario, Flores; dm Q45) Run by hospitable Magdalena and family who also have an alternative beauty salon-cafe nearer the lake, this low-key hostel is in a typical old house with garden at the rear. The dorms are pretty basic with bathrooms behind a

partition, but it's kept clean. Guest kitchen available.

Hostel Los Amigos
HOSTEL $

(Map p244; ☑ 7867-5075; www.amigoshostel.com; Calle Central, Flores; dm Q70-90, r with/without bathroom Q320/180; @) Far and away the most popular backpackers haven in El Petén, this hostel has grown organically in its 13 years of existence and now includes various sleeping options, from six- and 10-bed dorms to a treehouse. All the global traveler's perks are here in abundance: herbal steam bath, pool table, hammocks, heaping helpings of organic food, yoga and cut-rate jungle tours.

Despite the good-time atmosphere, it's lights out after 10, but the fun goes on in an ingeniously soundproofed night lounge upstairs. A new annex around the corner is quieter, with seven originally designed rooms.

Hospedaje Doña Goya
HOSTEL $

(Map p244; ☑ 7867-5513; hospedajedonagoya @yahoo.com; Calle Unión, Flores; dm Q40, s/d Q120/160, without bathroom Q90/120; 🔊) This family-run guesthouse makes a fine budget choice. Though ultra-basic, the sheets are clean, the fans work, the water's hot and the paint's fresh. Dorms, too, are spacious and spotless. Best of all is the roof terrace with a palm-thatched shelter and hammocks.

Hotel El Peregrino
HOTEL $

(Map p244; ☑ 7867-5701; peregrino@itelgua.com; Av La Reforma, Flores; s/d Q120/160, without bathroom Q70/120; 🞰) El Peregrino is an older, family-run place with home cooking in the front *comedor* (basic, cheap eatery). Large rooms with tile floors and powerful overhead fans line up along plant-festooned corridors – no views here.

Posada de la Jungla
HOTEL $

(Map p244; ☑ 7867-5185; lajungla@martsam.com; Calle Centroamérica 30, Flores; s/d Q120/180, with air-con Q190/280; 🞰🔊) Worth considering is this slender, three-story building with front balconies. Though a bit cramped, rooms are comfortably arranged, with quality beds.

Hotel Aurora
HOTEL $

(Map p244; ☑ 7867-5516; aldeamaya@gmail.com; Calle Unión, Flores; dm Q40, s/d Q75/150; 🞰@🔊) This backpacker haven's got a jungle theme, with banisters made to look like climbing vines. Rooms are plain, airy and well scrubbed, with screened windows, and most have some kind of view. A super roof terrace features an open-air shelter slung with hammocks. Guest kitchen available.

Hotel Santa Bárbara
HOTEL

(☑ 7926-2813; http://radiopeten.com.gt; s/d/tr Q200/400/500; 🞰🔊) Part of a trio that includes a museum (p245) and cafe, this is a perfect retreat from the hubbub of Flores on an islet just five minutes west by *lancha* (small motorboat; included in price). Three comfy cabins with big beds and tile floors overlook the lake past a garden brimming with coconut palms and a ceiba tree. Highly recommended.

La Casona del Lago
HOTEL $$$

(Map p246; ☑ 7952-8700; www.hotelesdepeten.com; Calle Litoral al Lago Petén Itzá, Santa Elena; s/d/tr Q625/780/925; P🞰@🔊🞰) The horseshoe shape here allows all the rooms to enjoy the vista of Lago de Petén Itzá and Isla de Flores. At the center of the horseshoe is the lovely terrace, complete with swimming pool and hot tub. Rooms are equally appealing, with sparkling white tiles and ocher-colored walls.

Green World Hotel
HOTEL $

(Map p244; ☑ 7867-5662; greenworldhotel@gmail.com; Calle 30 de Junio, Flores; s/d Q125/175, with air-con Q205/275; 🞰@🔊) This low-key shoreline property features an interior patio and an upper sundeck overlooking the lake. Compact, low-lit rooms have safes, enormous ceiling fans and good hot showers – number 8, with its rear balcony, is by far the nicest.

Hotel Flores de Petén
HOTEL $

(Map p244; ☑ 4718-2635; Calle Sur, Flores; s/d/tr Q125/170/200; 🔊) The first hotel you reach coming off the causeway has bright and spacious rooms with cut-rate furniture and a terrace for lake-gazing. The steady flow of traffic from Santa Elena means you'll probably be up early.

La Posada de Don José
HOTEL $$

(Map p244; ☑ 7867-5298; Calle del Malecón & Calle Fraternidad, Flores; dm Q60, s/d Q175/250, without bathroom Q125/175; 🞰🔊) Near the northern tip of the island, this is an old-fashioned establishment (check the lobby for a portrait of the founder) with rocking chairs scattered around a plant-laden patio and a friendly family that knows your name. The lake level has reclaimed the *malecón* (jetty) here, making the rear terrace infinitely more peaceful than further down. Besides the neat little rooms, there's a spacious fan-cooled dorm in back.

Hospedaje Yaxha
HOSTEL $$

(☑ 5830-2060; www.cafeyaxha.com; Calle 15 de Septiembre, Flores; dm/s/d Q60/150/200) A haven for archaeologists, historians and fans of pre-Hispanic cuisine, Café Yaxha (p250) now offers a clean and simple place to lay your head. There's a four-bed dorm, private rooms with bath and an apartment – all with quality mattresses and ceiling fans.

Mayaland Plaza Hotel
HOTEL **$$**

(Map p246; ☎7926-4976; mayalandplaza@yahoo.com; 6a Av & 4a Calle, Santa Elena; s/d/tr Q225/285/375; P✱❄@✱) The spacious comfortable rooms are set colonial-style around a peaceful courtyard. All services are on hand, including a recommended restaurant and travel agent.

Hotel La Casona de la Isla
HOTEL **$$**

(Map p244; ☎7867-5203; www.hotelesdepeten.com; Calle 30 de Junio, Flores; s/d/tr Q390/450/550; ✱@✱) Popular with package travelers, this has a Caribbean flavor. Small-ish rooms line a long veranda facing a pool with a rock garden and adjacent lake-view deck for sunset dining. The most appealing units, 31, 303 and 304, have windows facing the lake.

Hotel Petén
HOTEL **$$**

(Map p244; ☎7867-5203; www.hotelesdepeten.com; Calle 30 de Junio, Flores; s/d/tr incl breakfast Q380/480/600; ✱@✱✱) Rooms are cheerily decorated here with a dash of chintz. Definitely choose the lake balcony units as they cost no more than interior ones. A good-sized swimming pool straddles the courtyard and rear deck, and the restaurant-bar opens on a lakeside terrace.

Casazul
BOUTIQUE HOTEL **$$**

(Map p244; ☎7867-5451; www.hotelesdepeten.com; Calle Unión, Flores; d/tr Q440/496; ✱✱) As the name suggests, it's blue all over, from the plantation-style balconies to the nine individually decorated, spacious and comfortable rooms. A couple have their own balconies and everyone can enjoy the beautiful top-floor terrace.

Casa Amelia
BOUTIQUE HOTEL **$$**

(Map p244; ☎7867-5430; www.hotelcasamelia.com; Calle Unión, Flores; s/d Q350/450; ✱@✱) Standing tall along Flores' western shore, the Amelia offers bright, stylish chambers with lake views; rooms 301 and 302 are best, opening on the superb balustraded roof terrace.

Hotel Santana
HOTEL **$$**

(Map p244; ☎7926-5123; www.santanapeten.com.gt; Calle 30 de Junio, Flores; s/d/tr Q385/500/600; ✱@✱✱) A tropical fantasy, the Santana holds a commanding presence at Flores' southwest corner, with a popular terrace restaurant and its very own ferry dock. Rooms are generously sized with wicker furniture and lime green walls, and if you get one out back, you'll have a great balcony facing Isla Santa Bárbara.

Hotel La Mesa de los Mayas
HOTEL **$$**

(Map p244; ☎7867-5268; mesamayas@hotmail.com; Av La Reforma, Flores; s/d Q125/200, with air-con Q150/250; ✱✱) Standing alongside a narrow alley, the Mesa is terrific value. Rooms are neatly furnished, with pyramidal headboards, checkered bedspreads and reading lamps; some feature plant-laden balconies.

Hotel Villa del Lago
HOTEL **$$**

(Map p244; ☎7867-5131; www.hotelvilladelago.com.gt; Calle 15 de Septiembre, Flores; s/d/tr Q290/341/390; ✱@✱) Behind the odd Grecian facade there's a cool, breezy interior that's long on potted plants and patio furniture. Comfortable, airy rooms have bright decor and big ceiling fans; lake-view units are pricier. Breakfast is served on the delightful upper terrace.

Hotel Petenchel
HOTEL **$$**

(Map p244; ☎7867-5450; escalofrio_puga@hotmail.com; Calle Sur, Flores; s/d Q120/180, with air-con Q150/230; ✱@) Just off the causeway, this comfy hideaway has eight spacious rooms, all with firm beds, green paint and high arched ceilings, set around a lush garden. Get breakfast burritos at the attached cafe, called Escalofrío ('chill').

Hotel La Unión
HOTEL **$$**

(Map p244; ☎7867-5531; gulzam75@hotmail.com; Calle Unión, Flores; s/d Q150/180; ✱) Considering its location on the waterfront, this family-run property is quite a deal, with cozy decor, quality beds and nicely tiled bathrooms (surcharge for lake-view units), and there's a superb rear terrace. The drawback is that the waterfront promenade turns into a cruising zone each evening with the attendant noise and exhaust. The hotel doubles as an agency for reliable shuttle service.

Hotel Isla de Flores
HOTEL **$$$**

(Map p244; ☎2476-8775; www.hotelisladeflores.com; Av La Reforma, Flores; s/d Q544/616; ✱✱✱) This newish option sports an understated tropical style that's highly appealing. Hardwood beams frame bone-white walls with floral motifs that are echoed on cool stone floors, and large firm beds back up on painted headboards. Though it doesn't stand on the lake shore, the plank-deck roof terrace, with a small pool, commands fantastic views over the whole island.

Enjoy mojitos and fusion cuisine in the equally stylish street-level cafe.

Hotel del Patio
HOTEL **$$$**

(Map p246; ☎7926-0104; http://hoteldelpatio.com.gt; cnr 8a Av & 2a Calle, Santa Elena; r Q780; P❋🕾❄) Shady corridors lined with terracotta floors wind around a stunning courtyard, centered on a gurgling fountain. Rooms are tasteful and comfortable, though not quite as luxurious as the courtyard.

Hotel Maya Internacional
HOTEL **$$$**

(Map p246; ☎7926-2083; www.villasdeguatemala.com; Calle Litoral del Lago, Santa Elena; s/d/tr incl breakfast Q465/550/670; P❋@🕾❄) One of the best reasons to stay in Santa Elena is this tropical-chic resort spreading over a landscaped marsh by the waterfront. The big-top dining room is the center of activity; an adjacent wooden deck with a small infinity pool is great for sunset daiquiris. A boardwalk snakes through tropical gardens to reach the 26 thatch-and-teak rooms. Rooms 49 to 54 have the best lake views.

Ramada Tikal
HOTEL **$$$**

(Map p244; ☎7867-5549; www.ramadatikal.com; Playa Sur, Flores; s/d Q700/745; P❋@🕾❄) This glossy business-class lodging holds a commanding presence at the southwest corner of the island. Rooms are luxuriously appointed with iguana motifs and feature lake-view balconies. Leisure moments can be spent soaking in the outdoor or indoor pools or downing daiquiris in the bar.

Hotel Petén Espléndido
HOTEL **$$$**

(Map p246; ☎7774-0700; www.petenesplendido.com; 1a Calle 5-01, Santa Elena; s/d/tr Q784/880/976; P❋🕾❄) Standing alongside the causeway with its own marina, the most formal hotel in the region pulls out all the stops, featuring room safes, bathroom telephones and great balcony views. Rooms could be bigger, but they're definitely comfortable and a couple of good restaurants and a poolside bar can keep you happy. If you're flying in, hook up a free shuttle from the airport.

🍴 Eating

As might be expected, Flores is rife with tourist-oriented joints pitching a bland mélange of 'international' fare to the package crowd. Nevertheless, a few local gems rise above the pack.

Las Mesitas
GUATEMALAN **$**

(Map p244; El Malecón, Flores; snacks Q5-10; ☺3-10pm) Every evening, but especially Sundays, there's a street party on the waterfront promenade, as local families fix enchiladas (actually *tostadas* topped with guacamole, chicken salad and so on), tacos and tamales, and dispense fruity drinks from giant jugs. All kinds of cakes and puddings are served, too. Everyone sits on plastic chairs or low barrier walls.

Cool Beans
CAFE **$**

(Map p244; ☎5571-9240; Calle 15 de Septiembre, Flores; breakfast Q25-35; ☺7am-10pm Mon-Sat; 🕾) Also known as Café Chilero, this laid-back place is more clubhouse with snacks than proper restaurant, featuring salons for chatting, watching videos or laptop browsing. The lush garden with glimpses of the lake makes a *tranquilo* spot for breakfast or veggie burgers. Be warned – the kitchen closes at 9:01pm sharp.

Restaurante El Mirador
GUATEMALAN **$**

(Map p244; ☎7867-5246; Parque Central; set menu Q25; ☺7am-10pm Mon-Sat) Refreshingly not aimed at foreign travelers, this traditional eatery does toothsome home cookin'. You'll find such hearty options as *caldo de res* (beef stew), served with all the trimmings, *fresco* (fruit drink) included, in a bright lunch hall that looks over the treetops. It's next to the basketball court on the Parque Principal.

Café/Bar Doña Goya
CAFE **$**

(Map p244; El Malecón, Flores; breakfast Q35-50; ☺6:30am-10pm; 🕾) Doña Goya's is good for an early breakfast or sunset snack, with a pretty terrace facing the lake. Toward the weekend, it blends into the nightlife scene along this stretch of the promenade, with occasional live music.

Restaurante Mijaro
RESTAURANT **$**

(Map p246; ☎7926-1615; www.restaurantemijaro.com; 6a Av, Santa Elena; meals Q25-40; ☺7am-10pm) You'll find good home cooking at this locally popular *comedor* (cheap eatery) a few blocks south of the causeway, with an airy thatch-roofed garden area. Besides the grub, they do good long *limonadas* (lime-juice drink).

⭐Terrazzo
ITALIAN **$$**

(Map p244; Calle Unión, Flores; pasta Q70-80; ☺8am-10pm Mon-Sat) Inspired by a chef from

TIKAL & FLORES, GUATEMALA FLORES & SANTA ELENA

Bologna, this Italian gourmet restaurant covers a romantic rooftop terrace. The fettuccine, tortellini and gnocchi are all produced in house, the pizzas (made of seasoned dough) are grilled rather than baked, and the fresh mint lemonade is incredible. All this, and the service is the most attentive in town.

Antojitos Mexicanos   STEAK $$
(Map p244; Calle Playa Sur, Flores; grilled meats Q50-60; ⊙7-10pm) Every evening at the foot of the causeway these characters fire up the grill and char steak, chicken and pork ribs of exceptional quality. Their specialty is *puyazo* (sirloin) swathed with garlic sauce. Sit outside facing the twinkly lights on the lake or, if it's raining, inside under a tin roof. Staff behave with all the formality of an elegant restaurant. Also known as 'Don Fredy'.

Raíces   STEAK $$
(Map p244; ☑7867-5743; Calle Sur, Flores; mains Q90-175; ⊙noon-10pm) A broad deck and a flaming grill are the main ingredients at this stylish lakefront restaurant-bar, possibly the prettiest setting in Flores for dinner. Char-grilled meats and seafood are the specialty; they also do wood-oven pizzas.

Restaurante El Peregrino   GUATEMALAN $$
(Map p244; ☑7867-5115; Av La Reforma, Flores; mains Q40-60; ⊙7am-10pm) Part of the hotel of the same name, this humble *comedor* (dining room) serves heaping helpings of home-cooked fare such as pork-belly stew and breaded tongue. Ask for the daily lunch specials (Q25).

Café Arqueológico Yaxha   CAFE $$
(Map p244; ☑4934-6353; www.cafeyaxha.com; Calle 15 de Septiembre, Flores; mains Q45-70; ⊙6:30am-10pm) Apart from the usual egg-and-bean breakfasts, what's special here are the pre-Hispanic and Itzá items – pancakes with *ramón* seeds, yucca scrambled with *mora* herbs, chicken in *chaya* sauce.

Restaurante El Puerto   SEAFOOD $$
(Map p246; 1a Calle 2-15, Santa Elena; mains Q90-100; ⊙11am-11pm) Seafood is the star attraction at this breezy, open-air hall by the lakefront in Santa Elena, with a well-stocked bar at the front. It's an ideal setting to enjoy shellfish stews, *ceviches* or the famous *pescado blanco* – whitefish from the lake.

La Luna   MEDITERRANEAN $$
(Map p244; ☑7867-5443; cnr Calle 30 de Junio & Av 10 de Noviembre, Flores; mains Q95-135; ⊙noon-11pm Mon-Sat; ☑) Favored by foreign visitors, this restaurant cultivates a tropical ambience with low-lit patio dining. Aside from the usual steak and pasta dishes, Spanish cuisine is their strong suit (the owner hails from the mother country): go for the gazpacho.

♀ Drinking & Nightlife

Flores' little Zona Viva is traditionally the strip of bars along Calle Sur, but there's plenty of action around the bend, along the lakefront promenade north of Hotel Santana.

Qué Pachanga   CLUB
(Map p244; El Malecón, Flores) One of a pair of lively nightspots round the west side of the island, this room gets heavy most evenings, as young Guatemalans decked out in their tightest possible jeans gyrate to a continuous barrage of throbbing reggaetón and *cumbia* (Colombian dance tunes).

El Trópico   BAR
(Map p244; Calle Sur, Flores; ⊙4:30pm-1am Mon-Sat) Longest running of the bars along the southern bank, El Trópico supplies tacos and *cerveza* (beer) to a mostly older Guatemalan clientele. The candlelit terrace is a nice spot to start the night, as the lights of Santa Elena reflect pleasingly off the lake. Many Gallos later, the pulse picks up and DJs work the crowd.

Jamming   BAR
(Map p244; Calle Sur, Flores) One of several nightlife venues along the southern bank, Jamming sports a reggae theme though there's more beer guzzling than ganja smoking. It attracts a younger set of middle-class Guatemalans.

Mi Disco   DISCO
(Map p246; 4a Calle, cnr Calzada Virgilio Rodríguez Macal, Santa Elena; ⊙Mon-Sat) 'El Mi' is Santa Elena's major disco, a cavernous hall with a big stage for salsa combos. If you'd rather croon than dance, head here on Monday to Wednesday evenings as they are reserved for karaoke.

🛍 Shopping

Castillo de Arizmendi   HANDICRAFTS
(Map p244; Parque Central, Flores; ⊙9am-6pm) A monument to Martín de Ursúa Arizmendi y Aguirre, who snatched the island from the Maya in 1697, the castle on the main plaza's north side houses a series of shops with local handicrafts, particularly tropical hardwood carvings by artists from El Remate working in mahogany, cedar and *chicozapote*.

Metroplaza Mundo Maya MALL
(Airport Rd, Santa Elena) This modern shopping mall is opposite Mundo Maya International Airport. The main reason to travel out here is to use the Banco Industrial ATM, the most reliable one around.

ℹ️ Information

ATM (Calle 30 de Junio, Flores) The only ATM in Flores is at the Fotomart convenience store, opposite Capitán Tortuga.

Banco G&T Continental (Maya Mall Petén, 1a Calle 6-17, Santa Elena; ⊙10am-7pm Mon-Sat, to 6pm Sun) Has a Visa ATM.

Banco Industrial (Metroplaza Mundo Maya, 1a Calle, Santa Elena; ⊙9am-4pm Mon-Fri, 10am-2pm Sat) In the shopping mall opposite the airport, this is Santa Elena's most reliable ATM.

Banrural (Av Flores) Just off the Parque Central, changes US dollars, cash and traveler's checks.

Comisión de Turismo Cooperativa Carmelita Agency (☑7867-5629, 7861-2639, 7861-2641; www.turismocooperativacarmelita.com; Calle Centro América, Flores) Flores agency for this Carmelita-based cooperative of trekking guides.

Hospital Privado Santa Elena (☑7926-1140; 3a Av 4-29, Zona 2, Santa Elena) Emergency service available.

Inguat (Map p244; ☑2421-2800, ext 6303; info-ciudadflores@inguat.gob.gt; Calle Centro América, Flores; ⊙8am-4pm Mon-Sat) The official Inguat office provides useful maps and information.

Inguat (☑7926-0533; info-mundomaya@ inguat.gob.mx; Aeropuerto Internacional Mundo Maya; ⊙7am-noon & 3-5pm) The airport branch of the official tourist office.

Martsam Travel (☑7832-2742, in the US 1-866-832-2776; www.martsam.com; Calle 30 de Junio, Flores) Central America–wide operator specializing in custom-designed tours; supports ecotourism initiatives and community involvement.

Police Station (☑7926-1365; Calle Límite 12-28, San Benito)

Post Office (Map p246; 4a Calle & 4a Av, inside Centro Comercial Karossi, Santa Elena; ⊙8am-5pm Mon-Sat)

Proatur (Tourist Police; ☑5414-3594; proatur. peten1@gmail.com; Calle Centro América)

Tikal Net (Calle Centroamérica, Flores; per hr Q10; ⊙8am-9pm) Internet access as well as domestic and international phone calls.

ℹ️ Getting There & Away

AIR

Aeropuerto Internacional Mundo Maya is on the eastern outskirts of Santa Elena, 1.2 miles from the causeway connecting Santa Elena and Flores. **Avianca** (www.avianca.com) has two flights daily between here and Guatemala City. The Belizean airline **Tropic Air** (☑7926-0348; www.tropicair.com; Airport) flies once a day to/from Belize City, charging around Q1500 each way for the one-hour trip.

CAR & MOTORCYCLE

Several car-rental companies have desks at the airport.

Hertz (☑3724-4424; www.guatemalarentcar. com; Airport)

Tabarini (☑7926-0253; www.tabarini.com; Airport)

SHUTTLE MINIBUS

Maayach Expeditions offers a shuttle service at 8am (Q150), picking up passengers from their hotels; purchase tickets at **San Juan Travel** (Map p244; ☑4068-7616; Calle Playa Sur, Flores). San Juan Travel operates shuttle minibuses to Tikal (one way/round trip Q50/80). There are five departures between 4:30am and 1pm. Most hotels and travel agencies can book these shuttles and they will pick you up where you're staying. Returns leave Tikal at 12:30pm, 3pm and 5pm. If you know which round trip you plan to be on, ask your driver to hold a seat for you or arrange one in another minibus. If you stay overnight in Tikal and want to return to Flores by minibus, it's a good idea to reserve a seat with a driver when they arrive in the morning.

ℹ️ Getting Around

A taxi from the airport to Santa Elena or Flores costs Q30. *Tuk-tuks* will take you anywhere between or within Flores and Santa Elena for Q5 to Q10; the *tuk-tuk* service stops after 7pm.

BUS & MICROBUS

Long-distance buses use the Terminal Nuevo de Autobuses in Santa Elena, located 1 mile south of the causeway along 6a Av. It is also used by a slew of *aka expresos* (microbuses), with frequent services to numerous destinations. Second-class buses and some micros make an additional stop at 5a Calle, in the market area (Map p246; the 'old' terminal) before heading out. You can reduce your trip time by 15 minutes by going straight to the market, though the vehicle may be full by then. As always, schedules are highly changeable and should be confirmed before heading out.

BUS & MICROBUS

DESTINA-TION	COST (Q)	TIME (HR)	FREQUENCY	CONNECTIONS
Belize City	160	5	**Línea Dorada** (☏ 7924-8535) leaves at 7am, returning from Belize City at 1pm.	The bus connects with boats to Caye Caulker and Ambergris Caye.
Bethel/La Técnica (Mexican border)	45	4-4½	**AMCRU** (☏ 3127-6684) runs 12 microbuses to Bethel between 4:15am and 4:30pm, eight of which continue on to La Técnica.	
Carmelita	40	4½	Two Pinitas buses at 5am and 1pm from the market.	
Cobán				Take a bus or minibus to Sayaxché, where connecting microbuses leave for Cobán.
El Ceibo/La Palma (Mexican border)	40	4	El Naranjo–bound microbuses depart every 20 minutes, from 4:20am to 6:30pm, stopping at the El Ceibo junction, where there are shuttles to the border (Q10, 15 minutes). Five of these go to El Ceibo (Q45).	At La Palma, on the Mexican side, you can find transport to Tenosique, Tabasco (one hour), and onward to Palenque or Villahermosa.
El Remate	20	45min	ATIM microbuses leave every half-hour from 6:30am to 7pm.	Buses and minibuses to/from Melchor de Mencos will drop you at Puente Ixlú junction, 1.2 miles south of El Remate.
Guatemala City	130-225	8-9	**Línea Dorada** (☏ 7924-8535) runs four 1st-class buses between 6:30am and 10pm (Q225). **Autobuses del Norte** (☏ 7924-8131) has buses at 9pm and 10pm (Q180). Fuente del Norte runs at least 11 buses between 4am and 10:30pm (Q130), including five deluxe buses (Q180),	
Melchor de Mencos (Belizean border)	50	2	Microbuses go about every hour from 5am to 6pm. Línea Dorada Pullmans en route to Belize City depart at 7am (Q40).	
Poptún	30	2	Microbuses, via Dolores, every 10 minutes 5am to 7pm.	
Puerto Barrios	115	6		Take a Guatemala City–bound Fuente del Norte bus. Change at La Ruidosa junction, south of Río Dulce.
Río Dulce	100	4		Take a Guatemala City–bound bus with Fuente del Norte or Línea Dorada.
San Andrés/San José	8	35-40min	Microbuses depart around every 15 minutes, from 5am to 6:40pm, from the left side of the terminal entrance.	
Sayaxché	23	1½	Microbuses depart about every 15 minutes from 5:35am to 5pm.	
Tikal	30	1¼	Six microbuses by ATIM between 6:30am and 3pm, the last returning at 5pm.	You could also take the Uaxactún-bound bus (Q40) at 2pm, which is slower.

Understand
Belize

BELIZE TODAY **254**

With stable government and a growing travel industry, Belize is striving to preserve it's precious natural resources while building a solid economy.

HISTORY **256**

Today's independent Belize is only a little more than three decades old, but its history is rich with ancient civilizations, piracy, slavery and intercultural mixing.

ANCIENT MAYA **266**

The experts shed some light on the mystery of ancient Maya practices and beliefs.

PEOPLE OF BELIZE **273**

Belize may be small, but its people come in all creeds and colors.

RHYTHMS OF A NATION **277**

The music of Belize is as rich and varied as its people.

BEYOND RICE & BEANS **280**

From johnnycakes to habanero sauce, *ceviche* to gibnut, here's the best of Belizean cooking.

WILD THINGS **284**

Wildlife-watchers, bird nerds and floral freaks will be amazed by the vast biodiversity found in tiny Belize.

LAND & ENVIRONMENT **290**

Like most countries, Belize struggles to balance the demands of economic development with the conservation of its natural environment.

Belize Today

To the casual observer, Belize seems to be flourishing, with compulsory primary education, a relatively stable democracy, a thriving tourism industry and an economy that is plugging along. Indeed a sufficient proportion of Belizeans are pleased enough with the way the country is being run to re-elect the government for a third time in 2015. However, not everyone in Belize has seen the benefits of this progress and poverty remains widespread, especially in rural areas.

Best on Film

Mosquito Coast (1986) Harrison Ford and River Phoenix star as members of an American family in search of a simpler life in Central America.
Apocalypto (2006) Mel Gibson's visually arresting – if not historically accurate – Maya thriller.
Curse of the Xtabai (2012) Belizeans are quite proud of this feature-length horror film, the first to be 100% filmed and produced in Belize using local scenery, cast and crew.

Best in Print

Beka Lamb (Zee Edgell; 1982) A heart-wrenching novel about a girl's coming-of-age amid political upheaval.
The Last Flight of the Scarlet Macaw (Bruce Barcott; 2008) An unflinchingly honest account of Sharon Matola's fight against the construction of the Chalillo Dam on the Macal River.
Jaguar (Alan Rabinowitz; 1986) A first-person account of two years living among the Maya and the jaguars.

Tourism

Tourism is the country's top source of employment and investment. The challenge moving forward seems to be one of balancing the needs of the tourism industry with Belizeans' desire – expressed time and again – to protect the environment.

While the benefits of tourism for the country as a whole are acknowledged by Belizeans at nearly every level of society, Belize does not yet have the infrastructure to support the massive numbers of tourists that arrive each year. The most contentious tourism-related issue today concerns cruise-ship passengers.

Belize is among the most popular stops on the Caribbean cruise-ship circuit, but many Belizeans believe these day visitors do not contribute enough to the local economy to justify their impact on environment and infrastructure. The past few years have seen increasing opposition to opening new areas to cruise-ship passengers and the issue has come to a head with the development of Harvest Caye near Placencia by the Norwegian Cruise Lines company.

Distance from the cruise terminal at Belize City has meant, until now, Placencia and other southern towns have been mostly immune to cruise crowds. But with the opening of the Harvest Caye facility, on cruise days thousands of passengers will disembark on the tiny island and many are likely to find their way to Placencia's streets, dramatically altering the laid-back vibe.

Local groups also raised environmental concerns about the impact the facility would have on the delicate reef and local manatee populations, but despite protests, the government has given the facility the green light and it was scheduled to receive its first ships in 2016.

Most Belizeans are proud of their natural heritage and recognize that the goals of environmental conservation and economic prosperity are not mutually exclusive. But the best way to pursue those goals seems certain to remain the subject of much debate.

Persistence of Poverty

Despite the growth in tourism, economic prosperity remains elusive for most Belizeans. A few entrepreneurs have made big money, and a small middle class survives from business, tourism and other professions. But many more Belizeans live on subsistence incomes in rudimentary circumstances. In 2013 an estimated 41% of the population lived below the poverty line.

Unemployment has reached 14% in recent years. And labor – whether washing hotel sheets, cutting sugarcane or packing bananas – is poorly paid when compared with the high cost of living. Although Belize has the second-highest per capita income in Central America, this does not reflect the huge disparity that exists between rich and poor.

The Petroleum Economy

When Prime Minister Dean Barrow called a snap election for late 2015, many observers attributed the decision, at least in part, to the political turmoil in Venezuela. What does social strife in a distant South American nation have to do with the Belizean electorate you may ask? The answer, of course, is petroleum and its importance to the local economy.

Under a regional development program Petro Caribe, founded by the late Venezuelan president Hugo Chavez, Belize receives fuel from Venezuela but only pays half the selling price up front, with the other half being converted into a low-interest long-term loan. The profits from retailing the imported fuel are then fed into government coffers and have permitted the Barrow government to spend on a range of major infrastructure projects around the country.

In early 2015, polls suggested that the ruling United Socialist Party (PSUV) in Venezuela was facing defeat in parliamentary elections, a scenario that would throw future subsidized oil trading into jeopardy. Facing the prospect of one of the government's major revenue streams drying up, putting the brakes on the local economy and bringing an end to spending on popular projects, Barrow bought forward the elections from 2016.

His gamble paid off, with the UDP winning with an increased majority and Barrow being reappointed for an unprecedented third successive term. Shortly afterwards, the PSUV did indeed suffer a heavy defeat in the parliamentary elections, but whether the new parliament will halt the Petro Caribe program remains to be seen.

POPULATION: **370,300**

AREA: **8867 SQ MILES (22,965 SQ KM)**

GDP: **US$1.699 BILLION**

INFLATION: **1.2%**

ANNUAL VISITORS IN 2013: **294,177 (OVERNIGHT), 677,350 (CRUISE SHIP)**

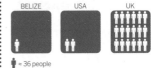

population per sq mile

= 36 people

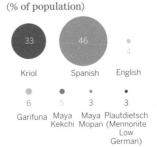

languages
(% of population)

Kriol 33 · Spanish 46 · English 4 · Garifuna 6 · Maya Kekchi 5 · Maya Mopan 3 · Plautdietsch (Mennonite Low German) 3

if Belize were 100 people

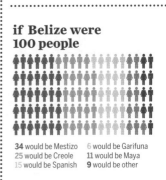

34 would be Mestizo
25 would be Creole
15 would be Spanish
6 would be Garifuna
11 would be Maya
9 would be other

History

Don't be fooled into believing that Central America's youngest independent nation is short on history. Though independence came only in 1981 (peacefully, we might add), many Belizean families trace their connection to the land back for many generations. Most Belizeans have a story to tell about the role played by their relatives in the creation of the nation they now proudly call home.

From Lordly Realm to Lost World: Ancient Maya

Belize hosted one of the great Mesoamerican civilizations of ancient times, the Maya. The Maya created vibrant commercial centers, monumental religious temples and exquisite artworks. They possessed sophisticated knowledge about their earthly and cosmological environments, much of which they wrote down. The Maya thrived from roughly 2000 BC to AD 1500, before succumbing to domestic decline and alien assault. The stone foundations of their lordly realm became a lost world submerged beneath dense jungle.

The Maya ranged across Central America, from the Yucatán to Honduras, from the Pacific to the Caribbean. They were not ethnically homogeneous but only loosely related, divided by kinship, region and dialect. The different communities sometimes cooperated and often competed with one another, building alliances for trade and warfare.

Archaeological findings indicate that Maya settlements in Belize were among the oldest. In the west, Cahal Pech, an important commercial center between the coast and interior, was dated to around 1200 BC. In the north, majestic Lamanai, a major religious site for more than 2000 years, was founded as early as 1500 BC. In Belize today, three distinct Maya tribes still exist: the indigenous Mopan in the north; the Yucatec, who migrated from Mexico, also in the north; and the Kekchi, who migrated from Guatemala, in the west and south.

The Maya were organized into kingdoms, in which social and economic life was an extension of a rigid political hierarchy. At the top

History Books

Thirteen Chapters of a History of Belize by Assad Shoman

Belize: A Concise History by PAB Thomson

The Caste War of the Yucatán by Nelson Reed

TIMELINE	2400 BC	2000 BC–AD 250	AD 250–1000
	The earliest known settlement in Belize is at Cuello in Orange Walk. It predates even the Preclassic period, and some archaeologists attribute the settlement to Maya predecessors.	The earliest sedentary Maya communities are formed during the Preclassic period. Among the earliest Maya settlements are Cahal Pech in Cayo and Lamanai in Orange Walk.	The Classic period of the Maya civilization is characterized by the construction of cities and temples and other artistic and intellectual achievements. The population reaches around 400,000.

were the king – or high lord – and his royal family, followed by an elite stratum of priests, warriors and scribes; next came economically valued artisans and traders; and finally, holding it all up were subsistence farmers and servant workers. The system rested on a cultural belief that the high lord had some influence with the powerful and dark gods of the underworld, who sometimes took the form of jaguars when intervening in human affairs. This view was reinforced through the ruling elite's elaborately staged power displays, a temple theater of awe.

Even before the germ-ridden Europeans arrived, the cultural underpinnings of Maya society were already coming undone. A prolonged drought had caused severe economic hardship, leaving the impression that the kings and priests had somehow lost their supernatural touch. It was left to the Spanish, however, to officially cancel the show.

Possibly the most impressive of the Maya kingdoms in Belize was at Caracol, in the western Mountain Pine Ridge. At its height, in the 6th and 7th centuries, Caracol was a major urban metropolis, with more than 100,000 residents. It boasted first-rate jewelers and skilled artisans, an intricately terraced agriculture system, a prosperous trading market, and 40 miles of paved roads (considerably more than it has today). According to the story carved by Maya artists into commemorative stone, the king of Caracol, Water Lord, defeated his chief rival, Double Bird, king of Tikal, in a decisive battle in AD 562, ushering in a long period of Caracol supremacy in the central highlands. The pictographic stone inscriptions also suggest that Water Lord personally sacrificed Double Bird to further emphasize the Caracol triumph. Perhaps this had something to do with the still-simmering feud between Belize and Guatemala.

In the 1500s, the jaguar kings were forced to take cover in the rainforest when the sword-wielding Spanish arrived in Belize with the aim of plundering Maya gold and spreading the word of God. The Maya population of Belize at this time numbered about a quarter of a million, but their ranks were quickly decimated by as much as 90%, from the lethal combination of the disease and greed of the Spanish. In the 1540s, a conquistador force based in the Yucatán set out on an expedition through much of present-day Belize, down the coast and across to the central highlands. Disappointed by the lack of riches uncovered, they left a bloody trail of slaughtered victims and abandoned villages in their wake. Religious sites, such as Lamanai, were forcibly converted to Catholicism.

In the early 1600s, the Maya finally staged a counteroffensive that successfully drove out the few Spanish settlers and missionaries that had decided to stay. Weakened and fearful, the Maya did not return to the now desolate old cities, choosing instead to stay huddled in the remote interior.

Joyce Kelly's *An Archaeological Guide to Northern Central America* offers the best descriptions of the Maya sites of Belize, along with those in Guatemala and Mexico.

HISTORY FROM LORDLY REALM TO LOST WORLD: ANCIENT MAYA

900–1000	1000–1600	1540s	1638
The great Maya civilization declines, possibly as a result of drought, disease or environmental disaster. Large urban centers come under stress and their populations disperse throughout the region.	During the Postclassic period, the Maya civilization continues to develop, although populations are not as concentrated. Political and cultural centers migrate to northern Belize and the Yucatán.	Spanish conquistadors sweep through northern and western Belize, attempting to establish strongholds in Chetumal near Corozal, Lamanai in Orange Walk, and Tipu in Cayo.	British Baymen 'settle' Belize when former pirate Peter Wallace lays the foundations for a new port at the mouth of the Belize River, on the site of today's Belize City.

The virtually unexplored Glover's Atoll is named for the pirate John Glover, who hung out there in the 1750s; there are supposed to be pirate graves on Northeast Caye.

Baymen of the Caribbean: British Settlement

When Columbus accidentally bumped into the continental landmass soon to be known as the Americas, his Spanish royal patrons Ferdinand and Isabella had it made. Soon, Aztec gold and Incan silver overflowed in the king's coffers, making Spain a transatlantic superpower. In 1494 the Treaty of Tordesillas established an exclusive Iberian claim on the region, declaring New World riches off-limits to old-world rivals. But the temptations were too great, and the hiding places too many. Spain's spoils were set upon by British buccaneers, French corsairs and Dutch freebooters. In times of war, they were put into the service of their Crown as privateers; at other times, they were simply pirates.

Belize emerged as one of several Caribbean outposts for Britain's maritime marauders. In the early 17th century, English sea dogs first began using the Bay of Honduras as a staging point for raids on Spanish commerce; henceforth the Brits in the region came to be known as Baymen.

The Belizean coast had several strategic advantages from a pirate's perspective. The land was both bountiful and uninhabited, as the Spanish had already driven the Maya out but never bothered to settle in themselves. It was just a short sail away from the heavily trafficked Yucatán Straits, where – if luck be with ye – the Treasure Fleet might

THE FIRST MESTIZO

In 1511 the Spanish ship *Valdivia* was wrecked at sea when a reef ripped through its hull. About 15 survivors drifted for several days before making it to shore in northern Belize, where they were promptly apprehended by anxious Maya. Just to be on the safe side, the locals sent 10 to the gods and kept five for themselves.

One of the captives was conquistador Gonzalo Guerrero, a skilled warrior and apparently not a bad diplomat either. Guerrero managed to win his freedom and a position of status with the Maya chief at Chetumal. He became a tribal consultant on military matters and married the chief's daughter; their three children are considered the first *mestizos* (mixed-race Spanish and Amerindian) in the New World.

Eight years later, Hernán Cortés arrived in the Yucatán and summoned Guerrero to serve him in his campaign of conquest. But Guerrero had gone native, with facial tattoos and body piercings. He turned down the offer, saying instead that he was a captain of the Maya. Cortés moved on in his search for gold and glory. Guerrero, meanwhile, organized Maya defenses in the wars that followed. It would take the Spanish more than 20 years to finally defeat the Maya of Yucatán and Belize.

1638–40	1667	1724	1717–63
Maya rebellion finally drives out the Spanish for good, although they never relinquish their claim on the territory. The Maya population drops dramatically due to war, drought and disease.	Britain and Spain sign a treaty that grants freedom of trade, as long as Britain agrees to control piracy. The result is an increase in logging and the acceleration of settlement of Belize.	The first African slaves are recorded in Belize. Slaves are put to work cutting logwood and mahogany, as well as doing domestic work and farming.	Spanish attacks attempt to end British extraction of hardwoods. Finally, the Treaty of Paris gives Britain the right to cut and export logwood, but the Spanish still claim the land.

be gathering in Havana or the Silver Train passing through on its way from Panama. And the shoreline, concealed behind thick mangroves and littoral islands, offered protective cover, while the long barrier reef was a treacherous underwater trap that kept Spanish war galleons at a distance.

For the sake of historical record, the year 1638 was made the official founding date of a British settlement at the mouth of the Belize River. It was around then that a Scottish pirate captain, Peter Wallace, decided to organize the building of a new port town. Legend has it that he laid the first foundations of what became Belize City with woodchips and rum bottles, presumably empty.

Meanwhile, the Baymen found yet another activity to annoy the Spanish crown – poaching its rainforest. The settlement became a rich source of hardwoods, especially mahogany, much valued by carpenters, furniture-makers and shipbuilders back in Britain. In addition, the lowland forest was abundant in logwood trees, which provided a valuable dye extract used to make woollen textiles.

By the 18th century, Britain's monarch finally had a navy and merchant fleet to match Spain's. Privateers were no longer needed, and pirates were a nuisance. In 1765 Jamaican-based British naval commander Admiral Burnaby paid a visit to the rough-hewn Baymen and delivered a code of laws on proper imperial etiquette: thieving, smuggling and cursing were out; paying taxes and obeying the sovereign were in.

As the British settlement became more profitable, the Spanish monarch became more irritable. Spain's armed forces made several unsuccessful attempts to dislodge the well-ensconced and feisty squatters. With the Treaty of Paris, in 1763, Spain instead tried diplomacy, negotiating a deal in which the Brits could stay and harvest wood as long as they paid rent to the Spanish Crown and promised not to expand the settlement. The Baymen did neither.

Spain finally got the better of the Baymen in 1779, burning down Belize City in a surprise attack and consigning the prisoners to slavery in Cuba. The conflict reached a decisive conclusion in 1798 at the Battle of St George's Caye when a squadron of 30 Spanish warships was met and turned back by the alerted Baymen operating in smaller but faster craft. From this point, Spain gave up trying to boot the Brits from Belize. And the battle made such a good story that it eventually inspired a national holiday (Battle of St George's Caye Day).

In Living Color: British Honduras

In the 19th century, modern Belize began to take form, largely shaped by its economic role and political status in the British Empire, where it was

Colonial Sights

Government House (Belize City)

Museum of Belize (Belize City)

St John's Cathedral (Belize City)

1786	1798	1832	1838
The Convention of London gives loggers the right to fell the forest, but not to establish any agriculture or government. However, an informal group of magistrates governs and agriculture exists.	During the seven-day Battle of St George's Caye, British Baymen and Creole slaves defend their settlement from Spanish invasion, finally ending Spanish claims on the territory.	A group of Garifuna from Honduras settle in present-day Dangriga. This ethnic enclave was previously deported from the British-ruled island of St Vincent, after being defeated in the Carib Wars.	According to the Abolition Act, slavery is outlawed throughout the British Empire, including Belize. Former slaves are unable to own property and are dependent on their ex-masters for work.

officially dubbed British Honduras. At first it was administered from Jamaica, but later was made a Crown Colony with its own appointed royal governor. Belizean society was an overlapping patchwork of British, African, Maya and Spanish influences. It was a haven for refugees and a labor camp for slaves, a multicultural but hierarchical Crown Colony in living color.

At the top of the colonial social order were the descendants of the Baymen. In earlier times, their outlaw ancestors comprised an ethnically mixed and relatively democratic community. But as the colony grew larger and ties with the empire stronger, an oligarchy of leading families emerged. They may have descended from anti-establishment renegades, but now they were all about aristocratic manners. They touted their white, cultured British lineage, and used the Crown's authority to reinforce their status. By order of His Majesty's Superintendent for British Honduras, they alone were given political rights in colonial affairs and private entitlement to the forest and land. This elite colonial cohort managed to hold sway until the early 20th century.

As the economy was centered on timber exports, strong bodies were needed to perform the arduous labor of harvesting hardwoods from the dense rainforest. As elsewhere in the Americas, African slaves provided the muscle, along with much sweat and pain. By 1800, the settlement numbered about 4000 in total: 3000 black slaves, 900 mixed-race coloreds and free blacks, and 100 white colonists. Slave masters could count, and acted shrewdly to stay on top. Male slaves were kept divided into small work teams based on tribal origins. They were forced to do long tours of duty in remote jungle camps, separated from other teams and from their families. Slave women performed domestic chores and farm work. Interracial separation, however, did not mean interracial segregation, as mixed-race Creoles (descendants of African slaves) would eventually make up nearly 75% of the population.

In 1838 slavery was abolished in the British Empire. The plight of Afro-Belizeans, however, did not much improve. They were forbidden from owning land, which would have enabled them to be self-sufficient, and thus remained dependent on the white-controlled export economy. Instead of slaves, they were called 'apprentices' and worked for subsistence wages.

In 1872 the Crown Lands Ordinance established Carib Reserves and Maya Reserves, which stripped the Garifuna and Maya of their property rights.

When the timber market declined in the 1860s, landowners diversified their holdings by introducing fruit and sugarcane. One persistent historical narrative has it that slave life in Belizean logging camps was more benign than the harsh conditions that existed on Caribbean sugar plantations. While this may be so, the facts remain that Belize experienced four major slave revolts between 1760 and 1820, and re-

1847	1854	1862	1865
Spanish, *mestizo* and Maya peoples engage in the War of the Castes in the neighboring Yucatán Peninsula. The violence sends streams of refugees into Belize.	A new constitution establishes a Legislative Assembly of 18 elected, property-holding members, thus consolidating British political control of the territory.	The settlement in Belize is declared a Crown Colony and named British Honduras. Initially it is administered from Jamaica, but a separate royal governor is appointed soon after.	The Serpon sugar mill – the country's first steam-powered mill – is built on the Sittee River, ushering in an era of economic development.

corded a high annual incidence of runaways, suggesting instead that repressive inhumanity may come in different packages.

Toward the mid-19th century, British colonists finally came into contact – and conflict – with the indigenous Maya. As loggers penetrated deeper into the interior, they encountered the elusive natives, who responded with hit-and-run assaults on the encroaching axmen.

At this time in the neighboring Yucatán Peninsula, an armed conflict broke out among the lowly Maya, second-class *mestizos* and privileged Spanish-descended landlords. The bloody War of the Castes raged for over a decade and forced families to flee. Caste War refugees more than doubled the Belize population, from less than 10,000 in 1845 to 25,000 in 1861.

The movement of peoples redefined the ethnic character of northern Belize. *Mestizo* refugees, of mixed Spanish-Indian stock, brought their Hispanic tongue, corn tortillas and Catholic churches to scattered small-town settlements. Yucatecan Maya refugees, meanwhile, moved into the northwestern Belizean forest, where they quickly clashed with the logging industry. In 1872 the desperate Maya launched a quixotic attack on British colonists at Orange Walk, in what was a fierce but futile last stand. Diminished and dispirited, the remaining Maya survived on the territorial and social fringes of the colony.

Emory King's *The Great Story of Belize* is a fun read, and quite detailed, even though it has come under criticism for glamorizing the swashbuckling ways of the early British settlers.

Patience & Resistance: Belizean Independence

Belize remained a British colony until 1981, rather late for the West Indies. Spain and France lost most Caribbean possessions in the early 19th century, while Her Majesty's island colonies were liberated in the 1960s. With its deep ethnic divisions, a unifying national identity formed slowly, and the Belizean independence movement displayed more patience than resistance.

As the 19th century closed, the orderly ways of colonial life in British Honduras showed signs of breakdown. The old elite was becoming more isolated and less feared. Its cozy connections to the mother country were unraveling. By 1900 the US surpassed Britain as the main destination of the mahogany harvest; by 1930 the US was taking in 80% of all Belizean exports.

The colonial elite's economic position was further undercut by the rise of a London-based conglomerate, the British Estate and Produce Company, which bought out local landowners and took over the commodity trade. Declining timber fortunes caused colonial capitalists to impose a 50% wage cut on mahogany workers in Belize City, which provoked riotous protests and the first stirrings of social movement.

1871	1927	1931	1950
A new constitution establishes a nine-member Legislative Council, which governs the colony alongside the lieutenant governor.	Successful international trading ties give rise to a prosperous Creole elite, which gains formal means of power when several representatives are appointed to the Legislative Council.	The deadliest hurricane in Belizean history hits on September 10, when the country is celebrating the national holiday. Belize City is destroyed, as is most of the northern coast; 2500 people die.	A severe economic crisis sparks anti-British protests, and the pro-independence movement is launched under the leadership of George Price and the People's United Party (PUP).

In 1984, 18-year-old David Stuart became the youngest person to receive a McArthur Genius Award for his work in cracking the Maya hieroglyphic code, which he had been working on since the age of 10.

During the first half of the 20th century, Belizean nationalism developed in explosive fits and starts. During WWI, a regiment of local Creoles was recruited for the Allied cause. The experience proved both disheartening and enlightening. Ill-treated because of their dark skin, they were not even allowed to go to the front line and fight alongside white troops. They may have enlisted as patriotic Brits, but they were discharged as resentful Belizeans. Upon their return, in 1919, they coaxed several thousand into the streets of Belize City in an angry demonstration against the existing order.

It was not until the 1930s that a more sustained anticolonial movement arose. It began as the motley 'Unemployed Brigade,' staging weekend rallies in Battlefield Park in Belize City. The movement fed on the daily discontents of impoverished black workers, and spewed its wrath at prosperous white merchants. It soon was organizing boycotts and strikes, and shortly thereafter its leaders were thrown into jail.

Finally, in the early 1950s, a national independence party, the People's United Party (PUP), became politically active. When WWII caused the sudden closing of export markets, the colony experienced a severe economic crisis that lasted until well after the war's end. Anti-British

BELIZEAN STARS & BARS

At the end of the US Civil War, several thousand Confederate soldiers chose not to return to their defeated and occupied homeland. The rebels instead accepted an invitation to resettle under the British flag in Belize.

The white colonial elite of Belize sympathized with the Southern cause during the conflict. During the war, they supplied the Confederacy with raw materials and guns. After the war, colonial officials enticed the war veterans with promises of land grants and other economic incentives. It was hoped that these expatriate Americans could help rejuvenate the Belizean economy, which suffered from a decline in timber exports, by sharing their expertise of the plantation system.

As many as 7000 American Southerners made it to Belize in the 1860s, mostly arriving from Mississippi and Louisiana, with the dream of recreating the Old South in tropical climes. Their initial attempts to cultivate cotton, however, were dashed by the inhospitable steamy jungle climate. They had better luck with sugarcane. The Confederate contribution to the colonial economy was notable, as Belizean sugar exports between 1862 and 1868 increased four-fold, from 400,000lb to 1,700,000lb.

But the move did not go smoothly. The American newcomers had run-ins with the local white landowners, who resented their presence and privileges, and with the local black workforce, who refused to submit and serve. All but a couple of hundred of the Confederate contingent eventually cashed out and returned home.

1961	1971	1972	1975
Hurricane Hattie devastates Belize, killing hundreds of people and destroying Belize City. British naval troops arrive to control widespread violence and looting.	In response to the devastation wrought by Hurricane Hattie, a new inland capital is established at Belmopan. The new National Assembly building is designed to resemble a Maya temple.	Jacques Cousteau takes his research ship *Calypso* to the Blue Hole, bringing unprecedented publicity and kicking off its popularity as a destination for divers and snorkelers.	Young activist attorneys Said Musa and Assad Shoman begin an intensive campaign to obtain international support for an independent Belize.

demonstrations spread all across Belize, becoming more militant and occasionally violent. Colonial authorities declared a state of emergency, forbidding public meetings and intimidating independence advocates.

In response, the PUP organized a successful general strike that finally forced Britain to make political concessions. Universal suffrage was extended to all adults and limited home rule was permitted in the colony. The imperial foundations of the old ruling elite crumbled, as the colony's ethnically divided peoples now danced to a common Belizean drum beat.

Full independence for Belize was put off until a nagging security matter was resolved. Spain never formally renounced its territorial claim to Belize, which was later appropriated by Mexico and Guatemala. In the 19th century, Britain signed agreements with both claimants to recognize the existing colonial borders, but the one with Guatemala did not stick.

Guatemala's caudillo (Spanish/Latin American military dictator) rulers remained very preoccupied with the perceived wealth of British Honduras. The 1945 Guatemalan constitution explicitly included Belize as part of its territorial reach. Britain, in turn, stationed a large number of troops in the west. Guatemala barked, but did not bite. By the 1960s, the border threat was stabilized and the demand for independence was renewed.

Belizeans waited patiently. In 1964 the colony became fully self-governing, installing a Westminster-style parliamentary system. In 1971 the capital was relocated to Belmopan, a geographic center symbolically uniting all regions and peoples. In 1973 the name was officially changed from the colonial sounding British Honduras to the more popular Belize. And in September 1981 Belize was at last declared an independent nation-state within the British Commonwealth. Even Guatemala recognized Belize as a sovereign nation in 1991, although to this day it maintains its territorial claim.

In 1988 the Duke of Edinburgh and WWF head, Prince Philip, was on hand to celebrate the creation of the Cockscomb Basin Wildlife Sanctuary, the world's first wildlife sanctuary for the jaguar. By 1998 the protected realm of the Belizean jungle's king eventually reached more than half a million acres.

Return of the Jaguar King: Contemporary Belize

Independence did not turn out to be a cure-all. The angry nationalists that led Belize to independence turned into accommodating capitalists. The country had a small economy whose fortunes were determined beyond its control in global commodity markets. Belizeans eventually discovered that rather than remain vulnerable to exports, they had something valuable to import: tourists. The rise of ecotourism and revival of Maya culture has reshaped contemporary Belize, and cleared the jungle overgrowth for a return of the jaguar king.

1981	1991	1994	1998
After years of anticolonial and pro-independence political movements, Belize receives formal international recognition of its independence. George Price (PUP) is the first prime minister.	Guatemala finally recognizes Belize as a sovereign, independent state. Tensions continue, however, as the neighbor to the west refuses to relinquish its territorial claim over parts of Belize.	The United Kingdom withdraws military forces, with the exception of the British Army Training & Support Unit, which is established to assist the new Belize Defence Force.	Promising to 'Set Belize Free,' the People's United Party (PUP) takes the national elections, winning 26 of 31 seats in the House of Representatives. Party leader Said Musa becomes prime minister.

Belizean politics were long dominated by the founder of the nationalist People's United Party (PUP), George Price. His party won nearly every parliamentary election, consolidating political independence and promoting a new middle class. In 1996, at the age of 75, Price finally stepped down with his national hero status intact; the PUP, however, looked vulnerable.

The party was tainted by corruption scandals: missing pension funds, selling off of public lands and bribery. Supporters argue that other parties' politicians are guilty of similar crimes.

The frail economy inherited at the time of independence was slow to recover. Many Creoles began to look for work outside the country, forming sizeable diaspora communities in New York and London. As much as one-third of the Belizean people now live abroad. Meanwhile, civil war and rural poverty in neighboring Guatemala and Honduras sent more refugees into Belize, whose demographic profile changed accordingly, with Spanish-speaking *mestizos* becoming the majority ethnic group. From the time of independence, the Belize nation has doubled in size, from 150,000 in 1981 to 333,200 in 2010.

Belize was an ideal candidate for a green revolution. Wide swaths of lowland rainforest were unspoiled by loggers, while sections of the interior highland had never even been explored by Europeans. The jungle hosted a rich stock of exotic flora and fauna, feathered and furry, while just offshore was the magnificent coral reef and mysterious Blue Hole, which Jacques Cousteau had already made famous.

A Tourist Ministry was created in 1984, but it was not until the 1990s that the government began to recognize ecotourism as a viable revenue source and invested in its promotion and development. Infrastructure associated with various sites improved, small business loans became available, training programs were organized for guides, and a bachelor's degree in tourism was created at Belize University.

Over the next decade, more than 20 sites from the western mountains to the eastern cays were designated as national parks, wildlife sanctuaries, forest reserves and marine preserves. More than 40% of Belizean territory received some form of protective status, including 80% of its pristine rainforest. The number of visitors rose steadily, from 140,000 in 1988 to more than one million in 2010. By the end of the 1990s, tourism was Belize's fastest-growing economic sector, surpassing commodity exports.

The eco-craze coincided with archaeological advances to spur a revival of Maya culture. In the 1980s significant progress was made in cracking the Maya hieroglyphic code, enabling researchers to gain deeper insights into this once-shrouded world, while NASA satellite

In 2008 the Belize and Guatemala governments signed an historic agreement to refer their territorial conflict to the International Court of Justice, pending approval from their electorates. The referenda – which must be held in both countries simultaneously – have not been scheduled due to the volatile political climate in Guatemala.

2002	2006	2008	2011
The purpose-built Tourism Village opens in Belize City to welcome cruise-ship passengers to Belize. The following year, the tiny country hosts more than half a million cruise-ship tourists.	Black gold. After more than four years of exploration around the country, oil is discovered in commercially viable quantities in the Mennonite village of Spanish Lookout.	Led by Dean Barrow, the United Democratic Party (UDP) overwhelmingly defeats the PUP in countrywide elections, capturing 25 out of 31 seats in the House of Representatives.	Under pressure from local residents and hotel owners, the Belize Tourism Board decides against the development of a new cruise-ship port on Placencia peninsula.

technology revealed over 600 previously unknown sites and hidden temples beneath the Belizean rainforest. In 2000 the government allocated nearly $30 million to support excavation projects. A lost culture became a live commodity. Maya descendants re-engaged with traditional ceremonies, craft-making, food preparation and healing techniques, often in response to tourist curiosity. However, the commercial aspects of cultural revival can be controversial, and one doesn't have to look far for examples where tourism and sanctity clash. One example concerns Cayo's Actun Tunichil Muknal cave, which is at once a sacred spot to the Maya and a top tourist attraction. After one visitor dropped a camera, fracturing an ancient human skull, cameras were banned from the cave. This example, among others, begs the question of how to promote cultural tourism while avoiding a carnival atmosphere.

In contemporary Belize, the new understanding of the Maya past fostered a changed attitude in the Maya present. The Maya culture is no longer disparaged at the fringe of society, but now is a source of pride and a defining feature of Belizean identity.

2012	2012	2015	2016
While the the United Democratic Party (UDP) loses several seats in the general election, it holds onto its majority with 17 seats to the PUP's 14.	Eccentric computer millionaire John McAfee's bizarre antics in San Pedro and Orange Walk put the nation briefly in the international spotlight.	Prime Minister Dean Barrow of the UDP wins an unprecedented third straight election after calling a snap early election.	Norwegian Cruise Line (NCL) announces the opening of controversial island cruise-ship development Harvest Caye for late 2016.

Ancient Maya

Though the Maya population of Belize is small (around 10% of the nation's population), imagining contemporary Belize without the Maya would be difficult. From the Cayo District's Caracol (which covers more area than Belize City and still boasts Belize's tallest structure) and Xunantunich to smaller archeological sites stretching from the nation's far north into its deep south, remnants of ancient Maya glory abound.

Preclassic Maya Sites

Cuello
(Orange Walk)

Lamanai
(Orange Walk)

Cerro Maya
(Corozal)

Caracol (Cayo)

Altun Ha
(Belize District)

Creation Story

Nearly all aspects of Maya faith begin with their view of the creation, when the gods and divine forebears established the world at the beginning of time. From their hieroglyphic texts and art carved on stone monuments and buildings, or painted on pottery, we can now piece together much of the Maya view of the creation. We can even read the precise date when the creation took place.

In AD 775, a Maya lord with the high-sounding name of K'ak' Tiliw Chan Yoat (Fire Burning Sky Lightning God) set up an immense stone monument in the center of his city, Quirigua, in Guatemala. The unimaginative archaeologists who discovered the stone called it Stela C. This monument bears the longest single hieroglyphic description of the creation, noting that it took place on the day 13.0.0.0.0, 4 Ahaw, 8 Kumk'u, a date corresponding to August 13, 3114 BC on our calendar. This date appears over and over in other inscriptions throughout the Maya world. On that day the creator gods set three stones or mountains in the dark waters that once covered the primordial world. These three stones formed a cosmic hearth at the center of the universe. The gods then struck divine new fire by means of lightning, which charged the world with new life.

This account of the creation is echoed in the first chapters of the *Popol Vuh,* a book compiled by members of the Maya nobility soon after the Spanish conquest in 1524, many centuries after the erection of Quirigua Stela C. Although this book was written in their native Maya language, its authors used European letters rather than the more terse hieroglyphic script. Thus the book gives a fuller account of how they conceived the first creation:

> This is the account of when all is still, silent and placid. All is silent and calm. Hushed and empty is the womb of the sky. These then are the first words, the first speech. There is not yet one person, one animal, bird, fish, crab, tree, rock, hollow, canyon, meadow or forest. All alone the sky exists. The face of the earth has not yet appeared. Alone lies the expanse of the sea, along with the womb of all the sky. There is not yet anything gathered together. All is at rest. Nothing stirs. All is languid, at rest in the sky. Only the expanse of the water, only the tranquil sea lies alone. All lies placid and silent in the darkness, in the night.
>
> All alone are the Framer and the Shaper, Sovereign and Quetzal Serpent, They Who Have Borne Children and They Who Have Begotten Sons. Luminous they are in the water, wrapped in feathers...They

For a lively discussion of Maya religion and the creation, pick up a copy of *Maya Cosmos* by David Freidel, Linda Schele and Joy Parker.

are great sages, great possessors of knowledge...Then they called forth the mountains from the water. Straightaway the great mountains came to be. It was merely their spirit essence, their miraculous power, that brought about the conception of the mountains.

Popol Vuh: The Sacred Book of the Maya

The Maya saw this pattern all around them. In the night sky, the three brightest stars in the constellation of Orion's Belt were conceived as the cosmic hearth at the center of the universe. On a clear night in the crisp mountain air of the Maya highlands, one can even see what looks like a wisp of smoke within these stars, although it is really only a far-distant string of stars within the M4 Nebula.

Maya Cities as the Center of Creation

Perhaps because the ancient Maya of northern Belize didn't have real mountains as symbols of the creation, they built them instead in the form of plaza-temple complexes. In hieroglyphic inscriptions, the large open-air plazas at the center of Maya cities are often called *nab'* (sea) or *lakam ja'* (great water). Rising above these plastered stone spaces are massive pyramid temples, often oriented in groups of three, representing the first mountains to emerge out of the 'waters' of the plaza. The tiny elevated sanctuaries of these temples served as portals into the abodes of gods that lived within. Offerings were burned on altars in the plazas, as if the flames were struck in the midst of immense three-stone hearths. Only a few elite persons were allowed to enter the small interior spaces atop the temples, while the majority of the populace observed their actions from the plaza below. The architecture of ancient Maya centers thus replicated sacred geography to form an elaborate stage on which rituals that charged their world with regenerative power could be carried out.

Many of the earliest-known Maya cities were built in Belize. The earliest temples at these sites are often constructed in this three-temple arrangement, grouped together on a single platform, as an echo of the first three mountains of creation. The ancient name for the site known today as Caracol was Oxwitza' (Three Hills Place), symbolically linking this community with the three mountains of creation and thus the center of life. The Caana (Sky-Place) is the largest structure at Caracol and consists of a massive pyramid-shaped platform topped by three temples that represent these three sacred mountains.

The Belizean site of Lamanai is one of the oldest and largest Maya cities known. It is also one of the few Maya sites that still bears its ancient name (which means Submerged Crocodile). While other sites

Books on Maya Art & Architecture

Maya Art & Architecture by Mary Ellen Miller

The Ancient Maya by Robert J Sharer

The oldest known copy of the Popol Vuh was made around 1701–03 by a Roman Catholic priest named Francisco Ximénez in Guatemala. The location of the original Popol Vuh from which Ximénez made his copy, if it still survives, is unknown.

THE HERO TWINS

According to the Popol Vuh, the Lords of Xibalba (the underworld) invited Hun Hunahpu and his brother to a game in the ballcourt. Upon losing the game, the brothers were sacrificed and the skull of one of them was suspended from a calabash tree as a show of triumph.

Along came an unsuspecting daughter of Xibalba. As she reached out to take fruit from the tree, the skull of Hun Hunahpu spat in her hand, thus impregnating her. From this strange conception would be born the Hero Twins, Hunahpu and Xbalanque.

The Hero Twins would go on to have many adventures, including vanquishing their evil half-brothers. Their final triumph was overcoming Xibalba and avenging the death of their father – first by fooling the Lords, and then by sacrificing them. After this, the twins ascended into the sky, being transformed into the sun and moon.

Mara Vorhees

The Maya likely used their counting system from day to day by writing on the ground, the tip of the finger creating a dot. By using the edge of the hand they could make a bar, representing the entire hand of five fingers.

were abandoned well before the Spanish Conquest in the 16th century, Lamanai continued to be occupied by the Maya centuries afterward. For the ancient Maya, the crocodile symbolized the rough surface of the earth, newly emerged from the primordial sea that once covered the world. The name of the city reveals that its inhabitants saw themselves as living at the center of creation, rising from the waters of creation. Its massive pyramid temples include Structure N10-43, which is the second-largest pyramid known from the Maya Preclassic period and represents the first mountain and dwelling place of the gods.

The Maya Creation of Mankind

According to the *Popol Vuh,* the purpose of the creation was to give form and shape to beings who would 'remember' the gods through ritual. The Maya take their role in life very seriously. They believe that people exist as mediators between this world and that of the gods. If they fail to carry out the proper prayers and ceremonies at just the right time and place, the universe will come to an abrupt end.

The gods created the first people out of maize (corn) dough, literally from the flesh of the Maize God, the principal deity of creation. Because of their divine origin, they were able to see with miraculous vision:

> Perfect was their sight, and perfect was their knowledge of everything beneath the sky. If they gazed about them, looking intently, they beheld that which was in the sky and that which was upon the earth. Instantly they were able to behold everything... Thus their knowledge became full. Their vision passed beyond the trees and the rocks, beyond the lakes and the seas, beyond the mountains and the valleys. Truly they were very esteemed people.
> *Popol Vuh: The Sacred Book of the Maya*

In nearly all of their languages, the Maya refer to themselves as 'true people' and consider that they are literally of a different flesh than those who do not eat maize. They are maize people, and foreigners who eat bread are wheat people. This mythic connection between maize and human flesh influenced birth rituals in the Maya world for centuries.

Maya Kingship

The creation wasn't a one-time event. The Maya constantly repeated these primordial events in their ceremonies, timed to the sacred calendar. They saw the universe as a living thing. And just like any living thing, it grows old, weakens and ultimately passes away. Everything, including the gods, needed to be periodically recharged with life-bearing power or the world would slip back into the darkness and chaos that

---

GUIDE TO THE GODS

The Maya worshiped a host of heavenly beings. It's practically impossible to remember them all (especially since some of them have multiple names), but here's a primer for the most powerful Maya gods.

Ah Puch God of Death

Chaac God of Rain and Thunder

Itzamma God of Priestly Knowledge and Writing

Hun Hunahpu Father of the Hero Twins, sometimes considered the Maize God

Hunahpu & Xbalanque The Hero Twins

Ixchel Goddess of Fertility and Birth
Mara Vorhees

AMAZING MAIZE

No self-respecting Maya, raised in the traditional way, would consider eating a meal that didn't include maize. They treat it with the utmost respect. Women do not let grains of maize fall on the ground or into an open fire. If it happens accidentally, the woman picks it up gently and apologizes to it. The Maya love to talk and laugh, but are generally silent during meals. Most don't know why; it's just the way things have always been done. As one elder explained, 'For us, tortillas are like the Catholic sacramental bread: it is the flesh of god. You don't laugh or speak when taking the flesh of god into your body. The young people are beginning to forget this. They will someday regret it.'

existed before the world began. Maya kings were seen as mediators. In countless wall carvings and paintings, monumental stone stelae and altars, painted pottery and other sacred objects, the Maya depicted their kings dressed as gods, repeating the actions of deities at the time of creation.

A common theme was the king dressed as the Maize God himself, bearing a huge pack on his back containing the sacred bits and pieces that make up the world, while dancing them into existence. A beautiful example of this may be seen on the painted *Buena Vista Vase,* one of the true masterpieces of Maya art. Discovered at Buenavista el Cayo, a small site in the Cayo District of Belize, right on the river (north side) close to the border with Guatemala, it is now one of the gems of the Maya collection housed in the Department of Archaeology, Belize City. These rituals were done at very specific times of the year, timed to match calendric dates when the gods first performed them. For the Maya, these ceremonies were not merely symbolic of the rebirth of the cosmos, but a genuine creative act in which time folded in on itself to reveal the actions of the divine creators in the primordial world.

In Maya theology, the Maize God is the most sacred of the creator deities because he gives his very flesh in order for human beings to live. But this sacrifice must be repaid. The Maya, as 'true people,' felt an obligation to the cosmos to compensate for the loss of divine life, not because the gods were cruel, but because gods cannot rebirth themselves and need the intercession of human beings. Maya kings stood as the sacred link between their subjects and the gods. The king was thus required to periodically give that which was most precious – his own blood, which was believed to contain the essence of godhood itself. Generally, this meant that members of the royal family bled themselves with stingray spines or stone lancets. Males did their bloodletting from the genital area, literally birthing gods from the penis. Women most often drew blood from their tongues. This royal blood was collected on sheets of bark paper and then burned to release its divine essence, opening a portal to the other world and allowing the gods to emerge to a new life. At times of crisis, such as the end of a calendar cycle, or upon the death of a king and the succession of another, the sacrifice had to be greater to compensate for the loss of divine life. This generally involved obtaining noble or royal captives through warfare against a neighboring Maya state in order to sacrifice them.

Altar 23 from Caracol shows two captive lords from the Maya cities of B'ital and Ucanal, on the Guatemala–Belize border, with their arms bound behind their backs in preparation for sacrifice, perhaps on that very altar. If this were not done, they believed that life itself would cease to exist.

The beauty of Maya religion is that these great visions of creation mirror everyday events in the lives of the people. When a Maya woman

When the Spaniards arrived, Christian missionaries zealously burned all the Maya hieroglyphic books they could find. Only four are known to have survived and are held in Dresden, Madrid, Paris and Mexico City.

The Maya hieroglyphic writing system is one of only five major phonetic scripts ever invented – the others being cuneiform (used in ancient Mesopotamia), Egyptian, Harappan and Chinese.

rises early in the morning, before dawn, to grind maize for the family meal, she replicates the actions of the creators at the beginning of time. The darkness that surrounds her is reminiscent of the gloom of the primordial world. When she lights the three-stone hearth on the floor of her home, she is once again striking the new fire that generates life. The grains of maize that she cooks and then forms into tortillas are literally the flesh of the Maize God, who nourishes and rebuilds the bodies of her family members. This divine symmetry is comforting in a world that often proves intolerant and cruel.

Maya Hieroglyphic Writing

More than 1500 years prior to the Spanish Conquest, the Maya developed a sophisticated hieroglyphic script capable of recording complex literary compositions, both on folded screen codices made of bark paper or deer skin, as well as texts incised on more durable stone or wood. The importance of preserving written records was a hallmark of Maya culture, as witnessed by the thousands of known hieroglyphic inscriptions, many more of which are still being discovered in the jungles of Belize and other Maya regions. The sophisticated Maya hieroglyphic script is partly phonetic (glyphs representing sounds tied to the spoken language) and partly logographic (glyphs representing entire words), making it capable of recording any idea that could be thought or spoken.

Ancient Maya scribes were among the most honored members of their society. They were often important representatives of the royal family and, as such, were believed to carry the seeds of divinity within their blood. Among the titles given to artists and scribes in Maya inscriptions of the Classic period were *itz'aat* (sage) and *miyaatz* (wise one).

Counting System

Maya arithmetic was elegantly simple: dots were used to count from one to four, a horizontal bar signified five, a bar with one dot above it was six, a bar with two dots was seven etc. Two bars signified 10, three bars 15. Nineteen, the highest common number, was three bars stacked up and topped by four dots.

The Maya didn't use a decimal system (which is based on the number 10), but rather a vigesimal system (that is, a system that has a base of 20). The late Mayanist Linda Schele used to suggest that this was because they wore sandals and thus counted not only their fingers but their toes as well. This is a likely explanation, since the number 20 in nearly all Maya languages means 'person.'

To signify larger sums, the Maya used positional numbers – a fairly sophisticated system similar to the one we use today and much more advanced than the crude additive numbers used in the Roman Empire. In positional numbers, the position of a sign and the sign's value determine the number. For example, in our decimal system the number 23 is made up of two signs: a 2 in the 'tens' position and a 3 in the 'ones' position; two tens plus three ones equals 23.

If you are curious about how scholars unlocked the secrets of Maya hieroglyphics, read Michael Coe's *Breaking the Maya Code*. It reads like a detective novel.

In the Maya system, positions of increasing value went not right to left (as ours do) but from bottom to top. So the bottom position showed values from one to 19 (remember that this is a base-20 system so three bars and four dots in this lowest position would equal 19); the next position up showed multiples of 20 (for example, four dots at this position would equal 80); the next position represents multiples of 400; the next, multiples of 8000 etc. By adding more positions one could count as high as needed.

Such positional numbers depend upon the use of zero, a concept that the Romans never developed but the Maya did. The zero in Maya numbering was represented by a stylized picture of a shell or some other object – but never a bar or a dot.

Calendar System

The Maya counting system was used by merchants and others who had to add up many things, but its most important use – and the one you will most often encounter during your travels – was in writing calendar dates. The ancient Maya calendar was a way of interpreting the order of the universe itself. The sun, moon and stars were not simply handy ways of measuring the passage of time, but living beings that influenced the world in fundamentally important ways. Even today, the Maya refer to days as 'he.' The days and years were conceived as being carried by gods, each with definite personalities and spheres of influence that colored the experience of those who lived them. Priests carefully watched the sky to look for the appearance of celestial bodies that would determine the time to plant and harvest crops, celebrate certain ceremonies, or go to war. The regular rotation of the heavens served as a comforting contrast to the chaos that characterizes our imperfect human world.

In some ways, the ancient Maya calendar – still used in parts of the region – is more accurate than the Gregorian calendar we use today. Without sophisticated technology, Maya astronomers were able to ascertain the length of the solar year as 365.2420 days (a discrepancy of

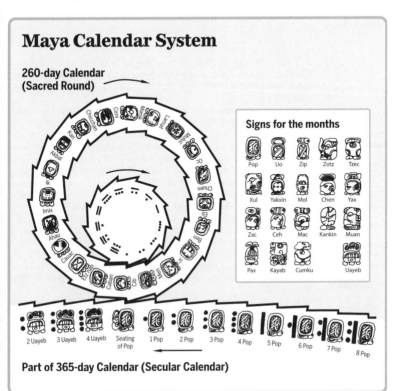

Maya Calendar System

260-day Calendar (Sacred Round)

Signs for the months

Pop, Uo, Zip, Zotz, Tzec

Xul, Yakxin, Mol, Chen, Yax

Zac, Ceh, Mac, Kankin, Muan

Pax, Kayab, Cumku, Uayeb

2 Uayeb, 3 Uayeb, 4 Uayeb, Seating of Pop, 1 Pop, 2 Pop, 3 Pop, 4 Pop, 5 Pop, 6 Pop, 7 Pop, 8 Pop

Part of 365-day Calendar (Secular Calendar)

HOW THE MAYA CALENDAR WORKED

The ancient Maya used three calendars. The first was a period of 260 days, known as the Tzolkin, likely based on the nine months it takes for a human fetus to develop prior to birth. The second Maya calendar system was a solar year of 365 days, called the Haab. Both the Tzolkin and Haab were measured in endlessly repeating cycles. When meshed together, a total of 18,980 day-name permutations are possible (a period of 52 solar years), called the Calendar Round.

Though fascinating in its complexity, the Calendar Round has its limitations, the greatest being that it only goes for 52 years. After that, it starts again and so provides no way for Maya ceremony planners to distinguish a day in this 52-year Calendar Round cycle from the identically named day in the next cycle. Thus the Maya developed a third calendar system that we call the Long Count, which pinpoints a date based on the number of days it takes place after the day of creation on August 13, 3114 BC.

Let's use the date of Friday April 1, 2011 as an example. The Maya Long Count date corresponding to this day is 12.19.18.4.10, 3 Uayeb 11 Oc.

The first number, '12,' of this Long Count date represents how many *baktuns* (400 x 360 days or 144,000 days) that have passed since the day of creation (thus 12 x 144,000 = 1,728,000 days). The second number, '19,' represents the number of *katuns* (20 x 360 or 7200 days) that have passed, thus adding another 19 x 7200 = 136,800 days. The third number, '18,' is the number of *tuns* (360 days), or 6480 days. The fourth number, '4,' is the number of *uinals* (20 days), or 80 days. Finally the fifth number, '10,' is the number of whole days. Adding each of these numbers gives us the sum of 1,728,000 + 136,800 + 6480 + 80 + 10 = 1,871,370 days since the day of creation.

The Maya then added the Calendar Round date: the Haab date (3 Uayeb) and the Tzolkin date (11 Oc).

17.28 seconds per year from the true average length of 365.2422 days). The Gregorian calendar year works out to be 365.2425 days. Thus the Maya year count is 1/10,000 closer to the truth than our own modern calendar.

Maya astronomers were able to pinpoint eclipses with uncanny accuracy, a skill that was unknown among the brightest scholars in contemporary medieval Europe. The Maya lunar cycle was a mere seven minutes off today's sophisticated technological calculations. They calculated the Venus cycle at 583.92 days. By dropping four days each 61 Venus years and eight days at the end of 300 Venus years, the Maya lost less than a day in accuracy in 1000 years!

The ancient Maya believed that the Great Cycle of the present age would last for 13 *baktun* cycles in all (each *baktun* lasting 144,000 days), which according to our calendar ended on December 23, AD 2012, beginning a new cycle. The Maya saw the end of large cycles of time as a kind of death, and they were thus fraught with peril. But both death and life must dance together on the cosmic stage for the succession of days to come. Thus the Maya conducted ceremonies to periodically 'rebirth' the world and keep the endless march of time going.

The Maya never expected the end of this Great Cycle to be the last word for the cosmos, since the world regularly undergoes death and rebirth. Koba Stela 1 (the first stela from the site of Koba) records a period of time equivalent to approximately 41,341,050,000,000,000, 000,000,000,000 of our years! (In comparison, the Big Bang that is said to have formed our universe is estimated to have occurred a mere 15,000,000,000 years ago.)

Dr Allen J Christenson has an MA and a PhD in Pre-Columbian Maya Art and Literature, and works as a professor in the Humanities, Classics and Comparative Literature department of Brigham Young University in Provo, Utah. His works include *Popol Vuh: The Sacred Book of the Maya* (2003), a critical translation of the Popol Vuh from the original Maya text.

People of Belize

Belize is a tiny country, but it enjoys a diversity of ethnicities that is undeniably stimulating and improbably serene. Four main ethnic groups – *mestizo*, Creole, Maya and Garifuna – comprise 76% of the population. The remaining 24% includes East Indians (people of Indian subcontinent origins), Chinese, Spanish, Arabs (generally Lebanese), the small but influential group of Mennonites, and North Americans and Europeans who have settled here in the last couple of decades.

Mestizo

Mestizos are people of mixed Spanish and indigenous descent. Over the last couple of decades, *mestizos* have become Belize's largest ethnic group, now making up about 34% of the population. The first *mestizos* arrived in the mid-19th century, when refugees from the Yucatán flooded into northern and western Belize during the War of the Castes. Their modern successors are the thousands of political refugees from troubled neighboring Central American countries. While English remains Belize's official language, Spanish is spoken by more than half of the population; this has caused some resentment among Creoles, who are fiercely proud of their country's Anglo roots.

Creoles

Belizean Creoles are descendants of African slaves and British baymen, loggers and colonists. In the 1780s, after much conflict, the Spanish and the British finally reached an agreement allowing Brits to cut logwood from the area between the Río Hondo and the Belize River (essentially the northern half of Belize). Three years later, according to the Convention of London, the area was extended south.

The convention also permitted the British to cut mahogany, a hardwood that was highly valued in Europe for making furniture. In return, Britain agreed to abandon the Miskito Coast of Nicaragua, prompting 2214 new settlers to come to Belize and quadrupling its non-Maya population. Three-quarters of the newcomers were slaves of African origin.

2000 BC–AD 250

The oldest Maya sites in Belize – including Cahal Pech and Lamanai – date to the Preclassic period of this indigenous civilization.

16th Century

By now dispersed and depopulated, the Maya nonetheless resist the Spanish attempts to convert and conquer them. Early Spanish explorers do not stay.

17th Century

Belize becomes a popular hideaway for British Baymen, who eventually establish settlements along the coast and move inland.

1786

Britain cedes the coast of Nicaragua, bringing to Belize an influx of African slaves – the beginning of today's Creole population.

1832

After being deported from St Vincent and migrating from Honduras, a group of Garifuna settles in present-day Dangriga.

1847

Spanish, *mestizo* and Maya peoples engage in the War of the Castes in the neighboring Yucatán Peninsula, sending streams of refugees to settle in Belize.

1958

After being driven out of Mexico, the first group of Mennonites settles in Belize.

BILEEZ KRIOL

Although English is the official language of Belize, when speaking among themselves many locals use Kriol (Creole). According to one local journalist, Kriol is 'di stiki stiki paat,' or 'the glue that holds Belize together.' While this patois sounds like English, most anglophones will have a hard time understanding it. It is a language that 'teases but just escapes the comprehension of a native English speaker,' as one frustrated American traveler so aptly stated.

Kriol derives mainly from English, with influences from Mayan and West African languages, as well as Spanish. Linguists claim that it has its own grammatical rules and a small body of literature, as well as speaking populations in different countries – criteria that determine the difference between a dialect and a language.

In 1995 the National Kriol Council was established to promote Kriol language in Belize. The council believes that the use and recognition of the language can solidify national identity and promote interaction and cooperation among different ethnic groups. Kriol is used by more than 70% of the population; not only by Creoles, but also many Garifuna, mestizos and Maya who speak Kriol as their second language. The council believes that a better understanding of Kriol will actually improve local English. As people recognize that Kriol is a different language – and not just improper English – both children and adults will make the effort to learn the differences in grammatical construction.

This influx of slave labor was convenient for the loggers. Mahogany is a much larger tree than logwood, and it is more scattered in the forest, meaning that its extraction required more labor. Thus it was that mahogany played a key role in the creation of the Afro-Belizean population. After several generations of mixing with the loggers and other colonists, the so-called Creoles became the most populous ethnic group in Belize.

Belizean Creoles now form only about 25% of Belize's population, but theirs remains a sort of paradigm culture. Racially mixed and proud of it, Creoles speak a fascinating and unique version of English: it sounds familiar at first, but it is not easily intelligible to a speaker of standard English. Most of the people you'll encounter in Belize City and the center of the country will be Creole.

Maya

The Maya of Belize make up almost 11% of the population and are divided into three linguistic groups. The Yucatec Maya live mainly in the north; the Mopan Maya in the southern Toledo District; and the Kekchi Maya in western Belize and also in the Toledo District. Use of both Spanish and English is becoming more widespread among the Maya. Traditional Maya culture is strongest among the Maya of the south.

Garifuna

Garifuna History, Language & Culture of Belize, Central America & the Caribbean by Sebastian Cayetano, gives an easily understood overview of the Garifuna people and their culture.

In the 17th century, shipwrecked African slaves washed ashore on the Caribbean island of St Vincent. They hooked up with the indigenous population of Caribs and Arawaks and formed a whole new ethnicity, now known as the Garifuna (plural Garinagu, also called Black Caribs).

France claimed possession of St Vincent in the early 18th century, but eventually ceded it to Britain according to the Treaty of Paris. After prolonged resistance, the Garifuna finally surrendered in 1796, and Britain decided to deport them. Over the course of several years, the Garifuna were shuffled around various spots in the Caribbean, with many dying of malnutrition or disease. Finally, 1465 of the original 4000-plus deportees arrived at the Honduran coastal town of Trujillo. From here, these people of mixed Native American and African heritage began to spread along the Caribbean coast of Central America.

The first Garifuna arrived in Belize around the turn of the 19th century. But the biggest migration took place in 1832, when, on November 19, some 200 Garifuna reached Belize in dugout canoes from Honduras. The anniversary of the arrival is celebrated as Garifuna Settlement Day, a national holiday.

Today the Belize Garifuna number around 20,000, about 6% of Belize's population, most of whom still live in the south of the country, from Dangriga to Punta Gorda. The Garifuna language is a combination of Arawak and African languages with bits of English and French thrown in.

The Garifuna maintain a unique culture with a strong sense of community and ritual, in which drumming and dancing play important roles. The dügü ('feasting of the ancestors' ceremony) involves several nights and days of dancing, drumming and singing by an extended family. Its immediate purpose is to heal a sick individual, but it also serves to reaffirm community solidarity. Some participants may become 'possessed' by the spirits of dead ancestors. Other noted Garifuna ceremonials include the *beluria* (ninth-night festivity), for the departure of a dead person's soul, attended by entire communities with copious drumming, dancing and drinking; and the *wanaragua* or *jonkonu* dance, performed in some places during the Christmas-to-early-January festive season.

Garifuna culture has been enjoying a revival since the 1980s, due in no small part to the *punta* rock phenomenon. In 2001, Unesco declared Garifuna language, dance and music to be a 'Masterpiece of the Oral and Intangible Heritage of Humanity' – one of the initial selections for what has become the cultural equivalent of the World Heritage list.

The Mennonites

It almost seems like an aberration, an odd sight inspired by too much sun: women in bonnets and drape-like frocks; blond-haired, blue-eyed men in denim overalls and straw hats; the whole family packed onto a horse-drawn carriage, plodding along the side of the highway. In fact, it is not something your imagination has conjured up; you're looking at Belizean Mennonites.

The Mennonites originate from an enigmatic Anabaptist group that dates back to 16th-century Netherlands. Like the Amish of Pennsylvania, the Mennonites have strict religion-based values that keep them

Experts estimate that the number of Belizeans living overseas is roughly equal to the number of Belizeans living at home.

Progressive Mennonite Groups

Blue Creek (Orange Walk)

Spanish Lookout (Cayo)

WHAT THEY BELIEVE IN BELIZE

Ethnicity is a big determinant of religion in Belize, with most *mestizos*, Maya and Garifuna espousing Catholicism as a result of their ethnic origins in Spanish- or French-ruled countries or colonies. Catholicism among Creoles increased with the work of North American missionaries in the late 19th and early 20th centuries. Approximately a quarter of Belizeans are Protestants, chiefly Anglicans and Methodists. Today the number of Pentecostalists and Adventists is growing due to the strength of their evangelical movements. Mennonites also constitute a small minority.

Among the Garifuna, and to a lesser extent the Maya and Creoles, Christianity coexists with other beliefs. Maya Catholicism has long been syncretized with traditional beliefs and rites that go back to pre-Hispanic times, while some Creoles (especially older people) have a belief in *obeah,* a form of witchcraft.

Belize's tradition of tolerance also encompasses Hindus, Muslims, Baha'i, Jehovah's Witnesses and a small (but eye-catching) number of Rastafarians.

isolated in agricultural communities. Speaking mostly Low German, they run their own schools, banks and churches. Traditional groups reject any form of mechanization or technology (which explains the horse-drawn buggies).

Mennonites are devout pacifists and reject most of the political ideologies that societies have thrust upon them (including paying taxes). So they have a long history of moving about the world trying to find a place to live in peace. They left the Netherlands for Prussia and Russia in the late 17th century. In the 1870s, when Russia insisted on military conscription, the Mennonites upped and moved to isolated parts of Canada. After WWI the Canadian government demanded that English be taught in Mennonites' schools and their exemption from conscription was reconsidered. Again, the most devout Mennonites moved, this time to Mexico. By the 1950s Mexico wanted the Mennonites to join its social security program, so once again the Mennonites packed up.

The first wave of about 3500 Mennonites settled in Belize (then called British Honduras) in 1958. Belize was happy to have their industriousness and farming expertise, and the settlements expanded.

Today Belize has many different Mennonite communities. The progressives – many of whom came from Canada – speak English and have no qualms about using tractors or pickup trucks; other groups are strongly conservative and shun modern technologies.

Conservative Mennonite Groups

....

Shipyard (Orange Walk)

....

Little Belize (Corozal)

Belize has been good to the Mennonites and in turn the Mennonites have been good to Belize. Mennonite farms now supply most of the country's dairy products, eggs and poultry. Furniture-making is another Mennonite specialty and you'll often see them selling their goods at markets. They are also accomplished house builders, constructing houses within their communities and then loading them onto massive tractor trailers to be delivered to clients around the country.

Rhythms of a Nation

Belize knows how to get its groove on. You'll hear a variety of pan-Caribbean musical styles, including calypso (of which Belize has its own star in Gerald 'Lord' Rhaburn), *soca* **(an up-tempo fusion of calypso with Indian rhythms) and, of course, reggae (with Belize being represented by exceptionally talented Tanya Carter). But what's most special about the Belizean music here is the styles that are uniquely homegrown.**

Punta & Punta Rock

Musicians and linguists speculate that '*punta*' comes from the word *bunda*, which means 'buttocks' in many West African languages. The word derivation is not certain, but it is appropriate. Heard at any sort of celebration or occasion, this traditional drumming style inspires Garifuna peoples across Central America to get up and shake their *bunda*.

The crowd circles around one couple, who gyrate their hips while keeping the upper body still. Traditionally, it is associated with death and ancestor worship, which explains why the dance is often performed at funerals and wakes.

Punta rock was born in the 1970s, when *punta* musician Pen Cayetano, a native of Dangriga, traveled around Central America and came to the realization that Garifuna traditions were in danger of withering away. He wanted to inspire young Garifuna people to embrace their own culture instead of listening to and copying music from other countries – and so he invented a style that is cool, contemporary but uniquely Belizean. He added the electric guitar to traditional *punta* rhythms and so was born *punta rock*.

Punta rock can be frenetic or it can be mellow, but at its base are always fast rhythms designed to get the hips swiveling. Like traditional *punta,* the dance is strongly sexually suggestive, with men and women gyrating their pelvises in close proximity to each other. The lyrics are almost always in Garifuna or Kriol, which differs from traditional *punta.*

Cayetano's Turtle Shell Band spread the word, and the rhythm, to neighboring Guatemala, Honduras (both with their own Garifuna populations), Mexico and even the USA (where there are sizable Belizean and Garifuna communities). Ideal Castillo, Mohobub and Mime Martinez are all members of the Turtle Shell Band who went on to enjoy success in their solo careers.

Andy Palacio was a leading ambassador of *punta rock* until his untimely death in 2008. Palacio was known for mixing the Garifuna sound with all sorts of foreign elements, including pop, salsa and calypso beats. He deserves the credit for widening the audience for *punta rock* and turning it into the (unofficial) national music of Belize.

One of Belize's biggest modern sensations is Supa G, who provides a fusion of *punta rock,* techno and a spot of Mexican balladeering. His songs include amusing takes on Belizean society and culture.

Originally from Hopkins, Aziatic has blended *punta* with R&B, jazz and pop, earning him an international audience, particularly in the US, where he now lives.

Pen Cayetano is a polymathic figure who started the *punta rock* musical phenomenon, but he also does oil paintings portraying the Garifuna culture.

After musician Andy Palacio's untimely death, an estimated 2500 people descended on his home village of Barranco, where he was laid to rest following a Catholic Mass, a Garifuna ceremony and an official state funeral.

In the liner notes of the album *Paranda*, Aurelio Martínez writes, 'I feel very proud to be in the same album with such great *paranderos*. And in a symbolic way I feel like they are passing me the torch to carry on the tradition. To me this is more than a Grammy.'

Paranda

Shortly after the Garifuna arrived in Central America, they started melding African percussion and chanting with Spanish-style acoustic guitar and Latin rhythms. The result is known as *paranda,* named after a traditional African rhythm that is often at the root of the music. Unlike *punta rock, paranda* is totally unplugged, played on wooden Garifuna drums, acoustic guitars and primitive percussion instruments, such as shakers and turtle shells. It combines fast rhythms and lyrical melodies.

Although musicians have been playing *paranda* since the 19th century, it was not recorded and therefore rarely heard outside Garifuna communities. It's a genre of folk music that is in danger of dying out, as very few young musicians are making new *paranda* music. In the mid-1990s, producers from Stonetree Records recognized the importance of making a recording before the great *paranderos* passed, which resulted in the so-called Paranda Project – an album featuring eight of the most esteemed *paranda* musicians from Belize and Honduras. The Belizean master of *paranda* was the late Paul Nabor, who was born in Punta Gorda in the 1920s. The next generation of the genre is led by Honduran-born Aurelio Martínez, who also served as his country's first black congressman. The title of Martínez' album *Garifuna Soul* gives a good idea of what *paranda* is all about.

Brukdown

In the 18th and 19th centuries, most of the hard labor of logging – the intensive cutting and heavy lifting of the massive mahogany trees – was carried out by African slaves and their descendents. Here, in the logging camps of the Belize River valley, workers soothed their weary bodies and souls by drinking, dancing and making their own unique music, known as *brukdown.*

Belize's most prominent Creole music, *brukdown* is deeply rooted in Africa, with layered rhythms and call-and-response vocals. Back in the camps, it was normally played by an ensemble of accordion, banjo, harmonica and a percussion instrument – usually the jawbone of a pig, its teeth rattled with a stick. Nowadays, modern musicians might add a drum or an electric guitar.

Like the Garifuna music, *brukdown* is predominantly a rural folk tradition that is rarely recorded. The exception is the so-called King of Brukdown, Wilfred Peters, and his band Mr Peters' Boom & Chime. Mr Peters made music for more than 60 years before his death in 2010, and became a national icon and the country's best-loved Creole musician. In 1997 Queen Elizabeth II awarded him an MBE for his cultural contributions.

GARI-FUSION

In contemporary Belize there has been a resurgence of Garifuna music, popularized by musicians such as Andy Palacio, Mohobub Flores and Adrian Martinez. These musicians have taken many aspects of traditional Garifuna music and fused them with more modern sounds. Andy Palacio's last album, *Watina,* was a collaboration with other musicians, known as the Garifuna Collective. Each track on the album is based on a traditional Garifuna rhythm, and all of the songs are in the Garifuna language, which is a novelty itself. Rooted in musical and folkloric tradition, the album exhibits remembrance of the past and hope for the future of the Garifuna people.

Umalali, which means 'voice' in the Garifuna language, is the name of an album created by the Garifuna Women's Project. In 2002, Garifuna women from all around Central America met in the village of Hopkins to record their most beloved songs and musical stories. Their voices were then layered on top of the rhythms and instrumentation of the Garifuna Collective, fusing many elements of the rich but endangered culture.

THREE KINGS OF BELIZE

Three men, three geographic regions, three cultures, three musical traditions. What these men have in common, besides their native land, is their passion for an art that is fading.

Three Kings of Belize is a documentary by Katia Paradis (2007) that follows three pre-eminent musicians, each considered the 'king' of his genre. Paul Nabor was a legendary Garifuna *parandero* from Punta Gorda, Wilfred Peters was a Creole *brukdown* accordionist from Belize City, and Florencio Mess is a traditional Maya harpist living in the farming village of San Pedro Columbia. The film captures the artists in their homes, interacting with their families, recalling stories from their lives and, of course, making music.

The recurring theme – expressed by all three – is a frustration, and perhaps a fear, that young people no longer make this music. There is a sense that when the original artists of traditional genres die, their music might die too. But *Three Kings* is not just about frustration or fear. It is wistful, perhaps, but ultimately accepts that nothing is eternal.

In June 2010, Wilfred Peters died at the age of 79. Hundreds of people attended his funeral, including the prime minister and the leader of the opposition – proof that music is greater than politics. The local newspaper noted that the funeral service was 'far from a solemn occasion,' with plenty of *brukdown* beats to accompany the hymns. 'The service concluded with a rising rendition of *brukdown* music with the cathedral's bells tolling in the background,' it said.

Another state funeral was held in Punta Gorda for Paul Nabor who died in October 2014 at the age of 86. The event, which also included a Garifuna ceremony, drew Belizeans from all over the country to the deep south. The event was followed by a concert featuring many artists influenced by the *paranda* legend.

If Mr Peters was the King of Brukdown, the Queen of Brukdown is undoubtedly Leela Vernon. A resident of Punta Gorda, Leela Vernon is a high-energy singer and dancer. In addition to making four albums, she has also started a dance group to preserve traditional Creole dance.

Kungo Muzik

'This muzik is one of the heart beats felt out of Afrika coming by way of Belize.' So says Brother David Obi, better known in Belize as Bredda David. And he should know, as he created the fast-paced fusion of Creole, Caribbean and African styles known as *kungo muzik*.

Maya

The Maya have been making music for thousands of years. In contemporary Maya music, bones and rattles are used for percussion, while instruments include whistles, flutes and horns made from conch shells. The *ocarina* is an ancient wind instrument, something like a flute with a wider body and 10 to 12 finger holes. The same types of instruments have been found as artifacts at archaeological sites all around Central America.

Originally from Guatemala, Pablo Collado is a Maya flautist who now resides in Benque del Carmen. His new-age-style music is light and relaxing, often incorporating sounds that mimic nature, such as the gurgling of water or the calls of birds or insects.

Also popular among the Maya is the marimba, a percussion instrument that resembles a xylophone, except it is made of wood and so produces a mellower sound. Marimba music is used during Maya religious ceremonies.

Stringed instruments like the guitar, violin and harp are used in Maya ceremonial and recreational music. Crafted from native woods like mahogany or cedar, harps were traditionally carved with animal symbols, representing the Maya gods. Florencio Mess not only plays the Maya harp, but also makes these instruments by hand in the traditional style. His music – based on age-old melodies and rhythms – has been called 'a living connection to ancient Maya culture.'

Top Albums

Best of Punta Rock
by Pen Cayetano and Mohobub Flores

Bumari
by Lugua Centeno

Garifuna Soul
by Aurelio Martínez

Brukdown Reloaded
by Mr Peters' Boom & Chime

Beyond Rice & Beans

A staple of Belizean cuisine, rice and beans comes in two varieties: 'rice and beans,' where the two are cooked together; and 'beans and rice,' where beans in a soupy stew are served separately in a bowl. Both variations are prepared with coconut milk and red beans, which distinguishes them from other countries' rice and beans. You're bound to eat a lot of rice and beans (or beans and rice) while you are in Belize, but Belizean cuisine has more depth than would first appear.

Seafood

Rice and Beans (www.riceand beansindc. blogspot.com) is a blog about mindful eating, written by a Belizean ('I love me some spicy food') with organic roots ('I want my food straight from the dirt').

When it comes to seafood in Belize, lobster plays the starring role. Distinguished from the American and European lobster by their lack of claws, the Caribbean crustaceans are no less divine, especially when grilled. Lobster is widely available in coastal towns, except from mid-February to mid-June, when the lobster season is closed.

Conch (pronounced 'konk') is the large snail-like sea creature that inhabits conch shells. Much like calamari, it has a chewy consistency that is not universally appreciated. During conch season, from October to June, it is often prepared as *ceviche* (seafood marinated in lemon or lime juice, garlic and seasonings) or conch fritters (and it's considerably cheaper than lobster).

Aside from the shellfish, the local waters are home to snapper, grouper, barracuda, jacks and tuna, all of which make a tasty filet or steak.

Belizeans really know how to prepare their seafood, be it barbecued, grilled, marinated, steamed or stewed. A common preparation is

JOHNNYCAKES

There is no more satisfying Belizean breakfast than a fresh-baked johnnycake with a pat of butter and a slice of cheese. These savory biscuits – straight from the oven – steal the show when served with eggs or beans.

Ingredients
2lb flour
6 teaspoons baking powder
½ cup shortening
½ cup margarine
1 teaspoon salt
2 cups coconut milk or evaporated milk

Method
Sift dry ingredients. Heat oven to 400°F. Use fingertips or knife to cut margarine and shortening into flour. Gradually stir in milk with a wooden spoon. Mix well to form a manageable ball of dough. Roll out dough into a long strip and cut into 1½in to 2in pieces. Shape into round balls and place on greased baking sheets. Flatten lightly and prick with a fork. Bake in hot oven for 10 minutes or until golden brown.

'Creole-style,' where seafood, peppers, onions and tomatoes are stewed together.

Meat & Poultry

Seafood is popular on the coast (and especially in tourist towns), but most often the main course in Belize comes from a chicken. Poultry serves as an accompaniment for rice and beans, a stuffing for burritos and *salbutes* (a variation on the tortilla), and a base for many soups and stews.

Belizeans do not eat a lot of beef, but they do love cow-foot soup. This is a glutinous concoction of pasta, vegetables, spices – and an actual cow's foot. Cow-foot soup is supposed to be 'good for the back'; in other words, an aphrodisiac.

Pastries

Almost every town in Belize has at least one shop where the shelves are lined with sweet and savory pastries to make you drool. If you're looking for a quick, tasty and cheap snack, you can't go wrong at the local bakery. Grab a tray and a pair of tongs and make your selection from the delectable treats on display.

While these pastries are pretty to look at and delicious to eat, they are not the best in Belizean baked goods. That title belongs to fresh-baked johnnycakes, or biscuits, smothered in butter, beans or melted cheese. Johnnycakes are the quintessential breakfast in Belize, but they are also served throughout the day as a snack or side dish.

Every cuisine in the world includes some version of fried dough, usually topped with fruit or sugar. In Belize they are stuffed then fried and are called fry jacks. Again, it can be served sweet or savory, usually for breakfast but also throughout the day.

Maya Specialties

Maya meals are sometimes on offer in the villages of southern Belize and in Petén, Guatemala. *Caldo* is a hearty spicy stew, usually made with chicken (or sometimes beef or pork), corn and root vegetables, and served with tortillas. *Ixpa'cha* is steamed fish or shrimp, cooked inside a big leaf. The Maya also make Mexican soups-cum-stews such as *chirmole* (chicken with a chili-chocolate sauce) and *escabeche* (chicken with lime and onions).

Garifuna Specialties

Garifuna culinary traditions come from St Vincent. When the Garifuna people came to Belize, they brought their own traditions, recipes and even ingredients, meaning that cuisine is one more way that Garifuna culture is unique.

One of the most important staples, cassava, is a starch, like a sweet potato, used to make cassava bread. A *varasa* is like a tamale, but it's made from a fruit that is a cross between a banana and a plantain, picked while it's still hard and cooked until it's soft.

A 'boil-up' is a stew of root vegetables and beef or chicken. This is the dish that is most common on restaurant menus, although it is traditionally prepared for Garifuna Settlement Day.

Other Garifuna specialties feature fresh fish, bananas or plantains, and coconut milk. *Alabundiga* is a dish of grated green bananas, coconut cream, spices, boiled potato and peppers, served with fried fish fillet (often snapper) and rice. *Sere* is fish cooked with coconut milk, spices and maybe some root vegetables. Possibly the most beloved Garifuna dish, *hudut* is made from plantain, cooked until tender, mashed with

Restaurants for Foodies

Aji Tapas Bar (San Pedro)

Running W Steakhouse (San Ignacio)

Hidden Treasures (San Pedro)

Rumfish (Placencia)

Cerros Beach Resort (Cerros)

Palmilla Restaurant (San Pedro)

BEYOND RICE & BEANS MEAT & POULTRY

Food Festivals

Lobster Festivals (Placencia, Caye Caulker, San Pedro)

Fish Fest (Punta Gorda)

Cashew Festival (Crooked Tree)

Chocolate Festival of Belize (Punta Gorda)

SHARP ON THE TONGUE

Belizean meals are not usually very spicy, but your table and your meal are always enlivened by the inimitable presence of Marie Sharp's fiery sauces, accurately labeled 'Proud Products of Belize.'

Marie Sharp got into the hot-sauce business in 1981. One season she and her husband found themselves with a surplus of habanero chili peppers at their family farm near Dangriga. Hating to see them wasted, Marie experimented with sauce recipes in her own kitchen. She felt that other bottled hot sauces were often watery and sometimes too hot to be flavorful. She wanted one that would complement Belizean cuisine and would not have artificial ingredients. She tried out some of her blends on her friends and family, and by far the favorite was one that used carrots as a thickener and blended the peppers with onions and garlic.

Once she had her formula, Sharp embarked on a guerrilla marketing campaign, carrying samples of the sauce, along with corn chips and refried beans, door-to-door to shopkeepers all over Belize. When proprietors liked what they tasted, Marie asked them to put the sauce on their shelves and agreed to take back the bottles that didn't sell. The sauce, initially bottled under the name Melinda, caught on and was soon not only in stores but also on restaurant tables all over the country.

Marie bottled the sauces from her kitchen for three years, finally bringing in a couple of workers to help her mix the zealously guarded formula. She eventually hybridized her own red habanero pepper – a mix of Scotch bonnet and Jamaican varieties – which contributes to the distinctive color of her sauces. She opened her own factory in 1986 with two three-burner stoves and six women to look after her pots, and moved to her current factory outside Dangriga in 1998.

Today Sharp's hot red-habanero sauces come in six heat levels: 'Mild,' 'Hot,' 'Fiery Hot,' 'No-Wimps-Allowed,' 'Belizean Heat' and 'Beware.' Make sure to try the new 'Smoked Habanero' variety.

Sharp also produces a range of mixed sauces (habaneros with prickly pears or citrus fruit), pepper jellies and tropical-fruit jams.

'*Belikin*' is Mayan for 'road to the east' and the main temple of Altun Ha is pictured on the label of Belikin beer.

a big mortar and pestle, then cooked with local fish like snapper and coconut milk.

Snacks

Just like their Caribbean and Central American neighbors, Belizeans like to cook with habaneros, jalapeños and other peppers. Most restaurants have a bottle of hot chili sauce on the table next to the salt and pepper so guests can make their meals as spicy as they like.

In small towns, the best breakfast is usually found at the local taco vendor's cart, where tortillas stuffed with meat and lettuce are sold. Other Mexican snacks are also ubiquitous, including *salbutes, garnaches, enchalades* and *panades* – all variations on the tortilla, beans and cheese theme (*salbutes* usually add chicken, *panades* generally have fish). You'll also come across burritos and tamales (wads of corn dough with a filling of meat, beans or chilies).

Drinks

If you want to know what tropical paradise tastes like, sample the fresh fruit juices that are blended and sold at street carts and kiosks around the country. Usually available in whatever flavor is seasonal (lime, orange, watermelon, grapefruit, papaya and mango), they're delicious and refreshing – and healthy!

In recent years, Belize has started catering to coffee drinkers with its own homegrown beans, even though Belize lacks the high altitudes that benefit other Central American coffee-growing countries. On a *finca* (farm) in Orange Walk, a local company called Gallon Jug is producing shade-grown beans for commercial distribution. Caye Coffee in San Pedro gets its beans from Guatemala, but roasts them in its facility right in San Pedro, producing such popular blends as Belizean Roast and Maya Blend.

Belikin is the native beer of Belize. You'll be hard-pressed to find any other beer available, as there are severe import duties levied on foreign brews. Fear not, however, as Belikin is always cold and refreshing. Belikin Regular is a tasty lager, but Belikin also brews a lower-calorie, lower-alcohol beer, called Lighthouse Lager, as well as Belikin Stout and Belikin Premium.

In a Caribbean country that produces so much sugarcane, it's not surprising that Belize's number one liquor is rum. The country has four distilleries; the Travellers distillery in Belize City has won several international awards with its thick, spicy One Barrel rum. Visitors can take a tour of the factory and sample all the company's varieties.

Cuba libre (lime, rum and coke) and piña colada are the most popular ways of diluting your fermented sugarcane juice. But according to Belize bartenders, the national drink is in fact the 'panty-ripper' or 'brief-ripper,' depending on your gender. This concoction is a straightforward mix of coconut, rum and pineapple juice, served on the rocks.

Books for Cooks

....

Mmm... A Taste of Belizean Cooking
by Tracy Brown da Langan

....

Foods of the Maya
by Nancy and Jeffrey Gerlach

BEYOND RICE & BEANS DRINKS

Wild Things

Belize's sparse human population and its history of relatively low-key human impact have yielded a vast diversity of animal and plant species. The country has an admirable conservation agenda, pursued by governments and nongovernmental organizations (NGOs) since Belizean independence in 1981. This has led to the nation becoming a top destination for anyone interested in the marine life of the coral reefs, the vegetation and animal life of the forests, or the hundreds of bird species that soar, flutter and swoop through the skies.

Jaguar: One Man's Struggle to Establish the World's First Jaguar Preserve is the story of American zoologist Alan Rabinowitz' efforts to set up what has become the Cockscomb Basin Wildlife Sanctuary.

Animals

Land Mammals

Felines

Everyone dreams of seeing a jaguar in the wild. Jaguars are found across the country, and live in large expanses of thick forest. The largest populations and most frequently reported sightings are near Chan Chich Lodge and at the Río Bravo Conservation & Management Area in Orange Walk. You also might see their tracks or the remains of their meals in Cockscomb Basin Wildlife Sanctuary, which was established in Stann Creek as a jaguar reserve in the 1980s. But although Belize has healthy numbers of the biggest feline in the western hemisphere (which measures up to 6ft long and 250lb in weight), your best chance of seeing one is still at the Belize Zoo.

Belize has four smaller wildcats, all elusive like the jaguar: the puma (aka mountain lion or cougar), almost as big as the jaguar but a uniform gray or brown color (occasionally black); the ocelot, spotted similarly to the jaguar but a lot smaller; the margay, smaller again and also spotted; and the small, brown or gray jaguarondi.

Monkeys

The endangered black howler monkey exists only in Belize, northern Guatemala and southern Mexico. Its population has made a comeback in several areas, especially in the Community Baboon Sanctuary in Belize District, established in the 1980s to protect this noisy animal. The sanctuary is now home to some 3000 individual monkeys. Other places to see and hear howlers include Lamanai in Orange Walk; Cockscomb Basin Wildlife Sanctuary in Stann Creek; Chan Chich and Río Bravo in Orange Walk; and Tikal National Park in Guatemala. The howler's eerie dawn and evening cries – more roars than howls – can carry 3 miles across the treetops.

Less common are the smaller, long-tailed spider monkeys, though you may still spot some in similar areas.

Other Land Mammals

Visitors and residents alike are often surprised to learn that the national animal of Belize is Baird's tapir (sometimes called the mountain cow). The tapir is related to the horse, but it has shorter legs and tail, a stouter build and small eyes, ears and intellect. Baird's tapir is a herbivore and – interestingly – a daily bather. It tends to be shy, so it's infrequently spotted and likely to run like mad when approached.

You have better chances of catching sight of a peccary, a wild pig that weighs 50lb or more. There are two types, whose names – white-lipped peccary and collared peccary – define their differences. Both types of peccaries are active by day and they travel in groups, making them relatively easy to check off your wildlife list. Be aware that these meanies can run fast. If you get in the way of a pack of wild peccaries, experts advise you to climb a tree (they can't catch you up there).

Resembling a large spotted guinea pig, the *gibnut* (or *paca*) is a nocturnal rodent, growing up to 2ft long and weighing up to 22lb, that often lives in pairs. You might see a *gibnut* in the wild, and you are also likely to see one on the menu at your local Belizean restaurant. The agouti is similar but diurnal and more closely resembles a rabbit, with strong back legs. The tayra (or tree otter) is a member of the weasel family and has a dark-brown body, yellowish neck and 1ft-long tail. The coatimundi (or quash) is a cute, rusty-brown, raccoon-like creature with a long nose and ringed tail that it often holds upright when walking. It's not uncommon to see coatimundi in daylight on the sides of roads or trails. Also in the raccoon family is the nocturnal kinkajou (or nightwalker), mainly a tree-dweller.

Wildlife Watching

Community Baboon Sanctuary

Río Bravo Conservation & Management Area

Shipstern Nature Preserve

Gales Point Manatee or Swallow Cave

Cockscomb Basin Wildlife Sanctuary

WILD THINGS ANIMALS

Marine Life

West Indian manatees inhabit the waters around river mouths, in coastal lagoons and around the cays. The sure-fire places to spot these gentle, slow-moving creatures are Southern Lagoon, near Gales Point Manatee village, and Swallow Caye, off Belize City. Manatees are the only vegetarian sea mammals in existence. Typically 10ft long and weighing 1000lb, adults eat 100lb to 150lb of vegetation each day (especially sea grass). Only a few hundred manatees survive in Belizean waters.

Belizean waters are home to the world's largest fish. Whale sharks grow up to a whopping 60ft (although the average length is 25ft) and weigh up to 15 tons. They hang out at Gladden Spit, near Placencia. Between March and June – usually during the 10 days after a full moon – these filter-feeding behemoths come in close to the reef to dine on spawn. Fun fact: whale sharks can live up to 150 years.

Other sharks – nurse, reef, lemontip and hammerhead – and a variety of rays often make appearances around the reefs and islands. Sharing the water with the larger animals is a kaleidoscope of reef fish, ranging from steely-eyed barracuda and groupers to colorful parrotfish, angelfish and butterfly fish. The fish frolic amid a huge variety of coral formations, from hard elkhorn and staghorn coral (named because they branch like antlers) to gorgonian fans and other soft formations. Belizean waters host more than 500 species of fish and 110 species of coral, plus an amazing variety of sponges.

Reptiles

The protected green iguana is a dragon-like vegetarian lizard that is often spotted in trees along riverbanks. You can also see it in iguana houses at Monkey Bay Wildlife Sanctuary in Belize District and at the San Ignacio Resort Hotel.

Belize is home to two species of crocodile: the American crocodile and Morelet's crocodile, both of which are on the endangered species list. The American usually grows to 13ft and can live in both saltwater and freshwater. The smaller Morelet's crocodile, which grows to 8ft, lives only in fresh water. Belizean crocs tend to stick to prey that's smaller than the average adult human. Still, it's best to keep your distance.

Hawksbill, loggerhead, leatherback and green sea turtles can be seen in the waters of Belize. They live at sea and the females come ashore only to lay their eggs. Sea turtles are victims of poaching and egg hunting, as their eggs are believed by some to be an aphrodisiac. However, while all sea turtles are endangered, the hawksbill, which was hunted for its shell, is the only one currently protected in Belize. Turtle-viewing outings are organized in the May to October laying season from Gales Point Manatee village.

Up to 60 species of snake inhabit the forests and waters of Belize, but only a handful are dangerous. The nasties include the poisonous fer-de-lance (commonly known as the yellow-jaw tommygoff), which is earth toned and a particular threat to farmers when they're clearing areas of vegetation; the coral snake, banded with bright red, yellow and black stripes; the tropical rattlesnake; and the boa constrictor, which kills by constriction but can also give you a mean (but venomless) bite.

'One perceives a forest of jagged, gnarled trees protruding from the surface of the sea, roots anchored in deep, black, foul-smelling mud, verdant crowns arching toward a blazing sun...Here is where land and sea intertwine, where the line dividing ocean and continent blurs.' Klause Rutzler and Ilka Feller, *Scientific American*, March 1996

Birds

Ornithologists have identified 590 bird species in Belize, 20% of them winter migrants from North America. You're likely to see interesting birds almost anywhere at any time, although February to May are particularly good months. Wetlands, lagoons, forested riverbanks and forest areas with clearings (the setting of many jungle lodges and Maya ruins) are good for observing a variety of birds.

Sea Birds

Magnificent frigate birds constantly soar over the coastline on pointed, prehistoric-looking wings that have a span of up to 6ft. They have difficulty taking off from the ground, so their method of hunting is to plummet and catch fish as they jump from the sea. They often hang out around fisherfolk and other birds so that they can swoop in on discarded or dropped catches. Males have red throats that are displayed during courtship.

MIND THE MANATEES

Belonging to a unique group of sea mammals comprising only four species worldwide, manatees are thought to be distantly related to elephants. However, with at least 55 million years separating the two, their kinship is only apparent in a few fairly obscure anatomical similarities and a broadly similar diet. Like elephants, manatees are herbivores and require huge amounts of vegetation each day. Grazing on a wide variety of aquatic plants, a large adult can process as much as 110lb every 24 hours, producing a prodigious amount of waste in the process – fresh floating droppings (similar to a horse's) and almost continuous, bubbling streams of flatulence are useful ways to find them. (Not too appetizing, but it does make them easier to spot.) The best places for a chance to observe manatees are around 'blowing holes' or *sopladeros* (deep hollows where manatees congregate to wait for the high tide).

Manatees are reputed to have excellent hearing, but they're most sensitive to fairly high-frequency sounds, such as their squeaking vocalizations. Apparently, the engine of a motorboat is not a high-frequency sound, which means that quiet approaches are often rewarded with good viewing, although sadly it also makes the manatees vulnerable to collisions with motorboats.

Swooping and soaring with the frigate birds are neotropic cormorants, brown pelicans, nine species of heron, eight species of tern and six species of gull. The rare red-footed booby bird lives at Half Moon Caye.

Raptors & Vultures

Raptors are predators that usually hunt rodents and small birds. The most common species in Belize include the osprey (look for their huge nests atop houses and telephone posts), peregrine falcon, roadside hawk and American kestrel. Most of these birds of prey are territorial and solitary. The majestic harpy eagle is rarely seen in the wild, but is a resident at the Belize Zoo, as is the ornate hawk eagle, which is a beautiful large raptor with a black crest, striped tail and mottled breast.

Inland along the sides of the road and flying overhead you'll see large turkey, black and king vultures. Their job is to feast on dead animals. The turkey vulture has a red head, the king has a black-and-white color scheme with a red beak, and the black vulture appears in black and shades of gray.

Other Well-Known Birds

The national bird of Belize is the keel-billed toucan. This is the species of Toucan Sam, the hungry bird who knows to 'follow your nose' to find the fruit loops. A black bird with a yellow face and neck, it has a huge multicolored bill. The 'keel bill' is actually very light and almost hollow, enabling the bird to fly with surprising agility and to reach berries at the end of branches. Toucans like to stay at treetop level and nest in holes in trees. They are surprisingly aggressive and are known to raid other birds' nests for breakfast.

The beautiful scarlet macaw, a member of the parrot family, is highly endangered. Belize's small population of the bird – possibly under 200 – lives most of the year in remote jungles near the Guatemalan border, but from January to March they can be seen at the southern village of Red Bank, where they come to eat fruit.

The jabiru stork is the largest flying bird in the Americas, standing up to 5ft tall and with wingspans of up to 12ft. Many of the 100 or so remaining Belizean jabirus gather in Crooked Tree Wildlife Sanctuary in April and May.

You'll also have the chance to see (among others) many colorful hummingbirds, kingfishers, motmots, parrots, woodpeckers, tinamous, tanagers and trogons.

Plants

Belize is home to more than 4000 species of flowering plant, including some 700 trees (similar to the total of the USA and Canada combined) and 304 orchids. Nonspecialists can usefully distinguish three chief varieties of forest in the country: coastal forests (19%), moist, tropical broadleaf forests (68%), and pine and savannah (13%).

Coastal Forests

Coastal forests comprise both the mangrove stands that grow along much of the shoreline and the littoral forests slightly further inland. Mangroves serve many useful purposes as fish nurseries, hurricane barriers and shoreline stabilizers, and they are credited with creating the cays: when coral grows close enough to the water surface, mangrove spores carried by the wind take root on it. Mangrove debris eventually creates solid ground cover, inviting other plants to take root

---

Bird-watching

Crooked Tree
(Belize District)

New River
(Orange Walk District)

La Milpa
(Orange Walk District)

Red Bank
(Stann Creek)

In 2004 Belize finally got its own birding guide with the publication of the comprehensive *Birds of Belize* by H Lee Jones, which is well illustrated by Dana Gardner.

The tropical broadleaf is often called rainforest, although technically only far southwestern Belize receives enough rain to officially support rainforest.

and eventually attracting animal life. There are four common species of mangrove: red, buttonwood, white and black.

Trees of the littoral forests typically have tough, moisture-retaining leaves. They include the coconut palm, the Norfolk Island pine, the sea grape and the poisonwood, the sap of which causes blistering, swelling and itching of the skin, as well as (happily) the gumbo-limbo, with its flaky, shredding bark that acts as an antidote to poisonwood rashes. The sandy bays off the coast are covered in sea grass, including turtle grass, manatee sea grass and duckweed sea grass.

Tropical Broadleaf Forest

Tropical broadleaf grows on thin clay soils where the principal nutrients come not from the soil but from the biomass of the forest – that is, debris from plants and animals. Buttressed trunks are a common phenomenon here. These forests support a huge diversity not only of plants but also of animal life.

One of the fascinating elements of these forests is their natural layering. Most have at least three layers: ground cover (a ground or herb layer); a canopy layer formed from the crowns of the forest's tallest trees; and, in between, shorter subcanopy or understory trees. Throughout the layers grow hanging vines and epiphytes, or 'air plants,' which are moss and ferns that live on other trees but aren't parasites. This is also the habitat for more than 300 species of orchid, including the national flower, the black orchid.

The national tree in Belize is the majestic mahogany, known for its handsome hardwood. Also important is the ceiba (the sacred tree of the Maya), with its tall gray trunk and fluffy kapok down around its seeds. The broad-canopied guanacaste (or tubroos) is another tree that can grow more than 100ft high, with a wide, straight trunk and light wood used for dugout canoes (its broad seed pods coil up into what look like giant, shriveled ears). The strangler fig has tendrils and branches that

---

MAYA MEDICINE

The Maya have not only long depended on the forest for food and shelter, but also for hygiene and healing. These days in Belize, tour guides are quick to recommend an herbal remedy for everything from stomach ills to sexual failures. But there are only a few remaining healers who are skilled and knowledgable in the science of Maya medicine. If you are curious about this holistic and natural approach to medicine, consult a professional (eg at the Chaa Creek Rainforest Medicine Trail in Cayo).

Among the natural remedies used by Maya are the bark of the Guava tree *(Psidium guajava)*, which is made into a tea that is used to treat diarrhea and dysentery. Another useful bark tea used as a remedy for stomach complaints is that of the Bay cedar *(Guazuma ulmifolia)*. Stomach ulcers are treated with a tea made from Skunk root *(Petiveria alliacea)*.

Maya medicine goes well beyond stomach complaints. Oil from the Cohune palm *(Orbignya cohune)* is used to moisturize the skin. A tea made of thorns from the Cockspur tree *(Acacia cornigera)* is a natural remedy for acne, while healers use the bark of the tree to relieve some snake bites.

One traditional Maya remedy that has become mainstream knowledge throughout Belize is that of the gumbo-limbo tree *(Bursera simaruba)*, which is usually found growing near the nasty poisonwood. While poisonwood can cause an itchy rash, the inner bark of the gumbo-limbo tree provides rapid relief.

BELIZE'S WORLD HERITAGE SITE

In 1996 Unesco designated the Belize Barrier Reef Reserve System a World Heritage site. The World Heritage listing covers seven separate reef, island and atoll areas, not all of which include bits of the barrier reef. The seven sites were recognized for demonstrating a unique array of reef types (fringing, barrier and atoll) and a classic example of reef evolution; for their exceptional natural beauty and pristine nature; and for being an important habitat for internationally threatened species, including marine turtles, the West Indian manatee and the American crocodile. These are the seven sites:

➡ Bacalar Chico National Park & Marine Reserve (Ambergris Caye)

➡ Blue Hole Natural Monument (Lighthouse Reef)

➡ Half Moon Caye Natural Monument (Lighthouse Reef)

➡ Glover's Reef Marine Reserve (Central Cayes)

➡ South Water Caye Marine Reserve (Central Cayes)

➡ Laughing Bird Caye National Park (Central Cayes)

➡ Sapodilla Cayes Marine Reserve (Punta Gorda)

surround a host tree until the unfortunate host dies. The flowering calophyllum, sometimes called the Santa Maria tree, is used for ship-building, while its resin has medicinal uses.

Pine & Savannah

The drier lowland areas inland from Belize City and the sandy areas of the north are designated as lowland savannah and pine forest. Growth here is mostly savannah grasses and Honduran and Caribbean pine, as well as Paurotis palm, giant stands of bamboo, and some oak and calabash.

The Mountain Pine Ridge is a fascinating phenomenon. As you ascend these uplands, the forest changes abruptly from tropical broadleaf to submontane pine, due to a transition to drier, sandier soils. Predominant species include Mexican white pine, Pino amarillo (or Mexican yellow pine) and Hartweg's pine.

The best all-in-one wildlife guide is *Belize & Northern Guatemala: The Ecotravellers' Wildlife Guide* by Les Beletsky, offering helpful descriptions along with full-color drawings and photographs.

Land & Environment

Happily, the Belize government and the populace have recognized that their country's forests and reefs are natural treasures that need to be preserved – not only for their intrinsic ecological value, but also for attracting tourism. Early on, the government developed a large network of national parks and reserve areas; however, these areas are only as inviolable as the degree to which the community is able to protect them.

Enviro-mental NGOs

Belize Audubon Society (www. belizeaudubon.org)

Oceanic Society (www.oceanic-society.org)

Programme for Belize (www.pfbelize.org)

Toledo Institute for Development & Environment (www.tidebelize. org)

Wildlife Conservation Society (www.wcs.org)

National Parks & Protected Areas

About 44% of Belizean territory, a little over 4062 sq miles, is under official protection of one kind or another. Belize's protected areas fall into six main categories:

➡ **Forest reserve** Protects forests, controls timber extraction, and conserves soil, water and wildlife resources.

➡ **Marine reserve** Protects and controls extraction of marine and freshwater species; also focuses on research, recreation and education.

➡ **National park** Preserves nationally significant nature and scenery for the benefit of the public.

➡ **Natural monument** Protects special natural features for education, research and public appreciation.

➡ **Nature reserve** Maintains natural environments and processes in an undisturbed state for scientific study, monitoring, education and maintenance of genetic resources; not usually open to the general public.

➡ **Wildlife sanctuary** Protects nationally significant species, groups of species, biotic communities or physical features.

Ecotourism

Belize practically invented the concept of ecotourism. Its ecolodges allow guests to live in luxury but also in harmony with the creatures and plants in their midst, while its educational tours and activities allow travelers to learn about the forest and the reef without harming the fragile ecosystems. Conscientious enterprises minimize their environmental impact by employing alternative and renewable energy sources; avoiding destruction of surrounding habitats; effectively managing waste and employing recycling programs; and using locally grown produce whenever possible. Dedicated entrepreneurs also give back to the community by employing local people and investing in local causes, thus sharing the wealth.

Ecotourism depends on a precarious balance: welcoming tourists, but not too many of them; allowing access to natural sights, but not too much access; maintaining an infrastructure to support the visitors, but not having too much infrastructure. Belize is constantly struggling to maintain this balance, with varying degrees of success.

➡ Forest cover in 1980: 75.9%

➡ Forest cover in 2014: 60.3%

There is no doubt about the economical boon of tourist dollars flowing from visiting cruise liners; however, the recent increase in cruise-ship traffic in Belizean waters has worried many conservationists and citizens, who view the huge numbers of tourists as disturbing wildlife and overwhelming the infrastructure.

Development along the coast caters to the growing demands of tourists. A recent study suggests that as much as 80% of coastal property is foreign-owned, with construction planned or underway. Construction of buildings and pavement of the roads on Ambergris Caye has dramatically changed the aesthetics and the atmosphere of that island, once a sleepy outpost and now a destination for package-tourists and partiers. In a recent struggle, San Pedro developers petitioned to eliminate the protected status of the southern portion of Bacalar Chico National Park & Marine Reserve. To the relief of many, the petition was rejected.

Of course, there is no hard and fast rule about how many tourists are too many or how much development is too much. Many Belizeans compare their country to Cozumel or Cancún and they are proud of the way that ecotourism is preserving their paradise. On Ambergris, few locals would stop the construction of condos and resorts that is taking place up and down the coast. It's predominantly the expats – who came to Belize to 'escape civilization' – who complain about the rampant level of development. Locals, by contrast, appreciate the influx of cash into the economy – the jobs, the roads, the restaurants – not to mention the constant flow of tourists who keep bringing money to spend.

Deforestation

Despite the impressive amount of protected territory, deforestation in Belize has been slow and steady since independence. Agriculture and aquaculture, development and illegal harvesting all contribute to the felling of the forests, which is taking place at a rate of 0.6% per year.

This contradiction is a result of poor management and monitoring. Protection requires money and even at the best of times Belizean governments are short of cash. Underfunding means understaffing, which impedes the fight against poaching and illegal extraction.

There is a perception in Belize that illegal Guatemalan immigrants are responsible for many of these incursions into protected areas. The ongoing territorial dispute between Guatemala and Belize exacerbates the situation, as some Guatemalan peasants are taught to believe they have a right to hunt and harvest there.

Energy Management

The problem of power is certainly not unique to Belize. Like many other countries, Belize consumes more than it can produce, and its consumption is increasing by 10% to 15% per year. Historically, Belize has imported much of its electricity from Mexico, although the country is implementing a multi-prong strategy to reduce this dependency.

Hydro

Two plants harness the power of the Macal River in Cayo to produce hydroelectric power. Built in 1995, the Mollejon Dam is limited by the storage capacity of its reservoir, but since 2006, the huge Chalillo Dam has fed both plants. The dam has the advantage that it can generate power in the evening (peak consumption hours), when imported electricity is more expensive. The construction of the Chalillo Dam sparked massive controversy, as critics voiced concerns about the damage inflicted on wildlife habitats in the river valley, as well as the financial viability of the project.

Cogeneration

A byproduct of the processing of sugarcane, *bagasse* is also a fuel. In 2009 the sugar industry opened a cogeneration facility that would

---

Ecolodges

Cerros Beach Resort (Corozal)

Chan Chich Lodge (Orange Walk District)

La Milpa Lodge (Orange Walk District)

Black Rock Lodge (Cayo District)

Thatch Caye Resort (Central Cayes)

Cotton Tree Lodge (Deep South)

LAND & ENVIRONMENT DEFORESTATION

The highest peak in the Maya Mountains is Doyle's Delight (3687ft), named after Arthur Conan Doyle, author of The Lost World. He wrote, 'There must be something wild and wonderful in a country such as this, and we're the men to find it out!'

BELIZE'S PROTECTED AREAS AT A GLANCE

PROTECTED AREA	FEATURES
Actun Tunichil Muknal	spectacular cave with ancient Maya sacrificial remains
Bacalar Chico National Park & Marine Reserve	northern Ambergris Caye barrier reef and surrounding waters
Blue Hole Natural Monument	400ft-deep ocean-filled sinkhole home to sharks
Caracol Archaeological Reserve	Belize's biggest and greatest ancient Maya city
Caye Caulker Marine Reserve	barrier reef reserve with plentiful marine life
Cockscomb Basin Wildlife Sanctuary	large rainforest reserve for jaguars, with huge range of wildlife
Community Baboon Sanctuary	forest sanctuary for black howler monkeys
Crooked Tree Wildlife Sanctuary	wetland area with huge bird population
Gales Point Wildlife Sanctuary	inland lagoons with Belize's largest colony of manatees
Gladden Spit & Silk Cayes Marine Reserve	barrier reef and island reserve visited by whale sharks
Glover's Reef Marine Reserve	beautiful atoll with coral-filled lagoon and seas swarming with marine life
Guanacaste National Park	small forest park centered on huge guanacaste tree
Half Moon Caye Natural Monument	lush bird-sanctuary atoll island with spectacular underwater walls offshore
Hol Chan Marine Reserve	waters off Ambergris Caye with the famous Shark Ray Alley Protected Area
Laughing Bird Caye National Park	island on unusual faro reef in waters full of marine life
Mayflower Bocawina National Park	rainforest park with hills, waterfalls, howler monkeys and hundreds of bird species
Mexico Rocks	Belize's newest marine reserve covers a particularly vibrant area of reef just offshore from Ambergris Caye
Monkey Bay Wildlife Sanctuary	small private sanctuary on savannah and tropical forest
Mountain Pine Ridge Forest Reserve	upland area with rare pine forests and many waterfalls
Nohoch Che'en Caves Branch Archaeological Reserve	stretch of Caves Branch River running through caverns
Port Honduras Marine Reserve	inshore islands and coastal waters important for marine life
Río Bravo Conservation & Management Area	large rainforest reserve with great wildlife diversity
Sapodilla Cayes Marine Reserve	beautiful barrier reef islets with healthy coral and abundant marine life
Shipstern Nature Reserve	wetlands and rare semideciduous hardwood forests with diverse wildlife, including wood-stork colony
South Water Caye Marine Reserve	large reserve encompassing parts of barrier reef and inshore islands
St Herman's Blue Hole National Park	small rainforest park with cave and swimming hole
Swallow Caye Wildlife Sanctuary	small island with permanent manatee population
Temash-Sarstoon National Park	rainforests, wetlands and rivers with huge variety of wildlife
Turneffe Atoll Marine Reserve	protects one of the most pristine areas of the Mesoamerican reef system

ACTIVITIES	BEST TIME TO VISIT	PAGE
caving	year-round	p164
diving, snorkeling, birdwatching, wildlife-watching	year-round	p85
diving, snorkeling	Dec-Aug	p125
exploring ruins, birdwatching	year-round	p180
diving, snorkeling	year-round	p109
hiking, wildlife-watching, plant identification, river-tubing	Dec-May	p206
wildlife-watching, birdwatching, horseback riding	year-round	p69
birdwatching, walking, canoeing, horseback riding	Feb-May	p72
manatee and turtle watching, birdwatching, fishing, sailing	year-round	p80
diving, snorkeling, kayaking	Mar-Jun	p34
diving, snorkeling, swimming, fishing, sailing, kayaking	Dec-Aug	p198
birdwatching, swimming, plant identification	year-round	p158
diving, snorkeling, birdwatching, kayaking	Dec-Aug	p126
diving, snorkeling	year-round	p85
diving, snorkeling	Dec-Aug	p34
hiking, birdwatching, swimming	year-round	p195
diving, snorkeling	year-round	p87
birdwatching, wildlife-watching, canoeing, caving	year-round	p79
walking, swimming, birdwatching, horseback riding	year-round	p178
river-tubing	year-round	p159
diving, snorkeling	Dec-May	p225
birdwatching, wildlife-watching, trail hiking, canoeing	year-round	p139
diving, fishing, kayaking, snorkeling, swimming	Dec-May	p225
wildlife-watching	year-round	p149
diving, snorkeling, birdwatching, kayaking	Dec-May	p197
swimming, caving, hiking, birdwatching	year-round	p160
manatee watching	year-round	p109
wildlife-watching, walking, boat trips	Dec-May	p225
diving, snorkeling	year-round	p123

BLACK GOLD

Early in the millennium, the possibility of sweet crude oil in Belize caused dollar signs to start flashing inside the minds of Belizean officials and international prospectors. Eighteen oil companies obtained licenses for exploration all around the country, sometimes without conducting an environmental impact survey or campaigning for community involvement.

After several years, the Irish-owned Belize Natural Energy (BNE) found what they were looking for in Spanish Lookout: oil fields with commercially viable quantities. In 2010, BNE discovered another oil field near Belmopan.

Conservationists fear the environmental degradation that may result from further oil exploration and extraction. There is also significant overlap between the petroleum map and the protected-areas map, threatening the sanctity of these spots. In the wake of the 2010 oil spill in the Gulf of Mexico, an umbrella group of NGOs called for a ban on all off-shore drilling, especially in the Belize Barrier Reef, which has been designated as a World Heritage site.

Under pressure from local communities and conservationists, in 2007 the government of Belize instituted a 40% tax on oil production profits, declaring that the 'petroleum fund' would be used to improve education, fight poverty and strengthen the Belizean dollar. Several years down the line, however, there are concerns about the success of this fund, with the local press asserting the revenues – estimated to be in the hundreds of millions of dollars – have been 'absorbed by the government for its day-to-day operating expenses.'

supply 13.5 megawatts to the national grid, in addition to powering the sugar mill and other industry facilities.

Bruce Barcott investigates the construction of the Chalillo Dam, and the efforts of Sharon Matola (founder of the Belize Zoo) to stop it, in his fascinating book *The Last Flight of the Scarlet Macaw*.

Solar

Solar power is becoming more viable on a small scale, but it does not yet offer a feasible solution for the energy needs of the country. Solar power is still relatively expensive and – significantly – it can't produce power at night. That said, it has become a popular alternative for some ecolodges and even some villages that are off the grid. In 2011 the government of Belize signed an agreement with the University of Belize to construct photovoltaic panels, which generate solar electricity. Proponents of alternative energy are hopeful that the so-called Photovoltaic Project might lead to a long-term, large-scale commitment to solar energy.

Survival Guide

DIRECTORY A–Z 296

Accommodations....... 296

Customs Regulation 297

Electricity 297

Embassies &
Consulates 297

Etiquette 297

Food & Drink.......... 298

GLBTI Travelers........ 298

Health................ 298

Insurance............. 300

Internet Access........ 300

Legal Matters 300

Maps................. 200

Money................ 300

Opening Hours 301

Post..................301

Public Holidays.........301

Safe Travel.............301

Telephone 301

Time 302

Toilets................ 302

Tourist Information 302

Travelers with
Disabilities............ 302

Visas................. 303

Volunteering 303

Women Travelers 304

Work 304

TRANSPORTATION ..305

GETTING
THERE & AWAY........ 305

Entering the Country.... 305

Air 305

Land 305

Sea 306

GETTING
AROUND 307

Air 307

Bicycle 307

Boat 307

Bus 308

Car & Motocycle........ 308

Golf Carts 309

Hitching &
Ride-Sharing........... 309

Local
Transportation 310

Directory A–Z

Accommodations

Cabañas & Cabins

These two terms are pretty well interchangeable and can refer to any kind of free-standing, individual accommodations structure. You'll find cabins in every class of accommodations: they can be made of wood, concrete or brick, and be roofed with palm thatch, tin or tiles. They may be small, bare and cheap, or super-luxurious and stylish, with Balinese screens, Japanese bathrooms and Maya wall hangings. Locales vary from beachside, riverside or jungle to on the grounds of a hotel alongside other types of accommodations.

Camping

Belize does not have many dedicated camping grounds (though San Ignacio has two), but some (mainly budget) accommodations provide camping space on their grounds, and some national parks such as Cockscomb Basin offer camping.

Guesthouses

Guesthouses are affordable, affable places to stay, with just a few rooms and usually plenty of personal attention from your hosts. Most are simply decorated but clean and comfortable. Rooms usually have a private bathroom with hot water. You'll find guesthouses in towns or on the coast or cays. Some guesthouses (also called B&Bs) provide breakfast.

In the southern Toledo District, the **Toledo Ecotourism Association** (TEA; ☑702-2119; www.teabelize.org) runs an excellent village guesthouse program that enables travelers to stay in the area's Maya villages, and there's a similar program at Maya Center.

Hotels

A hotel is, more or less, any accommodations that generally doesn't give itself another name (although some smaller hotels call themselves inns). You'll find hotels in villages and towns of all sizes. Some offer lovely rooms and extra amenities like a restaurant or a pool.

Lodges

In Belize the term 'lodge' usually means an upmarket

GREEN ACCOMMODATIONS

Ecotourism means big business in Belize, and sometimes it seems like every hotel, hostel, lodge, resort and guesthouse is a friend and protector of Mother Earth. But attaching 'eco' to the front of a name does not necessarily make it so. This prefix may mean that the enterprise is taking serious steps to reduce its environmental impact, whether by practicing recycling, implementing alternative energy, participating in conservation programs or educating its guests. On the other hand, it may mean nothing more than a remote location or rustic accommodations. Most likely, the truth is somewhere in between.

Many lodges, resorts, hostels and guesthouses *are* implementing 'ecopolicies' (with varying degrees of effectiveness). Look for the 🍂 (sustainable) icon in the listings.

resort-style hotel in a remote location, be it in the Cayo jungles or the offshore cays. Most lodges focus on activities such as diving, fishing, horseback riding or jungle or river adventures, aiming to provide comfortable accommodations and good meals to sustain their guests between outings. Many lodges have gorgeous island, beach or forest settings, and they tend to be on the expensive side, due mainly to their high standards and wide range of amenities.

Rental Accommodations

In main tourist destinations such as San Pedro, Caye Caulker and Placencia, there are houses and apartments for rent for short stays or by the week or month. If you plan a long stay, you'll certainly cut costs by renting your own place. Look out for real estate or rental offices in these towns and plan ahead: these places can get booked up in season.

Customs Regulations

Duty-free allowances on entering Belize:

➡ 1L of wine or spirits

➡ 200 cigarettes, 250g of tobacco or 50 cigars

It is illegal to leave the country with ancient Maya artifacts, turtle shells, unprocessed coral and fish (unless you have obtained a free export permit from the Fisheries Department). It is also illegal to take firearms or ammunition into or out of Belize.

Electricity

110V/60Hz

Embassies & Consulates

A few countries have embassies in Belize. Many others handle relations with Belize from their embassies in countries such as Mexico or Guatemala, but may have an honorary consul in Belize to whom travelers can turn as a first point of contact.

Australian Embassy (☑55-1101-2200; www.mexico.embassy.gov.au; Rubén Darío 55, Mexico City) The Australian embassy in Mexico handles relations with Belize.

Canadian Honorary Consulate (☑223-1060; cdncon.bze@btl.net; 80 Princess Margaret Dr, Belize City; ☺9am-2pm Mon-Fri)

German Honorary Consulate (☑222-4369; seni@cisco.com.bz; Mlle 3.5 Western Hwy, Belize City)

Guatemalan Embassy (☑223-3150; embbelice1@minex.gob.gt; 8 A St, Kings Park, Belize City; ☺8:30am-12:30pm Mon-Fri)

Honduran Embassy (☑224-5889; embajadahonduras.belice@gmail.com; 6 A St, Kings Park, Belize City; ☺9am-noon & 1-4pm Mon-Fri)

Mexican Embassy (☑822-0406; www.sre.gob.mx/belice; Embassy Sq, Belmopan; ☺8am-5pm Mon-Fri)

Mexican Consulate (☑223-0193; consular@embamex.bz; cnr Wilson St & Newtown Barracks Rd, Belize City)

Netherlands Honorary Consulate (☑223-2953; mchulseca@btl.net; cnr Baymen Av & Calle Al Mar, Belize City)

UK High Commission (☑822-2146; http://ukinbelize.fco.gov.uk; Embassy Sq, Belmopan; ☺8am-noon & 1-4pm Mon-Thu, 8am-2pm Fri)

US Embassy (☑822-4011; http://belize.usembassy.gov; Floral Park Rd; ☺8am-noon & 1-5pm Mon-Fri)

Etiquette

Dress

Apart formal occasions, such as going to church, dress in Belize is generally very casual even when heading out to eat or for drinks. However, Belize remains a conservative nation and very revealing outfits may be frowned upon in some areas.

Greetings

Don't be shy about making eye contact and greeting strangers on the street. Belizeans are friendly! The most common greeting is the catch-all 'Aarait?' ('Alright?'), to which you might respond, 'Aarait, aarait?'

Queues

Belizeans for the most part are firm in respecting queues. Where there is a turn system for services, respect the order. This is especially important at taxi ranks; while you may not be able to see a physical line, the drivers know whose turn it is, so ask before jumping into a vehicle.

Food & Drink

See p280 for more information on the cuisine of Belize.

GLBTI Travelers

GLBTI travelers should be advised that male homosexuality is illegal in Belize, although female homosexuality is legal. Tourists have not been prosecuted for homosexuality, but local people have been arrested and jailed. Generally speaking, Belize is a tolerant society with a 'live and let live' attitude. But underlying Central American machismo and traditional religious belief, as well as legal prohibitions, mean that same-sex couples should be discreet. Some useful resources:

Gay Travel Belize (☑635-0518) A GLBTI focused travel agency based in San Pedro. Its Facebook page has useful tips for GLBTI travelers.

International Gay & Lesbian Travel Association (www.iglta. org) General information on gay and lesbian travel in Latin America.

Purple Roofs (www.purpleroofs. com) Includes some listings in San Pedro and the Cayo District.

Undersea Expeditions (www. underseax.com) Gay and lesbian scuba-diving company that sometimes offers live-aboard trips to the Blue Hole.

Health

Travelers to Central America need to be concerned about food- and mosquito-borne infections. While most infections are not life-threatening, they can certainly ruin your trip. Besides getting the proper vaccinations, it's important that you pack a good insect repellent and exercise great care in what you eat and drink.

Before You Go
HEALTH INSURANCE

Medical facilities in Belize are not of the highest standard – make sure to check your travel insurance covers major medical emergencies, hospitalization and evacuation.

MEDICATIONS

It is a very good idea to carry a medical and first-aid kit with you, in case of minor illness or injury:

➡ antibiotics

➡ antidiarrheal drugs (eg loperamide)

➡ acetaminophen/paracetamol (Tylenol) or aspirin

➡ anti-inflammatory drugs (eg ibuprofen)

➡ antihistamines (for hay fever and allergic reactions)

➡ antibacterial ointment (eg Bactroban) for cuts and abrasions

➡ steroid cream or cortisone (for poison ivy and other allergic rashes)

➡ bandages, gauze, gauze rolls

➡ adhesive or paper tape

➡ scissors, safety pins and tweezers

➡ thermometer

➡ pocketknife

➡ insect repellent containing DEET for the skin

➡ insect spray containing permethrin for clothing, tents and bed nets

➡ sunblock

➡ oral rehydration salts

➡ iodine tablets (for water purification)

➡ syringes and sterile needles

Bring medications in their original containers, clearly labeled. A signed, dated letter from your physician describing all medical conditions and medications, including generic names, is also a good idea. If carrying syringes or needles, be sure to have a physician's letter documenting their medical necessity.

In Belize
AVAILABILITY & COST OF HEALTH CARE

Not surprisingly for a small, developing country, medical care in Belize is not of the highest standard. It is also fairly expensive compared to neighboring countries – expect to pay around US$70 for a visit to a private doctor and around US$500 per night for hospitalization in a private clinic.

The cheapest health care can be found at the network of public hospitals and clinics throughout the country, but they are often overcrowded and sometimes have issues with supplies and equipment. Many visitors and expats with insurance prefer to go

EATING PRICE RANGES

The following price ranges refer to a standard meal – rice, beans, meat or fish and a side. Only the fanciest places tend to have service charges, but tipping is always appreciated.

$ less than BZ$15

$$ BZ$15–35

$$$ more than BZ$35

RECOMMENDED VACCINATIONS

Since many vaccines don't produce immunity until at least two weeks after they're given, visit a physician four to eight weeks before departure. Note that some of the recommended vaccines are not approved for use by children and pregnant women; check with your physician.

VACCINE	RECOMMENDED FOR	DOSAGE	SIDE EFFECTS
Hepatitis A	all travelers	one dose before trip with booster six to 12 months later	soreness at injection site; headaches; body aches
Hepatitis B	long-term travelers in close contact with the local population	three doses over a six-month period	soreness at injection site; low-grade fever
Chickenpox	travelers who've never had chickenpox	two doses one month apart	fever; mild case of chickenpox
Measles	travelers born after 1956 who've had only one measles vaccination	one dose	fever; rash; joint pain; allergic reaction
Tetanus-diphtheria	all travelers who haven't had a booster within 10 years	one dose lasts 10 years	soreness at injection site
Typhoid	all travelers	four capsules by mouth, one taken every other day	abdominal pain; nausea; rash
Yellow fever	required for travelers arriving from yellow-fever-infected areas in Africa or South America	one dose lasts 10 years	headaches; body aches. Severe reactions are rare.

directly to private clinics, the best of which are located in Belize City. Another option, popular with expats in Belize, is to head across the border to Chetumal in Mexico where quality health care is far cheaper.

For emergencies situations it's recommended to have comprehensive insurance that covers evacuation to medical facilities outside Belize.

ENVIRONMENTAL HAZARDS

The major annoyance that almost all travelers are likely to encounter is biting insects. Sand flies (no-see-ums) are a real problem on some islands and mosquitoes pretty much everywhere. Bring quality repellent from home.

TRAVELER'S DIARRHEA

To prevent diarrhea, avoid tap water unless it's been boiled, filtered or chemically disinfected (with iodine tablets); only eat fresh fruit or vegetables if cooked or peeled; be wary of dairy products that might contain unpasteurized milk; and be highly selective when eating food from street vendors.

If you develop diarrhea, be sure to drink plenty of fluids, preferably an oral rehydration solution containing salt and sugar. A few loose stools don't require treatment, but if you start having more than four or five stools a day, you should start taking an antibiotic (usually a quinolone drug) and an antidiarrheal agent (such as loperamide). If diarrhea is bloody, persists for more than 72 hours or is accompanied by fever, shaking chills or severe abdominal pain, you should seek medical attention.

MOSQUITOES & TICKS

To avoid mosquito and tick bites, wear long sleeves, long pants, hats and shoes or boots (rather than sandals). Use insect repellent that contains DEET, which should be applied to exposed skin and clothing, but not to eyes, mouth, cuts, wounds or irritated skin. In general, adults and children over 12 years should use preparations containing 25% to 35% DEET, which last about six hours. Children between two and 12 years of age should use preparations containing no more than 10% DEET, which will usually last about three hours. Products containing lower concentrations of DEET are as effective, but for shorter periods of time.

For additional protection, you can apply permethrin to clothing, shoes, tents and bed nets. Permethrin treatments are safe and remain effective for at least two weeks, even when items are laundered. Permethrin should not be applied directly to skin.

TAP WATER

In major urban areas tap water in Belize is considered safe to drink. Outside larger cities and towns, hotels may use wells or rainwater collection tanks in which case water should be boiled or treated.

Many hotels will provide drinking water for guests.

Insurance

Travelers should take out a travel insurance policy to cover theft, loss and medical problems. Some policies specifically exclude 'dangerous activities,' which can include scuba diving, motorcycling and even trekking. Check that the policy you are considering covers ambulances as well as emergency flights home.

You may prefer a policy that pays doctors or hospitals directly rather than requiring you to pay on the spot and claim later. If you have to claim later, make sure you keep all documentation.

Worldwide travel insurance is available at www. lonelyplanet.com/travel-insurance. You can buy, extend and claim online anytime – even if you're already on the road.

Internet Access

Belize has plenty of internet cafes, with typical rates ranging from BZ$4 to BZ$8 per hour. Many hotels and lodges also provide computers where their guests can access the internet.

For those traveling with laptops and smartphones, most accommodations also have wireless access in the rooms or in common areas, as indicated by the 🛜 icon. This access is fairly reliable, but is easily overburdened if there are several people working simultaneously.

Public wi-fi hot spots have not really taken off in Belize

and there are few places outside hotels and restaurants to get online.

Belize's highly unpopular blocking of VOIP protocols was finally lifted by the government in 2013, meaning internet telephony programs are now able to be used throughout the country.

Legal Matters

Drug possession and use is officially illegal and, if caught in possession of larger amounts of marijuana or possession or use of any other illicit drugs, offenders will generally be arrested and prosecuted.

Persons found having sex with a minor will be prosecuted; the age of consent for both sexes is 16. Travelers should note that they can be prosecuted under the law of their home country regarding age of consent, even when abroad.

You are not required to carry ID in Belize but it's advisable to do so. If arrested, you have the right to make a phone call. The police force does not have a reputation for corruption as in many countries in Central America, and it is highly unlikely that you will be stopped and hassled or asked for a bribe.

For detailed information on the Belize legal code, check out the Belize Legal Information Network (www. belizelaw.org).

Maps

Lonely Planet maps will enable you to find your way to many of the listed destinations, but if you'd like a larger-scale, more detailed travel map, you cannot beat the 1:350,000 *Belize* map, published by International Travel Maps of Vancouver.

Another high-detail map is German firm Borch's laminated 1:500,000 *Belize* road map, which also includes Ambergris Caye and Caye

Caulker at 1:250,000 and individual maps of all the main Maya ruins.

Divers should check out Franko Maps' laminated dive side map, which has a full-colored tropical fish identification card on the back.

Money

ATMs are widely available; credit cards are accepted at most hotels, restaurants and shops.

Currency

The Belizean dollar (BZ$) is pegged to the US dollar at two to one (BZ$1 = US$0.50). Nearly every business in Belize accepts US dollars and prices are sometimes quoted in US dollars at upscale resorts and hotels.

Taxes & Refunds

Hotel room tax is currently 9%. Restaurant meals are subject to a 12.5% sales tax. Some hotel owners quote prices with taxes already figured in.

Tipping & Bargaining

Tipping is not obligatory but is always appreciated if guides, drivers or servers have provided you with genuinely good service. Some hotels and restaurants add an obligatory service charge to your check (usually 10%), in which case you definitely don't need to tip.

Hotels Belizeans generally don't tip in hotels but baggage porters appreciate a small gratuity.

Restaurants Rounding up the check by somewhere between 5% and 10% is usually a suitable tip.

Taxis Tips are usually not expected.

Tour guides In high-volume areas, tour guides are used to receiving tips for good service

Bargaining is not common in Belize with the notable exception of outdoor souvenir markets where everything is negotiable. When business is slow, it's possible to obtain a discount on hotel rooms, golf-cart rentals and other tourism services, although this is usually limited to a quick back-and-forth rather than hard-edge bargaining.

Opening Hours

Outside of banks, phone companies and government offices, you'll generally find most opening hours to be flexible. Restaurants and bars tend to keep longer hours during high season, but will also close early if they wish (if business is slow etc).

Banks 8am to 3pm Monday to Thursday and 8am to 4pm or 4:30pm Friday

Pubs and bars noon to midnight (or later)

Restaurants and cafes 7am to 9:30am (breakfast), 11:30am to 2pm (lunch) and 6pm to 8pm (dinner)

Shops 9am to 5pm Monday to Saturday, some open Sundays

Post

The Belize postal service has branches all over the country and offers fairly slow normal mail and a far better express service. Express mail sometimes needs to be sent from a different counter or office.

Public Holidays

Many of Belize's public holidays are moved to the Monday nearest the given date in order to make a long weekend. You'll find banks and most shops and businesses shut on these days. Belizeans travel most around Christmas, New Year and Easter, and it's worth booking ahead for transportation and accommodations at these times.

New Year's Day January 1

Baron Bliss Day March 9

Good Friday March or April

Holy Saturday March or April

Easter Monday March or April

Labor Day May 1

Sovereign's Day May 24

National Day September 10

Independence Day September 21

Day of the Americas October 12

Garifuna Settlement Day November 19

Christmas Day December 25

Boxing Day December 26

Safe Travel

Belize has fairly high levels of violent crime but most areas frequented by travelers are safe and by taking basic precautions visitors are unlikely to experience any serious problems. The most likely issues for travelers involve opportunistic theft both while out and about and from hotel rooms.

In order to minimize the risks:

➡ Keep your bag in the overhead rack or under your seat on long-distance buses rather than at the back of the bus.

➡ Make sure windows and doors lock correctly in your room, especially in remote

beachside huts, and use hotel safes where provided.

➡ Ask hotels and restaurants in major urban areas to phone a trusted taxi.

Telephone

Belize has no regional, area or city codes. Dial a seven-digit local number from wherever you are in the country.

Country code	☏501
Directory assistance	☏113
Emergency	☏90, ☏911
International access code	☏00
Operator assistance	☏115

Mobile Phones

Local SIM cards can be used in most unlocked international cell phones with the notable exception of phones from some operators in the US.

International cell phones can be used in Belize if they are GSM 1900 and unlocked. You can buy a SIM pack for

Media

Newspapers Belize's most read paper is *Amandala*, a twice-weekly publication with a left-wing slant.

Radio Love FM is Belize's most widely broadcast radio station, with spots at 95.1 MHz and 98.1 MHz, while KREM FM (www.krembz.com) plays a modern selection of music at 91.1 MHz and 96.5 MHz.

TV There are two main commercial TV stations: Channel 5 (www.channel5belize.com) and Channel 7 (www.7newsbelize.com).

Weights & Measures

The imperial system is used. Note that gasoline is sold by the (US) gallon.

Smoking

Still permitted in most public places in Belize, including in bars and restaurants. Within establishments there are rarely designated smoking and nonsmoking areas.

US$10 from DigiCell distributors around the country.

If your cell phone is not compatible with the local network or locked to your phone company, you'll need to activate international roaming, which can be costly – around US$2.50 to US$3 per minute of calls. Check with your service provider back home about coverage in Belize.

If you're staying for more than a week or two, a cheap phone with a prepaid SIM card can be had for less than BZ$80. Many car-rental companies provide free phones with vehicles.

Time

Belize uses North American Central Standard Time (GMT/UTC minus six hours), same as in Guatemala and central Mexico. The Mexican Caribbean state of Quintana Roo, which shares its southern border with Belize, is one hour ahead (UTC minus five hours), which is important to note if flying in or out of Cancún.

Belize and Guatemala do not observe daylight saving, so there is never any time difference between them, but Mexico – with the exception of Quintana Roo – does observe daylight saving from the first Sunday in April to the last Sunday in October, so Belize is one hour behind central Mexico during that period.

When it's noon in Belize, it's 10am in San Francisco, 1pm in New York, 6pm in London and 4am the next day in Sydney (add one hour to those times during daylight saving periods in those cities).

Toilets

Public toilets are rare in Belize, although many businesses will lend you their services without a fuss.

ONLINE RESOURCES

Belize Tourism Board (http://www.travelbelize.org/accommodation) The Belize Tourism Board has a helpful accommodations page.

Lonely Planet (lonelyplanet.com/belize/hotels) Recommendations and bookings.

Airports and museums generally have toilets, but not all bus terminals have facilities.

Tourist Information

Belize Tourism Board (BTB; Map p58; ☑227-2420; www.travelbelize.org; 64 Regent St; ⏰8am-5pm Mon-Thu, 8am-4pm Fri) The official tourist agency has information offices in Belize City and San Pedro.

Belize Tourism Industry Association (BTIA; Map p58; ☑227-1144; www.btia.org; 10 North Park St, Belize City; ⏰8am-noon & 1-5pm Mon-Fri) An independent association of tourism businesses, actively defending 'sustainable ecocultural tourism.' The Belize City office provides information about the whole country and it also runs small information offices in some key destinations. The website has a plethora of information.

Travelers with Disabilities

Belize lacks accessibility regulations and many buildings are on stilts or have uneven wooden steps. You won't see many ramps for wheelchair access and there are very few bathrooms designed for visitors in wheelchairs.

More difficulties for wheelchair users come from the lack of footpaths, as well as plentiful rough and sandy ground. With assistance, bus travel is feasible, but small planes and water taxis might be a problem.

Not to put too fine a point on it – Belize is a very challenging destination for

visitors with limited mobility. But while Belize definitely lacks facilities for travelers with disabilities, it has no shortage of extremely helpful locals who are generally more than willing to lend a hand to assist travelers with special needs get around.

Visitors with limited mobility do come to Belize. Accommodations suitable for wheelchair users include the **Radisson Fort George Hotel** (Map p58; ☑223-3333; www.radisson.com; 2 Marine Pde Blvd; r BZ$545-621; P @ ⛱ ⚤) in Belize City; **Corona del Mar** (Map p86; ☑226-2055; www.coronadelmarhotel.com; Coconut Dr; r BZ$298-414; ⚤) and **Sun Breeze Hotel** (Map p92; ☑226-2191; www.sunbreeze.net; 8 Coconut Dr; r BZ$376-496; ⚤) on Ambergris Caye; **Costa Maya Beach Cabanas** (Map p110; ☑226-0432; www.costamayabelize.com; Front St; r BZ$130-180, ste BZ$260-400; ⚤) on Caye Caulker; **Orchid Palm Inn** (Map p130; ☑322-0719; www.orchidpalminn.com; 22 Queen Victoria Ave; s/d BZ$77/94; P @ ⚤) in Orange Walk; **Hok'ol K'in Guest House** (Map p142; ☑422-3329; www.corozal.net; 89 4th Ave; s/d with fan BZ$77/104, with air-con BZ$92/120; @ ⚤) in Corozal; **El Rey Inn** (Map p156; ☑822-3438; www.elreyhotel.com; 23 Moho St; r BZ$80, with air-con BZ$120-160; P ⚤) and the **Bull Frog Inn** (Map p156; ☑822-2111; www.bullfroginn.com; 25 Half Moon Ave; s/d BZ$180/213; P ⚤) in Belmopan; **Jungle Huts Resort** (Map p191; ☑665-8966, 522-0185; junglehutsresort@gmail.com; 4 Ecumenical Dr; d from BZ$86, cabañas & suites

BZ$158; (P ⊠) in Dangriga; and **Turtle Inn** (☑523-3486, in USA 800-746-3743; www. turtleinn.com; cottages BZ$638-2038, villas BZ$1300-3858; P ⊠ ⊠) in Placencia.

There are a number of useful organizations and websites for travelers with disabilities, though there's little information that is specific to Belize:

Access-Able Travel Source (www.access-able.com) Has good general information.

Global Access Disabled Travel Network (www.globalaccess news.com) Good website with interesting general travel information.

Mobility International (www. miusa.org) US-based website that advises travelers with disabilities or mobility issues; you can organize a mentor and someone to help you plan your travels.

Download Lonely Planet's free **Accessible Travel guide** from http://lptravel. to/AccessibleTravel.

Visas

Entering Belize is a simple, straightforward process. You must present a passport that will be valid for at least three months from the date of entry. Officially, visitors are also required to be in possession of an onward or return ticket from Belize and funds equivalent to BZ$120 per day for the duration of their stay in the country, but it's rare for tourists to be required to show these.

Visitor Visa

For most nationalities, visas are issued upon entry for up to 30 days.

Information on visa requirements is available from Belizean embassies and consulates, and the **Belize Tourism Board** (www.travelbelize.org). At the time of writing, visas were not required for citizens of EU, Caricom (Caribbean

---

Community) and Central American countries, nor Australia, Canada, Hong Kong, Israel, Mexico, New Zealand, Norway, Singapore, Switzerland and the USA. A visitor's permit, valid for 30 days, will be stamped in your passport when you enter the country. In most cases this can be extended by further periods of one month (up to a maximum of six months) by applying at an immigration office (there's at least one in each of Belize's six districts). For further information you can contact the **Immigration & Nationality Department** (☑822-3860; Dry Creek St; ⊗8am-noon & 1-5pm Mon-Thu, to 4:30pm Fri) in Belmopan.

Volunteering

There are a lot of opportunities for volunteer work in Belize, especially on environmental projects. In some cases, you may have to pay to participate (costs vary).

Belize Audubon Society (Map p58; ☑223-4987, 223-5004; www.belizeaudubon.org; 16 North Park St) Invites volunteers who are available to work for at least three months to assist in the main office or in education and field programs. Divers can volunteer for marine

---

research projects. For rural sites, volunteers should be physically fit and able to deal with rustic accommodations.

Belize Wildlife & Referral Clinic (Map p174; ☑632-3257; www.belizewildlifeclinic.org) Offers short-term internships in wildlife medicine for veterinary and non-veterinary students. Various scholarships and work exchanges are available for students with sincere interests and skills, and the clinic is flexible and always interested in speaking with potential interns and long-term volunteers.

Oceanic Society (☑in USA 800-326-7491; www.oceanic-society.org; Blackbird Caye; 5-day research programs BZ$5400) ✎ Paying participants in the society's expeditions assist scientists in marine research projects at the society's field station on Blackbird Caye and elsewhere.

Cornerstone Foundation (www. cornerstonefoundationbelize. org) This NGO, based in San Ignacio, hosts volunteers to help with AIDS education, community development and other programs. Most programs require a two-week commitment, plus a reasonable fee to cover food and housing.

Monkey Bay Wildlife Sanctuary (☑822-8032; www. belizestudyabroad.net; Mile 31.5 George Price Hwy) ✎

PREVENTING CHILD SEX TOURISM IN BELIZE

Tragically, the exploitation of local children by tourists is becoming more prevalent throughout Latin America, including Belize. Various socioeconomic factors make children susceptible to sexual exploitation, and some tourists choose to take advantage of their vulnerable position. Sexual exploitation has serious, lifelong effects on children. It is a crime and a violation of human rights.

Belize has laws against sexual exploitation of children. Many countries have enacted extraterritorial legislation that allows travelers to be charged as though the exploitation happened in their home country.

Responsible travelers can help stop child sex tourism and exploitation by reporting it to websites such as the CyberTipline (www.cybertipline.com). You can also report the incident to local authorities and, if you know the nationality of the perpetrator, to their embassy.

Travelers interested in learning more about how to fight sexual exploitation of children can find more information through End Child Prostitution & Trafficking (www.ecpat.net).

Monkey Bay's programs provide opportunities in education, conservation and community service. It also has many links to other conservation organizations in Belize.

Earthwatch (www.earthwatch. org) Paying volunteers are teamed with professional scientific researchers to work on shark conservation projects.

Help for Progress (www.help forprogress.interconnection.org) A Belizean NGO that works with local community development organizations in fields such as education, gender issues, citizen participation and environment.

Maya Mountain Research Farm (☑630-4386; www.mmrfbz. org; ☎) ✦ The 70-acre organic farm and registered NGO in Toledo offers internships for those interested in learning about organic farming, biodiversity and alternative energy.

Plenty International (www. plenty.org) Opportunities for working with grassroots organizations (such as handicraft cooperatives) and schools, mostly in the Toledo District.

ProWorld Service Corps (www. proworldvolunteers.org) Like a privately run Peace Corps, ProWorld organizes small-scale, sustainable projects in fields such as healthcare, education, conservation, technology and construction, mostly around San Ignacio in Cayo.

Volunteer Abroad (www. volunteerabroad.com) A sort of clearing house for volunteer opportunities around the world. The database includes a few dozen organizations that work in Belize.

Women Travelers

Women can have a great time in Belize, whether traveling solo or with others. Of course, you do need to keep your wits about you and be vigilant, as does any solo traveler. Keep a clear head, and keep in mind that excessive alcohol will make you vulnerable.

If you don't want attention, try to wear long skirts or trousers and modest tops when you're using public transportation and when on solo explorations. Some men can be quite forward with their advances or even aggressive with their comments. Such advances are rarely dangerous: be direct, say no and ignore; they're likely to go away. A bicycle can be an asset in this scenario: you can just scoot.

Avoid situations in which you might find yourself alone with unknown men at remote archaeological sites, on empty city streets, or on secluded stretches of beach. For support and company, sign up for group excursions or head for places where you're likely to meet people, such as guesthouses that serve breakfast, backpacker lodgings or popular midrange or top-end hotels.

Work

Unemployment and underemployment are rife in Belize so visitors should think twice before taking on paid work that could be filled by a local.

In order to legally work in Belize, a work permit must be obtained from the Labor Department in the district where the business offering employment is located. Note that the US$1200 fee means that taking on an odd job to earn some extra drinking money is not a particularly viable option.

Transportation

GETTING THERE & AWAY

Travelers can get to Belize by land, sea or air. Overland, travelers might enter Belize from Guatemala or Mexico. Boats also bring travelers from Honduras and Guatemala. Air carriers service Belize from the USA, Panama and El Salvador. Flights, cars and tours can be booked online at lonelyplanet.com/bookings.

Entering the Country

Entering Belize is a simple, straightforward process. You must present a passport that will be valid for at least three months from the date of entry. Officially, visitors are also required to be in possession of an onward or return ticket from Belize and funds equivalent to BZ$120 per day for the duration of their stay in the country, but it's rare for tourists to be required to show these.

Air

Airports & Airlines
Philip Goldson International Airport (BZE; www. pgiabelize.com), at Ladyville, 11 miles northwest of Belize City center, handles all international flights. With Belize's short internal flying distances, it's often possible to make

---

a same-day connection at Belize City to or from other airports in the country.

The following airlines fly to and from Belize:

American Airlines (☑223-2522; www.aa.com; Philip Goldson Hwy) Direct flights to/from Miami, Charlotte and Los Angeles.

Avianca (☑225-2163; www. avianca.com) Direct flights to/from Houston and San Salvador in El Salvador.

Copa Airlines (www.copaair. com) Flights three times weekly to Panama.

Delta Airlines (☑225-2010; www.delta.com) Direct flights to/from Atlanta and Los Angeles.

Southwest Airlines (☑225-4902; www.southwest.com) Direct flights to Houston Hobby airport.

Transportes Aeros Guatemaltecos (www.tag.com.gt) Regular flights between Belize and Guatemala City via Flores.

Tropic Air (☑226-2012; www. tropicair.com) Flights to Flores, Guatemala; Merida and Cancún in Mexico; Roatan and San Pedro Sula in Honduras.

United Airlines (☑822-1062; www.united.com) Direct flights to/from Houston, New York and Chicago.

Land

Mexico
There are two official crossing points on the Mexico–Belize border. The more frequently used is at Subteniente López–Santa Elena, 9 miles north of Corozal Town in Belize and 7 miles from Chetumal in Mexico. The all-paved Philip Goldson Hwy runs from the border to Belize City.

The other crossing is at La Unión–Blue Creek, 34 miles southwest of Orange Walk Town near the Río Bravo Conservation and Management Area. The road between

LAND DEPARTURE TAX

When departing Belize by land, non-Belizeans are required to pay fees that total BZ$37.50 (US$18.75) in cash (Belizean or US dollars). Of this, BZ$7.50 is the Protected Areas Conservation Trust (PACT) fee, which helps to fund Belize's network of protected natural areas.

Blue Creek and Orange Walk was under construction at the time of research and should be a nice, wide paved highway by the time you read this.

BUS

Mexican bus company ADO runs excellent air-conditioned express bus services nightly from Cancún (BZ$102, 10 hours) and four times a week from Merida (BZ$102, 10 hours) to Belize City via Corozal and Orange Walk. The Cancún bus stops in Playa del Carmen and can drop passengers directly at Cancún airport on the return leg. The buses do not enter Chetumal town in either direction.

Many regular Belizean buses ply the Philip Goldson Hwy between Belize City and Chetumal. In Chetumal, buses bound for Corozal Town (BZ$4, one hour), Orange Walk Town (BZ$8, two hours) and Belize City (BZ$14 to BZ$16, four hours) leave from the north side of Nuevo Mercado, about 0.75 miles north of the city center. Leaving from Belize, buses mostly depart in the morning, while from Chetumal, afternoon departures are more common.

Additionally, an air-conditioned tourist bus (BZ$50, three hours) runs daily between the San Pedro Beze Express Water Taxi Terminal and Chetumal.

CAR & MOTORCYCLE

To bring a vehicle into Belize, you need to obtain a one-month importation permit at the border. This obliges you to take the vehicle out of Belize again within the validity of the permit. To get the permit you must present proof of ownership (vehicle registration) and purchase Belizean motor insurance (available for a few US dollars per day from agents at the borders). Permit extensions can be obtained by applying to the **Customs Department** (☏227-7092) in Belize City. In the unlikely event that a Mexican or Guatemalan car-rental agency permits you to take one of their vehicles into Belize, you will also have to show the rental documents at the border.

It's not unusual to see US license plates on cars in Belize, as driving from the USA through Mexico is pretty straightforward and car rental in Belize can be expensive. The shortest route through Mexico to the crossing point between Chetumal and Corozal is from the US–Mexico border points at Brownsville–Matamoros or McAllen–Reynosa, a solid three days' driving.

You are required to obtain a temporary import permit for your vehicle at the border when you enter Mexico; as well as the vehicle registra-tion document you'll need to show your driver's license and pay a fee of around US$50. You'll also have to buy Mexican motor insurance, also available at the border.

Guatemala

The only land crossing between Belize and Guatemala is a mile west of the Belizean town of Benque Viejo del Carmen at the end of the all-paved George Price Hwy from Belize City. The town of Melchor de Mencos is on the Guatemalan side of the crossing. The border is 44 miles from the Puente Ixlú junction (also called El Cruce) in Guatemala, where roads head north for Tikal (22 miles) and southwest to Flores (18 miles). The road is now fully paved.

BUS

Two companies run express buses to/from Guatemala. From the San Pedro Belize Express Water Taxi terminal in Belize City, you can go to Flores (BZ$50 to BZ$60, five hours) at 10am and 1pm. From Flores there are frequent connections to Guatemala City.

You can also take any of the frequent westbound Belizean buses to Benque Viejo del Carmen and then use the local service to the border.

Sea

It's now possible to arrive in Belize by boat from all three of its neighboring countries.

SEA DEPARTURE TAX

The only fee you have to pay when leaving Belize by sea from Placencia is the BZ$7.50 (US$3.75) Protected Areas Conservation Trust (PACT) fee. It's payable in cash (Belizean or US dollars).

Those leaving from Punta Gorda or using the water-taxi service from Caye Caulker/San Pedro to Chetumal are required to pay the regular departure tax of BZ$37.50 plus a BZ$2.50 facility fee before leaving Belize.

ENTERING BELIZE BY SEA

FROM	TO	FREQUENCY	DURATION	PRICE (BZ$)
Chetumal, Mexico	Caye Caulker	daily	2½hr	110
Chetumal, Mexico	San Pedro	daily	2hr	100
Livingston, Guatemala	Punta Gorda	daily	30min	50
Puerto Barrios, Guatemala	Punta Gorda	twice daily	45min	50-60
Puerto Cortés, Honduras	Placencia	weekly	4hr	130

GETTING AROUND

Transport in Belize is cheap and occasionally efficient. A useful website offering updated schedules and other transport-related info is http://belizebus.wordpress.com.

Air Two companies (Maya Island and Tropic Air) fly between all major towns in Belize. Planes are small, flights are short and fairly affordable, although ticket prices are on an upward trajectory. Both companies enjoy good safety records.

Boat Caye Caulker and Ambergris are serviced by ferries from Belize City, and there is also a boat from Corozal to Ambergris with a possible Sarteneja stop. No regular boats to the smaller islands and cays, but passage can be arranged with a private boatman from Dangriga, Hopkins or Placencia, or through resorts and hotels.

Bus Most travel in Belize is done by bus. All towns from Corozal to Punta Gorda are serviced by one or more of a bewildering variety of private bus services, and you can usually flag down a bus on the highway.

Car Belize drives on the right side of the road. All major highways are paved, but few have decent shoulders and painted dividing lines. Speed bumps are common but not all are marked.

Air

Airlines in Belize

Belize's two domestic airlines, **Maya Island Air** (☎223-1140, 223-1362; www.mayaislandair.com) and **Tropic Air** (☎226-2012; www.tropicair.com), provide an efficient and reasonably priced service in small planes on several domestic routes, with plenty of daily flights by both airlines on the main routes:

➡ Belize City–Dangriga–Placencia–Punta Gorda

➡ Belize City–Caye Caulker–San Pedro

➡ Belize City–San Pedro–Corozal

➡ Belize City–San Pedro–Orange Walk

➡ Belize City–Belmopan (Tropic Air only)

➡ Belmopan–Caye Caulker–San Pedro (Tropic Air only)

➡ Belize City–San Ignacio (Tropic Air only)

Belize City flights use both the Philip Goldson International Airport and the Municipal Airstrip, about 12 miles from the international airport; flights using the Municipal Airstrip are usually significantly cheaper than those using the international airport.

Bicycle

Most of Belize, including all three of the main highways, is pretty flat, which makes for pleasant cycling, but traffic on the main highways does tend to travel fairly fast; make sure you're visible if riding along these roads. Belizeans use bicycles – often beach cruiser–type bikes on which you brake by pedaling backward – for getting around locally, but you don't see them doing much long-distance cycling unless they're into racing.

Bikes are available to rent in many of the main tourist destinations for around BZ$20 per day. You don't usually have to give a deposit. It may be possible to purchase a used bike from one of these rental companies for longer-term use.

Boat

There are several boat services operating between the mainland and the islands (mainly Caye Caulker and Ambergris Caye). Lodges and resorts on the smaller islands usually arrange transportation for their guests.

Otherwise, getting to and around Belize's islands and reefs is a matter of taking tours or dive-and-snorkel trips, using boats organized by island accommodations or chartering a launch. As a rough rule of thumb, launch charters cost around BZ$200 per 10 miles. They're easy to arrange almost anywhere on the coast and on the main islands.

Regular services include the following:

Belize City–Caye Caulker–San Pedro At the time of research, two different companies handled this route nearly a dozen times a day, so there are plenty of options.

Corozal–Sarteneja–San Pedro The **Thunderbolt** (☎631-3400) has a monopoly on this route, with a daily service in each direction.

Dangriga–Central Cayes Not exactly offering a regularly scheduled service, but there is a handful of water taxis that make the run frequently. It's easy to arrange and cheaper to share.

Placencia–Independence The **Hokey Pokey Water Taxi** (☑665-7242) travels between Placencia and Independence, saving travelers a long road detour between Placencia and Punta Gorda.

River boats are an efficient way to get to some inland destinations, including the Maya ruins at Lamanai.

Bus

To the untrained eye, the Belize bus system still seems to be in chaos. However, all you need to know is that there are regular buses plying the regular routes, and that they charge – more or less – the same prices.

Following are the three main bus routes, all of which originate in Belize City:

Philip Goldson Hwy (Northern Hwy) From Belize City to Orange Walk and Corozal (and on to Chetumal, Mexico). There are half a dozen companies servicing this route, and between 25 and 30 buses a day going in each direction.

George Price Hwy (Western Hwy) From Belize City to Belmopan, San Ignacio and Benque Viejo del Carmen. Several companies service this route, resulting in a regular service that runs in both directions every half-hour throughout the day.

Hummingbird and Southern Hwys Buses from Belize City and Belmopan head down the Hummingbird Hwy every hour or so, stopping in Dangriga then continuing on to the Southern Hwy to Independence and Punta Gorda. Other regular services run from Dangriga to Hopkins and Placencia.

Most Belizean buses are old US school buses.

Regular-service buses stop anywhere to drop off and pick up passengers. Express buses have limited stops and are usually less crowded. They cost a bit more but they save a lot of time, especially on longer trips, so it's worth the extra few dollars.

A variety of smaller bus companies serve villages around the country. They often run to local work and school schedules, with buses going into a larger town in the morning and returning in the afternoon.

Occasional breakdowns and accidents happen with Belizean buses, but their track record is at least as good as those in other Central American countries. Luggage pilfering has been a problem on some buses in the past. Carry valuables with you on the bus and give your stored baggage to the bus driver or conductor only, and watch as it is stored. Be there when the bus is unloaded to retrieve your luggage.

Car & Motorcycle

Having a vehicle in Belize gives you maximum flexibility and enables you to reach off-the-main-road destinations and attractions (of which there are many) without having to depend on tours and expensive transfers. Though car rental is costly in Belize, it doesn't look so exorbitant when you consider the alternatives, especially if there are three or four people to share the expenses.

Belize has four asphalt-paved two-lane roads: the Philip Goldson Hwy between Belize City and the Mexican border north of Corozal; the George Price Hwy between Belize City and the Guatemalan border near Benque Viejo del Carmen; the Hummingbird Hwy from Belmopan to Dangriga; and the Southern Hwy, which branches off the Hummingbird Hwy a few miles from Dangriga and heads south to Punta Gorda. Connecting the Western Hwy just south of Belize City with the Southern Hwy just west of Dangriga, the unpaved Manatee Hwy will will save you a few miles but isn't recommended for cars without 4WD and actually takes longer.

Most other roads are one- or two-lane unpaved roads. The most oft-used roads are kept in fairly good condition, but heavy rains can make things challenging. Off the main roads you don't always need a 4WD vehicle, but you do need one with high clearance.

Driving Licences

If you plan to drive in Belize, you'll need to bring a valid driver's license from your home country.

Fuel & Spare Parts

There are plenty of fuel stations in the larger towns and along the major roads. At last report, regular gasoline was going for around BZ$8 to BZ$9 per US gallon. Premium (unleaded) is a few

---

DRIVING DISTANCES BETWEEN BELIZE & USA

From Subteniente López–Santa Elena border crossing to US–Mexico border points:

Brownsville–Matamoros 1257 miles

McAllen–Reynosa 1267 miles

Laredo (Texas)–Nuevo Laredo 1413 miles

El Paso–Ciudad Juárez 1988 miles

Nogales (Arizona)–Nogales 2219 miles

CLIMATE CHANGE & TRAVEL

Every form of transport that relies on carbon-based fuel generates CO_2, the main cause of human-induced climate change. Modern travel is dependent on airplanes, which might use less fuel per mile per person than most cars but travel much greater distances. The altitude at which aircraft emit gases (including CO_2) and particles also contributes to their climate change impact. Many websites offer 'carbon calculators' that allow people to estimate the carbon emissions generated by their journey and, for those who wish to do so, to offset the impact of the greenhouse gases emitted with contributions to portfolios of climate-friendly initiatives throughout the world. Lonely Planet offsets the carbon footprint of all staff and writer travel.

cents more. Spare parts and mechanics are most easily available in Belize City, although San Ignacio, Belmopan and Orange Walk Town also have parts suppliers. Check the Belize Yellow Pages (www.yellow pages.bz).

Hire

Generally, renters must be at least 25 years old, have a valid driver's license and pay by credit card.

Most car-rental companies have offices at Philip Goldson International Airport as well as in Belize City; they will often also deliver or take return of cars at Belize City's Municipal Airstrip or in downtown Belize City. Rental possibilities are few outside Belize City, but it is possible to rent cars in San Ignacio and Placencia.

Rental rates, including taxes, insurance and unlimited mileage, generally start at around BZ$110 a day for an economy vehicle with 4WD and air-con. If you keep the car for six days, you'll often get the seventh day free.

Most rental agencies will not allow you to take a vehicle out of the country. One agency that allows cars to be taken into Guatemala and Mexico is **Crystal Auto Rental** (☑223-1600; www.crystal-belize.com; Mile 5 Philip Goldson Hwy; ⊗7am-5pm) in Belize City.

Insurance

Liability insurance is required in Belize. There are occasional police checkpoints on the main highways, where you may be required to produce proof of it – you face possible arrest if you can't. You won't be able to bring your own vehicle into Belize without buying Belizean insurance at the border, but rental companies always organize the necessary insurance for you.

Road Hazards

Outside Belize City, traffic is wonderfully light throughout the country, but there are some potential hazards to be aware of:

➡ On the main roads, watch out for erratic and dangerously fast driving by others. Drive defensively.

➡ Watch for speed bumps (also known as sleeping policemen): these are sometimes well signed, but sometimes not signed at all.

➡ Off the major highways, most roads are unpaved: be careful of potholes.

➡ After a lot of rain, some roads may become impassable; make inquiries before you set out, and if you're in doubt about whether you'll get through a stretch, don't risk it.

➡ Always have water and a spare tire, and always fill your tank before you head off into the back country as gas stations can be few and far between and off-road driving can use more fuel than expected.

Road Rules

➡ Driving in Belize is on the right-hand side of the road.

➡ Speed limits are 55mph on the open highway, and either 40mph or 25mph in villages and towns.

➡ Seat belts are compulsory for drivers and front-seat passengers.

➡ Mileposts and highway signs record distances in miles and speed limits in miles per hour, although many vehicles have odometers and speedometers that are calibrated in kilometers.

Golf Carts

If you're spending some time at the beach and you can't fathom being dependent on your own leg power, you might consider renting a golf cart. It's relatively inexpensive (compared to a car) but it still gets you to the beach and back without causing you to break a sweat. The golf cart is a popular form of transportation in Placencia, San Pedro and – to a lesser degree – Caye Caulker. Both gas-powered and battery-powered golf carts are available: gas goes further and faster, but battery is better for the planet. Expect to pay about BZ$100 to BZ$130 per day for a four-seater.

Hitching & Ride-Sharing

Hitchhiking is never entirely safe in any country and in Belize, like anywhere, it's

MAIN DRIVING ROUTES

In 2012 the Belizean government renamed the country's two main highways. The Northern Hwy was changed to Philip Goldson Hwy and the Western Hwy to George Price Hwy. Note that many locals still use the old names when giving directions.

Philip Goldson Hwy Belize City to Orange Walk Town (1½ hours, 57 miles), Corozal Town (2¼ hours, 86 miles) and Santa Elena (Mexican border; 95 miles, 2½ hours).

George Price Hwy Belize City to Belmopan (1¼ hours, 52 miles), San Ignacio (1¾ hours, 72 miles) and Benque Viejo del Carmen (Guatemalan border; 80 miles, two hours).

Hummingbird and Southern Hwys Belmopan to Dangriga (1½ hours, 55 miles), Hopkins (two hours, 63 miles), Placencia (3½ hours, 98 miles) and Punta Gorda (4½ hours, 148 miles).

imperative that you listen to your instincts and travel smart. Travelers who decide to hitchhike should understand that they are taking a small but potentially serious risk. You're far better off traveling with another person, and never hitchhike at night. Also keep in mind that buses in Belize are cheap and fairly efficient; you might decide that a bus is a safer and more comfortable bet.

Hitchhiking is a fairly common way for Belizeans to get around. In a country where vehicle owners are a minority and public transportation is infrequent to places off the main roads, it's common to see people trying to catch a lift at bus stops or at speed bumps, where traffic slows down. If you too are trying to get some place where there's no bus for the next three hours, it's likely that you'll soon get a ride if you hold out your hand and look friendly. Offering to pay a share of the fuel costs at the end of your ride never goes amiss. But always be aware of the potential risks.

Local Transportation

All of Belize's towns, including the parts of Belize City that most visitors frequent, are small enough to cover on foot, although for safety reasons you should take taxis for some trips within Belize City. Taxis are plentiful in all mainland towns and are also an option for getting to places out of town, although asking taxis to venture beyond their normal work area can be fairly expensive.

Bicycling is an enjoyable way of getting around local areas and bikes can be rented for around BZ$20 per day in many tourist haunts (and are free for guests at some accommodations). On the cays, of course, you get around by boat if you're going anywhere offshore.

Behind the Scenes

SEND US YOUR FEEDBACK

We love to hear from travelers – your comments keep us on our toes and help make our books better. Our well-traveled team reads every word on what you loved or loathed about this book. Although we cannot reply individually to postal submissions, we always guarantee that your feedback goes straight to the appropriate authors, in time for the next edition. Each person who sends us information is thanked in the next edition – the most useful submissions are rewarded with a selection of digital PDF chapters.

Visit **lonelyplanet.com/contact** to submit your updates and suggestions or to ask for help. Our award-winning website also features inspirational travel stories, news and discussions.

Note: We may edit, reproduce and incorporate your comments in Lonely Planet products such as guidebooks, websites and digital products, so let us know if you don't want your comments reproduced or your name acknowledged. For a copy of our privacy policy visit lonelyplanet.com/privacy.

OUR READERS

Many thanks to the travellers who used the last edition and wrote to us with helpful hints, useful advice and interesting anecdotes:

Amanda Bresnan, Anne-Marie Schuurman-Kleijberg, Chandelle Mackenzie, Edwin Schuurman, Frank Sciberras, Holly Frazer, Jo Hillier, Julian De Vita, Katja Grosse-Sommer, Linda Cassidy, Marcia Matheson, Mary Klinck, Nick Case, Sabrina Bernhardt, Sara Steinhoffer

WRITER THANKS

Alex Egerton

Big thanks go out to Oscar 'Gallina' Gilede for outstanding driving/nature-guiding in tough terrain, and to Carito for the permission. Also big ups to the many supremely accommodating Belizeans all over the country, in particular Debbie Morrison in the north; Elly out on the cays; and all at the Turneffe Atoll Sustainability Association. Finally a big shout to Nick, Olga, Juan Lasso, Paul, Bailey and Mara Vorhees.

Paul Harding

Many people in Belize helped with advice, information or just a good chat over a cold Belikin. Thanks in particular to Vitali and Nick around Belmopan; Mike, James and Daniel in San Ignacio; Eric and friends in Hopkins; and Ernesto and Aurora in Maya Center. Big thank you to Bailey at Lonely Planet and my legendary co-author Alex. Most of all, and as always, thanks to Hannah and Layla at home for your love and patience.

ACKNOWLEDGMENTS

Climate map data adapted from Peel MC, Finlayson BL & McMahon TA (2007) 'Updated World Map of the Köppen-Geiger Climate Classification', *Hydrology and Earth System Sciences*, 11, 1633–44.

Cover photograph: Jaguar, Frans Lanting / Getty Images ©.

THIS BOOK

This 6th edition of *Belize* was researched and written by Alex Egerton, Paul Harding and Daniel C Schechter. The previous two editions were written by Mara Vorhees and Joshua Samuel Brown. This guidebook was produced by the following:

Destination Editor Bailey Johnson

Product Editors Kate Chapman, Amanda Williamson

Senior Cartographer Mark Griffiths

Assisting Cartographers Valentina Kremenchutskaya, Alison Lyall

Book Designer Wibowo Rusli

Assisting Editors Victoria Harrison, Helen Koehne, Catherine Naghten, Lauren O'Connell, Kristin Odijk

Cover Researcher Naomi Parker

Thanks to Liz Heynes, Andi Jones, Kate Mathews, Karyn Noble, Kirsten Rawlings, Kathryn Rowan, Luna Soo, Angela Tinson, Tony Wheeler

Index

A

accommodations 296-7, *see also individual locations*
activities 22, 23-5, 38-43, *see also individual activities, locations*
  birdwatching 22, 71-2, 79, 80, 81, 114, 126, 139-40, 147, 168, 195, 214, 225, 231, 287, **13**
  boat tours 32, 66, 71, 72, 85, 93-4, 107, 114, 122, 123, 132, 146, 149, 194, 200, 217, 224-5
  cave-tubing 159
  caving 39, 159, 160, 164-5, 232, **40**
  cycling 91, 114, 206, 307, 310
  day spas 91-2, 114, 210
  diving 9, 20, 31-7, 85, 86-9, 109, 111, 123-4, 125-6, 195-9, 200, 203, 208-10, 220-1, 225, **2**, **36**
  fishing 14, 41-2, 81, 91, 112, 113-14, 123-4, 195-9, 200, 210, 219, 220, **14**
  Garifuna drumming 11, 199-200, 202-3, 219-20, 275, 277, **11**
  hiking 13, 38-9, 68-9, 114, 160, 195, 207
  horseback riding 39, 41, 159, 176, 184, 200, **40**
  manatee-watching 80, 89-90, 108-9, 112
  river-tubing 41, 228, 207
  sailing 42-3, 90-1, 112-13, 200, 208-10
  snorkeling 10, 20, 31-7, 57, 85, 87, 89, 112, 123, 125, 126, 195-9, 200, 208-10, 219, **10**, **33**
  swimming 90, 113

Map Pages **000**
Photo Pages **000**

---

  turtle-watching 80-1, **36**
  water sports 9, 41, 43, 79, 90-1, 113, 198, 200, 203, **9**, **43**
  yoga 93, 176-7
  zip-lining 159, 175, 195, 228, 232
Actun Tunichil Muknal 164-5
Aguacaliente Wildlife Sanctuary 225
air travel 305, 307
airlines, domestic 305
airlines, international 307
airports 305
along the Coast Road 80-1
Altun Ha 12, 74-5, **74**, **12**
Ambergris Caye 10, 84-108, 84-109, **86**, **5**, **10**
  accommodations 95-100
  activities 87-93
  drinking & nightlife 103-4
  festivals & events 95
  food 100-3
  history 84-5
  shopping 104-6
  sights 85-7
  tourist information 106-7
  tours 93-5
  travel to/from 107
  travel within 107-8
animals 284-7, *see also howler monkeys, iguanas*
  jaguars 77, 139, 206-7, **16**
  manatees 80, 89-90, 108-9, 112
  turtles 80-1, 85, 109, 286, 126, 198, **36**
area codes 19
around San Ignacio **174-5**
around the Deep South 227-32
art galleries, *see* museums & galleries

B

Bacab Adventure & Eco Park 68-9

Bacalar Chico National Park & Marine Reserve 85
Ball Court, Lamanai 137
Baron Bliss 56
Barton Creek Cave 175, **21**
bathrooms 302
beaches 20
  Cucumber Beach 76
  The Split 109
Belize Botanic Gardens 183
Belize Central Prison 76, 77
Belize City 54-68, **54**, **58**
  accommodations 60-2
  activities 57
  drinking & nightlife 63-4
  entertainment 64
  festivals & events 60
  food 62-3
  history 55
  shopping 64
  sights 55-7
  tourist information 65-6
  tours 57, 59
  travel to/from 66-7
  travel within 67-8
Belize District 48, 52-81, **53**, **54**, **58**, **74**
  accommodations 52
  along the Coast Road 80-1
  Belize City 54-68
  climate 52
  food 52
  highlights 53
  northwest of Belize City 68-75
  travel seasons 52
  west of Belize City 75-80
Belize Zoo 16, 77-8, **16**
Belmopan 154-8, **156-7**
  accommodations 154-5
  activities 154
  drinking & nightlife 157-8
  entertainment 158
  food 155-7
  history 154
  sights 154

---

  tourist information 158
  travel to/from 158
  travel within 158
Benque Viejo del Carmen 186-7
Big Falls & around 227-9
big five 90
birds 286-7
birdwatching 22, 287, **13**
  Aguacaliente Wildlife Sanctuary 225
  Caye Caulker 114
  Copper Bank 147
  Crooked Tree Wildlife Sanctuary 71-2
  Gales Point 80, 81
  Half Moon Caye Natural Monument 126
  Mayflower Bocawina National Park 195
  Monkey Bay Wildlife Sanctuary 79
  Red Bank 214
  Río Blanco National Park 231
  Río Bravo Conservation & Management Area 139-40
  San Ignacio 168
  Shipstern Conservation Management Area 149
black howler monkeys 16, 284, **16**
  Belize Zoo 77
  Blue Creek 232
  Burrell Boom 68-9
  Cockscomb Basin Wildlife Sanctuary 207
  Community Baboon Sanctuary 69-70
  Lamanai 136
  Mayflower Bocawina National Park 195
  Tikal 239
  Uaxactun 241
Bliss, Henry Edward Ernest Victor 56, 57
Blue Creek 232

Blue Hole National Park 160
Blue Hole Natural Monument 9, 125, **8-9**
boat tours 32, *see also* boat travel, sailing
  Ambergris Caye 93-4
  Bacalar Chico National Park & Marine Reserve 85
  Belize City 66
  Caye Caulker 114, 122
  Chetumal 123
  Corozal Town 146
  Crooked Tree Wildlife Sanctuary 72
  Dangriga 194
  Hopkins 200
  Orange Walk Town 132
  Placencia 216
  Punta Gorda 224-5
  Rancho Delores 71
  San Pedro 107
  Shipstern Conservation Management Area 149
boat travel, *see also* boat tours, *individual locations*
  travel to/from Belize 306-7
  travel within Belize 307-8
books 254
  archaeology 257
  architecture 267
  art 267
  birdwatching 287
  Cockscomb Basin Wildlife Sanctuary 284
  cooking 283
  environmental issues 294
  Garifuna people 274
  history 256, 261
  Maya people 272
  religion 266
  wildlife 289
brukdown 278-9
Bullet Tree Falls 182-3
Burrell Boom 68-9
bus travel
  to/from Mexico 306
  to/from Guatemala 306
  within Belize 308
business hours 301

Map Pages **000**
Photo Pages **000**

butterfly farms
  Butterfly Farm & Guesthouse 230
  Chaa Creek Natural History Center & Butterfly Farm 183
  Green Hills Butterfly Ranch 174
  Orchid Garden Eco-Village 76
  Shipstern Conservation Management Area 149
  Tropical Wings Nature Center 186

C
Cahal Pech 165, 167
calendar system 271-2
canoeing, *see* water sports
car travel 308-9, 310
Caracol 11, 180-1, **180**, **2, 11**
cathedrals, *see* churches & cathedrals
cave-tubing 159
caves 20
  Actun Tunichil Muknal 164-5
  Barton Creek Cave 175, **21**
  Blue Creek Cave 232
  Che Chem Ha 187
  Nohoch Che'en Caves Branch Archaeological Reserve 15, 159, **15**
  Río Frio Cave 179
  St Herman's Cave 160, **15, 40**
  Tiger Cave 79
caving 39, **40**
  Actun Tunichil Muknal 164-5
  Blue Creek Cave 232
  Nohoch Che'en Caves Branch Archaeological Reserve 159
  St Herman's Cave 160
Caye Caulker 11, 108-22, **110, 11**
  accommodations 115-19
  activities 109, 111-14
  drinking & nightlife 121
  festivals & events 115
  food 119-21
  history 108
  shopping 121
  sights 108-9
  tourist information 121-2
  tours 114-15
  travel to/from 122
  travel within 122

Cayo District 49, 151-87, **152-3, 156, 166, 174-5, 180, 185**
  accommodations 151
  around Belmopan 158-60
  Belmopan 154-8
  climate 151
  food 151
  highlights 152-3
  Hummingbird Highway 160-2
  northwest of San Ignacio 182-3
  San Ignacio 165-73
  southeast of San Ignacio 173-81
  southwest of San Ignacio 183-7
  travel seasons 151
  travel to/from 154
  west of Belmopan 162-5
Cayo Esperanto 122-3
cell phones 18, 301-2
Central Cayes 32, 195-9
Cerro Maya 147-8
Chaa Creek 183
Chaa Creek Natural History Center & Butterfly Farm 183
Chan Chich Lodge 133, **21**
Che Chem Ha 187
child welfare 304
children, travel with 44-7, 94
chili farms 162
Chiquibul Roads 174
chocolate farms
  Ajaw Chocolate 167
  Che'il Chocolate Factory 205
  Cotton Tree Chocolate Factory 219
  Eladio's Chocolate Adventure 230
  Ixcacao Maya Belizean Chocolate 226
  Miguel Choco's Farm Tours 228
churches & cathedrals
  Assembleas de Dios Church 109
  Baron Bliss Tomb 57
  Catholic Church, Caye Caulker 109
  Catholic Church, San Pedro 86
  Lamanai 137, 138
  St John's Cathedral 56-7
  St Paul's By-the-Sea 142
  Yarborough Cemetery 57

cinema 254
climate 18, 23-5, 78, **18**, *see also individual locations*
climate change 309
Coastal Rd 80-1
Cockscomb Basin Wildlife Sanctuary 13, 206-7, 263-5, **13**
colonial sites 259
Community Baboon Sanctuary 16, 69-71, **16**
Consejo 148
consulates 297-8
Copper Bank 147-8
coral reefs 31-7
Corozal Town 141-7, **142**
  accommodations 143-5
  activities 143
  drinking & nightlife 146
  festivals & events 143
  food 145-6
  history 141
  shopping 146
  sights 141-3
  tourist information 146
  travel to/from 146-7
costs 19
counting system, Maya 270-2
Creole drummers 219
Creole people 273-4
Cristo Rey 174-8
Crooked Tree 71-3
Crooked Tree Wildlife Sanctuary 13, 71-2, **13**
Cuello 131
cultural centers
  García Sisters' Place 175
  House of Culture 86
  Lebeha 199-200
  Living Maya Experience 227-9
customs regulations 297
cycling 307, 310
  Ambergris Caye 91
  Caye Caulker 114
  Cockscomb Basin Wildlife Sanctuary (Ignacio's Bike Trail) 206

D
Dangriga 190, 192-4, **191**
  accommodations 192-3
  activities 192
  drinking & nightlife 193
  festivals & events 192
  food 193

shopping 194
sights 190
day spas
   Ambergris Caye 91-2
   Caye Caulker 114
   Placencia 210
Deep South, see Toledo District
deforestation 291
departure taxes 306
disabilities, travelers with 302-3
diving 9, 20, 31-7, **2**, **36**
   Ambergris Caye 86-9
   Blue Hole Natural Monument 125
   Boca del Rio 86
   Caye Caulker 109, 111
   Central Cayes 195-9
   Cypress Garden 86
   Esmeralda 87
   Hol Chan Cut 86-7
   Hol Chan Marine Reserve 85
   Hopkins 200
   Lighthouse Reef 124
   Long Caye 125-6
   Mexico Rocks 87
   Placencia 208-10
   Punta Gorda 220-1
   Sapodilla Cayes Marine Reserve 225
   Shark Ray Alley 87
   Sittee Point 203
   Turneffe Atoll 123-4
   Tackle Box Canyons 86
   Tres Cocos 85-6
   Tuffy Canyons 86
drinks 282-3

E

economy 254-5
ecotourism, see sustainable tourism
El Pilar 182-3
El Remate, Guatemala 241-3
electricity 297
embassies 297-8
emergencies 19
energy 291, 294
environment 287-9, 290-4
environmental issues 88, 290-1, 294
ethnicities 273-6
etiquette 297
events, see festivals & events
exchange rates 19

F

ferry travel 149
festivals & events 23-5, 134, 281, **25**
   Fiesta de Carnaval 95
   Garifuna Settlement Day 11, 192
   La Ruta Maya 42
   lobster season 95, 115, 211
   September Celebrations 24, 60
Fiesta de Carnaval 23, 95
films 254
fish feeding 88
fishing 14, 41-2, **14**
   Ambergris Caye 91
   Caye Caulker 112, 113-14
   Central Cayes 195-9
   Gales Point 81
   Hopkins 200
   Placencia 210
   Punta Gorda 219, 220-1
   Turneffe Atoll 123-4
Flores, Guatemala 50, 243-52, **234**, **244**
   accommodations 246-9
   activities 245
   drinking & nightlife 250
   food 249-50
   shopping 250-1
   sights 244-5
   tourist information 251
   tours 245-6
   travel to/from 251, 252
   travel within 251-2
food 269, 280-3, 298, see also individual locations
'Free Zone' 144

G

Gales Point 80-1
Gales Point Wildlife Sanctuary 80
gardens, see parks & gardens
Garifuna drumming 11, 219-20, 275, 277, 278, **11**
   Hopkins 199-200, 202-3
   Punta Gorda 219-20
galleries, see museums & galleries
Garifuna people 260, 274-5
   Dangriga 190, 192
   drumming 11, 275, 277, 278, **11**
   festivals 24, **25**
   food 281-2

Hopkins 199-200
   music 278
   Settlement Day 24, 192, **25**
   Seine Bight 213
Garifuna Settlement Day 24, 192, **25**
gay travelers 298
geography 287-9, 290-4
gibnuts 285
Gladden Spit 34
Glover's Atoll 258
Glover's Reef 9, 37, 198-9, **9**
golf carts 309
Green Hills Butterfly Ranch 174
Green Iguana Conservation Project 167
green iguanas 285, **46**
   Belize Zoo 77
   Blue Creek 232
   Caye Caulker 109
   Cockscomb Basin Wildlife Sanctuary 207
   Lamanai 138
   San Ignacio 167
Guanacaste National Park 158-9
Guatemala 233-52, **234**, **236-7**, **244**, **246**
   accommodations 233
   border crossings 306
   climate 233
   El Remate 241-3
   Flores 243-51
   food 233
   highlights 234
   language 235
   money 235
   Santa Elena 243-51
   Tikal 234-40
   travel seasons 233
   travel to/from 173, 232, 306
   Uaxactun 241
   visas 235
   Yaxhá 240-1

H

Half Moon Caye Natural Monument 17, 126, **2**, **17**
Hattieville 76-7
health 298-300
hieroglyphics 262-5, 270-1
High Temple, Lamanai 137
hiking 13, 38-9
   Blue Hole National Park 160
   Burrell Boom 68-9

Caye Caulker 114
Cockscomb Basin Wildlife Sanctuary 207, **13**
Mayflower Bocawina National Park 195
historic buildings
   Belize Central Prison 76, 77
   Clock Tower 142
   Clock Tower, Punta Gorda 219
   Court House 57
   Flagpole Plaza 131
   Fort Barlee 142
   Fort George Lighthouse 57
   Government House 57
   Independence Plaza 131
   Municipalidad 245
   Old Customs House 141
   St Paul's By-the-Sea 142
   Swing Bridge 56
   Town Hall 142-3
history 256-65
   ancient Maya 256-7, 266-72
   British rule 258-61
   Guatemala, relations with 264
   independence 261
   recent 263-5
   US, relations with 262
hitchhiking 309-10
Hol Chan Marine Reserve 32, 85, 86-7
holidays 301
Hopkins 16, 199-203, **199**, **16**
horseback riding 39, 41, **40**
   Cristo Rey 176
   Hopkins 200
   Nohoch Che'en Caves Branch Archaeological Reserve 159
   Xunantunich 184
hot sauce farms
   Hot Mama's 162
   Marie Sharp's Factory 190, 192, 194
howler monkeys 16, 284, **16**
   Belize Zoo 77
   Blue Creek 232
   Burrell Boom 68-9
   Cockscomb Basin Wildlife Sanctuary 207
   Community Baboon Sanctuary 69-70
   Lamanai 136

howler monkeys continued
Mayflower Bocawina National Park 195
Tikal 239
Uaxactun 241
Hummingbird Highway 15, 160-2, **15**
hurricanes 78

I

iguanas 285, **46**
Belize Zoo 77
Blue Creek 232
Caye Caulker 109
Cockscomb Basin Wildlife Sanctuary 207
Lamanai 138
San Ignacio 167
immigration 305
insurance
car 309
health 298
travel 300
internet access 300
internet resources 19
environment 290
food 280
itineraries 26-30, **26**, **27**, **29**, **30**

J

Jaguar Temple, Lamanai 137
jaguars 77, 139, 206-7, **16**
johnnycakes 280

K

kayaking, see water sports
Kekchi people 217
Blue Creek 232
Big Falls 227-8, 229
San Pedro Columbia 229-30
kitesurfing, see water sports
kungo muzik 279

L

La Isla Bonita, see Ambergris Caye
La Milpa 139
La Ruta Maya 23, 42
Lamanai 12, 135-9, **136**, **12**
languages 255, 274

Laughing Bird Caye Faro Reef System 34-5
legal matters 105, 300
lesbian travelers 298
LGBTI travelers 298
Lighthouse Reef 37, 124-5, **2**, **36**
literature 254
archaeology 257
architecture 267
art 267
birdwatching 287
Cockscomb Basin Wildlife Sanctuary 284
cooking 283
environmental issues 294
history 256, 261
Maya people 272
religion 266
wildlife 289
Little Belize 140
live-aboard boats 32
lobster season 24, 95, 115, 211
Long Caye 125-6
Lubaantun 229-30, **230**

M

maize 269
Manatee Highway 80-1
manatee-watching 108-9, 285
Ambergris Caye 89-90
Caye Caulker 112
Gales Point 80
Swallow Caye Wildlife Sanctuary 108-9
maps 300
marine reserves, see also national parks & reserves, wildlife reserves
Bacalar Chico National Park & Marine Reserve 85
Caye Caulker Marine Reserve 109
Hol Chan Marine Reserve 85
Port Honduras Marine Reserve 225
Sapodilla Cayes Marine Reserve 225
Swallow Caye Wildlife Sanctuary 108-9
marriage 105
Mask Temple, Lamanai 136-7
Maya Center 205-6
Maya calendar system 241

Maya counting system 270-2
Maya hieroglyphic writing 270
Maya Mountain Research Farm 231
Maya people 14, 256-7, 260, 266-72, 274, **14**
Deep South 217
food 281
Maya Center 205-6
medicine 288
music 279
Toledo District 217
Maya sites 14, 22, 266
Actun Tunichil Muknal 164-5
Altun Ha 12, 74-5, **74**, **12**
Barton Creek Cave 175
Cahal Pech 165, 167
Caracol 11, 180-1, **180**, **2**, **11**
Cerro Maya 147-8
Cuello 131
El Pilar 182-3
Lamanai 12, 135-9, **136**, **12**
La Milpa 139
Lubaantun 229-30
Nim Li Punit 227-8, **227**
Nohmul 131
Santa Rita 141-2
Tikal 50, 234-40, **234**, **236-7**
Uxbenka 231
Xunantunich 12, 185-6, **185**, **12**, **28**
Mayflower Bocawina National Park 195
measures 301
Mennonites 140, 164, 275-6
mestizos 273
Mexico
border crossings 305-6
travel to/from 123, 147, 305-6
mobile phones 18, 301-2
money 18-19, 300-1
Monkey Bay 79-80
monuments
Baron Bliss Tomb 57
Chaos Oasis 230
Drums of Our Father's Monument 191
Mopan Maya people 14, 217, **14**, see also Maya people
Maya Center 205
San Antonio 230-1
motorcycle travel 308-9

mountain biking, see cycling
Mountain Pine Ridge Area 178-80
museums & galleries
Banquitas House of Culture 131
Belize Archives Department 154
Benque Viejo House of Culture 187
CBS Museum & Visitor's Center 70
CCIT 239
Corozal Museum 142
George Price Center for Peace & Development 154
Gulisi Garifuna Museum 190
Image Factory 56
Lamanai Museum 137
Museo Santa Bárbara 245
Museo Lítico 245
Museo Sylvanus G Morley 239
Museum of Belize 55-6
Old Belize Exhibit 75-6
Pen Cayetano Studio Gallery 190
Sa'c Tunich 175
music 22, 277-9

N

national parks & reserves 290-4, see also marine reserves, wildlife reserves
Bacalar Chico National Park & Marine Reserve 85
Blue Hole National Park 160
Guanacaste National Park 158-9
Mayflower Bocawina National Park 195
Río Blanco National Park 231
Spanish Creek Rainforest Reserve 70
Temash-Sarstoon National Park 225-6
nature parks, see wildlife reserves
nature reserves, see wildlife reserves
newspapers 301
Nim Li Punit 227-8, **227**
Nohmul 131
Nohoch Che'en Caves

Branch Archaeological Reserve 15, 159, **15**
Northern Belize 49, 127-50, **128**, **130**, **136**, **142**
  accommodations 127
  climate 127
  Corozal District 140-50
  food 127
  highlights 128
  history 129
  Orange Walk District 129-40
  travel seasons 127
Northern Cayes 31-2, 49, **82**-126, **83**, **86**, **92**, **110**
  accommodations 82
  Ambergris Caye 84-108
  Caye Caulker 108-22
  climate 82
  food 82
  highlights 83
  other northern cays 122-6
  San Pedro 84-108
  travel seasons 82
  travel to/from 84

O
oil 294
Old Belize 75-6
Old Northern Highway 73-5
opening hours 301
Orange Walk Town 129-35, **130**
  accommodations 132-3
  drinking & nightlife 134-5
  food 133-4
  history 130
  sights 131
  tourist information 135-6
  tours 132
  travel to/from 135-6

P
paranda 278
parks & gardens
  Bacab Adventure & Eco Park 68-9
  Battlefield Park 57
  Belize Botanic Gardens 183
  BTL Park 57
  Green Iguana Conservation Project 167
  Masewal Forest Garden 182
  Poustinia Land Art Park 186-7
  Tropical Wings Nature Center 186

passports 305
Placencia 15, 208-17, **209**, **15**
  accommodations 211-14
  activities 208-10
  drinking & nightlife 216
  food 214-16
  shopping 216
  tourist information 216-17
  travel to/from 217
  travel within 217
planning 18-19
  Belize's regions 48-50
  budgeting 19
  calendar of events 23-5
  cell phones 18
  children 44-7
  climate 18, 23-5, 78, **18**
  exchange rates 19
  highlights 6-7, **6-7**
  internet resources 19
  itineraries 26-30, **26**, **27**, **29**, **30**
  languages 18
  mobile phones 18
  money 18
  opening hours 19
  telephone services 18
  time 18
  travel seasons 18, 23-5
  visas 18
plants 287-9
Plum Caye 197-8
politics 254-5
Popol Vuh 266-7
population 255
Port Honduras Marine Reserve 225
postal services 301
public holidays 301
punta 277
Punta Gorda 218-25, **220**
  accommodations 221-3
  activities 219-20
  festivals & events 221
  food 223-4
  shopping 224
  sights 219
  tourist information 224
  tours 220-1
  travel to/from 224-5
  travel within 225
punta rock 277

R
radio 301

Rancho Dolores 71
Red Bank 214
red-footed boobies 126
religion 255
reserves, *see* national parks & reserves
ride-sharing 309-10
Río Blanco National Park 231
Río Bravo Conservation & Management Area 139-40
river-tubing 41, *see also* water sports
  Big Falls 228
  Cockscomb Basin Wildlife Sanctuary 207
road distances 310

S
safe travel 65, 301, 303
sailing 42-3, *see also* boat tours
  Ambergris Caye 90-1
  Caye Caulker 112-13
  Hopkins 200
  Placencia 208-10
San Antonio 230-2
San Ignacio 17, 165-73, **166**, **174-5**, **17**
  accommodations 168-70
  drinking & nightlife 172
  entertainment 172
  food 170-2
  shopping 172
  sights 165-6, 167
  tourist information 172-3
  tours 167-8
  travel to/from 173
  travel within 173
San José Succotz 185-6
San Miguel 229
San Pedro 84-108, **92**, **28**
  accommodations 95-100
  activities 87-93
  children, travel with 94
  drinking & nightlife 103-4
  festivals & events 95
  food 100-3
  history 84-5
  shopping 104-6
  sights 85-7
  tourist information 106-7
  tours 93-5
  travel to/from 107
  travel within 107-8
San Pedro Columbia 229-30

Santa Elena, Guatemala 243-52, **246**
  accommodations 246-9
  activities 245
  drinking & nightlife 250
  food 249-50
  shopping 250-1
  sights 244-5
  tourist information 251
  tours 245-6
  travel to/from 251, 252
  travel within 251-2
Santa Rita 141-2
Sapodilla Cayes Marine Reserve 225
Sarteneja 149-50
sauce farms
  Hot Mama's 162
  Marie Sharp's Factory 190, 192, 194
Seine Bight 213
September celebrations 24, 60
Shark Ray Alley 10, 87, **10**
Sharp, Marie 190, 192, 194, 282
Shipstern Conservation Management Area 149
Silk Cayes Marine Reserve 34
Sittee Point 203-5, **199**
Sittee River 205
smoking 301
snorkeling 20, 31-7, **10**, **33**
  Ambergris Caye 89
  Bacalar Chico National Park & Marine Reserve 85
  Belize 57
  Blue Hole Natural Monument 125
  Caye Caulker 112
  Central Cayes 195-9
  Half Moon Caye Natural Monument 126
  Hol Chan Marine Reserve 85
  Hopkins 200
  Placencia 208-10
  Punta Gorda 219
  Shark Ray Alley 10, 87
  Turneffe Atoll Marine Reserve 123
South Water Caye 197, **43**
South Water Caye Marine Reserve 32
Southern Belize 50, 188-232, **189**, **191**, **199**, **209**, **218**, **220**, **227**, **230**

Southern Belize *continued*
accommodations 188
climate 188
food 188
highlights 189
Stann Creek District 190-217
Toledo District 217-32
travel seasons 188
travel to/from 190
Southern Cayes 34-5
Spanish Creek Rainforest Reserve 70
Spanish Creek Wildlife Sanctuary 71
Spanish Lookout 164
spelunking, *see* caving
spice farms 228
St Herman's Cave 160-1, **15**, **40**
stand-up paddleboarding, *see* water sports
Stann Creek District 190-217
Stela 9, Lamanai 137
sustainable tourism 22, 35, 290-1
Belize Wildlife & Referral Clinic 162
Maya Mountain Research Farm 231
Río Bravo Conservation & Management Area 139-40
Spanish Creek Rainforest Reserve 70
Toledo Ecotourism Association 222
Universal Healing Institute & Retreat 161
Ya'axché Conservation Trust 219
swimming **46**
Ambergris Caye 90
Caye Caulker 113

T
TEA 222, 296
telephone services 18, 301-2
Temash-Sarstoon National Park 225-6
Thatch Caye 197-8
Tikal, Guatemala 50, 234-40, **234**, **236-7**

accommodations 239-40
activities 239
food 240, 240-1
sights 235-9
tourist information 240
tours 239
travel to/from 240
time 18, 302
Tobacco Caye 195-7
Toledo District 217-32, **218**, **220**, **227**, **230**
around Punta Gorda 225-7
around the Deep South 227-32
Punta Gorda 218-25
travel to/from 218
toilets 302
Toledo Ecotourism Association 222, 296
tourist information 302, 303, *see also individual locations*
transportation 305-310
travel seasons 18, 23-5, *see also individual locations*
travel to/from Belize 19, 305-6
travel within Belize 307-310
Tres Cocos 85-6
Turneffe Atoll 35, 37, 123-4
turtles 80-1, 85, 109, 286, 126, 198, **36**
TV 301

U
Uaxactun, Guatemala 241
Unesco World Heritage Sites 289
Bacalar Chico National Park & Marine Reserve 85
Blue Hole Natural Monument 9, 125, **8-9**
Glover's Reef 9, 37, 198-9, **9**
Half Moon Caye Natural Monument 17, 126, **2**, **17**
Laughing Bird Caye 34-5
Sapodilla Cayes Marine Reserve 225
South Water Caye 197, **43**

South Water Caye Marine Reserve 32
Tikal Tikal 50, 234-40, **234**, **236-7**
Uxbenka 231

V
vacations 301
vaccinations 299
visas 303
volunteering 203-4, 303-4
Arcas 245
Belize Wildlife & Referral Clinic 162
Project Ix-Canaan 241
Spanish Creek Rainforest Reserve 70

W
water sports 9, 41-3, **9**, **43**
Ambergris Caye 90-1
Barton Creek Cave 175
Caye Caulker 113
Central Cayes 198
Dangriga 192
Glover's Reef 9, 198
Hopkins 200
Monkey Bay Wildlife Sanctuary 79
Sittee Point 203
waterfalls
Barquedier Waterfall 160
Big Rock Falls 179
Five Sisters Falls 179
Río On Pools 179
Thousand Foot Falls 179
weddings 105
weights 301
west of Belize City 75-80
wildlife 284-9
wildlife programs
Belize Wildlife & Referral Clinic 162
Green Hills Butterfly Ranch 174
Green Iguana Conservation Project 167
wildlife reserves, *see also* marine reserves, national parks & reserves
Aguacaliente Wildlife Sanctuary 225
Biotopo Cerro Cahuí 241

Caye Caulker Forest Reserve 109
Chaa Creek Natural History Center & Butterfly Farm 183
Cockscomb Basin Wildlife Sanctuary 13, 206-7, 263-5, **13**
Community Baboon Sanctuary 16, 69-71, **16**
Crooked Tree Wildlife Sanctuary 13, 71-2, **13**
Gales Point Wildlife Sanctuary 80
Hol Chan Marine Reserve 32
Monkey Bay Wildlife Sanctuary 79
Shipstern Conservation Management Area 149
Silk Cayes Marine Reserve 34
South Water Caye Marine Reserve 32
Spanish Creek Wildlife Sanctuary 71
wildlife watching 20, 285, *see also individual animals*
windsurfing, *see* water sports
women travelers 304
work 304

X
Xunantunich 12, 185-6, **185**, **12**, **28**

Y
Yaxhá, Guatemala 240-1
yoga
Ambergris Caye 93
Cristo Rey 176-7

Z
zip-lining
Big Falls 228
Blue Creek 232
Cristo Rey 175
Mayflower Bocawina National Park 195
Nohoch Che'en Caves Branch Archaeological Reserve 159
zoos 77-8

Map Legend

Sights

- Beach
- Bird Sanctuary
- Buddhist
- Castle/Palace
- Christian
- Confucian
- Hindu
- Islamic
- Jain
- Jewish
- Monument
- Museum/Gallery/Historic Building
- Ruin
- Shinto
- Sikh
- Taoist
- Winery/Vineyard
- Zoo/Wildlife Sanctuary
- Other Sight

Activities, Courses & Tours

- Bodysurfing
- Diving
- Canoeing/Kayaking
- Course/Tour
- Sento Hot Baths/Onsen
- Skiing
- Snorkeling
- Surfing
- Swimming/Pool
- Walking
- Windsurfing
- Other Activity

Sleeping

- Sleeping
- Camping

Eating

- Eating

Drinking & Nightlife

- Drinking & Nightlife
- Cafe

Entertainment

- Entertainment

Shopping

- Shopping

Information

- Bank
- Embassy/Consulate
- Hospital/Medical
- Internet
- Police
- Post Office
- Telephone
- Toilet
- Tourist Information
- Other Information

Geographic

- Beach
- Gate
- Hut/Shelter
- Lighthouse
- Lookout
- Mountain/Volcano
- Oasis
- Park
- Pass
- Picnic Area
- Waterfall

Population

- Capital (National)
- Capital (State/Province)
- City/Large Town
- Town/Village

Transport

- Airport
- Border crossing
- Bus
- Cable car/Funicular
- Cycling
- Ferry
- Metro station
- Monorail
- Parking
- Petrol station
- Subway/Subte station
- Taxi
- Train station/Railway
- Tram
- Underground station
- Other Transport

Note: Not all symbols displayed above appear on the maps in this book

Routes

- Tollway
- Freeway
- Primary
- Secondary
- Tertiary
- Lane
- Unsealed road
- Road under construction
- Plaza/Mall
- Steps
- Tunnel
- Pedestrian overpass
- Walking Tour
- Walking Tour detour
- Path/Walking Trail

Boundaries

- International
- State/Province
- Disputed
- Regional/Suburb
- Marine Park
- Cliff
- Wall

Hydrography

- River, Creek
- Intermittent River
- Canal
- Water
- Dry/Salt/Intermittent Lake
- Reef

Areas

- Airport/Runway
- Beach/Desert
- Cemetery (Christian)
- Cemetery (Other)
- Glacier
- Mudflat
- Park/Forest
- Sight (Building)
- Sportsground
- Swamp/Mangrove

OUR STORY

A beat-up old car, a few dollars in the pocket and a sense of adventure. In 1972 that's all Tony and Maureen Wheeler needed for the trip of a lifetime – across Europe and Asia overland to Australia. It took several months, and at the end – broke but inspired – they sat at their kitchen table writing and stapling together their first travel guide, *Across Asia on the Cheap*. Within a week they'd sold 1500 copies. Lonely Planet was born.

Today, Lonely Planet has offices in Franklin, London, Melbourne, Oakland, Beijing and Delhi, with more than 600 staff and writers. We share Tony's belief that 'a great guidebook should do three things: inform, educate and amuse'.

OUR WRITERS

Alex Egerton

Belize District, Northern Cayes, Northern Belize A journalist by trade, Alex has been coming to Central America for almost two decades and has spent extended periods residing in colorful towns along the Caribbean. He has a keen interest in the unique culture of the region, especially in the expressive music and dance of traditional communities, and is constantly working on polishing up his *punta* moves. When not on the road for work, Alex can probably be found at home in the mountains of Colombia planning his next escape to the Northern Cayes and craving fryjacks smothered with habanero sauce. Alex also wrote the Understand and Survival Guide sections.

Paul Harding

Cayo District, Southern Belize As a writer, photographer and person with chronic itchy feet, Paul has traveled a good part of the world in the past two decades, usually in search of adventure, islands and beaches. Belize ticks all the boxes: Caribbean coast and cays on one side, remote jungle on the other. On this research trip, Paul river-tubed through caves, zip-lined over jungle canopies, explored Mayan ruins, snorkeled on the reef, sampled hot sauces and inspected many cabanas. He has contributed to more than 50 Lonely Planet guides to countries as diverse as Australia, Iceland, Vanuatu and India. Paul also wrote the Plan section.

Daniel C Schechter

Guatemala A native New Yorker, Daniel has been poking around Latin America for so long it sometimes makes more sense to him than his place of birth. After living in Colombia and Puerto Rico, he called Mexico home for more than a decade. During that time he spanned the Mundo Maya on various forays, discovering and writing about such places as Campeche, Calakmul and Tikal, and cultivating an enduring interest in Classic Maya history. Daniel currently lives in the Netherlands, where he blogs on cycling (http://netherlandsbikeways.blogspot.nl).

Published by Lonely Planet Global Limited
CRN 554153
6th edition – October 2016
ISBN 978 1 78657 110 6
© Lonely Planet 2016   Photographs © as indicated 2016
10 9 8 7 6 5 4 3 2 1
Printed in China

Although the authors and Lonely Planet have taken all reasonable care in preparing this book, we make no warranty about the accuracy or completeness of its content and, to the maximum extent permitted, disclaim all liability arising from its use.